Major Equipment Procurement

Books by Joseph Auer and Charles Edison Harris

Computer Contract Negotiations
Major Equipment Procurement

Major Equipment Procurement

Joseph Auer
President
International Computer Negotiations, Inc. (ICN)
Winter Park, Florida

Charles Edison Harris, Esq.
Attorney at Law
Orlando, Florida

VNR VAN NOSTRAND REINHOLD COMPANY

Library of Congress Catalog Card Number: 82-8372
ISBN: 0-442-20870-7

Published by Van Nostrand Reinhold Company Inc.
135 West 50th Street
New York, New York 10020

Van Nostrand Reinhold Company Limited
Molly Millars Lane
Wokingham, Berkshire RG11 2PY, England

Van Nostrand Reinhold
480 Latrobe Street
Melbourne, Victoria 3000, Australia

Macmillan of Canada
Division of Gage Publishing Limited
164 Commander Boulevard
Agincourt, Ontario M1S 3C7, Canada

15 14 13 12 11 10 9 8 7 6 5 4 3 2

Library of Congress Cataloging in Publication Data

Auer, Joseph.
 Major equipment procurement.

 Bibliography: p.
 Includes index.
 1. Industrial equipment—Purchasing. 2. Capital
investments. I. Harris, Charles Edison. II. Title.
HD39.3.A9 .1982   658.7′2   82-8372
ISBN 0-442-20870-7   AACR2

To
Dick Brandon

and

Sidney Segelstein

Who tragically lost their lives
during 1981

PREFACE

This book provides the knowledge necessary for a user to plan, negotiate, and document a major equipment procurement. Although vendor marketing and legal personnel will probably find it fascinating "defensive" reading, this is a book written for companies that acquire and use equipment. As such, it is designed with one central focus in mind: how to help the user optimize the financial and legal aspects of a major equipment acquisition.

Because many fine texts have been written on the separate subjects of equipment contracts, negotiating skills, and financial analysis, this book is not intended to be an academic treatise on any of these areas. Rather, it is designed to combine these and other subjects into practical tools that can be applied effectively in an actual transaction. Although concept and theory are discussed where appropriate, most of this book is based upon what the authors call "truth from the trenches"—cold, hard experience that can only be gained from success and failure at the negotiating table.

The factors that cause a particular equipment acquisition to be "major" vary considerably from transaction to transaction. For purposes of this book, the authors consider an equipment procurement to be "major" if it involves any of the following elements: (i) a significant financial commitment by the user (whether for a single item or a group of related items); (ii) equipment that is critical to the user's operations or business; or (iii) equipment that poses significant legal, operating, or other risks to the user or its customers or employees. Nevertheless, many of the factors discussed in this book are applicable to equipment acquisitions that do not measure up to any of these standards. Consequently, equipment users and their professional advisors should find this book helpful in planning, negotiating, and documenting a wide range of acquisitions that are too important or complex to be covered by a user purchase order or standard form vendor contract.

Because negotiating is critical to every stage of the equipment procurement process, the initial chapters of this volume focus on negotiating skills. Chapter 1 explores why many users fail to negotiate, and why this naive approach leads to disastrous results. Chapter 2 reinforces this discussion by offering vivid examples of the classic vendor sales ploys that are used in actual equipment marketing efforts. Chapter 3 follows with an explanation of basic user negotiating skills, while Chapter 4 offers a detailed explanation of the procurement process from a negotiating perspective.

The remaining chapters of the book provide advice and guidance on understanding, negotiating, and documenting specific equipment acquisitions. Chapter 5 offers a comprehensive analysis of one of the most potent, and least understood, weapons in the user's acquisition arsenal—the request for proposal. Providing technical background for later discussions, Chapters 6 and 7 focus on the legal principles involved in equipment contracts—including an overview of patents, copyrights, and trade secrets. The ensuing chapters cover a wide variety of legal and financial issues involved in selecting, drafting, and negotiating specific types of equipment agreements; used equipment contracts, third party leases, rental agreements, installment purchases, general procurement agreements, and user form contracts are among the areas discussed. Because the procurement process does not end when the equipment is installed, the final chapter explains the critical role of a good contract administration program. Although example provisions are interspersed throughout the text, the Appendix includes additional provisions, an extensive contract checklist, and excerpts from a user request for proposal.

Many of the vendor ploys and negotiating tactics discussed in this book were initially explored by the authors in early volumes of *Computer Negotiations Report (CNReport),* a monthly newsletter published by Sunscape International, Inc., Orlando, Florida. Because most of this material and virtually all of our suggestions are based upon actual negotiating experience, the fact settings and example provisions in this book have been altered where appropriate to mask the identity of the parties participating in the negotiations.

No book is ever possible without the support and assistance of a great many people. As always, our deepest thanks go to our families, for their encouragement, their patience, and their understanding. Only a child can appreciate how many missed baseball games it takes to make a chapter of a book. We are also grateful to Suzanne Hedgecock, who typed (and retyped) our manuscript while managing a law office and a business consulting firm. We continue to be indebted to Larry Hager, our Editor-in-Chief, whose foresight and persistence led to our first book as well as this one. Finally, we offer our appreciation to the thousands of managers and executives who have supported *CNReport* and our respective professional firms. Their procurement triumphs and failures provided the impetus for this volume and the examples necessary to benefit their colleagues in future transactions.

JOSEPH AUER
CHARLES EDISON HARRIS

CONTENTS

1
THE RATIONALE FOR NEGOTIATING

Most business executives already have the basic skills necessary to negotiate—or at least learn to negotiate—a sound major equipment transaction. The user's executives employ these skills every day in their own personal transactions. Take that new car the user's senior manager purchased at the end of the last model year. He test drove a dozen models. Checked out several makes and a number of local dealerships. Poured over the test results in consumer and automotive magazines. Studied all the gas mileage and interior space data published by the United States government. In fact, he even assessed the repair cost figures published by consumer groups and the insurance industry. Finally, armed with an arsenal of statistics, he set out to drive his bargain.

When the auto dealer's smoothest salesman began his sweetest pitch, the manager crisply replied, "I'm interested in that blue sedan over there, sticker number CP-899, but only if you add the optional equipment on this note sheet and the total price, less tax and tag, is $9,685." As the car salesman began his histrionics, the manager whipped out his pocket calculator and calmly said, "Please, I'm not interested in all that. The price I gave you is precisely $125 over your invoice price, not considering any retains or special factory incentives you may be getting. That's calculated on the basis of a dealer invoice multiplier of .82, plus freight."

After the usual sales gamesmanship, which the manager both anticipated and ignored, the salesman agreed to the deal and the manager executed the dealer's installment sales contract. Now the contract contained some potentially obnoxious provisions, but the manager was not terribly worried. After all, the written warranties in the contract were backed by the recent federal law that clarified and strengthened warranties of all types. And the warranty waiver provisions of the contract would be overridden in part by state law and in part by the implied warranties and strict product liability imposed by a variety of state and federal court cases. The car did turn out to be somewhat of a lemon at first, but the manager just stopped paying and called the bank that purchased the installment sales contract from the dealer. Under the new FTC regulations abolishing the holder-in-due-course doctrine in these situations, the bank shared responsibility for the mess. Once the bank threatened to make the auto dealer buy back the installment sales contract, the dealer fixed things up in a hurry. And now the car is running like a dream. The car dealer's repair shop has also improved, since the state started licensing mechanics, the local courts threw out blue book fixed rate charges, and the newspaper began publishing a list of consumer complaints received by dealers through the county consumer action agency.

The user's manager also received a pretty good interest rate on his car loan, despite the state of the economy. He tried his local bank and credit union, but found that, for once, the car dealer's own indirect loan rate was lower because of a particularly good arrangement between the dealer and its bank. He looked into leasing, both closed and open end, but finally settled on the 48-month loan deal offered by the car dealer, largely because the downpayment was low and he decided to keep the car for some time and then give it to his daughter for college. In making all these comparisons, the manager had no concerns about misrepresentation of finance charges, thanks to the protection of Regulation Z, the federally-mandated truth-in-lending law, and the related truth-in-leasing regulations.

As this simple example suggests, most business executives are becoming increasingly sophisticated buyers of consumer goods. They proceed with the caution they deem appropriate to the situation, from the proverbial distrust of buying from a used car salesman to the well-known confidence of dealing with an old family friend. These business executives research their proposed purchases in great detail by reading reports and surveying colleagues. Barraged by horror stories about the nonperformance and hazards of their favorite consumer items, they expect to receive and enforce a variety of implied and express warranties. Annoyed by having to pay increasingly expensive bills for unnecessary or faulty repairs, they select their auto mechanic and appliance repairman with the care once reserved for the family doctor. And throughout, the business executive is supported by increasing governmental regulation, intervention, and assistance.

Despite the business executive's increasing ability to negotiate sound consumer purchases, something strange often occurs when the executive goes to work and considers a major equipment acquisition. The executive can plan, negotiate, and optimize the acquisition of a new car costing several thousand dollars, or even a console television costing a few hundred dollars. But for some reason, the executive cannot or will not apply the same basic negotiating skills—plus some additional expertise to be sure—to the acquisition of a new data processing or manufacturing system costing hundreds of thousands, if not millions, of dollars.

To the cynic convinced of the innate corruption of the American business executive, the reason for this disparity might be said to be that the executive cares more about saving $1,500 of his or her own money on a new car purchase than on saving $150,000 on the firm's major equipment acquisition. Although caring—or, more properly, being motivated about optimizing the transaction—is one part of the equation, the reasons that the executive fails to effectively negotiate the equipment transaction are much more complex. Notwithstanding this complexity, most of the reasons relate to one simple factor: far too often, major equipment negotiations have been and are the exclusive game of the vendor, not the user. When it comes to negotiating or documenting a major equipment transaction, the vendor generally supplies the bat and the ball, and also makes up and enforces the rules of the game.

THE REASONS USERS DECIDE NOT TO NEGOTIATE

The historical dominance of the vendor in most major equipment transactions creates a number of basic problems for the user. All of these problems tend to cause the user to do business with the vendor on the vendor's terms, conditions, prices, and forms.

First, the vendor is highly experienced and skilled in negotiating and drafting equipment contracts. The vendor has a professional sales and negotiating team whose full time responsibility is (and has been for some time) optimizing the vendor's position in equipment transactions. In contrast, the user is seldom sophisticated in acquiring major equipment. Major equipment negotiations represent an unusual event for most users and for their legal and accounting advisers. When compared to the vendor's professional negotiating team, the user's staff members suffer from a serious lack of experience, confidence, technical understanding of equipment contracts, interdisciplinary training, and negotiating skills.

Second, the user is almost always overly impressed with the vendor, its system, and/or the idea of applying advanced technology to solve the user's ills. Although fewer and fewer users are burdened with the glassy stares and children-on-Christmas-morning grins that used to afflict company executives acquiring their first computer system or other state-of-the-art device, most users still suffer unknowingly from vestiges of this disease.

Equipment sales representatives are trained to exploit the "three R's" when dealing with a user. Rapport, rationale, and relationship are the key ingredients used by the vendor's marketing representatives to shape the user's thinking and close the deal. The vendor's marketeer builds personal rapport with key members of the user's staff, subtly placing the transaction on a personal basis that can be warmed by dinners, sporting events, and pleasant office conferences. The sales representative listens for the user's "hot buttons" and, employing those items and the vendor's current marketing pitch, creates and reinforces the user's rationale for acquiring the vendor's system. Here, the vendor offers to educate the user's key executives, to let them see the true light about the future in the user's particular industry, and to permit them to be privy to the vendor's own "secret" plans to provide even greater advances in the near future. User trips to the vendor's manufacturing plants and systems planning or "think tank" offices are key parts of impressing the user. Often this effort is carried out simultaneously on two different management levels. The user's top executives are whisked away, perhaps on the vendor's private jet, to meet with the vendor's president or other key officers and to receive a high level executive briefing on the future of a particular segment of their industry. At or about the same time, the user's operations managers are touring the vendor's manufacturing and research facilities. By the time these and similar activities are completed over a period of months, all levels of user management are completely impressed with the vendor, and thoroughly convinced of the critical need to proceed with the transaction.

Once the vendor's marketing representative has created the necessary rapport and rationale, the third R—relationship—is a foregone conclusion. The user's key executives and staff feel comfortable with the vendor's representatives, both personally and professionally. All of the user's officers are impressed with the vendor's technology and with its assessment of and commitment to the future. As a result, they are pleased to have a warm and professional relationship with the vendor. Indeed, they are proud to be associated with the vendor and with its people, technology, and systems.

Third, the user is far too busy to spend the time and expense necessary to plan, negotiate, and document a complex equipment acquisition. The user's executives and managers have a business to run, problems to solve, and daily deadlines to meet. They are understaffed and, quite likely, underpaid. A new operating system is supposed to be a solution, not an additional problem requiring hundreds of hours of planning and negotiating. Once a management decision has been reached to proceed with a new system, everyone on the user's management team wants the equipment installed and operating at the earliest possible date.

With this lack of time and with this sense of urgency, the user's managers are tremendously pleased that the vendor is willing to simplify the process and do much of their work for them. For example, the vendor's systems experts will help determine the user's needs and design several alternative solutions. The vendor's financial experts will prepare analyses showing how much more or less the proposed systems will cost compared to the user's present equipment. The vendor will even call in third-party leasing firms to make proposals if it seems such an approach would be advisable for the user. The vendor's sales representative will present a nicely worded proposal summarizing the final conclusions mutually agreed upon by him or her and the user's operations staff, in a format that can be sent directly on to the user's senior management for approval. And finally, the vendor's representative will present a succinct form contract for signature, with a few neatly typed additions or addenda to meet the user's special needs. In sum, the vendor offers a neatly packaged solution that is easy to accept and difficult to refuse.

Fourth, unlike the vendor's representatives, the user's managers have no immediate incentive to negotiate aggressively. The vendor's key participants in the transaction are usually paid on a commission or bonus plan that provides a clear financial incentive to complete the transaction on a basis that is favorable to the vendor. Although the user's executives may also participate in a bonus plan, their compensation is unlikely to bear any meaningful relationship to whether the user does or does not optimize a given equipment acquisition. This disparity in personal incentive and aspiration level permeates the transaction from the start and must be affirmatively overcome by the user's representatives as the negotiations continue.

Fifth, the vendor enjoys an information advantage. It not only understands the negotiating process inside out; it also manipulates that process to give it considerable inside information concerning the user's needs, weaknesses, and "hot buttons." The vendor's sales effort almost invariably involves a survey of the user's needs and problems. Although many vendors emphasize their generosity in providing staff assistance for preliminary surveys and other studies, these staff efforts are generally a critical part of the vendor's marketing plan. The preliminary studies permit the vendor's staff to have full access to the user's existing equipment and personnel, to view all the user's problems, and to develop good rapport (and even co-author their report and recommendations) with the user's staff. On the other hand, the user gains no similar right to survey the vendor's operations and view its practices and problems. As one user executive put it not long ago, "The problem with this whole survey approach is that we open up our kimono to them without getting anything in return except a more effective sales effort." In reality, of course, the vendor's surveys do benefit the user by permitting the vendor to design a better and more accurate proposal. Ideally, however, the user's negotiating position would be enhanced if it had the technical and staff expertise to conduct its own objective surveys, forcing all competing vendors to bid on the basis of information supplied through a good request for proposal (RFP) procedure.

Sixth, the traditional acquisition process emphasizes vendor and equipment evaluation and selection at the relative expense of contract negotiation and drafting. Historically, users have allocated time and money toward the evaluation and selection phases of an acquisition rather than the negotiation and documentation phases. (As suggested above, this user approach and other traditions in the acquisition process have been largely set and reinforced by vendor influence and emphasis.) Consequently, if a user determines that negotiation and documentation deserve greater emphasis in a particular transaction, the user must literally fight an uphill battle against the traditional way of doing business. (Fortunately, this tradition is changing.)

Finally, the user simply does not see the need for lengthy, costly negotiations with the vendor. If anything, the user is convinced that such negotiations are not necessary and possibly counterproductive. The user may admit that the vendor's contract should be reviewed by the user's attorney (perhaps the day before or the day of contract execution), but this review is a far step from full contract negotiations.

The user's attitude in this regard is actually not too surprising. Consider the following summary of the user's assessment of the situation:

- The user trusts the vendor. The user is impressed with the vendor's people, its technology, and its comprehensive and professional approach to the user's present and future problems.
- The user sincerely wants to have a long and warm relationship with the vendor, and believes that such a relationship will have bottom-line results for the user's business.
- The user has seldom if ever negotiated a major equipment transaction and has little idea of how to go about it.
- The vendor has offered the user its standard form agreement that far larger customers have signed without change. In fact, the vendor has even made a few concessions because of the "close relationship" between the vendor and user. If the user thumbs its nose at all this, the system may be delayed and the user's critically important "relationship" with the vendor is certain to be damaged.
- Negotiating the contract at this point will take considerable time. It will delay installation, perhaps significantly if the negotiations cause the user to lose its place in the equipment delivery queue. The time required to negotiate the contract will also delay all the other priority projects being handled by key members of the user's staff. The user's attorneys will also have to be involved, adding to legal fees and possibly blowing the whole deal.

- Whatever benefits might result from the negotiations just do not seem to be worth the risk, time, cost, and hassle. The vendor has already made several good concessions. The transaction is favorable from a financial and technical standpoint. The vendor always puts the burden of justifying any further changes to its form contract squarely on the user. Documenting and articulating the need for any such changes will be complicated and time-consuming, particularly since the vendor's marketeer will likely assert all the reasons why the changes are not really necessary.
- The user's past experience with the vendor has been reasonably good. A few problems have occurred, but most were worked out satisfactorily. Indeed, the great majority of the past problems were probably as much the user's fault as the vendor's. And the vendor's senior management has personally committed that the user's account will receive high priority so that past problems will not recur.

THE REASONS WHY NEGOTIATING IS CRITICAL

Despite these rationalizations, the need to negotiate most major equipment transactions is very real. The reasons why aggressive negotiations are critical are discussed below.

First, the only acceptable reason for failing to negotiate a major contract is seldom present in most situations. The sole valid reason for not negotiating an equipment acquisition or disposition is because the user sincerely believes that the total significance of the project to the user does not merit spending the time and money necessary to negotiate and document the transaction on a professional basis. In practice, users enter into myriad agreements that do not deserve or require a full blown negotiating effort. Ordinarily, such agreements involve relatively minor financial commitments and products or services that are comparatively unimportant to the user's operations—in effect, contracts that pose little financial or operating risk to the user.

Some equipment agreements fall into this category. Most major equipment contracts, however, are considerably more critical to the user, both in terms of financial commitment and operating significance. In today's business environment, many of the user's operations—data processing and manufacturing, for example—are likely to be essential to its continued survival. Few large users would be able to continue to do business on a profitable basis if they were to suffer a massive data processing or operational failure for any substantial period of time. And virtually all users, large or small, would suffer serious disruptions and losses in the event of continued problems with major equipment.

Because most major equipment transactions involve large financial commitments by the user, the transactions not only offer opportunities for risk and avoidance, they also offer significant opportunities for both hard and soft dollar savings. Even where the vendor involved refuses to discount its equipment, a sophisticated user can obtain valuable soft dollar commitments through aggressive negotiations. Where the vendor discounts its equipment on a regular but seldom publicized basis, the user can also achieve direct financial benefits by lowering the acquisition price through effective negotiations. Regardless of whether the savings involve reduced equipment prices or vendor commitments to supply services or software at reduced expense or no charge at all, the value flows to the user's bottom line.

User personnel sometimes ask how large the potential savings on a given transaction should be before the user should attempt to optimize its financial position through negotiations. The answer is obviously one that varies with the size of the user, its earnings, and its overall financial condition. An aggressive user that strives to achieve every possible financial savings in its operations will pursue even relatively small amounts, while a more staid and mature firm may require larger potential savings before it will strive for financial optimization of the transaction.

For some years, the authors have suggested a relatively simple formula to user executives who pose the question noted above. The formula is based on the following inquiry: "If you could save your entire annual salary for your company, would your senior management be appropriately impressed?" The formula, then, is that it is always worth negotiating an equipment acquisition where the potential hard and soft dollar savings exceed the annual salary of the manager handling the transaction. In practice, most users are amazed at how many major equipment acquisitions fall within this test. Although generalizations are difficult, and perhaps even misleading, thousands of major equipment transactions involve potential hard and soft dollar savings equal to 10% and more of the total contract price. Where the system involves any size or significance for the user, or the user is shifting from one vendor to another, the potential for saving more than the annual salary of the user's chief negotiator or manager is almost assuredly present. Where the transaction involves used equipment, particularly that acquired from a broker or dealer, a similar potential for savings often exists.

Second, relying on "rapport" and "relationship" in a significant business transaction is foolhardy at best. Despite the warm feeling that the user's personnel may have when dealing with the vendor's sales staff and senior executives, the fact remains that the sales representative's very livelihood depends on selling equipment and maximizing income for the vendor. Even in the most ideal world of business ethics, the salesman is likely to look out for the vendor—and himself—first. If the salesman can achieve increased commissions and management recognition by lulling the user to sleep and achieving higher profits for the vendor, he is rather certain to do so. Recorded history does not appear to document those sales representatives who, faced with such an opportunity, voluntarily gave away the vendor's profits and their own commissions in order to preserve or create a warm relationship with the user.

Even if the value of rapport and relationship with the vendor can be considered meaningful during the local tenure of a particular vendor sales manager, personnel and relationships change over time. The vendor's warm and friendly sales representative may be transferred, and the vendor's senior management may be replaced or retired. Yet, long after these individuals have moved on, the user will be left with its equipment and its standard vendor form agreement. Any remnants of the supposedly valuable relationship will simply be warm memories, with no binding legal effect.

A similar result often occurs when the vendor finds that business reasons dictate the adoption of new procedures and policies. In such circumstances, the vendor will almost always implement its new policies crisply and efficiently, regardless of any pleasant relationship that may have existed previously. Quite appropriately, the vendor's obligation to its shareholders will take precedence over whatever unwritten commitments may have been made at the vendor's local branch level or, indeed, at its senior management level.

Third, developing a mutually agreeable equipment contract based on documented vendor "deliverables" is a perfectly valid business goal. The purpose of a negotiated agreement is to describe and document a proposed transaction in a fashion that is understandable and acceptable to both parties. For the contract to do its job as a legal document, it should cover all aspects of the transaction and clearly specify the promises and obligations of each party. The simple fact is that virtually all vendor form agreements fail to meet this test. Most vendor contracts are blatantly one sided documents that clearly indicate the user's responsibilities, omit or minimize the vendor's obligations, and eliminate or limit the vendor's liability for nonperformance. If nothing else, the vendor's standard agreement should be modified to document exactly what the vendor is responsible for doing, when the vendor is obligated to do it, and what liability the vendor will face if it fails to meet its promises. To leave these basic matters to interpretation, or to the oral promises or side letters of the vendor's branch manager, is remarkably unprofessional.

Fourth, far from damaging the supposed relationship between the vendor and user, an active negotiating stance by the user is likely to increase the vendor's respect for the user and build a longer term, more professional association between the two firms. Although the user's initial efforts at negotiating may create trauma for both the user and the vendor, once the user has established that it intends to follow professional contracting principles in its major equipment procurements, the user is likely to face more honest vendor appraisals and sales efforts, fewer vendor ploys, and more realistic initial price concessions.

Fifth, failing to employ professional contracting and negotiating procedures may create serious career problems for the user employees involved. Admittedly, being the first advocate of extensive user negotiations may not be a particularly popular position for most managers. Initial user efforts at bringing equality to the bargaining table are often rocky, and the responsible managers may well be criticized for delaying or even killing the deal, increasing costs, and ignoring other corporate priorities. Because lawyers are frequently used as the butt of all corporate problems, or at least of all delayed transactions, the user's inside or outside corporate counsel is particularly likely to experience criticism over his or her efforts to employ valid negotiating strategies. These problems may be exacerbated if the vendor's sales representative successfully executes a divide and conquer maneuver in which he, or one of his senior management officers, convinces the user's senior management that the vendor's marvelous solution to the user's problems is being delayed by the recalcitrance of certain user managers or attorneys.

On the other hand, ignoring professional contracting procedures offers a much more certain future for the user managers involved: sooner or later, it is likely to cost them considerable embarrassment or, more critically, their jobs. Failing to properly negotiate and document a transaction as important as a major equipment acquisition ultimately leads to problems. A given user or manager may have a record of "no problems" or of working out all its problems as a result of its warm relationship with the vendor. But statistically, the user or manager that pursues such practices is merely waiting for its turn.

In some instances, the ultimate decline and fall of the user and its operations or procurement manager occurs when problems arise in the installation or operation of the system, and the user's remedies prove to be nonexistent. In other situations, the difficulty occurs when senior management finally recognizes that the user has been leaving tens of thousands of dollars lying on the negotiating table in transaction after transaction. In still other cases, the career disaster occurs as a result of some alleged "misunderstanding," generally based upon the fact that a critical oral promise allegedly made by the vendor was somehow excluded from the written contract. Regardless of the scenario, the result is generally the same. Senior management either removes the responsible manager outright or, more likely, becomes initially disenchanted with the manager and subsequently biased against him or her. Within a few weeks or months, particularly if similar incidents surface, senior management reaches a decision to retire, reassign, or replace the manager.

Despite these and other arguments in favor of negotiating major equipment contracts, many users fail to appreciate just how subtle and manipulative vendor sales practices can be. Although these users admit that other companies may be deceived by vendor marketing efforts, they refuse to believe that their own decision-making has been and is anything other than objective and farsighted. The authors have discovered that one of the better methods of conveying the critical need to negotiate is to spotlight some of the more popular sales efforts or "ploys" used by equipment marketing representatives. When presented with an explanation of these sales strategies, most users recognize that they have been victimized by one or more of the ploys in past acquisitions. Consequently, the following chapter presents a chilling compilation of popular vendor marketing techniques, taken from the pages of actual negotiating sessions. In an appropriate preview of subsequent sections of this book, the chapter also offers suggestions concerning user remedies and tactics that can be used to avoid, deflect, or minimize each of the vendor ploys discussed in the chapter.

2
POPULAR VENDOR PLOYS

Most equipment vendors devote considerable resources toward training their marketing personnel. Equipment sales representatives receive education in technology, finance, marketing, and psychology. They engage in role playing, map out detailed marketing plans covering both short and long range objectives, and enjoy significant second position experience before even calling on a user as its principal account representative. Regardless of the informal, friendly attitude conveyed by the vendor's salesperson, most equipment marketing efforts are neither informal nor friendly. Rather, they are precise strategic exercises involving the detail and discipline of any military campaign.

Although vendor marketing representatives employ a wide variety of general negotiating strategies, some of the more popular sales efforts are particularly effective when applied in major equipment transactions. Where important equipment acquisitions are involved, users succumb to sales ploys that they would dismiss out of hand in other contexts.

Several factors contribute to the effectiveness of vendor ploys in most equipment negotiations. In some instances, all of these factors may influence a user's decision-making. In other situations, only a single issue may make the difference.

First, the user generally trusts the vendor and its marketing representatives. As noted in Chapter 1, vendor marketeers devote substantial emphasis toward building rapport and relationship with the user. When these efforts are successful, as they frequently are, the user's trust of the vendor exceeds reasonable bounds and borders on gullibility. As a result, the user seldom asks the vendor for verification or written confirmation of sales promises.

Second, the user normally has high respect for the vendor's technical expertise and leadership. Because the user seldom feels qualified to question the vendor's abilities (after all, the user has probably selected the vendor at least in part because of its excellence), the user accepts vendor statements at face value, whether the representations relate to technical matters or contracting practices. This user trait is often exacerbated by the fact that the user has had relatively little experience in acquiring major items of equipment on a professional basis.

Third, the user generally needs an immediate solution to a pressing problem. The user's technical evaluation of alternative types of equipment may have taken far too long, leaving management impatient for immediate delivery once the system selection has been made. In other situations, financial constraints may have postponed the new acquisition beyond the operating capabilities of the old equipment, leaving a critical need to implement the new system as soon as possible. In other circumstances, the apparent immediacy of the user's need may be heightened by the simple human factor of impatience: once management has approved the new system, the user's operations personnel and end user staff can hardly wait to get their hands on the improved capabilities, especially the more exotic bells and whistles.

Fourth, users often move too quickly when they perceive, or are offered, what appears to be a bargain. Despite the old adages of "you can't get something for nothing," "there's no free lunch," and "if it looks too good to be true, it may be," most users leap when offered any realistic price concession or soft dollar savings by the vendor. User personnel like to believe that they are highly qualified business negotiators capable of driving a hard bargain in a technical acquisition that is most important for their company. However, as noted above, user negotiators are seldom capable of living up to this self-perception. Because of this fact, and several of the other factors noted above, relatively inexperienced user negotiators are tremendously pleased with any financial concession offered by the vendor or any other financial analysis that indicates that the acquisition recommended by them will save money or provide an improved price/performance ratio.

Fifth, as noted in Chapter 1, most user executives do not have adequate time to devote to major equipment negotiations. They and their professional advisors are burdened with a variety of pressing business matters. They are too busy putting out fires and killing rats and snakes to manage their own areas of responsibility effectively, let alone embark on a drawn-out series of acquisition negotiations. As a result, these key user participants subconsciously (and perhaps consciously) want the acquisition process to be smooth and short. Consequently, they tend to react too favorably when presented with an acquisition methodology that satisfies these goals.

Although most of the more successful vendor ploys are based upon some combination of the factors outlined above, the ploys themselves come in all shapes and sizes and in varying degrees of iniquity. Some ploys simply involve honest marketing skills, honed to perfection and applied in an environment where the vendor owns the bat, ball, and gloves. Other ploys involve excessive sales puffery and misrepresentation by omission. Still other ploys go beyond any reasonable propriety and include known misrepresentations.

Fortunately, most major equipment marketing representatives are seldom guilty of anything more than overly-aggressive puffery, omission of certain relevant facts, and refusal to document promises in the written contract. Unfortunately, vendor sales ploys can be devastatingly effective without the application of any more treacherous tactics.

Although admittedly lacking any scientific data to document the claim, the authors estimate that at least one of the ploys described below is used in at least 80% of all major equipment acquisitions consummated in the United States each year. The authors also suspect that the successful implementation of one or more of the following ploys is either the deciding factor, or one of several deciding factors, in the successful closing of at least half of these acquisition transactions. If these estimates are correct, and the authors firmly believe that they are, a thorough understanding of these ploys should be of significant value to any user engaging in major equipment negotiations.

Because any user that appreciates the intricacies of these ploys will enjoy an improved position at the negotiating table, the following compilation has been placed early in this volume, in the hope of providing immediate benefit to a reader engaged in actual negotiations. This early discussion also provides valuable background for, and insight into, subsequent chapters of this book, particularly those dealing with negotiating skills, strategies, and tactics.

THE "WE DON'T NEED TO WRITE THAT DOWN, YOU CAN TRUST ME" PLOY

In this ploy, the vendor manipulates the personal relationship between its marketing people and the user's staff to justify leaving various vendor commitments out of the written vendor/user agreement. By employing this carefully developed personal relationship, the vendor's marketeer convinces the user's staff to rely upon oral promises and side letters, in lieu of firm contractual commitments, to document various vendor obligations.

The vendor's tools for this rather subtle ploy are the "three R's" of selling: rapport, rationale, and relationship. As noted in Chapter 1, vendors hire marketing people who can use these tools very well—personnel who can manipulate that rapport to create supposedly long-term personal relationships with the user's key managers. Once this has been established, well-trained marketing personnel can easily establish a long-term business relationship with the user. The key is helping the user's staff—now personal and professional friends of the vendor's marketing personnel—rationalize how and why they should do business with the vendor.

Once personal relationships are established, normally very cautious business-men and women will accept a local salesman's oral assurances on a wide variety of technical and legal points, ranging from why a particular system is needed to why a given point need not be included in the contract. In essence, the "trust" resulting from the personal relationship makes all of the vendor's ploys easier to accomplish.

As a result of the rapport, rationale, and relationship developed by well-trained marketing personnel, major equipment "negotiating" sessions are often filled with echos of the industry's fairy tales: "Oh, don't worry about writing that down, we'll take care of it here at the local level," or "We can't put that in the contract because of government auditing problems; but don't worry, we'll honor our promise to take care of it." The list goes on and on. The amazing thing is not that the vendor's personnel try to rationalize this kind of approach to "contracting," but that so many users accept the vendor's position.

User staff personnel often ask why they should worry about a reputable vendor's failing to stand behind this type of oral representation. To the typical staff person—particularly one who has such a personal relationship with the vendor's representative—the vendor has always been an honorable company and, consequently, can be relied on to continue to meet its commitments, whether oral or written. The answer is easy: conditions—and commitments—often change over time.

In some cases, it may turn out that the vendor's local marketing representative never had the authority to make the commitment and the vendor simply cannot accept the economic or practical burden of fulfilling the promise. In other situations, the vendor may change its original position in an effort to offset reduced earnings or intimidate the user into upgrading its system or, perhaps, as retaliation for the user's purchases of used equipment from a broker. In yet other situations, it may turn out that the original oral understanding was really a misunderstanding and the vendor claims, quite legitimately, that it never agreed to take the requested action.

The absurdity of allowing a personal relationship to influence a critical acquisition decision is often sadly demonstrated by the change in the relationship that occurs when either the vendor's representative or the user's manager leaves his or her respective company for another position: The supposedly long-term personal relationship evaporates. The after-hours socializing stops, the friendship (to the extent it ever really existed) dwindles away, and the only remnant that survives is the vendor's one-sided, standard form contract signed by the user.

From a legal standpoint, the key rule in dealing with this vendor ploy is very simple: "if it's not written into the contract, it's not part of the deal." Business transactions involving thousands, if not millions, of dollars should be handled on a businesslike basis. The user's negotiators should draft a good contract. Then and only then should they worry about being "good guys" and maintaining a personal relationship. Too many users forget that personal relationships—and personnel—come and go, particularly in the equipment sales area. But as these personnel, and their personal relationships, rise and fall, the actual parties to the contract—that is, the companies—remain legally obligated. And the legal obligations are based upon the written agreement, not upon the oral assurances of the vendor's former marketing representative.

In this regard, two related points should be mentioned. First, the user should never, ever sign the vendor's standard form agreement. Second, the user should always involve its attorney or other professional advisors early enough in the negotiations to allow them to offer meaningful suggestions and help mold the transaction. Although these two points are so basic they almost should not need to be mentioned, the authors continue to be amazed at the number of large national and regional companies that either sign the vendor's standard form contract with no changes, or that incorporate some minor changes into the standard form without the advice of their attorney.

From a personal conduct standpoint, a pair of rules should be helpful in dealing with this vendor ploy. First, wherever possible the user should avoid the establishment of any "personal relationships" between the vendor's marketing personnel and the user's key staff. Second, if personal relationships appear to be impossible to avoid, the user should take additional, conscious steps to ensure objectivity in the decision-making process. The best possible approach is for the user's staff to recognize that their objectivity (and, consequently, their career development) will be best served by maintaining professional rather than personal relationships with the vendor's marketing representatives. Ideally, this rule need not preclude occasional after work cocktails to discuss business matters nor even a social event from time to time. The difficulty, however, is that once such quasi-social meetings occur, the line is hard to draw. In reality, therefore, the safest and most professional approach is to eliminate the problem by eliminating the possibility. Business should be conducted in a business setting and other invitations should be politely refused. Where some social contact seems mandatory, the associated risks can, to some extent, be reduced by ensuring that a second or third staff person (who does not socialize with the vendor's salesman) is involved in all decision-making evaluations and decisions.

These rules apply to virtually all levels within the user's organization. Although technical experts on the user's staff may not actually be the "decision-makers" in the user's next equipment acquisition, their analyses of specifications and performance may be critical to the user's decision. And their recommendations may be colored if the vendor has successfully established the desired rapport and social relationship. The same risks exist at the line, staff, and executive management levels, all the way up through the chief executive officers of the respective organizations.

THE "YOU'RE GETTING OUR BEST PRICE" PLOY

In this ploy, the vendor's marketing representative convinces the user's negotiators that the user is getting the vendor's very best price. The implication, of course, is twofold. First, since the user is being offered the vendor's best price, further negotiations to achieve additional price concessions would be a waste of time. Second, because the vendor has already cut its profit on the transaction to the bone, the user should not expect to receive soft dollar and contractual concessions from the vendor. In this regard, the vendor's marketeer may note that the quoted best price is based upon the vendor's standard contract and not on some lengthy document that alters "traditional" liability relationships and includes dozens of other vendor concessions.

This ploy is effective against big companies and small firms alike. Large users are susceptible to the ploy because they are already impressed with their own size and clout with their vendors. Equipment vendors play on this corporate ego and have to do little further convincing that the quoted price is the best price. Vendors will even feed a large company's corporate ego by comparing that firm's negotiating advantages to the disadvantages faced by smaller users. "Mr. Adams, we recognize we're dealing with one of our largest customers," says the vendor's marketeer. "We would never think of having you pay the same price we quote to our smaller customers. They just don't have the same purchasing power. So rather than beat around the bush, we've quoted you our best price from the start." The amount of money and contractual protection left on the table by large users as a direct result of this "ego inflation" can be staggering.

Smaller users can also be victimized by this same approach. Here, the vendor's marketeer convinces the user's staff that, because of their personal relationship, their strong negotiating ability, or the importance of this transaction to the vendor, the vendor is giving the user its very best price—a price that is seldom available to much larger users and virtually never offered to smaller firms. In this approach, the vendor's representative says, "Because this transaction is especially important to us and to our senior management, and because your negotiating team has a strong reputation for driving a hard bargain, we've quoted you our very best price from the outset. I hope you appreciate the fact that this is a significant discount. I know for a fact that [insert the names of a few Fortune 500 companies] have not been offered this price, despite their size. But we want your business and we want to expedite this transaction to meet your installation deadlines." The vendor's representative may also assure the user's staff that the vendor's standard form contract, which the user has the audacity to ask to modify, has been accepted virtually unchanged by a number of named national firms. In some situations, the salesman is simply misrepresenting the situation—something that can be checked out by a series of telephone calls to the supposed signers. In many other cases, the salesman will be all too correct. Some of the nation's largest users leave the most contractual protection, and the most money, lying on the negotiating table.

Regardless of the user's size, the vendor should be required to back up its best price puffery in writing with a "most favored nation" (sometimes called a "most favored user") provision in the contract. (See Chapter 8 and Appendix B.) If the vendor will agree to include such a provision in the contract, the user will gain meaningful contractual protection (and peace of mind). If the vendor balks at such a provision, the user may learn a great deal about the candor of the vendor and the relative importance that the vendor really attaches to the user's business.

Consider the following situation, where the vendor began by saying, "John, this is obviously our very best price. As you know, you get our best price and we can't sell it for less than that amount, even to a company of your size." Unlike most users, however, Mr. John Williams replied, "Great; if that's the case, I'm sure you won't mind a contract provision that states that you are selling us your system for the maximum allowable discount, which will give us the minimum total price. Furthermore, since you have represented the fact verbally, let's put in writing that this system has not been sold for less money to anybody else; and, if at a later date we find out that you have sold it to somebody for less money prior to our date of signing, we will be entitled to a retroactive discount."

As might be expected, a request for this kind of provision normally separates puffery from reality. When a user negotiator asks for this one, he or she really finds out if the vendor is telling the truth. If a vendor puts this provision in the contract, the user can pretty well be assured that the vendor has undertaken a high-level review of the negotiations to make sure that the user is in fact being given the maximum allowable discount. If the vendor is not willing to put this provision into an agreement after making grandiose verbal representations, the user has a simple remedy: throw the vendor's negotiators out of the office.

This dramatic action usually results in one of two things happening, once the vendor finishes up its gamesmanship relating to being tossed out of the user's office. If the vendor was serious about being willing to offer the user the vendor's "best price," it may go somewhere to regroup, figure out a way to save face, and come in with the discount and the "most favored user" clause. In doing so, however, the vendor may restructure the transaction in an effort to scramble the actual discount or protect itself with respect to other favored users. On the other hand, the vendor may come back with a considerably different story and an absolute refusal to provide the most favored user clause. If this is the reaction, the user should probably ignore the vendor's stated rationale for being unable to provide such a clause and zero in on the relevant question: why won't the vendor supply the clause in writing? The reason, of course, may be that the vendor really does have a firm policy against such provisions. However, the more likely reason may be that the vendor has offered a better discount to another user; in essence, the larger (or smaller) user firm was not so "favored" after all.

THE "HERE'S EVERYTHING YOU NEED FOR ONE LOW PAYMENT" PLOY

This ruse can be more simply described as "attractive packaging can be expensive." In this ploy, the user's friendly, easy-to-do-business-with equipment sales representative comes in and says, "Mr. Smith, we can do everything your data processing people asked for in their last report. With our new system, we can eliminate your quarter-end bottleneck, provide audio response, add the in-house time-sharing capability, and so on (and on). We've gotten together with your people and our regional staff and designed one comprehensive package that solves all those problems, includes the new hardware, and provides a wealth of software, systems, and education benefits. Most importantly, the monthly cost for the next five years is below your previous projections! Just sign here and we can ship the system this week."

This ploy has a number of risks. First, the user may be rushed into acquiring hardware, software, or systems support that it may not need. Because of the financial and operating benefits of the vendor's total package, the user may not stop and analyze each package component to determine whether it is really needed or, indeed, whether anyone has even studied the issue. For example, in one situation, the vendor's package included completely new peripherals in order to upgrade the user's entire shop to the vendor's newest series. However, once the user slowed things down and carefully analyzed each component of the package in terms of its own needs, it determined that its existing peripherals could do the job quite well, with one or two exceptions. Consequently, a number of the new peripherals "recommended" by the vendor and the user's own data processing staff were "re-evaluated" and deleted from the package at a substantial savings.

Second, even if the package components are all beneficial to the user, it may be pushed into acquiring the complete system without considering alternative methods of obtaining each component. Software and systems support offer particularly costly examples. The vendor's package on one $6 million hardware acquisition included roughly $250,000 of software and systems support to be financed along with the hardware under the third-party lease. Thus, the user would have been paying a substantial interest rate for seven years in order to finance a component that it ordinarily would have paid for as the services were performed. By separating the software and systems component from the financing package (a rather difficult task, given the vendor's varying explanations) and purchasing the software and support for cash as needed, the user saved money—not a fortune, to be sure, but enough to pay for some additional programming and education benefits.

The third risk is that the user may end up paying more for the package than it would have if it had negotiated each item separately. Like your local new car dealer, your friendly equipment salesman often finds comfort in hiding behind "one low package price." The salesman's hope, in each case, is that the buyer will find the total price so attractive that it will not ask why the dealer is selling undercoating or rather plain floor mats for twice the price those same items are available for elsewhere. And the user's manager will not ask why the financing in the vendor's package is almost a full percentage point higher than that available from a competing leasing company or why the time sharing costs in the package are considerably above the rates charged by competing service bureaus.

The basic solution to this ploy is to assess each item of the proposed transaction separately. A user should never accept the vendor's package without breaking out and analyzing each component in terms of need, cost, source, and acquisition (or financing) method. It takes time and effort to break apart a vendor's nice, easy package, particularly when the vendor offers resistance, red herrings, and frankly misleading responses every step of the way. The results, however, are often quite surprising—and usually rewarding.

In analyzing the price for each component, the user may find that the price being charged for some items is in excess of the vendor's normal negotiated price for those items. The price being charged for other items (especially financing) may be above the rates being charged by competitive sources. The user may also find that the total package price includes some "grossed up" costs or other amounts that do not seem directly related to any desired component. These "funny numbers" often represent methods of booking sales that will return desired commissions or marketing credits to the vendor's local office or salesman. In some instances, the user may be able to negotiate a better deal by helping the marketing representative build these credits or other amounts (software and trade-in credits are particularly popular items in this area) into the transaction; however, to protect itself, the user must be aware of exactly what is happening and what amounts are involved.

THE "PRICE PROTECTION CONTRACT" AND "PRICE INCREASE COMING" PLOYS

Experienced vendor marketing personnel look at price increases as great opportunities to book a lot of business without having to negotiate any contracts. Although a number of variations exist, the strategy in each case usually involves the "price increase coming" or "price protection contract" ploys.

The "Price Protection Contract" Ploy

In its most basic form, the "price protection contract" ploy works like this: the vendor's marketing representative tells his customer, "You are a great customer and we're here to look after your best interest. We want to give you the capability to protect your company from the price increases we expect to announce later this year. Why don't we evaluate your equipment needs for the next 12 to 24 months and get the items you may need on order now, before the price increase takes effect?" (This ploy is even more effective if the vendor can convince the user that this approach will also allow the user to have a good position on the vendor's production and delivery schedule.) If the user seems hesitant, the vendor often offers reassurance by noting, "Of course, since the contracts are for price protection only, they can be cancelled by you at any time." Alternatively, the vendor may state that 90 days notice is required for this type of cancellation.

This approach holds several risks for the user. First, the user almost always signs the price protection contract without any serious negotiations over price or terms. In most cases, the user simply signs the vendor's standard form agreement, without additions or deletions. Needless to say, the user leaves important legal, financial, and substantive concessions lying on the table.

Second, the user generally signs the contract without carefully considering whether the equipment involved is really needed or, if it is, whether the mode of acquisition proposed is in the user's best interests. As a result, the user often ends up with equipment that is not needed or with a high-cost rental agreement when a third-party lease would be preferable.

Third, the user often executes the contract without proper review and approval by its senior management and board of directors. This oversight can be particularly hazardous if the transaction "blows up" in the future or if a board member learns of the contract indirectly.

Fourth, cancelling the contract may be considerably more difficult than executing it. In far too many cases, the contract used simply does not contain any mention of cancellation. Although the vendor's marketing representative may nevertheless permit cancellation in the future, the binding legal agreement does not require the vendor to do so. If the user decides to change vendors or take other action against the incumbent vendor, the vendor may resurrect the price protection contract and threaten to enforce it. More than one user has learned this lesson the hard way. Although the user might well claim "fraud in the inducement" in such a situation, few users can readily afford the time, trouble, and expense of litigating this type of issue.

The "Price Increase Is Coming" Ploy

The "price protection contract" ploy is generally used when the user and vendor are not in the middle of negotiations on a new acquisition or other transaction. However, when negotiations are in progress, the vendor may use a related strategy known as the "price increase coming" ploy.

Like its relative, this ploy can cost the user money. In implementing this strategy, the vendor strives to convince the user that the most important factor in the transaction is for the user to avoid an impending (and sometimes already announced) price increase. Consequently, the user drops its guard and fails to pursue other concessions that might be more valuable than the savings from avoiding the price increase.

In one example of this ruse, the vendor's marketing representative said, "If we can get this contract signed and into Atlanta by March 31, you'll avoid the 6% price increase that goes into effect then." In subsequent negotiations, the marketing representative demonstrated that a 6% savings on $1 million of equipment would be a handsome $60,000. In an effort to collect this savings, the operations manager talked his company into proceeding with the transaction by the deadline set by the vendor. In doing so, the user executed the vendor's standard form contract and purchased the system at list price (the "old" list, to be sure). What the user's manager overlooked was that, at the time, the vendor's "standard" discount on the system was about 12%. If the user had waited for the price increase, negotiated a good contract, and obtained the then-standard discount, it actually would have saved somewhat over $60,000. Indeed, the user might have been able to negotiate the contract and achieve the standard discount before the price increase, thereby saving about $120,000, if it had not been so preoccupied with the vendor's "price increase coming" ploy.

A minor variation on this ploy involves the vendor's announcement that prices have already gone up, officially, but the user can still buy at the old prices if the contract can be signed within the next 24 to 48 hours. This variation involves all the hazards mentioned above, plus the additional risk that the user will make a rash, and probably imprudent, decision to acquire the equipment without taking the time to conduct a careful analysis of its overall equipment needs.

The easiest way for a user to avoid both of these ploys is to develop two firm rules. First, the user should never sign a "price protection contract" without full review, approval, and negotiations. Second, the user should never be rushed into acquiring any item of major equipment, particularly when the vendor seems to be dangling a carrot. To borrow from an old axiom, the user should beware of vendor representatives bearing gifts.

The vendor, after all, is out to make a profit. Trite as it may seem, if the deal seems too good to be true, it may well be just that. Contrary to the marketing representative's opinion, slowing the transaction down may be the best possible strategy for the user. This is particularly true where discounts may be available. Many vendors, including some that claim otherwise, offer discounts that increase in direct proportion to the time elapsed since introduction of the equipment.

THE "TRY IT, YOU'LL LIKE IT" PLOY

In this ploy, the vendor's sales representative comes in and says, "Hey, we've got a new machine. Since you are an important, big account, we want to bring one of the first of these devices to your site to show you how it works and to use it as a demonstration to others in the area." The marketeer continues, "Of course, since this is a new product, there will be only a minimal obligation on your part. You just pay for the maintenance, but there won't be a charge for the hardware itself."

The way this ploy actually works is this: first, a contract is signed for the equipment. Second, a side letter is generated which states that no rent will be paid for some period of time, and that the contract itself can be cancelled at the end of this period if the user does not want to continue using the equipment. Third, the salesperson works hard to be sure that the device performs well and that those who are using it like it. Fourth, by the end of the trial period, the user's personnel have come to depend upon the equipment and have "sold" it internally so that it stays and payments begin. Assuming that the equipment is good, the people like it, and it does the job on a cost/performance basis, who loses? Nobody perhaps; but the vendor has again walked away with a standard form contract without any negotiations and the user has left further financial and contractual optimization on the table.

The user could have achieved a better deal by negotiating originally, but it relaxed its guard because it grabbed at the "something for nothing" instead of simply seeking the best acquisition method. This ploy succeeds so frequently because it is easier to take what's being offered, especially when it's "almost free," than to be creative and negotiate what the user really needs.

The impact of this little truism was demonstrated to a fairly large user. The marketing representative was offering some new manufacturing control equipment on a demonstration basis, for "maintenance only" payments. The user's manager tried to insert some additional provisions in the vendor's standard contract covering the equipment. The marketing representative was "incensed" that the user would demand "additional concessions" when the vendor was being good enough to provide the latest equipment at "virtually no cost." The manager backed off, the contract was not cancelled after the trial period, and some months later the user paid out several thousand dollars in "cancellation" fees as a result of not insisting on a rather routine provision in the form contract it had signed.

Although not really a part of this ploy, the vendor may also enjoy substantial marketing benefits from utilizing a major user's shop as a demonstration site for a new device. To some extent, of course, the user is compensated for this by paying for maintenance only during the trial period. The user is also able to test the machine for its own purposes. Nevertheless, a user should not be afraid to ask for additional concessions in this type of situation, particularly where the arrangement may result in significant local marketing advantages for the vendor.

To avoid the pitfalls involved in this ploy, the user should apply a basic rule: "Don't sign any contract, cancellable or not, unless it contains all necessary financial and legal considerations." (See the "We Don't Need To Write That Down, You Can Trust Me" ploy, above.) This rule is particularly important where the vendor seems to be offering something for nothing, or almost nothing.

Even where the user has fallen for this ruse and signed a "cancellable" standard form contract, a rather simple cure exists: Notwithstanding the fact that the user wants the equipment, it should cancel—or threaten to cancel—the contract. Then, once the user has the vendor's undivided attention and at least some semblance of a negotiating position, it can offer to sign a new contract that contains adequate user protection. In executing this remedy, the user should be prepared to ignore the vendor's initial wails of dismay and comments about the user's lack of honor. Once the vendor quiets down and gets over having its ploy deflated, it will probably execute the new contract. After all, the vendor wants the user to keep the system.

THE "HOT BUTTON" PLOY

Vendor marketing representatives are highly trained to sell on "hot buttons"—the four or five things that the user believes are most important. From an objective standpoint, the user's hot buttons may not be the most critical factors in the acquisition. The important point to the vendor's sales representative is that the user believes that its hot buttons are the key factors.

For example, the scenario may go like this: the vendor's marketeer says, "Mr. Bogner, our equipment can handle your problems in this manner, within these budgetary constraints; we can deliver the entire system, including conversions, within your time frame and the system will provide this performance level. Can we do business?" If the points mentioned are the main substantive concerns of the user—its "hot buttons"—more often than not there will be a "yes" response. The vendor's representative then provides the vendor's standard form agreement and says, "Great; sign here and we can have the system shipped by 5 p.m. tomorrow." The user signs because its primary concerns at that time are in the four or five areas that the vendor has so carefully met.

Unfortunately, the user often finds out later on in the relationship that, in its haste to satisfy its hot buttons, it overlooked some extremely important points (for example, it paid more than it needed to or it neglected to gain adequate contractual protection). In essence, the user finds that it got sidetracked by a bad case of tunnel vision, compliments of a great sales job by the vendor's marketing representative.

This ruse has a number of variations. In some situations, the vendor uses a financial hot button to convince the user's comptroller to sign the contract. With profits and earnings down, the financial officer is searching for additional sources of income and more effective cost controls. The vendor's marketing representative gets wind of this problem while trying to sell new equipment to the user. The vendor and a third-party leasing firm structure a lease that allows the user to trade in its existing equipment, acquire the "new and better system," and—most important to the comptroller—actually improve the user's net earnings by several cents per share during the first year of the step-transaction lease. (This vendor approach was particularly effective during the 1974–75 and 1980–81 recessions.)

When the vendor uses this ploy, the new equipment may actually be just what the user needs. On the other hand, it may not be. The problem is that the vendor is manipulating the user to acquire important, expensive equipment on the basis of an inadequate decision-making process.

Ironically, the hot button approach may not only lead to a bad acquisition, it may also fail to satisfy the very hot button that caused the user to jump into the transaction in the first place. For example, in the financial hot button scheme mentioned above, the user's independent public accountants may step in and refuse to allow the additional net income to be reported on the user's public financial statements without at least some footnote disclosure of the unusual source. Given this position, management might have preferred not to have entered into the transaction in the first place. (This unfortunate result occurred more than once during 1974–75.)

The hot button ploy is rather easy to overcome if the user's management is willing to follow one basic rule. The rule is simple, and directly related to basic consumer affairs: "Don't buy on impulse." As any retail merchandiser will readily admit, impulse buying is an important factor in retail consumer sales. Regardless of whether impulse buying is appropriate justification for purchasing a new tie or a hanging plant, it has no place in a decision to acquire a multimillion dollar system that is critical to the user's operations.

A major equipment transaction is hard enough for the user to optimize when the negotiations proceed along a carefully structured plan. The odds against the user are virtually insurmountable when hot buttons overpower the user's normal decision-making process.

THE "FORM CONTRACT" PLOY

In the form contract ploy, the vendor's marketing representative strives to make the contract the smallest, least significant part of the acquisition transaction. In implementing this approach, the vendor's salesman works to make the closing of the transaction a mere formality. The vendor's form contract—which contains the only legally-binding vendor commitments—is treated almost as an afterthought or, in the words of one marketeer, an "oh, by the way."

Although the form contract ploy can be used effectively by virtually any vendor, it is most easily employed by the large established equipment manufacturers. These firms are generally better able to develop the sense of "trust" or "relationship" that increases the user's willingness to sign the vendor's agreement with few or no questions asked. Rightfully or wrongfully, the user is more likely to act on the basis of the "business reputation" of the larger firms, thereby relegating the contract to a minor role. On the other hand, the same user is more likely to question the staying power and business ethics of the smaller, less established vendors, thereby increasing the importance of the contract when these firms are involved.

Implementing this ploy is relatively simple, once the vendor sales representative has his or her standard form agreement and a typical user. Ordinarily, the marketing representative uses one or more of the following techniques:

- Downplay the importance of the contract at every possible point. Overlook it, if possible. If the user raises the matter, postpone it (e.g., leave the contracts at the sales office, put them "in preparation" or "in typing," or promise them next week).
- Where possible, make the contract signing event very casual (e.g., "Bill, I'll drop by at 10 on Monday to get your signature on the agreement." or "Why don't we play golf Saturday morning? That way I can bring the contract along for your signature and we can have the gear shipped Tuesday.").
- Never give the user's attorney or senior management the form agreements in advance. If the user insists on getting the agreement during or before negotiations, try to keep the forms on the desk of the user's operations manager (e.g., "John, keep these until we get the deal worked out. Then I'll go with you to see your president and your attorney. That way, I can present the terms and explain the agreements.").
- If the user insists on receiving copies of the agreements in advance, try to omit some of the equipment schedules or supplements and all of the software and maintenance agreements. (Knowing users will recognize that some of the largest vendors put the most onerous terms in the supplements. Maintenance and software agreements are also famous for their "gotcha" provisions.)
- Present the form agreement at an opportune moment. Often, this will be when the marketeer has just met the user's "hot buttons," where he or she has otherwise created a good sense of urgency in the user, or where the marketeer has maximized his or her "relationship of trust" with the user.
- When the data processing manager presents the form contracts to his or her attorney (or to senior management), be sure the sales representative goes along. Ideally, have the sales representative stay while the attorney or senior manager "reviews" the contract. This approach forces a sense of urgency on the lawyer or manager, thereby limiting the detail of his or her review. In addition, it permits the sales representative to use his or her superior knowledge of the equipment and related technical terminology to confuse the attorney or manager and, in many situations, to make him or her feel adequate to challenge the vendor's position.
- Once the contract is signed by the user, never volunteer to give the user a copy. This technique downplays the importance of the contract. In addition, it keeps the user from being able to review the contract (for the first time or more carefully) and possibly revoke it between the date the user signs the agreement and the date the vendor accepts the contract at its home office. Although most vendors voluntarily give the user a copy of the agreement once it is fully accepted, a few do not. The latter group uses this technique to make it difficult for the user—or its attorney—to "check the agreement" in the event of a subsequent dispute.

This ploy can be a valuable sales tool for the vendor for any of several reasons. First, it enables the vendor to avoid the problems associated with long, drawn-out contract negotiations. If the user will accept the vendor's form agreement, the sales representative can close the transaction quickly, "while he is hot." Extensive contractual negotiations increase the risk that a user will back out of the proposed transaction. For example, the user's attorney may point out legal or business concerns that cause the user to rethink the proposal (due to legal, financial, or performance factors). At the same time, while the attorneys are negotiating the legal points, the user's comptroller may have time to reconsider his or her analysis and recognize that the user overlooked an important alternative method of obtaining a better price/performance ratio.

Second, the ploy enables the vendor to use its own standard form agreement to document an important, expensive transaction. As thoughtful users recognize, a vendor's form agreement is almost always an artfully worded document designed to give maximum protection to the vendor and minimum protection to the user. If no changes are made in this agreement, the user will be at an extreme disadvantage in the event the system malfunctions or the vendor otherwise fails to meet its marketing commitments. The form contract ploy serves as an excellent method of ensuring that the commitments made by the vendor's marketing representative are not part of the contract and, therefore, not part of the deal.

Even if the user insists on having the vendor's form agreement "reviewed by counsel," this ploy can help the vendor minimize its contractual commitments. By treating the contract almost as an afterthought, the vendor's marketeer can virtually lock up the sales campaign before giving the agreement to the user or its attorney. If the sales representative is adept, the user will be fully and firmly committed to the acquisition before the user's attorney is ever brought into the picture. The user will then be on the sales rep's side, urging the user's counsel not to "blow the deal" by "rewriting the whole agreement." When the user's management has this vendor-created sense of urgency, counsel seldom has the time (or the strength and patience) to effect meaningful changes in the vendor's agreement. As a result, the user receives some contractual protection, but the vendor still remains in a superior legal position.

Third, the ploy enables the vendor's sales representative to separate the negative impact of the vendor agreement from the positive impact of his or her marketing pitch. As suggested above, vendor agreements contain little for the user except disclaimers of vendor liability. These disclaimers generally conflict with the marketeer's assertions of "We're the best people in the world, with the best equipment and maintenance anywhere, and we will do anything for you, our valued customer." Consequently, the sales representative's job is made easier if the user does not have a copy of the vendor contract at the outset. If the user does obtain a copy of the contract (for example, by special request or because of an earlier transaction), the vendor's representative can still obtain similar but less effective benefits by downplaying the importance of the contract by such asides as "Oh, we'll get to that later" or "Let's leave that one for the lawyers." In each case, the basic goal is the same: Keep the user's attention focused on the sales pitch, not on the contract; don't let the user look for the marketeer's representation in the agreement. (After all, it probably won't be there.)

Avoiding the form contract ploy is relatively easy, if the user is willing to follow a few simple rules. First, the user should always obtain copies of all relevant vendor contracts, supplements, and schedules (including equipment, software, and maintenance agreements) at the very outset of negotiations. Of course, if the user employs a good RFP technique, the vendor will have supplied copies of all such documentation as part of its initial proposal.

Second, the user must ensure that all participants on its negotiating team review the vendor's contracts before negotiations begin (which means before the vendor's marketeer makes any serious presentations to the user's staff). It is essential for all members of the user's negotiating team—operations, legal, financial, and senior management—to understand just what commitments the vendor has and has not made in its proposed form contract. For example, this technique permits the user's operations manager to interrupt the vendor's sales presentation and ask, "Will you place that precise commitment in the written agreement?"

Third, the user's legal staff should review the vendor's form agreements and prepare all necessary changes and addenda (or an alternative agreement) as far as possible in advance of the proposed contract signing. Even if the user's attorneys cannot yet draft all relevant provisions (due to existence of continuing negotiations on substantive matters), this approach gives the user's lawyers time to "neutralize" and "counteract" the pro-vendor form agreement. This process of neutralizing the onerous effect of the pro-vendor provisions in the form agreement, and drafting the dozens of pro-user provisions required to counteract it, can be a painstaking and time-consuming task, particularly if the user's attorney does not have an extensive "data base" or form file of pro-user provisions. The user should never be rushed into signing anything—much less the vendor's form agreement—without adequate review by legal counsel. In this regard, the user must avoid the vendor's sense of urgency ploys and keep the acquisition in proper perspective. In effect, the user's negotiators must remember that neither the nation nor their company is likely to fail if their attorney takes a few extra days to review and redraft a vendor form agreement. On the other hand, rushing into the transaction, on the wings of the vendor's biased form agreement, may cost the user thousands, if not millions, of dollars—and it may also cost the user negotiators their careers.

THE "UNFORTUNATELY, I'LL HAVE TO GET ANY CHANGES APPROVED BY CORPORATE" PLOY

This ploy is particularly effective when used by a major vendor against an inexperienced user. In the basic version of this ploy, the vendor's marketeer indicates that, as much as he or she would like to meet the user's demands, the matters desired by the user must be approved by "corporate"—a difficult and time-consuming task. The ploy places substantial pressure on the user by forcing it to "sell the vendor." If the user fails to meet the necessary burden of proof, the vendor wins.

Experienced vendor marketing personnel generally use this ploy in one or more of the following situations:

- The user wants to write things down;
- The user wants to change the vendor's form agreement;
- The local vendor marketing representative is over-committing (or has already over-committed); or
- The marketing representative wants to test the user's seriousness or desire for real negotiations.

This ploy has a number of advantages for the vendor representative. First, it is logical and, therefore, relatively easy to use. Second, it can be used to enhance other "sense of urgency" ploys. Third, the ploy can be employed to present the marketeer as a "good guy" or a "nonnegotiator." In essence, the vendor's representative emphasizes his or her own willingness to do everything possible for the user, but continually stresses the problems in dealing with the vendor's corporate or legal departments. The marketeer stresses, "I don't want to go to the well too many times, so let's make sure we have all your demands [with emphasis on "all" and "demands" to stress the user's unreasonableness] before I stick my neck out for you." Finally, the ploy can be used to bolster the vendor's trust or relationship oriented ploys. Again the vendor stresses the problems of getting things through "corporate" or "legal," but readily offers an oral or local commitment of support, resources, or special terms. By using hurt, confused body language, the vendor's representative can convey ideas such as, "You obviously don't trust me, despite our fine personal relationship, or you wouldn't make me try to get these demands through corporate, especially since I've already told you we can handle these matters at the branch level."

The effectiveness of this ploy can be traced to one of three characteristics. First, the ploy constantly forces the user to justify its negotiating position. In the process, the user's negotiators waste time and professional talent on relatively minor points and, in the process, are slowly worn down.

Second, the ploy allows the vendor to hide behind the shield of its "standard way of doing business." The user is therefore placed in a defensive position and must constantly ask whether this position really is unnecessarily onerous, as alleged by the vendor. This uncertainty is likely to be particularly strong where the user and/or its professional advisors have little experience in sophisticated equipment negotiations. Even experienced user lawyers find it difficult to continue to stand up to allegations by the vendor's marketing representative and the user's management that the user's attorneys are "blowing the deal."

Third, the ploy allows the vendor to emphasize that the vendor's standard form agreement is the easiest, fastest, and best way for the user to obtain the necessary equipment, "especially since our contract has been accepted without change by Fortune 500 companies considerably larger than yours." (Unfortunately, the vendor's representative may be telling the truth, but that's no reason to compound the error.)

Fourth, the ploy causes the user to disclose its entire "shopping list" at the outset to keep the nice-guy vendor representative from having to "endure the pain" of going to corporate or legal more than once. As a result, the user loses effective "salami" or "slice at a time" negotiating strategies and the vendor has time to quietly plan ways to maneuver around the concessions desired by the user. In addition, the user finds it strategically difficult to add to its shopping list during later negotiations. (The marketeer invariably says, "You told me I had all your demands. Do you mean I've got to go back to corporate with this?" And, the inexperienced user often gives in.)

Finally, the ploy enables the vendor to use the benefits from the "limited authority" negotiating technique. With this tactic, the vendor's representative can probe the depths of the user's concerns without divulging the vendor's final position. In addition, the marketeer can use a silent "bad guy" to be responsible for the bad news that the user's position will not be accepted (thereby effectively implementing the "good guy, bad guy" tactic and also preserving the local "relationship").

Despite these problems, this ploy can be effectively dealt with by an experienced user. The following suggestions may be helpful.

First, the user should recognize the ploy for what it is: an excellent way to sign up a user quickly, with little hassle and few formal vendor commitments.

Second, the user must recall that "if it's not part of the contract, it's not part of the deal." The user should refuse to accept side letters and "local" vendor promises in lieu of formal contractual agreements.

Third, the user should keep in mind that most major equipment acquisitions involve sizeable amounts of money and serious business risks for the user. Anything that involves such factors deserves to be fully studied, negotiated, and documented. Haste does make waste, especially in major equipment acquisitions.

Fourth, the user should prioritize its negotiating shopping list and plan its negotiating strategy. The user's negotiators should ensure that they are not tricked into spreading out their entire wish list at the first negotiating session.

Fifth, the user should remember the dangers of permitting the vendor to use the limited authority ploy. The user should not negotiate if the vendor will not provide the necessary senior management and legal personnel, or at least direct access to such individuals.

Sixth, the user should use a good RFP process and make certain that the vendor agrees to provide deliverable commitments in the bid proposal. At the same time, the user should generally avoid giving away its entire shopping list by including a GSA-type standard user agreement with its RFP. (See Chapter 5.)

Seventh, the user should make clear that it has no intention of signing, or even seriously considering, the vendor's standard form agreement. Wherever the vendor's marketing representative asserts that something is covered in the standard vendor agreement, the user should ask that the marketeer quote the applicable provision, without self-serving (and non-binding) explanations, and then ask how the provision involved provides adequate protection to the user.

If the user's negotiators remain calm and recognize the vendor's attempt to use this ploy, they may be able to turn it against the vendor. In this technique, the user must insist that the vendor's sales representative "get clearance from corporate." This approach can provide the following benefits.

First, the vendor will be forced to increase the level of corporate and legal involvement in the negotiations, possibly involving high level vendor personnel who can offer alternatives and concessions not known to, or available from, local marketing personnel.

Second, the user can better determine the final negotiating authority on the vendor's side.

Third, any concessions gained with "corporate" or "legal" vendor approval will have more validity, thus improving the likelihood of appropriate contractual coverage and actual vendor performance.

Fourth, negotiations will be placed on a more formal and businesslike basis, thereby reducing the effectiveness of the marketeer's "personal relationship" tactics.

Finally, the user will be able to turn around the vendor's "sense of urgency" ploys by indicating that, in light of the short time, the vendor should bring its top lawyer and contract signer down for the negotiations. As a result, these vendor representatives will be on site and in a frame of mind to address reasonable user demands. Alternatively, the vendor's marketeer will be forced to admit that the deadline is not so urgent after all and that alternative negotiations will have to be arranged later on when the proper vendor personnel can be made available.

THE "TRADE-IN CREDIT" PLOY

The trade-in credit ploy is generally employed against a user that is concerned about the additional expense that may be involved if the system being acquired must later be traded in or upgraded during the term of the lease or the useful life of the purchased equipment. The ploy is very simple: the vendor merely emphasizes that trade-in credits will be made available to the user if the user elects to trade the equipment in on other equipment manufactured or supplied by the same vendor.

This ploy is particularly effective for several reasons. First, it is based on reason and financial substance: a valid trade-in credit can be a financially attractive benefit to the user. In contrast, most of the other vendor ploys discussed in this chapter are based more on interpersonal relationships and emotion than on substance. For example, consider the sense of urgency involved in the "There's a Price Increase Coming" ploy or the user naivete and trust involved in the "You're Getting Our Best Price" ploy. Second, the trade-in credit ploy can quiet user concern about being "locked in" by a long-term lease or purchase. The financial value offered by the trade-in credit can make the user's financial staff less concerned about the expense of the transaction "because there's an out if we need to upgrade." Similarly, the trade-in credit can reduce the line manager's concern about future state-of-the-art developments. By giving everyone an apparent "out" to go to new equipment, the ploy allows the vendor to lower current system costs by proposing a longer lease than the user might otherwise be willing to accept.

This ploy is dangerous to the user for several reasons. First, the ploy may cause the user to overlook the basic question of whether it wants to be "locked in" to one vendor. To be sure, a real trade-in credit may offer the user flexibility in upgrading and moving to new state-of-the-art systems, but the credit is generally available only if the new equipment is manufactured or supplied by the original vendor. For example, a legitimate Vendor A trade-in credit may help the user upgrade to a new or larger Vendor A product, but it may not do much if the user desires to switch to a new Vendor B product. (Some trade-in credits offered by third-party leasing companies may allow the user to change from one manufacturer to another. However, the same leasing firm must be used and, as outlined in Chapter 10, this limitation may give rise to some "funny numbers.") As suggested above, the ploy may also help the vendor's marketeer "lock in" the user with a longer lease or an outright purchase. In this situation, the offered trade-in credit makes the user more willing to accept the longer lease term or the purchase.

The second basic danger in the trade-in credit ploy is that the credit may not be properly documented in writing. If the user is particularly naive, the vendor will not even offer to place language guaranteeing the credits into the contract. (In this approach, the vendor is likely to emphasize the "vendor's trade-in policy" as if the policy were etched in granite.) When this occurs, of course, the "credits" only exist through the continued generosity of the vendor.

If the user follows basic contracting principles, of course, the vendor will include the basic credit provision in the agreement. However, the vendor's first choice will be to use extremely vague language that does little to pin down the amount of the "guaranteed" credit. For example, the provision may simply state, "If Customer wishes to upgrade the equipment at any time during the term of this lease, Customer may return the equipment to the Vendor, as provided herein, and receive a trade-in credit to be used on any other equipment purchased or leased from the Vendor, in accordance with Vendor's then existing trade-in policies." The problem here is that only the vendor has any control over what the "then-existing trade-in policies" will be.

If the user is more sophisticated and demands more specificity, the vendor's marketing representative may finally "give in" by offering a "guaranteed" trade-in credit "formula." (This fairly minimal concession is often given only after substantial gamesmanship in which the vendor's marketeer uses body language, telephone calls to "corporate" or "legal," or false concern to emphasize the alleged importance of allowing the user to win this point.) Although this formula may at first appear to be a firm guarantee, two problems generally exist. First, the "guaranteed formula" may be more flexible than it at first appears. This flexibility for the vendor, and the concurrent risk for the user, generally results from adding one or two hedge phrases, such as "pursuant to vendor's policies," to an otherwise complicated and valid formula. Second, and perhaps more likely, the credit will eventually be applied against a purchase or lease price that is above the then-market rate. This point represents the critical danger, and no user should seriously value any trade-in credit without being aware of this risk.

This key problem can be best demonstrated with an example. Acme Company, the user, acquires a system from Vendor, Inc. by purchase or third-party lease. A detailed trade-in credit formula is included in the agreement. Later Acme decides to trade the system in on the new vendor machine. At that point, the formula is used and a trade-in credit of approximately $200,000 is calculated (about 20% of the purchase price of the new equipment). Being somewhat experienced in equipment negotiations, Acme is aware that Vendor has been routinely discounting the system by approximately ten percent (10%). Putting 20 and 10 together, Acme confidently asks for a total discount and trade-in credit of 30%. "Impossible," explains Vendor's sales representative. "We are not allowed to mix discounts and trade-in credits. See, it says right here in the credit formula that the credit will be applied to Vendor's published prices for the new equipment. After all, we have to have some fixed amount against which to apply the credit."

In an even more frequent variation on this example, Acme Company is not even aware of what discount, if any, Vendor may be offering on the system. Consequently, Acme pays the full list price for the system, or perhaps list less a very small discount, and Vendor's marketeer proudly explains that Acme is receiving the full benefit of the trade-in credit. Assuming Vendor is offering some discount on the system at the time (a practice that varies widely among vendors and within one vendor from time to time), one of two things is happening: either Acme is getting the standard discount (without knowing it) and not getting the trade-in credit, or Acme is getting the trade-in credit but not getting the discount routinely being offered to others.

Despite the risks that may be involved in a vendor's offer of trade-in credits, the user can take several steps to "lock in" the value being offered by the vendor. First, in assessing the vendor's proposal, the user should place only limited value on the offer of trade-in credits. To be sure, the credits should be sought and tied down if they are available. But the user should recognize that the ultimate value of the benefits may be somewhat questionable, if, for example, the user desires to switch vendors or the risks set forth above cannot be minimized. This recognition by the user is particularly important where the user is comparing alternative proposals from brokers or third-party sources that may not be able to offer trade-in credits.

Second, the user should make every effort to see that the trade-in credit provision in the contract is as specific as possible. All "hedge" provisions should be eliminated, and the final language should be approved by the user's procurement manager and legal counsel.

Third, the user should ensure that the credit provision specifically provides that the trade-in credit will be fully available despite the application of any other discount from or credit against the base or list price. A "most favored user" provision may provide some protection in this area. Additional protection will also result from careful consideration of the language used to describe the "base" or "list" price against which the credit will be applied.

Finally, when the time comes to apply the trade-in credits to a new acquisition, the user should take the approach of the experienced new car buyer: Ignore the trade-in credits initially and negotiate the best possible discount without the credits. (In this step, accurate information from professional negotiators and other users concerning currently available vendor discounts can be invaluable.) Then and only then should the user consider or subtract the trade-in credits. The user should thereafter negotiate each amount separately, to the extent possible under the vendor's alleged policies. If the vendor refuses to permit application of both discount and trade-in credit, the user should protest loudly and, if at all possible, call off the negotiations (for the time being, of course; like the tax collector, the vendor will be back). Substantial user complaints about the vendor's failure to keep its word can be effective at this point, as can legalistic allegations of "fraud in the inducement."

If the vendor consistently refuses to allow the user the benefit of both the discount and the credit, the user should seriously explore the possibility of disposing of the old equipment on the open market, in lieu of pressing for the trade-in credits, and then demanding the full vendor discount on the system. (This alternative is generally considered by sophisticated users in any event.) If practical, this approach may lower the net cost of the new system to the user and, at the same time, prevent the vendor from receiving a veritable windfall by refusing to allow the user the benefit of both the standard discount and the previously earned trade-in credits. Even if this approach is not practical, the user that seriously threatens to follow this alternative may find the vendor more willing to reconsider its previous "policy" against permitting the use of both a discount and a trade-in credit. In this regard, the user should remember that some vendors are seriously interested in weakening or destroying the third-party market in their used equipment. Direct sale of the old equipment by the user not only threatens to reduce the vendor's profit on the user's new acquisition; it also threatens to reduce or eliminate the vendor's potential profit on a possible sale or lease by the vendor to the party that purchases the user's old system.

THE "RIGHT TO SUBSTITUTE AND OTHER SHELL GAMES" PLOY

One of the more popular uses of this ploy involved the market for used IBM 370/158 computer systems during 1978. However, the ploy has been used effectively in connection with other computer systems, and other equipment, both before and after the example referenced in this discussion.

Despite the reduction in used 370/158 prices that occurred in 1977, user demand for 370/158's exceeded the available supply. IBM was unable to provide 158's on delivery schedules acceptable to many users and, of course, the delivery timeframes for the then new 303x series were even longer.

As a result, many users with increasing IBM processing requirements turned to the used market for 370/158's. In the used equipment sector, this increased user demand escalated prices on 158's to just under new equipment levels (discounted to reflect the ITC and free-maintenance-for-one-year benefits that could then be obtained with new equipment).

The increased demand for 158's (coupled with the long delivery timeframes for 303x systems) also inflated the premiums being offered for 158 and 303x delivery positions. Despite IBM's previously announced policies designed to eliminate the "futures market" in IBM delivery positions, methods of evading these restrictions had already surfaced, particularly where the positions were held by larger lessors or users.

As the prices and premiums for 370/158 equipment increased dramatically, brokers and dealers flocked into the market to enjoy the profits involved. With significant amounts being thrown at anyone even claiming to have a 370/158, the temptation for sellers to be overly optimistic about their ability to find a 158 became very strong.

Of course, knowledgeable users required that a broker or dealer demonstrate the availability of a given system. This was and is generally accomplished by having the broker or dealer supply the serial number and present location of the proposed system. (In ordinary times, this approach generally scares off the brokers that have not actually tied down a system. This technique also allows the user to determine whether competing brokers or dealers are making proposals on the same or different equipment.)

However, in the 370/158 market during early 1978, this approach was not adequate. Encouraged by the high profit potential involved, some otherwise reputable brokers and dealers utilized a new variation of the old "now you see it, now you don't" shell game. In essence, they began selling (actually, committing to sell) the same equipment twice.

The ploy they used works like this. Early in the negotiations, the vendor gives in to the user's demand that the vendor supply the serial number for the particular equipment (a 370/158 in the example) being proposed. The vendor may also encourage the user to visit the current installation site and inspect the maintenance log for the equipment. At this point, the user begins to relax and forget about the possibility that the vendor may be offering a phantom system.

The problem arises when the vendor supplies the contract (or letter of intent) for the previously identified equipment. The agreement lists the particular equipment by serial number, but adds that the vendor may elect to supply "substitute" or "equivalent" equipment. This right of substitution is generally set out as inconspicuously as possible (often parenthetically or in an asterisked footnote). Once the vendor has the right to substitute, it can continue to offer the previously identified equipment to the highest bidder and, in the meantime, search for a "substitute" machine to supply to the first user.

Unfortunately, the first user may have no idea that its system has been provided to another customer until it is too late to obtain a replacement from another source. If the vendor has been careful, the user's contract will not contain firm delivery dates or, alternatively, will contain delivery dates but no liquidated damages or other serious consequences for vendor nonperformance. The vendor will continue to promise a substitute system in the near future and, because of the continued shortage of available systems, the user will have no real alternative. Moreover, the vendor will probably have a substantial deposit that the user readily offered months earlier when the vendor offered to supply the serial-number-identified system.

The substitution of a "phantom" system can be particularly dangerous where the user has negotiated the contract on the basis of the vendor's initial promise to supply a particular serial-number-identified system. For example, the user may be more willing to provide a large deposit to "tie up" specifically identified equipment. In addition, the user may be less concerned about optimizing contractual protection in such areas as delivery dates and vendor default. Moreover, although the user may demand the right to inspect the serial-number-identified equipment (perhaps within ten days after executing the agreement), it may not provide for similar rights with respect to any substitute equipment. In effect, the user may negotiate a contract for a specifically identified machine rather than a contract for a machine that the vendor merely hopes to find in the marketplace. The two agreements are seldom the same.

To minimize the risks involved in this ploy, a user must take additional steps to "tie up" the promised equipment and the vendor. These steps must be taken regardless of whether the user believes it is dealing with a "reputable" broker or dealer. The following matters should be covered in the binding user/vendor agreement and in any letter of intent or deposit receipt:

- The equipment should be identified by serial number and present location.
- The vendor should represent and warrant either that the vendor is the present owner of the identified equipment, free and clear of any and all liens (subject to specific exceptions listed), or that the vendor has the unqualified and binding right to buy the identified equipment. These warranties should be made applicable not only as of the date the user/vendor agreement is signed, but at all times between the date the agreement is signed and the date the equipment is accepted by (and, if applicable, title passes to) the user.
- The vendor should represent and warrant that the identified equipment is not, and will not be, under contract for sale, lease, or supply to any person or firm other than the user. As suggested above, this warranty should be continuous between the date of the user/vendor agreement and the date of user acceptance.
- The vendor should agree that no equipment may be substituted for the specifically identified equipment without the express prior written consent of the user. Alternative inspection and acceptance standards should be imposed for any such approved substitute.
- The agreement should contain meaningful delivery and performance dates, with corresponding penalties for vendor nonperformance. Even if user protection is relaxed where the vendor actually supplies the identified machine, substantial penalties should be imposed in the event the vendor provides a substitute machine and fails to meet delivery or acceptance criteria.

THE "WE CAN'T DO IT FOR YOU BECAUSE THE GSA WON'T LET US" PLOY

In this ploy, the vendor's sales representative cuts off the user's efforts to optimize a particular aspect of an acquisition by simply saying, "Look, we would really like to do that for you, but our GSA contracts with the federal government say we can't give anyone, even a favored customer like your firm, a better deal than we give to them. So our hands are tied; as much as we would like to do it for you, we just can't. As you can suspect, we wouldn't want to break a contractual commitment to the U.S. Government which is, of course, our biggest customer."

This ploy is simple and effective for several reasons. First, few users understand—or try to understand—what the vendor's General Services Administration (GSA) commitments really are. Second, few users seriously want to ask the vendor to break a contractual agreement with Uncle Sam. (After all, it's almost un-American!) Third, most users have little or no idea of the legal methods a vendor can use to get around its GSA commitments to offer special benefits to a business customer. Finally, many users feel that they have obviously done a good job of negotiating if they have even asked for a benefit beyond those offered to the federal government; consequently, they back off to a compromise position as soon as the GSA ploy is raised.

The important point to remember is that the GSA "shield" is often used by vendor marketing personnel purely as a negotiating tactic, without regard to whether or not the concessions could actually be provided. Indeed, most vendor commercial marketing people do not even know what specific concessions their company has made to the federal government. Government contracting is traditionally the responsibility of a separate vendor division, such as the "Federal Equipment Division." Although the vendor's attorneys and senior marketing personnel may be trained in the vendor's GSA standards (and a few GSA clauses may be included in the salesman's "optional clause" notebook), vendors generally prefer to keep these concessions away from their business account sales force, lest the clauses find their way into too many commercial agreements.

The best way to counter the GSA ploy is to employ the four keys to success in any negotiations: know your opponent's position; get the facts and use them to your advantage; listen carefully; and maintain a high aspiration level.

A good response to the GSA ploy is simply to ask the vendor to supply a copy of the actual contractual terms and conditions given to the GSA. (The standard, blank GSA purchase and rental agreements are public documents generally available from government contracting offices.) Following this step has several advantages. First, it puts the vendor's sales representative off guard and on the defensive (he or she may even be exposed for previously handing out erroneous or misleading information). Second, it causes the marketeer to realize that, unlike other users, this user will not sit still for hollow representations. Third, it may supply the user with the desired GSA language which in itself may be an excellent provision to incorporate into the user's agreement.

Regardless of whether the user obtains the vendor's precise GSA commitments, it should ask the vendor, "Are you representing that you can't give us anything better than you give the government, or are you offering to give us the same deal that you have agreed to give the government?" Most vendors do not like to answer this one, and the technique can be very effective for the user. First, if the vendor refuses to make concessions similar to those given the GSA, the user can focus on "why?" (This approach can be particularly devastating to the vendor's consistent assurances that the user's account is valued highly by the vendor.) Second, if the vendor agrees to grant its basic GSA commitments to the user, the user will at least obtain significant concessions above and beyond the vendor's standard form contract (and also above most user drafted agreements).

The user's real goal, however, should be to legally optimize the acquisition agreement without regard to the vendor's GSA commitments. Three basic techniques are available.

First, the user should listen to exactly what the vendor is saying about its GSA commitments. In most instances, the vendor's GSA ploy is factually based upon a "most favored nation" provision in the vendor/GSA contract that says that the vendor will not grant any other user in a similar transaction a better deal than the government received in its transaction. If this is the case in the user's situation, the easiest approach may be to make the user's transaction unique. In effect, this approach keeps the user's "special" transaction from being "similar" to the vendor/GSA transaction.

Many vendors and users type into the agreement the fact that the particular acquisition involves a "test site" or the "first ABC/999 installed in _____ area" or configured in a certain manner, and so on. The key is to make the user's specific transaction different. Most vendor attorneys and senior marketing people are well aware of this technique. If they are pressed hard enough and they want the sale badly enough, they can probably provide the language necessary to establish the transaction as "unique."

Second, the user should remember that the most favored nation concept has two sides: benefit to the user and consideration or payment to the vendor. If the user needs a particular concession that the vendor claims cannot be provided free, "due to GSA restrictions," the user should look for some soft dollar consideration to compensate the vendor for the benefit. The essence of this approach is to "pay" for the benefit with consideration that does not adversely impact the user. For example, one major equipment manufacturer implements this approach with a clause that provides that the vendor has the right to utilize the user's system for tests, time sales, demonstrations, and site tours (sometimes adding language that the vendor's time will be equal to the user's time).

The major risk in this approach is that the user's "soft dollar" consideration may turn out to be very expensive if the vendor chooses to strictly enforce the user's commitment. For example, most of the soft dollar "demonstration site" clauses offered by vendors do not include any restrictions on the vendor's use of the user's system. The clauses are purposefully vague, in order to allow the vendor to convince GSA auditors that the value of the "demonstration site" far outweighs the value of the benefit provided to the user. This vagueness can backfire if the user and vendor have a falling out and the vendor demands to use the equipment to the maximum extent permitted by the language of the agreement.

The best protection for the user in this area is a soft dollar clause drafted by the user's counsel. That provision should strictly limit the vendor's use of the equipment to times and dates permitted by the user or, at least, to specified periods when excess or unused machine time is expected to be available. The provision should also include adequate language to protect the user from liability or loss of proprietary information that may result from site tours, time sales, or demonstration use. (Reference to the indemnification and liability waiver provisions in the vendor's standard agreement may offer interesting insight for this purpose.)

Third, the user should ask the vendor to supply specified services or equipment support with a guarantee that the work will be completed within a maximum number of hours or a maximum price. For example, if the user needs 2,000 electronic cash registers installed and converted to its new system, it might have the vendor agree to perform the installation and conversion at the normal hourly rate for its programming or systems support people. (So far, no GSA problems.) In addition, the user might have the contract include a representation by the vendor that under no circumstances will the installation and conversion work take more than 50 hours of vendor time, but, if it does, the vendor will complete the work at no additional expense to the user. (This technique is particularly popular with a major equipment manufacturer that is well known for refusing to negotiate on prices.) Here again, however, the user should be sure that its own attorney drafts the clause; the vendor's draft may not really commit the vendor to make the conversion. (Many such clauses merely provide that the vendor will "assist" the user in the conversion.)

Some users may feel that the GSA evasion techniques suggested above are unethical or immoral because they essentially make the user a party to defrauding the Federal government. That point should not be overlooked. But these same users should recognize that in many, many cases the vendor may write up a transaction internally on a financial basis totally different from that shown in the user/vendor contract. As any experienced equipment marketeer knows, a business user may receive a greater discount or a better package than the government gets, but the vendor can write the transaction up internally to show that the vendor is getting far greater consideration than it received from the government. This practice is by no means unusual in the industry, although many users do not even recognize that they are or could be benefiting from it.

The important point is that the GSA ploy should be exposed for exactly what it is in most cases: a highly effective vendor marketing technique. Users that wish to do so can benefit by utilizing the avoidance tactics mentioned above. Users that prefer not to beat the government can still use these techniques during the negotiating stage to draw out the vendor and determine its real interests and negotiating parameters. For example, if a vendor is willing to provide a benefit through a GSA avoidance provision, the vendor may be willing to offer a benefit of equal value through a concesssion that would not conflict with the vendor's GSA commitments. Whatever approach is ultimately adopted, the user should have the information necessary to make an intelligent decision on whether to use a GSA avoidance provision. In the final analysis, the user can make a decision concerning the advisability of using a GSA avoidance technique only if the user understands the GSA ploy and the methods that can be used to deflate it.

Most of the issues involved in executing and avoiding the GSA ploy are also present in a related marketing effort based upon the federal antitrust laws, or upon the vendor's previous granting of "most favored nation" commitments to various users. In all three cases, the vendor's approach is the same: the vendor would be happy to grant the desired price or other concession to the user, but the vendor cannot do so without violating: (a) prior GSA commitments; or (b) various antitrust restrictions on predatory and other unfair pricing practices; or (c) the most favored nation provisions in the vendor's agreements with other users.

In each case, the vendor's concern may be real and valid rather than mere sales puffery. However, in each case, the user's answer should also be the same: Most of these problems can be disposed of, or at least alleviated, by making the user's transaction unique. As suggested above, vendor attorneys have substantial experience in drafting an agreement or configuring a transaction in a manner that will create the degree of uniqueness necessary to preclude problems in any of these three areas. The user, however, must be prepared to exert the negotiating pressure required to cause the vendor to grant the desired concession and document the transaction accordingly.

THE "WE CAN'T DO IT FOR YOU BECAUSE WE'D BE SETTING A PRECEDENT" PLOY

This popular ploy is often used to counter virtually any user request for a vendor concession. In this ploy, the vendor's sales representative explains that, if the vendor granted the user's request, the vendor would be "setting a precedent" and would be forced to offer similar concessions to all (or at least some) other users.

In some respects, this vendor approach is similar to the "We Can't Do It for You Because the GSA Won't Let Us" ploy. Indeed, the "We Can't Do It for You Because We Would Be Setting a Precedent" ploy is a somewhat more ambiguous extension of the negotiating strategy inherent in the GSA ploy.

Because the "Setting a Precedent" ploy is so ambiguous and flexible, it is particularly hard to rebut or overcome. The essence of the problem is that most users do not have the information necessary to challenge the vendor claim that forms the heart of the ploy. In effect, the vendor's representative states, "We've never given that concession to anyone and, if we gave it to you in this situation, we'd then have to offer it to everyone who asked for it." In the first place, the user does not know whether the vendor has or has not granted the same or a similar concession to another user. In addition, the user does not know whether the vendor really would have a "precedent" problem if it did determine to grant a new concession in the present negotiations. (For example, the vendor may view all such prior "concessions" to be negotiable items in all subsequent acquisitions. On the other hand, the vendor may have a policy of not viewing any prior concession as a "precedent" in any subsequent transaction.)

Because the user lacks the information mentioned above, it is effectively at the mercy of the vendor from a negotiating standpoint. The user must either accept the vendor's statements as true or reject them as false, with little or no opportunity for independent verification.

Despite this basic problem, several user strategies can be used to counter this vendor ploy. Among these are the following.

First, the user should demand that the vendor provide a list of all other concessions or "precedents" previously granted by the vendor. In this approach, the user should show apparent interest in the vendor's so-called "problem" of precedent setting concessions. The user's negotiator should ask the vendor's sales representative, "You mean you would really have a precedent problem if you granted this concession? Does your firm really take things so seriously? Do you keep track of this kind of thing?" Usually, the vendor's representative will unsuspectingly pick up the friendly challenge and go to great lengths to explain the vendor's supposed "policy" in this area, perhaps with a few references to previous "precedent" problems. At an appropriate point in this explanation, the user should respond by asking the vendor's representative for a detailed list of all prior vendor concessions or "precedents." In effect, the user should explain, "Look, you said you kept track of this kind of thing and that your company has a policy of granting any prior concession to any user that subsequently asks for it. Before we can negotiate further, we're certainly going to need a list of all available previous concessions."

At this point, the vendor's representative is likely to counter with some denial, expression of disbelief, or claim of ignorance. If the marketeer claims not to see the logic of the user's reasoning, then it may be beneficial for the user to press for the original concession on the ground that the vendor does not (after all) have a "precedent" problem or any related policies. On the other hand, if the vendor's representative claims that he does not have a list of prior concessions, or that he "doesn't think" any such prior concessions have been granted (a very unlikely event), then the user should respond by calling off the negotiations until the vendor can produce a knowledgeable representative who does have this type of information. In this regard, the user's negotiator might observe, "How can you possibly talk about precedents and what you can or can't do if you don't even have a list of what prior concessions have been granted?" Most major equipment vendors have preapproved contract changes and addenda. However, a user must have a strong negotiating posture in order to access these materials.

Second, the user should threaten to obtain the precedents from other sources. In a variation on the above approach, the user can simply break off negotiations in order to research and obtain information concerning the vendor's prior concessions from other parties. The most likely sources of information about prior vendor concessions are other users, user groups, specialized publications, and professional negotiators and advisors. Of course, the user should preferably access these sources before the negotiations begin. However, deadlocking the negotiations in order to access these sources on an immediate basis can still be effective. Moreover, the mere threat by a user to break off negotiations for this purpose can be an important user strategy even if the user does not attempt to collect meaningful information.

Third, if the vendor's representative insists that the vendor has never granted a particular concession or series of concessions, the user should consider asking the vendor to include a "most favored nation" provision in the vendor/user agreement. (See Appendix B.) As noted above, this language essentially states that, if the vendor has granted any user a better price or concession during a specified period (generally beginning before the execution date and continuing for some stated time thereafter), then the vendor will automatically provide (or at least offer) the same concession to the user. This type of provision can be made to apply to the entire vendor/user agreement or to only certain designated sections of the agreement. The latter approach can be particularly useful in countering the vendor's claim that a specific provision requested by the user would create an unacceptable precedent.

One additional caveat should be noted. Some vendor sales representatives will offer to avoid the supposed "precedent" problem by suggesting that the requested concession be granted through some form of "side letter" signed by the vendor representative or branch manager. Regrettably, many users jump at this "opportunity" and agree to the side letter approach. In general, the vendor's marketeer has a very good reason (from his standpoint) for not wanting to put a side letter concession into the formal contract. Usually, the reason involves the fact that the vendor's contract review group will never see the side letter and/or the fact that the side letter will have no legal or binding effect on the vendor.

Virtually all vendor agreements have an "integration" provision that states the contract itself is the only binding agreement among the parties, and that no other documents or promises will be binding unless formally incorporated into the contract or executed as an amendment to it. Thus, the side letter may not have any legal effect unless it is incorporated by reference in the contract. Moreover, most vendor sales representatives do not have actual authority to bind the vendor legally. As a result, most vendor/user contracts are executed by a vendor vice president or similar officer rather than by the marketing contact. In contrast, most vendor side letters are executed by a vendor employee who does not have legal authority to sign such a commitment on behalf of the vendor.

If the side letter approach is the only real alternative available to a user, the user should follow two strict rules. First, the side letter should be formally incorporated into, and attached to, the primary written agreement or a written amendment thereto. Second, if at all possible, the side letter should be signed or countersigned by the same vendor officer that signs the vendor/user agreement or amendment on behalf of the vendor.

THE "THAT'S NOT THE WAY WE FIGURED THE DEAL" PLOY

This effective vendor ploy is perhaps best explained by using an example of the technique in action. Consider the following scenario:

After extensive preliminary presentations, demonstrations, and some early negotiations, the vendor's representative drops off the form agreement for signature or the usual cursory review by the user's attorney. The user and its counsel review the contract and present the vendor with a list of changes and additional provisions.

Upon receipt of the user's changes and provisions, the vendor's sales representative immediately springs the ploy. Alternatively, the marketeer graciously accepts the user's list, observes that the list will undoubtedly cause delays and problems, and leaves. In this approach, the vendor's representative triggers the ploy later, often after some delay to increase the user's sense of urgency.

Regardless of the timing involved, the ploy itself is based upon a very simple response by the vendor's representative: "Hey, this just isn't in the deal. This is not the way we put the deal together when we initially priced it." With some elaboration, the marketeer's response can be expanded to include the following: "When we initially presented our proposal to you, you said you were in a hurry. We've done everything possible to accommodate you. But we've based everything up to now on our standard documentation. Now you're telling us we have to redraft our entire agreement and spend days, and thousands of dollars worth of lawyer time, to finish this off. It's just not in the deal, at least not at the price we've quoted you. Listen, all these provisions you've suggested increase our legal risks and our cost of sales. We can't do all this and give you the price and terms we've quoted. How much is all this really worth to you; I mean, how much are you really willing to pay to add all this unnecessary material to the contract?"

The essence of the vendor's position is based upon several points. First, the user should feel guilty for "springing" its "lengthy" list of contractual changes on the vendor "at the last minute." Second, the contractual changes and additions suggested by the user will take time and money to negotiate (both for the user and the vendor). Third, the changes and additions will weaken the protection afforded to the vendor by its form agreement, thereby increasing the vendor's risk of liability in the event of nonperformance of its obligations under the agreement. Fourth, because of the vendor's greater cost of sales and legal liability, the user should not expect to receive the supposedly favorable price and terms previously quoted by the vendor. Finally, the user should, therefore, "back off" and accept the "original deal" with few, if any, changes to the vendor's form agreement. (Although the vendor's representative will argue that the user should permit the vendor to increase the contract price to accommodate the user's changes, in most instances the marketeer really prefers, and is striving to achieve, a rapidly closed transaction, using the vendor's standard agreement, rather than an increase in price and protracted negotiations and drafting.)

The problems with this vendor approach should be obvious, but often are not. The basic fallacies in the vendor's arguments can be demonstrated by several comments on each of the points discussed above.

First, the user should seldom have any reason for feeling guilty about "springing" its list of contractual changes "at the last minute." In most instances, the vendor's representative does everything possible to postpone or avoid giving the user's attorney all the documentation for review. Even where the user has had all vendor form agreements for some time, and could have (and, indeed, should have) started contractual negotiations sooner, the vendor has generally brought the problem down on itself by presenting an unrealistic, overly-one-sided set of form documents.

Second, the user's changes will, indeed, take time and money to negotiate. But both parties are likely to share the blame for not starting this process earlier. Moreover, the negotiations will involve additional time and money for the user as well as the vendor. The vendor is not the only party that will "suffer" from this approach.

Third, the user's changes may well weaken the vendor's legal position and result in a more equitable document. But these changes will create financial liability or loss for the vendor only if the vendor fails to perform. Without the changes, the user will face virtually all the risk of vendor nonperformance even though the user is far less able than the vendor to correct or ensure performance of the vendor's equipment. If the user's changes really create a significant financial risk for the vendor, that fact alone should immediately signal the user to accept the financial risk of its own nonperformance, why should the user accept that risk?

Fourth, even if the vendor really did not expect to negotiate when it quoted the price, some question exists as to what gave the vendor the right to make this assumption in this case. (The sad answer, of course, is that far too many users do not negotiate.) In addition, even if negotiations will increase the vendor's cost of sales on this particular transaction, the vendor should consider the user to be such a valued account as to be ready and willing to spend a few more dollars to get the user's business. In any event, the margin of gross profit on most major equipment transactions, even those that are supposedly quoted at a very attractive rate, is quite wide enough to pay for a few days or even weeks of vendor negotiations.

Finally, the vendor's position on price-versus-risk is simply misguided. When banks price for risk, they charge a higher interest rate on loans where the borrower's financial condition (a matter outside the bank's control) poses a higher risk of loss to the bank. Here, however, the vendor wants to charge the user more because of a risk that is essentially within the vendor's control, not the user's. Moreover, if the vendor refuses to concede this point, the user's position is very simple: it will not do business without an adequate, negotiated agreement. If the vendor wants to raise the price, and quite likely lose the deal in the process, fine; but the user intends to negotiate. Signing the vendor's standard form agreement is simply not an alternative, in so far as the user is concerned.

To avoid this vendor ploy altogether, a user should follow good negotiating and scheduling tactics that prevent the vendor from ever raising the issue in the first place. This approach requires that the user alert the vendor at the outset that contractual changes and additional provisions are likely to be required. A good RFP technique is one of the best ways of providing advance warning on this issue.

To counter this ploy once the vendor has started to implement it, the user should simply stand firm and insist on both the initial price (or, preferably, a better and even lower, negotiated price) and the changes and additions to the form agreement. In taking this approach, the user should consider, and selectively utilize, the counterarguments to the vendor's position, set out above. The vendor's representative is likely to follow up with the usual dramatic, sense-of-urgency comments discussed throughout this chapter. The user should be ready for these histrionics, and be prepared to ignore them. Once the vendor's marketeer realizes that the user will not budge (a point that can often be made effectively by the user's president in a brief but threatening meeting with the vendor's personnel), serious negotiations are likely to be held on a timely and productive basis.

3
GENERAL NEGOTIATING SKILLS

Negotiation is an art. The key trait that distinguishes an outstanding negotiator in any field is the individual's ability to apply basic negotiating skills to achieve a successful objective in a constantly changing competitive environment.

Like the other arts, however, successful negotiation requires a thorough knowledge of underlying principles and techniques. Without this knowledge, a negotiator is unlikely to be effective, much less outstanding. Armed with these tools, a negotiator has a realistic opportunity to learn and practice the subtle creative talents that distinguish the true professional in this important area.

Before entering the highly competitive arena of equipment contract negotiations, the user's negotiators must gain an overview of the basic bargaining strategies that are valuable in any negotiating session. As noted earlier, this book does not attempt to serve as a textbook on negotiating skills. Many other volumes have been written on the general subject of negotiations, and these texts can and should be referred to by the user's negotiators. Three particularly interesting books are *The Art and Skill of Successful Negotiation* by attorney John Ilich (Englewood Cliffs, NJ: Prentice-Hall, Inc., 1973), *The Negotiating Game* by Dr. Chester L. Karass (New York: Thomas Y. Crowell Co., 1970), and *Fundamentals of Negotiating* by New York lawyer Gerald I. Nierenberg (New York: Hawthorn Books, Inc., 1973). The last book combines revised and expanded versions of Nierenberg's earlier books entitled *The Art of Negotiating* and *Creative Business Negotiating*. A practical layperson's guide to negotiating is Herb Cohen's *You Can Negotiate Anything* (Secaucus, NJ: Lyle Stuart, Inc., 1980). Perhaps the best book on the subject is *Getting to Yes* (Boston: Houghton Mifflin Co., 1981), by Roger Fisher and William Ury. Written by the leaders of the Harvard Negotiation Project, this relatively short book zeroes in on which negotiating strategies lead to mutual agreement—and which do not. Although based on academic research, it is a highly readable volume.

The discussion of basic negotiating strategies set forth in this chapter is designed to serve two purposes. First, it is intended to provide an overview of selected negotiating skills that are often utilized in major equipment negotiations. Second, it is designed to expand on the negotiating strategies discussed in the more general textbooks and explain how those skills can be used in an equipment transaction.

MOTIVATING HUMAN BEHAVIOR

In order to be as successful as possible in the negotiating ring, a negotiator must understand the factors that motivate human behavior. This is particularly true for users engaging in equipment negotiations because most vendor representatives have received sophisticated training in negotiating techniques and strategies—including human motivation from a bargaining standpoint. Understanding human motivational behavior can help the user's negotiating team recognize and avoid vendor marketing ploys and, at the same time, help the team members gain a better understanding of their own actions and desires. Consequently, the user should ensure that the members of its negotiating team have had a "short course" in the basic factors that motivate human behavior and decision-making.

At the most basic level, human behavior is motivated by a desire to satisfy certain physical and psychological needs. Professor Abraham Maslow listed seven of these needs in a famous ranking known as Maslow's Hierarchy of Needs. (See Fig. 3-1.) According to Maslow, we seek to satisfy our needs in the following order:

1. Physiological Needs
2. Safety and Security Needs
3. Need for Love and Belonging
4. Need for Self-Esteem
5. Need for Self-Actualization
6. Need for Knowledge and Understanding
7. Aesthetic Needs

To be effective in negotiations, the user's team members must recognize which needs the vendor's representatives may be seeking to satisfy during the negotiations. If the user's representatives are unaware of these needs, certain of the user's negotiating tactics may backfire because they inadvertently threaten the very needs the vendor's negotiators wish to satisfy. On the other hand, if the user's negotiators recognize the vendor's needs, the user's team can design its tactics in a manner that will reinforce the basic needs of the vendor's negotiators and management and thereby enhance the effectiveness of the user's negotiating efforts.

In Maslow's Hierarchy, physiological needs are those that satisfy the basic human drives relating to hunger, fatigue, shelter, sex, and the like. Safety and security needs include such goals as

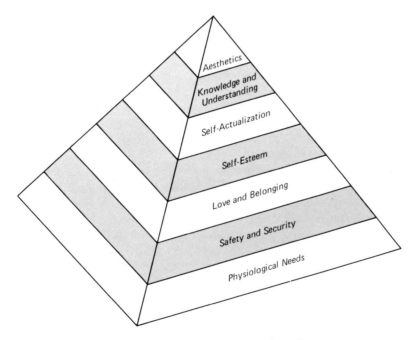

Fig. 3-1.   One depiction of Maslow's needs.

job security, safety and security in our daily lives, and freedom from fear and uncertainty. Although some negotiations instructors overlook these two categories of needs, both of these human desires can be involved in equipment negotiations. For example, a negotiator may over-react if he feels that an approach is threatening his job security (and, therefore, his ability to satisfy the physiological needs of himself and his family). On a less basic level, the negotiator may also be adversely influenced if he feels that the negotiations are improperly altering his usual meal schedule or causing extensive fatigue (that may lead to illness). Indeed, long hours of negotiations may even adversely impact family and social life, thereby affecting the first, second and third needs included on Maslow's list.

Love and belonging needs and the need for self-esteem are usually considered to be the most critical motivational factors related to contract negotiations. Love and belonging needs are the desires to be loved, to be part of the group, to have friends, a family, a sweetheart. The need for self-esteem is the related desire to attain a good reputation, status, independence, domination, and freedom. In the context of equipment negotiations, the need for self-esteem is directly related to the concept of "saving face." Human behavior is such that when we are put in a "face losing" situation, most of us tend to become intransigent in our position. We may or may not be "right," but we are not about to lose face by giving in to our opponent's consistent efforts to prove us wrong. Consequently, a good negotiator seldom tries to cause his opponent to lose face. Rather, the negotiator shifts gears and allows the opponent room to maneuver and come up with an alternative plan that will satisfy the negotiator's goal and enable the opponent to save face.

This point has been vividly demonstrated, favorably and unfavorably, in numerous equipment negotiating sessions. In one session, the vendor's regional marketing director was continually boxed into a corner by the user on a pricing issue. Finally, the marketing director exploded with, "You've implied we're crooks every time we offer you anything. Well, we're not about to lower our price now to prove you right. To hell with you." In another session, a similar pricing road-block occurred during the negotiations. This time, however, the user's professional negotiator proposed a break and left the room with the vendor's district marketing representative. The user's negotiator proposed a very simple approach to the marketing representative in a low-key, one-on-one session: "Look, your price is just not going to be acceptable. Can't we figure out a way to reconfigure the deal so you can better meet the user's needs?" After some discussion, the vendor's representative offered to change some of the components and the acquisition method in order to give the user a more attractive package. The vendor's sales representative never did change his "final" price on the initial proposal (thus saving face), but the alternative proposal saved the user money without causing the salesman to lose face.

The need for self-actualization is the desire to become everything one is capable of becoming. The need to know and understand is the desire to satisfy basic curiosity, to learn, and to under-stand one's life and surroundings. In the negotiating context, neither of these needs at first appears particularly relevant. However, both needs may be indirectly involved. For example, both of these needs can be threatened if a member of the vendor's negotiating team is unable to comprehend a given provision or if he is consistently spoken down to or treated with condescension.

The aesthetic need is the basic desire for order, balance, and the finer things in life. In nego-tiations, this need can be found in the participant's desire for a clean, neat, and quiet negotiating room.

The aesthetic need, and virtually all of Maslow's other needs, can also be linked to a very basic factor present in virtually all equipment negotiations: money. Regardless of one's own per-sonal philosophy, the fact remains that money can buy many of the things that will satisfy (in whole or in part) most, if not all, of Maslow's needs in our contemporary society. Consequently, when the user threatens the vendor representative's commission, the marketeer may overreact across the board. Obviously, a user cannot acquiesce to the marketeer's desire to maximize his commission income. However, the user can recognize that, given two equal alternatives, it may be more effective to press for the alternative that will preserve or increase the salesperson's commission.

Utilizing Maslow's needs as a starting point, every member of the user's negotiating team should strive to recognize the basic motivational needs of the vendor's negotiators and management representatives. If the user's negotiators can learn to recognize these needs, they will be able to design negotiating strategies that will cause the user's proposals to appear to meet the vendor's needs. At the same time, the user's negotiators should be able to manipulate alternative proposals (that are less favorable to the user) in a manner that will make them seem inconsistent with the vendor's motivational needs, thereby increasing the relative attractiveness of the user's primary proposal.

BODY LANGUAGE

A solid understanding of the art of reading body language—or nonverbal communication—can be an effective tool in recognizing the motivational needs of the vendor's negotiators. More generally, basic training in body language is an essential prerequisite for anyone interested in mastering professional negotiating skills. Consequently, the user's negotiating team should make an early commitment toward developing the talents necessary to recognize and interpret nonverbal communication. The following paragraphs present an overview of this important technique, with particular emphasis on gestures likely to be encountered in equipment negotiations.

At the outset, several caveats should be noted.

First, a person does not acquire the skills necessary for reading body language overnight. Although the basic concepts are rather easy to grasp, the sophistication necessary for full utilization of this negotiating tool develops much more slowly. In many respects, achieving fluency in body language requires a level of practice not unlike that necessary to learn a foreign language.

Second, body language gestures generally come in clusters. The movements in these clusters must be assessed together. Failure to include all linked movements may lead the viewer to an erroneous conclusion.

Third, a given body language cluster may include "congruent" and "incongruent" gestures. Understanding the relationship, if any, among various congruent and incongruent gestures within a cluster is essential.

Fourth, gesture clusters must be compared to the subject's verbal communication. Although the relative congruence among gestures may be more valuable than the relative consistency between a gesture cluster and the individual's spoken words, both the verbal and nonverbal communication must be analyzed together.

Fifth, body language is not an infallible tool, for several reasons. Some practitioners of the art of reading this silent language are simply not trained adequately enough to obtain an accurate assessment. Some body language "speakers" use movements that are unusual; that is, gesture clusters that translate abnormally, thereby conveying or resulting in an erroneous interpretation. (The risk of an erroneous interpretation is particularly high where differing cultures are involved.) Other body language "speakers" are themselves students of the art and, as such, enjoy contriving and conveying silent messages that are designed to deceive a negotiating opponent. (Despite this fact, many experts in the field suggest that it is impossible, or at least foolhardy, to use body language in an offensive or deceptive mode.)

These points should be carefully considered in the context of equipment negotiations. Many vendor marketing representatives have received good body language training, both in the classroom and at the negotiating table. These individuals are quite capable of "reading" the gestures made by the user's key executives. In addition, they are capable of generating false body language communication to keep the user's negotiating team off base.

The vendor's likely advantage in body language can mean several things to the user. First, the user's negotiating team may be giving its position away through inadvertent and ill-understood body movements. Second, the user may be missing an opportunity to generate false body language to use as an affirmative negotiating tool. Third, the user may be overlooking an opportunity to read the body language generated by the vendor's representatives. (Despite this final point, however, the user must always recognize that the vendor may be superior at the body language game. Therefore, the risk of false readings and improper conclusions always exists for the user.)

One of the more effective methods of learning to read body language is to set aside a few minutes each day to observe the gestures of others. Airport and other waiting rooms, restaurants, and business meetings can serve as particularly valuable training grounds. Another helpful technique is to acquire a good text on the subject. One of the easiest-reading, yet relatively sophisticated, books in the field is *How to Read a Person Like a Book* by Gerard I. Nierenberg and Henry H. Calero (New York: Hawthorn Books, Inc., reprinted 1978).

To assist the reader interested in gaining a brief look at the art of reading body language, the following section contains a "primer" of individual gestures. As suggested above, this glossary of body language gestures must only be used as a starting point for further training and practical experience. In addition, the individual gestures should only be evaluated in the context of a gesture cluster. Members of the user's negotiating team should attempt to test the following gesture explanations in "real life" situations in order to gain an initial appreciation for the degree of accuracy that can be expected. In addition, team members should have a debriefing after each vendor negotiating session to discuss, among other things, their observations concerning the body language utilized by vendor and user negotiators.

One additional comment should be noted. Many management and professional-level individuals find the concept of body language to be something akin to astrology and reading tea leaves. As a result, these individuals refuse to take the time necessary to determine whether or not the art of nonverbal communication might be a valuable negotiating tool. Based upon the authors' lecturing and seminar experience, the most difficult part of learning body language is overcoming the natural aversion to believing that the technique has any possible value. Once a manager is willing to give the idea a chance, he or she is generally surprised at the potential value of achieving fluency in nonverbal communication. Indeed, initial skeptics are often among the most avid students of the body language glossary set out below.

Defensiveness, Confrontation, and Suspicion

Crossed Arms; Arms Crossed on Chest. These gestures are among the most basic and universal signs of defensiveness, disagreement, or suspicion, sometimes in connection with insecurity. Clenched fists or fingers grasping the biceps evidence an even stronger negative attitude.

Crossed Legs; Action of Crossing Legs or Ankles. These actions are generally a sign of disagreement or increased competitiveness or confrontation; however, they also may be only a habit of comfort or boredom.

One Leg Over a Chair Leg; Feet on Desk; Straddling a Chair with Chairback to Listener. All of these actions may evidence lack of cooperation, hostility, or aggression. Superiority, dominance, and lack of concern may also be involved. These gestures can be misleading because of the initial (and erroneous) suggestions of informality, cooperation, and friendliness.

Touching or Rubbing the Nose; Rubbing the Eye. Although less clear than some of the gestures mentioned above, these movements may also suggest an adverse or negative reaction, particularly when supported by other confrontation or defensive gestures. Chair squirming, movements toward the door, and clockwatching may also reinforce these actions. (Of course some nose itching and eye rubbing is purely physical and carries no "message.")

Slumping or Leaning Backward in Chair. The action of slumping or leaning backward in a chair, or tilting a chair backward on its rear legs, may be a sign of confrontation disbelief, or defensiveness, especially when coupled with crossed arms or hands in the pockets. This gesture often evidences the "show me" attitude found at the outset of a sales presentation by a marketing representative.

Openness and Evaluation

Openness of Hands; Unbuttoning of Coat; Uncrossing of Arms, Legs, or Ankles. Each of these movements may be strong evidence of openness and willingness to listen (and possibly agree). The removal of a coat by a businessman may also be meaningful. All of these gestures are most likely to convey the suggested message if they occur in the presence of the listener, sometime into the conversation or negotiations.

Hands on Hips. When supported by other gestures, this action may signal readiness and openness. However, the gesture can also evidence superiority in some situations.

Tilted or Cocked Head. This gesture is one of the most basic and universal signs of affirmative interest and honest evaluation.

Chin, Beard, or Mustache Stroking; Other "Hands or Fingers on Cheek" Gestures. These gestures often evidence thought, evaluation, and consideration of the material being presented.

Leaning Forward at Desk or in Chair; Sitting on Edge of Chair. Except where the gesture involves boredom, the action of moving or tilting the head or body forward at a desk or in a chair may show interest, openness, and serious consideration. Facial squinting, nose-bridge pinching, and hands-to-face gestures are supportive of this interpretation. Sitting on the edge of a chair in a leaning forward position, often shows intense interest and potential agreement.

Confidence and Superiority

Finger Steepling. Finger steepling consists of joining the fingertips of both hands, with palms apart (in the appearance of a "church steeple"). The action generally conveys a superior, confident, or smug attitude. (Nierenberg and Calero report that the higher an executive feels he is, the higher he will hold his hands while steepling.) Obviously, steepling is a very easy gesture to contrive in an effort to throw an opponent off balance.

Handling an Object and Placing It Carefully on a Desk. The careful study and placement of an object, especially a favored item, within a desired location may evidence superiority (in a territorial or property sense) and a sense of control. (Handling the object alone, without placement, may simply show evaluation or even boredom.)

Positioning by Height. Elevation generally involves a message of superiority and position. Standing "above" a seated individual, seeking the higher of several chairs, and even rocking forward from heel to toes while standing may evidence such an attitude. Although the action is not used substantially today, a sharp clicking of the heels while standing may convey a similar impression. (Note that where increased height is not a viable option, choosing a seat at, or near, the head of the conference table may suggest a similar message.)

Leaning Backward with Hands Clasped Behind Head. This action is one of the basic gestures of an individual who feels "in control."

Authority Stance. The classic military, maitre d', or first sergeant stance (chin high and forward, chest out, feet firmly planted and perhaps rocking with deliberation, hands often behind the back) is a rather firm sign of actual or contrived superiority. Although the female version of this authority stance is often less formal and exaggerated, the basic physical signs are similar to the more traditional male model.

One Leg Over a Chair Leg; Feet on Desk; Straddling a Chair with Chairback to Listener. As noted above, these gestures may evidence superiority or dominance as well as hostility or lack of cooperation.

Nervousness and Frustration

Clearing the Throat. A brief clearing of the throat may suggest unease, nervousness, or anxiety. However, the action may also be unrelated to apprehension. Most users are already aware of the basic differences between the two types of coughs. Changes in voice inflection, stuttering, and using "ah," "you know," and "okay?" may also show nervousness.

Arms Spread Wide with Palms on or Hands Gripping Table. This stance may suggest substantial frustration and annoyance, particularly when reinforced by previous gestures or contemporaneous verbal communication. Anxiety and nervousness may also be evident. This posture is sometimes seen where a negotiator is making a frustrated, last ditch effort to convince an opponent.

Whistling. Although various types of whistling can convey vastly different meanings, relatively quiet, under-the-breath whistling in a negotiating environment may indicate nervousness or concern.

Wringing Hands; Fidgeting, Shifting Position While Seated. These actions are among the more well recognized signs of nervousness or frustration. Depending upon the other gestures in the cluster, these actions may also suggest a degree of boredom.

Putting Out or Ignoring a Lighted Cigarette. Nierenberg and Calero assert that, in business negotiations, "lighting up" a cigarette is not a sign of tension or nervousness. Rather, they say that a nervous or tense negotiator either puts out a lighted cigarette or permits it to burn (without smoking it further). The authors' negotiating experience confirms this interesting assessment.

Hands or Fingers Covering the Mouth While Talking. Mumbling or speaking "through" a hand or fingers covering the mouth may indicate concern, anxiety, or nervousness. It may also suggest a lack of candor or truthfulness. (Users should not confuse this gesture with talking through or behind steepling fingers, which may evidence superiority, gamesmanship, or smugness.)

Acceptance and Agreement

Openness. As suggested above, many of the gestures associated with openness may evidence a willingness to agree. In some situations, these gestures may be part of an acceptance or agreement gesture cluster.

Removing Barriers; Moving Closer. Movement closer together physically often coincides with movement closer together on the issues. In both senses, the "gap" is closed. This physical movement may occur as two negotiators turn or move toward one another, or as one negotiator gets up from his desk chair, rounds his desk, and chats with the sales representative sitting in a guest chair. Reinforcement by the listener at this point can further solidify the evidence of agreement. (Moving closer for confidential discussions should not be misinterpreted as necessarily evidencing agreement.)

Touching. Depending upon the individuals involved and the other gestures in the cluster, touching or grasping the listener's arm or shoulder may evidence potential or actual agreement or a willingness to pull closer on the issues at hand.

Sitting on the Edge of a Chair. As noted above, sitting on the edge of a chair, perched forward, suggests intense interest and often indicates a willingness to act. Depending upon the other gestures involved, the action may signal potential agreement and acceptance. In other contexts, however, it can evidence boredom, disgust, or a readiness to leave.

PSYCHOLOGICAL NEGOTIATING LEVERAGE

Several sections of this book discuss the disparity in negotiating leverage faced by most users. Although numerous factors contribute to the relative inequality faced by users at the bargaining table, one of the more pervasive elements involves the user's failure to appreciate the relationship between timing and psychological negotiating leverage.

In virtually any effective negotiations, the leverage enjoyed by the respective parties ebbs and flows during the course of the negotiations. One party may be (or appear to be) "in command" at the outset of the discussions. This strong leverage may fall considerably at a later point, perhaps when the first meeting is held to discuss the acceptance test or warranty provisions. This type of fluctuation in relative negotiating leverage occurs both on a "macro" scale and on a "micro" scale. Thus, the leverage held by a party varies across the entire acquisition process, from the bid and RFP stage through the award phase and into the contract bargaining stage. And, on the "micro" level, leverage fluctuates within a given negotiating session, from the opening remarks through the deadlock or successful completion of the meeting involved.

At the "macro" level, the user's procedures and timing can have a significant impact on the relative negotiating leverage of the vendor and the user. This impact can be demonstrated by considering the negotiating leverage enjoyed by the respective parties in three alternative examples. This leverage is depicted in the three graphs shown in Figs. 3-2, 3-3, and 3-4. In each graph, the "100%" symbol at the top of the verticle axis represents the theoretical "maximum possible leverage" at the time in the equipment acquisition process.

Figure 3-2 represents a typical scenario where the user has little or no experience in acquiring important equipment and effectively feels outmanned and outclassed at each stage of the acquisition process. This situation might be compared to that where an individual applies for his or her first bank loan at a large, impersonal financial institution. In that setting, the potential bor-

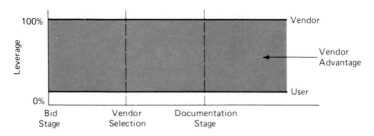

Fig. 3-2. Psychological negotiating leverage in an acquisition involving an inexperienced user.

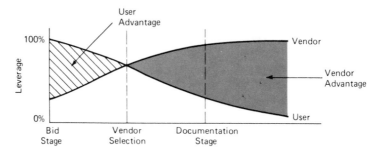

Fig. 3-3. Psychological negotiating leverage in an acquisition in which the user has a high sense of urgency.

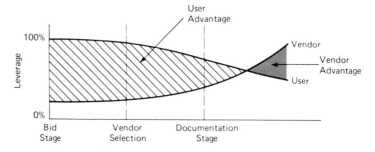

Fig. 3-4. Psychological negotiating leverage in an acquisition in which the user applies professional negotiating techniques.

rower walks into the bank and softly asks the loan officer, "You, uh, wouldn't possibly be able to loan me some . . . uh; could I perhaps get a small loan to, uh. . . ." In the major equipment context, the situation is not much better, even though the spoken words may be more coherent. In the equipment acquisition, the user thinks (often subconsciously), "If I really do everything right and try not to act too stupid, maybe this large, sophisticated vendor will favor me by selling our firm an impressive new system that will improve our operations and enhance my career. I certainly hope I don't do anything wrong or rock the boat in getting this contract signed."

This user attitude was pervasive only a few years ago, particularly among medium-size and smaller companies. Fortunately, fewer and fewer users have this timid outlook today. Despite this improvement, however, many users still suffer from occasional attacks of this negotiating weakness, either in specific bargaining sessions or particular acquisitions. Other users enjoy negotiating leverage somewhat higher than that shown in Fig. 3-2 but still lack meaningful negotiating confidence. As a result, the relative leverage disparity is not as severe as that in Fig. 3-2, but the graph trend line is still flat throughout all stages of the acquisition.

Figure 3-3 depicts the situation where the user is relatively informed, but has a real or perceived sense of urgency for some reason. In this example, the user has high negotiating leverage at the beginning of the acquisition process because competing vendors see an opportunity to make a quick sale (or other transaction) with relatively high profits. These vendors recognize the user's sense of urgency and feel that, once the user has made an equipment and/or vendor selection, the contract will be signed with few or no negotiations concerning terms or price. (After all, they say, the user wants to expedite the transaction.) Consequently, the user has a great deal to offer the competing vendors and, as a result, the vendors are aggressively seeking the user's business.

In this setting, the user's negotiating leverage drops from the theoretical maximum at the bid or RFP stage to almost zero at the outset of the contract bargaining phase. The drastic swing effectively occurs when the user awards the bid; that is, when the user selects the particular vendor that will supply the equipment involved. At this point, the selected vendor realizes that the user has a sense of urgency to complete the transaction. Now, however, the competition from the other vendors is gone. The user has selected one vendor and essentially said, "We have to get this equipment up and running as soon as possible." The result: high negotiating leverage for the vendor and low leverage for the user.

Figure 3-4 represents the setting where the user follows good negotiating procedures and does not have (or refuses to divulge) a sense of urgency. In this situation, the user has strong negotiating leverage at the bid or RFP stage, again because various vendors are actively competing for the user's business. When the primary vendor is selected, the user's leverage drops somewhat, and the vendor's equity increases, because the user has played its hand and reduced its options. Unlike the prior example, however, in this situation the user has followed sound negotiating practice by naming several "zone of consideration" vendors that may have an opportunity to provide the equipment if the user's negotiations with the primary vendor prove to be unsuccessful. In addition, because the user does not have a sense of urgency, the primary vendor recognizes that the user is prepared to commit substantial time and resources to the contract negotiations. Because the vendor realizes that the user is serious about engaging in thorough negotiations, the vendor feels that it will have to be prepared to make concessions or face at least some risk of losing the user's business.

As the document negotiations progress, the user becomes more and more willing to compromise the remaining and/or less important issues and execute the agreement. Ordinarily this user attitude results from a combination of two factors. First, the user has met many of its expected negotiating goals and does not feel compelled to negotiate further on the as yet unresolved points. Second, despite the user's lack of a sense of urgency, the time consuming nature of the negotiations has taken its toll on the user's willingness to continue the discussions (to the exclusion of other pressing business demands). Consequently, the relative leverage of the two parties converges and the agreement is executed. After the contract signing, the user's negotiating leverage generally drops still further, as the vendor holds the ace cards of delivery, successful installation, and ongoing maintenance.

These examples reinforce several points concerning user negotiating tactics. First, a strong user aspiration level is critical to success at the negotiating table. If the user fails to have confidence and refuses to set and follow solid negotiating goals, it will be much like the uneducated loan customer going into the bank for his or her first loan. In equipment negotiations, as well as in personal borrowing, meaningful experience and knowledge of what to expect are important factors in creating and conveying a strong sense of confidence.

Second, the user's leverage posture can be strongly affected by the negotiating procedures and timing adopted by the user. If the user follows procedures that effectively "lock in" (or guarantee the business for) a single vendor early in the acquisition process, the user will have little chance to achieve or regain meaningful negotiating leverage. Simply put, once the vendor and the equipment are selected—once the contract is "awarded"—the user suffers a severe drop in psychological negotiating leverage. For the user to achieve or retain reasonable leverage, vendor uncertainty—indeed, vendor fear—must exist. The vendor or, ideally, several vendors must feel that, unless concessions are made to the user during the negotiations, the user will decide to do business with another source. This vendor uncertainty or fear creates the essential vendor willingness to seek a compromise at the contract negotiating table in order to obtain the user's business.

Third, most users lose their negotiating leverage before even getting to the contract bargaining phase of the acquisition process. As a result, the user's attorneys and other negotiators are forced to seek key contractual and financial concessions with little or no bargaining equity.

Unfortunately, most equipment acquisitions occur through the following user steps: evaluation, selection, and negotiation. Users spend considerable time on the evaluation and selection phases of this process, only to find that, for some reason, they lack the necessary negotiating leverage to achieve reasonable concessions in the negotiation stage. In reality, the three acquisition steps listed above would be far more accurately described as: evaluation, selection, and "begging." For, despite their rationalizations otherwise, most users end up "begging" far more than "negotiating" at the contract bargaining stage of the acquisition process.

To achieve any effective negotiating leverage, the user's advocates must attempt to create a sense of uncertainty in the mind of the vendor, even though the vendor is, at this point, quite certain that the user has no real alternative and will sign the agreement in any event (once the user's negotiators finish their orations and recognize the futility of their efforts). As a result, the user's negotiators are forced to employ such strategies as purposefully deadlocking and breaking off negotiations in an effort to suggest that, despite all prior indications, the user just might consider doing business with another vendor.

The futility faced by many user attorneys can be demonstrated by offering a hypothetical user conversation as an example. Although somewhat extreme, the following statement effectively summarizes the practical effect of many user acquisition efforts: "Mr. Vendor, our user company spent six months preparing our RFP which, as you know, we issued five months ago. We received 12 bids and devoted another four months to evaluating all of the proposals. At that point, we narrowed the field to four vendors and continued our evaluation using benchmark tests. Last week, we recommended to senior management and the board of directors that we do business with your firm and accept your proposal. Today, our president advised me that our recommendations were accepted in full and we are authorized to implement your proposal as soon as possible. Now, let's negotiate the agreement!"

Despite the contrived nature of this example, the point is clear: Effective negotiations require leverage. Unless the user retains, or at least appears to retain, something that the vendor wants (i.e., the user's final commitment to do business with the vendor), it will be difficult or impossible for the user to have the necessary leverage in the critical contract bargaining phase of the equipment acquisition process.

PERSONAL NEGOTIATING POWER AND THE SELECTION OF USER TACTICS

Just as psychological negotiating leverage varies over time for each corporate party to the negotiations, personal negotiating power (PNP) is also wavelike or cyclical, even for the best negotiators. The negotiating power held by an individual negotiator ebbs and flows over time for a number of reasons, both personal and professional. Negotiators have good days and bad and, within each category, have strong periods and weak. Because negotiating is indeed a practiced art, in some instances the negotiator's plan of attack works flawlessly, creating a thrust or winning a point with the same artistic poise of the best sculptor or professional athlete. In other circumstances, the negotiator's efforts may be less rewarded and fall far short of the desired mark, perhaps stifled by a superior opposition, or killed by the implementing negotiator's own lack of creative juices at the critical moment.

An experienced negotiator will constantly study and assess the PNP of his or her opponent throughout each bargaining session, using the perceived PNP level to select the negotiating tactics to be employed. Decisions concerning which negotiating tactics should be employed at a particular time are among the most difficult of any in the negotiating process, and neither the study of PNP nor any other single action will provide a perfect answer at any given point in time. However, the relative PNP level of the opposing negotiator will give even an inexperienced user negotiator a valid starting place in considering the tactics to be employed. As in the study of body language, the user's assessment of PNP levels must be considered in the context of the total communications and gesture "cluster" being projected by the opponent at a given time. Moreover, the user must be particularly alert to any incongruence that may appear to exist in the complete cluster.

The PNP level is an effective tool because, as a negotiator experiences changes in his PNP curve, he reacts more or less strongly to Maslow's needs. (See Fig. 3-1.) In effect, a reasonably direct relationship exists between the relative height of a negotiator's PNP curve and his sensitivity to negotiating tactics or concessions that meet, or appear to meet, the different need levels included in Maslow's hierarchy. For example, if a negotiator is enjoying a strong PNP, he will generally be relatively self-confident and assured. As such, he is unlikely to be concerned about the dangers of pure failure in his mission. Rather, he is likely to be considering the minor details and personal items that will optimize his sense of superiority and achievement. Translated into Maslow's hierarchy of needs, the negotiator is unlikely to be concerned about basic physiological or safety and security needs (such as shelter and food), which rank most important on Maslow's list. In contrast, the negotiator is likely to be motivated by, or drawn to the more subtle and sophisticated needs, such as aesthetic and artistic needs, which rank as the last satisfied on Maslow's list.

By recognizing this relationship between PNP and Maslow's needs, a good user negotiator can judge which negotiating tactics will be more or less effective at a given point in a bargaining session. For example, where the PNP held by the vendor's negotiator is high, and the individual is therefore unlikely to be motivated by Maslow's most basic needs, the user's negotiator should not waste time employing a tactic that is solely designed to knock his opponent off his feet (e.g., by threatening the entire transaction and, thus, the opponent's commission or job). The application of such a tactic would probably have little serious effect at that point. The opponent's high PNP would cause him to brush the user's threats aside, recognizing them for what they are: a weak and ill-timed effort to change the course of the bargaining session. The failure by the user's negotiator in this type of effort, and the concomitant success by the vendor's representative in perceiving the weakness in the user's attempt, will only serve to increase the PNP held by the vendor's negotiator.

Where the PNP of the vendor's negotiator is high, the user's negotiator would be far better advised to employ a more sophisticated tactic designed to appeal to one of Maslow's higher level (less basic) needs. In such a situation, the user's negotiator might appeal to the vanity, sense of fairness, or drafting expertise of the vendor's representative. With his PNP high, the vendor's negotiator is likely to have the self-confidence necessary to permit him to react favorably to the user's pleas that a particular provision is simply inconsistent, unfair, or incorrectly drafted.

Conversely, when the PNP of the vendor's negotiator is relatively low, the individual will ordinarily be susceptible to bargaining tactics that appeal to the more basic needs on Maslow's list. Intense surprise, deadlocking the discussions, and threatening to disengage the vendor can all be useful tactics in such a situation. On the other hand, the vendor's negotiator is not likely to be interested in, or to react favorably to, user tactics that relate to the more sophisticated needs in Maslow's hierarchy. With his mind on weakness and potential failure, the vendor's negotiator will be far more concerned about basic motivational factors, such as financial and job security, than about the "finer things in life." (Obviously, the examples used above are somewhat extreme, for purposes of demonstrating the concepts involved. In reality, the distinctions are usually much more subtle.)

The relationship between PNP levels and user tactics is not limited to the PNP of the vendor's negotiator. In many instances, the ability of the user's negotiator to employ a given tactic successfully is directly related to the PNP enjoyed by the user's negotiator himself at the time he attempts to implement the tactic. As might be expected, various negotiating tactics require different levels of negotiating power, leverage, or equity to execute. The amount of PNP necessary to implement a particular tactic successfully depends on several factors, including the difficulty or sophistication of the tactic, the importance of the financial or other substantive points involved, and the PNP of the opposing negotiator. This last factor is interesting, because it accurately suggests that the PNP enjoyed by one negotiator may be more or less inversely proportional to the PNP held by the opposing negotiator at a given point in time. If this relationship were perfect, the PNP of both opposing negotiators could be represented by a single trend line or sine wave, with the area above the curve representing the relative PNP of one negotiator and the area below the curve representing the PNP of the opposing negotiator. (See Fig. 3-5.)

In reality, the PNP relationship is by no means perfect, and any suggestion otherwise is an extreme oversimplification of an otherwise useful theory. However, in many instances, the inverse PNP relationship between opposing negotiators is present, at least to a degree. When one negotiator enjoys a relatively high PNP, the opposing negotiator suffers from a relatively low PNP, and vice versa. These complementary relationships may not be immediately apparent in a particular session, due to the time delay that often occurs between the rise of one negotiator's PNP and the fall in the PNP of the opposing negotiator. However, as the time axis is spread out, the relationship ordinarily becomes more pronounced.

The existence or lack of existence of this inverse relationship also bears on the question of which bargaining tactics should be selected by the user's negotiator. Many of the stronger tactics available to the user's negotiator require a relatively strong PNP level to be successfully implemented (e.g., purposefully deadlocking negotiations or making strong and surprising demands). Many of these same tactics are most effective where the PNP of the vendor's negotiator is relatively low, and his susceptibility to the more basic of Maslow's needs is therefore relatively high. If the relationship between the PNP of the user's negotiator at that time bears an inverse relationship to the PNP of the vendor's negotiator, the user's representative will be in a partic-

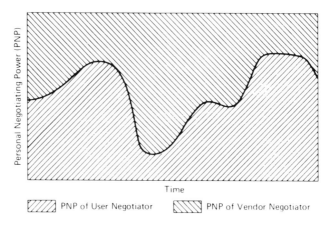

Fig. 3-5. Theoretical interrelationship of personal negotiating power (PNP) of vendor and user negotiators.

ularly good position to employ the strong tactic; that is, the user's negotiator will enjoy the high PNP necessary to employ the tactic effectively, and the vendor's negotiator will suffer from low PNP, thereby maximizing the effectiveness of the tactic from the user's standpoint.

In contrast, if the relationship between the PNPs of the opposing negotiators does not equal or approach an inverse proportion, then the ability of the user's negotiator to employ the tactic will be somewhat impaired. For example, if in the situation described both opposing negotiators suffer from relatively low PNPs, the signals from assessing the two PNP levels would be incongruent. The low PNP level of the vendor's negotiator would suggest that the strong user tactic could be successfully employed. However, if implementation of the tactic requires the user's negotiator to have a high PNP level, the user's representative may be unable, or (more likely) less able, to employ the tactic successfully. In such a situation, the user's negotiator should recognize the potential value of executing the tactic but, at the same time, realize that optimum application of the tactic may not be possible at that point in the bargaining process, due to the weakness in the PNP held by the user's negotiator himself.

NEGOTIATING HARMONICS

Optimum equipment negotiations involve the mutual dampening of each opponent's aspiration levels to a common level that is acceptable to both parties. Negotiating deadlocks of varying duration generally occur when both parties to the negotiations have strong aspiration levels and are pressing hard for their respective goals. Although successful negotiations can be held without any intervening deadlocks on specific issues, the majority of meaningful major equipment negotiations involve one or more deadlocks, at least if both parties are pursuing appropriately strong aspiration levels. As one experienced user negotiator put it, "How would you feel if you completed negotiations on a major acquisition without a single deadlock? It just might suggest you didn't do your job very well."

Where these deadlocks occur, maintaining a strong aspiration level becomes even more critical. If negotiations are to continue to a successful conclusion, the deadlock must be broken by compromise or concession. And, if one party weakens its aspiration level too much at this critical point, the other party may achieve an excessive negotiating victory in the form of a compromise or concession that is more than what would have been necessary to break the deadlock and continue the negotiations.

Put another way, at the point of deadlock, each negotiator must consider the potential compromises and concessions that his or her side might make to break the deadlock. If the negotiator does not have a strong aspiration level at that point, he or she may offer an excessive concession, in effect "giving away" more than would have been necessary to break the deadlock and get the negotiations moving again. (The art of knowing just how much to concede, of course, involves far more than simply having a strong aspiration level; however, this factor is a critical element in that art.)

These general concepts can be demonstrated by reviewing an example of perhaps the most basic of all negotiating objectives: price. Traditionally, most vendors have two key levels in their price negotiations. The first is an absolute minimum acceptability level dictated by the minimum profit that the firm's management is willing to accept (viewed both in the context of the specific transaction and user, and in the context of the vendor's full range of business). The second vendor price level is an aspiration level that is dictated by: (1) the vendor's desire to achieve more than the minimum acceptable profit; and (2) the vendor negotiator's personal incentive to maximize vendor profits in order to achieve higher compensation under the vendor's profit-oriented sales compensation plan.

Conversely, most users concentrate on a single level in their price negotiations: an acceptability level. Despite the profit orientation of most user companies, the general corporate goal of maximizing profits seldom flows directly through to the user's side of the equipment negotiating table.

To some extent, this disparity between vendor and user aspiration levels may exist because the applicable user department has already received management approval to acquire given equipment at a given price (usually the vendor's published price or, possibly, the published price less some discount already offered by the vendor). Indeed, in many user companies, serious negotiations do not even begin until this management approval has been received. In other situations, the user expenditure is a replacement expense which fits into an already existing budget and needs no further justification to management. In either case, the user's negotiators have little reason to press for a lower price; after all, to do so might "make waves," "ruin the relationship" with the vendor, or drag out the negotiations and thereby postpone the delivery date.

The user's relatively weak aspiration level with respect to price may also exist in part because the user's negotiators seldom have a personal, financial incentive to optimize the price paid by the user. As noted in Chapter 1, even user companies that have an incentive bonus plan for their managers seldom utilize a compensation system that offers the kind of direct, commission-oriented incentive available to most equipment marketing representatives. Regardless of the dedication of a user's negotiators, the fact remains that a vendor negotiator, who stands to pocket additional cash as a result of optimizing the vendor's price position, will have a considerably stronger price aspiration level than the user's salaried employee. This difference in incentive can be particularly onerous to the user when the negotiations drag on after business hours. At that point, the vendor's representative is still "fired up" and ready to maximize his or her commission. The user's salaried employee, on the other hand, is generally participating in the negotiations as an added duty, and may well feel that the time spent negotiating is detracting from his or her already heavy workload. In other words, negotiations are part of a vendor marketeer's job description, which gives him or her incentive to put in as much time as necessary to optimize the deal; negotiations are not normally part of the user manager's job description and in this case his or her incentive may be to complete the transaction as quickly as possible and get back to his or her "regular" job, even if it means making some unnecessary concessions.

The concept of negotiating harmonics and the importance of relative aspiration levels can be seen in the accompanying graphs that depict various stages in a price negotiating session.

In Fig. 3-6, the horizontal line at $1.0 million represents the vendor's (internal and proprietary) acceptability level (VAL). However, in this example the vendor has quoted a price to the

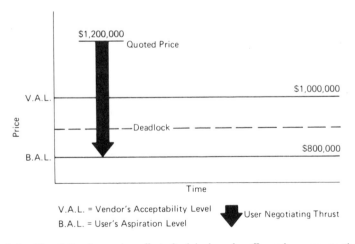

Fig. 3-6.   Negotiating harmonics: effect of original vendor offer and user counterthrust.

user of $1.2 million, representing the vendor's aspiration level. The user has countered with a price of $800,000, which represents the user's (buyer's) original acceptability level (BAL). (The downward vertical arrow, or vector, represents the user's thrust through the vendor's acceptability level to the buyer's aspiration level of $800,000.) At this point in the negotiations, given firm representations on both sides, an interim impasse or deadlock has been created; that is, the vendor cannot accept less than $1.0 million, but the user has offered only $800,000.

In Fig. 3-7, this interim deadlock is broken by a vendor counteroffer of $1.1 million. This is a critical point in the negotiations for most users. Far too frequently, the user mistakenly believes that this vendor counteroffer represents the vendor's acceptability level. However, because of the two vendor incentives discussed earlier, the vendor seldom counters with its VAL. In this example, the vendor's counteroffer is actually $100,000 over its minimum price or VAL.

If the user in Fig. 3-7 does not have a strong aspiration level (as is the case, for example, of a "one deadlock" user), the user will generally agree to the vendor's offer of $1.1 million. But this early and excessive user concession will leave a significant amount of money on the bargaining table—largely because of the user's inability to strive consistently to optimize the price through multiple, strong-aspiration-level probes (offers). If the user in Fig. 3-7 has a moderate-to-strong aspiration level, the user may counter with some other offer; for example, an offer of $1.0 million (which is the VAL in the example situation). Even though this amount represents the vendor's minimum acceptability level, the vendor's desire to achieve a high profit will probably cause the vendor to "stand pat" at $1.1 million and, if the deadlock continues, to offer or agree to "split the difference" for a final price of $1,050,000. Although the user in this example would be receiving a far better price than the initial vendor offer of $1.2 million, the final price would still be $50,000 above the VAL. (In effect, the user would be "splitting" its own money.)

In this situation, an experienced user would probably counter the vendor's $1.1 million offer and/or the vendor's $1.05 million "split the difference" offer with a counter thrust of $900,000. (See Fig. 3-8.) At this point, splitting the difference in a compromise would yield a final price of $1,000,000-exactly on the VAL.

Of course, in reality, the user seldom if ever knows the vendor's minimum acceptability level or the degree to which a vendor offer exceeds its VAL or a user offer is less than the VAL. The important point is that, if aggressive price negotiations continue over a reasonable period of time, with multiple interim deadlocks, the mutual dampening effect shown in Fig. 3-9 is likely to occur and, as a result, the final price is more likely to approach the VAL. How close the final price actually comes to VAL will depend on a variety of factors, including the time devoted to price

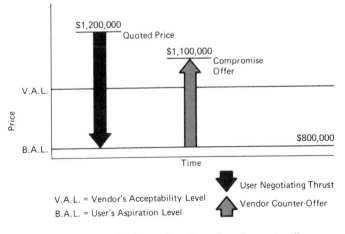

Fig. 3-7. Negotiating harmonics: effect of vendor counteroffer.

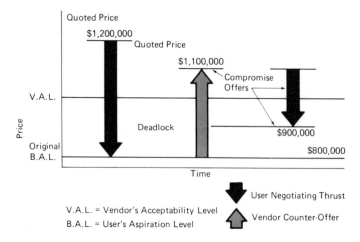

Fig. 3-8.   Negotiating harmonics: effect of further counterthrust by user.

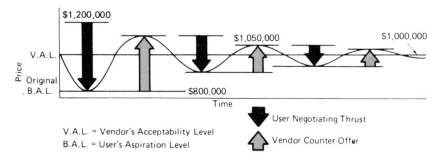

Fig. 3-9.   Negotiating harmonics: dampening oscillation effect of alternative vendor and user offers and counteroffers.

negotiations, negotiating skills held by the user, the relative goals of the two parties, and even good old-fashioned "luck." But a key prerequisite, both initially and at each interim deadlock point along the way, will be the degree to which the user has achieved and maintained a strong aspiration level throughout the price negotiations.

BASIC NEGOTIATING TACTICS

Although most negotiators develop a repertoire of effective tactics only after years of experience, individuals with fewer years at the bargaining table can and do learn to apply basic negotiating tactics with relative ease. These basic tactics enable the beginning negotiator to make resonable progress in active negotiations while still developing the more sophisticated skills that come only with continued practice and experience. As the introduction to this chapter cautioned, the present volume is not intended to be a general primer on negotiating skills. Nevertheless, certain basic tactics are particularly useful in equipment negotiations—so useful, in fact, that the vendor's representatives are likely to employ them if the user's negotiators do not do so first. Utilizing these basic tactics can assist the user's negotiators in meeting their bargaining goals and objectives. At the same time, recognizing and defending against these same tactics can help the user's negotiators deflate the efforts of vendor negotiators to achieve bargaining victories of their own. Because these basic negotiating tactics are important tools to vendor and user alike, and because some or all of these tactics are present in most equipment bargaining sessions, a brief overview of each is outlined below.

When employed properly, these and other negotiating tactics are linked actions that permit a user to implement or achieve a particular strategy. In essence, tactics are the "battles" that permit the user to win the strategic "war." Consequently, it is not enough for the user's negotiators to recognize and learn to utilize individual negotiating tactics. In addition, they must master the art of designing and applying clusters or chains of tactics to achieve one or more strategic objectives. One of the skills that marks the professional negotiator is the individual's ability to scan the horizon and look ahead, both within and beyond a specific bargaining session, constantly changing and updating the tactic clusters that will be executed as the negotiations ensue.

Breaking Off Negotiations

As the previous section on aspiration levels suggests, a user must be willing and able to break down negotiations in order to achieve a negotiating goal or, at least, to determine the vendor's acceptability level with respect to that goal. If the user's negotiating team is unable or unwilling to break off negotiations to achieve its objectives, the user probably has no business "negotiating" in the first place.

Although the truth of this position has been demonstrated over and over in major equipment negotiations, many users still refuse to accept it. These users cry, "That's not the way we do business. We have a very good relationship with our vendor that we have to preserve. We can't risk making them mad."

The problem, of course, is that these users have not been through the necessary "attitude adjustment," suggested in Chapter 4. They overlook the very basic point that the vendor wants to sell its equipment at least as much, if not more, than the user wants to buy it. They also overlook the fact that equipment vendors and salespeople all have defined earnings and sales goals. They need the user's business to achieve those goals.

Actually, most user representatives probably believe that all these points are true. The difference lies between the users who are willing to test these points, by being willing to break down negotiations, and those who are not willing to do so.

In many situations, the only way for the user to really determine how much the vendor will or will not bend on a given point is to purposefully break off negotiations. As one experienced user put it, "Throw the rascals out of your office until they have a better frame of mind on the issue." Depending upon the subject involved and the state of the negotiations, this strategy can be implemented in a number of ways: politely suggesting a four-hour recess; indicating that since no progress is being made, everyone might try again next week; or firmly (and perhaps forcefully) telling the vendor's representatives to leave, without giving any indication as to when, or whether, negotiations might continue. (This last technique can be particularly effective when used at 4:00 A.M. during an all-night session that the vendor feels is leading to a next-day contract signing ceremony.)

Once the user has determined to utilize this tactic, it must be willing to take a deep breath and stand pat. In effect, the user must be willing to "expect the worst" insofar as the vendor's reaction is concerned. The potential for a severe vendor reaction (or overreaction) is particularly great if this is the user's first attempt at implementing this negotiating tactic with a particular vendor.

To minimize the effect of the vendor's reaction to this user tactic, the user's negotiators should clear the approach with senior management and key members of the user's operations staff. Receiving this advance clearance from all key user representatives is critical, for the vendor's salesperson will be likely to confront every possible user contact with the allegation that the user's negotiators are "blowing the deal" despite the vendor's good faith and best offer. Most vendor marketeers are quite adept at formally or informally going outside of the user's normal chain of command to make this point. One of the user's best defenses to this tactic is for the user's president or other key manager to advise the vendor (when contacted outside the chain of command) that the user's negotiating team is handling all aspects of the transaction—period.

Another favorite vendor reaction to the user's decision to break off negotiations temporarily is for the vendor to threaten to break off negotiations permanently. This threat is sometimes staged by having key vendor representatives very obviously cancel local hotel reservations, accelerate travel plans, and the like. In other situations, the vendor's salesperson may appear to call the factory and advise them to release equipment earmarked for the user to another party. In still another alternative staging, the vendor's representatives may become silent and sullen, slowly packing up their papers and mentioning "how good it could have been" if the transaction had been consummated.

Users implementing this tactic should expect all this and more. The key to success, however, is for the user to ignore it all. Time is on the user's side. The vendor's representatives may pack up and leave. But, like the swallows of Capistrano, they will be back. And, despite all the histrionics, it is highly doubtful that, in the meantime, the country, the vendor, or the user will have failed because the negotiations have taken a few extra sessions.

Employing Informal Communication

One of the most effective, but frequently overlooked, negotiating tactics is that of informal communication. This tactic involves just what its name denotes: informal discussions among negotiators from the various sides, outside the formal meetings and bargaining sessions. Some of the most experienced negotiators in the business are convinced that more substantive concessions are granted, and more deadlocks broken, through informal communications than through any other negotiating tactic. As one particularly salty negotiator explained, "Those bargaining sessions are just for show and to frame the issues. I make all my deals over two fingers of scotch in the bar. The worst deadlock I ever experienced was against a teetotaler who wanted to discuss everything in the conference room."

As this comment suggests, for the informal communications tactic to be effective, it must represent a distinct contrast from the formal negotiating discussions. This contrast can be as vivid as having discussions in a smoke-filled bar or as minor as engaging in informal conversation in an office hallway or the corner of a meeting room. The key in each setting is that the spotlight is off, thus allowing two negotiators who were at each other's throats at the formal bargaining session to exchange quiet inquiries on "what it's going to take" to effect a compromise. (The compromise itself may then be formally announced, or "negotiated" at a subsequent public conference.) As a result, both negotiators can agree to a compromise without losing face or self-esteem in the process. Neither side is forced to "eat crow" or "cave in" in the sunlight of a formal bargaining session. Indeed, the compromise resulting from the formal bargaining session may even be designed in a manner that precludes either side from being cast in the losing position.

Although the informal communication tactic can be implemented by almost any member of the user's negotiating team, the user and vendor negotiators engaging in the informal communications should share two traits: (1) they should be viewed by one another as being trustworthy and credible; and (2) they should have apparent and actual authority to make, or at least seriously influence, the decisions reached by their respective negotiating teams. If the negotiators lack mutual trust, they will be unable to offer candid alternatives without fear that their opponent will expose and ridicule their suggestion at the next bargaining session. If one or both negotiators lack the ability to make commitments on behalf of their respective clients, the informal sessions will represent nothing more than an information exchange. Such an informal exchange of information can be valuable in itself, of course, and may be the first stage of a more substantive informal communication session. But the value of the informal communications tactic will be impaired if the participating negotiators cannot make at least tentative commitments on behalf of their respective parties. Because of the credibility and negotiating authority required, particularly experienced members of each negotiating team are often selected for informal communication sessions.

The informal communication process becomes a tactic, rather than a mutual approach, depending upon the timing with which it is employed. For the user's negotiating team to gain maximum advantage, it must recognize when the compromises to be reached during the informal communications would be most likely to favor the user. This point may be when the PNP of the user's participating negotiator exceeds the PNP of the vendor's participant by a reasonable amount, and the user's psychological negotiating leverage appears to be high. Informal communications will seldom be effective or even possible if a significant disparity exists between the PNP of the vendor and user participants. In such a situation, the negotiator with the low PNP is likely to recognize his or her weakness and either be extremely wary or refuse to participate.

Using the Good Guy/Bad Guy Technique

Because of its popularity in television detective shows, the Good Guy/Bad Guy negotiating strategy is sometimes called "The Streets of San Francisco Technique." In the television version, Lieutenant Bad Guy has the suspect in the interrogation room and is verbally abusing him about the head and shoulders. After this has gone on for some period of time, with the Lieutenant being extremely unreasonable, he leaves the room. Then along comes Inspector Good Guy. He offers the suspect a cigarette, a cup of coffee, and so on. He explains to the suspect that they don't really want to be nasty to him but they have a job to do and just want the facts. It's a basic negotiating tactic that has been used for centuries.

This approach can also be very successful in equipment negotiations. In the most basic method of implementing this tactic, the user's team must select one of its negotiators to be the Bad Guy. Although inherently nice people can be effective bad guys, it is easier for this role to be assigned to the member of the team who, in the eyes of the vendor, is most likely to be "Mr./Ms. Obnoxious" in the user's organization. Lawyers and rather haughty members of senior management are generally good candidates for this honor. Once the Bad Guy is selected, another team member must be chosen to be the Good Guy. A negotiator who is known to be relatively warm and friendly to the vendor, or who is well trained in effecting compromises, may be a sound candidate for a Good Guy.

In the early phases of the particular negotiations, the vendor's negotiators should be forced to deal with the Bad Guy. The Bad Guy, of course, takes a most unreasonable negotiating attitude. For example, he poses a lengthy list of vendor concessions that must be met before any agreement will even be seriously considered by the user. As the Bad Guy continues his unreasonable demands, the vendor's representatives will attempt to deal with him—to determine how best to nullify, compromise, or meet his list of user requirements. As the vendor's personnel become fully involved in trying to satisify or negate the Bad Guy, the user's Good Guy enters the picture. He suggests to the vendor that, despite all these problems, perhaps some compromise can be reached.

One particularly effective technique is for the Bad Guy to take an unimportant concession from the bottom of the user's list and blow it up all out of proportion. After the vendor has butted heads with the Bad Guy on this point, the Good Guy steps in and suggests that this point be conceded in exchange for two or more other points that are important to the user. (Of course the degree of importance of the various negotiating points should only be known by the user's negotiating team.) If this strategy is implemented well, the vendor's negotiators may be so happy to get away from the Bad Guy and have someone reasonable to deal with (the Good Guy) that they may readily agree to the alternative proposal.

Of course, users should be aware that this negotiating technique is well known to, and often used by, most vendor marketing teams. Very often a vendor will bring in someone from outside the local marketing office to be the Bad Guy. In this way, the vendor's local people can remain the Good Guys and not disturb the carefully created "relationship" with the user's staff.

Users should also remember that inflating the relative importance of negotiating concessions is likely to be a two-edged sword. Vendors have been known to take a particular concession that they could easily grant and pretend that it would be impossible to provide. Once the user has focused on that point, the vendor concedes it for one or more other points that are more critical to the vendor. Because of their generally superior negotiating skills, many vendors are able to implement this strategy in the middle of the user's efforts to effect its own Good Guy/Bad Guy maneuver. Members of the user's negotiating team should be continually aware of this risk and avoid the dangers of becoming overly cocky in their efforts to implement this negotiating tactic.

Taking the Offensive

One of the most basic and valuable negotiating techniques involves taking the offensive. Despite the fact that most users agree with this statement in theory, few users fully understand how to implement the theory in actual negotiations.

Very simply, taking the offensive in negotiations means seizing the momentum and precluding the vendor from regaining it. However, far too many users believe that taking the offensive means "coming on strong"—for example, using loud words, pounding on the table, and issuing controversial or nonnegotiable demands. Although all these techniques can help a sophisticated user gain or maintain the offensive, these actions generally do little to help most users. The reason is simple: these techniques involve dramatic, overt threats or polarizing actions. Such actions are likely to make most vendor representatives react in a manner that will ultimately work against the user—for example: (1) by showing annoyance and possibly deadlocking the negotiation as a ploy; (2) by coming on even stronger, thus overpowering the unsuspecting user; (3) by remaining very calm and cautious, thereby causing an insecure user to be even more so; or (4) by completely diverting the discussion to another area, where the vendor can more subtly and effectively gain or regain the offensive. In each case, the vendor realizes that the user is trying to take the offensive. Thus, the vendor is able to react, usually through the application of superior negotiating skills.

To implement this negotiating tactic correctly, the user should always attempt to gain the offensive as early as possible during the negotiations. However, "as early as possible" does not mean before the user can effectively seize and maintain the momentum. Timing is critical, as is the negotiating technique actually used.

One good technique for taking the offensive is for the user to concentrate on the vendor's weak negotiating points. This approach forces the vendor to devote more time and attention to its weak areas (both in preparation and in actual negotiating sessions.) Because the vendor must devote unexpected and excessive resources to bolstering its own weak points, it has less time to concentrate on its strong points or on the user's weak points. Indeed, some of the vendor's strong points may become weaker, due to lack of adequate vendor attention and support. When this happens, the user can add these items to its list of vendor weak points and further solidify its control.

Another useful method of gaining the offensive is for the user to zero in on the language used by the vendor's marketing representative. Vendor marketing personnel generally use broad, glowing terms to describe their products, services, and support. Vendor product brochures and magazine ads ordinarily do the same, although in somewhat more restrained terms. When this happens, the user has an excellent tool to use in gaining the offensive.

To utilize this methodology, the user must force the negotiating discussions to concentrate on the precise words used by the vendor. If the vendor claims, "We're committed to maintaining your new equipment in top shape," the user might zero in on "committed" and "in top shape." In doing so, the user would ask such questions as, "Just what do you mean by commitment? Will the contract specify the number of field engineers assigned to our site? Will the term of the maintenance contract run a full seven years? Will you contractually agree to maintenance and lease credits if the system ever fails to have 98% uptime in any month? Will you commit to replace any gear that fails to have at least 90% uptime in any calendar quarter? Let's take a look at the language you use in your standard maintenance contract to see if it reflects your commitment." And so on.

Once the momentum is gained, the user must constantly strive to reinforce its position. Although experienced negotiators can generally retain the offensive by mixing both aggressive and conservative postures on various issues, inexperienced users would be better advised to stick to a positive course of action. Therefore, the user should take the offensive throughout each negotiating session.

Generally, it is easier to gain the offensive at the outset of negotiations than to regain it after it has been lost. Nevertheless, most vendor marketing personnel are excellent negotiators (whether they appear to be or not) and are quite capable of shifting gears and issues to regain any momentum that the user may have seized.

One of the more vulnerable positions for the user is the period immediately after the user has actually gained the offensive. During this period, the user may tend to be overly proud and self-confident of its victory in seizing the momentum. Sophisticated vendor negotiators are aware of this weakness and will attempt to utilize this period of user overconfidence to regain the offensive. Vendor negotiators can employ a number of techniques at this point; for example, subtly turning the discussion to the user's weak points, volunteering a strong pro-user vendor concession (previously planned by the vendor for use at some point during the negotiations), or simply blowing the user "out of the saddle" by employing strong, aggressive language. (As suggested above, experienced negotiators are far better able than inexperienced negotiators to use strong language to gain or regain the offensive.)

A similar user weak point often exists at the outset of each negotiating session, particularly at the session immediately following the meeting where the user first gained the offensive. The user should remember that, to be effective, the momentum must be maintained and reinforced at each new meeting. As in the initial negotiating session, the best time for reinforcement is at the outset of each new meeting (including the first few minutes of any session that is reconvened after a break for lunch or dinner).

Using Surprise as a Tactic

The element of surprise can be an effective user tactic and, as such, should be included in the arsenal of every experienced negotiator. However, like anger, surprise must be used purposefully to achieve maximum results and avoid potentially negative counter effects.

Although many definitions of tactical surprise exist, perhaps the best and most basic is any planned negotiating maneuver which thrusts sudden and unexpected change on a negotiating opponent. The library of possible surprise maneuvers contains thousands of volumes and good negotiators choose those elements which they can best master personally. (As in all negotiating tactics, the negotiator must select those methods of implementation that are most natural and effective for the individual involved. As suggested above, negotiating is both a learned skill and a practiced art, but a good negotiator recognizes his or her weaknesses and selects those strategic tools which maximize the strengths.) The following actions offer a good cross section of examples of the surprise tactic:

- Sudden display of temper.
- Unanticipated, obvious change in voice pitch, speed, or volume.
- Unexpected display of emotion, or the introduction of an emotional issue into the negotiations (e.g., an issue that the implementing negotiator can legitimately get "worked up" over).
- Unplanned change in negotiators, often based on a variation of the "good guy/bad guy" routine described above.
- Total and unexpected change of subject and focus, either in the middle of ongoing discussions or after a planned break or brief rest room intermission.
- Sudden deadlock of negotiations either short-term or longer (e.g., overnight).
- Sudden walk-out, where the implementing negotiator simply leaves the room for a short period (either with or without also using one of the other examples mentioned above).

Most users have little difficulty recognizing how to utilize surprise as a tactic. However, the question of when to use the tactic generally presents more of a problem. Users that have previously attempted to use tactical surprise often complain that the effort was ineffective or, at best, brought a "ho-hum" reaction from the vendor's negotiators. Oftentimes, this user disenchantment stems from the fact that the user injected surprise into the negotiations at precisely the wrong time.

As noted earlier in this chapter, the personal negotiating power (PNP) held by a given negotiator is cyclical, ebbing and flowing over time in a sinelike course. The key time for a negotiator to utilize surprise as a tactic is when his or her personal negotiating power has peaked and is on the ebb. Using surprise as a tactic when the negotiator is at the height of his or her negotiating power is, quite simply, a waste of resources. Because the negotiator is already at or near the top of his or her negotiating power, the introduction of surprise at this point may actually have little effect. On the other hand, waiting until the negotiator is at his or her weakest negotiating power may pose real risks in the use of surprise as a tactic. To be implemented successfully, tactical surprise requires reasonable amounts of negotiating power and credibility. If the negotiator waits until he is in his weakest position before utilizing surprise, he may not have the negotiating strength necessary to pull out of the valley. Indeed, in this weakened position, the user may be susceptible to unplanned uses of temper or surprise in a last ditch effort to do anything to turn the tide.

Waiting until the last possible moment to employ surprise also poses substantive risks for the negotiator. Despite the fact that negotiating power is cyclical, a good negotiator strives to minimize both the depth and duration of the downward cycle. If the negotiator waits too long to employ tactical surprise, both the depth and duration of the downside curve may be more extreme, thus increasing the user's exposure to potentially adverse compromises and vendor ploys that prey on a weakened user negotiator.

When it is implemented successfully, tactical surprise strengthens the user's individual negotiating power, giving the negotiator additional time to achieve concessions and employ other tactics that require strong negotiating position for effective implementation. In effect, tactical surprise tends to extend the upward cycle of the negotiating power curve, either in terms of height or duration or both. (See Fig. 3-10.) But ultimately that curve will also begin to ebb, thereby requiring the user to again employ surprise or another tactic that offers similar negotiating advantage.

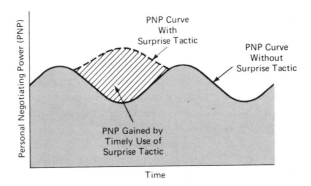

Fig. 3-10.   Increased personal negotiating power (PNP) resulting from timely user execution of the surprise tactic.

Applying the *Fait Accompli* Tactic

Fait accompli is a French phrase that roughly translates as "the deed is done" or "the thing is accomplished." In the context of negotiations, the term also describes a negotiating tactic that generally involves a bold action that is designed to place one party in a superior bargaining position.

In equipment negotiations, this tactic can be employed by both the vendor and the user. In both situations, the person utilizing the strategy effectively tells the other party (by words and/ or actions) to "take it or leave it!" For example, the vendor's marketing representative may dramatically give the user the vendor's standard form agreement and say, "This is the contract we use and we just don't modify it. Even Ford signs this form agreement." Alternatively, the vendor's marketeer may say, "This is our absolute best price. If this won't get the business, you've just lost one heck of an opportunity." On the other side, the user may employ the tactic by saying, "Look, we won't do business unless you come in under $550,000. If you can't break that, forget it." In each situation, the implication is "do business on my final terms or we call off the negotiations"; in effect, "take it or leave it" or "we've been through the negotiations; the deal is done—either we do business on these terms or we don't do business at all." Because of the implication of finality, this tactic is related to the strategy of breaking off negotiations, discussed above. However, the *fait accompli* technique can be far more subtle and refined.

When the *fait accompli* tactic is employed carefully, it can be extremely effective. The strategy is particularly useful:

- To "overpower" a weaker opponent. In this use, the party with the bargaining advantage uses the tactic to intimidate a weaker party into promptly closing the transaction.
- To catch an ill-prepared party "off-guard." Here the party using the tactic effectively disarms a poorly prepared negotiator. The latter party signs because he is afraid of losing the deal—and he is too poorly prepared to understand otherwise.
- To enhance a time dependent or "sense of urgency" marketing ploy. Here, too, the weaker party is afraid not to close—on the ground that the offer really may not be available for long.
- To wrap things up or bring matters to conclusion when further negotiations either are not desired or are not permitted due to a shortage of time.

In each situation, the tactic works because it says, "Now it's up to you. We've given our best offer. You can agree and save the deal. Or you can balk and blow all the advantages you've negotiated up to this point." The party hit with the strategy is faced with a number of fears: the fear of personal failure, concern about business or personal rejection, and fear of failing to meet his company's needs by completing the transaction.

The *fait accompli* tactic is often used as a one shot or "killer" close technique; that is, when victory can be gained by making one (or one more) dramatic move. The tactic can also be used before the closing to force the opponent into some action or reaction. In this mode, the approach is effective to break open negotiations that are wandering or those that have dragged to a virtual standstill. (In such a situation, any action may be better than no action at all.) Finally, as suggested above, the *fait accompli* technique can be used to force a deadlock or a break off in negotiations. In this use, the negotiator deliberately polarizes the discussions either by posing an ultimatum or final offer that obviously will not be accepted or by countering the other party's *fait accompli* move with his own *fait accompli* ultimatum. When both sides use the tactic at the same time, a deadlock often results.

Despite these potential advantages, the *fait accompli* tactic is not without risks. The basic problem in the *fait accompli* approach is what to do if the tactic fails to work. The technique is primarily effective because of its "poker game bluff" impact. However, sometimes the other side refuses to buy the bluff and calls instead. Because of this risk, a negotiator who uses this technique must always have a fall back position—and a route to get there without losing face. Saving face is important from a psychological standpoint (remember Maslow's needs), but it is also important if the negotiator is to retain credibility. Retaining credibility, and maintaining an effective "bluff" capability, is particularly critical if the negotiator will face his or her opponent again in the future, as is often the situation with an incumbent vendor.

Another potential disadvantage of the *fait accompli* tactic is the resentment and bitterness that it may engender in the members of the opposing negotiating team. As the saying goes, "no one likes an ultimatum," and some negotiators may become particularly resentful when confronted with a blatant use of the *fait accompli* tactic. This risk can seldom be eliminated, in part because the reaction of opposing negotiators can never be judged with perfection. Nevertheless, the risk can be moderated by: (1) recognizing that resentment may occur; (2) avoiding any steps that might cause opposing negotiators to lose self-esteem; and (3) employing the informal communication tactic where appropriate to soften the subsequent effects of the *fait accompli* approach.

Jumping the Hurdles One at a Time

This negotiating technique is called a variety of clever names, such as "The Salami," "One Slice at a Time," and "Going Through the Tunnel." Many experienced negotiators simply refer to it as "Jumping the Hurdles One at a Time." Whatever the name, the technique is essentially a method of gaining or maintaining negotiating strength and direction. In the context of equipment negotiations, the key to the approach is for the user to disclose its negotiating goals to the vendor "one step at a time" and thereby force the vendor to fully address, and accept or reject, each of these negotiating goals on a separate basis.

This technique has a number of advantages. First, it helps the user gain and maintain control of the negotiations. Because only the user is aware of its full "shopping list," the vendor is far less able to map a comprehensive negotiating strategy and control the negotiations. On the other hand, the user can manipulate its separate negotiating points and disclose, withhold, or compromise them as may be necessary to maximize negotiating advantage.

Second, the strategy permits the user to add a further issue at virtually any point in the negotiations. Because the vendor is not aware of the length of the user's "shopping list," the user can raise additional points that occur to the user during the negotiations without being subject to the standard vendor criticism concerning the user's "bad faith" for adding points "at the last minute."

Third, the approach puts pressure on the vendor and keeps it off balance. For the two reasons suggested above, this negotiating technique keeps the vendor from being able to accurately assess the user's negotiating position. From a practical standpoint, this drives most vendor marketing representatives "right up the wall" and gives a psychological advantage to the user.

Fourth, the strategy permits the user to assess and react to the vendor's position with maximum flexibility. In essence, the user is able to analyze the vendor's reaction to various user concerns and vary further negotiating thrusts accordingly.

Fifth, the technique often increases the likelihood that the vendor will agree to specific user negotiating points. If the vendor is aware that negotiations will continue to other points only if the agreement is reached on the specific subject under consideration, the vendor may be more likely to reach early and meaningful agreement on the issue. In addition, if early agreement can be reached on some minor issues, it may set the stage and chemistry for further agreement on other points.

Sixth, the methodology weakens the effectiveness of various vendor ploys designed to keep the user off guard. The tactic is particularly effective to stifle the "Unfortunately I'll Have to Get Any Changes Approved By Corporate" ploy discussed in Chapter 2. Similarly, the technique helps the user determine where final negotiating authority lies in the vendor's organization.

Seventh, this approach lets the vendor know that the user is playing professional ball. The formal structure used to implement the tactic shows that the user intends to take the negotiations seriously and to pursue each point with vigor.

Finally, the technique helps keep the user's own negotiating team "on track." In effect, the structured approach involved lessens the risk that the user's representatives will lose direction and end up thoughtlessly considering a variety of issues with little or no sense of priorities. The "one at a time" negotiating technique is particularly effective when coupled with an agenda or other document that contains ground rules for the negotiating session. Under this approach, the user opens the negotiations by gaining vendor agreement on a set of basic "rules of the game" that will govern all sessions.

Such an agenda might contain the following ground rules among others:

1. The parties will strive for agreement on a point by point basis.
2. Both parties will be open and candid on any points of disagreement; however, a problem solving approach will be used in an effort to reach mutual agreement on each point.
3. The parties will avoid irrelevant discussions that do not contribute toward the goal of reaching mutual agreement on the issue under discussion.
4. The meeting will adjourn if agreement cannot be reached on key issues under discussion or if vendor or user personnel do not have authority to firmly commit to any such issue.
5. If applicable, any unresolved items will be discussed first at the next meeting, before other issues are considered.
6. In the event mutual agreement is not reached on an issue deemed important by the user, the user reserves the right to break off negotiations with the vendor and enter into, or continue, discussions with alternative vendors that are within the "zone of consideration." (See Chapters 4 and 5.)

This tactic of using "ground rules" permits the user to establish the "Jump the Hurdles One at a Time" strategy early during the negotiations, with minimum difficulty and with maximum psychological advantage. When the ground rules are part of a written agenda, the user can also refer back to them later on, if necessary, to reinforce the negotiating strategy.

Several other techniques are also available that will permit the user to maximize the effectiveness of this negotiating tactic.

First, the user should continue to make the vendor feel that the user may break off negotiations if the specific point under consideration cannot be resolved. This technique forces the vendor to take the "one step at a time" approach seriously. Some users make this point by keeping alternate vendors in the "zone of consideration," ready for immediate negotiations if the primary session deadlocks. Other users simply explain that the entire purpose of focusing on one issue at a time is "to determine if there is any rationale for continuing the negotiations." As one user negotiator explained to the vendor, "Look, your time is valuable; our time is valuable. Before we clutter up the session with a lot of issues, or waste time working through the contract, we want to know if you are willing to reach agreement on a number of issues that we think are critical to this entire deal."

Second, the user should mix and match the priorities of issues brought up for discussion. By not considering its shopping list in the order of priority, the user maximizes its ability to keep the vendor confused concerning the user's ultimate negotiating strategy and goals.

Third, the user should selectively table issues where this approach seems advantageous for the user; at the same time, the user should refuse to table other issues when desirable for the vendor's convenience. This approach also keeps the vendor off base. In addition, it permits the user to determine if and when several points will be considered at once or left pending (often for the purpose of effecting a compromise or trade-off).

Fourth, the user should recognize in advance that the vendor may do everything possible to avoid the "one step at a time" approach, either at the outset of negotiations or during later sessions. In this regard, the user should predetermine to reject out of hand any standard vendor comments concerning the desirability of "going to the well only once, with the whole package." This vendor strategy is a variation of the "corporate authority" ploy where the vendor urges the user to present its entire position at once so the vendor's marketing representative will only have to "go to corporate headquarters" one time to gain approval of the negotiated transaction. (See Chapter 2.) Although there are a number of effective counters to this vendor ruse, two are especially effective. First, simply say "no" and refuse to accept the idea. Second, listen attentively and then ask the sales representative why the user's account is not worth the trouble of "going to corporate headquarters" on all the critical issues, one at a time or otherwise (or bringing someone into the negotiations who has final negotiating authority for the vendor).

Using the Agenda as a Strategy

As the previous section suggests, one of the more subtle negotiating tactics available to a competent user is the development of a formal agenda for each important bargaining session. An agenda prepared by the user has several advantages.

First, it forces the user's negotiating team to review its priorities, goals, and objectives in the context of a particular proposed meeting. Even where a negotiations position paper has been developed, many users fail to prepare adequately for specific bargaining sessions. In many situations, the user's negotiators are only generally aware of the points or questions they intend to cover at a particular meeting; they have given little or no thought to the order of the meeting or the psychological advantages that might be obtained by bringing issues up in a specific fashion.

Second, an agenda strengthens the ability of the user's team to control the negotiating session, thereby enhancing the user's potential ability to accomplish its own objectives. Control of the negotiating environment can be a critical advantage, particularly where the control permits the user's team to implement a planned user strategy or to block a vendor-attempted negotiating ploy. In this regard, a carefully designed agenda permits the user to sequence the topics to be discussed in a manner that eliminates subsequent "bulges" and allegations of surprise with respect to deferred items. As the initial portion of Chapter 8 suggests, the user's ability to achieve negotiating success may be related to its skill in controlling the order in which various linked issues are discussed. The failure to consider related issues together may permit the vendor to allege surprise later in the negotiations, thereby causing the discussions concerning the deferred item or items to "bulge" way out of proportion. Figures 3-11 and 3-12 demonstrate this problem. In Fig. 3-11, the user fails to control the discussion of related issues through an agenda or other tactic. Despite the potential for agreement reached on issue A, the potential for disagreement on issues B and C increases, even though (actually, because) those issues are not discussed along with issue A. In Fig. 3-12, all three issues are negotiated, or at least considered, together or in a controlled sequence. As a result, the average potential for agreement on the three issues is improved.

Third, an agenda generally throws most vendors off balance, for few users have the sophistication to prepare any type of agenda, not to mention a good one. By catching the vendor off guard, the agenda strengthens the user's ability to implement its own strategies and weakens the vendor's efforts to utilize various negotiating ploys. This psychological advantage enhances the user's ability to control the bargaining session, as mentioned above.

Fourth, the agenda can be used as an indirect method of getting the user's point across on a specific bargaining issue. Similarly, the agenda can be utilized as a subtle tool to implement, or reinforce, a particular user negotiating strategy. The mere promulgation of the agenda by the

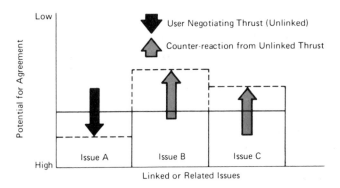

Fig. 3-11. Reduction in average potential for agreement resulting from user's failure to negotiate related issues in a concurrent or sequential manner.

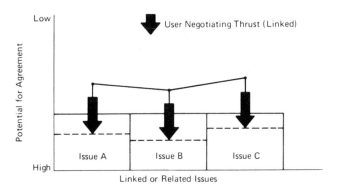

Fig. 3-12. Increase in average potential for agreement resulting from user's decision to negotiate related issues in a concurrent or sequential manner.

user, and the acceptance of it by the vendor, permits the user to achieve a preliminary negotiating victory: the vendor admits, directly or indirectly, that the user's concerns are worth addressing. Beyond this point, the specific language and organization of the agenda can be employed to implement or reinforce particular user negotiating strategies.

The key in using an agenda strategically is to appreciate the subtleties involved. For example, consider the following outline of a longer agenda that was actually used in one bargaining session involving computer equipment:

AGENDA

Potential Supplier: XYZ Corporation
Date: June 1, 1980

PRELIMINARY

I. *Meeting arrangements and schedule*

  A. Introductions
  B. Ground Rules
  C. Meeting Objectives
    1. Potential Supplier Intentions/Needs
    2. User Intentions/Needs
  D. Agenda Review
  E. Agreement Potential

II. *Vendor's representations and commitments*

  A. Vendor's Presentation of Its "Deliverables"
    1. Inclusion of Vendor Proposal in Agreement—Penalties.
    2. Inclusion of Benchmark Results in Agreement—Penalties
    3. Acceptance Criteria—Penalties.
      a. Hardware
      b. Software—Operating
      c. Software—Application
    4. On-Going Performance Criteria—Penalties.
      a. Maintenance
      b. Systems Support
      c. Hardware—Current and Future
      d. Operating Software—Current and Future Revisions
      e. Application Software
      f. Crisis Management Methodology
  B. User's Explanation of Its Concerns—If Any
    1. Resolution of Concerns (If Possible)
    2. No Resolution—Continuation Decision by User (If Applicable)
  C. Agreement on Vendor's Ability to Perform (including warranties and remedies acceptable to User)

III. *Break—caucus—user continuation decision*

WORK SESSION—IF APPLICABLE

I. *Vendor payment aspirations*

  A. Review of Vendor Concessions
  B. Review of Payment Schedule vs. User Risks (at various timeframes)

II. *Caucus—user continuation decision—meeting resumption* (if applicable)

III. *Vendor's ability to meet user's critical needs*

    A. ITC Warranty

    B. Emergency Hardware Replacement

    C. Delivery Standards and Detailed Installation Plan

    D. Installation Hours

    E. Damages for Late Delivery, Installation, or Acceptance

    F. Interim Equipment

    G. Free Documentation Copies

    H. Guaranteed Maintenance for "System Life"

    I. Performance Bond

    J. Price Warranty

       [*Note: The above points are examples only; the Agenda should list principal contractual points or concessions deemed necessary by the User.*]

IV. *Caucus—user continuation decision—meeting resumption (if applicable)*

V. *Vendor's presentation of contractual documents to substantiate vendor's representations*

    A. Presentation and Review of Documents by Vendor's Counsel

    B. Comment by User's Counsel

    C. Conceptual Agreement (If Possible)

    D. Assignment of Drafting Responsibilities and Completion Dates

INGREDIENTS FOR SUCCESS—IF APPLICABLE

I. *Review remaining tasks, responsibilities, and timeframes*

II. *Review points of agreement and consider any remaining problems*

III. *Schedule contract signing or outline objectives for next meeting*

In the above example, the vendor is referred to as a "potential" supplier. This phraseology can have a disarming effect, particularly if the vendor otherwise believes that it is the sole source being considered by the user. The "Ground Rules" section in the sample agenda allows the user's lead negotiator to explain that the user is ready and willing to do business and, indeed, to execute an agreement (see "Agreement Potential" and the final "Ingredient for Success" in the agenda), but if agreement cannot be reached to user's satisfaction in this session, the user can and will immediately call in the next "potential" supplier. Going further, the agenda requires the vendor to present its "deliverables." Later, the vendor will be asked to place all of these items in the vendor/user agreement. If the vendor refuses to do so at that point, it will be in the position of backing off from earlier commitments. This subtle step toward "positioning" the vendor is repeated several times in the agenda.

Primarily by referring to various "caucus" break points, the agenda also emphasizes that negotiations may be broken off at any time if acceptable vendor concessions are not forthcoming. At the same time, the agenda serves as a constant reminder that an executed agreement is possible if certain listed points can be resolved. In practice, it is this combination "carrot and stick" approach that makes the agenda particularly valuable as a user strategy.

Using Environment as a Tactic

Most experienced negotiators agree that the time and place of negotiations can have a material impact on the outcome of a particular bargaining session. Fortunately, many users of major equipment have the flexibility to control the negotiating environment to their benefit. Unfortunately, few users seriously attempt to do so, primarily because they refuse to recognize the ultimate importance of this control or because they feel the entire subject is too insincere or manipulative.

Despite these concerns, the basic rule is very simple: Whenever practicable, a user should strive to select and control the time, place, and environment of all negotiating sessions.

Time. As contemporary time management courses suggest, most individuals have certain periods during the day when they perform best. Each member of the user's negotiating team should assess his or her personal traits and determine those times when the individual is most likely to excell in the negotiating arena. Although these primary periods are unlikely to coincide for all members of the team, the periods may overlap and, in any event, a majority or primary period can be determined for the team as a whole. When at all possible, important negotiating sessions should be scheduled only during this period.

Other factors, however, can also impact the effectiveness of the team during the primary negotiating period or during any other bargaining session. Fatigue, travel, and meals are the three outside factors likely to be the most significant. Consequently, the potential effect of these three factors should always be considered in scheduling important negotiations.

Fatigue. Fatigue obviously affects a negotiator's mental sharpness and ability to recognize and defuse vendor ploys. Moreover, it reduces the negotiator's ability to employ tactics. In many individuals, fatigue also reduces patience and increases the potential for uncontrolled anger. When fatigue is related to overwork, it may also signal an actual or potential lack of preparation. Because of these and other negatives, the negotiating team should avoid scheduling negotiating sessions when the team as a whole, or one or more key team members, is suffering from fatigue.

Travel. Travel often results in temporary fatigue, even where the distance is relatively short and the negotiator has made many business trips before. When negotiations must be linked with travel, the team should strive to allow adequate rest and adjustment time before the actual conference. Although the ability of different individuals to bounce back after traveling obviously varies, one of the best general methods of reducing the potential effects of negotiating trips is to travel during the afternoon and early evening of one day and schedule the negotiations for a primary period on the following day. For most negotiators, one of the worst schedules involves travel late into the night on the day before an early morning bargaining session.

Time and rest are not the only important factors associated with travel. The quality of travel can also be a critical element. Particularly during times of economic decline, many users insist that all employees travel tourist class and not exceed stated per diem amounts for room and board. Although these budgetary constraints should not be dismissed lightly, they also should not be applied indiscriminately, particularly when the travel is directly linked to negotiating a multimillion dollar equipment acquisition. When viewed in the proper perspective, first class travel costs very little. Yet the value of that travel can be substantial in a negotiating context.

The authors generally recommend that all members of a user's negotiating team travel first class on all key trips. Regardless of whether the additional amenities and service are "worth" the higher cost when viewed in terms of wider seats or somewhat better food, first class travel reduces fatigue and the potential for outside annoyance. (Being headquartered in Orlando, the authors have often used the example of flying to New York City on Eastern Airlines—the "Official Airline of Walt Disney World"—with dozens of tired children wearing Mickey Mouse ears and alternately shrieking or crying.) In addition, first class travel has a subtle but important psychological advantage. Very simply, it makes the negotiator feel that his or her company is willing to spend a little more money to ensure his or her comfort and convenience. First class travel tells the employee, "You're important to this company and you're on an important assignment where we want you to be at your best so you can do your best." This subtle "pat on the back" can do a great deal to give a negotiator that extra drive and edge necessary to gain and keep a high aspiration level and a strong psychological negotiating advantage.

Food. At its most basic level, food affects metabolism. Lack of food—particularly at "normal" mealtimes—can distract attention and bring on or increase fatigue. Consequently, a negotiating schedule should make proper allowance for meals.

However, assuring adequate intake is not the only metabolic problem. For most individuals, food temporarily dulls the senses as digestion ensues. Although some negotiators conduct their best performances over a lengthy dinner, most individuals perform relatively poorly for about an hour after a medium-to-heavy lunch or dinner. To minimize this problem, the authors recommend that users avoid scheduling key negotiating sessions immediately after lunch or dinner. Where meals must be scheduled during lengthy negotiations, the schedule should provide for a caucus session or other noncompetitive period immediately after a meal.

If the intensity of the negotiations does not permit this luxury, the user's negotiating team should exercise basic dietary restraint. The rules are relatively simple, and can be put to good use at formal dinners or conference table box lunches. The first and foremost rule is to eat lightly. By reducing intake, a negotiator minimizes the lethargic or "full and sleepy" feeling that so often follows more extensive meals. The second rule is to avoid rich foods. Light, easily digested meats like chicken or fish will generally have less impact on sharpness than fatty red meats or rich casserole dishes and desserts. The third rule is controversial to some: Avoid alcohol (including beer and wine). Regardless of one's personal views toward drinking, the fact remains that alcoholic beverages dull the senses. And dull senses have no place in the negotiating arena. Although exceptions certainly must be made from time to time, the authors suggest that a negotiator not consume any alcoholic beverage within two to three hours before a negotiating session. Ideally, a negotiator should have an alcoholic drink only at the end of the day's bargaining and debriefing sessions. Even then, moderation must be exercised if negotiations will resume early the following day.

Place. The best place to negotiate is wherever the user's negotiating team can optimize its control of the bargaining process. Every experienced negotiator recognizes the physical negotiating environments that seem to reinforce his or her ability to achieve negotiating success. For some negotiators, the golf course, the hood of a car, or a luncheon table at the club offers the best environment. For others, a formal conference room in their own or their client's offices provides the only secure location. For still others, the offices of their opponent maximize the negotiator's opportunity for success. The key point to remember is that, in most instances, users have the luxury of being able to pick the negotiating site. To waive this right, or to exercise it carelessly, is an unforgiveable error.

Because the best place to negotiate is largely influenced by the personalities and preferences of the user's negotiators, generalizations concerning selection of the proper physical environment are somewhat difficult. (Indeed, the authors sometimes disagree between themselves over the selection of the best negotiating site in a particular transaction.) Nevertheless, the following factors are relevant to any consideration of the proper physical environment.

General location. At the outset, the advantages and disadvantages of negotiating at home, at the opponent's location, or at a neutral third site should be assessed. Because the pros and cons of a particular site may vary depending upon the stage the negotiations are in at the time of a given bargaining session, the user may need to reassess this matter from time to time as the negotiation process continues to progress.

For many user representatives, negotiating on the user's home court provides substantial benefits. Negotiating is a team sport and, in a simplistic sense, the home team advantage can be just as applicable in business bargaining sessions as it is in football, baseball, or hockey contests. Negotiating on the user's home ground improves the user's ability to control such critical factors as travel, food, fatigue, and physical surroundings. Home court negotiating also permits the user's team to avoid the psychological and physical problems associated with adapting to a new and temporary physical environment. In addition, it maximizes the team's access to other user resources, including staff support personnel, files, and final decision makers. Negotiating at the user's home offices also permits one or more user senior executives to "set the tone" and lay down the ground rules for the negotiations, both at the outset and as discussions continue.

Despite these advantages, home court negotiating also offers potential problems. Unless the user's negotiating team executes substantial discipline, the press of ongoing business at the user's site is difficult to channel or otherwise control. As a result, home office negotiations are often plagued by persistent interruptions and pressures that cause distractions and morale problems for the user's negotiators. (Just watching other work pile up on the user's desk may cause this problem.) Negotiating on the user's home court also makes it more difficult for the user to implement certain limited authority and deadlock tactics. If the negotiations are being held at the user's headquarters, the user's negotiators may be less able to assert that they cannot gain management approval on a particular matter until a later date or time. Moreover, as a general principle, it is easier to walk out, or threaten to do so, than it is to throw someone out. Thus, while the user's negotiators have numerous methods of "packing up to leave" at the vendor's site or at a neutral site, this flexibility is not present when the negotiations are held at the user's offices. Finally, when the user negotiates at home, the vendor's ability to pull an "end run" and attempt to influence or undermine the user team's negotiating authority is enhanced, simply because of the vendor's proximity to the user's senior executives.

Because of these disadvantages, some experienced negotiators prefer to negotiate at the vendor's offices, at least during certain stages of the acquisition process. When properly orchestrated, negotiations at the vendor's site ensure that the proposed transaction will have high visibility within the vendor organization. This visibility provides two benefits to the user. First, it gives the user negotiators an opportunity to meet with senior management or marketing representatives within the vendor organization, thereby increasing the user's ability to effect a substantive compromise on important issues. Second, this visibility places the spotlight on the vendor's negotiators, exposing them to substantial pressure and criticism if, for example, the user's negotiators walk out (just before a scheduled lunch with a vendor executive vice president). Holding negotiations at the vendor's site also makes it more difficult for the vendor to implement various limited authority ploys. For example, the vendor's negotiators are less able to complain about "going to corporate," being unable to make a given decision, or being unable to locate a particular informational or human resource. Particularly where the user negotiators are experienced business travelers, bargaining at the vendor's site can improve the user's focus and reduce the fatigue associated with marathon negotiating sessions. As noted above, lengthy negotiations at the user's site create time pressures and interruptions for the user's negotiators. By negotiating at the vendor's offices, the user's negotiators can eliminate many of their day-to-day interruptions and devote their full attention to achieving an optimum transaction. Because the negotiators are out of town for a stated duration, they can avoid some of the morale problems that can and do arise from the cancelled meetings, unreturned telephone calls, and late night sessions (where family dinners are either late or abandoned) that plague home-site negotiating sessions.

Nevertheless, negotiating at the vendor's site can create serious problems for the user. Naive user negotiators are likely to be overwhelmed by the vendor's attention, interest, and apparent dedication, as the vendor puts on its finest game of show and tell, factory tours, and management luncheons. This danger is particularly great: (1) early in the negotiation process, when an appropriately impressed user may decide that the vendor is so wonderful that formal negotiations are not necessary (see Chapter 1); and (2) when the user's negotiators are inexperienced, again raising the risk that they will determine not to proceed with proper negotiating principles. As suggested above, negotiating at the vendor's site may also cause problems relating to travel, fatigue, and inability to control the physical environment. While these problems cannot be totally controlled, an experienced user negotiator can make the best of the out of town setting (for example, by traveling first class, ignoring home office pressures, and taking every opportunity possible to run back to the hotel for a refreshing shower or nap).

Negotiating at a neutral third site has many of the advantages and disadvantages discussed above. The problems and benefits of traveling to a site away from distractions are present. Both sides are still able to execute limited authority ploys. Both parties face the disadvantage of being unable to access resource people, files and management. Neither party has the immediate ability to control the physical advantage, although the party making the reservations and meeting arrangements may seize this opportunity. (Even at a neutral location, the host sets the tone for the negotiations.)

Physical environment. The physical environment of the negotiating arena can be as important as the city in which the negotiations are held. Most experienced negotiators have favorite surroundings and key team members should be canvassed to determine likely conference facilities. When the negotiations will be held in the user's city, a good conference room in the offices of the user or its attorneys or professional negotiators is often the best site. However, as noted above, the advantages associated with negotiating at the user's headquarters can be quickly overcome if key team members are frequently interrupted by telephone calls and meetings with associates. Consequently, any user conference room must be effectively cut off from interruptions relating to day-to-day work assignments. The key goal should be to select a meeting room that (to the user's team) will feel familiar, avoid distractions, and minimize interruptions. The decor of the conference room or other negotiating location should also be considered by the user's team. Where possible, the appointments should be reasonably rich in order to instill self-confidence in the user's negotiators and convey a sense of user strength and control to the vendor's representatives. Generally, room must also be provided for breaks and team caucuses. Where the user is in control of the location, the vendor's team may be assigned pleasant but somewhat substandard caucus rooms. Conversely, the user's team may be permitted to caucus in the main conference room or in a first class nearby location. To avoid distractions and interruptions, the user's caucus location should not be the office of a member of the user's negotiating team.

To the extent permissible within environmental guidelines, the temperature of all meeting rooms should be cool to cold for maximum mental sharpness. Lighting should be good and, where possible, the same type of lighting (e.g., cool ray fluorescent) that the user's team members are used to working under.

Seating arrangements in the main conference or meeting rooms should also be considered. Chairs should be relatively comfortable to slightly uncomfortable, with the latter sometimes necessary to avoid drowsiness during long bargaining sessions. If the meeting room contains windows, whether curtained or not, the vendor's negotiators should generally be seated facing the glare and distractions of the outside world. (Users should recognize that a factor as simple as glare can change the negotiating environment. An office or meeting room with bright sunlight may be a pleasant meeting place, but if the seating arrangements and window coverings are placed in a fashion that creates glare for one side or the other, or that precludes one negotiator from clearly seeing into the eyes of his or her opponent, tension is created, and the parties without the glare problems will enjoy superior negotiating control.)

The shape of the table must also be assessed, as different table designs create, or assist in creating, different negotiating environments. For example, a round table generally conveys a "collegial" feeling: It has no obvious head or sides. (Fig. 3-13.) Such a table can reduce tension and infer that all seated at the table are colleagues and approximate equals. On the other hand,

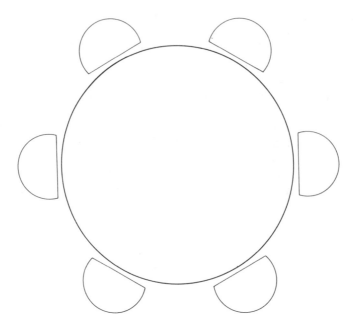

Fig. 3-13.   A round negotiating table facilitates agreement by creating a collegial feeling.

a rectangular table usually has a clearly defined head, and those seated around it ordinarily gravitate toward their respective sides and (especially at larger tables such as those found in board rooms) the seats acceptable to their position in the relative pecking order. (Fig. 3-14.)

Although many fine negotiators suggest that a round meeting table and other pro-agreement environmental factors should be the standard setting for any bargaining session, the authors caution most users not to utilize such an arrangement in major equipment negotiations, particularly during early stages of the negotiating process. As Chapters 1 and 2 emphasize, most users have a serious problem gaining equality at any bargaining table, due to the vendor's sophisticated efforts to utilize a warm relationship and various ploys to lull the user into a sense of happiness,

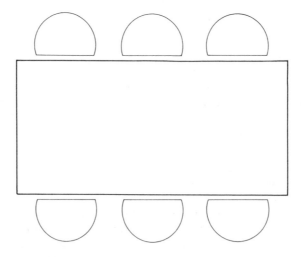

Fig. 3-14.   A rectangular negotiating table generally creates tension by emphasizing the opposing sides.

wonderment, and security. A round negotiating table or an informal office seating area only reinforces the vendor's efforts to let relationship overshadow reality. Consequently, in most instances, a more formal seating arrangement will better serve the user's interests, by emphasizing the user's negotiating strength, position, and equality. Once this critical user positioning has been made, the user's team can more safely employ alternative seating arrangements and other environmental factors to signal concession, agreement, and the like.

Regardless of the table shape selected, the arrangement of opposing negotiators at the table can also affect the negotiating environment. Where the table has an obvious head, many lead negotiators prefer to seize that seat in order to optimize their control of the meeting and the negotiations. (The head of even a rectangular table varies depending upon the room layout and seating order. In some situations, the functional head of a rectangular or free form table may be in the middle of one side rather than at either end.) Other lead negotiators, generally those with strong experience and confidence levels, prefer to select a position in the middle of the table, actually forcing one of the vendor's negotiators to sit in what soon becomes a "hot seat" at the traditional head of the table. These negotiators use their superior negotiating abilities to develop and impose dominance from an unexpected location in a successful effort to keep the vendor's negotiators on the defensive.

Where a rectangular table is involved, the feeling of tension is heightened if each party's negotiators sit on one side of the table. In contrast, a more collegial feeling can be gained by informally mingling the negotiators around the table without "seizing sides." However, if pushed to an extreme, this approach can create severe tension; for example, where the user's negotiators choose alternate seats around the entire table, forcing all of the vendor's negotiators to be separated from one another. Such an extreme approach is seldom recommended, but where it is employed it is likely to create a substantial impact.

As this example suggests, the user should also consider the relative seating arrangements for the members of its own team. Personal preferences should generally control this decision. For example, where the user's lead negotiator is not the team attorney, the negotiator may prefer for the attorney to sit to his or her right (thereby facilitating handwritten notes if the lead negotiator is right handed), with the user's chief technical advisor to his or her left (again to facilitate communications during the bargaining session). In contrast, the negotiator may feel that such an approach weakens his or her eye contact with these key team members and that, therefore, they should be seated across the table or at an angle. The only "right" answer is that the seating arrangements should maximize the ability of the lead negotiator and the other team members to communicate and negotiate effectively.

Physical surroundings must also be considered where the negotiations are held in an executive's office rather than in a conference or meeting room. For example, in an executive's office, a couch or chair grouping around an end or coffee table conveys informality, warm business relationship, and likely agreement. In contrast, seating which places the executive in his or her desk chair, across a broad desk from the visitor sitting in a relatively straight back chair facing the desk, creates a formal and slightly strained position that enhances the superiority and control of the executive. This feeling of superiority can be enhanced if the guest chairs at the desk are relatively soft and low, thereby giving the executive a height advantage even while all parties are seated.

Ideally, the executive offices of the user should include enough meeting rooms and arrangements to permit the user's negotiators to select and control alternative environments as needed. For example, the offices should contain at least two small meeting rooms, one with a round table and one with a rectangular table. A larger, more dramatic meeting room should also be available to upgrade "important" sessions. This room is often most effective when it has an unusual shaped table, such as an octagon or free-form design. Tables such as these usually permit alternative seating arrangements that can be made more or less collegial as desired. The area should also include private offices where smaller (often preliminary) meetings or brief follow-up sessions can be held. These offices should ideally include both formal "across the desk" seating arrangements and informal conversation groupings. One effective informal arrangement for an executive office involves four chairs around a small round or square meeting table—much the same layout found in many residential breakfast areas. The desk layout in one such office might include a setting in which the executive sits with his or her back to a window, thereby placing the traditional two guest chairs facing the window. Blinds or drapes can then be used to create glare or visual comfort for the executive's visitors.

All of these environments have only one goal: to give the user's negotiators the best possible tools in their efforts to optimize the user's bargaining position. By selecting and controlling these environments, the user can create a meeting that maximizes the opportunity for business relationship and agreement or that stresses differences and suggests the need for continuing efforts to bring the parties closer together.

Psychological environment. In addition to controlling the physical negotiating environment, the user should also strive to control the psychological environment. The user can employ a number of subtle strategies toward this end, all of which are designed to increase the user's sense of control, confidence, and dominance at the relative expense of the vendor. Although these strategies are employed more easily when the user is negotiating on its own ground, most can be implemented at any location.

Particularly in drawn-out bargaining sessions, the user should strive to keep its team members feeling fresh. Adequate sleep is desirable, of course, but not always possible. Where sleep is restricted and the bargaining sessions are long, the user should attempt to rotate the members of its team in and out of the negotiating conferences. Members that are rotated out should relax and take a legitimate break from the pressure of the negotiating arena. A good shower, a fresh change of clothes, and a few minutes of "feet up rest" or a catnap can substantially rejuvenate an experienced negotiator. The ability of a negotiator to achieve this relaxation may depend on both location and commitment. For example, if the negotiations are being held at the user's offices, and the negotiator lives nearby, a quick trip home for dinner and some time with his or her spouse and children can be highly effective (assuming that family circumstances actually make such time relaxing—an assumption that, in all seriousness, may not always be valid). However, this technique can contribute to additional tension, rather than relaxation, unless the negotiator and his or her spouse preplan the dinner and make a mutual commitment toward creating a quick, relaxing break. Where the negotiator lives too far away from the negotiating site to go home for a break, relaxation may still be possible at a company cafeteria, lounge, or athletic facility. In important marathon negotiations where relaxation for the user's negotiators would otherwise be difficult, the user should rent one or more nearby hotel rooms, either to be shared for temporary rest and relaxation or to be checked into for living accommodations for the duration of the negotiations. Where the negotiations are held at a location other than the user's city, a similar approach should be employed, with the user's hotel accommodations being close enough to the vendor's facilities to permit user negotiators to rotate back to the hotel for rest and relaxation.

Ideally, while the user is slowly rotating its team members in and out of the negotiations, it should also attempt to keep all vendor participants fully occupied to preclude them from partaking of similar rest and relaxation. This strategy can be implemented by ensuring that all of the vendor's negotiators always have some reason to be present at the conference table or at a private vendor caucus. For example, the user can direct a lengthy or involved question to a given vendor representative or request that the vendor's negotiators use a planned break to call headquarters to clarify a point. As in the case of rotating team members in and out for rest and relaxation, keeping the vendor's negotiators at least partly busy during scheduled breaks, including meal periods, can increase the user's psychological negotiating advantage.

When the negotiations are held at the offices of the user or its attorneys, the user should maintain a bright and cheery environment for as long into the night as negotiations continue to progress at a satisfactory level. Particularly if the vendor seriously hopes to execute an agreement that evening or by some other early deadline, the user can contribute a (sometimes deliberately false) sense of hope by keeping secretarial staff available for typing last minute changes. Moreover, the user can drastically alter this apparently favorable environment to evidence displeasure at a particular vendor position or the overall progress of the negotiations. For example, the user can send all secretarial personnel home, cut back on lighting, and shut down copiers and other office equipment. These actions can have almost the psychological impact of deadlocking the negotiations, while at the same time permitting the conference to continue at a somewhat strained level.

Regardless of the techniques employed, the user should recognize the importance of controlling the negotiating environment and take steps to ensure that control throughout the negotiating process. Admittedly, some users find the authors' suggestions concerning the affirmative use (or, as some allege, manipulation) of environmental factors to be unprofessional or even unethical. Although these views must be respected, the authors firmly believe that the recognition and employment of environmental factors, within reasonable limitations, is an acceptable and advisable user tactic. Experienced vendor negotiators are well aware of the advantages of controlling the negotiating environment. In most instances, if the user does not attempt to control environmental factors in its favor, the vendor will strive to turn those same factors against the user.

Reversing Vendor Boilerplate Provisions

Most vendor standard form agreements include a number of "boilerplate" provisions that are extremely one-sided. These provisions provide significant protection to the vendor and few, if any, benefits to the user. Indeed, many of these provisions may pose significant risks for the user.

One of the more difficult problems faced by user negotiating personnel is the question of how to change these "boilerplate" provisions to make them less onerous. This problem is particularly acute when the user's negotiating team and/or attorney has only limited experience in dealing with the particular vendor or with equipment contracts in general.

One effective method of dealing with these standard provisions is to "turn them around" and make them equally applicable to the vendor and the user. For example, consider the following provision taken from a standard vendor agreement: "In no event will Vendor be liable for any indirect, special, or consequential damages arising out of this Agreement or the use of any equipment, programs, documentation, and services provided in this Agreement."

Ideally, the user might wish to hold the vendor liable for indirect or consequential damages arising out of the vendor's default under the agreement. However, few users are able to achieve this negotiating goal, due to the severe risk "consequential damages" could pose to the vendor. (Users with significant bargaining power are able to achieve this objective in some instances, depending upon the vendor involved. See Chapter 8.)

For most users, the realistic negotiating goal with respect to this provision would be to "turn it around" so that it provides protection to the user as well as the vendor. This approach can be implemented easily as follows: "In no event will Vendor or Customer be liable for any indirect, special, or consequential damages arising out of this Agreement or the use of any equipment, programs, documentation, and services provided in this Agreement."

Similarly, consider the following provision excerpted from the same vendor form agreement: "Vendor will not be liable for any failure or delay in performance due in whole or in part to any cause beyond Vendor's control." Because of the user's affirmative contractual obligations to prepare the data processing site and perform certain other tasks, it makes sense for the user to turn this provision around as well. Here, however, the user may also wish to make substantive changes in the language of the provision in order to make it more precise and give the vendor less leeway. In one actual negotiating session, the user's attorney initially proposed the following "turn around" language: "Neither Vendor nor Customer shall be liable for any failure or delay in performance due in whole or in part to any cause beyond such party's control."

Interestingly, as the user's attorney had suspected, the vendor's lawyer did not want to accept this provision. The vendor's lawyer did not object to giving the user (as well as the vendor) the benefit of some form of "force majeure" or "Act of God" clause. Rather, the vendor's attorney felt that the language was too broad, now that it applied against the vendor as well as the user. As a result, the vendor's attorney suggested that the parties draft a new, more detailed, and more restricted, force majeure clause that would apply to both sides. The following provision was the result:

> No failure or omission on the part of either party hereto to carry out or observe any of the terms or conditions of this Agreement shall give rise to any claim against such party or be deemed to be a breach of this Agreement by such party if such failure or omission arises from any cause or causes reasonably beyond the control of such party. Without limiting the generality of the foregoing, the following causes affecting such party or others having business dealings with such party shall be deemed to be reasonably beyond the control of such party: strikes, lockouts or other industrial disturbances, war, blockades, insurrections, riots, natural disasters, restraints of or by governments, orders or requirements of any civil or military power, civil disturbances, major breakages or damages to or substantial destruction of critical machinery, facilities, equipment or lines that substantially or materially curtail production or operations, shortages, curtailment or other inability to obtain any material or equipment used in or needed for compliance with this agreement, and interruption or delays in transportation.

The same vendor form agreement also contained the following provision:

Customer will be in default under any of the following events or conditions:

(a) Nonpayment or nonperformance of any obligation of Customer in this Agreement and the continuance of such nonpayment or nonperformance for a period of thirty days after Vendor's written notice thereof to Customer.

In the same negotiating session described above, the user's attorney wished to include a "vendor default" provision in the agreement. As is far too frequently the case, the standard vendor form agreement overlooked this item, containing instead a provision describing only events of "customer default." In addition, the user's attorney wanted to limit the standard "customer default" language to ensure that the user would not be held in default as a result of technical noncompliance with a minor contractual obligation. The user's attorney met both of these goals by initially adopting the "customer default" provision and applying it to the vendor, as follows: "Vendor will be in default upon any of the following events or conditions: (a) Nonpayment or nonperformance of any obligation of Vendor in this Agreement and the continuance of such nonpayment or nonperformance for a period of thirty days after Customer's written notice thereof to Vendor."

When presented with this proposal, the vendor's attorney did two things. First, he agreed that a "vendor default" provision could be added to the agreement. Second, he suggested that both the "customer default" and the "vendor default" provisions be modified from the language contained in the vendor's standard form agreement. In effect, the vendor's attorney was willing to impose the form contract language (with all its risks and ambiguities) on the user, but he was not willing to impose comparable language on the vendor. Consequently, the vendor's attorney suggested that the following language be used in both the "customer default" and the "vendor default" provisions:

[Customer or Vendor] default occurs upon any of the following:

(a) Nonpayment of any obligation hereunder and the continuance thereof for a period of thirty days after [Vendor's or Customer's] written notice to [Customer or Vendor] of such event and of [Vendor's or Customer's] intention to declare such a default.

(b) Substantial nonperformance by [Customer or Vendor] of any other obligation or liability arising from this Agreement resulting in a material breach of this Agreement and the continuance thereof for a period of thirty days after [Vendor's or Customer's] written notice to [Customer or Vendor] of such event and of [Vendor's or Customer's] intention to declare such a default.

These examples demonstrate that turning around selected vendor standard-form provisions can have two major benefits for the user:

First, causing the pro-vendor provision to "cut both ways" may permit the user to gain the same contractual protection or rights that the vendor is attempting to achieve for its own benefit in its standard form agreement.

Second, turning the provision around may cause the vendor to admit that its standard form contract language is overly broad, thereby opening the door to reasonable negotiations concerning a more precise alternative. Although these negotiations may help the vendor to some extent by limiting the particularly adverse or risky form contract language (as it is turned around and made to apply to the vendor), the user will receive the same benefits: The vendor's own attorney will help the user's lawyer limit and "clean up" the overly broad language contained in the standard agreement, as it applies to the user as well as the vendor. Active participation by the vendor's attorney on a provision that "cuts both ways" can be particularly helpful where the governing law for the agreement is that of the vendor's state rather than the user's state.

In some situations, the user may derive an extra dividend from carefully implementing this tactic. This benefit occurs where the type of provision involved really provides more benefit or protection to the vendor than to the user. For example, a provision relating to "nonpayment" is substantively more likely to benefit the vendor than the user, because the vendor is unlikely to have payment responsibilities under the contract. Therefore, if the user turns the vendor's standard default-for-nonpayment provision around so it "cuts both ways" and the vendor then weakens the provision (for example, by providing for 30 days notice rather than 10, or by requiring that the notice include a stated intention to declare a default), the weakening of that provision will be more valuable to the user than to the vendor.

FINAL NEGOTIATING AUTHORITY

Most equipment negotiations involve several people on two or more sides. In many transactions, the individuals involved cycle in and out of the negotiating process. New names and faces are introduced and new strategies are exploited.

At the outset, the user's representatives must strive to determine who the primary negotiators are and who has final negotiating authority. Regardless of the puffery, one individual on each negotiating team usually has the responsibility of making all final decisions in the negotiations.

To a lesser extent, several subordinates may have the semifinal responsibility (subject to being overruled by the chief negotiator) of making or recommending substantive decisions in selected specialty areas, such as law and accounting.

To succeed in any negotiating effort, the user must reach the person with final negotiating authority. From a practical standpoint, reaching this individual may also require successfully targeting the subordinates who have the responsibility of making final recommendations in key areas.

In many negotiations, there is no direct announcement of who has final negotiating authority. Even where some idea of seniority can be gleaned from the names and titles passed out during the introductions, the person with final authority may not even be present! Sometimes, this is the result of a conscious effort not to waste the senior individual's time on preliminary matters; other times, this is the point of a careful strategy designed to give the senior person a new crack at the transaction. The latter approach is often used in implementing the limited authority negotiating ploy.

The best rule for the user is not to proceed with serious discussions until the person with final negotiating authority is identified and present. Any other approach wastes the time of the user's negotiators and risks exposing the user's strategy to a person who can carefully record the user's position for later analysis, but who cannot agree to any substantive concessions. Equipment sales representatives are particularly adept at masking the true identity of the senior decision maker or, alternatively, keeping that individual away from the scene of the actual negotiations. As a result, users too often waste their time on local or district representatives who, not too surprisingly, keep telephoning the vendor's regional or national manager or lawyer before making any binding commitments.

The difficulty of exposing the vendor's senior negotiator varies considerably from transaction to transaction. As might be expected, the task is generally more difficult where the user is unfamiliar with the vendor's organization. However, care must be exercised even where a vendor/ user relationship has existed, as vendor staff changes may alter negotiating authority overnight. The following approaches may be helpful in identifying the vendor representative with final negotiating authority.

First, the user's negotiating team should obtain a copy of the vendor's local, regional, or national organizational charts and check the names and titles of the individuals who are involved in the user's transaction. Titles and positions can be misleading, but the chart will provide a starting place. The chart's information should then be bolstered through informal discussions with the vendor's marketing representative.

Second, the user's team should determine who will be signing the contract for the vendor. The person who has legal authority to bind the vendor often has the final responsibility for the terms and conditions of the transaction. In this regard, the user should be certain to distinguish between the person who can "sign but not bind" and the person who can "sign and bind." In the former case, the signature is mechanical at best and the agreement is not effective until accepted and executed at headquarters. A similar approach can be followed with the vendor's attorney. In effect, the user should determine who, if anyone, the vendor's attorney must talk to in order to gain clearance for major changes.

Third, the user should demand that the vendor's contract signer and attorney be present for the negotiations and closing. The user's principal representative should emphasize that the transaction will only be consummated if the vendor formally executes the contract at the user's offices. This approach not only forces the vendor to identify the contract signer; it also places that individual on the user's home field.

Fourth, the user's negotiators should split the vendor's team up one or two members at a time, and explore relatively easy issues in considerable depth. A negotiator with little or no negotiating authority will shy away from making any serious commitments. The body language "spoken" by vendor negotiators under these circumstances can also be helpful in determining the strong party or parties on the vendor's team.

Fifth, the user's team members should endeavor to catch the vendor's negotiators off guard with a series of unexpected or aggressive moves. These sudden user actions often result in an immediate reaction by the vendor's team, generally under the relatively obvious leadership of the vendor's principal negotiator.

Finally, the user should also consider taking the simplest approach of all: ask. Under this direct methodology, the user's principal negotiator should indicate at the outset of negotiations that the user's team has no time to waste on frivolous discussions—that the user is prepared to strive toward a prompt agreement if serious, frank negotiations can be undertaken. The user's representative should then indicate that the user will not proceed with discussions until the person with final negotiating authority for the vendor is present. This direct approach can also be productive in setting a firm tone for the negotiations, thereby enhancing the user's ability to seize and maintain control.

Where the user employs a good RFP procedure, the question of final negotiating authority can be raised in the RFP document. In this approach, the RFP may contain a direct question concerning vendor negotiating and approval authorities. Alternatively, the RFP may indicate that both the RFP and the eventual contract must be executed on behalf of the vendor by the same executive, who must also participate in the formal contract negotiations at the user's site or other designated location. In addition to providing good evidence of who has final negotiating authority for the vendor, this approach tends to reduce the level of puffery in the vendor's proposal and to increase the level of vendor commitment at an early stage in the negotiation process.

For users with more timid hearts, the direct approach can also be implemented in less obvious ways. For example, one subtle method merely requires a user representative to ask which of the vendor's personnel should be invited to the contract signing cermony or to some proposed celebration dinner. If the user sets the mock scenario with care, the list of names is likely to include the vendor's principal negotiator. To narrow the list further, the user's representative can continue the ruse by discussing alternative seating arrangements for the hypothetical dinner party, thereby gaining additional insight into the vendor's pecking order.

DANGERS IN THE LAST HOURS OF NEGOTIATIONS

The last few hours of lengthy equipment negotiations may well be the most dangerous for the user. Although a number of potential problems can occur during this period, most, if not all, result from fatigue and an unnecessary feeling of urgency.

Even when carefully trained, the members of a negotiating team can lose their sharp edge when exposed to the grinding pace of virtually around-the-clock negotiations. Accuracy is likely to be sacrificed, thereby opening the way for errors in such basic matters as equipment lists and proofreading. Perhaps more importantly, judgment may also be impaired. The user's lawyer, for example, may not understand the full business or legal impact of a provision proposed by the vendor's marketing representative or attorney. The user's financial expert may not appreciate the interest expense of adding relatively inexpensive programming and education services into an 84-month equipment lease.

The fatigue resulting from long-term bargaining may also take some of the "fight" out of the user's negotiating team. As the hours draw on, dinners are missed, families are not seen, other work piles up on the desk, and the members of the team begin to wonder whether the entire transaction is worth all of this effort. As a consequence, they may not pursue a given point with the vigor required to achieve the user's negotiating objectives. Compromise may be effected far sooner than during earlier stages of the negotiations.

The vendor is aware of all of these possibilities and ordinarily manipulates the fatigue factor during this critical period so that it will have the maximum detrimental effect upon the user and its negotiating team. Carefully placed comments by the vendor can increase the feeling of fatigue by the user's negotiators. Offhand remarks concerning the missed dinners, the late hours, the "wife and kids," and the volume of other work that must be piling up, all drive home the fatigue factor.

In some situations, the vendor may actually save critical points until late in the negotiating session in an effort to allow fatigue to minimize the user's resistance. This approach can be particularly effective when the user has proposed that its attorney review the entire document and negotiate each important point along the way. In this situation, the vendor will spend considerable time discussing points that are actually quite minor from the vendor's standpoint. (This may be done by suggesting that the standard form agreement be reviewed first, followed by the user's lengthy addendum. Alternatively, the vendor may suggest that "sticky" points be passed over until the "easier" changes are discussed.) The user's negotiator then spends substantial time and energy arguing the less critical points. When the important points are finally reached, the user's negotiator may well be too tired, from a physical and mental standpoint, to achieve optimization of the contractual provisions for the user.

The fatigue factor can be most effective for the vendor when it is bolstered by a sense of urgency. Salesmen in all walks of life are aware of the fact that timing can be critical to a successful closing. The creation of a false sense of urgency is as effective in the equipment business as it is in the real estate industry. In both situations, the purchaser's sense of judgment and care is adversely affected by an intense feeling, falsely created by the vendor, that it in the best interests of the purchaser to close the transaction at the earliest possible time (or within some time frame deemed appropriate by the vendor). Unfortunately, however, haste makes waste in most fields of endeavor and equipment negotiations are no exception, at least as far as the user is concerned. When haste and fatigue are put together, judgment and drive are most certain to be impaired.

Nevertheless, the problems of fatigue and urgency can be reduced and controlled by the user in most situations. Although the solutions can be utilized to minimize the effects of these factors at any stage of the negotiating process, they are particularly effective during the critical last few hours of lengthy bargaining.

First, and perhaps most important, the user must recognize the problem—and its complexity. Members of the user's negotiating team must appreciate the fact that fatigue can and will occur and that it will adversely affect their performance. Team members must also understand that the vendor will probably create a false sense of urgency at some point during the negotiating process. Furthermore, the members must recognize that both fatigue and a sense of urgency may be used by the vendor as affirmative negotiating strategies, particularly during the final hours of the negotiating process. All of these points should be discussed by the negotiating team prior to the time that formal bargaining sessions begin with the vendor.

Second, the user's negotiators should determine at the outset to minimize the effect of the vendor's false sense of urgency. This can be done in a number of ways, but one of the most effective methods is to ensure that all user participants recognize that the proposed transaction is at least as important to the vendor as it is to the user. With this in mind, the user's negotiators should appreciate that, if pressed, the vendor will do everything possible to bring the negotiations to a successful conclusion. Regardless of what the vendor's representative says, his or her proposal is almost certain to be left open until the user either executes the agreement or finally rejects the transaction once and for all. A second method of minimizing the sense of urgency is to place the transaction in a proper perspective from the user's standpoint. In this regard, the easiest rule is for user team members to remember that neither their company nor the country is likely to fail if the agreement is not signed by the date demanded (or threatened) by the vendor.

Third, the user's negotiating team should be alert to vendor efforts to divert negotiating priorities from critical issues to insubstantial subjects. As suggested earlier, an agenda prepared by the user can be an effective method of gaining and maintaining control of individual bargaining sessions.

Fourth, the user's team should strive to control the effects of fatigue, using the environmental factors suggested earlier in this chapter. One of the best methods of controlling the fatigue of the user's negotiators, and often increasing the fatigue of the vendor's negotiators, is to bring in someone fresh. The interjection of an alert, impeccably dressed "varsity squad" replacement at a mature stage of the bargaining session can: (1) provide an element of surprise; (2) help the user maintain or regain control; (3) permit the newcomer to address "tired" issues with more clarity of mind and better results; and (4) extract meaningful concessions from the vendor's negotiators.

Finally, the team should adopt an affirmative tactic to turn the fatigue factor against the vendor. As noted previously, this technique can be particularly effective when the vendor's representatives are negotiating out of town, away from their home base. By turning the effects of fatigue against the vendor's negotiators, the user generally gains two advantages. First, the fatigue and confusion faced by the vendor's representatives increases the user's relative bargaining position and weakens the vendor's ability to use fatigue to its own advantage. Second, by causing the user's negotiators to focus on the fatigue factor, the approach keeps the user's team members constantly alert to, and more immune from, the vendor's efforts to use fatigue and a sense of urgency as affirmative negotiating tactics.

4
THE NEGOTIATION PROCESS

The key to understanding the negotiation process is appreciating just how long and complex it is. In essence, the "negotiation process" is the "acquisition process," viewed from a *negotiating* perspective.

When asked to describe the acquisition process, user representatives generally provide a variety of responses, based upon their own experience and point of view. Attorneys tend to describe the process in terms that focus on the agreements and the formal bargaining sessions over alternative contractual provisions. Financial experts outline the process by referring to the principal economic and analytical steps, such as cost justification, lease-purchase analysis, and payment calculation. Equipment and procurement professionals key on the technical and production factors, such as equipment selection, installation, and immediacy of delivery. General management has a somewhat broader view, often encompassing financial and production concerns, but seldom focusing on legal details or risks.

In reality, of course, all of these factors are involved in the acquisition process. However, if the user is to optimize its position, two other points must be recognized and achieved. First, the acquisition factors from the various professional areas (e.g., legal, financial, technical, and management) must be melded together, assessed, and applied at *each stage* of the acquisition process. Second, the individual factors and the entire acquisition process must be considered from a *negotiating* perspective.

If each functional or professional area is permitted to view the acquisition process from its own perspective, the user will never achieve the unity of communication, understanding, and advocacy that is necessary to counter the vendor's professional negotiating team. The user's representatives must work together to develop a unified view of the acquisition, from the user's goals to the specific contract provisions. Similarly, the user's negotiators must recognize that *every stage* in the acquisition process involves an opportunity for the user to strengthen or weaken its position vis-a-vis the vendor. "Negotiating" does not begin the first time the parties sit down at the table to discuss price or contractual provisions. Negotiating, in a "positioning" sense, begins the first time the vendor and the user communicate with one another, in person or in writing. Thus, each stage of the acquisition process, and each factor deemed important by each member of the user's negotiating team, must be viewed as one piece of a jigsaw puzzle that is designed to optimize the user's position in the transaction. Equipment selection, financial analysis, contractual bargaining, and all the other steps must be considered on two levels: first, what substantive points are desired by the user; and second, what actions must be taken by the user to improve its ability to achieve those points. If the user determines all the substantive points desired by it, without positioning itself in the process, the user will be at a serious disadvantage once it moves to the more traditional contract bargaining phase of the acquisition. Put very simply, *effective negotiation* requires "positioning" throughout all stages of the acquisition process.

The importance of this point can perhaps best be appreciated by considering the steps involved in the acquisition process. Asked to reach some consensus on the most basic steps in the acquisition process, many users would probably be willing to settle for the five stages shown in Fig. 4-1. Indeed, these same users might be willing to expand this basic outline to the degree of detail shown in Fig. 4-2.

Both of these outlines are perfectly reasonable methods of explaining certain aspects of the acquisition process. However, both lack one critical component: a negotiating perspective. Figures 4-1 and 4-2 essentially present views of the acquisition process that fail to include the negotiating or "staging" steps that are necessary to optimize the user's position. As such, both outlines are as incomplete as a photograph taken through a filter that absorbs all light in the red wavelength. The objects are still in the photograph, but the color and feeling are drastically distorted.

Figs. 4-1 and 4-2 seem to suggest that most or all of the "negotiating" occurs in Stage III: the "analysis and negotiation of vendor proposals." In reality, Stage III does involve negotiating in the traditional sense (i.e., bargaining over alternative contractual provisions). But most of the negotiation process occurs—or, at least, should occur—before Stage III is ever reached. In a well-planned acquisition, the most difficult and time consuming steps in the negotiation process take place in Stages I and II of Figs. 4-1 and 4-2.

Viewed purely from a negotiating perspective, the acquisition process can be outlined as shown in Fig. 4-3. Of course, this view of the total process is also distorted, as it only keys on the negotiating elements. In essence, Fig. 4-3 presents the view of the acquisition process that was blocked by the red filter mentioned above. Consequently, a complete view of the acquisition process emerges only when the more traditional steps outlined in Fig. 4-1 are merged with the negotiating steps shown in Fig. 4-3. This merger is depicted in Fig. 4-4. This figure clearly demonstrates the point made above: although the two processes overlap throughout, the most complex steps in the negotiation process occur during Stages I and II of the more traditional view of the acquisition process.

Why do most users fail to view the acquisition process from the perspective shown in Fig. 4-3 or Fig. 4-4? The reasons vary, but several common factors can be identified.

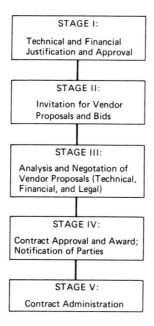

Fig. 4-1.   Summary view of the acquisition process: traditional perspective.

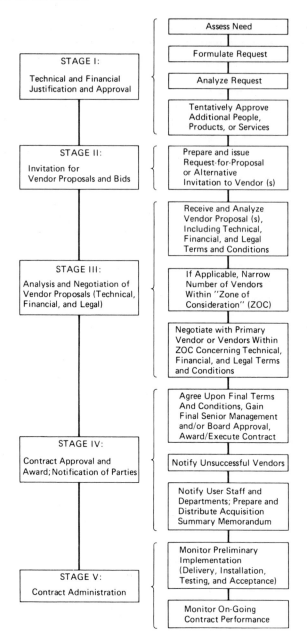

Fig. 4-2. Expanded view of the acquisition process: traditional perspective.

First, as noted above, most individuals view the acquisition process from their own vantage point, based upon their background and expertise. Although this fact causes the acquisition process to be perceived and described in terms of legal, financial, and technical issues, it seldom results in a "negotiating" view of the process. The reason is relatively simple: Few users have any staff or professional experts that specialize in *negotiations*. Although a user's legal advisors may be fair contract negotiators, they rarely have the unique blend of general negotiating ability *and* technical, financial, and legal knowledge necessary to view and direct the entire transaction

THE ACQUISITION PROCESS:
NEGOTIATING PERSPECTIVE

1. Form Negotiating Team
2. Begin Data Collection
3. Obtain Preliminary Approvals
4. Complete Data Collection
5. Determine Contractual Approach (Results or Resources)
6. Establish Goals and Objectives
7. Prioritize Objectives
8. Draft Preliminary Negotiations Position Paper
9. Obtain Further Approvals
10. Consider Equipment Acquisition Alternatives
11. Draft and Issue RFP or Invitation-for-Bids; Hold Bidders' Conference
12. Update Negotiations Position Paper
13. Reevaluate Goals and Objectives
14. Obtain Further Approvals
15. Select Zone of Consideration (ZOC) Participants and Conduct "Formal" Negotiations, Using ZOC Approach
16. Update Negotiations Position Paper
17. Prepare Final Contractual Documents for Execution
18. Obtain Final Approvals and Award Contract
19. Execute Documents
20. Prepare and Distribute Final Report or Acquisition Summary Memorandum
21. Evaluate and Document Vendor Compliance or Noncompliance
22. Conduct and Document Ongoing Contract Administration

Fig. 4-3.   Sequential view of the acquisition process: negotiating perspective.

from a negotiating perspective. As a result, each area—technical, financial, and legal—emphasizes its own skills and the only "negotiations" that occur take place during the few contract bargaining sessions that the user's attorney is allowed to hold before he or she is blamed for unnecessarily delaying the transaction.

Second, as Chapter 2 and other portions of this book explain, a "sense of urgency" permeates far too many major equipment acquisitions. When this sense of urgency is present, the user's general and technical management focus on one thing: how soon the equipment can be ordered, installed, and operating. Driven by this single concern, user personnel have little time for, or interest in, the time-consuming formalities involved in the negotiating steps shown in Fig. 4-3.

Third, even where a sense of urgency is not present, the negotiating steps outlined in Fig. 4-3 require substantial user effort throughout the acquisition process. Because the level of effort required is high, and the process itself rather alien, most users fail to appreciate all of the steps involved. Even where a user has some understanding of the entire process, it often fails to execute all of the steps, generally rationalizing that special circumstances of some kind either preclude the need for, or do not permit the execution of, one or more steps. Although perhaps honestly applicable in certain instances, this rationalization process often becomes a self-fulfilling prophecy that governs all future acquisitions made by the user.

Fourth, users simply do not understand how to identify or execute the negotiating steps involved in the acquisition process. As suggested above, the negotiating side of the process is generally foreign ground to the user, except for the traditional "contract bargaining" session, and the sources of user-oriented information on how to proceed effectively are slim or nonexistent. (Obviously, the last point is one of the key factors that led to this book.)

THE ACQUISITION PROCESS:
COMBINED PERSPECTIVE

STAGE I: TECHNICAL AND FINANCIAL JUSTIFICATION AND APPROVAL
1. Form Negotiating Team
2. Begin Data Collection
3. Obtain Preliminary Approvals

STAGE II: INVITATION FOR VENDOR PROPOSALS AND BIDS
1. Complete Data Collection
2. Determine Contractual Approach (Results or Resources)
3. Establish Goals and Objectives
4. Prioritize Objectives
5. Draft Preliminary Negotiations Position Paper
6. Obtain Further Approvals
7. Consider Equipment Acquisition Alternatives
8. Draft and Issue RFP or Invitation-for-Bids; Hold Bidders' Conference

STAGE III: ANALYSIS AND NEGOTIATION OF VENDOR PROPOSALS (TECHNICAL, FINANCIAL, AND LEGAL)
1. Update Negotiations Position Paper
2. Reevaluate Goals and Objectives
3. Obtain Further Approvals
4. Select Zone of Consideration (ZOC) Participants and Conduct "Formal" Negotiations, Using ZOC Approach

STAGE IV: CONTRACT APPROVAL AND AWARD; NOTIFICATION OF PARTIES
1. Update Negotiations Position Paper
2. Prepare Final Contractual Documents for Execution
3. Obtain Final Approvals and Award Contract
4. Execute Documents
5. Prepare and Distribute Final Report or Acquisition Summary Memorandum

STAGE V: CONTRACT ADMINISTRATION
1. Evaluate and Document Vendor Compliance or Noncompliance
2. Conduct and Document Ongoing Contract Administration

Fig. 4-4.   Sequential view of the acquisition process: combined perspective merging Figs. 4-1 and 4-3.

This chapter is dedicated to a discussion of the acquisition process from a negotiating perspective. As such, it keys on the "staging" steps that must be taken to optimize the user's position in the acquisition. Particular emphasis is placed on the early negotiating steps that can substantially improve the user's equity once it reaches the more traditional "bargaining table" phase of the acquisition process. Because this chapter focuses on the negotiating side of the acquisition process, the steps and skills outlined below must be considered and applied in the practical context of the more traditional view of the acquisition process, such as that outlined in Fig. 4-1 or Fig. 4-2. Because the traditional steps listed in those figures are familiar to most users and explained in a number of other sources, they are omitted from the detailed discussions in this chapter.

THE NEGOTIATING TEAM

As the preceding discussion suggests, melding the skills and views of various professional disciplines greatly improves the user's ability to engage in meaningful contract negotiations. Perhaps the most effective method of achieving this blending of skills is to organize a user negotiating team. Negotiation is a team sport, requiring all the specialized skills, communication ability, team spirit, and gamesmanship found in any professional sporting event. Structured properly and deployed in an effective and timely manner, the user negotiating team can play a critical role in bringing equality to the bargaining table.

Forming the Team

For the user's negotiating team to be effective, it must be organized at an early date, preferably as the first step in preparing for a specific acquisition. (See Fig. 4-3.) Some users avoid this approach on the ground that it wastes valuable staff and professional time too early in the transaction. These users fear that naming the team members at an early date will cause the entire acquisition planning cycle to be run "by committee" and, perhaps worse, by a committee that includes lawyers, accountants, and professional negotiators.

In most situations, these fears are misplaced. Although the negotiating team members should be selected at the beginning of the negotiation process, all members do not have to be directly involved in all stages of the process. Particularly during the early phases of equipment and vendor selection, the team may wish to assign substantial responsibilities to team subcommittees, or to individual team members, and other staff and professional advisors who do not serve as permanent members of the team.

At the time the negotiating team is formed, general responsibilities should be assigned to each member. These responsibilities will ordinarily follow the professional and technical expertise of each of the team representatives. For most negotiations, the team should include members with primary responsibilities in each of the following areas: legal, financial, operations or production (technical and management, either together or separately), and company management. In many situations, various "end users" of the equipment should also be included on the negotiating team or made available as team resource individuals.

Operations. Depending upon the equipment being procured, the user's operations division, or a comparable technical area, should ordinarily be well represented on the negotiating team. Although a single team member can sometimes handle this area acceptably (particularly when additional staff members are available as team resources), two technical or operating representatives are generally advisable. One of these teams members should have considerable technical expertise in the system involved. The other should have departmental or divisional management responsibilities. This combination assures that the team will be able to assess specific technical problems and, at the same time, appreciate overall goals and problems in the applicable department or division. Where a negotiating team includes only a single operations representative, the risk is that the individual involved will either be technically deficient or unable to understand the broad management issues faced by the division.

Despite the value of having the team include both technical and management representatives from the applicable operations area, care should be taken to ensure that the team does not become top heavy with technical personnel. Failing to appreciate the role of the team, some users expand its membership to include several technical experts and two or three management representatives, all from the operations division. Although these individuals may have important parts to play in the acquisition process, they generally should not be included as formal members of the negotiating team. For the team to be effective, it must remain relatively small and manageable. Perhaps more importantly, it must be "interdisciplinary" and not dominated by any one area or profession. Where additional expertise is required, special team resource individuals can be named. These resource persons can report to the team through one or more team members, or through direct oral or written presentations. Resource subcommittees can be used to facilitate this process, with each subcommittee being chaired by a team member and staffed by resource individuals who may be members of the subcommittee but not the negotiating team.

Financial. For the team to be effective in assessing vendor proposals and various acquisition alternatives, it must include a qualified accountant or other financial analyst. To maximize objectivity, this individual ideally should not be an employee or officer of the operations or technical division referred to above. Many users assign a member of their corporate accounting or financial planning department to the team for this purpose. In some situations, an independent accountant may be used.

Regardless of the source, the financial member of the team should have considerable experience in assessing alternative methods of acquiring and financing equipment and other products. Where the user is a public company or otherwise subject to various pronouncements of the accounting regulatory bodies, the financial team member must also appreciate the impact that alternative acquisition methods may have on the user's financial reporting obligations. In addition, the member should be capable of assessing, or at least communicating with experts concerning, the tax aspects of various acquisition methods.

Legal. Despite the fact that many users execute major equipment contracts (involving millions of dollars, critical company functions, and significant potential liability) without any meaningful involvement by their attorneys, such agreements are legally binding documents of immense importance and, as such, should never be signed without prior, thorough review by competent legal counsel. For the user's attorney to have a realistic opportunity to shape the acquisition documents, the lawyer must be a full member of the negotiating team. Regardless of his or her professional expertise, an attorney cannot draft or negotiate effectively, or appreciate all aspects that must be covered in the contract, unless he or she is granted adequate time and information to do so.

Ideally, the legal member of the user's negotiating team should be an attorney with considerable experience in drafting and negotiating major equipment contracts. If the user is unable to retain counsel with this level of experience, the user should seek an attorney with drafting and negotiating experience in other areas, such as mergers and acquisitions or real estate. Most major equipment acquisitions are complex transactions that involve—or should involve—extensive documentation. Consequently, an attorney with experience in negotiating and handling complex contracts will be more effective than a lawyer with little background in such matters.

If the legal member of the team has strong negotiating talents and reasonably good interdisciplinary training (particularly as a result of prior major equipment negotiations), the lawyer may be a good choice as chairperson of the negotiating team. Alternatively, the attorney may be assigned primary responsibility for orchestrating the formal bargaining sessions, while another member serves as team chairperson.

Company Management. A member of upper-middle or senior management of the user should be included on the negotiating team, even if the person cannot take the time to attend all team meetings and negotiating sessions. This management representative is important for several reasons. First, the senior manager can ensure that the acquisition is consistent with overall company goals and objectives, both short and long term. Second, the management member can provide input as the proposed transaction is structured. This advice may enable the team to shape the acquisition in a manner that offers significant financial or policy advantages to the company. Particularly where leasing is involved, the user may have considerable flexibility in structuring the financial side of the acquisition. Company management is generally in the best position to assess the impact that a proposed acquisition approach may (or should) have on the company's financial and operating goals and management policies.

Adding a representative of top management to the negotiating team also has another advantage. It minimizes second guessing. Many equipment acquisitions are financial and political "hot potatoes" (just ask all the managers who have lost their jobs over what hindsight called a "bad deal"). By having a senior management official plugged in from the start, the negotiating team not only has the advantage of management input—it also has the advantage of prior management commitment. From a practical standpoint, management will be far less likely to second guess the acquisition at a later date if a senior manager has actually participated in the acquisition process. In this regard, a five-minute explanation of the transaction to management just before the contract is signed is no substitute for actual involvement from the beginning.

Adding a member of company management to the negotiating team also reduces the likelihood that the vendor will attempt to "go around" the team to senior management if the negotiations deadlock or otherwise turn against the vendor. In addition, the management member may provide a psychological advantage to the user during the negotiating process. For example, the management member can serve to remind the user that the company places considerable importance on the acquisition and on the successful outcome of the negotiations. The management member of the team can also add immediate strength to team decisions, particularly decisions to deadlock negotiations or reject a given vendor proposal.

Assignments. As the members of the negotiating team are selected, the assignment of technical responsibilities should not overlook possible areas of intrateam conflict or confusion. For example, the team should agree on which member or members will be primarily responsible for assessing the tax aspects of the transaction (including the contractual language and the financial and accounting benefits) and who will be responsible for gaining outside review (if desired) by other members of user management or by the user's outside consultants and experts in law, accounting, and other fields.

Once all technical assignments are clarified, preliminary role playing responsibilities should be discussed. More detailed and specific role playing assignments should generally be delayed until later in the negotiating process, in preparation for actual bargaining sessions.

Adjusting Mental Attitude

In providing professional negotiating assistance to users, the authors have consistently found that one of the more difficult obstacles to overcome is the user's basic attitude toward the negotiations. In most situations, the user has a relatively friendly, close relationship with the vendor. As a result, the user is generally less than objective in analyzing the vendor's proposals, promises, and provisions. Because the user basically trusts the vendor, or at least the vendor's local marketing representative, the user is more susceptible to the vendor's negotiating and sales ploys. (See Chapter 2.)

If the user's negotiating team is to have any real chance of achieving equality at the negotiating table, the team members must constantly strive to achieve maximum objectivity in dealing with the vendor. For all but the most professional and experienced user negotiating teams, achieving the necessary level of detachment and objectivity generally requires a substantial attitude adjustment. In essence, the user's team members must learn—and seriously believe—that the vendor and its representatives are adversaries (although friendly ones, to be sure) that can and will seek to take financial and contractual advantage of the user at virtually every opportunity. The vendor can supply meaningful information and expertise. Indeed, the vendor can and often should be a professional "partner" in achieving the user's business goals. But everything the vendor says, does, or suggests must be doubted, independently verified, and documented before the user relies on it for any purpose.

The authors have grappled with numerous techniques to effect the attitude adjustment that is so critical for many users. A tough analysis of the vendor ploys explained in Chapter 2 is often a useful method of instilling a healthy respect for user objectivity. A list of attitude adjustment points is also productive. Set out below is one such list of attitudinal reminders, written in the context of a memorandum to the user's negotiators, from the user's professional advisors. User negotiators may find it helpful to review this list of attitude adjustment points (or a similar list prepared by the user for specific vendor negotiations) just before entering a negotiating session.

Memorandum to User Negotiators:

You are the potential buyer; the vendor is the seller. The vendor needs your business at least as much as you need its product or services—maybe more.

In most instances, the vendor or the vendor's sales representative cannot afford to lose your account.

There are many, many pressures on vendors and their sales personnel for goal performance at various times. These pressures can work to your advantage.

If negotiations "break down," the vendor will almost always come back, and very probably, with a better plan. Indeed, purposefully "breaking off negotiations" can be a very effective technique for the user.

Causing a vendor to "bring in its top brass" is almost always to the user's advantage, so long as the user remains "unimpressed" with the vendor's show of force.

Although vendor representatives are normally very capable of masking their feelings and reactions to negotiating situations, these representatives nevertheless have significant anxieties about most negotiations.

The vendor will attempt to create a sense of urgency in virtually all situations. On the other hand, "haste makes waste" for the user. Generally speaking, a user should never place a time limit on how long it may take to obtain maximum contractual protection at an optimum contractual price. Even where the user faces serious time limitations, the vendor should not be made aware of this fact.

Vendor promises and benefits should never be accepted or even seriously considered unless they are documented by clearly-written contractual commitments.

Vendor management is generally paid on profitability.

In nearly every case, you do have other alternatives to the vendor or vendors you are negotiating with. Even if you would strongly prefer to do business with the vendor you are negotiating with, the existence of these other alternatives should continually be kept in your mind and in the vendor's mind.

Most vendors are not particularly experienced in negotiating with professional negotiators who are well-versed in the vendor's position and techniques. Similarly, most vendors are not experienced in negotiating with customers who are truly well prepared.

Regardless of your own tactical decisions concerning strategies and timing, the vendor should be continuously reminded that negotiations will come to a successful conclusion only when you and your professional advisors are fully satisfied and the agreement has been completely documented in writing.

You should be prepared to ignore the vendor's claim of "that's absolutely the best deal we can give you," especially when this plea is made early in the negotiating process.

In most instances, you should consider multiple acquisition methods. In contrast, the vendor will probably try to cause you to have tunnel vision on the method presented by its representatives.

Regardless of your own feelings about the outcome of individual negotiating sessions, you must always strive to keep a high level of confidence and aspiration. Visible confidence and strength can do much to solidify your negotiating position.

Your negotiations will be enhanced by thorough preparation and planning, substantial knowledge of your needs and negotiating position, a strong desire for contractual protection and optimization, and an affirmative mental attitude.

Facilitating Communications

One of the more pervasive problems faced by user negotiating teams is the inability of various team members to communicate with one another. The authors refer to this problem as the "buzz word ineffective communications syndrome." This difficulty arises when the user finally assembles its negotiators, only to discover that each team member is speaking what amounts to a foreign language.

The basic problem is a failure of communications. The user's technical people talk in terms of "throughput," "cooling beds," "tag axles," "cycles per hour," "64K dynamic RAM," and "emulator." Its lawyers toss out "indemnify and hold harmless," "limitation of implied and express warranties," "notwithstanding any other term of this agreement," and "conditions for attornment." The finance executive adds "ITC," "APR," "residual value," "unamortized balance," and "net income before securities transactions, taxes, and extraordinary items." The user's top managment, who may be confused by the entire conversation, pointedly remarks, "Look, tell me one more time how this deal is going to save us three cents per share this year, cut our production time in half, and provide us assurance that we can get out of the deal in twenty-four months if the Finley merger comes through." A few years ago, quite a few chief executive officers might have also asked, "By the way, is this thing newer than the gear Jones, Ward, and Williams (the guys at the club) have?" Fortunately, at least, the last inquiry is becoming less frequent.

Unless these internal communications problems can be solved, the user's negotiating efforts will be seriously impaired. In far too many situations, the user's technical personnel and legal counsel never do fully understand one another. As a result, the user leaves valuable protection lying on the negotiating table—not because the negotiator was unable to gain the desired concession (although he will certainly be so blamed later on), but because he never realized that the provision was even necessary in the first place. This problem and others like it are made worse by the fact that, all the while, the vendor's interdisciplinary negotiating team will be standing by, watching the user's communications problems with a carefully-masked smile. After all, the vendor's team solved these communication problems several dozen deals ago.

These language difficulties are made worse by the age-old problem of pride. Few people are willing to admit that they are so uninformed that they cannot even grasp the language being used to discuss the situation. This is particularly true when such an "admission of ignorance" must be made in front of a group, before a superior officer, or before the vendor's staff. Attorneys, accountants, and other "professional" people are probably the worst offenders in this regard; they absolutely hate to appear "stupid" in a crowd. Technical staffers often compound this dilemma; they dogmatically refuse to believe that their presentation could be unclear to anybody. The situation is even worse in those firms where there is an inherent but unstated dislike, envy, or mistrust among the lawyers, accountants, and technical representatives.

The easiest, most direct way to minimize this problem (for it is seldom eliminated) is simply to open the necessary lines of communication. The following steps can be helpful in achieving this goal.

First, the user's negotiating team leader should openly admit and discuss the communications problem. Team members should be encouraged to ask questions relating to language problems. At the same time, they should be asked to anticipate the problems that may be faced by others and to volunteer explanations before questions must be asked.

Second, the team leader should make certain that opportunities exist for proper intrateam communication. Team discussions should be scheduled before and after all negotiating sessions to allow language problems to be brought out and covered. Signals should be arranged that can be used to break up negotiating sessions with the vendor when team members must get together to discuss a language problem (or any other point).

Third, the team leader should encourage each team member to become familiar with the basic terms used by other members of the team. Few lawyers have the time to become operations or production experts, and vice versa, but some professional interchange is both possible and necessary. The attorney member of the user's negotiating team should read or scan the basic trade publications. He should also be knowledgeable in the financing area. Conversely, the user's technical and financial team members should understand the basic legal problems involved in an equipment acquisition.

Fourth, the user should provide the nontechnical members of its negotiating team with a ready reference guide that can be used, without asking anyone, to gain the meaning of various terms and phrases. Some users provide this assistance by making available a published technical dictionary, such as Charles J. Sippl's *Data Communications Dictionary* (New York: Van Nostrand Reinhold Co., 1976). Others do so by drafting a comprehensive memorandum that sets forth the technical details of the proposed transaction in layman's language. This approach can be extremely valuable to the user's attorney, particularly if a brief glossary of terms is included or if all "foreign" words are explained parenthetically.

Whatever approach is employed, the communications problem faced by the user's negotiating team must be recognized and minimized at an early date. If this is not done, the user's team may actually risk doing more harm than good.

DATA COLLECTION

Once the negotiating team has been organized, the first and most basic step in the acquisition process is determining the user's requirements. Whether viewed from a negotiating or technical perspective, this step essentially involves data collection. Before the user's negotiating team can move effectively to the bargaining table, the user's goals must be thoroughly defined and understood by all applicable staff personnel in the user's organization. Moreover, before these goals can even be formulated, the user's negotiating team must have adequate background information concerning the user's needs, problems, and potential solutions. In essence, the user's negotiating team must know what it is striving to achieve, and why, before it can develop and implement the negotiating strategies necessary to get there. Data collection is critical to the overall success or failure of the user's negotiating efforts because most major equipment negotiations are won or lost on the basis of two factors: (1) which team has the better information; and (2) which team is better able to apply and manipulate that information in the context of the specific negotiations. Far too frquently, users leave important considerations on the negotiating table because the issues and needs were never properly defined and presented at the outset. As inexcusable as it may be to fail to achieve contractual optimization due to a lack of negotiating expertise, it is even more inexcusable to leave a specific need out of the contract due to the fact that the negotiators never realized that the matter was important in the first place.

The data collection process can be described in any number of ways, depending upon the degree of detail desired. Some users divide the process into the collection of *internal* and *external* information. Others describe data collection according to the technical or functional areas involved, e.g., *data processing, end-user department, financial,* and so on. Still other users allocate the process into *user* and *vendor* stages, subdividing each into more detailed technical areas. Although all of these approaches are perfectly valid, the following section describes the data collection process in terms of *general information* and *economic factors*. This approach permits a relatively brief overview of the process of collecting general information (which most users are familiar with), while devoting additional emphasis to assessing economic factors (which most users seldom do in the context of equipment negotiations).

Obtaining General Information

For most users, the data collection process should begin with a survey directed to a variety of user representatives: operations management and technical staff, senior company management, the ultimate end users or "customers" of the applicable user division, and the like. The goal should be to collect problems, objectives, priorities, and needs covering a wide range of technical, financial, legal, and management issues. Despite the belief held by some user representatives that they can individually supply "all the answers" in these diverse areas, the fact remains that the necessary breadth of opinion on these wide-ranging issues simply cannot be provided by one or two individuals within the user organization.

The information collection process varies from transaction to transaction and from user to user. Consequently, no firm outline of the mandatory steps involved in the process can or should be formulated. Nevertheless, the following areas should generally be included, or at least considered, in most acquisitions.

Acquisition Justification Factors. In many respects, the process of collecting general information overlaps with, and can be made an integral part of, the traditional process of assessing and justifying the proposed acquisition (e.g., cost-benefit analyses and feasibility studies). Much of the information required to determine the need for and cost of the proposed system is equally important from a negotiating viewpoint. Unless the members of the user's negotiating team have a full and complete understanding of the reasons for, and the strengths and weaknesses of, the proposed acquisition, they will not have the background information necessary to optimize the transaction, regardless of the negotiating expertise displayed at the bargaining table.

Existing Contract Files. One of the most frequently overlooked data collection sources is the user's own equipment contract files. As a part of the survey process, the user's staff should analyze its previously-executed equipment agreements (hardware, software, systems, and maintenance) to determine what problems have arisen, and what facts have changed. This review should include all contract-related documents and materials, such as "side letters," vendor proposals, presentation letters, marketing brochures, and benchmark test criteria and results. In each situation, the promise of the contractual commitment should be compared to the actual performance. Problems should be documented and solutions tentatively proposed. Although this step is particularly important where the user will be negotiating with the same vendor, the technique can also be instructive where a new vendor will be involved in the upcoming negotiations.

Vendor Relationship History. As an adjunct to the formal document review, the user's staff should prepare a narrative chronology of the user's past relationships with relevant equipment vendors. The discipline involved in this technique can be quite educational. The resulting historical perspective can refresh memories, educate new members of management and of the negotiating team, and pinpoint previous problems that might otherwise be overlooked. The old adage that "history repeats itself" is as applicable to major equipment as it is to the world at large. Remarkably, users that experienced serious problems with one vendor only a few years ago walk into the same or a very similar problem with a new vendor. Users seem particularly prone to forget past problems when they are in the process of changing back to a previous vendor. Somehow, these users only seem to recall the problems caused by the most recent vendor. The difficulties involved in the prior relationship with the new proposed vendor have faded from view, only to arise once again when the new relationship has been consummated. (See Chapter 13.)

Other Equipment Users. Once the user begins to frame its requirements, the data collection process should be expanded to include other users that have had experience with the same vendor(s) and/or equipment that the user proposes to engage in the upcoming negotiations. Most users recognize that other firms are extremely valuable sources of information and advice on a variety of equipment performance topics. However, far too many users fail to appreciate that their fellow users can be particularly good sources of negotiating and acquisition information. The key in seeking this type of information is to zero in on the users' past problems, negotiating oversights and failures, and negotiating successes. To be sure, many users are not too eager to talk about their errors, omissions, and failures. But most will come around if the user takes a professional, low key approach of "we can all learn from common successes and failures." A workshop or training session environment, such as that found at conventions, users' group meetings, and seminars, often offers the best setting for a candid information exchange.

Other External Sources. In addition to fellow users, several other sources of external information should be considered. Trade publications offer a wealth of information concerning industry developments, rumors, and opportunities. This information often can and should affect the user's negotiating strategies. Consequently, every member of the user's negotiating team should read, or at least scan, several of these publications throughout the acquisition process (and, preferably, all year). The fact that the technical members of the team read these publications does not preclude the need for other team members to at least review them. As noted above, the negotiating team approach is interdisciplinary, requiring the maximum possible understanding of all functional areas by all members of the team. Moreover, part of the value of the team approach is that one member may view a particular item in a negotiating perspective that might not be readily apparent to other members of the team.

In addition to considering the more traditional industry publications, the user's data collection efforts should include several specialized newsletters (e.g., *Computer Negotiations Report*) or similar services designed to supply current insight about vendor ploys, practices, and pricing. Even more than the usual industry periodical, these publications are likely to supply advice or cautions that will directly affect the user's negotiating strategies.

When the size and importance of the proposed acquisition warrants such an approach, as it often does, the user's data collection process should also include the retention of one or more professionals specializing in major equipment acquisitions and contract negotiations. This suggestion is by no means a general endorsement of retaining a consultant. The user's need for one or more consultants should be viewed as neutrally as possible, based upon the degree to which the user would benefit from external professional assistance that cannot be supplied internally or through the user's regular attorneys or accountants. Applying these criteria, most users benefit more from professional advice concerning how to approach and structure the negotiating process (that is, "how to negotiate") than from counsel about how to select a vendor or a particular system. If the user determines that professional advice should be solicited, the relationship ideally should be initiated during or before the data collection phase of the acquisition process. Although initiating such a relationship later in the process is certainly better than doing without professional advice altogether, an earlier engagement often precludes the user from making positioning errors that will be difficult or impossible to cure at a later point. Moreover, earlier involvement is often less expensive in the long run, both in terms of the professional's total fee and the aggregate savings achieved in the acquisition.

Assessing Economic Factors

As the general information collection process outlined above is executed, the user's negotiating team must also assess the external economic factors that may be relevant to the proposed acquisition. Since World War II, America has experienced several recessionary cycles of varying severity. In recent years, these recessionary periods have involved considerable economic uncertainty and such previously unknown factors as "stagflation." Not too surprisingly, the external economic environment can have a significant effect upon equipment negotiating and acquisition strategies. Consequently, an astute user must constantly assess the relative impact that then-current economic conditions may have on the respective operations and goals of the vendor and the user.

From a practical standpoint, the user need not attempt to predict future economic events with precision. Rather, the user's goal should be to recognize future economic trends and translate those factors into related vendor and user practices. The important step is for the user to recognize the likely bottom-line costs of various vendor and user problems—and to adjust the user's acquisition plans and negotiating strategies accordingly.

The following sections review a number of potentially-adverse economic factors and analyze their possible impact on the user. (In practice, of course, these generalizations must be carefully tailored to actual economic events and the specific needs of the vendor(s) and user involved.) Subsequent sections explain various user strategies that may be useful in responding to these and related economic factors.

Higher Interest Rates. Higher prime and related interest rates may impact the user in several areas, including the following.

Higher vendor prices. High interest rates increase costs for the vendor and its suppliers. Eventually these costs are passed along to the user in the form of higher prices. In some instances, primarily involving products, the impact to the user may actually occur after rates have begun to subside.

Higher lease and installment purchase rates. By definition, higher rates drive up the cost-of-money factor in financing leases. This problem can be particularly troublesome when the vendor purposefully ignores the rising rates, thus "low-balling" the user in the sales campaign, only to demand a far higher rate at the contract signing.

Increased competition for available funds. As higher interest rates slow the economy and the ready availability of credit, some leasing companies may be unable to gain adequate financing. As money tightens, banks and other lending sources are likely to become more selective in making loans to lessors and/or users. Smaller leasing companies and smaller users may have difficulty gaining the desired funds, particularly if either party evidences weak financial condition. Higher interest rates, of course, put an increased financial burden on the firm paying those rates.

A user or lessor capable of paying 10% to 12% for funds may be placed into financial difficulty by sustained rates of 18% to 25%.

Increased leasing demand. Higher interest rates often increase user demand for leased equipment. Despite the higher implicit rates included in the lease calculations, leasing—and particularly third-party leveraged leasing—can offer rate advantages over comparable purchase transactions. In addition, as interest rates rise and credit becomes tight, users may prefer to "finance" their equipment acquisitions through leasing in order to leave their regular bank lines and similar credit sources free for other purposes.

Increased purchasing pressure. Just as higher interest rates may cause more users to favor leasing, the higher rates may also cause vendors to favor user purchasing. Given the high interest rates vendors must pay if they fund their operations through outside loans, vendors prefer to use internally generated funds instead of third-party loans for this purpose. The incentive to use internal funds causes many vendors to cut back on leasing in order to use the lease financing dollars to fund ongoing operations. This pressure does not exist, however, where the vendor traditionally sells or assigns its leases at a discount to a third-party financing source, such as a bank. Nevertheless, the tight credit that is likely to be associated with higher interest rates may reduce the vendor's ability to continue to sell or assign its leases in this manner. If such a credit crunch occurs, the vendor generally has little choice but to reduce its leasing efforts or to finance the leases internally. (Of course, internal financing may be a viable alternative if the lessor/vendor can extract a high enough rate from the user and the lessor/vendor has a ready source of capital for its leasing and ongoing operations.)

Increased demand for used equipment and lease renewals. As high interest rates and tight credit make the financing of new equipment more expensive and/or more difficult, many users may determine to postpone a new equipment acquisition for 6 to 18 months, when (the user hopes) interest rates will be more reasonable. Users that adopt this approach implement it by retaining, and in some cases upgrading, their existing systems. If these systems are purchased, the eventual trade-ins are delayed. If the systems are leased, the leases are generally extended or otherwise renewed. These user actions reduce the supply of used equipment flowing into the marketplace, driving up demand and price for some items. Because of the higher demand for leased equipment, the higher cost of acquiring new equipment, and the relative reduction in available used equipment, lessors may be less willing to routinely renew existing leases. Indeed, users attempting to renew leases that do not have a renewal provision with a specified maximum rent may find themselves renewing at, or only slightly below, the existing (prime term) rental rate.

Higher Costs and Prices. Increased costs associated with inflationary factors in the economy can cause such results as the following.

Higher vendor prices. As in the case of interest rates, higher component and labor expenses raise the cost of the product or service to the user. As this "future inflation factor" grows, the user may be able to economically justify moving a given acquisition to an earlier date, or paying a slightly higher price at present to avoid further increases in the future. Similarly, higher future costs may justify accepting a high interest rate, due to the fact that future inflationary price increases may outweigh any anticipated decline in interest rates.

Increased risk of economic failure for vendors. As the cost of components, money, and labor increases, some vendors find themselves caught in a cash flow and/or profit squeeze. Marginal suppliers may be unable to adjust prices fast enough to survive, particularly in highly-competitive product fields.

Shortage or Capacity Economy. A shortage or capacity economy develops when demand for goods equals or exceeds the available productive (factory, for example) capacity. This situation often occurs during the later stages of an economic recovery. When demand exceeds not just available supply (in warehouses and the like), but also exceeds existing productive capacity, a number of results can occur.

Higher prices. As every economics student has learned, when demand exceeds supply, prices increase. When the only way to increase supply is through the construction of additional plant and machinery (as opposed to simply increasing output in an existing assembly line), prices tend to climb even more. As noted above, the user is then faced with price increases of a direct (for example, equipment list price increases) and an indirect (for example, price increases resulting from higher-cost purchased components used in the equipment) nature. In this scenario, "premiums" above list price may develop. An example of this effect in a very limited product line can be found in the premiums offered on certain IBM computer systems during the late seventies.

Lack of supply. In some instances, certain systems or components may simply be unavailable (or unavailable at a feasible cost). When this occurs, the user may be forced to alter its business plans by substituting less desirable equipment. This problem may be more acute where component manufacturers begin selling directly to users as well as to original equipment manufacturers (OEMs).

Increased risk of vendor nonperformance. Where supply is a problem and windfall premium prices abound, timely vendor performance may be a problem. Some vendors may have difficulty performing due to their inability to obtain or produce an adequate supply of the necessary products. Indeed, some vendors may fail because of this problem. Other vendors may try to juggle orders in order to fill the more profitable orders first, while delaying the less profitable orders until supply comes closer to demand. The latter situation is more likely to occur where premiums are being paid or where used equipment is being acquired through third-party sources.

Seller's market or "take it or leave it" syndrome. A capacity economy is a seller's market. Despite the fact that users are becoming more sophisticated in their negotiating techniques, the vendor's marketing representative can, and most likely will, become much harder to bargain with in a capacity economy. Matters that were previously negotiable with only moderate prodding become nonnegotiable "take it or leave it" items. This vendor attitude affects both price and contractual protection issues. In this environment, the traditional vendor ploys thrive. Even where shortages do not exist with respect to all categories of the vendor's equipment, the "seller's market" syndrome is likely to spill over and affect the vendor's willingness to negotiate for any and all of its products and services.

Recommended User Responses. Despite the problems brought on by a period of increasing costs and/or diminishing supplies, the user can take several steps to minimize the impact of this type of economy on its operations. A few suggestions are summarized below.

Recognize the problem. As always, the most basic step is to recognize the problem. In the present context, this means recognizing the economic conditions that are likely to change in the future and appreciating the potential impact of these changes on the user's equipment operations and negotiations. Keeping track of the economy through reading several different economic reports or through consulting the user's economists should meet the first half of the problem-recognition step. The summary of factors set out above, coupled with a thoughtful analysis of the user's three or five year future business plan, should suffice for the second half of this step. In this regard, the user should be particularly careful to review each vendor and supplier separately. As noted above, the economic changes are likely to have a more severe impact in newly established or otherwise marginal vendors.

Exercise additional care in selecting vendors. Because of the increased risk of vendor economic failure, the user should exercise additional care in selecting potential vendors and other suppliers. Increased importance should be placed on the vendor's financial condition and staying power, particularly in the context of an inflationary economy with rapidly increasing interest rates and costs. Because of the increased problems of short supply and high demand, the user should also consider the ability and willingness of the vendor to deliver the desired equipment within the required time frame. The vendor's past practices and reputation in this area can be particularly instructive. If the vendor fails to deliver on schedule during periods of adequate supply, the user should expect the worst in a capacity economy.

Emphasize contractual protection against vendor default. Because of the increased risk of vendor nonperformance, the user should try to put teeth into the vendor/user agreement to guard against vendor default. More specific performance deadlines, multiple date or checkpoint schedules, liquidated damages, and user cancellation provisions can all assist the user. At the same time, the user should strive to eliminate any standard vendor form contract provision that may grant inappropriate protection to the vendor. One example of such provisions is the "force majeure" section found in some contracts that absolves the vendor from liability for nonperformance where the failure to perform is due to events beyond the vendor's control. Many such sections particularly reference the failure of any supplier to provide component parts. Whether the vendor should have to pay damages in this type of situation is open to debate. However, in most such instances, the user should at least have the right to cancel the order after a reasonable period and look for an alternative source of supply.

Advance the planning cycle. To minimize the price and supply problems involved in an adverse economic scenario, the user should advance its planning cycle and study its future equipment needs to determine if certain acquisitions or dispositions can or should be moved up or delayed. For example, it may be advantageous for the user to acquire a system sooner in order to avoid later supply or pricing problems. On the other hand, it may be possible for the user to continue to utilize an existing system until both the demand and the price for the system increase, thereby permitting the user to trade or sell the used equipment at a meaningful premium. Indeed, in some situations, the user may be able to acquire a new system early and retain the old system until the demand for it increases, perhaps using the old system for testing, training, or conversion work.

Recognize and counteract traditional vendor ploys and shortage economy marketing techniques. As the previous discussion suggests, the user must be alert to the vendor ploys and tactics associated with a "seller's market." Ploys relating to future price increases and supply problems are especially popular (and, unfortuantely, sometimes based on fact). To minimize the impact of these ploys, the user can and should analyze the relationship between a given economic event, such as an increase in the prime rate, and the true impact of that event on the user's proposed acquisition, such as the cost of senior debt financing for a third-party lease. For example, the user should remember that interest rates for five-to-seven year money may not increase as rapidly as the short-term prime rate. The user should also recognize that certain leveraged leasing techniques can provide an effective annual percentage rate below prime, even where the user obtains or shares the investment tax credit.

THE CONTRACTUAL APPROACH: RESULTS VERSUS RESOURCES

At this point in the negotiation process, the natural user tendency is to move toward the formulation of acquisition goals and objectives. However, before this step can be accomplished, the user's negotiating team must consider and agree upon the *contractual approach* that will be utilized in the acquisition. To accomplish this task, members of the user's negotiating team must understand the difference between "contracting for resources" and "contracting for results."

When a user is contracting for resources, it is generally agreeing to procure specified people, products, or services. Consequently, the documentation in such a transaction is designed to ensure that the user receives the agreed upon resources (people, products, or services), but little or nothing is said about results, that is, about whether or how those resources will meet the user's needs. To be sure, the user contracting for resources may go to great lengths to ensure that the agreement contains certain warranties that the equipment will perform according to the manufacturer's specifications or that the equipment will achieve certain initial "uptime" percentages. But this type of engineering specification is seldom directly related to the user's needs or desired results.

On the other hand, when a user is contracting for results, it is generally agreeing to have the vendor provide specified resources that will achieve stated results at the end user or customer level. In effect, the vendor is representing that the equipment will not only meet technical specifications but will also perform certain defined user functions.

From a conceptual standpoint, if a user is contracting for resources and the given people, products, or services fail to meet the vendor's generic specifications for them, the vendor (rather than the user) faces the liability for nonperformance—assuming, of course, that the user has extracted reasonable warranties from the vendor. But if the user is contracting for resources and the resources meet all relevant vendor specifications but fail to provide the desired level of end user or customer service, the user (rather than the vendor) has the problem. This latter result does not occur, of course, if the user is contracting for specified results rather than resources.

The key difference between contracting for resources and contracting for results is whether the vendor or the user will have *responsibility* if the equipment functions according to certain generic engineering specifications but fails to "do the job" anticipated and required at the end user or customer level. A user can validly determine to accept this responsibility (by contracting for resources) or to force the vendor to accept it (by contracting for results). However, the user should make this decision knowingly, with full appreciation of the consequences involved. This type of knowledgeable decision can be made only if the user fully understands the results required by its end users or customers and the potential risks associated with achieving those results through use of the vendor's equipment or other resources. In most instances, the vendor is in a far better position to warrant that its resources can achieve the desired results. (However, the vendor has a right to expect a reasonably detailed, written description of the desired results and at least some protection against failure caused by the user.) In some situations, the user may be in a better position to ensure that the vendor's resources will be able to achieve the results desired by the user. In the latter case, the vendor has a valid argument that the agreement should cover resources rather than results, unless the user can point to narrow areas where the vendor can reasonably expect to have responsibility for ensuring that the equipment will in fact provide the results desired at the end user or customer level.

Because of the substantially increased liability (and risk of nonperformance) and the problems associated with distinguishing the vendor's duties from those of the user, most vendors prefer to contract for resources rather than results. For similar reasons, sophisticated users prefer to contract for results wherever the vendor will agree to do so. This is particularly true where, as in the majority of cases, the user has effectively contracted with its own end users or customers to provide results rather than resources.

To contract for results, a user must be capable of saying, "I'll accept the system when it works" (at the end user or customer level). Although this requirement may seem abundantly simple at first glance, for the approach to be successful the user must also be capable of defining two key words in detail: "system" and "works." Defining these two words is 90% of the job.

As this statement suggests, the user's decision to contract for resources or results has a substantial effect on the type of preparation required before entering the negotiating arena. If the user elects to contract for resources, it accepts a much heavier burden that the selected resources will in fact meet its specific operating requirements. Consequently, the user must devote additional effort toward analyzing its technical requirements and the operating specifications for the equipment being considered. On the other hand, if the user determines to contract for results, it attempts to shift to the vendor much of the burden of ensuring that the people, products, and services supplied under the contract will actually meet the operating requirements involved. Consequently, the user must spend considerable time determining, defining, and documenting the results desired by its various customers or departments. Although equipment and other product specifications remain important, particularly as methods of assessing and verifying vendor representations concerning the results that they supposedly can and will provide, the main concern becomes how to define and describe the desired results in a binding legal agreement.

Because these two methods—results and resources—require substantially different emphasis during the preparation phase of the negotiating process, the user's team must face the results-versus-resources question at an early stage of preparing for a particular acquisition. In most instances, this consideration should occur prior to, in connection with, or immediately after the data collection phase described above. The decision can be postponed beyond this point, particularly if both alternatives are considered simultaneously, but formal external steps, such as RFP preparation or contract bargaining, should not be instituted until the team has reached agreement on this issue. As suggested above, of course, "agreement" on this issue may include a decision to use the resources approach for some items and results approach for certain other items. The critical point is that the team should formally determine which approach will be used and proceed accordingly in preparing to negotiate and acquire the respective items involved.

ACQUISITION GOALS AND NEGOTIATING OBJECTIVES

Formulating Goals and Objectives

Once the contractual approach has been determined, the negotiating team should develp and document the user's acquisition goals. If the user is contracting for resources, the team should define the resources required and ensure that the applicable published specifications for the products will meet the user's needs. If the user is contracting for results, the team should define the desired level of acceptability to the end user level, remembering that the vendor will be responsible for warranting that the products can and will actually provide this level of service. If a combination approach is used (for example, a contract that spells out minimum equipment specifications and also includes vendor warranties concerning results of conversions and the total system operation), both approaches should be pursued simultaneously.

As the user's broad acquisition goals are formulated, the negotiating team should begin defining and documenting the basic contractual, financial, and technical objectives necessary to meet the acquisition goals. In this process, the team must translate general acquisition goals into more specific contractual, financial, and technical objectives. Later, these specific objectives must be further transformed into language that can be utilized in, or incorporated into (as an addendum or exhibit), the actual vendor/user contract.

The importance of this step in the negotiating process cannot be overemphasized. Although equipment contracts "fail" or create subsequent problems and exposure for users for a variety of reasons, the authors firmly believe that a substantial percentage of these problems can be traced in whole or in part to the respective user's failure to develop adequate goals and objectives before moving to the formal bargaining sessions. The problems created by such a failure are pervasive. For example, if the user has not accurately quantified its own requirements, the user's attorney has little hope of drafting solid contractual provisions covering equipment performance standards. Moreover, where the user's team has not clearly documented its own goals and objectives, the vendor's sales representatives are able to discuss user concerns in general rather than specific terms, thereby avoiding any detailed response that might in the long run prove to be less acceptable to the user. When this happens, the vendor's general response on a given issue seems more or less "reasonable" to the user, because the user has not taken the time and trouble to determine for itself what a "satisfactory" vendor response is, or should be, on the issue involved.

The facts of life concerning this step of the negotiation process are very simple. If the user's negotiating team makes every effort to prepare for an acquisition through competent and thorough data collection, analysis, and documentation, it will stand a reasonable chance to achieve its goals by applying its negotiating skills at the bargaining table. On the other hand, if the user's team enters formal negotiations without the necessary precommitment to preparation, it may fail in its mission regardless of the negotiating skills brought to bear in the individual bargaining sessions.

"If the formulation of detailed acquisition goals and negotiating objectives is so critical to success," one might ask, "why do so many users fail to do an adequate job?" The answer is simple. Doing an adequate—much less extensive—job of documenting user goals and objectives is a difficult, time-consuming, and painful job that requires a significant corporate and managerial commitment. It takes substantial time and effort to do the job right. Faced with on-going business responsibilities and conflicting time demands from a host of different areas, most user representatives are unwilling or unable to devote the time and resources necessary to do the job correctly. Some users, of course, fail to appreciate the need to devote so much preparation time to this area. Others recognize the theoretical importance of documenting goals and objectives, but rationalize that special circumstances permit or require the step to be omitted "in this one instance." (As suggested above, this rationalization often afflicts all future acquisitions as well.) Still other users appreciate the importance of this step, but justifiably conclude that shortages of time and resources beyond their control only permit an incomplete job to be done. Regardless of the reason, or the reasoning, the result is the same: an inadequate job of developing and documenting user goals and objective leads to an inadequate contract and acquisition. Recognition and correction of this basic truth would save equipment users millions of dollars each year.

In most situations, the process of defining general goals and setting specific objectives requires considerable assistance from non-team members, primarily other user departments and outside experts. Particularly where large or extremely critical acquisitions are involved, the negotiating team should use this process both to obtain valuable technical and professional assistance and to gain sign-off commitments from relevant end users. (See "The Departmental Approval Process," below.) Involving these end users and obtaining their approval at this stage in the negotiating process serves two major purposes. First, it enhances the user's ability to define the problem and establish comprehensive goals and objectives. Second, it minimizes the likelihood that the end users will engage in second guessing and other exercises in hindsight later in the negotiating process.

In defining the user's goals and objectives, the negotiating team should avoid making a decision on the specific acquisition method that will be used. Although one or more members of the team may believe that the user will ultimately determine to use a specific acquisition method (for example, a third party lease), the team should maintain maximum flexibility at this stage in the negotiating process by considering all reasonable acquisition alternatives. As long as a particular acquisition method meets the user's general acquisition goals and specific negotiating objectives, it should remain open for consideration and assessment during much of the negotiating process. Frequently, the user should be willing to consider various acquisition methods through and including the RFP phase of the negotiating process. (An obvious exception to this approach exists, of course, where special user circumstances dictate that a specific acquisition method be utilized.)

The language utilized to document the user's acquisition goals and negotiating objectives is not particularly critical, as long as the approach is both understandable and comprehensive. Goals and objectives may be expressed in varying degrees of specificity, but goals should be phrased in terms of acquisition purpose and objectives should be phrased in terms of specific negotiating efforts. Put another way, acquisition goals should state key solutions or factors that the acquisition is expected to achieve (e.g., reasons for the acquisition). Negotiating objectives should state the legal, financial, and technical specifics that will be included in the contract in order to achieve the broader acquisition goals. For example, the user's negotiating team might determine that one of its acquisition goals is to improve system uptime to a specified level. (Note that stating this goal without specifying the desired level of performance would be an exercise in inadequate goal definition.) Based upon this goal, the user's team might develop as specific negotiating objectives a 95% uptime acceptance test provision, a 90% or 95% maintenance and rental credit provision, a one-hour minimum maintenance response time provision, and a system replacement ("lemon") provision.

Prioritizing Objectives

Once the user's negotiating team has defined its basic goals and objectives for the acquisition, the negotiating objectives must be prioritized or ranked according to relative importance.

Some negotiating objectives are more important than others in virtually any acquisition. The objective of minimizing certain types of operational and financial risks falls into this category. The importance of other objectives varies in each acquisition, depending upon such factors as the particular needs of the user, the past performance of the vendor, and the risk/cost factors involved in any failure of performance. The objectives of maximizing price concessions and gaining an investment tax credit (ITC) warranty might fall into this category.

Prioritizing objectives forces the user's personnel to consider seriously the relative importance of all relevant issues—before the formal bargaining sessions begin. Such a careful analysis permits all members of the user's negotiating team to agree on the assigned priorities before entering the negotiating arena. As a result, members of the team are less likely to misunderstand one another—and inadvertently give away an important point—at the negotiating table. Advance prioritizing of objectives also helps keep the user's negotiating team "on track" during the heat and confusion of actual negotiations. Important goals are readily delineated as such, and can be treated accordingly. Less critical goals can be given less time and talent, as desired. In this regard, prioritizing effectively reduces the user's susceptibility to a favorite vendor negotiating technique where the vendor trades a user concession on a major vendor issue for a vendor concession on a minor user issue. In this approach, the vendor argues vigorously against a very minor concession demanded by the user and then finally "gives in." In doing so, the vendor either gains a corresponding concession from the user on an issue of major importance to the vendor, or claims that extraction by the user of the vendor's concession (and others like it) precludes the vendor from being able to agree to any of the user's other (and considerably more important) requests. The user, having fought a strong and successful, albeit misguided, battle for an insigificant point, wins the battle and loses the war.

A number of methods can be employed to rank the user's goals and objectives. Some firms utilize an informal conference where members of the negotiating team and the user's operations staff discuss the objectives and, following some debate, agree on interim, and then final, priorities. Depending on the degree of formality and recordkeeping desired, minutes or other notes of the meeting may be retained for future reference.

If all of the members of the negotiating team are reasonably well trained, the priority ranking approach described below can offer a sound method of assigning relative priorities to the user's objectives. Even if the team does not use the priority ranking that results from this technique, the ranking experience itself is often educational; in many cases, team members appreciate for the first time the difficult value judgments involved—and the differing values assigned to objectives by various team members.

The priority ranking technique requires that each member of the negotiating team assign a sliding-scale value to each negotiating objective. Values are assigned from a predetermined ranking table, such as the following:

Rank	Priority
1 to 3	Critical issue; deadlock negotiations if necessary to achieve objective.
4 to 7	Important issue; strive to achieve objective in some acceptable form but negotiate as required.
8 to 10	"Oh, By The Way" issue; attempt to achieve objective, but do not waste negotiating strength and equity on this issue.

Other ranking tables can also be used. Some users prefer ranking each objective on a scale of from one to four as follows:

Rank	Priority
1	Critical issue
2	Important issue
3	Minor issue
4	Limited issue with little or no value

Although the scale employed is not critical, the authors generally recommend use of a one-through-ten or similar scale so that team members will have an opportunity to rank issues within a given priority. For example, under this approach a "critical issue" could be assigned a value of "one" or "three." With a more limited scale, the only acceptable ranking would be "one." The same ranking-within-a-ranking can also be achieved by using a two-step process and a one-through-four scale. Under this approach, objectives are initially ranked into four categories, using the one-through-four scale set out above. Then objectives are ranked within each scale value by assigning a further one-through-four rank to each objective receiving, for example, a rank of "one" during the first ranking step.

Once all of the objectives have been ranked, the ranking scores for each objective are averaged and a "composite" or "team" rank is assigned to each objective. The objectives are then reordered according to the new team rank.

As suggested above, the final step is the most important. In this step, team members review the new rankings, discuss their respective reasons for assigning their own ranking to each particular objective, and then rerank all the objectives as a result of the team discussions. In many instances, team members will concur with the composite ranking assigned to the objective. In other situations, a team member with particular expertise in a given area may assign a much higher rank to an objective. For example, the team attorney may feel that minimizing a rather innocuous legal risk is absolutely essential. The discussion and reranking phase of the prioritizing process allows team members to fully consider disagreements of this nature. As such, the process avoids the possibility that the relative "ignorance" of several team members will outweigh the expertise of another member on a given issue. At the same time, the technique avoids unnecessary discussion on the issues where agreement is easy to reach.

To implement the ranking approach, one member of the team should be assigned to prepare a list of negotiating objectives. All members of the team, and perhaps other user staff personnel, should contribute to this list. (User checklists, such as those published in this volume, offer a useful starting point.) These objectives should then be arranged at random (alphabetical order generally results in a random priority order) on a ranking sheet or on several sets of 3″ x 5″ file cards.

A ranking sheet or set of file cards should then be provided to each team member. Each member should be instructed to write his or her rank for each objective on the sheet or on each card. Finally, the "team" rank should be determined, as explained above.

Set out below is an example priority ranking sheet taken from an educational workshop conducted by the authors. To provide realism, the sheet is based upon certain "user assumptions" in the hypothetical acquisition:

- The user intends to purchase the new system.
- The new system involves a conversion.
- The current system is badly overworked.
- The user has had no experience with the new system.
- The user is interested in maximizing financial savings.
- The new system will be maintained by the vendor.

The user objectives included in the example ranking sheet are not intended to be a complete acquisition checklist. Most users will have a considerably larger number of objectives on their actual ranking sheet.

Example Ranking Sheet The User Corporation

Priority Rank	Negotiation Objective
_____	Right to move system.
_____	Title transferred to user on Acceptance.
_____	Software source code available to user (in escrow or direct).
_____	All vendor proposals and benchmark test results included in contract.
_____	Investment Tax Credit warranty by vendor.
_____	Order modification possible up to thirty (30) days prior to shipment at no penalty.
_____	User has unconditional right to use system.
_____	User can transfer software license with sale, lease, or transfer of system.
_____	User can seek maintenance from non-vendor source.
_____	User assumes all risk of loss until Acceptance.
_____	User has right to delay delivery for up to ninety (90) days without penalty.
_____	User can modify system and add attachments at no penalty (maintenance).

_____ Equipment malfunction credits available after Acceptance (credits against maintenance price).
_____ Equipment refurbishment warranty.
_____ Price protection prior to Acceptance.
_____ Liquidated damages imposed for late Acceptance.
_____ Most favored nation price provision.
_____ Selected peripherals (list types) available on consignment.
_____ Hardware configuration warranty.
_____ Liquidated damages imposed for late delivery.
_____ Complete Acceptance test included.
_____ Minimum purchase price.
_____ No maintenance charges imposed during warranty period.
_____ Eliminate all pro-vendor warranty limitations.
_____ Specific trade-in schedule included in contract.
_____ Vendor warrants system will perform to published specifications (with stated penalties.)
_____ Major unit replacement available if serious malfunction continues after Acceptance.
_____ Vendor to supply ten sets of all documentation at no charge.

As in the seminar where this example was used, there is no "right" or "wrong" answer to prioritizing this list of objectives. Each user must reach its own assessment of priorities in each acquisition. The important point is that the user's negotiating team engage in a formal prioritizing exercise before proceeding further in the acquisition process.

EQUIPMENT ACQUISITION ALTERNATIVES

Most users are generally aware that most equipment can be acquired through a number of different methods and financing vehicles. Too frequently, however, many of these users fail to fully evaluate these acquisition alternatives in the context of a specific proposed transaction. As a result, they leave dollars, flexibility, and contractual protection on the negotiating table. One of the most frequent user oversights in this area involves the failure to appreciate the full range of acquisition alternatives and the manner in which these alternatives interrelate.

Although many other factors can be involved in a thorough consideration of acquisition alternatives, three basic options should be considered in most situations:

- New versus used equipment.
- Purchase versus rental acquisition method.
- Single vendor source versus multiple vendor sources.

While each of the three choices listed above can be phrased as "A versus B," each of the three alternatives involves a continuum rather than polar extremes. The full range of alternatives can be best described on a three-dimensional coordinate system, by plotting each of the three alternative sets along the appropriate axis. When this approach is employed, an "Acquisition Alternative Matrix," such as that shown in Fig. 4-5, results.

Utilizing this matrix, the user can "plot" a point on each decision axis. For example, the user may determine to acquire new, refurbished, or used equipment, or some combination of new and used, used and refurbished, new and refurbished, or the like. Similarly, the user may decide to purchase, lease, or rent the components or to utilize some combination of these basic acquisition

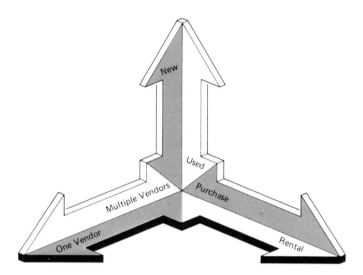

Fig. 4-5.   Three-dimensional matrix depicting equipment acquisition alternatives.

methods (not to mention a full range of variations, such as installment purchase, third-party lease, and rental with purchase options). Moreover, the user can determine to utilize any number of vendors for each of the alternatives noted above.

As in any three dimensional matrix, once the user's decisions are plotted on each axis the resulting "decision point" can be determined in the matrix solid or cube. Recognizing the large number of plotting or position alternatives in the matrix cube is often helpful in dramatizing the full range of equipment acquisition alternatives available to the user.

For example, the user may determine to "finance" the purchase of certain manufacturing equipment (through an installment purchase or third-party lease) due to its anticipated long life and the expense of a rental arrangement. On the other hand, the user may also decide to rent some extra equipment required during the installation process from a third-party vendor (because it may not be needed after the installation effort) and to rent additional and control equipment where state-of-the-art improvements are expected on a recurring basis (in order to maximize upgrade flexibility). At the same time, the user may decide to buy some older "work-horse" components at a bargain price, acquiring this equipment from another user or from a broker.

As this example suggests, the user's negotiating team must assess the full range of acquisition alternatives at a relatively early stage of the negotiating process. To make this assessment, all members of the negotiating team must understand the basic advantages and disadvantages associated with each of the available alternatives.

In assessing alternative acquisition methods, the user should carefully consider the changes enacted by the Economic Recovery Tax Act of 1981. Signed by President Reagan on August 13, 1981, this important law altered existing tax depreciation rules, replacing them with a new Accelerated Cost Recovery System (ACRS) that generally ignores salvage values and shortens the periods over which business assets may be written off for tax purposes. The 1981 Act also made a number of important changes in the investment tax credit (ITC) and created a new tax "safe harbor" for equipment leases. Transactions that meet the requirements for this "safe harbor" will be deemed to be leases for tax purposes, even though they do not meet a number of conditions that were previously required for a tax lease. (For example, a "safe harbor" lease can grant the user a fixed-price, or even bargain-price, purchase option at the end of the lease term.)

The general effect of the 1981 Tax Act was to make leasing a more preferable acquisition method (at least for *tax* purposes), and to facilitate the transfer of ITC benefits to corporations that can utilize the benefits to offset current taxable income. (During 1982, considerable Congressional opposition developed over the alleged "windfalls" permitted by "safe harbor" leasing. Readers are urged to consult with their tax advisors to determine the status of applicable regulations before relying on any "safe harbor" lease.)

The relative advantages and disadvantages of rental and direct lease agreements, installment purchase contracts, and third-party leases are explored in Chapters 10 and 12. Chapter 10 also highlights the ITC and "safe harbor" lease provisions contained in the 1981 Tax Act.

The following outline provides an overview of the relative advantages and disadvantages of various *equipment, acquisition,* and *vendor* alternatives. Although the actual benefits and detriments involved in each alternative will vary from acquisition to acquisition and from user to user, the outline should provide a useful framework for negotiating team members interested in reaching their own decisions on each of the issues involved. (The following discussion assumes the continued availability of "safe harbor" leasing under the 1981 Tax Act.)

1. EQUIPMENT CHOICES
A. New Equipment

Advantages	Disadvantages
• May offer state-of-the-art technology	• Higher cost may outweigh processing advantages
• May offer maximum Investment Tax Credit (assuming user can utilize)	• Delivery schedules and availability may delay installation
• May offer better warranties, lower maintenance costs and fewer maintenance problems	• New system or programs may not be proven or fully debugged, problems may result
• Can add to company or executive status and image	• Higher status of new system may color acquisition decision
• Often can be acquired with "less hassle" and more confidence	

B. Used Equipment

Advantages	Disadvantages
• Cost is generally much lower; may offer better price/performance ratio	• System may be old and subject to aging problems
• System and software may be thoroughly proven and debugged	• Processing speed, memory, and the like may not be state-of-the-art
• May be available on faster delivery schedule; may become productive more rapidly	• Warranties generally short; maintenance costs may be high
• Maintenance records available for inspection	• Acquisition may require more complex contract and increase user "hassle" and apprehension
• May offer more applications software	• Investment Tax Credit generally not available or very limited

2. ACQUISITION CHOICES
A. Rental

Advantages	Disadvantages
• Offers maximum flexibility	• Cost is comparatively very high
• Offers short term commitment	• Price may increase on short notice (e.g., 90 days)
• Generally provides direct interface with manufacturer	• Generally offers no residual value (unless purchase option credits exercised)

- Often includes maintenance at no extra charge and maximizes service
- Payments deductible; minimizes asset/liability problems and related accounting uncertainties (e.g., FASB 13)
- May offer purchase option credits

- Generally requires fixed payment schedule with no financial flexibility
- Vendor generally has less room for financial or soft dollar concessions

B. Lease

Advantages

- Cost generally lower than rental alternatives; leveraged lease methods may offer particular advantages
- Payment stream can be tailored to user's needs (step up, step down, and so on)
- Offers excellent vehicle for pass-through of investment tax credit and other tax benefits, particularly after adoption of Economic Recovery Tax Act of 1981 (and its "safe harbor" for tax leases)
- May be effective "financing" vehicle, regardless of accounting treatment required; can also offer tax and balance sheet advantages if payments are deductible
- May be more flexible than outright purchase

Disadvantages

- Term generally longer than rental alternatives
- Upgrade or equipment change during term may be difficult or expensive
- Generally no residual value, although Economic Recovery Tax Act of 1981 now permits end-of-term purchases at pre-determined (and even bargain) prices
- Accounting and tax treatment may be uncertain or inconsistent, although Economic Recovery Tax Act of 1981 now permits "safe harbor" lease qualification for *tax* purposes
- May involve third parties and more removal from manufacturer

C. Installment Purchase

Advantages

- Offers compromise between straight purchase and lease or rental
- Depending on interest rates and user's internal rate of return, may be more effective financing vehicle than lease and more profitable than outright purchase
- Some tax aspects may be positive; permits user to show increased assets and liabilities
- Once all payments made, permits total user control over asset; may offer resale or residual value
- Generally involves fewer legal restrictions and user commitments than third-party lease alternative

Disadvantages

- Financing arrangements impose more restrictions than outright purchase alternative
- Depending on interest rates and user's internal rate of return, cost of financing may be excessive
- May now be less attractive than a lease with a bargain end-of-term purchase option (under "safe harbor" lease rules contained in Economic Recovery Tax Act of 1981)
- Some tax aspects may be negative
- Financing may preclude upgrade arrangements
- Involves payment of interest and risk of reduced resale value without affording user the limited term flexibility found in lease alternatives

D. Straight Purchase

Advantages

- Total cost often low, particularly when compared to rental
- May offer residual or resale value
- Some tax aspects of ownership may be positive
- Permits total user control over the asset (subject to maintenance and software constraints)
- No continuing relationship with leasing company

Disadvantages

- Capital outlay may be excessive, particularly when compared to "safe harbor" lease alternative
- Vendor or market action may drastically reduce residual or resale value expectations
- Some tax aspects of ownership may be negative
- To upgrade, may require sale or lease to others; trade-in may be expensive
- To protect investment, may need long-term vendor commitment on software and maintenance

3. VENDOR CHOICES
A. Single Vendor

Advantages

- Permits convenience of "one-stop shopping"
- Reduces problems involved in meshing obligations of multiple vendors
- Requires fewer contractual complexities than multiple-vendor alternative
- May offer increased flexibility for upgrades and trade-ins on system as a whole
- May permit better standardization and support

Disadvantages

- Often increases price
- May preclude processing advantages available in assembling custom hardware/systems
- May preclude advantages available in seeking special software or service support
- May reduce soft dollar concessions offered by vendor
- Restriction of total number of user/vendor relationships may reduce user flexibility in future acquisitions

B. Multiple Vendors

Advantages

- Often offers price advantages
- May improve processing through assembly of custom hardware/systems
- Improves present and future vendor competition and willingness to offer concessions
- Increases user's available vendor sources for future acquisitions
- May increase negotiating and technical experience of user's staff

Disadvantages

- Requires increased user "hassle" and apprehension
- Requires careful meshing of vendor responsibilities
- May reduce total vendor commitment to user's account
- May reduce upgrade and trade-in flexibility on certain components and on system as a whole
- May create component compatibility problems

THE NEGOTIATIONS POSITION PAPER

Once the team has prioritized its negotiating objectives and completed its analysis of acquisition alternatives, it should prepare a negotiations position paper that summarizes the user's goals and objectives and sets forth the team's approach to both the acquisition and the related negotiations. Preparation of this document provides discipline and organization that can be critical to the team's success during the actual negotiations. Much like the budgeting process, this step is valuable both in terms of the resulting report and in terms of the understanding that is gained by preparing the report. Once completed, the position paper should be approved by the same level of the user's corporate management that will be responsible for approving the final user/vendor transaction and documentation. The position paper will then serve as the team's road map and "portfolio" as the negotiations ensue.

As major developments and changes occur during the negotiating process, the position paper should be updated and reapproved by all user participants, including management. The process of updating the position paper can be an excellent debriefing tool for the user's negotiating team after several days (or even hours) of heated bargaining sessions. To be sure, updating the document requires time. However, as in the case of the initial draft, the mental discipline required to complete the update often causes team members to focus on issues, alternatives, and solutions that might otherwise be overlooked. In addition, the updating process ensures that all user participants will be kept abreast of changes in the user's objectives and strategies that may occur during the negotiating process. Far too frequently, users fail at the bargaining table because they are not prepared to be there. The negotiations position paper can serve as a key element in the user's preparations for a specific acquisition.

As suggested above, a good negotiations position paper should be capable of serving as a stand-alone summary of the user's acquisition goals and negotiating objectives and strategies. Consequently, each position paper must be tailored to the specific circumstances of a particular acquisition. Nevertheless, the following outline of a position paper employed by one user in a relatively typical transaction may offer guidance to users interested in preparing their own papers:

1. General Business Information:
   A. Name and Address of User Department Acquiring System.
   B. Names, Titles, Addresses and Phone Numbers of Personnel: (1) on the User's Negotiating Team (including the User's Counsel); and (2) Otherwise Involved in the Approval Process (including senior management).
   C. Names, Titles, Addresses and Phone Numbers of User's Professional Negotiators and Advisors.

2. General Equipment Information and User's Overall Objectives:
   A. Summary of User's Existing Equipment and Other Resources (including basic contractual terms).
   B. Summary of Proposed Equipment and Resources (including any suggested trade-in or similar alternatives).
   C. Summary of User's Overall Equipment and Resource Objectives (including replacements, upgrades, time frames, and alternatives).

3. Vendor Information:
   A. Name of Existing Vendor, and Names, Titles, Addresses, and Phone Numbers of Local and Regional Vendor Marketing Personnel.
   B. Names of All Proposed or Alternative Vendors (including where possible the marketing personnel data specified above).
   C. Summary of User's Relationships with Various Vendors (including past problems, actual or potential favoritism, and—if possible—a dollar value assessment of the "benefit" of maintaining certain subjective "relationships" with the incumbent or other vendors).

4. Financial Considerations:
   A. Summary of Proposed Acquisition/Financing Methods (including primary and secondary goals and the reasons therefor; lease-versus-purchase analyses and similar exhibits may be attached).
   B. User's Tax Considerations (including Investment Tax Credit impact and goals).
   C. User's Depreciation Method (if applicable).
   D. Assessment of User's Internal Rate of Return (for purposes of permitting future reassessment of alternative acquisition methods).

5. Timing Goals and Considerations:
   A. Alternative and Fall-back Negotiating Positions.
   B. Assessment of Penalties and Risks Involved in Various Alternatives.
   C. Assessment of Risks Involved in Event of Vendor Default.
   D. Preliminary Negotiating Schedule(s).

6. User's Prioritized Goals and Objectives:
   A. List of User's Goals and Objectives (listed in order of priority).
   B. Summary of Vendor's Inducements/Offers to User (financial, legal, and technical).
   C. Current Estimate of Degree to Which Vendor's Inducements/Offers Meet User's Desired Goals and Objectives.

      D. Appendix Showing Legal and Contractual Issues to be Contained in User's Request for Proposal (alternatively, the Appendix may include a draft of the full Request for Proposal).

7. Negotiating Considerations:

      A. Assessment of User's Negotiating Posture (including user's willingness to take a hard line position or break off negotiations).

      B. Expected Role of User's Negotiating Team, Other Staff, and Experts in the Negotiations (including a summary of staff assignments and responsibilities).

      C. Current Assessment of Possible Vendor and Equipment Alternatives (to provide possible alternatives to be pursued or threatened in the event of a breakdown in negotiations with primary vendor).

8. Signature Blocks for:

      A. User Staff Preparing the Position Paper.

      B. Any Other Negotiating Team Members.

      C. Senior Management Personnel Who Will Finally Approve the Transaction.

THE DEPARTMENTAL APPROVAL PROCESS

Preparing for any proposed acquisition involves, or at least should involve, considering various operating requirements and commitments and reviewing and revising myriad contractual provisions. Although these tasks are usually the primary responsibility of the user's negotiating team, other user departments may also have important input concerning certain provisions or matters. All too frequently, users fail to gain this interdepartmental input in advance. As a result, the user department involved is forced to accept the provision or other matter ("live with it") after the contract is signed or, if the department is slightly more fortunate, to review and attempt to change the negative language or other commitment at the very last minute before the agreement is executed.

This process is risky, unprofessional, and—most of all—unnecessary. Despite the hectic pace of most major equipment negotiations, proper planning and procedures can permit advance review of key contractual sections and other commitments by selected user departments and, if necessary, outside experts or advisors. The following discussion outlines how this review can be orchestrated.

As is often the case, the first step is recognizing the importance of doing the job right. Several major incentives are involved.

First, most vendor/user agreements include at least some provisions that require the user to take action prior to, or immediately after, the agreement is executed. For example, the delivery section may require that the user furnish insurance on the equipment during shipment from the vendor's factory to the user's site. The installation section may require that various site improvements be completed prior to the time the equipment is delivered. The payment section may require that downpayment checks be issued or that notes or security agreement forms be executed as of specific dates. The list goes on and on. Ordinarily, the actual implementation of these items will not all be the responsibility of the user's negotiating team. Other user departments will be involved. If these other departments are not permitted to review the relevant contractual provisions in advance, the related user obligations may not be performed within the time, or in the manner, specified in the contract.

Second, similar problems often arise with provisions that require user implementation at a later point in the transaction. Again, failure to involve the responsible user departments at the outset may leave a serious information gap. This communications problem may place the user in default under the agreement, resulting in a full gamut of risks from needless embarrassment to serious liability.

Third, the failure to have selected provisions reviewed in advance by key user departments generally ensures that the sections involved will be less than optimum. The risk that the provisions will be substantively defective from the user's standpoint is increased where the section covers a narrow topic that is not within the direct province of a member of the user's negotiating team. Matters involving insurance, invoice processing, and equal opportunity/affirmative action contracting requirements are likely problem areas.

Fourth, leaving key user departments out of the advance approval process increases the probability that one or more of these groups will engage in second guessing or other hindsight exercises at a later date, particularly if anything goes wrong. Even if not fully justified, this type of after-the-fact finger pointing can taint the entire acquisition process and bring other decisions made by the user's negotiating team into question or disregard.

The second step in properly handling interdepartmental review is to determine the contract provisions or other matters that should be considered in advance by other user departments. As suggested above, these matters will ordinarily be those that are not directly within the expertise of a member of the user's negotiating team. For example, most technical data processing provisions will receive sound advance review by one of the team members from the operations department, or from a nonteam colleague selected by the team member. On the other hand, if some site preparation matters will be handled by the user's real estate department, and that department is not represented on the negotiating team, a problem may arise unless proper review procedures are followed. Many users have already implemented formal interdepartmental "contract review" procedures that offer excellent guidance in selecting the departments and at least some of the provisions that should be involved. In a few instances, these procedures will be adequate to provide all necessary interdepartmental review. In most situations, however, the complexity of a major equipment transaction will require modified or additional procedures.

The third step in establishing an adequate interdepartmental review process is to schedule the review period or periods and transmit the necessary information. Many users postpone this step, rationalizing that the provisions involved will be modified by further negotiations and that little benefit would be served by distributing premature drafts or vendor standard form provisions. Consequently, as the bargaining process heats up, little or no time is left for interdepartmental review and the entire process is ignored ("there just wasn't time") or overlooked. To minimize these problems, the user's team should alert all relevant departments of the proposed transaction and the impending contract review at a responsible date. This early warning can often be in the form of a transaction summary based upon excerpts from the user's negotiations position paper, which outlines the proposed acquisition. If preliminary or final provisions are available, these can and should be circulated at this point. In some instances, excerpts from documents proposed by the vendor may be used. Where appropriate, a covering memorandum should outline the enclosures and indicate whether the recipient should review and respond to the enclosed provisions or await further drafts. Once this formal avenue of communication has been opened, subsequent provision changes can be conveyed by messenger, telephone, or telecopier as the negotiations move toward execution of the formal agreement.

The final step in this review process is to document all responses. One member of the negotiating team should be assigned responsibility for coordinating and documenting all interdepartmental approvals. A brief checklist offers one of the better methods of handling this task. The checklist should include the department involved, the various drafts reviewed, and the approvals or comments received (including relevant dates and staff members involved).

REQUEST FOR PROPOSAL PROCEDURES

Once the user has reached this stage of the negotiation process, it can focus on formally involving the vendor, or several competing vendors, in the acquisition. Although vendor personnel may have been involved during earlier phases, perhaps by supplying technical information or making the proverbial informal sales call or survey, the first formal interface with the vendor on a specific acquisition generally occurs, or at least should occur, during the request for proposal (RFP) or invitation for bids stage. It is only at this stage, after the substantial efforts outlined above, that the user is ready to release to the vendor the equipment specifications and other standards for the acquisition. Any invitation for bids and, indeed, any communication with the vendor, that occurs prior to this point is based upon incomplete information and assessment. Consequently, the best practice is for the user to limit its interface with vendor personnel until the RFP is released and to formalize the RFP process in a manner that clearly indicates that only the RFP contains accurate acquisition specifications.

The authors will be among the first to admit that not every major equipment acquisition justifies or even permits the use of a formal RFP. The preparation of a good RFP is a tedious, time-consuming job that requires a substantial commitment of resources. In determining whether an RFP seems advisable (or, indeed, mandatory) in a specific transaction, the user should consider such factors as the size and cost of the transaction, the processing and financial risks involved, the uniqueness of the desired equipment, and the degree of user commitment to a single source of manufacturer. In addition, the user should recognize that attempting to determinine whether an RFP is advisable is itself a difficult task. The assessment is made more difficult where, as is often the situation, the applicable user department is short on both time and staff and long on pending projects and commitments. Perhaps because of these factors, far too many users rationalize that an RFP is seldom if ever needed (or even possible) in their own equipment acquisitions. Although these users can recite all the academic reasons in favor of using an RFP, they quickly explain that special circumstances preclude the need for an RFP, or make preparation of an RFP impossible, in whatever proposed acquisition may then be under consideration. The unfortunate fact of the matter is that most of the managers behind these rationalizations have never drafted and issued a thorough RFP, and probably never will. They simply do not want to admit that they lack the professional discipline to do the detailed job required, or to demand the additional staffing necessary to use the RFP process.

Rather than attempt to pontificate on the fact that more users should utilize RFPs in more acquisitions (which they should), the authors simply suggest that, before concluding that an RFP is either unnecessary or impracticable in a given transaction, the user's negotiating team, or its operations or senior management, should seriously and objectively consider the potential benefits offered by applying the RFP process to that transaction. In some instances, the only compelling conclusion will be that an RFP is essential. In other cases, an RFP may be advisable but impossible. (Even then, the user may be able to apply certain RFP tactics successfully.) In still other instances, the benefits offered by the RFP process may be totally outweighed by other factors. The important point is that the potential benefits from the RFP process should be carefully assessed in the context of each proposed transaction, and dismissed only upon the presentation of compelling countervailing factors.

Assessing the Benefits

A well-prepared RFP offers a number of important benefits to the user. First, preparing and issuing an RFP forces the user's technical, legal, financial, and managerial staff to analyze all aspects of the proposed acquisition before negotiations begin with a given vendor or manufacturer. Properly handled, this process alone can save the user thousands of dollars (and may even indicate that the proposed acquisition is unnecessary). Second, the RFP puts the user squarely in the driver's seat during the critical early negotiations stage. Ordinarily, the vendor enjoys the initiative during this period and the user merely reacts to the vendor's marketing plan. Third, the RFP benefits both the user and the vendor by clarifying the user's needs in writing at the outset of the negotiating process. This clarification reduces later vendor or user misunderstandings and also makes it difficult for the vendor to claim later that it did not fully appreciate that the user really demanded a particular concession. Fourth, a good RFP enhances competition and improves the likelihood that all bidding vendors will offer substantive concessions. Even where the user knows that it must acquire a particular system to do business with a given vendor, an RFP can be beneficial in getting the only practical source in the proper frame of mind for negotiations. As one old pro in major systems procurement stated, "Putting your current vendor out there scraping for crumbs just like everyone else is probably one of the best ways possible to really get something you want from him, even though he's the only way you can actually go."

Handling the Complaints

A user that is considering using a formal RFP in a particular acquisition is likely to encounter some opposition from its incumbent vendor, particularly if the user has not followed the RFP approach in previous acquisitions. Although there are exceptions, most incumbent vendors—particularly those with cozy relationships—are unlikely to be very happy about going through a full-fledged RFP/bidding procedure. Even incumbent vendors that presently participate in a routine, ineffective RFP/bidding process are likely to object if a procompetitive three-part RFP approach is adopted. The RFP complaints most likely to be raised directly or indirectly include the following:

"Using an RFP Will Ruin our Relationship." In this approach, the vendor suggests that the good user/vendor relationship enjoyed during recent years will be destroyed if the vendor is forced to endure the time and expense of an RFP/bidding procedure. If the vendor is actually giving the user the best deal possible—voluntarily—this point may have some merit. However, this level of voluntary optimization by the vendor very seldom exists. In the vast majority of cases, a nice, cozy sole source relationship costs the user money, both in hard dollars and in soft dollar benefits.

Ironically, a good RFP process can actually strengthen the position of a competitive sole source incumbent vendor. During the RFP/bidding procedures, the incumbent vendor can once again demonstrate why the user is indeed fortunate to be served by the incumbent vendor, provide the user with substantive new benefits to demonstrate the vendor's commitment to the user's account, and quiet any charges leveled by competitors (often to the user's senior management) that the user is ignoring competitive proposals from other vendors in favor of sole sourcing to the incumbent vendor.

"Using an RFP Will Destroy Your Timetable." In this complaint, the vendor argues that the additional time required for the user's RFP procedures will add months to the acquisition process and negate any possibility that the user's essential timetable can be met. This argument should not be taken lightly. As suggested above, a good RFP process takes time, both to prepare the RFP itself and to analyze and optimize the various bids and proposals. In many situations, a user just embarking on the RFP approach may be forced to abandon the technique for near-term acquisitions and focus on implementing the program during later transactions.

The proper response to this problem, of course, is for the user to begin the RFP planning well in advance of any proposed acquisition. However, even where a shortage of time seems to exist, the user should consider two possibilities: First, the vendor may simply be trying to establish a "sense of urgency" that will force the user to abandon a technique that would result in increased competition for the incumbent vendor; and second, the user may actually save time, money, and headaches by ignoring the alleged time constraints, changing the system acquisition deadlines, and proceeding to implement an adequate RFP procedure.

"You Don't Have the Staff to Properly Prepare an RFP and Analyze the Various Responses." In this complaint, the vendor keys upon the difficulties involved in preparing a good RFP, reviewing the resulting bids, and making a sound decision. The vendor's suggestion is that an ill-prepared, poorly analyzed RFP/bidding procedure will result in a bad decision that will cost the user thousands of dollars. This warning is usually coupled with the thought that the RFP process will prevent the incumbent vendor from providing the careful planning, analysis, and insight that has essentially kept the user's operation going for the last few years.

The unfortunate fact is that, far too frequently, these warnings are correct. Many users do not have the personnel necessary to conduct a good RFP/bidding procedure. Many user departments do lack proper short- and long-range planning. Indeed, the only real "planning" in some user shops is that found in the vendor's marketing plan.

Regardless of whether the vendor's warnings in this area are based upon fact or fantasy, the user should still move to implement an adequate RFP procedure. If deficiencies exist in the user's organization, personnel training should take place on a priority basis. Where necessary, existing personnel should be replaced or competent RFP personnel added. Where time does not permit internal development of staff personnel with strong RFP experience, professional negotiators, consultants, or other experts should be retained to meet immediate needs and assist with training.

Conducting a truly competitive RFP process is not an easy task. It requires time and talent. However, a good RFP procedure can save a user thousands and thousands of dollars in a single acquisition. Indeed, the authors have found that a good RFP process, including proper planning and aggressive negotiations, can quite easily save a user at least ten percent of the total costs of a major equipment acquisition. In many cases, the savings are measured in multiples of that figure. From a bottom line standpoint alone, not to mention savings in time and frustration, that kind of savings can justify (and, in fact, mandate) a competent, well-paid RFP team.

Methods of implementing a strong RFP technique are discussed in considerable detail in Chapter 5.

Employing the Invitation-for-Bids Alternative

Where a user determines (hopefully for valid and objective reasons) that full RFP procedures are not possible in a particular acquisition, it should still consider utilizing an invitation-for-bids approach in lieu of a sole source or totally informal procurement process. Although the invitation-for-bids technique is unlikely to supply the substantial benefits available from the full RFP process, it can offer meaningful competitive advantages.

In the invitation-for-bids approach, the user essentially employs many of the RFP procedures, but does so on a much more limited scale. As used by the authors, the invitation-for-bids approach is simply a considerably abbreviated version of the RFP procedure. For example, the invitation-for-bids approach involves a formal user "request for bids" (RFB) that is forwarded to competing vendors. However, the RFB is considerably shorter and less detailed than a comparable RFP. The RFB may specify the particular equipment or other products being sought (thus involving a "resources" rather than a "results" approach), minimum acceptance and delivery criteria, and an outline of the user's procurement procedures. The RFB can be coupled with other procompetitive bidding practices, such as the bidders' conference and the "zone of consideration" (ZOC) approach. (See Chapter 5.) In the latter situation, the RFB can be an important method of creating the appearance of considerable competititon in an acquisition where one vendor (usually the incumbent) would otherwise feel that the transaction was essentially a sole source procurement. At the same time, the RFB avoids the detailed specifications and contractual standards involved in a good RFP. Because of this fact, the invitation-for-bids approach is not an acceptable compromise where the user is contracting for results rather than resources. For similar reasons, the invitation-for-bids technique should not be utilized in other complex transactions, even where the user is contracting for resources rather than results.

The dividing line between the RFP procedure and the invitation-for-bids approach is not much more distinct than the line between "mini" and "micro" computers. The important point is that, where a user determines that it cannot employ full RFP procedures due to time, resource, or other constraints, the user should nevertheless consider the possibility of employing a consciously restricted RFP—here called an invitation-for-bids or RFB—in order to achieve at least some of the competitive benefits available from the full RFP process.

FORMAL NEGOTIATIONS

Regardless of whether the user employs the full RFP procedure, a more abbreviated invitation-for-bids, or a sole source or informal procurement, at some point the user must sit down and "negotiate" various technical, financial, or contractual points with the vendor. Indeed, it is this stage—the formal bargaining process—that most users think of when they refer to "equipment contract negotiations."

At the risk of being redundant, it may be beneficial to point out once again that a user has no place entering into any formal bargaining sessions with the vendor until the negotiating stages outlined earlier in this chapter have been successfully completed. Put another way, before a user engages in any traditional "negotiations" or moves to the contract bargaining table, the user and its negotiators must:

- Form the user's negotiating team.
- Begin and complete the data collection process.
- Justify the proposed acquisition.
- Determine the contractual approach (results versus resources).
- Establish acquisition goals and negotiating objectives.
- Prioritize negotiating objectives.
- Prepare and update a negotiations position paper.
- Obtain preliminary departmental and senior management approvals.
- Prepare and issue an RFP or, at least, an invitation-for-bids.
- Follow RFP procedures to maximize competition (e.g., hold a bidders' conference).

Then and only then can the user move to the bargaining table with any real opportunity for success.

If an RFP is used and the ZOC process works well, the team may be able to conclude the formal contract soon after the primary vendor is selected. (See Chapter 5.) This is possible because, ideally, ZOC negotiations cover contractual as well as financial and technical issues. Thus, if the user has employed a thorough RFP (including legal matters) and the ZOC negotiations have considered and resolved all relevant RFP issues, the principal contractual points should be covered and agreed upon by the time that the ZOC negotiations are completed. Where this occurs, little additional time must be devoted to legal squabbling or drafting. Even where the agreed-upon concessions have not yet been committed to writing in the formal contract, the only principal requirement should be one of drafting and clarifying various provisions.

Practically, of course, few negotiations involve a perfect RFP/ZOC process. As a result, most acquisitions require considerable additional bargaining after the primary vendor is selected and before the formal agreement is executed. Where additional negotiating sessions are necessary to resolve contractual matters, financial concessions, or other issues after the primary vendor has been selected, the user must exercise particular care to maintain negotiating leverage with the vendor.

As Chapter 3 explains, the user's leverage generally drops significantly after the vendor determines that it has beaten all competition and is the user's primary (and probably sole) source. (See Fig. 3-3.) The most effective method of maximizing the user's negotiating leverage during this critical period is to create substantial uncertainty in the minds of the vendor's representatives. This uncertainty can be created by direct and indirect user comments, by an attitude of user smugness or assurance, and by actually keeping at least one other vendor source waiting in the wings. Even where the user has no intention of utilizing an alternative source, it is absolutely essential for the primary vendor to believe that the user might call in another source if the primary vendor balks at key points or negotiations otherwise fail to progress.

Once the user proceeds to formal negotiations, its negotiating team must be prepared to follow highly organized, disciplined procedures every step of the way. While preparation is the user watchword throughout the preceding stages of the negotiation process, organization, discipline, and control are the key commands at the bargaining table itself. Chapter 3 outlines many of the basic negotiating tactics utilized by experienced users. The following portion of this section highlights several additional keys to achieving success at the negotiating table.

Achieving and Maintaining Control

Control is important throughout the negotiating process, but it is essential once the negotiators move to the formal bargaining table. Control is valuable for one reason: It permits the negotiator to obtain his or her objectives and, thereby, to achieve his or her firm's acquisition goals. Control is not valuable as an end in itself, and the negotiator who attempts to maintain some degree of control without understanding where or how that control is directed may ultimately lose both the battle and the war.

Control at the negotiating table can be achieved through a number of means. Indeed, strategic control is seldom effectuated through a single tactic or effort. Users should consider the following methods of achieving and maintaining control.

Organization. The critical factor underlying most control strategies is organization. Admittedly, the world has witnessed some negotiators who are capable of sustaining control throughout a long negotiation purely on the basis of artistic skill, with little or no precommitment to organization. However, such artisans are few and far between, and the distances among them are littered with the remains of inexperienced negotiators who plunged into the fray without adequate organization and preparation.

Organization means different things in different contexts. For example, organization may require that a user carefully outline the points expected to be covered, the likely vendor reaction, the counterthrusts, and the expected trade-offs. Vendor representatives invariably use this type of organization, complete with role playing exercises and written execution plans, before embarking on most user sales calls or bargaining sessions. Organization in another context may demand studying prioritized objectives, predetermining roles, or detailing an agenda (see below). In yet another situation, organization may necessitate assigning arguments to different team members, scheduling meeting rooms to optimize environmental control, and avoiding (or scheduling) unnecessary interruptions. Whatever the context, and whatever the requirements, the user's negotiating team should not enter into the formal bargaining phase of the acquisition process without asking, very simply, "Are we organized? Have we completed all the organizational steps necessary to permit us to control the upcoming meetings?"

Agendas and Schedules. As noted in Chapter 3, a properly prepared agenda can be an effective method of gaining and maintaining control of an individual bargaining session. The agenda permits the user to determine what general areas will or will not be discussed at particular times. In addition, when carefully drafted the agenda can subtly mold the substance of the session, in effect serving as a user strategy in and of itself. The mere use of an agenda also makes an affirmative statement about the user's preparation and organization. The fact that a user has a well-prepared agenda strongly suggests that the user intends to maintain control. Just as an agenda can help the user control an individual bargaining session, a longer range schedule can facilitate control of the entire acquisition process. Because of the important opportunities offered by these items, the user should ensure that it is the sole source of agendas and schedules. Moreover, the user should affirmatively utilize these items for control purposes, even pulling and replacing previously distributed schedules where necessary to express displeasure or implement some other user tactic.

Urgency. Maintaining control requires that the user avoid, or at least strictly limit, any real or false sense of urgency. As Chapter 2 indicates, many vendor ploys are based upon creating or heightening a sense of urgency in the user. In addition, of course, the user often has a true sense of urgency in many instances: The user has delayed the acquisition for too long and needs the new equipment now! Regardless of the source or reason, when the sense of urgency is translated into haste, control is almost certain to slip from the user to the vendor. User negotiators involved in acquisitions with critical deadlines should be cognizant of this risk, and should be particularly alert for any of the early user rationalizations (e.g., "ordinarily, we would proceed this way, but we just don't have time in this case") that may suggest that control is turning into a stampede toward contract execution.

Minutes. Formal minutes of negotiating sessions and user discussions with competing vendor participants can be an interesting and somewhat unique method of enhancing control. Although this approach is admittedly not called for, practical, or affordable in every acquisition or negotiating session, it clearly places the user in the driver's seat by evidencing the seriousness with which the user views the proceedings. The potential advantages of this approach must be weighed against several possible negatives: the formal record may be costly to make and impractical to use, the presence of the reporter or recorder may stifle all productive discussions, and, unless notified in advance, the vendor may overreact and refuse to participate under such conditions (at least until the user makes clear just how firm its intention is to use the approach). Where this approach is implemented effectively, users generally employ one of two methods: tape recordings or a court reporter. Of the two techniques, the court reporter is by far the most costly and the most effective.

Concessions and Commitments. One of the disadvantages of using a negotiating team or, for that matter, any multinegotiator environment is that one person does not and practically cannot control all of the comments made by one side. As a result, one team member may blurt out a comment on a key point just as another team member (perhaps the user's lead negotiator) is preparing to offer a vital compromise. Effective control requires that the team come to grips with this possibility in advance and determine who will make key concessions and commitments. Although appointing a sole spokesperson may mechanically alleviate this problem, it may not improve the team's effectiveness at the bargaining table. One of the benefits of the team approach to negotiations is the multifaceted interplay of ideas and suggestions, and one of the strengths of a good team is the ability of all of its members to participate actively in the discussions. Ordinarily, the proper balancing of this issue can only occur after several strong role playing exercises or actual negotiating sessions, where the personalities and bargaining styles of the team members can be observed. When this approach is used, one team member generally emerges as the user spokesperson on key issues. (This individual need not be the chairperson of the negotiating team.) The attorney or general management representative on the team often enjoys this position.

In addition to controlling concessions and commitments at the bargaining table, the user must ensure that the negotiating team is in control of the entire acquisition process. For the team to have this control, the vendor must recognize that: (1) any and all management decisions concerning the acquisition will be made or recommended by the negotiating team; and (2) the vendor is not permitted to discuss or attempt to influence the acquisition at any other level of the user's organization (e.g., the end user department, the chief executive officer, or the board of directors). Assuming that the team has the necessary level of management or board commitment (which is the critical prerequisite), the user's negotiating team can assure the proper control by indicating the applicable constraints in a written communication directed to the vendor early in the acquisition process. Some users require all competing vendors to formally acknowledge these restraints, both at the outset of the acquisition process and in any RFP proposal. Dealing with the other side of this problem is equally important: "Loose lips sink ships" in equipment negotiations as well as international conflagrations. The user's negotiating team and senior management must seriously caution middle level managers, particularly those in the operations division and any end-user departments, not to discuss any aspect of a pending acquisition with any vendor personnel (including vendor maintenance personnel). Moreover, to maximize security, the user's negotiating team should follow the "need to know" approach and not permit any user staff members other than those with a clear "need to know" to have access to negotiating strategies, position papers, or assessments concerning the status of the transaction. In this regard, all memoranda circulated among user team members should be sealed and marked "confidential." User team members should also be cautioned not to discuss the negotiations or their personal perceptions around individuals who are outside the "need to know" circle of advisors.

Aspiration Level. As Chapter 3 indicates, maintaining a strong aspiration level and a high degree of confidence is conducive to sustaining momentum and control. Consequently, the user's team should strive to maintain these affirmative attitudes throughout the formal bargaining sessions. Interestingly, the relationship between control and aspiration/confidence level appears to involve dual feedback. While a high aspiration level facilitates control, effective control also reinforces self-confidence and often increases aspiration level. Conversely, a low aspiration/confidence level can reduce control, and in turn the diminished control can cause further diminution in the aspiration/confidence level.

Environment. Control can also be reinforced through environmental factors, as the discussion in Chapter 3 suggests. Environment can best influence the user's control, or the appearance of its control (which can often be equally important), when the negotiations are held in the user's offices in surroundings that are rich, elegant, and highly-businesslike. When the vendor enters such an arena, the office environment can and should "speak control." Confusion, disorganization, messy offices, and unprofessional rushing about should be eliminated (even if normally present!) in favor of a soft-spoken elegance in which every move is carefully orchestrated to indicate that the user is meticulous, professional, and capable of dealing with every aspect of the transaction, from coffee service to word processing to contract execution. Seat selection and body language must also be considered in any effort to use environment as a control factor.

Strategies and Tactics. As Chapter 3 and other portions of this book explain, a number of negotiating tactics can be used to seize and maintain control and momentum. All members of the user's negotiating team need to understand these tactics and appreciate when and how to employ them. Control tactics must not be wasted; rather, they must be played at precisely the right intervals in order to sustain personal negotiating power and psychological negotiating leverage.

Negotiating Concepts Before Specifics

One of the most dangerous things that a user can do is fall into the trap of negotiating specifics before the user or the members of its negotiating team have negotiated, or even considered, the concepts underlying those specifics. Yet most users, including some of the biggest and best in the business, literally spring this trap on themselves time after time.

What happens is relatively simple. When the vendor and user sit down to the negotiating table, the vendor's representative suggests that matters would probably be facilitated if the parties reviewed the vendor's standard contract section by section. The user far too frequently agrees and, even if the user has prepared an agenda or other tools to optimize its control of the negotiations, the discussion ultimately bogs down over specific user-proposed changes to the vendor's contract.

The problems with this approach are neither complex nor obvious.

First, the user is embroiled in proposing and negotiating specific changes to a form contract carefully prepared and refined by the vendor over a period of years. In this posture, the user is placed at a disadvantage at the outset. Any change proposed by the user is likely to be countered by the vendor, and a compromise weaker than that originally proposed by the user is almost certain to result.

Second, the vendor knows its contract inside out. Unless the user's negotiating team is particularly sharp, chances are high that the vendor can accept one user change and still be protected by another provision of the contract. Many sections of a standard vendor agreement are inter-related. As a result, for the user to negotiate meaningful changes in substance, it must implement specific amendments to each relevant section of the document. (Provisions relating to restrictions on use or transfer of the system are a good example. Relevant sections may include those relating to licenses, assignment, maintenance, transfer, right to move, and title.) The section-by-section review often proposed by the vendor directs the user's attention and negotiating efforts to one section at a time, reducing the likelihood that the user will drop back and consider all interrelated sections as a single substantive area.

Third, and most important, by negotiating specific changes to the vendor's form contract, the user is almost certainly conceding that the acceptable underlying concepts are those inherent in the vendor's standard agreement. At best, the user will achieve negotiated concessions to the specific language used by the vendor. Seldom, if at all, will the user be successful in raising, negotiating, or implementing conceptual changes and related linguistic amendments to the vendor's form agreement. The result of all this is that the user brilliantly argues and achieves vendor concessions on all the right *words,* only to find later that it failed to have the agreement based on the right *concepts.* To modify a trite phrase, the user wins the battle over words but loses the war over the conceptual substance of the transaction itself.

What the user should be doing, at the very outset, is considering and negotiating the basic concepts surrounding each issue. If, and only if, agreement is reached on these basic concepts, should the user proceed to negotiate the specific language that will be employed to document those concepts in the agreement.

Consider the example of user acceptance. Far too many vendor form agreements simply provide that the equipment will be deemed accepted on the date that the vendor certifies to the user that the system is installed and ready for use. In some less archaic cases, the vendor's standard contract provides for nominal acceptance testing of the hardware only. The usual reaction of an informed user to this type of provision is to draft and negotiate a more substantial acceptance test, generally either by amending the vendor's inadequate provision or by inserting a quasi-acceptable standard such as that used by the General Services Administration (GSA) in federal procurement agreements.

Although the results of this approach are certainly likely to be superior to accepting the vendor's standard form agreement, the approach fails to consider the basic conceptual question of why (or even "whether") the user wants an acceptance test in the first place and what, if anything, the user wants that test to achieve. An acceptance test can check the reliability (over a short period, to be sure) of hardware, all types of operating, applications, and special software, and even maintenance, as well as various combinations of those items. The test can also determine whether some or all of those items meet certain minimum standards of performance. In some transactions, it may be adequate to use an acceptance test that merely checks the performance and reliability of the new hardware being installed. In other instances, the test may need to cover the entire new system, including hardware, software, and maintenance. In still other circumstances, the only prudent acceptance test may be one that includes both existing and new systems in order to ensure adequate compatibility. Similar examples can be posed concerning other aspects of acceptance tests, including the issue of whether the test can or should include, or at least interface with, various postacceptance malfunction credits, which again may cover any combination of hardware, software, and maintenance. (Acceptance tests are discussed in more detail in Chapter 8.)

Negotiating the concepts first can provide real value to the user. Among the benefits from this approach are the following.

First, the approach forces the user through a more disciplined assessment of just what the user wishes to achieve from the transaction. This user effort to determine and describe the underlying substance of the transaction (or "intent" as the lawyers sometimes call it) can provide improved understanding to all members of the user's negotiating team. The user's attorney is often a primary beneficiary from this approach, due to the fact that most users tend to hamstring their lawyers from the outset by failing to provide them with adequate background information concerning the basic substance of the transaction and the associated business goals.

Second, utilizing this approach can improve the user's negotiating position. The usual section-by-section review of contractual provisions takes time and plays directly into the hands of a vendor intent on controlling the timing of the negotiations and implementing various "sense of urgency" ploys. When the user says "look, we really don't want to waste time on the contract or the detailed language unless and until we have agreed in full on the basic concepts," the vendor is forced off base. The user's firm comes across as a professional organization intent on fully negotiating the substance of the transaction on equitable terms. The user is in better control and the vendor is less able to utilize its "sense of urgency" ploys.

Finally, by negotiating the concepts first, the user is forced to step back several notches and consider what it is that the user is attempting to achieve in the transaction, or in one particular aspect of the transaction. In taking this broader view, the user may determine that the basic approach employed in the vendor's form agreement is incompatible with the user's needs and, indeed, the user's perception of the entire transaction. On the other hand, the user may find that the concepts embodied in some sections of the vendor's contract are perfectly acceptable, in which event the negotiations on those provisions can proceed to the specific language involved. The important point is for the user to determine at the outset which areas of the agreement need conceptual discussion, and then to pursue that discussion before becoming sidetracked with the "nits and nats" of specific contractual language.

Employing RFI Procedures

As the negotiation process moves toward, or into, the formal bargaining phase, the user's negotiating team should seriously consider employing the "request for information" (RFI) procedure. The RFI technique may be used in virtually any negotiating environment, from an RFP/ZOC approach to a sole source procurement. Extremely simple to implement, the RFI procedure merely involves a written request by the user that the vendor, or several competing vendors, supply written responses outlining the vendor's position on various points or questions posed by the user in the RFI.

The RFI approach offers several potential benefits to the user. Among these are the following.

First, the RFI helps the user document the vendor's position on selected negotiating issues, in advance of the actual bargaining sessions. This approach reduces the vendor's ability to change its position in the midst of the negotiations. In addition, it gives the user an opportunity to study the vendor's positions in a quiet office environment, outside the negotiating arena itself. In this environment, the user's negotiating team and consultants can make more considered judgments concerning various user compromises and strategies. (On the down side, the value of these benefits may be reduced somewhat if the vendor takes a "hard line" approach in responding to the RFI, perhaps as part of a deliberate effort to throw the user off guard and avoid disclosing the vendor's actual position on the issues involved until the face-to-face negotiating sessions. The natural tendency of a vendor to adopt such a stance may be minimized if the user clearly warns the vendor that, if the vendor's RFI responses are not deemed to be acceptable, actual negotiations will not ensue. This user threat is most effective if several other vendors—perhaps ZOC contenders—are waiting in the wings.)

Second, the RFI technique keeps the vendor busy. Although this user benefit may seem somewhat unusual at first glance, its importance cannot be overemphasized. As many of the ploys explained in Chapter 2 demonstrate, vendor sales personnel strive to create a false sense of urgency in the user, either to induce the user to select the vendor's equipment and proposal or to urge the user to sign the vendor's contract with few or no changes. As the contract negotiations commence, most users are extremely vulnerable to vendor "urgency" tactics. Because the RFI approach effectively sends the vendor "back to the drawing board" or, at least, back to the vendor's senior management or legal department, it reduces the ability of the vendor's sales representative to accuse the user of delaying the acquisition. Instead of playing the defensive role of the "bad guy" (which most users unwillingly play when the vendor's sales representative keeps hinting that the user's negotiating stance is delaying—or even endangering—the entire transaction), the user is able to explain to the vendor: "Look, don't talk to me. We told you our procedures include the RFI. We gave you our RFI schedule two days ago. When are you going to respond so we can proceed?" (Or, if the user wishes to reinforce its message, "When are you going to respond so we can determine whether it's worthwhile for us to proceed to the actual negotiation and drafting of the agreement?")

Third, the RFI procedure can be used to gain back some of the ground lost by a user that failed to employ a good RFP at the outset, or that utilized an RFP but failed to include legal and contractual issues in the specifications. Failure to utilize a strong, complete RFP process generally weakens the user's negotiating position, particularly where a sense of urgency has been created by the vendor or by the user's own operating problems. The RFI offers an opportunity for the user to cover selected RFP issues (for example, legal and contractual points) at a later time, after a full RFP approach would be impracticable. In this setting, the RFI technique is generally most effective if it is utilized after the RFP stage but before the formal bargaining stage of the user/vendor discussions. However, the RFI procedure can also be employed during the contract negotiations themselves, either because user delay precluded earlier use of the technique or because user strategies dictated this later timing (for example, as part of a user effort to throw the vendor off balance, perhaps in connection with a deliberate deadlock of the negotiations by the user).

Fourth, the RFI procedure adds an appropriate element of formality to the negotiations, thus elevating the professionalism of the user in the eyes of the vendor. By moving the negotiations away from psychological issues and onto specific contractual or other points and vendor "deliverables," the RFI technique reduces the likelihood that the vendor's sales representative will attempt to utilize traditional vendor negotiating ploys. In essence, the RFI procedure (and similar formalities, such as a user-prepared meeting agenda) generally increases the vendor's respect for the user's negotiating expertise. This respect can be critical in permitting professional, rational discussions on key issues.

Fifth, the RFI approach generally requires the vendor's sales representative to contact, and perhaps obtain approval from, the vendor's regional or senior management and/or legal counsel. Although this fact may create some delay and consternation, the delay itself can be beneficial in diffusing the sense of urgency created by the vendor, as noted above. Moreover, by forcing the vendor's sales representative to go to a higher level in the vendor organization, the RFI reduces the effectiveness of the popular vendor ploy known as the "Unfortunately, I'll Have to Get Any Changes Approved by Corporate" ploy (explained in Chapter 2). In addition, by gaining the involvement of higher executives in the vendor organization, the RFI procedure reduces the likelihood that the vendor's sales representative will "commit" to a concession that the vendor cannot—and ultimately will not—deliver. At the same time, the procedure places the user's key issues, as set out in the RFI, directly before higher level vendor officials who have the authority to commit to them.

Finally, and perhaps most important, the RFI technique increases the user's negotiating leverage. As far too many user attorneys have found over the years, users frequently lack any meaningful negotiating equity at the critical moment when contract negotiations begin. By that point in time, most users are fully committed to the particular vendor, the specific system, and the supposedly "critical" delivery date. Although the user's attorneys and negotiating team may do their best at achieving the user's negotiating goals, their efforts would be enhanced if they had additional negotiating leverage. That leverage can be achieved, at least in part, if certain key issues where the leverage is needed most are included in the RFI. This approach permits the user to say to the vendor, either directly or indirectly: "Frankly, our attorneys and management will not even consider sitting down and negotiating the agreement unless and until your people have indicated their willingness to make it worth our while to do so. You have our RFI schedule. Unless your responses to those requirements meet our needs, we don't see much point in wasting our time and money negotiating the contract. If your RFI responses are acceptable, fine, we'll proceed at an accelerated pace. If your position is negative, however, we'll proceed to other alternatives." Of course, this position is most effective when the user actually has, or appears to the vendor to have, the flexibility and willingness to actually pursue other vendors or sources.

Drafting a good user RFI is not difficult, once the issues or specifications to be used have been determined by the user's negotiating team. The covering documentation for the RFI specification schedule can be quite brief. For example, one user employed the following language:

To Vendor A:

In order to expedite our mutual desire to conclude our contractual arrangements, we will require your written response to certain issues outlined in the attached Request for Information. Please furnish your position on all of these matters, even though certain of the issues may have been discussed previously in informal meetings.

Upon receipt of satisfactory responses on these issues, we will be in a position to proceed directly to drafting the acquisition agreement. However, the submission of incomplete or unsatisfactory responses by your firm may delay our discussions or require that we proceed with other alternatives.

Please be assured that we appreciate your willingness to enable us to determine whether full contractual negotiations would appear to be mutually beneficial.

The RFI schedule or list of issues can cover virtually any subject or group of subjects, although the technique particularly lends itself to legal and contractual points. The only real requirement is that the language cause the vendor to take a clear written position on each matter. Language such as the following should suffice for each issue: "Specify whether Vendor A will warrant that it has good and clear title to the equipment, free and clear of all liens and encumbrances, and that Vendor A will have such title at the closing date." A more "questioning" approach can also be used: "Will Vendor A warrant that it has good and clear title . . . ?"

Drafting Provisions

Once formal bargaining table discussions begin, one of the more difficult strategic questions is the degree to which "negotiations" should be interrupted to permit new or alternative contractual provisions to be drafted by the attorney participants on the respective teams. The answer to this problem varies from situation to situation, depending upon such factors as the competence and styles of the attorneys involved, the time available, and the negotiating strategies of the respective parties. The authors recommend that, wherever practical, the drafting process should be postponed until after the parties have reached both conceptual (see above) and substantive agreement on the issues involved. The following points are among those that should be considered in reaching a decision in this area.

Agreement on Principles. Just as there is value in negotiating concepts before negotiating specifics, in most instances the user will save time, energy, frustration, and negotiating leverage by gaining agreement on the substance of key points before becoming bogged down in drafting and discussing specific contractual language. If agreement cannot be reached on the substance of all important issues, drafting actual provisions may be a waste of time. Moreover, delaying such drafting clearly indicates that the user recognizes this fact and has little intention of risking such a waste of resources until substantive agreement is reached on the important issues. In addition, substantive agreement on one issue early in the negotiations may be altered later in the discussions as issues are "traded off." If the provision relating to the first issue has already been drafted and agreed upon, the job will have to be done over again (plus, one or both attorneys will have already "played their hand" in divulging or agreeing to compromises on the specific language of the initial provision).

Attorney Participation. The effectiveness of the negotiating team approach depends upon the availability and participation of all team members most of the time. Particularly where the user's attorney is a key member of, or principal spokesperson for, its negotiating team, the vendor may suggest that, to expedite matters, the lawyers on both sides should excuse themselves and get started drafting or reviewing specific provisions. Alternatively, when the negotiations are ready to break for the night, the vendor may propose that the lawyers draft the necessary language "this evening" so the negotiations will not be delayed the next day. Although exceptions certainly exist, this approach is almost always detrimental to the user, sometimes critically so. The vendor's attorney is seldom a key member of the vendor's negotiating team. In contrast, the user's attorney is frequently a key participant on the user's team. Most vendor marketing personnel have experienced dozens of major equipment contract negotiations and have a good understanding of the legal principles and risks involved. On the other hand, most user team members have little experience and enjoy no meaningful legal background. Consequently, if the vendor can carve the user's attorney out of the active negotiations, either directly (by concurrent drafting sessions) or indirectly (through fatigue resulting from all-night drafting sessions), the vendor will gain a significant positioning victory.

***Fait Accompli* Drafting.** When two attorneys attempt to negotiate contractual provisions as the formal negotiations continue, they often have a tendency to become overly combative over rather inane points. Lawyers are trained advocates, of course, and when placed in a purely adversary position they may fight for every "the," comma, and semicolon in a given provision. When this problem occurs, it unnecessarily delays the negotiation process, polarizes the parties, and increases the all-too-popular social disdain for lawyers in general. On the other hand, when the parties have reached agreement on the substance of all key contractual provisions, and the attorneys have simply been asked to formalize the agreement in "legalese," the combative atmosphere often diminishes and the two attorneys are able to draft and discuss the necessary language in a more professional, cooperative manner. In effect, the lawyers recognize that the transaction is a *fait accompli,* and the only remaining step is for them to document the substantive understandings reached by the parties.

Timing. Good contractual provisions take time, not only for drafting, but also for careful proofreading and substantive review by all team members. Regardless of any other factors, the attorneys may not have any serious alternative to drafting and discussing the provisions as the formal negotiations ensue. Where this problem exists, it can be alleviated (but only slightly) by the use of provisions taken from previously-negotiated agreements between the same parties, master user contract provisions, and preliminary drafts prepared in advance of the formal bargaining sessions.

CONTRACT EXECUTION

As the negotiations draw to a close and the final contract documents are prepared, the user's negotiating team must continue to exercise a high degree of accuracy and care. Most major equipment agreements are complex documents, both technically and legally. If all members of the negotiating team do not remain alert through the execution stage, errors can and will occur. The following areas are among those that should be considered as the negotiation process moves into the contract award and execution stage.

Assigning Responsibility

Considerable disagreement exists over who is responsible for the accurate production of contract documents. Many user representatives feel that this task is solely the responsibility of the user's attorney, in cooperation with the vendor's lawyer. Other user executives hold this view, but admit that the technical or operations members of the negotiating team should review the equipment lists and possibly other areas of the agreement. Unfortunately, few user representatives recognize that all members of the negotiating team must share responsibility for the accuracy of the final contract documents. Every member of the team should read all final contracts, addenda, and schedules, page by page, before the documents are released to the user's executives for signature. The contract award, preparation, and execution phase is not a period in which most of the members of the user's negotiating team can relax, socialize, and celebrate the successful completion of the negotiations. Rather, it is a time when all members of the team actively ensure that the contract documents fully and correctly reflect the transaction that both parties worked so hard to achieve. The fact that the text of various provisions, and perhaps of the entire agreement, has been previously read and approved by team members (as it should be, where possible) does not eliminate the need for one final review of the execution copies.

Because of the importance attached to participation and review by all members of the user's negotiating team, some users document the agreement approval process by having all team members and any inside or outside experts sign a cover sheet attached to the principal file copy of the documents. This sheet lists the contracts, exhibits, schedules, and other materials involved, provides an indication of review and approval, and includes individual signature blocks containing name, title, and date. Some users expand this form to include documentation of any required corporate authority approvals (e.g., board approval, senior management approval, purchase order execution). Although many users find this procedure to be overly formal, it has considerable merit, not only in major equipment acquisitions but in other large transactions as well.

Determining the Proper Degree of Linkage

The question of agreement linkage is one that must be handled at some point in the acquisition process, preferably at an earlier time but certainly no later than the point of contract preparation and execution. "Linkage" in this context refers to the issue of whether various aspects of the transaction should be handled in separate contracts and, if so, whether these separate agreements should be legally "linked" in some manner (i.e., made conditioned upon one another).

As a general rule, separate, unlinked agreements pose greater risks to the user than a single contract. Separate agreements that are formally linked create somewhat greater risks for the user than a single agreement, but the risk differential is seldom as substantial.

The problem with separate, unlinked agreements is that a vendor default under one agreement may not cause a default under a related agreement. Thus, where the user has executed separate equipment and maintenance contracts, a vendor default on the maintenance contract would not necessarily preclude the user from being liable for all amounts due under the equipment contract, even though the maintenance default effectively destroyed the user's ability to utilize the equipment. Maintenance is not the only area in which concerns of this type may arise. Contracts involving multiple deliveries, preliminary services, conversions, and similar connected matters can create substantial user exposure if the vendor obligations are included in separate, unlinked documents.

Formally linking the separate documents generally reduces this exposure (e.g., by making the vendor's performance under one agreement a condition precedent to the user's obligation under another agreement, or by providing that a vendor default under one agreement is an automatic default under all linked agreements). Nevertheless, the protection afforded by formal linkage is only as good as the draftsmanship involved. Linking complex equipment agreements in all necessary areas is often difficult, and the failure to tie all relevant sections of two or more agreements together in the required detail may create exposure for the user.

On the other hand, attempting to place all aspects of a major equipment transaction into a single agreement that covers all people, products, and services is also a difficult task that requires more time and drafting talent than many users are able to provide. (See the discussion of master agreements in Chapter 11.) Attempting to use a single, broad agreement when the user's negotiating team cannot devote the drafting effort necessary may create substantive risks above and beyond those found in separate but linked agreements. Because of this fact, many users appropriately compromise by adopting the separate but linked approach. Although this solution may not be ideal from a textbook standpoint, it avoids many of the risks arising from the use of separate, unlinked contracts, without requiring the substantial drafting commitment associated with single, all-encompassing agreements.

Handling Corporate Authority and Contract Execution

In connection with preparing the final contract documents, the parties must determine who will actually execute the agreements. Several factors must be considered in this regard.

First, where possible the agreements should be fully executed at the negotiating site or some nearby location. Unless no other approach is practical, the user should not execute the contracts and deliver them to the vendor's sales representative for review and execution by the vendor at some distant headquarters location. Legally, of course, this approach is perfectly permissible. Unfortunately, however, some vendors take advantage of this remote signature and review process in order to cite, for the first time, certain provisions that "must be altered to comply with company policy." In effect, these vendors permit the local sales representative to make an apparent commitment that is vetoed at the vendor's regional or main headquarters before the vendor executes the contract. This ploy is generally successful because, as the vendor suspects, the user is so pleased to have the negotiations out of the way and the agreement apparently consummated that the user would not think of balking at the suggested change and reopening negotiations.

Second, the user must ensure that the persons executing the documents have valid corporate authority to do so. On the user's side, this step generally means complying with the user's corporate purchasing and execution requirements. Ordinarily, the agreement must be executed by an officer holding the title of vice president or higher. Depending upon the size of the transaction, the prior written approval of a higher officer, or prior approval by the board of directors, may also be required. The corporate authority question on the vendor's side may be more difficult, but generally: (1) the agreement should be signed by an officer with the title of vice president or above; (2) the vendor's attorney should be asked to represent that the officer has authority to execute the agreement and bind the vendor; and (3) if the issue is critical and authority questions arise, the vendor should be asked to supply a "secretary's certificate" (including an excerpt from a board resolution or the vendor's by-laws) indicating those vendor officers having contract execution authority. Most vendor marketing representatives and branch managers do not have valid corporate authority to bind the vendor. The corporate authority issue applies to all documents requiring execution, not merely the "main" contract. Any supplemental agreements must also be validly executed.

Third, the question of whether the contracts should be witnessed, sealed with the corporate seal, or notarized are largely questions of local law or business preference. Although such additional formalities are seldom if ever harmful, they are also seldom essential. At a minimum, however, the agreements should use standard signature blocks that follow good business and legal practice. The following format is suggested unless the user's counsel advises otherwise:

USER CORPORATION	VENDOR CORPORATION
By: (Signature) _____	By: (Signature) _____
(Typed Name)	(Typed Name)
Title: _____	Title: _____
Date: _____	Date: _____

Fourth, local practice and professional preference also varies on the question of whether exhibits, addenda, and other material incorporated into the agreement should be executed or, at least, initialed. Unless the user's counsel offers other advice, the authors generally recommend that all primary exhibits, schedules, and addenda be executed on the last page of each such item, using signature blocks similar to those shown above. In addition, the authors suggest that, in larger agreements, all pages of all contract documents (except for pages bearing signature blocks) be initialed and dated by the individuals executing the agreements on behalf of the respective parties. This recommendation is made more for reasons of accountability, identification, and control than for reasons of contract law. Of course, any insertions or changes to typed pages should be separately initialed in any event, in order to document that the change was made by mutual agreement.

Fifth, the question of how many executed sets of documents should be prepared must be reached. Some attorneys admittedly believe that only one executed set should be prepared, with copies being made and distributed from that one original. The rationale for this approach appears to be more related to archaic evidenciary concepts than to contractual requirements. The authors recommend that, unless local counsel provides other advice, multiple agreement sets be executed and distributed. Depending upon the user's corporate policies and the preferences expressed by the user's attorneys, it may be beneficial for the user's operations, legal, and finance departments to each receive an executed set of contract documents.

Notifying Participating Vendors

The contract award process should not be considered complete until the user has notified all unsuccessful vendors of the RFP outcome. Depending upon the type of negotiations being conducted (e.g., AOC or sole source) this notice may or may not be anticlimactic. Three points are important in this regard. First, the notice must be provided, preferably in writing, at some point simply as a matter of professional and business courtesy. Second, in order to maximize competition and optimize the user's psychological negotiating leverage, care must be taken not to provide the final notice until after the contract has been executed (remember the value of keeping alternative vendors "waiting in the wings," even if the existence of waiting vendors is more theoretical than real). Earlier notification will only reinforce the primary vendor's likely existing view that the user really has no viable alternative source of supply. Third, providing notice of the results of the RFP does not necessarily mandate disclosure of why the successful vendor was selected or what final terms and prices were agreed upon. Obviously, government users must comply with applicable procurement and disclosure laws in this area. Private users generally have more flexibility and should seriously consider either disclosing no information about price and terms or disclosing only such limited information as may enhance competition in the next procurement cycle.

THE FINAL REPORT

After the contract documents have been executed, the user's negotiating team should prepare a final report, which may be in the form of an update or amendment to the negotiations position paper, or in the form of an acquisitions summary memorandum. Regardless of the format, the report should provide a summary of the final transaction, including principal user and vendor obligations, and a reference or index to each of the contract documents. Where time and resources permit, the report may also provide or at least refer to a more detailed analysis of the contractual documents, perhaps including a detailed schedule of events and excerpts from relevant contract provisions.

Copies of the final report should be submitted to key individuals and departments, including members of the user's negotiating team and user departments responsible for administering the contract. Depending upon the assignment of reponsibilities in the user's organization, some or all of these reports may need to be accompanied by copies of the user/vendor agreement. As earlier sections of this chapter observe, some user obligations (such as those relating to delivery, financing, and insurance) may have to be implemented promptly after, and sometimes even before, the agreement is executed. Consequently, the final report, summary, and agreement excerpts or copies must be prepared and delivered at the time, or as soon as possible after, the agreement is signed. Of course, where preexecution responsibilities exist, the user's negotiating team must communicate with key user departments before the formal agreement is actually executed.

Depending upon the contract administration procedures employed by the user, copies of, or excerpts from, the acquisition summary memorandum can be suspensed for use in future administration activities. In addition, the acquisition summary memorandum and/or the final negotiations position paper can serve as an effective tool in a subsequent "quality review" or "transaction analysis" covering the acquisition. (See Chapter 13.)

CONTRACT ADMINISTRATION

As suggested at the outset of this chapter, the negotiation process continues through contract compliance and administration. Although various user experts and department staff can and should be primarily responsible for administering the contract, the user's negotiating team is generally the best entity to supervise implementation of the executed agreement. Various team members can be assigned primary responsibilities in monitoring their respective disciplines, with operations or procurement members having particular responsibility for delivery, installation, acceptance, maintenance, and use. Supplemented by representatives from key end-user departments, the team can also serve as an effective review and evaluation board, responsible for assessing the ultimate success of the procedures used in acquiring the system and documenting the various agreements. In exercising this responsibility, the team should rely heavily on the formal contract documents and the final negotiations position paper that supports the acquisition. Periodic evaluation meetings offer a good method of formalizing this review process.

If the user's contract administration efforts are to be meaningful in planning and negotiating future acquisitions, adequate documentation must be kept during the administration period. Logs covering system maintenance and malfunction credits can be useful as basic documentation, but these materials should be supplemented by a formal system that records all user complaints and problems, including the timing, substance, and quality of the vendor's reaction to each. Copies of all related correspondence should also be maintained in a separate contract administration file.

Contract administration is discussed in more detail in Chapter 13.

5
REQUESTS FOR PROPOSAL

As the preceding chapter explains, the negotiation process essentially coincides with the acquisition process. Thus, the user must constantly focus on positioning itself vis-á-vis the vendor, taking every opportunity to leverage its position and control the pending acquisition. One of the most important tools available for this purpose is a well planned and prepared request for proposal (RFP). The present chapter discusses the purpose and use of RFPs, with particular emphasis on negotiating and strategy issues. The substantive content of RFPs is also considered, along with practical aspects of the bid solicitation process.

In this regard, one caveat should be noted at the outset. Properly prepared, almost every RFP is unique: It must be to reflect the terms and conditions of the acquisition being considered by the user. Equally-fine RFPs may vary significantly in length, content, and organization.

Consequently, the general comments set out in this chapter should be viewed as generic guidelines rather than ultimate truths. The function and strategy of an RFP are far more important than the length, content, or layout of the RFP document (although the latter issues are, of course, relevant concerns).

In considering this chapter, readers should also refer to Appendix C, which sets forth actual RFP excerpts. Again, these excerpts are intended to serve as specific examples rather than boilerplate paragraphs that should be transferred to another user document.

PURPOSE AND USE

Basic Function

In its most basic function, an RFP describes what the user expects to receive in a transaction and how interested vendors should submit proposals. To serve this minimum purpose, the RFP must contain the specifications, documentation, and descriptions of the transaction necessary to give the vendor a thorough understanding of the user's requirements. In addition, the RFP must explain how the bid process will work—for example, where and when vendor proposals must be submitted, how inquiries will be handled, and when and how contract awards will be made. To increase the consistency (and, therefore, the value) of vendor proposals, the RFP should also describe what type of bid documents the user wishes to receive. Regardless of the level of detail or attachments desired by the user, the RFP should specify the content, organization, and format of vendor proposals, emphasizing that substance will be much more important than form and fluff.

User Discipline

One of the spin-off benefits of this basic function is the discipline that RFP preparation places on the user organization. As Chapter 4 emphasizes, most users fail to appreciate the length of the negotiation process and the magnitude of the preparation required to achieve success in the acquisition. A properly prepared RFP forces the user's staff to consider its requirements carefully, reduce them to writing, and publish them in an understandable manner. Although an RFP hardly ensures that the user will comprehend its plans and needs in perfect detail, the user discipline of preparing the document generally results in better specifications, fewer surprises, more comprehensive understanding of the transaction (and its goals and objectives), and greater organization in the acquisition process. These results are not unlike those that often occur in the annual budgeting process, where the discipline of researching, planning, assessing, and documenting may actually be far more important to the organization's success than the budget itself.

Because of this fact, a strong argument can be made that some form of RFP should be prepared in any major equipment acquisition, even where the user is employing a sole source solicitation. Under this theory, the value of preparing the RFP is substantial enough to justify the process, even though competitive proposals are not being sought. Of course, in this context the RFP also serves as an appropriate source document for the sole vendor, thereby minimizing at least some potential for misunderstanding.

Contract Base

As discussed below, a good RFP provides that any proposal submitted by the vendor will be attached to and incorporated into any contract that may ultimately be executed between the user and vendor. When this practice is followed, the vendor proposal becomes an excellent "contract base" for the binding documents. Because the entire proposal is technically included in the contract and is, therefore, "part of the deal," no time need be wasted over whether or not a given promise in the vendor proposal should be included in the agreement. If a commitment is in the vendor's proposal, it is ripe for restatement in the written contract. At the same time, incorporating the vendor's proposal into the agreement does not preclude the user from going beyond this base to include additional concessions and conditions in the contract. Thus, the vendor's RFP proposal provides the user with a written record of the vendor's "deliverables," while not precluding the user from negotiating further on these and other issues. This practice reduces the vendor's ability to hedge on what it will really agree to in the written contract. Because *everything* in the proposal will be incorporated into the ageement, the vendor cannot feign misunderstanding or subsequently claim that a particular proposal promise was not intended to be a formal contractual item.

The requirement that the winning vendor's proposal be incorporated into the resulting contract also offers a procedural benefit for the user: It tends to result in vendor proposals that are more specific, less sales oriented, and more valuable to the user than "casual" marketing proposals. Faced with the fact that the proposal will become part of a legally binding document, vendors generally omit the colorful fluff, boilerplate paragraphs, and hollow promises that otherwise clutter and confuse most marketing presentations.

Control Device

The RFP process also enchances the user's ability to control the negotiations—and, therefore, the entire acquisition process. By formalizing all aspects of the acquisition, particularly those relating to the vendor's interaction with the user, the RFP process keeps the user in the driver's seat. As Chapter 1 emphasizes, major equipment negotiations have been the exclusive ballgame of the vendor too long. A good RFP process does not guarantee the user a winning game, but it at least lets the user supply the bat and ball.

Competition Incentive

One of the least recognized, but most important, uses of an RFP is to increase vendor competition. The formality of a good RFP procedure generally optimizes competition among vendors. The process alone indicates that the user is serious about the acquisition, and that it intends to do everything possible to gain competitive prices, terms, and conditions. The *substance* of the RFP can also increase competition and the potential for vendor concessions. Consequently, the content and strategy of each RFP must be carefully reviewed to increase its value as an affirmative negotiating tool. Even where the user generally expects to do business with a single vendor, an RFP can create at least an aura of uncertainty in the vendor's mind—particularly in an incumbent relationship. (On the other hand, care must be taken not to "cry wolf" too often: If the RFP is to have any value, all competing vendors must feel that they have at least some meaningful chance to unseat the incumbent.) Negotiating considerations involved in the preparation and use of an RFP are discussed in the following section.

NEGOTIATING CONSIDERATIONS

An entire book could be written on using the RFP as a negotiating strategy and implementing the related tactics. The following paragraphs outline some of the more important negotiating tactics that should be followed in drafting and applying a good RFP. Examples of most of the suggestions set forth below can be found in the RFP excerpts in Appendix C.

Focus on Deliverables

Virtually all vendor form agreements contain some form of disclaimer, such as the following: "This Agreement represents the entire understanding and agreement between the parties and supersedes any and all prior oral and written proposals and communications." This language is usually accompanied by various implied warranty disclaimers, such as this example: "There are no express or implied warranties, including the implied warranties of merchantability and fitness for a particular purpose, not specified herein respecting this Agreement or the equipment, programs, documentation, and services provided."

Although any carefully drafted agreement should certainly exclude prior oral promises—for the protection of both parties—the vendor should never be allowed to feel that it can safely "promise the moon" during the sales campaign and then disclaim all the promises in the final agreement. If the RFP can be used to eliminate, or at least substantially reduce, the key vendor tactic of puffery, the user will have a far greater opportunity to achieve its acquisition goals and objectives.

As the Contract Base discussion suggests, above, one of the better methods of deflating this vendor tactic is by indicating that the user's RFP and the winning vendor's proposal will be incorporated into the resulting vendor/user agreement. This approach forces any thinking sales representative to focus on deliverables rather than "gee whiz" promises. The undeniable logic of this technique can be simply explained to squirming vendor marketing personnel as follows: "Your standard purchase agreement contains various disclaimers of warranties and representations. In addition, it specifically says that all prior communications from you, whether written or oral, will not be included in the contract. That means all your sales brochures, all your representations, and even your response to our RFP will be irrelevant. In effect, your agreement says if its not in the contract, its not in the deal. Well, if it won't be in the contract, or the deal, it shouldn't be considered in our evaluation process. If we can't rely on it in the contract, we shouldn't rely on it in making our decision." Three RFP provisions are particularly helpful in implementing this approach. The first provision merely cautions the vendors that the winning proposal will be included in the resulting vendor/user agreement.

All proposals, information, and responses from the bidder must be submitted in writing. Unless supplemental oral commentary is specifically requested by [name of user] in writing, oral communications will not be considered in connection with any bidding proposal. All proposals, information, and responses submitted by a bidder will be incorporated into and made a part of any final agreement between [name of user] and such bidder. No such information or other material should be submitted that cannot be so incorporated into the agreement. [NAME OF USER] RESERVES THE RIGHT TO DISQUALIFY ANY BIDDER THAT SUBMITS A PROPOSAL OR CONTRACT THAT DIRECTLY OR INDIRECTLY ATTEMPTS TO PRECLUDE OR LIMIT THE EFFECT OF THIS REQUIREMENT.

The second provision reinforces the impact of this prerequisite by turning around a popular vendor clause. Many vendor form agreements attempt to reinforce the vendor's grasp on an unsuspecting user by including a provision such as the following at the end of the contract: "User and its undersigned officer(s) hereby acknowledge that they have read this agreement, understand it, and agree to be bound by its terms and conditions." This provision insults the user's intelligence and offers little legal value to the vendor in most jurisdictions. But it can be turned around, expanded, and applied effectively in the user's RFP, as follows:

The signature page to bidder's proposal must contain the following representation by bidder for the proposal to be considered by [name of user]: "Bidder hereby represents and agrees as follows:

1. Bidder and its undersigned representatives agree that they have read the RFP for which this Proposal is being submitted, that they understand such RFP, and that this Proposal is responsive to, and complies with the instructions and conditions to the RFP.
2. Bidder understands and agrees that this Proposal (including any and all attachments, exhibits, and documents of Bidder referred to herein) must be included in any contract between Bidder and [name of user] covering the acquisition specified in this Proposal.
3. Bidder agrees to be bound by the representations, terms, and conditions contained in its Proposal.
4. Bidder agrees that the contract provision incorporating its Proposal into the agreement, if any, between [name of user] and Bidder shall state as follows: [Name of Bidder] hereby agrees that its Proposal(s) dated [insert date(s)], including any and all attachments and exhibits thereto and exhibits referred to therein, shall be and hereby are incorporated into this Agreement. [Name of Bidder] and [Name of user] agree that any provision of this Agreement or of any such Proposal that conflicts with the preceding sentence, or seeks to exclude any portion of such Proposal from this Agreement or from any express warranty or any warranty provided by statute or implied at law, shall be void and of no force or effect."

The third RFP provision that urges vendors to focus on deliverables covers the packaging of the vendor's proposal. This section essentially reminds the vendor that the user wants substance rather than colorful brochures and fancy bindings. The following provision offers an example of this approach:

Economy of Presentation. Bidder's Proposal shall be prepared simply and economically in strict accordance with the format and instructional requirements of the RFP. Each Proposal should provide a concise delineation of the Bidder's capabilities to satisfy the requirements of this RFP, with emphasis on completeness and clarity of content. Fancy bindings, colorful displays, and promotional material are neither required nor desired, unless they add substance to Bidder's Proposal.

Minimize Misunderstandings

Some vendors are notorious for submitting a winning proposal in an RFP competition and then, during final contract negotiations, claiming that there was a misunderstanding at the proposal stage about one or two key points. Ordinarily, the vendor confidently attributes this unfortunate misunderstanding to "unclear" or "ambiguous" language in the user's RFP. As a result, the user ends up negotiating about a concession that the user legitimately believed was already granted in the vendor's proposal. This result is frustrating and counterproductive for the user and, unfortunately, all too effective for the vendor.

Because of this potential for "disappearing deliverables," the user's RFP negotiating strategy should include several countervailing steps. First, the RFP should be comprehensive and clear. It should be drafted by a team that includes members with good technical and nontechnical writing skills. Once drafted, it should be reviewed by a wide range of user managers, including a member of upper management, the chief procurement officer, a key operations manager, and a staff manager and line manager in the functional area where the equipment being acquired will ultimately be utilized. In addition, of course, the draft should be critiqued by all members of the user's negotiating team.

Second, the RFP process should include a formal method by which vendors can seek clarification of questions and uncertainties. A two-stage approach is often helpful here. When this technique is employed, the RFP includes a process for the submission of written questions by competing vendors and the provision of written responses by the user, with copies of both questions and answers being supplied to all vendors. In addition, the RFP process includes at least one bidders' conference, where questions (preferably in writing) may be posed by vendors and answered by the user in the presence of all bidders. The complexity of this two-stage clarification program can vary significantly from transaction to transaction. For example, some users permit the written question submission phase to include an opportunity for competing vendors to submit alternative provisions to a user contract mandated by the RFP. Where this approach is followed, both the alternative suggested by the vendor and the user's response are provided to all competing vendors.

The following provisions indicate how one large user firm handled the clarification issue:

Bidder Inquiries. Any questions or other inquiries from Bidders concerning this Procurement must be submitted in writing to [name and address of user contact omitted]. Oral questions will not be answered. All written questions and inquiries from Bidders will be answered in writing, and copies of the response and the related inquiry will be forwarded to all Bidders. Receipt of each response must be acknowledged by each Bidder on the Addendum Acknowledgment Form submitted as a part of the Bidder's Proposal.

Bidders' Conference. A Bidders' Conference will be held at 1:30 P.M., local time in [location omitted], as shown on the Procurement Schedule. The purpose of this Conference is to discuss this RFP and entertain questions from Bidders. All questons must be submitted in writing. Attendance at the Conference is not mandatory, but is highly recommended.

Third, having made every effort at minimizing the possibility of confusion and maximizing the opportunity for clarification, the user should formally shift the duty to ask questions and resolve ambiguity to the vendor. One method of effecting this shift is to have the RFP require the vendor to include the following representation in its RFP proposal: "Vendor understands and agrees that: (a) it has an affirmative duty to inquire about and seek clarification of any question or other item in the RFP that Vendor does not fully understand or that Vendor reasonably believes is susceptible to more than one interpretation; and (b) the Proposal submitted by Vendor must explain any and all conditions, exceptions, or limitations included in any response by Vendor to any question or other item in the RFP."

Fourth, in some instances, it may be advantageous for the RFP to specifically indicate that each vendor submitting a proposal has an obligation to respond orally or in writing to user requests for clarification of the proposal within a specified period of time. (The RFI procedure discussed in Chapter 4 is one method of implementing this approach.) Although this language is theoretically inconsistent with the approach, suggested above, of shifting the clarification burden to the vendor, it is a practical necessity in any large-scale solicitation. This procedure can be implemented through an RFP provision such as the following:

In the event [name of user] determines that clarification of any proposal is necessary, it will advise the bidder in writing, indicating whether the bidder should supplement its proposal in writing or through oral commentary. The bidder shall thereafter have the greater of ten (10) calendar days or the period specified in the request for clarification to submit the supplemental information in the form requested. [Name of user] shall have the right, without further notice, to disqualify any bidder failing to comply with such a request within the deadline specified above. Copies of all requests for clarification shall be provided by [name of user] to all competing bidders and copies of all responses and supplements shall be included in the public proposal file for the respective bidder.

Finally, the RFP should include a provision indicating that vendors cannot rely upon oral comments or promises made by user representatives during the bid process. This language can often be blended with that governing written vendor inquiries. The following excerpt from a longer provision offers one example:

For purposes of this RFP, no bidder may consider any oral representations or statements by an officer, employee, or agent of [name of user] to be an official expression on its behalf, unless such representations or statements are made in a written communication from [name of user] executed by one of the duly-authorized officers listed on page ____ of this RFP. All questions, answers, and statements from [name of user] covering any substantive matter associated with this RFP shall be in writing and copies thereof shall be forwarded to all bidders by certified mail, return receipt requested.

Maximize the Appearance of Competition

As suggested above, the mere use of an organized RFP process is one of the best methods of injecting meaningful competition into an acquisition. The existence of an RFP tells vendors that, regardless of whatever other marketing efforts they may wish to make, the bid will not be awarded until the detailed RFP schedule has been met. The "formalized delay" that is thus imposed by the RFP is helpful in deflating vendor sense of urgency tactics and in increasing the user's control of the acquisition process. Both of these benefits also increase the competitive environment.

Within the RFP process itself, the bidders' conference is one of the better methods of increasing the appearance of competition. Among the practical and strategic advantages offered by the bidders' conference are the following: First, the conference permits the vendors to view their competition. If the user has staged the RFP well to this point, the conference room should be bulging with aggressive competitors. (Added psychological benefit can be gained if the conference room size is somewhat small for the number of competitors expected to attend.) As a result, all of the vendors should feel that substantive concessions and realistic pricing will be necessary to win the user's business. An incumbent vendor that has been a sole source for years will be especially concerned about the increased competition (even if it never materializes).

Second, the bidders' conference helps alleviate the usual criticism that the "deal is wired" or that one vendor enjoys an inside track with the user's evaluation team. Assuming that the user seriously wants to run an objective RFP process, the bidders' conference can do much to convince the vendors that the process will in fact be open, fair, and objective. Where a strong incumbent vendor is involved, this approach will increase competition by assuring other vendors that it is worth their time to bid; at the same time, the incumbent vendor is also likely to recognize this fact and bid more aggressively. In essence, because the procurement process *appears* to be more open and competitive, the bidders will treat it that way and bid more aggressively. Competition then becomes a self-fulfilling prophecy.

Third, questions submitted at the bidders' conference (or otherwise) may provide the user with meaningful input from other vendors, particularly where a strong incumbent vendor is involved. Even when carefully prepared, the RFP may be unnecessarily biased against a given vendor or manufacturer. Often this problem results when the user has had a lengthy relationship with a sole source or where the user's staff has been unfortunately biased by the marketing personnel of a particular vendor, usually the incumbent. The bidders' conference and any later question and answer process allow the user to receive valuable input concerning any perceived or actual bias. Some vendor complaints may be marketing ploys in themselves, of course, but other comments may be helpful to the user.

Fourth, the user's attitude at the bidders' conference can increase the feeling of competition. For this result to occur, user representatives at the conference should emphasize that the RFP is designed to solicit proposals that are highly responsive to the user's needs. In addition, the representatives should stress aspects of the RFP that deal with price, performance, concessions, and competitive submission requirements. These remarks should be bolstered by body language and voice inflections that exude confidence and a high aspiration level. Vendors attending the conference should come away feeling that: (a) the user is serious about a professional, fair, competitive RFP process; and (b) the user is in command of the acquisition—that is, the user knows what it wants and when and how it will be achieved.

Maximize the Opportunity for Vendor Commitments

Although the RFP should clearly specify the user's technical requirements, preferably in a generic manner, the document should also maximize the opportunity for participating vendors to volunteer legal and financial benefits to the user. The optimum strategies for achieving vendor commitments vary from procurement to procurement.

In some acquisitions, voluntary vendor commitments are most likely to occur where the RFP does not specify the exact standard or commitment desired by the user. Under this approach, the RFP poses a list of issues, guidelines, or minimum standards or amounts (much like the minimum bid figure used in some auctions). The items contained in the RFP put the vendor on notice that concessions or commitments are desired in specific areas, but the RFP does not indicate the expectation level held by the user. Consequently, if the user has truly maximized competition in the RFP process, at least some vendors are likely to offer concessions above and beyond those that the user might have obtained or requested if the RFP had specified the precise standard desired by the user. RFP procedures that include nonmandatory master contracts offer a case in point. If competing vendors believe that the master agreement contained in the RFP represents the user's "ideal" contract, they certainly will not volunteer contractual concessions beyond those specified in the master agreement. Rather, many vendors are likely to take the user's master agreement as an "extreme" and negotiate from that position to a position more acceptable to the vendor. On the other hand, if the RFP contains a list of contractual issues and questions rather than a master agreement, each vendor will be required to "bid" on the contractual issues by indicating the type of provision or concession that will be offered. This procedure may result in voluntary concessions from some vendors considerably above and beyond those that the user would have included in its own master agreement.

Although this approach can improve the user's ability to achieve meaningful concessions in some acquisitions, in other procurements it may create more delays than commitments. For example, if the RFP process is not competitive for some reason, all the vendors may respond to the RFP by submitting proposals that do not begin to measure up to the user's expectations on a particular issue. Of course, if this occurs, the user can always reject all bids, either generally or on certain components, and indicate that it will accept new proposals that offer more meaningful (and perhaps clearly specified) commitments on the issue in question. But this action extends the bid process, perhaps to unacceptable levels. Moreover, it may tend to polarize the vendors toward their initial proposals, making subsequent vendor concessions more difficult for the user to obtain.

Because of these problems, in some procurements it may be better for the user to strive to maximize vendor commitments through an RFP that includes specific standards or master provisions. This approach leaves no doubt as to the user's aspiration level. But, as noted above, it may cause vendors to view the standards as the user's "first shot" in the negotiations, thereby spurring the vendors to negotiate downward from that point. This natural vendor tendency can be controlled in two ways.

First, a user with particularly strong bargaining power (e.g., a government agency or a large user planning significant purchases) can indicate that the master contract or other standards contained in the RFP are *mandatory,* not optional, and that no bid will be accepted unless it contains vendor commitments on those items. Obviously, the user must be prepared to carry out this threat, by declining all bids if necessary to prove the point. (This task is easier if the user has time in the procurement process for a full rebid-cycle—a luxury that admittedly is somewhat rare.) To soften this approach somewhat, some users permit vendors to submit written alternative provisions for consideration. Vendor provisions that are accepted are then supplied to all bidders, through formal supplements to the RFP, and may be used by any vendor in lieu of the original provision mandated by the user. One state government user employed the following RFP language to implement this approach:

Attachment A is a contract that sets forth terms and conditions desired by the State. All bidders will be required to execute Attachment A. Bidders may recommend minor changes. All recommended changes must be submitted to the State prior to the submission of the bid proposals. The State reserves the right to accept or reject any changes. The State at its option may accept or reject any or all [proposed changes], or any parts thereof. Any recommended changes which the State accepts [will be provided in writing to all bidders and may, at each bidder's option, be used in lieu of the corresponding provision in Attachment A].

Second, the user can increase vendor acceptance of the RFP contract or other standards by penalizing any vendor that refuses to accept the user's document. For example, if the RFP contains a master agreement, the user can indicate that any alternative provisions which are not accepted in advance by the user (as outlined above) will be deemed to increase the vendor's bid by a predetermined amount indicated in the RFP. This approach essentially discourages changes to the master agreement by imposing a "liquidated bid adjustment" on each change. Thus, a vendor that has an excellent equipment price but proposes too many changes to the master agreement faces the risk that its bid will be rejected "on price" because of the total liquidated adjustment to its bid price.

Although discussed here in the context of discouraging vendor changes to a user-specified contract, this approach is also an interesting tool to use in quantifying the value of a given contractual provision. As Chapter 4 explains, determining the relative priorities of alternative negotiating objectives and contractual provisions is often difficult. The discipline required to assign a "liquidated bid adjustment" figure to each provision often sheds additional light on just how much a particular provision is "worth" to the user.

On the other side, this approach also offers theoretical consistency for the vendor. By assigning a "price" to each contractual change required by a vendor, this process also forces the vendor to determine the relative value of, or risk posed by, the user's standard provision or the vendor's alternative provision.

The following RFP language offers two examples of the liquidated bid adjustment approach. The actual RFP from which these examples were excerpted contained similar provisions for a number of contractual areas. Readers should note that the adjustment is only made for purposes of the user's analysis of the competing bids; thus, the user does not agree to pay the higher "adjusted" amount if the bidder's proposal is accepted. A particularly aggressive alternative to this approach can also be specified, where the amount actually paid by the user will be reduced if certain vendor-proposed contractual changes are accepted by the user (e.g., a lower uptime percentage in a continuing performance standard results in a specified reduction in the actual price, but not in the bid). This approach is discussed later in this chapter.

17. *Programming Support.* Section 34 of the Master Agreement included in Exhibit D specifies that the Bidder shall provide certain mandatory programming support. In the event Bidder is unable to accept this provision in whole or in part, it should so indicate, in which event the following applicable amounts will be added to Bidder's bid by [name of user] for purposes of evaluating competing proposals. Such additional amounts shall in no event be paid by [name of user] to the Bidder. Man-years indicated below are calculated in accordance with the Definition section of this RFP.

A. *Project Manager:*

1. If furnished for only 9 months, $9,187 will be added to bid.

2. If furnished for only 6 months, $18,374 will be added to bid.

3. If furnished for only 3 months, $27,561 will be added to bid.

4. If furnished for less than 3 months, $36,748 will be added to bid.

[The RFP provision repeated this approach for a conversion specialist, an operating systems analyst, and a communications specialist.]

29. *Most Favored Nation.* In the event Bidder does not agree to the Most Favored Nation provision contained in Section 45 of the Master Agreement included in Exhibit D to this RFP, the following applicable amounts will be added to Bidder's bid by [name of user] for purposes of evaluating competing proposals. Such additional amounts shall in no event be paid by [name of user] to Bidder.

A. If Bidder rejects Section 45 in full or reduces the period covered by Section 45 to less than six (6) months, from the twelve (12) months specified, $125,000 will be added to bid.

B. If Bidder reduces the period covered by Section 45 to not less than six (6) months, from the twelve (12) months specified, $65,000 will be added to bid.

C. If Bidder reduces the period covered by Section 45 to not less than nine (9) months, from the twelve (12) months specified, $30,000 will be added to bid.

In sum, neither of the approaches set forth above is necessarily correct in any given acquisition. In some instances, voluntary commitments will be maximized more through use of a list of contractual issues than through including a user-prepared master agreement. In other situations, the opposite may be true. And, in still other acquisitions, the combination effect of a master agreement and liquidated bid adjustments may achieve the best commitment level. The important point is that the user must recognize that the manner in which the RFP is drafted can and will have a direct effect on the vendor responses that the user receives. Consequently, wherever possible the user should strive to phrase its RFP document and structure its entire RFP process, in a manner that will cause competing vendors to make commitments or concessions above and beyond any minimum standards, guidelines, or provisions included in the RFP package.

Implement the ZOC Approach to RFP Negotiations

Considerable controversy exists as to whether extensive negotiations have any part in a competitive bidding procedure. Some users argue that negotiations are inconsistent with an RFP/bidding process. These users suggest that each vendor should study the RFP and submit a response and a proposed contract (or changes to the user's desired master contract). The user then balances the various responses, selects one, and executes the contract submitted by the vendor (or, just maybe, the master contract included in the user's RFP). This approach is particularly popular with government agencies and larger companies. Other users follow a similar approach, but agree that the user may negotiate contractual terms with the "winning" vendor. Some of these users believe that it is impermissible for the user to reject the winning bid, even if the contract negotiations are unsatisfactory for the user; other users feel that the winning bid can be rejected, and the second best bid considered, if the contract negotiations are not successful.

The solution to this controversy rests somewhat on the type of RFP procedure being employed by the user. For example, if the RFP contains neither a standard user contract nor an extensive list of legal-contractual issues, the user's unilateral acceptance of the standard form agreement proposed by the winning bidder would seem foolhardy at best. (Despite this fact, thousands of users take this approach each year, significantly undermining the value of their RFP effort.) Alternatively, extensive negotiations with the winning vendor may be less critical if the user's RFP has included a master agreement that is mandatory or that only permits changes that have been approved by the user or that results in predetermined liquidated adjustments to the bid price.

Where negotiations with one or more bidders appear to be advisable, the authors recommend that users employ a "zone of consideration" (ZOC) technique designed to increase competition further.

In the ZOC approach, the user reserves the right to hold as many negotiating "rounds" and to receive as many proposal revisions as the user may determine—either before or after narrowing the list of competing bidders. For example, the user might receive six proposals and immediately select one, execute the agreement, and be done with it. (See Fig. 5-1.) Alternatively, the user might receive six proposals and select three of those as being within the "zone of consideration." The user would then negotiate with each of these three vendors on price, performance, and protection, and either select one vendor or ask each of the three for a "best and final offer." In the latter case, the "final" offers would be further evaluated and, if possible, the winner selected. Alternatively the evaluation might lead to further negotiations and still another round of proposals. (See Fig. 5-2.)

The key benefit of the ZOC approach is that it maximizes competition and also maximizes the opportunity for the user to optimize specific points. Although a vendor may face further

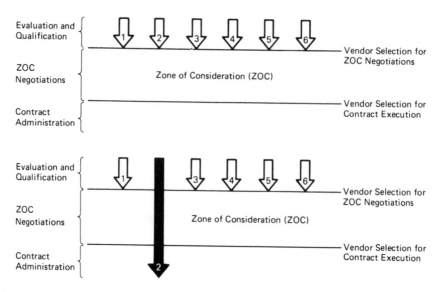

Fig. 5-1. Zone of consideration (ZOC) process involving immediate successful negotiation with a single ZOC participant.

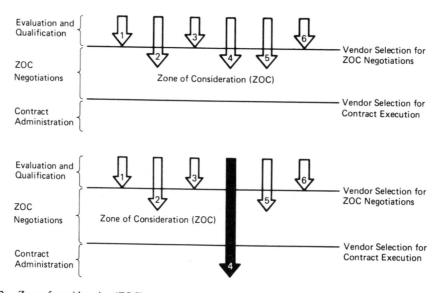

Fig. 5-2. Zone of consideration (ZOC) process involving sequential negotiations with multiple ZOC participants.

negotiations and demands for concessions, each proposal must be highly competitive because only the user controls the number of rounds of negotiations and proposals that will be permitted. In essence, only the user knows how long the RFP "tunnel" is. A vendor that holds back on the first proposal may find that the user has selected another vendor as the winner on the first round. Alternatively, the vendor may find that its proposal has not been included in the ZOC for the second round.

At the same time, the ZOC approach permits the user to review each proposal and negotiate further on specific costs and benefits. For example, a user might tell one vendor that it is within the ZOC for round two, but that the vendor is going to have to do considerably better on meeting the user's model acceptance test provision for the contract. The user might also explain that one aspect of the vendor's hardware configuration is really not wanted, but that additional education benefits are important to the user.

ALTERNATIVE APPROACHES

As the preceding sections of this chapter emphasize, there is no "best" method of preparing an RFP. Myriad alternative approaches exist, even for a single acquisition. Moreover, although each alternative carries with it certain advantages and disadvantages, the relative strengths and weaknesses can only be measured in the context of a particular acquisition *and* user.

Relevant Factors

At the risk of generalizing in an area where decisions can only be based on specifics, the following list outlines several factors that may be helpful in reaching preliminary conclusions concerning the best RFP approach. However, one caveat should be noted: As Chapter 4 explains, most users can conjure up any number of reasons *not* to use a good RFP in a given acquisition. The factors set forth below are designed to be relevant criteria that should be applied as objectively as possible. They are not intended to be the pegs on which weak-willed users hang their rationale not to employ a sound RFP (or their conclusion to utilize a shoddy one).

Time. A comprehensive RFP process takes time, both to prepare the documents and analyze the proposals. If the RFP includes particularly strict requirements, all bids may prove to be unresponsive, possibly resulting in a requirement to repeat the bid process with a revised RFP. Most users do not have the time necessary to prepare an RFP on anything other than a crash schedule that may well disrupt other user priorities. As a result, the user may have to ease into the RFP process, drafting a less-than-optimum RFP for one acquisition and then improving its RFP sophistication with each subsequent transaction.

Talent. In addition to time, a good RFP requires professional talent. An ill-prepared, poorly-planned, or biased RFP can lead to a bad user decision that may cost thousands of dollars over the life of the equipment. Many users do not have the personnel necessary to conduct a good RFP procedure, at least with respect to certain types of equipment. Where talent weaknesses exist, the user may need to seek outside assistance to train its personnel in RFP techniques or to participate in preparing the documentation itself. In addition, the user may have to weigh its priorities carefully to determine the level of RFP complexity that it can practically expect to employ in various acquisitions.

Financial Resources. As the discussion above suggests, a comprehensive RFP process requires considerable corporate resources. Particularly, where outside consultants must be retained, the user must be willing to devote the funds necessary to the task at hand. If the user's budget precludes such expenditures, a reduced RFP effort may be required, at least in some acquisitions.

Management Commitment. Even where the other factors above are present, a user is unlikely to achieve success in its RFP efforts without a strong commitment from its senior management. Indeed, without such a commitment, the user can seldom muster the time, talent, and financial resources necessary to draft, issue, and evaluate a comprehensive RFP. If the user's procurement or operations group lacks a firm commitment to the RFP in any acquisition, it may be better for the user to pursue a limited RFP or RFI approach that requires less time, people, and money than a full-blown RFP effort. In such an instance, employing a limited approach with success may result in more long-range satisfaction than pressing a complex RFP into certain failure.

Need. Despite the value of the RFP process, a complex RFP effort cannot be justified in every acquisition. The relative size and importance of each equipment acquisition must be judged to determine the relative degree to which an RFP and an acquisition agreement appear to be necessary. Generally, both the RFP and the related contract documentation will be most necessary in acquisitions that involve one or more of the following factors: (a) complex specifications, standards, or installation procedures; (b) sophisticated products, software, or services; (c) significant cost; (d) leveraged third-party financing; (e) operating performance critical to the user's business; or (f) complicated trade-ins, conversions, or upgrades. As these factors converge in any acquisition, the need for a comprehensive RFP ordinarily increases.

Common Requirements

Despite the wide range of alternatives possible in preparing an RFP, some elements are common to virtually all of them. These common requirements are outlined briefly below. (More extensive discussions of many of these factors also appear in subsequent sections of this chapter.) One caveat should be noted: Although the headings and divisions used below can be employed in virtually any RFP, the substance discussed in each area is more important than the divisions among areas. Thus, no hard-and-fast rule exists that an RFP must have separate Introduction and General Procedure sections, instead of a combined section that covers both subjects.

Introduction. Every RFP should include an introductory section that provides a brief overview of the acquisition. A "who-what-when-where-how" approach is often helpful here. Many users include a brief description of the user's business and the functions of the departments involved in the acquisition. Ordinarily, the overview will also explain the basic purpose of the equipment being acquired. Cross-references to specifications and subsequent portions of the RFP may or may not be provided. (Those who favor such cross-references assert that they facilitate early understanding of the transaction. Those who prefer to omit such references point out that they may only serve to confuse by encouraging bidders to skip back to the specifications and other areas without reading through the other preliminary material). Regardless of whether cross-references are used, a one or two page graphic depiction of the transaction or equipment can add a professional touch, where appropriate. Some users also include an index to all RFP documents in the introduction section.

General Procedures. Following this overview of the transaction, the RFP should outline the basic "rules of the road" for competing bidders. This section should generally include the following areas: (a) what the vendor has received or needs to receive to prepare and submit a responsive bid (e.g., the RFP documents, supplements, and any special studies required; (b) how vendor questions and inquiries will be handled; (c) where and when any bidders' conference will be held; (d) what constitutes a complete and responsive vendor bid; (e) when, where, and how a vendor bid must be submitted; and (f) if applicable, what alternative bid procedures are available (e.g., to submit a partial bid or to object to a mandatory provision). In addition, the General Procedures section should include a detailed schedule for the RFP process (unless this information is placed in a separate section).

The General Procedures section of the RFP offers the best area for the user to employ negotiating strategies to maximize competitive environment and the user's control over the acquisition. Consequently, this portion of the RFP should include most of the provisions discussed in the Negotiating Considerations section of this chapter, above. Among the provisions that are particularly helpful in this regard are those relating to written submissions and communications, incorporation of the RFP and winning bid into the vendor/user contract, and vendor compliance with RFP requirements.

Some users prefer for the General Procedures section to include any required definitions and a description of how the bids will be evaluated by the user. Although this approach is certainly acceptable, the authors prefer to place these items in separate sections. When included in the General Procedures section, both subjects add unnecessary clutter that may reduce the impact and effectiveness of the negotiating strategies being employed by the user in that area. Moreover, the user enjoys improved psychological positioning by placing the bid evaluation and award information after the bid specifications. In addition to being logical, this arrangement subtly reinforces the fact that no evaluation or award will be made until the vendor submits a bid that is responsive to the user's specifications and needs.

Specifications. The heart of every RFP must contain the specifications for the people, products, and services being acquired by the user. Thus, the Specifications section must include a detailed description of the *resources* or *results* desired by the user (see Chapter 4), including delivery, installation, and implementation. Some users prefer to introduce the detailed bid specifications with a comprehensive description of the user functions and systems applications involved in the acquisition. RFP specifications are discussed in more detail below.

Proposal Evaluation. Although an argument can be made that a user has no obligation to explain how it intends to evaluate competing vendor proposals, the authors strongly recommend that every RFP include a Proposal Evaluation section. From a negotiating strategy standpoint, this section offers the user an excellent opportunity to explain just how competitive a vendor must be to gain the user's business. Thus, the Proposal Evaluation section can and should outline the financial, technical, and legal factors that the user feels are particularly important. Where the user is employing liquidated bid adjustments, these matters can be described in the Proposal Evaluation section. Likewise, this section can explain other evaluation formulae, such as those necessary for total life cycle costing (TLCC). These specialized evaluation techniques are discussed in subsequent portions of this chapter.

Requirements and Approaches in Other Areas

Beyond the basic areas outlined above, any number of special requirements may also be included in the RFP. Key areas worthy of user consideration are outlined below.

Legal Requirements. Although a separate RFP section on legal issues may not be required in every acquisition, in most major procurements the RFP should cover legal specifications, just as it covers technical specifications. As the portion of this chapter on Negotiating Considerations points out, above, the legal section of an RFP can be approached in several different ways. The important point is that the user consider its legal objectives and adopt some appropriate method of including them in its RFP.

Principal alternative methods of handling user legal objectives in an RFP include the following:

Mandatory master agreement. The RFP contains a user-prepared standard agreement that the vendor must agree to use, without change. The contract documents used by the federal General Services Administration (GSA) offer the best example of this approach.

Master agreement with provision for approved changes. The RFP contains a user-prepared standard agreement, but permits vendors to submit suggested changes for consideration by the user. Any changes approved by the user are made available to all bidders and become acceptable (but not mandatory) alternatives for corresponding provisions in the user's agreement.

Master agreement with some mandatory provisions and some provisions subject to liquidated bid adjustments. The RFP contains a user-prepared standard agreement. Some provisions in the contract are mandatory and cannot be altered (or can only be altered by the user's prior agreement, as outlined in the preceding alternative). Other provisions can be altered or rejected, but changes result in liquidated adjustments to the vendor's bid, for evaluation purposes only, as described in the Negotiating Considerations section of this chapter, above.

Aspiration level master agreement. The RFP contains a user-prepared standard agreement, but merely indicates that vendors who fail to accept the document may be penalized by the user as it evaluates all relevant aspects of the vendor's bid. In essence, this approach uses the standard contract to specify the user's legal aspiration level, recognizes that vendors will propose changes to the agreement, and leaves to the user's discretion the degree to which any given vendor should be penalized for those changes.

Aspiration level or mandatory provisions. The RFP contains user-prepared provisions in selected areas, but does not include an entire agreement. In most acquisitions where this technique is used, these provisions are presented in the "aspiration level" style discussed above. However, some users specify that all or certain of the provisions are mandatory and cannot be altered (or can be altered only upon the conditions discussed under the mandatory contract headings, above). Even where most of the provisions included in this approach are aspirational rather than mandatory, boilerplate sections dealing with government-imposed standards (e.g., equal employment opportunity) are likely to be required rather than optional.

Legal/contractual issues. The RFP includes a list of legal or contractual issues, sometimes phrased as questions, rather than a standard contract or selected provisions. Each vendor is required to indicate the degree to which it is willing to accept the legal positions indicated. The user then evaluates the responses of all vendors on the various issues, and adds its assessment of the results to the general calculus being employed to select the winning proposal.

Price/Performance Measures. Particularly where generic specifications are employed, many users include price/performance measures in an RFP. Although many alternative approaches are available, the basic method of implementing this methodology is as follows. First, the user establishes a desired performance level for the equipment in its RFP. (Note that this level is *not* the minimum acceptable.) Second, each competing vendor submits published specifications or benchmark test results (as required by the user) to document the performance of its equipment in relation to the level of performance desired by the user. Third, the user assesses the degree to which the performance submitted by each vendor meets the level of performance desired by the user. As a result of this assessment, each vendor's bid price is increased *for purposes of the proposal evaluation only* by the amount specified through the application of an adjustment formula contained in the RFP. Although the technique is less frequently employed, some RFPs also provide for the opposite possibility. Thus, if the user believes that performance better than its desired level of performance should be rewarded, the RFP may permit stellar performance to reduce the amount of the bid price, again solely for purposes of the evaluation process.

This approach is obviously more effective where the performance of the equipment can be measured and documented. Electronic equipment, data processing systems, and certain categories of industrial/manufacturing equipment are among the principal examples. The following provision was utilized in an RFP issued for a data processing system that included significant on-line communications requirements.

Price Performance. It is desirable that each bidder propose a System that will exceed the Benchmark contained in Section VI of this RFP with a maximum transaction rate of fifteen (15) transactions per second on Phase V. The State attaches a value of $100,000 to this additional capability. For those bidders that do not attain the 15 transactions per second rate, the [name of user] shall automatically add to their costs in accordance with the following:

$$\frac{(15\text{-}n)}{(5)100,000} = \text{Cost added to Bidder's Proposal}$$

n = Number of transactions processed per second (maximum of 15 being credited)

System Availability and Reliability. As user sophistication increases, more and more users are including equipment availability and reliability criteria in their RFPs. This approach is often implemented by requiring competing vendors to supply verifiable reliability data from a minimum number of other users of the equipment, generally on forms included in the RFP package. This information is then compared to reliability standards determined by the user (or, in some instances, to the mean reliability of all of the vendors' equipment). These comparisons may be assessed with or without the liquidated bid adjustments noted above. In either event, the reliability levels of actual installed equipment form at least part of the basis for the user's evaluation decision.

Two points are particularly relevant in implementing this approach. First, the reliability data submitted by the vendors must itself be reliable. The validity of this information is generally increased if the user can contact the other users involved. In addition, because most vendors will submit data from their best sites, the number of other users from which information is collected must be large enough to avoid obvious bias in favor of the vendor. The type of equipment involved and the total number of installed sites will ordinarily affect the size of the sample necessary to achieve meaningful data. Generally, a larger installed base will necessitate a larger sample. Some users also bias the required sample in a manner that better reflects the size and nature of the user's operations (e.g., a user bank may limit the sample to other financial institutions).

Second, regardless of these efforts to create a useful sample, the user must remember that the statistical information collected is unlikely to reflect the actual reliability levels that can be expected by the user. This result occurs in most instances because only an unrealistically large sample would overcome the pro-vendor bias that naturally results when the vendors select the sites to be solicited. Despite this fact, the statistics can provide meaningful data on the *relative reliability* of the equipment offered by competing vendors.

The following excerpts from an actual RFP offer one method of implementing the approach outlined above.

8.2. *System Availability.* [Name of user] has determined that a minimum System Availability Level of 95% is required. (See Section 2, 13, and 46 of the standard agreement in Appendix D of this RFP.) However, a higher System Availability Level is desired. Bidder shall submit in Part IV of its Proposal system availability data (calculated in accordance with Section 13 of Appendix D) for ten (10) other users of the equipment proposed by Bidder. Such information shall include, for each such user:

(a) user name, address, and contact;

(b) exact equipment installed;

(c) period(s) equipment has been installed (preferably in excess of twelve (12) months);

(d) purpose and use of equipment at such user site, including total number of hours operated each month; and

(e) Monthly System Availability Level for the equipment, measured for the System as a whole, and presented for each calendar month from [insert date] to [insert date].

Utilizing the information submitted by all competing Bidders, the [name of user] shall compute a Combined Average System Availability Level for each Bidder. Based upon this information, the [name of user] shall add to each Bidder's Proposal a cost, if any, equal to the following:

(Installment Purchase Cost *plus* 60 months Average System Maintenance Cost) *times* (1.00 *minus* Combined Average System Availability Level for the respective Bidder) *equals* Liquidated Bid Increase for purposes of bid evaluation only.

In the event a Bidder fails to submit satisfactory data for ten (10) users, [name of user] shall make a liquidated bid adjustment to such Bidder's Proposal based upon an assumed Combined Average System Availability Level of 85%.

The liquidated bid adjustments made in accordance with the above procedure shall be applicable solely for purposes of evaluating the Proposals submitted by competing Bidders. In no event shall [name of user] be obligated to pay the amount of any such adjustment.

8.3 *System Reliability.* Bidder shall submit in Part IV of its Proposal system failure data (calculated in accordance with Section 13 of Appendix D) for ten (10) other users of the equipment proposed by Bidder. Such information shall contain the data set forth in Paragraph 8.2(a) through (d), above, and the Monthly System Failure Frequency for the equipment, measured for the System as a whole, and presented for each calendar month from [insert date] to [insert date]. Utilizing the information submitted by all competing Bidders, the [name of user] shall compute a Combined Average System Failure Frequency for each Bidder. Based upon this information, the [name of user] shall add to each Bidder's Proposal a cost, if any, equal to the following:

(Hourly System Cost) *times* (Combined Average System Failure Frequency, measured on an annual basis) *times* (five) *times* (.167) *equals* Liquidated Bid Increase for purposes of bid evaluation only.

For purposes of this formula:

(a) Hourly System Cost shall be computed as follows: (Installment Purchase Cost *plus* 60 Months Average System Maintenance Cost) *divided by* (720 *times* 60).

(b) An average Recovery Time of 10.80 minutes per System Failure shall be assumed.

In the event a Bidder fails to submit satisfactory data for ten (10) users, [name of user] shall make a liquidated bid adjustment to such Bidder's Proposal based upon an assumed Combined Average System Failure Frequency of 620 per year.

The liquidated bid adjustments made in accordance with the above procedure shall be applicable solely for purposes of evaluating the Proposals submitted by competing Bidders. In no event shall [name of user] be obligated to pay the amount of any such adjustment.

Preventive Maintenance Interruptions. The same approach outlined above can also be used to assess the relative amounts of time required for preventive maintenance. Although a good program of preventive maintenance should generally be encouraged rather than penalized, total preventive maintenance time can be a relevant factor in evaluating alternative equipment. One method of assessing relative preventive maintenance time is through the solicitation of other user data, as suggested above. Another method is through evaluation of published preventive maintenance specifications. Regardless of the source of the information utilized, the results of the analysis can be applied through the liquidated bid adjustment process outlined above or through subjective assessment by the user's negotiating team. One state agency employed the following formula in arriving at the amount to be added to the bid price of a responding vendor:

(Hourly System Cost) *times* (Average Number of
Preventive Maintenance Hours Per Year) *times*
(five) *equals* Cost to be Added to Vendor's Proposal

This user indicated that bidders not supplying the requested preventive maintenance information would have a liquidated bid adjustment imposed on the basis of a specified number of preventive maintenance hours per year.

One-Time Charge Analysis. Particularly where generic specifications are issued in a large acquisition, a comprehensive analysis of all major one-time charges is generally advisable. For example, equipment that has essentially comparable operating specifications and purchase prices may have widely different installation and site preparation costs (e.g., manufacturing equipment that will not fit existing plant space, data processing systems that require a shift from air to water cooling, and aircraft that necessitate new hangar and maintenance facilities). Consequently, many users solicit information concerning these one-time charges in their RFPs. Among the many types of charges that can be included in this analysis are the following:

- Equipment transportation costs.
- Equipment installation costs.
- Equipment return transportation costs.
- Support, overhead, or marketing costs and other expenses passed on to the user by the vendor.
- Programming costs (including conversions).
- Training costs.
- Construction costs for new buildings or facilities remodeling.
- Construction costs for new electrical lines or power connections.
- Construction costs for new cooling systems (e.g., air conditioning or liquid cooling facilities).
- Construction costs for Uninterruptible Power Supplies (UPS) for key operating or processing equipment.
- Purchase and installation costs for any special products necessary to use the equipment being acquired through the RFP (e.g., solid state frequency convertors, microprocessor control systems, custom maintenance equipment, pollution control units).
- One-time fees for software licenses, permits, royalties, or similar rights to use the equipment or other hardware or software.
- Lost production or development time resulting from installation, conversion, or testing delays.

Although these matters can be integrated into an RFP in several ways, one of the better techniques involves a table of one-time charges that must be completed by each vendor as part of its proposal. For this technique to be as useful as possible, the user must normally supply certain cost information or other assumptions to all vendors as a part of the RFP. For example, where air conditioning, water cooling, or building expansion costs may be incurred, the user should specify the dollar amount of, or formula to be employed in determining, those costs. On the other hand, where the costs of various extras will be determined by the vendor rather than the user, the better approach is to leave blank spaces on the cost sheet and place the full burden of providing relevant data on the vendor. The following table represents one method of implementing this approach.

Table A
One-Time Charges

BIDDER _____

Proposal Number _____

ONE TIME COSTS SUPPLIED BY BIDDER

1. Equipment Transportation Costs	$ _____
2. Equipment Installation Costs	$ _____
3. Equipment Return Transportation Costs	$ _____
4. Bidder's Support Costs	$ _____
5. Software Costs	$ _____
6. Training Costs	$ _____
7. Other One-Time Costs (Identify)	$ _____
TOTAL ONE-TIME COSTS SUPPLIED BY BIDDER	$ _____

ONE TIME COSTS [CALCULATED BY USER]

1. Air-Conditioning (Construction cost calculated in increments of 15 tons at $20,000.00 per 15 ton increment)	$ _____
2. Power (Construction cost calculated in increments of 30 power connections at $6,000.00 per 30 power connections)	$ _____
3. Raised Floor (Construction cost calculated in increments of square feet at $6.00 per square foot. Assumes use of existing titles and pedestals). Raised floor not using existing materials is $30.00 per square foot.	$ _____
4. UPS construction cost calculated in accordance with the following table:	$ _____

     100 KVA UPS—$175,000.00 $ _____

     200 KVA UPS—$250,000.00 $ _____

     400 KVA UPS—$300,000.00 $ _____

5. Additional floor space (calculated in increments of square feet at $63.00 per square foot (excluding raised floor and displacement costs)	$ _____
6. Cost of solid state frequency convertor including transportation and installation ($37,500.00 per unit)	$ _____
7. Plumbing (Construction costs on the basis of $25,000.00 per liquid cooled CPU)	$ _____
8. Displacement Costs (at a construction cost of $80.00 per square foot for office facilities)	$ _____
9. Other (if applicable)	$ _____
TOTAL ONE-TIME COSTS [CALCULATED BY THE USER]	$ _____

GRAND TOTAL ONE-TIME COSTS

$ _____

One of the more difficult one-time charge problems involves conversion programming. Where data processing or other programmable equipment is being acquired, it may or may not be compatible with the operations and applications software being utilized by the user. Conversions can almost always bridge the gap, by "converting" the existing programs to the new language or operating system. But conversion efforts can be remarkably expensive and time-consuming, as far too many users have found after the fact. (To paraphrase one computer marketing executive, "Sure, we can convert *anything.* The only questions are how long do we have and how much are you willing to pay!") In addition, convertibility is often oversold. Users are assured by the vendor that it has or will supply a conversion program, emulator, or black box that will either convert all necessary software in one pass or permit it to be translated each time it is utilized. In some instances, these programs and devices do a reasonably good job. But in many other situations disaster is more prevalent than success. Among the more common problems are efforts that do most of the job but not all, emulators that require so much machine capacity that processing fails, and programs that are simply filled with errors.

A comparison problem to oversold convertibility is exaggerated *compatibility*. Thus, a well-known manufacturer of mini-computers convinces all its XYZ-II customers that they can and should trade their existing machines for the latest state-of-the-art device, the XYZ-III. "You'll still be able to utilize all your existing programs and databases," the sales representative proudly announces. And the user signs, without any reference to compatibility in the contract. When the model III's are delivered, the user finds that some or all of its programs on data diskettes will not run on the new system. The sales representative explains, "Oh, we have a program that converts those for you. It will be available in about three months. In the meantime, we can convert your existing diskettes at our offices for only [insert any excessive price] each." (A major New York investment banking firm was among those caught in this trap in 1981.)

Because of these problems, any RFP involving equipment that may have compatibility or convertibility problems should be drafted with particular care. In addition to strong contractual provisions (or legal issue inquiries) on conversion and/or compatibility, the RFP should require vendors to present precise information on conversion costs and methods. As with other sections of the RFP, these data should be incorporated by reference into any final vendor/user agreement and be supported by appropriate vendor warranties. Some users supplement this approach by the liquidated bid adjustment process outlined above. Thus, one major data processing user included the following provision in its RFP:

Any conversion, simulation, or emulation of the [name of user's] existing ABC Data Base will limit the [name of user's] ability to share mutual software enhancements with certain existing firms and will also require additional support and development requirements. Therefore, in the event that a Bidder's proposal includes any use of a convertor, simulator, or emulator, the following costs will be added to such Bidder's base price bid:

Systems Assistance	$155,000
Documentation	65,000
Mutual Software Enhancements	180,000
TOTAL	$400,000

Operating Cost Analysis. Just as initial one-time charges for competitive equipment may vary materially, operating costs may be divergent enough to require careful comparison. In the current environment, where the equipment involved utilizes any form of fuel or energy, a detailed analysis of operating costs is almost mandatory. In the sixties, energy costs were seldom a material consideration, as long as other factors were favorable. Today, energy costs may still prove to be immaterial in light of total costs, or may be essentially the same for all suppliers, but energy has a much greater likelihood of being a key consideration. Equipment that uses or wastes other resources, such as water or minerals being processed, should also be subjected to an analysis of operating costs. The following examples provide a limited list of operating costs that may be relevant to an equipment acquisition:

- Energy Costs (e.g., gas, oil, or electricity);
- Water costs;
- Costs of other resources, minerals, or catalysts utilized in operating the equipment;

- Personnel costs involved in operating the equipment (e.g., single pilot versus pilot and copilot; human operator versus microprocessor control);
- Maintenance costs (including relative service and warranty levels);
- Ongoing license, permit, royalty, and similar fees for software or equipment;
- Costs of expendable parts and supplies (e.g., forms, paper, platens, ribbons, print wheels, and masks);
- Telecommunication and other interface costs;
- Tangible and intangible property taxes;
- Insurance costs.

Various methods exist for obtaining information about, and assessing, these and other operating costs. Although some users insist on analyzing these costs outside of the formal RFP process, the authors generally suggest that an RFP should solicit information about all principal operating expenses. (Merely determining *all relevant* operating expenses for myriad equipment produced by numerous vendors is often a difficult task in itself.) The following excerpts from two RFPs offer examples of this approach:

Example A:

Recurring "life cycle" costs of the equipment to be considered will include recurring costs of monthly installment purchase payments, equipment maintenance costs, environmental and support equipment maintenance costs, and power consumption and heat loss, both of which will be translated by the supplied rates into dollar amounts. The life cycle cost evaluation will consider the "power-on/cooling-on" period to be 720 hours per month. Rates to be employed will be as follows:

a. Cooling
   1. to air   — $.010/KBTU/HR
   2. to water   — $.006/KBTU/HR
b. Power
   1. 60 Hz   — $.06/KWH
   2. 400 Hz   — $.06/KWH

Example B:

For purposes of evaluating proposals, average anticipated operating costs will be calculated and spread over the three-year useful life of the fleet. Each proposal must include (see Bid Sheet 23) the total estimated fuel expense and the total estimated oil expenses (including oil use and charges) for the fleet over such three-year period, based upon an average mileage of 148,000 miles per vehicle. For such purposes, the following assumptions should be made concerning *average* fuel and oil costs over the period:

a. Fuel:
   1. Unleaded regular $2.05/gal.
   2. Regular (not unleaded) $1.90/gal.
   3. Diesel (#1 or 2) $1.78/gal.
b. Oil:
   1. Standard [insert codes] $1.80/qt.
   2. Premium [insert codes] $2.10/qt.
   3. Diesel   [insert codes] $2.10/qt.
   4. Synthetic [insert codes] $5.40/qt.

Weighting and Split Analysis Techniques. As the discussion on prioritizing in Chapter 4 indicates, all acquisition criteria do not generally have or deserve the same degree of importance in the user's appraisal process. Consequently, most experienced users employ a weighting system in evaluating the various portions of a vendor proposal. Some users approach the weighting issue very informally, subjectively determining the relative importance of different factors after all proposals have been received and reviewed. Other users employ a more sophisticated approach, documenting their analysis of all proposals on score sheets that specify the relative importance attributed to each issue. In some instances, these score sheets and the relative weights (ordinarily expressed as percents or points) are included in the RFP. The latter approach is subject to some disagreement among users and their advisors. Those in favor of the approach note that it permits each vendor to appreciate the degree of importance that the user attaches to various areas, and thereby indirectly increases the competitive environment. Those opposed to the technique assert that it unnecessarily places the user in a fishbowl, making the user more obligated to explain its decision-making process once the contract has been awarded.

Some users go beyond the weighting process to a split submission and analysis technique. In the latter approach, competing vendors each submit their proposals in two or more separate parts. The user then analyzes all proposals part by part. Vendors that submit sound proposals on part one are included in the group of finalists or ZOC contenders whose proposals are considered for part two. This process is repeated for each part of the proposal included in the split submission process.

One of the more popular methods of implementing this approach involves splitting the proposals into technical and financial packages. Another frequently-used option adds a third category of legal/contractual considerations. In each case, the RFP explains the process and advises vendors that their proposals will be reviewed sequentially by part, with successful completion of each partial review being a prerequisite for continued consideration in the RFP process.

The split submission and analysis technique offers three principal advantages for the user. First, it heightens the competitive environment. Because a vendor's complete proposal will be reviewed only if it is successful in meeting the minimum prerequisites for each stage, each vendor is required to focus considerable attention on the substance covered by the respective section. Second, the technique increases the user's control of the acquisition process. Because the user determines which proposals pass each stage of the split submission process, vendors have less ability to utilize ploys and other marketing techniques designed to create a sense of urgency and spawn an uninformed decision. Third, this control also keeps the user "on track," reducing the far too natural tendency to jump to conclusions or subjective judgments in the bid analysis stage of the RFP. (Bid format, evaluation, and selection are discussed in more detail later in this chapter.)

The following excerpts from an equipment RFP outline one rather limited method of implementing the split submission and analysis technique:

5.10. *PART I—TECHNICAL INFORMATION:* Part I of the Proposal shall address the technical requirements for the equipment, as set forth in Section VI. Three (3) complete copies of Part I must be submitted, clearly marked "Technical Data for Project ABHC-82-P."

No cost or expense information or comments concerning soft-dollar benefits shall be included in Part I, and the inclusion of such information in Part I may disqualify the Bidder.

* * *

5.25 *PART II—FINANCIAL INFORMATION:* Part II of the Proposal shall address the financial aspects of the acquisition, as set forth in Section VII. Three (3) complete copies of

Part II must be submitted, clearly marked "Financial Data for Project ABHC-82-P." Except where necessary to identify specific costs or cost alternatives, no technical information or performance data shall be included in Part II, and the inclusion of such information in Part II may disqualify the Bidder. Part II shall include the following mandatory tables, in the formats attached, and may also include any other financial information reasonably relevant to the user's assessment of total life cycle costs over the anticipated 60-month useful life of the equipment:

Table	Contents
A	One-Time Charges
B	Hardware
C	Software
D	Special Supplemental Hardware or Software
E	Optional Hardware or Software
F	Operating Costs
G	Cost Evaluation Matrix

* * *

8.1 *PROPOSAL EVALUATION:* All Proposals will be evaluated by a committee consisting of [membership omitted]. Proposals that, in the opinion of the committee, fail to meet the mandatory technical requirements specified in Section VI and presented in Part I of the Proposal shall not be considered further, and Part II of such Proposals shall be returned to the respective Bidders. Proposals that, in the opinion of the committee, meet the mandatory technical requirements specified in Section VI and presented in Part I of the Proposal shall be further evaluated with respect to Part II.

Prequalification of Bidders. One of the more difficult preliminary questions in many acquisitions is what vendors should be permitted or invited to bid. To be sure, in some acquisitions this problem is essentially nonexistent (e.g., where only a few viable suppliers exist, where "relationships" or other business considerations rightfully or wrongfully dictate the list of bidders, or where public bid procedures and advertised announcements permit any interested firm to bid). However, where questions do arise concerning the selection of acceptable vendors, they must generally be answered as a part of, or prior to, the RFP process.

In keeping with the split submission and analysis technique explained above, some users require the first part of each proposal to include vendor qualification information. Proposals from vendors deemed "qualified" are then evaluated further. Other users follow a similar approach on a more informal basis, requiring each proposal to include qualification information but evaluating that data more subjectively as part of an unsegmented assessment of the entire proposal.

Both of these techniques are somewhat unfair for the vendor, particularly where extensive RFP specifications and proposals are involved. Consequently, the authors generally recommend that, where prequalification of potential bidders is necessary or desirable, a preliminary questionnaire be employed for screening purposes. Depending upon the type of acquisition and number of potential vendors involved, this approach can be implemented in any of several ways. Where the user has already tentatively identified the proposed bidders, but desires to obtain confirming data prior to issuing the RFP, the prequalification questionnaire may be distributed only to those potential bidders already designated by the user. On the other hand, where the user has not already narrowed the field through subjective appraisals, the questionnarie may be sent to all available suppliers or to all vendors that reply to an advertisement or mailing announcing the solicitation. (Where a large number of suppliers is involved, a preliminary mailing of the announcement is generally more cost efficient than a mass distribution of the full questionnaire. Interested vendors that receive the announcement can then request a copy of the questionnaire.)

While this type of questionnaire should generally seek information concerning the ability of the vendor to submit a proposal that will be responsive and consistent with the user's needs, the questionnaire should not attempt to judge the substantive nature of the RFP response that will be received from the vendor. In effect, the screening questionnaire should qualify the vendor, not its proposal. The RFP should focus on the proposal and the vendor's ability to meet the technical requirements, prices, and terms desired by the user.

In this regard, "qualification" of a vendor should not be confused with acceptance. Qualification should merely indicate that the user feels that the submission of a proposal by the vendor, and an analysis of that proposal by the user, would be worth the time and money required to do the job. Despite the fact that a vendor has been found qualified through the preliminary screening process, the user should still be free to assess the relative qualifications of that vendor and other competing vendors to successfully implement the acquisition in accordance with the RFP and respective bid proposals. Moreover, prequalification should not be considered "binding" on the user in any way.

These caveats are appropriately reflected in the section on prequalification of suppliers contained in Preliminary Working Paper No. 2 of the American Bar Association's Coordinating Committee on a Model Procurement Code for State and Local Governments. The draft section and the associated commentary provide as follows:

3-402 *Prequalification of Suppliers.*

The [State] Purchasing Board may provide for prequalification of suppliers as responsible prospective contractors for particular types of supplies, services, and construction. Solicitation mailing lists of potential contractors of such supplies, services, and construction shall include but shall not be limited to such prequalified suppliers. Prequalification shall not foreclose a written determination:

(a) between the time of the bid opening or receipt of offers and the making of an award, that a prequalified supplier is not responsible; or

(b) that a supplier who is not prequalified at the time of the bid opening or receipt of offers is responsible.

COMMENTARY:

Prequalification is a system which may be adopted to ease the administrative burden incident to making the responsibility determinations required by Section 3-401(1) [Responsibility of Bidders and Offerors, Determination of Responsibility]. However, prequalification is *not* a conclusive determination of responsibility, and a prequalified bidder or offeror may be rejected as nonresponsible on the basis of subsequently discovered information. Similarly, a prior failure to prequalify will not bar a subsequent determination that a bidder or offeror is responsible with respect to any given procurement. Generally, prequalification will be based upon those factors considered in making of responsibility determinations.

Performance Bond Requirements. As part of the vendor qualification process, some users require all competing vendors to post mandatory bonds or cash deposits with their bid proposals. Although once limited almost entirely to the public sector, this approach is gaining increasing interest among private firms. Two principal techniques of implementing this approach are generally employed. In the first methodology, the vendor bond or deposit merely confirms the vendor's interest and provides a generally inadequate forfeiture in the event the vendor is selected but refuses to (or is unable to) execute the binding vendor/user agreement. In the second approach, the bond or deposit is tied to some substantive aspect of the vendor's commitment under the RFP, such as the vendor's ability to obtain installment purchase or leveraged lease financing or to cause the equipment to meet (or repeat) specified benchmark test results. In the latter use, the bond/deposit requirement becomes more important as a special remedy or liquidated damages (see Chapters 6 and 8). In addition, it adds considerable weight to the user's efforts to focus on vendor "deliverables" in a highly competitive and structured acquisition environment.

In one complicated equipment procurement involving generic specifications and extensive benchmark tests, the following requirements were outlined in the RFP:

Performance Bond. Each Bidder shall submit with its Proposal and at its own expense, a Performance Bond in the amount of Five Hundred Thousand Dollars ($500,000) issued by a reliable surety company licensed to conduct business in [insert name of state] in favor of [insert name of user]. In the event the acquisition contemplated by this RFP is awarded to the Bidder and a mutually-satisfactory contract is executed by and between Bidder and [insert name of user], and Bidder either (i) fails to supply the least financing outlined in Section 18(a) by the date specified therein or (ii) fails to cause the equipment to pass the Acceptance Tests specified in Section 24(d) by the date specified therein (subject to the extensions and conditions set forth in said Section 24(d), then the Bidder shall forfeit the Performance Bond and the full amount thereof shall be paid to [insert name of user]. The Bidder shall also forfeit the Performance Bond, and the full amount thereof shall be paid to [insert name of user] in the event that the acquisition contemplated by this RFP is awarded to the Bidder and the Bidder thereafter refuses to execute the Standard Contract attached as Exhibit D to this RFP (subject to such optional provisions as may be included in any Supplements to this RFP). Following satisfactory and timely completion of the conditions specified in clauses (i) and (ii), above, the Performance Bond shall be returned to the successful Bidder. Performance Bonds furnished by Bidders who are not awarded the acquisition will be returned.

Single and Multiple Bidder Responsibility. In many RFPs, users must face issues relating to single or multiple bidder responsibility. Thus, the user must determine whether a single successful bidder must have or accept responsibility for the entire acquisition or whether several bidders may each accept divided responsibility for separate portions of the procurement. Regardless of whether the user desires single or multiple bidder responsibility, the RFP should generally indicate the preference of the user and the flexibility accorded competing vendors. (Where a user is uncertain as to whether single or multiple responsibility will be practicable in an upcoming procurement, the vendor prequalification process can often be employed to collect relevant information.)

If the user desires, or at least is willing to accept, multiple bidder responsibility, several factors must be considered. These issues are discussed below.

First, the user must assess whether to issue a single RFP for the combined responsibilities or separate RFPs for each area. Generalizations are difficult without facts about each acquisition. However, the authors have found that, where practicable, a single RFP that covers all issues and subsets provides higher levels of competition and flexibility than several RFPs.

Second, regardless of whether single or multiple RFPs are issued, the user must determine which portions of the procurement can be set apart and bid upon separately. This decision should also consider the question of whether vendors bidding on portions of the acquisition should be permitted any flexibility in determining the products on which they wish to submit bids. Ordinarily, the user's approach in this area will be based upon the methods that appear most likely to provide competition on the largest number of components without creating undue confusion or bid assessment problems. In this regard, users must remember that, while proposal splitting may increase competition and the number of available suppliers, it can also create serious bid appraisal problems as users attempt to compare "apples to oranges."

Third, where multiple bidder responsibility is acceptable, the user must also determine the degree to which vendors responsible for separate areas will be required to coordinate or interface with one another. Even where multiple bidder responsibility is permitted, coordination and cooperation will normally be necessary, both during the RFP process and during implementation of the acquisition. Consequently, both the RFP and the vendor/user contracts should include requirements in this area.

Fourth, the user must determine whether it wishes to impose any evaluation penalty on vendors choosing to bid on the basis of multiple source responsibility. As noted below, reliance on separate vendors can increase implementation risks and expenses for the user. As a result, some users specify that single or multiple bidder responsibility will be acceptable, but impose a liquidated bid adjustment (increase) on each bidder that submits a proposal covering less than all people, products, and services covered by the procurement. Normally, this adjustment is imposed solely for purposes of the evaluation process and is not levied against vendors that legitimately subcontract certain portions of the procurement. With respect to the latter point, users must employ care to ensure that any subcontract, joint venture, or turnkey proposal is legally documented and supported by financially responsible parties so that the resulting single bidder responsibility is backed by substance as well as appearance.

Finally, the user must determine whether it wishes to have the flexibility to split its bid award among two or more vendors. Where such a division of the award may prove to be in the user's best interest, the RFP should reserve this right to the user and cover the various segmentation and interface issues discussed above. (Bid format, evaluation, and selection are discussed in more detail later in this chapter.)

As suggested above, dividing responsibility for implementing an acquisition among several vendors can create coordination problems and legal and financial risks for the user. Because of these difficulties, many users make single bidder responsibility a prerequisite in those acquisitions where it is possible to do so. Thus, vendor proposals that fail to cover all people, products, and services included in the RFP will be disqualified or deemed nonresponsive. This procedure can be implemented easily in the RFP, with a provision as basic as the following:

> Single bidder responsibility is required under this RFP. Each Bidder responding to this RFP must bid all equipment and services specified in Section III and, if awarded the contract, must be the sole contracting party with [name of user], responsible for all aspects of the procurement.

Some users go beyond this type of basic statement to cover potential problem areas or clearly identify the matters for which the successful bidder will be responsible. For example, one RFP included the following language cautioning about subcontracting practices:

> *Subcontracting.* The requirement for single-point responsibility in this procurement does not prohibit subcontracts or joint ventures provided that the single successful Bidder: (a) serves as the sole general contractor with [name of user]; and (b) assumes full responsibility for the performance of all of its subcontractors, joint venturers, and other agents; and (c) provides the sole point of contact for all activities through a single individual designated as Project Manager (see Section 5.7.1 of this RFP); and (d) submits information with its Proposal (see Section 7.2.3 of this RFP) documenting the financial standing and business history of each subcontractor and similar firm and submits copies of all subcontracts and other agreements

proposed to document such arrangement. Without limiting the foregoing, any such legal documents must: (i) make [name of user] a third-party beneficiary thereunder; and (ii) grant to [name of user] the right to receive notice of and cure any default by the successful Bidder under the document; and (iii) pass through to [name of user] any and all warranties, investment tax credit, and indemnities provided or offered by the subcontractor or similar party. (See Appendix F of this RFP for mandatory provisions.)

In another RFP, the user cautioned competing vendors that they must be "the single point of contact" for the following list of activities and services:

1. Submission of a plan for the physical installation of the Processor and peripherals contained in the bid. The bidder shall respond with both a written plan, by phase, including dates installation will begin and dates of installation completion, as well as scale drawings for each phase of proposed equipment in place showing, to scale, the relationship(s) to existing equipment and physical facilities.
2. Delivery of the Processor(s) and peripherals contained in the bid.
3. Delivery or recommended source of all mandatory software (as specified in Section 5.3) in their current release.
4. Equipment and programming ready and operational for acceptance testing.
5. Maintenance (Preventive and Remedial) for all equipment.
6. Maintenance for System Control Program.
7. Training for Data Center Managers, Analysts, Programmers, Operators, and other Agency personnel.
8. Systems Analyst support for program conversion, System Control Program installation, application, planning, etc.
9. Current reference manuals for processor, peripheral, and System Control Programs.
10. 370/158 Conversion.

Other variations in single and multiple bidder responsibility are also possible. One of the more difficult challenges occurs where the user clearly prefers to have single vendor responsibility, but no bidder seems qualified to provide all products and services required. Among the principal alternative solutions to this problem are the following:

• *New prime contractor.* The user calls in a new prime contractor that is not a competing bidder, and causes it to contract with the several successful bidders that will actually supply products and services under the RFP. Some users that adopt this approach prefer to negotiate and award the contracts with the various subcontractors; indeed, a smaller number of users insists on utilizing triparty agreements among the user, the prime contractor, and the subcontractor. Other users place the total responsibility for negotiating and optimizing the subcontracts on the prime contractor—a technique not unlike that employed in much real estate development. Regardless of the approach, the key is generally the strength and capability of the prime contractor and its ability to commit on behalf of, or marshal commitments from, the various subcontractors.

• *Single bidder as prime contractor.* The user selects a single bidder to serve as the prime contractor and also to supply its own products or services in the acquisition. The bidder selected for this responsibility may be the vendor supplying most of the products or services, or the vendor with the strongest management capabilities, or the vendor that evidences some other likely project management strength. Again, users that employ this procedure adopt different methods of implementing it. Reference should be made to the subcontracting alternatives outlined in the prime contractor discussion above.

- *Master multiparty contract.* No vendor serves as the prime contractor. Instead, the user employs a master multiparty contract executed by the user and all of the participating vendors. In essence, the user becomes its own general contractor, but utilizes a master agreement signed by all parties to minimize misunderstandings and the problems and risks associated with a multiple contractor environment. A master contract of this nature is a difficult document to draft. But, when carefully prepared, it can substantially reduce the fingerpointing and "responsibility gaps" that are otherwise likely to occur. Much like the RFP itself, the discipline of preparing this document is almost as enlightening and valuable as the end product that results.

- *Linked agreements.* The user contracts separately with each successful vendor, but links the various agreements to make them dependent upon one another in key areas (such as performance deadlines and default). This approach is often favored over the master multiparty agreement procedure because it requires substantially less drafting time and expertise, and because the contracts can be negotiated and settled separately, one agreement at a time. This relative simplicity also contributes to the biggest risk in utilizing this alternative: Despite the user's best efforts, the separate agreements may not be sufficiently linked in key areas.

- *Take-over-on-default agreements.* The user contracts separately with each supplier, with or without linking agreements. However, each agreement provides that, in the event a vendor defaults under its agreement with the user, the user may, upon notice to the vendor, elect to: (a) assign all of the user's contracts with other vendors to the defaulting vendor, thereby making that vendor financially responsible for assuming the user's payment obligations under those contracts; or (b) assume the obligations of the defaulting vendor, assign them to another supplier (in effect "covering" for purposes of contract remedy law), and proceed against the defaulting vendor for contractual damages. The latter approach is a rather standard alternative. The former approach is unusual to say the least. Essentially, it is a variation of a usual damages option. However, instead of forcing the user to prove its measure of damages, the procedure permits the user to say to the defaulting vendor, "Look, you defaulted on your part of this project. As a result, none of the other suppliers can meet their deadlines and the viability of the entire acquisition is doubtful. We'll start over, with another team. *You* pay the other vendors and do what you want with the equipment we ordered. You caused it; you deal with it."

Is this a realistic position for a user to take? In many respects, yes, it is. Is the position likely to be accepted readily by the vendors on a multisupplier project? No. In the first place, a vendor concerned about its own possible default would be disinterested in assuming the user's obligation under all the other user/vendor agreements. Second, the vendors that did not default might or might not be willing to look to the defaulting supplier, instead of the user, to pay the user's obligations under their agreements with the user.

Despite these valid points, this unusual approach can be successfully advocated in some acquisitions. It seems particularly appropriate to place this type of take-over-upon-default obligation upon a vendor that is clearly the largest supplier in the multivendor transaction. This vendor is likely to have the most critical role in the acquisition. In addition, it will probably be financially able to take over the user's obligations under the other user/vendor agreements. Where the other vendors express concern about this approach, principally from the standpoint of the financial capability of the defaulting vendor, the user may elect to remain secondarily liable for its obligations under the agreements assigned to the defaulting party. Even where the user retains this secondary liability, the psychological and financial pressure to perform that this approach places on the defaulting vendor can be significant.

Master RFP Programs. As user RFP experience continues to increase, more and more users are experimenting with a master RFP structure that involves plug-in modules for specific types of acquisitions. This cookbook approach can be expanded to cover virtually all aspects of the acquisition process, including RFP issuance and evaluation and contract drafting and administration.

In its most basic form, the master RFP structure involves a standard or common set of RFP procedures, carefully drafted to apply to a wide range of equipment and acquisition techniques. This umbrella structure is then supplemented in each procurement by one or more specific modules tailored to the type of equipment and/or acquisition method involved.

Although considerable time and expertise is required to design and draft a master RFP program, once the structure is in place it can save significant temporal and financial resources. Moreover, because it can be activated on short notice with little additional preparation, the master RFP process counteracts one of the primary factors leading most users to abandon any RFP effort: lack of time. The master RFP is generally most valuable to a large governmental or corporate user that has, or has the ability to create, a central procurement process.

Although the best master RFP programs are those carefully tailored to the specific needs of an individual user, the following areas are among those that should be considered in implementing this approach:

- Development of an umbrella structure that is as broad as possible in terms of the equipment being acquired and the acquisition method, yet reflective of the business needs of the issuing user.
- Development of modules for each major type of equipment, focusing primarily on technical requirements rather than acquisition methods or pricing alternatives.
- Development of modules for each major method of acquiring equipment (including purchase, rental, direct lease, third-party lease, and installment purchase), focusing primarily on acquisition structure and price.
- Development of modules to solicit supplemental pricing information in selected areas, when desired (e.g., installation costs and total life cycle costing).
- Development of modules, including legal/contractual criteria, in the form of standard user contracts, mandatory provisions, or legal/contractual inquiries and checklists.
- Development of supplemental implementation and evaluative criteria to support the master/module approach, including such matters as vendor selection criteria, bid evaluation standards, and instructions and checklists necessary to package existing modules and any required "custom" modules into a final RFP.

"Wiring the Deal." No review of alternative RFP approaches would be complete without mention of an item that is often whispered about, but seldom discussed openly: whether or not to "wire the deal." In raising this topic, the authors do not intend to condone clearly illegal or unethical practices that involve bid fixing, bribes, or illegal payments. Despite the continuing discussions over whether the Foreign Corrupt Practices Act attempts to legislate an overly-severe morality on American firms doing business overseas, the fact remains that the Act is the "law of the land." As such, it governs domestic activities as well as foreign corrupt practices, and imposes strict standards on all businesses with a class of equity securities registered under the Securities Exchange Act of 1934. All persons involved in a user's RFP procedures should be familiar with the constraints of the Foreign Corrupt Practices Act and any codes of ethics adopted by the user organization.

Despite this admonition, a user has considerable leeway in determining the degree to which it wants any procurement process to be open and competitive. It is within this context that the concept of "wiring the deal" becomes relevant. If the user truly wishes to optimize competition and permit any bidder to have a fair and equal chance at winning the contract, all RFP procedures should reflect that fact. However, not all users wish to have this degree of competition in every procurement. In some acquisitions, unbridled competition among all comers, qualified or not, would border on chaos and do little to serve the user's purposes. In other acquisitions, competition among more than a handful of firms may be inconsistent with the user's business goals and unnecessary to maximize the user's position in the transaction. In still other circumstances, the appearance of competition may best serve the user, by causing an incumbent vendor to stop resting on its laurels and become more responsive to the user's needs.

In each of these situations, the user is unlikely to employ RFP procedures that maximize competition or impose equal opportunity for all possible bidders. Rather, the user is more likely to narrow the field through a subjective or objective selection process, before releasing the RFP. Alternatively, the user may adjust its evaluation criteria in a fashion that increases the chances that a particular vendor will be able to submit a winning proposal.

As this discussion suggests, few RFPs are perfectly objective, even when the user is generally committed to a totally open procurement process. Rather than avoiding this issue, users should admit this imperfection and consciously strive to tailor the RFP to create the degree of openness and competition desired by the user. The result will generally be far superior than that which ensues from a confused, mixed effort at pretending to be competitive while secretly hoping not to be.

Thus, if the user has carefully concluded that its business interests would be best served by creating reasonable openness and a strong appearance of competition, while still utilizing specifications that favor the incumbent vendor, it should consciously adopt that approach and tailor its RFP accordingly. Alternatively, if the user believes that its position would be maximized by employing technical specifications and/or deadlines that place severe pressures on an incumbent vendor (perhaps one that has had strong political connections but weak performance), then the user should implement that approach in its RFP.

In advocating this conscious utilization of the RFP as a tool to achieve the user's business goals, three additional points should be noted. First, some users (and many more vendors) find the position advocated above to be unethical, immoral or, at least, unfair. The authors will appropriately leave those judgments to each reader, with one comment: No RFP process is completely "pure." Likewise, no vendor sales effort is totally free from bias. Recognizing these facts, users would do well to mold the RFP process in a *reasonable* manner that best serves the user's business needs.

Second, molding the RFP process in this manner does not mean taking undue advantage of vendors participating in the competition. To be sure, any RFP process that is molded or "wired" to meet user needs imposes an unequal opportunity on at least some bidders. However, if this inequality becomes too severe, the reaction from the disadvantaged vendors is likely to be loud and permanent. As one seasoned procurement officer explained, "You can create the *appearance* of competition only so long. Sooner or later, you've either got to offer an open procurement process or your incumbent vendor will be your only bidder." The point is simple: Vendors will compete in environments that involve some bias and reasonable molding, but they will not continue to participate in procurements where the RFP is repeatedly issued as a matter of form or as an effort to keep the incumbent honest.

Third, molding the RFP to meet the user's needs should not be confused with injecting bias into the user's *decision-making* process. Any judgments made by the user to mold the RFP process, to prefer one vendor over another, or to adopt specifications that favor one vendor or class of vendors should be made objectively, with the highest degree of care. Reasonable bias may be acceptable in the RFP itself, but it has no place in the decisions and judgments made by the user.

GENERAL DOCUMENTATION

As the previous section on Alternative Approaches suggests, every RFP should include certain general provisions and other documentation necessary to outline the acquisition and explain applicable procurement procedures. General documentation matters appropriate to a wide range of acquisitions are discussed below. Once again, the reader is cautioned that the items outlined below should not be accepted as mandatory in every RFP; in many instances, the user will be best served by utilizing the following discussion as a cookbook from which relevant provisions can be extracted and molded to the user's needs in a specific acquisition.

Document Index

Every RFP should include a table of contents or other index that outlines, and provides easy reference to, the full request for proposal. Where the RFP includes supplemental documentation, such as benchmark standards or additional specifications, these materials should be included in the index.

In addition to facilitating reference to specific portions of the RFP, the index serves two other purposes. First, it offers an overview of the RFP document and, more importantly, the entire RFP process. Ordinarily, this overview carries with it the strong psychological impression that the user is serious, knows what it is doing, and intends to implement a truly competitive procurement. Second, the index clearly specifies the scope of the RFP documentation, leaving no room for subsequent allegations that the vendor did not realize that a particular matter or document was included in the procurement process.

Although each RFP index must reflect the substance and organization of the particular procurement, the following example offers one relatively short method of approaching the contents/index area. This example was excerpted from an RFP utilized in a large-scale acquisition of wood processing equipment. The actual RFP from which this example was taken included additional detail (particularly in the area of specifications) that has been omitted below to facilitate presentation.

1. *Introduction*
   1.1 Background
       1.1.1   Government Service
       1.1.2   Social Services and Community Health
       1.1.3   Purpose of Proposed System
2. *General Requirements*
   2.1 Conditions of the RFP
       2.1.1   Vendor Queries
       2.1.2   Confidentiality
       2.1.3   Schedule of Events
       2.1.4   Vendor Response
       2.1.5   Vendor Selection
       2.1.6   Proposal Costs
       2.1.7   Vendor Documents
       2.1.8   Changes to Proposal
       2.1.9   Firm Prices
       2.1.10 Acceptance of Conditions
       2.1.11 Validation Demonstration
       2.1.12 Acquisition Agreements
       2.1.13 Terminology

3. *Application Description*
   3.1 Social Services and Community Health
       3.1.1   Background
       3.1.2   New Systems Development
       3.1.3   Capacity Requirements— Short Term
       3.1.4   Capacity Requirements— Medium/Long Term
   3.2 Government Services
       3.2.1   Background
       3.2.2   Network Node Location
       3.2.3   Capacity
       3.2.4   Expandability
       3.2.5   Minicomputer Requirements
4. *Terminal System Specifications*
   4.1 Off-Line Functions
       4.1.1   Source Data Entry
       4.1.2   Data Storage
       4.1.3   Report Printing
       4.1.4   System Log

Introduction

As explained above, every RFP should include an introduction section that provides an overview of the proposed acquisition. The following elements are often included in this section of the RFP:

User Background. To give all bidders at least a general understanding of the user's business, many RFPs include a brief description of the user corporation and, in some instances, the particular department involved in the procurement. The following statement offers one abbreviated example:

Acme Banks, Inc. is a registered multibank holding company headquartered in Metro, Florida. At December 31, 1981, it operated 14 subsidiary banks having 105 banking offices throughout peninsular Florida. At that date, Acme reported total assets of $2.6 billion and total deposits of $2.1 billion, making it the fifth largest banking organization in Florida. A copy of the Annual Report of Acme Banks, Inc. for the year ended December 31, 1981, is attached as Exhibit I to this RFP.

At present, Acme Banks, Inc. operates an on-line network of 54 Docubold automated teller machines, all of which are installed at branch office locations in Dade, Broward, and Palm Beach Counties. The company's ATM operations are managed by the Delivery Systems Group of Acme's Operations Division, headquartered in Podunk. Mr. John Jones, Vice President, heads the Delivery Systems Group and reports to Mr. F. J. Manuel, Senior Vice President, Operations. Mr. Manuel reports directly to Mr. D. Hale Oliver, President of Acme Banks, Inc. (Please refer to the organizational chart attached as Exhibit II to this RFP.)

Acquisition Overview. Most effective RFPs follow this user background with an overview of the proposed acquisition. This explanation can be extensive or limited, as the user may desire. The authors generally prefer a relatively brief summary of the acquisition, coupled with limited cross-references to other sections of the RFP document and, where practicable, a graphic depiction of the transaction. The following excerpt from a state government procurement offers one example:

INTRODUCTION

The State is interested in obtaining bids for a computer system with processing capabilities that meet the technical requirements of Section V and successfully complete all of the benchmark requirements of Section VI with required peripherals to implement and operate an online communications-oriented Wisconsin Vehicle/Driver Data Base System (WVDDBS) in the State. . . . The State anticipates acquisition of all equipment by the installment purchase method over a period of 60 months.

The objective of the State is shown in Figure 1.1, "Conceptual Hardware Overview." Some of this equipment presently exists [as indicated]. Detailed equipment requirements are specified in Paragraph 5.2.1.

The Conceptual Hardware Overview referenced as "Figure 1.1" in the above excerpt is reproduced as Figure 5-3 in this text.

Definitions. Whether included at the outset or the conclusion of the document package, a detailed RFP should include a definitions section or glossary that defines key terms. Ordinarily, the definitions section of the RFP can be substantially excerpted from the definitions provision of the proposed user/vendor agreement, or vice versa. Indeed, where the proposed contract is included as an exhibit to the RFP, the RFP definitions section can merely cross-reference to the applicable contractual provision.

Some users feel that an extensive definitions section in the RFP represents overkill and undue complexity. Although the formality gained by employing a strong definitions section can increase the appearance of high user control, reducing the size or scope of the definitions provision, or eliminating it altogether, is seldom fatal, as long as the RFP remains clear. As noted earlier in this chapter, the critical standard is for the RFP to provide the detail necessary to avoid misunderstanding or, equally important, the appearance of misunderstanding.

Where limited definitions are employed, clarity can be gained by including terms that refer to various departments within the user organization. Although these references are often described and explained as "terms of art" within the proposed vendor/user agreement, repeating the terms and the descriptions in the RFP is both professional and helpful in avoiding misun-

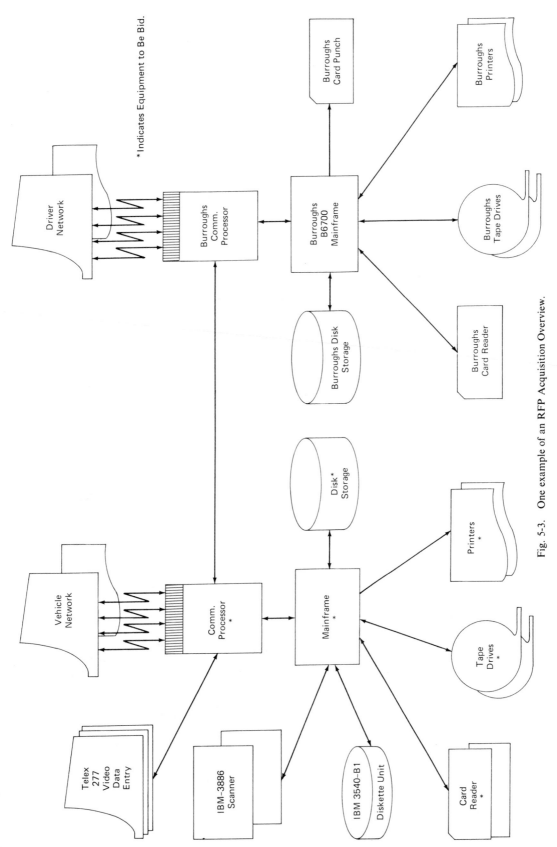

Fig. 5-3. One example of an RFP Acquisition Overview.

*Indicates Equipment to Be Bid.

derstanding. The following example shows the limited definitions utilized in a draft RFP for intelligent data entry, printing, and communications equipment.

APPENDIX E   *Definitions*

Words used in this RFP have the meaning set out in this definition list unless otherwise indicated.

ACQUISITION AGREEMENT	The Agreement or Agreements between the successful vendor and [the user] for the acquisition and servicing of the equipment and services sought in the RFP
CONTINUOUS AVAILABILITY	The equipment must provide all its function during normal working hours without interruption for service or maintenance
CRT	Cathode Ray Tube Terminal (see Video Display Terminal)
CSA	Canadian Standards Association
CW	Child Welfare
DDS	Data Decision sheet—the main input and change document for the Social Allowance program
DO	District Office
EVALUATION TEAM	The group of individuals appointed on behalf of [the user] to assess and select proposals submitted pursuant to this RFP
FST	Federal Sales Tax
IS	Income Security
ISD	Information Services Division of [the user]
N/A	Not Applicable to this item
Prior Contact Checks	When a client comes into a District Office, a check is made to see if this client has had previous contact with departmental services
PROPOSAL	The response of each vendor to this RFP, made in accordance with the provisions and conditions of this RFP
RDE	Remote Data Entry
RFP	Request for Proposal
RFP Close Date	Date responses are due to the Purchasing Branch of [the user]
T & M	Time and Materials. For items indicated with "T & M" the vendor will not enter into a maintenance agreement and service is on a time and materials basis
VENDOR	Suppliers of data processing equipment and services invited to respond to this RFP
VIDEO DISPLAY TERMINAL	The equipment consisting of a video screen and keyboard

This same RFP included several other "terminology" definitions designed to clarify the relative gradations of "mandatory" and "optional." The following language was employed for this purpose:

Terminology.

Throughout this RFP, terminology is used that describes the importance to the objectives of this RFP, of each requirement. Such terminology is as follows:

—*"must," "mandatory," "required"*—A requirement that must be met in a substantially unaltered form in order for the proposal to receive consideration.

—*"should," "desirable"*—A requirement having a significant degree of importance to the objectives of the RFP.

—*"optional"*—A requirement not considered essential to the application, but for which preference may be given.

As in any situation where "terms of art" are employed, the approach above requires that the user have a clear understanding of the definitions involved. In addition, the user must make a thorough analysis of the RFP document, before its release, to ensure that all terms are properly utilized.

Acquisition Method. Whether included in the acquisition overview, in the definition section, or elsewhere, the RFP should describe the method or methods of acquisition proposed to be used. This requirement is easily met where, for example, the user recognizes at the outset that all equipment will be acquired through the straight purchase method. The complexities arise where the user prefers, or at least is willing, to consider alternative methods of acquisition for all or certain equipment. In the latter event, the RFP should state the alternatives that are desired or acceptable, and establish the guidelines and submission and evaluation standards that will be utilized. (See the discussion of bid format, evaluation, and selection, below.) Among the critical points that should be covered are those designed to ensure that an "apples to apples" comparison of the various bids can be made. The following excerpt indicates how one user described this area in a procurement where the method of acquisition for the primary equipment was fixed, but alternative approaches were available for certain additional components:

3.0 *METHOD OF ACQUISITION*

User shall acquire the system configuration by the Installment Purchase method. The acquisition of additional equipment may be by the Lease with Option to Purchase Method or by exchange or expansion to the Installment Purchase Contract by amendment and will be predicated on new and presently unknown requirements which may arise during the initial contract period or subsequent thereto.

3.1.1. The *Installment/Purchase Method* means the acquisition and full use and benefit of the equipment for sixty (60) months in exchange for payment by the User to Bidder of a sum certain in sixty (60) monthly payments; and, upon the expiration of said period of time, all rights, title, and interest in the equipment shall be automatically vested in the User.

3.1.2 The *Lease with Option to Purchase Method* means the acquisition and full use and benefit of the equipment for a certain period of time in exchange for payment by the User to Bidder of a sum certain in equal monthly payments. At any time during said lease period the User may elect to obtain all rights, title, and interest in the equipment in exchange for a sum certain.

Bidder Qualification. Unless the matter is effectively handled through a preliminary qualification procedure (e.g., a proposed bidder's questionnaire), the RFP should outline the corporate, financial, or other qualifications required for a vendor to participate in the bid process. Depending upon the type of equipment being acquired and the user's specific needs, these qualification standards may cover such areas as the following:

- *Financial standing.* Minimum financial requirements, such as asset size, net worth, earnings, or the posting of a deposit or performance bond.
- *Prior performance.* Satisfactory completion of a specified minimum number of similar equipment installations at other user sites (or certain categories of user sites).
- *Line of business or method.* Ability to meet the user's desired acquisition or delivery method, often coupled with a demonstration of past performance (for example, a vendor that does not lease its equipment should not be permitted to participate unless it can be responsive to the user's desired acquisition method, either alone or in permitted participation with a leasing firm).
- *Governmental regulations.* Compliance with applicable governmental bidding requirements, such as those relating to disclosure of ownership interests, qualification to do business within a state, and local firm preference.
- *Location.* Ability to meet any user-imposed locational requirements, such as those relating to the site of the vendor's distribution or service centers.
- *Substantive responsiveness.* Ability to meet any minimum substantive prerequisites imposed by the RFP, such as processing power, delivery deadlines, or technical support.

Some users prefer not to include items of substantive responsiveness in the bidder qualification portion of the RFP. These users assert that a bidder's ability to meet any substantive requirements of the RFP should be outlined in, and judged upon, the specifications section of the document. Thus, under this approach, any bidder capable of meeting the nonsubstantive prerequisites should be permitted to submit a proposal, which will then be judged by the user as to its relative responsiveness on the specifications and other substantive matters. This approach is certainly logical and, presumably, any vendor unable to submit a competitive proposal would elect not to do so. Nevertheless, other users assert that neither the user nor the vendor is served by permitting the submission of proposals that do not even meet minimum substantive requirements. This position is also logical, particularly as it strives to eliminate obviously unacceptable proposals. In reality, the distinction among approaches probably has little practical importance due to the fact that few vendors will go to the time and trouble to submit an unresponsive proposal. Regardless of which approach is used, the key goal should be to ensure that any substantive prerequisites are clearly stated, either in the bidder qualification section or in the specifications section of the RFP. This emphasis on minimum substantive standards dissuades unresponsive submissions and, more importantly, reinforces the user's efforts at formalizing its control of the RFP process.

Acquisition Schedule. The RFP should also include a schedule outlining key dates in the acquisition process. While the user's needs will again dictate the precise format followed for the schedule, sufficient detail should be included to preclude any vendor from claiming that it did not understand a particular deadline or submission date. The schedule can also be utilized to reinforce the user's control of the acquisition process and to employ offensive negotiating tactics. In this regard, the entire acquisition schedule can and should serve many of the same purposes as an agenda for a specific bargaining session. (See Chapter 3.)

The following schedule offers one example:

SCHEDULE OF EVENTS

August 7, 1981	Release Specifications.
August 14, 1981	Bidders Conference (9:30 A.M.), [Location Omitted].
August 14, 1981	Last day for written inquiries as specified in Paragraph 3.2.
August 14, 1981	Last day for bidders' first recommended changes to Attachments A thru D, as specified in Section III.

September 4, 1981	Last day for bidders' final recommended changes to Attachments A thru D, as specified in Section III.
September 25, 1981	Proposals due and closing date and time for objections to the RFP in accordance with Paragraph 8.14. (1:00 P.M.), [Location Omitted].
September 25, 1981	Proposal and Cost Opening (1:30 P.M.). The proposal and cost opening shown above will be a public proposal and cost opening at [Location Omitted].
October 2, 1981	Begin evaluating bidder proposals.
November 6, 1981	Announce Apparent Qualified Bidders.
November 12, 1981	Closing date for objections to selection of Qualified Bidders in accordance with Paragraph 8.14.
November 16, 1981	Start Benchmark of apparent low qualified bidder(s).
November 24, 1981	Notify bidders of Evaluation Committee recommendations.
November 30, 1981	Closing date for objections to Evaluation Committee recommendations in accordance with Paragraph 8.14.
December 18, 1981	Recommendation to Board of Directors.
March 18, 1982	Site preparation complete (Facilities Readiness Date).
March 31, 1982	Delivery Date.
April 14, 1982	Conversion Complete.
April 21, 1982	Installation Date; Begin Acceptance Testing.
May 21, 1982	Complete Acceptance Testing (refer to Section 28 of Contract).

Confidentiality. Unless the user has some overriding reason not to do so, the RFP should include a strong confidentiality provision. Many users omit such a requirement because they fail to see any pressing need for confidentiality and they believe that vendors may be offended by the language involved. In the first instance, the need for confidentiality may not become apparent until after the RFP has been released. Consequently, rather than risk embarrassing subsequent disclosure the user should include the confidentiality restriction at the outset. The issue of vendor concern about such a provision is really beside the point. Any vendor interested in gaining the user's business will be willing to live with such a provision, particularly if it contains reasonable exceptions or a prior approval process (which, for example, can be used to release information to any other participating parties or subcontractors). The following example utilizes this approach:

42. *Confidentiality.* This RFP and any and all information supplied by User or obtained by Bidder in connection with the preparation and submission of any proposal hereunder is confidential and proprietary to the User and shall not be disclosed or used by the Bidder except as permitted in this Paragraph 42. In the event Bidder is required to release this RFP or any of the information referred to hereinabove to any third party for the purpose of preparing or submitting any proposal hereunder, Bidder shall first seek from such party its written consent to be bound by the provisions of this Paragraph 42. No other disclosure or use of this RFP or such information shall be made without the prior written consent of the User.

The provisions of this Paragraph 42 shall not apply to any portion of this RFP or the information referred to above that is released to the public by the user or that the Bidder can reasonably demonstrate that it obtained from public sources.

Contract Attachments. As outlined in the Alternative Approaches section, above, some users include mandatory or "model" contracts in, or as attachments to, the RFP. When this approach is utilized, the general documentation section of the RFP may be employed to describe the documents and outline the methods, if any, that may be used by the bidders to propose changes or objections to the model agreements. Some users prefer to place this information in a separate section of the RFP, often headed "Legal Specifications" or "Legal Requirements." The following excerpt outlines one method of including this material in the general information section of the RFP. (As noted in the Alternative Approaches section, a variety of other methods can be employed in presenting legal/contractual issues in the RFP.)

2.0 GENERAL CONTRACTS

Attachments A, B, C, and D are contracts which set forth the terms and conditions required by [the user] unless [the user] accepts bidder proposed changes as hereinafter provided.

2.1 Attachment A is an Installment Purchase Contract containing the terms and conditions to be used for the acquisition of equipment, programming, maintenance, and bidder support of the evaluation configuration. Attachment C is a contract containing the terms and conditions to be used for acquisition of Licensed Software.

2.2 Attachments B and D are contracts that may be used to acquire additional equipment and provide for separate maintenance service. These contracts are defined as follows:

a. Attachment B—Lease with Option to Purchase additional equipment

b. Attachment D—Maintenance Service

2.3 Bidders may submit proposed written changes to Attachments A, B, C, and D which the bidder desires [the user] to consider in accordance with the established schedule contained in Paragraph 3.0. Bidders are required to provide the value of each proposed contract change and a brief explanation as to why the change is requested. Value shall be defined as the cost or savings to [the user], and the advantage to [the user] of the proposed change. Proposed contract changes that do not include specific values and brief explanations as to reason for the change will be subject to rejection. [The user] reserves the right to accept or reject any proposed contract changes.

2.4 All bidders will be notified in writing of all proposed contract changes that are acceptable and all proposed contract changes that are not acceptable to [the user]. Those proposed contract changes that are acceptable to [the user] may be used by any bidder. The use of proposed contract changes that bidders have not been notified by [the user] as being acceptable to [the user], will be grounds for rejecting and disqualifying the bidder's response.

2.5 It is mandatory that Attachment A, B, C, and D be submitted with the bid and signed by the bidder. All Attachments must contain the signature of a corporate official who is authorized to act on behalf of the corporation. [The user], at its option, may award Attachments A and C to different bidders. Attached contracts contain blank spaces with underline to allow the bidder to provide certain specific items. Failure to supply data in all such spaces provided may subject the bid to rejection. Any spaces left blank will be assumed to be zero. The following Attachments contain space for bidder supplied data:

Attachment A:	*Attachment B:*
Paragraph Number 7.a.(2)	Paragraph Number 7.g
Paragraph Number 7.a.(3)	Paragraph Number 9.b
Paragraph Number 7.b	Rider C

Paragraph Number 9.g
Paragraph Number 11.a.(2)
Riders B through G

Attachment C:
Rider B, Pages 1 and 2 if applicable.

Attachment D:
Paragraph Number 7.d.
Rider C.

Inquiries, Oral Responses, and Other Matters. The general documentation provisions of most RFPs should also cover a number of matters relating to vendor/user communications, such as bidder inquiries, the bidders' conference, and the validity (if any) of oral communications between vendor and user representatives. These areas are discussed, and example provisions are outlined, in the previous section of this chapter on Alternative Approaches.

SPECIFICATIONS

Results Versus Resources

Before any technical specifications can be prepared for the RFP, the user must address the basic question of whether it intends to contract for "results" or "resources." As Chapter 4 explains, a user that is contracting for *resources* is generally agreeing to procure specified people, products, or services. Consequently, the acquisition documentation keys on the desired people, products, or services and little, if anything, is said about the results—that is, about whether these resources will actually meet the user's needs. In contrast, a user that is contracting for *results* is generally agreeing to have the vendor provide specified resources that will achieve stated results at the end user or customer level. Thus, the documentation focuses beyond technical specifications to the question of whether the people, products, or services will perform defined user functions.

This distinction in contractual approach becomes critical in the specifications section of the RFP. If the user is contracting for resources, the specifications must be phrased in terms of resources. On the other hand, if the user is contracting for results, the specifications must go beyond the resources involved and describe the specific results required. Where a combination approach is used, of course, the specifications must address both resources and results.

As Chapter 4 suggests, it is generally more difficult to prepare specifications for a *results* procurement than for a *resources* transaction. The reason is simple. In an acquisition of resources, the user's task is essentially limited to assessing and describing the people, products, or services that are desired. But in a results procurement, the user must not only be capable of determining what results are desired; it must also be able to define how those results will be measured and when they will be deemed to be achieved. Because a results procurement essentially states "the user will accept the system when it works," the RFP and the associated contractual documents must define both "system" and "works."

Generic Versus Specific

In most acquisitions, the user must also face the question of whether its RFP specifications should be generic or specific. Both alternatives involve a number of subtle shadings.

In a generic procurement, the user avoids specifying any particular make or model of equipment and, where practicable, software. Instead, the user specifies the processing capabilities required in broad terms that permit diverse vendors to submit proposed systems. In a specific procurement, the user describes the particular hardware and software desired, by make and/or model number, and accepts proposals from any firm able to supply the specified systems.

In reality, of course, many procurements involve the middle ground between these extremes. For example, a user that relies on IBM operating systems may issue specifications for IBM or IBM-compatible equipment. Alternatively, another user may employ the specific approach for a central processor unit and utilize the generic approach for all peripheral hardware. Yet another user may issue a generic RFP for the acquisition as a whole, but include specifics for certain individual components (e.g., an aircraft that must utilize avionics made by a named firm; fleet vehicles that must have tires manufactured by a specific supplier).

The following issues are among those that should be considered by a user in determining whether to employ a generic or a specific procurement process.

Time and Talent. Developing generic specifications ordinarily requires considerably more time and talent than employing specific, vendor-oriented criteria. This additional time is particularly likely to be required where the user has essentially been relying on the incumbent vendor to supply the necessary specifications as part of the vendor's "planning" assistance to the user. (Of course, this "planning" assistance is one of the most effective parts of the vendor's marketing program.) Many users simply lack the time and staff resources to do a proper job of preparing generic specifications.

Competition. With several exceptions, explained below, competition among vendors is generally enhanced by use of a generic RFP. By taking the time and effort necessary to develop general specifications, the user signals participating bidders that it is serious about implementing an open, highly-competitive procurement. Vendors that otherwise might be reluctant to bid are therefore more likely to submit proposals. Moreover, because the generic process offers relatively higher freedom for vendors to submit custom-designed or unusual systems, all vendors are more likely to use design and marketing creativity to optimize their submissions.

As noted above, the general rule that generic procurements heighten competition includes several exceptions. For example, where generic specifications result in too much competition, some vendors may actually be discouraged from submitting proposals. This result usually occurs where the generic RFP spawns a high volume of diverse competitors with little certainty about the equipment or system actually desired by the user. Generic specifications may also lessen competition where the vendors seriously doubt that the user is interested in a generic, open procurement process. When this occurs, the vendors perceive the effort at generic specifications to be little more than a smokescreen to disguise what amounts to a "wired" or sole source acquisition. Competition may also be reduced where the user attempts to employ generic specifications in a procurement that really deserves more specific vendor-oriented criteria. The use of generic specifications when the user really prefers a particular product line or operating system (e.g., IBM), only confuses the issue and invites an overabundance of useless bids. In situations of this kind, the user would generally improve its position by specifying the desired vendor or operating system and then drafting the RFP in a manner that will encourage the submission of proposals by a wide variety of competing *sources*.

Availability. As the preceding paragraph suggests, the user's business or operational needs sometimes limit the equipment capable of doing the job to that furnished by a single vendor or supplier. Where the desired equipment is only available from one or a small number of sources, the use of generic specifications is likely to be a waste of time for the user and vendors alike. However, as suggested above, where multiple sources are available, or where compatible equipment can serve the user's needs, the RFP can still be drafted in a manner that provides the competitive benefits of a generic procurement.

Total Life Cycle Costing

Another significant issue in developing the specifications for any major equipment acquisition is the question of whether the user intends to employ "total life cycle costing" (TLCC).

As a procurement process, TLCC involves assessing competing systems on the basis of the sum total of all direct, indirect, recurring, nonrecurring, and other related costs—including the costs of unreliability—incurred, or estimated to be incurred, in the design, development, production, operation, maintenance, and support of the system over its anticipated useful life span to the user. Put more simply, TLCC involves evaluation on the basis of all known or reasonably estimated costs over the full useful life of the equipment, rather than comparison on the basis of acquisition cost (and, in some situations, basic maintenance costs).

For most users, TLCC is a radically different procurement procedure. TLCC is a complex, difficult undertaking that requires considerable time and effort from the user. Because of the resources required to implement the TLCC approach, it is not practicable for all users or for all acquisitions. However, where it can be applied effectively, TLCC may cause the user to reach acquisition decisions totally different from those that would be agreed upon under more traditional acquisition/maintenance cost evaluation techniques. The basic principles involved in the TLCC approach are outlined below.

Usefulness. TLCC is most likely to be a justifiable evaluation tool in procurements having some combination of the following elements: (a) equipment involving major interrelated systems; (b) equipment having high on-going or operating costs, such as maintenance, fuel, or staff support; (c) equipment having high down-time or inadequate performance costs, such as manual back-up lost production, or customer liability.

TLCC can also provide benefits beyond the evaluation process. For example, because it accents the trade-offs among reliability, performance, and acquisition costs, TLCC can be a helpful system design tool. In addition, TLCC can improve on-going system management and budgeting procedures, providing a better understanding of the costs involved after the acquisition date. Finally, TLCC can help user management reach more informed decisions concerning the levels of cost and reliability that are desired.

Scope. For many years, the federal government considered "life cycle costs" (LCC) under a major procurement process known as "A-109." The A-109 approach required that federal agencies review both direct and indirect acquisition and ownership costs in reaching an evaluation decision. Thus, an LCC assessment included such indirect equipment costs as installation, training, and conversion, as well as more traditional direct acquisition costs. The LCC methodology also considered these factors for all major components involved in the procurement, not merely for one or two principal items.

The TLCC concept encompasses the LCC analysis of A-109, but goes further to include a detailed assessment of reliability and performance costs. TLCC considers more than out-of-pocket costs paid by the user to various contractors. TLCC also assesses the hard and soft costs incurred by the user as a result of reliability and performance problems. Thus, while A-109's LCC approach expands the user's evaluation process to include direct and indirect operating expenses as well as initial acquisition costs, the TLCC procedure broadens the user's horizon further by adding a wide range of "user impact costs."

Reliability. The techniques required to determine and measure the user costs of poor equipment reliability vary considerably from acquisition to acquisition, depending upon such factors as the type of equipment, acquisition method, and useful life involved. However, the following factors are generally among those that should be considered.

On-going payment, depreciation, and maintenance costs. Virtually all equipment involves some on-going expense associated with the rental, lease, or depreciation of the components. In most instances, maintenance costs will also be involved. If the system fails to perform acceptably, and these costs continue without abatement, the user suffers from direct operating costs without any offsetting productive benefit.

On-going staff and overhead costs. Similarly, most equipment has certain direct and indirect staff costs associated with its normal operation. Other overhead is also involved, such as building facilities, air conditioning, basing, and general administrative costs. In most instances, these expenses continue regardless of whether the equipment is operating at the desired level of reliability. In many situations, these costs encompass user departments in addition to the unit responsible for operating the equipment.

Costs of unavailable services. Whenever normally productive equipment becomes unavailable because of reliability or performance problems, the user suffers some loss of productivity or capacity. The relative cost and seriousness of this loss obviously varies from industry to industry and from acquisition to acquisition. For example, in the banking industry, the nonavailability of computer hardware may preclude the processing of customer checks, which may in turn cause the bank to miss its "midnight deadline" or cash letter delivery deadline, with resultant losses of hundreds of thousands of dollars.

"Covering" costs. When critical equipment is not available, many users find it necessary to "cover" by temporarily or permanently procuring alternative or backup equipment. (Indeed, as explained in Chapter 6, "covering" in the event of equipment failure is one method of pursuing user remedies under general contract law, and may even be necessary to ensure that the user takes the steps required to mitigate its damages.) In some instances, the user may "cover" by renting temporary equipment. In other situations, the user may replace the lost capacity by retaining an outside service company to provide the equipment and perform the tasks. Where high reliability is critical and/or serious problems are anticipated, the user may go one step further and procure backup equipment to produce on- or off-site redundancy. Regardless of the method employed by the user, the equipment utilized to "cover" must generally be capable of sustaining the user operations otherwise served by the problem equipment and providing enough extra capacity to permit the user to catch up for any period during which production ceased (or occurred at reduced levels). The equipment and personnel capacity required for these catch-up operations can often be significant, particularly if the user is unable to arrange covering equipment soon after the deficiency or other problem arises.

Recovery and reconstruction costs. Depending upon the industry involved, equipment reliability may also create data and information recovery problems. Where data processing or other programmable equipment is being evaluated, the user should consider the potential costs associated with recovery or manual reconstruction of data files, source programs, and customer records. Where recovery or reconstruction costs are particularly high, the user may choose to reduce them by employing dual backup or some form of "running parallel." However, while these approaches may reduce recovery and reconstruction costs, they are likely to involve significant costs of their own that should be considered in the TLCC evaluation process.

Diagnosis costs. Even where the equipment is covered by maintenance, reliability problems create diagnosis costs for most users. Few users can face continued reliability problems without assigning their own staff personnel to the diagnosis and correction effort.

Explanation costs. Reliability weaknesses have a remarkable ability to surface in the executive suite. Even where the problems are dealt with effectively and efficiently at the operating level, senior management often becomes involved. (Indeed, in some instances the problems may be so severe that senior management becomes a vocal participant at a very early and most inconvenient date.) In addition to creating potential "career costs" for the operating managers responsible for the reliability problems, the involvement of senior management generally spawns an amazing volume of meetings, memoranda, and explanations at all levels.

Integrity costs. Equipment that suffers from continuing reliability problems often creates a wide cross section of what the authors call "integrity costs"—expenses that result from the fact that no one is willing to place a high level of trust in the equipment involved. Of all the TLCC factors, integrity costs are perhaps the most difficult to isolate and quantify. Yet, they are as real and ever present as ongoing maintenance expenses. Consider, for example, the manager who informally maintains her own manual set of records because she consistently finds her communications down when she needs information most. Or consider the purchasing officer who always maintains an extra inventory of critical forms because the company's printers tend to malfunction on key jobs, requiring reruns at the last minute. Finally, consider the customer who generally tries not to use a particular company's products or services—unless absolutely necessary—because of the annoyances caused by equipment failures and delays.

Implementation. As the preceding discussion suggests, employing TLCC is a complex and difficult task. At the RFP stage of the acquisition process, the TLCC approach requires that the user execute a number of steps designed to provide comprehensive information about all costs that are, or at least should be, relevant in the procurement evaluation process. These steps frequently provide the user with more information about its own internal operations than it ever dreamed was possible—or necessary. Although no magic formula exists for the steps that should be employed for this purpose, in most instances, the user should pursue the following areas:

- Assess proposed system design to predict system reliability and availability.
- Identify reliability problem areas.
- Identify ongoing costs in other areas.
- Test the impact of any practicable system design changes on reliability and other ongoing costs.
- Study degraded operating modes and quantify impact on the user (and its customers).
- Study equipment failure possibilities and quantify impact on the user (and its customers).
- List all relevant TLCC costs derived from the above analysis.
- Convert TLCC costs to RFP specifications, employing liquidated bid adjustments to the extent desired.
- Develop the TLCC evaluation matrix to be used in analyzing vendor responses to the RFP.

BENCHMARK TESTS

For many types of equipment, benchmark tests offer an interesting evaluation opportunity. Unfortunately, many users do a poor job of implementing benchmark standards or otherwise fail to draft benchmark provisions that adequately protect the user's interest. Although an extensive discussion of the technical aspects of benchmark tests is beyond the scope of this book, several factors deserve mention in the context of this volume.

For purposes of this section, a benchmark test is any performance or operational demonstration of the equipment (or of comparable equipment) that is made and documented prior to contract signing (or, at least, acceptance) and is repeated on the equipment after contract signing as part of the installation and acceptance test procedures. The purpose of the test is to verify that the equipment being acquired will, once installed, perform in accordance with the actual operating specifications demonstrated in the initial test. In some instances, the first test may be run solely for purposes of providing a record (or "benchmark") of the normal and expected performance of a proven system. In other circumstances, the initial test may itself be designed to prove the operating capabilities of a custom of newly developed system.

Some vendors create their own definition of a "benchmark test" that replaces the dual test procedure outlined above with a single demonstration. Thus, vendor salesmen tell users, "Don't worry about that question, we'll benchmark it." In these instances, the salesman means that the vendor will test the application in question on comparable equipment already installed elsewhere, or on the equipment actually being acquired, but not both. In effect, the "benchmark test" in this context is merely a single demonstration of equipment performance in which the system must pass certain stated minimum criteria to be acceptable to the user. In effect, these stated criteria form a condition precedent that must be met for the user to proceed with the acquisition.

This type of demonstration is a perfectly acceptable sales practice that may provide meaningful benefits to the user. However, it does not involve a true benchmark test where the standard or benchmark is created in one test and compliance with the standard is verified in another, separate test. From a practical standpoint, semantics in this area are less important than the specific tests or demonstrations desired by the user in a particular acquisition. In some acquisitions, a two-stage true benchmark may be the only viable alternative. In other transactions, a single performance demonstration as part of the acceptance test may be adequate.

This section focuses upon the true, two-stage benchmark test, although many of the comments have some applicability to the single demonstration approach noted above. For additional information concerning equipment demonstrations, reference should be made to the discussion of acceptance provisions in Chapter 8.

Comparability

For a benchmark test to have value for the user, both demonstrations must be conducted on the same equipment, or on equipment that is comparable in all material respects. One of the best approaches is for the preinstallation test and the postinstallation test to be conducted on the same equipment—that being acquired by the user. Often, this procedure can be implemented by having the initial test performed at the vendor's factory on the actual equipment being designated for delivery to the user. The second test is then performed at the user's site, following installation.

In many circumstances, this approach is not possible (e.g., the specific equipment being ordered has not yet been produced or cannot practicably be assembled and made ready for testing at the distant site). In such situations, the initial test is generally performed on equipment that is said to be comparable to the equipment being acquired by the user. Where this approach is employed, the comparability of the equipment is absolutely essential. If the initial test is performed on equipment that varies in any material operating detail from that being acquired by the user, either the user or the vendor or both will experience an unnecessary and potentially costly surprise when the test is rerun on the equipment installed at the user's site.

Comparability problems frequently arise where the equipment involved is available with a large number of components or options (e.g., disk drives, tapes, accessories) that may vary from one user to another. Where this diversity exists, the user or vendor site selected for the initial test may have different components or options than the equipment being acquired by the user. Indeed, it may be difficult or impossible to locate an initial test site that has the same equipment configuration as that ordered by the user. Where such differences exist, the user should devote particular care toward understanding and documenting the operational aspects of the alternative systems. Vendor sales representatives are notorious for minimizing any such differences, principally because of their desire to "get the user signed up." These marketeers rationalize—all too correctly in many instances—that if problems do arise at acceptance the user will be too committed by that time to back out of the transaction.

Design

Many benchmark tests also suffer from inadequate design. As the above discussion of comparability suggests, a benchmark test is only as valuable as the information that it provides to the user. If the test does little more than demonstrate a few clever bells and whistles, it may provide far more value to the vendor's marketing plan than to the user's program of quality control.

The best protection in this area is very simple: never permit the vendor to design the specifications for a benchmark test. Although the vendor's personnel may need to participate in some aspects of the design process, the benchmark test should be devised by the user to meet and prove its own requirements. Unfortunately, most vendor-designed demonstrations and benchmark tests are seriously biased to favor the equipment's best attributes and to minimize or avoid its weaker areas. Users that fail to appreciate this fact, often because of their warm relationship with the vendor, are simply ignoring reality.

Generalizing about the proper design of benchmark tests is difficult, at best, as each test must be tailored to the specific equipment, user, and transaction involved. Perhaps the one key element for success in the design of benchmarks is adequate participation by all necessary members of the user's staff. As in the case of acceptance tests, the best benchmark tests are designed as a cooperative, creative effort by a cross section of technical, financial, legal, and management representatives. Although the technical details of the benchmark must obviously be left to the user's operations specialists, the general design and logic of the test can and should be considered and critiqued by all members of the user's interdisciplinary negotiating team or an alternative group having similar breadth and experience.

Contractual Connection. Once the benchmark test is designed, it must be legally connected to the contract. Interestingly, some users fail to appreciate that merely placing the benchmark test into the agreement may not provide any real protection or benefit to the user. One of the more classic examples of this fact was demonstrated in a contract executed by a multinational communications firm. The agreement contained a reasonably good test, but failed to state what would happen if the equipment failed to pass the test. Indeed, the contract did not even contain an affirmative obligation by the vendor to perform the test. At the same time, the agreement carefully provided that the user would have to pay for the equipment 30 days after delivery by the vendor to the carrier. The moral of the story is simple: For a benchmark test, acceptance test, or any other condition to be an operative, binding part of the vendor/user agreement, it must be made effective by appropriate contractual language. Plugging the test on as "Addendum A" to the agreement may not be enough. In most acquisitions, the vendor/user agreement should specifically cover such basic matters as the following:

- Detailed description and explanation of the test.
- Responsibilities and duties of each party, including an affirmative obligation by the vendor to conduct, or cooperate in, the benchmark.
- Actions to be taken, and remedies to be available, in the event the equipment fails to pass the full benchmark satisfactorily.

BID FORMAT

The two most important rules concerning the format of vendor bids are very simple. First, whatever the format desired, it should be clearly specified in the RFP released by the user. Second, although many alternatives are possible, the format selected by the user should optimize its ability to understand and compare competing vendor proposals. These points are explored further below.

Mandatory Format

One of the most basic errors that a user can make in any complex procurement is permitting vendors to determine the format of their own proposals. Failing to mandate bid format weakens the user's psychological position by evidencing its inexperience and by reducing its control over the acquisition process. In addition, permitting vendors to select their own format often causes the proposals to be more valuable as marketing aids for the vendor than as analytical tools for the user. Even where the proposals are not filled with marketing puffery, few bids will be submitted in the same format, thereby heightening the likelihood of omission and essentially precluding "apples to apples" comparisons by the user.

Mandatory bid format need not preclude the submission of supplemental information as part of a vendor's proposal. Thus, the RFP can specify the precise bid format that must be followed, while at the same time permitting a vendor to supply additional material. When this approach is followed, the user's position is generally enhanced if the RFP indicates where and how such supplemental information may be included. At a minimum, all supplemental materials should be made a part of the vendor's proposal which, in turn, will be incorporated by reference into the vendor/user contract.

For the mandatory bid format requirement to be meaningful, the RFP should clearly indicate that vendor proposals failing to meet the minimum standards will be deemed to be nonresponsive and returned to the submitting vendor. In order to preclude inadvertent noncompliance from disqualifying a particularly competitive proposal, some users provide various methods of curing the deficiency. One popular method permits the user to return such bids for correction and resubmission within a strict time limit. Although minor deficiencies can be waived by the user—and most RFPs include a provision identifying that user right—the user's negotiating position is generally enhanced by returning the bid for correction. Although the return process requires time, it evidences the user's intention to enforce its RFP requirements strictly. Moreover, the procedure reduces the user's tendency to ignore the deficiency and attempt to evaluate the bid anyway—an approach that often leads to biased judgments and, ironically, plays directly into the hands of vendor marketeers who purposefully submit proposals with minor format deviations that enhance the vendor's position.

Format Requirements

The mandatory format requirements included in the RFP should require submission by the vendor of all information necessary for the user to make an informed decision. Obviously, the data and materials required will change from procurement to procurement, depending upon a variety of factors including the type of equipment, acquisition method, and specific purposes involved. As the section on Alternative Approaches, above, suggests, the format of vendor proposals will also depend in part upon the RFP approach adopted by the user (e.g., whether the RFP includes a model contract or requires split submission of technical and financial proposals).

General Organization. One state agency employed the following approach in specifying the general layout and organization of vendor proposals. (References to specific paragraphs of the RFP have been omitted.)

Bid Format

VOLUME I—GENERAL INFORMATION

1) Executive Summary.

2) Supplemental Bid Sheets.

3) Exceptions from Supplemental Bid Sheets.

4) Performance Bond.

5) Addenda Acknowledgement Forms.

VOLUME II—TECHNICAL INFORMATION

1) Bidder commitment to Prime Contractor requirement.

2) Customer list.

3) Tables A and B.

4) Training program.

5) Delivery schedule.

6) Installation and delivery.

7) Environmental and site requirements, including Table D.

8) Responses to all other paragraphs in Section V not listed above.

9) Descriptive literature.

10) Conversion plan.

VOLUME III—BENCHMARK INFORMATION

Responses to each paragraph in Section VI

VOLUME IV—CONTRACTS

1) Signed Installment Purchase Contract.

2) Signed Lease with Option to Purchase Contract.

3) Signed Licensed Software Contract.

4) Signed Maintenance Contract.

The same state agency RFP included comments concerning the physical preparation of the bid package, and the submission of optional materials, as follows:

Each volume shall include a contents page plus a tab index to precede each section within a volume. Multiple volumes are acceptable provided each is properly identified. There is no intent to limit or restrict a bidder from including additional information, however, it should be placed in the back of the appropriate volume and be identified. Bid organization and format specified above will provide for ease of evaluation and continuity of each bid. Bidder's responses should be preceded by quoting the paragraph reference and the specific requirements from the RFP.

* * *

Each bid shall be prepared simply and economically, providing a straightforward, concise delineation of bidder's capabilities to satisfy the requirements of this RFP.

Fancy bindings, colored displays, and promotional materials are not desired. However, technical literature and photographs of bid equipment may be included in the bid. Emphasis in each bid shall be on completeness and clarity of content.

Supplemental submissions. As suggested earlier in this chapter, the RFP format standards should also prohibit oral discussions and govern supplemental submissions or amendments. Although oral representations can generally be restricted with a simple provision, as noted above in this chapter, amendments and supplemental materials are somewhat more difficult. At the outset, the user must determine whether vendors will be permitted to submit amendments, corrections, or supplemental information after the bid deadline and, if so, what submission procedures will be utilized. In addition, the user must reach similar decisions with respect to any amendments or supplements to the RFP that the user may issue before bids are submitted (or, in rare events, after the bid deadline).

The following provision offers an example of one approach in this area:

Amendments to RFP.

The User reserves the right to issue addenda, supplements, and amendments to this RFP at any time before executing the contract with the successful Bidder. The User will mail copies of any such materials to each Bidder's last known address by certified mail, return receipt requested, and will also attempt to orally notify the local marketing representative of each Bidder. All such materials will be issued in writing. Each Bidder must acknowledge receipt of such materials by returning the Amendment Acknowledgment Form that will be enclosed. Each Proposal must also include an acknowledgment of the Bidder's receipt of this RFP and all addenda, supplements, and amendments on Exhibit F. Each addendum, supplement, or amendment shall specify the time by which, and the manner in which, the Bidder must respond to the change. In the event the change is unacceptable to the Bidder, it may withdraw its Proposal by submitting written notice to the User by the indicated deadline.

Amendments to Proposal.

The user will accept addenda, supplements, and amendments to a Bidder's Proposal that are submitted in response to, and in accordance with the requirements of, any RFP change issued by the User pursuant to the above procedures. The User may also elect, but shall not be required, to accept other addenda, supplements, or amendments to a Proposal that are submitted by a Bidder on an unsolicited basis. All addenda, supplements, and amendments (whether solicited or unsolicited) submitted by a Bidder: (i) shall include the cover page specified at Exhibit M; (ii) shall be executed on behalf of the Bidder by a representative who is authorized to contractually bind the Bidder; and (iii) shall become a part of and incorporated into the Bidder's Proposal and any resulting contract with the User. In the event any unsolicited addendum, supplement, or amendment to a Bidder's Proposal is rejected by the User, the Bidder shall have the right to withdraw its Proposal by providing written notice to the User within the earlier of (i) ten (10) days after the User provides notice of its rejection to the Bidder; or (ii) the date the User executes the contract with the successful Bidder.

"No Bid" Responses. Any comprehensive discussion of bid formats must include a comment concerning "no bid" situations. In order to preclude misunderstandings and allegations of lost documents, the RFP packages should either be delivered by registered or certified mail, return receipt requested, or delivered in person through a procedure that includes documented receipts. Where the latter approach is employed, some users require all vendors to pick up and sign for the RFP packages at the user's offices or at a preliminary bidders' meeting. In addition to providing ready verification that the bidders have received the RFPs (which may be quite important where short bid submission deadlines are involved), this procedure subtly reinforces the user's apparent control in the acquisition process.

Assuming that a vendor receives an RFP but does not elect to submit a proposal, a standard procedure should be provided for the vendor to submit a formal "no bid" response. Some users include a special form for this purpose, facilitating a timely reply from vendors electing not to participate in the procurement competition. Other users expand this approach somewhat and include a master RFP acknowledgment sheet. This form can be used by a vendor to indicate whether or not it intends to submit a bid, on all or any permissible part of the RFP. By soliciting a bid or no bid response from each vendor, this form adds additional assurance that all RFP packages have been accounted for, and facilitates the user's efforts to assess which vendors can be expected to submit bids.

Schedules and Exhibits. To facilitate "apples to apples" comparisons, and further the user's control over the acquisition process, the RFP should require vendor proposals to utilize standard schedules and tables, designed by the user, wherever possible. Standard tables can often be the single most important factor in obtaining competitive proposals that can be analyzed fairly, quickly, and equally.

Although many users employ mandatory schedules in such basic areas as equipment lists and prices, most fail to exploit the advantages that standard tables offer in other areas. Assuming that the user's staff has an appropriate level of creativity, schedules and tables can be designed for most technical and financial data, including installation and other one-time charges (discussed above in this chapter), performance standards, and maintenance costs. In addition, schedules can also be designed to facilitate review of substantive matters in other areas. For example, some users include a legal or contractual schedule that requires each vendor to outline its responses to each provision in the user's proposed model contract. The following format offers one example of such a schedule (entries are omitted):

PROVISION IN USER CONTRACT	VENDOR RESPONSE (COMPLETE 1 COLUMN ONLY)		
	ACCEPTED	REJECTED	MODIFIED
(Insert summary of or excerpted Provision)	(Insert "X" if applicable)	(Insert "X" if applicable)	(Insert exact modified language *and* explanation)

Some users employ a similar schedule, but add a further column in which the vendor must explain its rationale for any proposed modification or outright rejection. Other alternative schedules can also be used to achieve similar goals.

Although the user can seldom control the precise format in the same manner available for tables and schedules, standard exhibit requirements can also facilitate comparative analysis and user control of the acquisition process. At a minimum, the RFP should specify the exhibits required to be submitted.

Where practicable, the RFP should also detail the order of various documents within the exhibits. For example, if a vendor is required or permitted to submit printed product brochures or specification sheets in a particular exhibit, the RFP should indicate the order in which the material should be submitted, and specify any index or explanatory information that may be desired.

Bidding and Page Numbering. Few things are more annoying than receiving complex bids that are substantively comparable but impossible to use from a practical standpoint. Consequently, the RFP should specify not only the substance but also the physical preparation of vendor proposals. The two most basic points in this area involve binding and page numbering.

Page numbering is the easier of the two. If the vendor proposal is to be discussed by any two or more representatives of the vendor or the user, it must have some reasonable page numbering system. Remarkably, many proposals do not. The authors prefer a sequential numbering system that runs from the outside cover through the last page of the last exhibit. Others accept a numbering system that runs section-by-section or volume-by-volume. While the latter approach facilitates vendor preparation of proposals, it can be confusing and result in complex page references. The advantage of this system can be meshed with the advantages of the full sequential numbering approach by using an automatic numbering stamp to overprint the entire Proposal from cover to cover. This provision is similar to that used by the Securities and Exchange Commission for documents filed with it: the materials can have any printed page numbering system as long as one copy is overstamped with sequential numbers from front to back, including the exhibits.

Binding requirements are somewhat more controversial. Most vendors have their own proposal submission binders and materials; conversely, most users have their own preferences concerning the physical presentation style that is most convenient. The authors generally prefer 3-hole punched materials, inserted in ring binders. This type of presentation facilitates the insertion of additional information, as well as the temporary removal of materials for copying. It also permits the inclusion of a variety of different brochures, schedules, and typewritten pages. Presentations of this nature are ordinarily far more convenient than permanently bound materials (e.g., continuous plastic rings or forged plastic strips) or pages temporarily clamped with plastic along one side. The uniformity of the binder size itself makes storage and analysis of the proposals somewhat easier. (After the RFP process is completed, relevant materials can be removed from the binders and filed or microfilmed.) Where the size of the proposal does not warrant insertion in a 3-ring binder, the authors generally prefer that the materials be held by a single staple in the upper left corner—a simple "binding" perhaps, but one that is adequate and convenient.

Regardless of the presentation style preferred by the user, the important point is that the user's preference should be clearly indicated in the RFP. Specifying the binding technique will reduce user frustrations, facilitate storage and analysis of the proposals, and serve as further evidence of the user's control over the acquisition process.

BID EVALUATION AND SELECTION

As in other areas of the acquisition process, no single method of evaluating competitive bids is necessarily best. Rather, the evaluation procedures following by the user will ordinarily vary, depending upon such factors as the type of equipment, the acquisition method, the size of the transaction, and the specific needs of the user. Despite this diversity of approaches, the user will be best served by clearly outlining its evaluation methodology in advance. Whatever selection procedures are employed, they should be organized and understood at the outset, before the RFP is designed and issued. Because this approach permits the user to mesh the RFP with the evaluation standards, it reduces the gaps and oversights that may otherwise occur. In addition, by further tightening the user's apparent and actual control over the acquisition process, the procedure increases the user's negotiating leverage.

The following pages outline a number of factors that should be considered by a user in designing the evaluation and selection phase of an acquisition. Although most of the factors noted will be relevant in virtually any acquisition, they should be tailored to meet the specific needs of each transaction.

Published Evaluation Standards

Perhaps the first evaluation factor that should be considered is whether the evaluation standards employed by the user should be published as part of the RFP or other information supplied by the user. Government users must of course comply with applicable procurement procedures. Private users normally have more flexibility.

Publication of the proposed evaluation standards can be beneficial for the user. For example, publication tends to increase the general level of competition by emphasizing the user aspiration level that must be met by a competing vendor. Publication also spotlights the issues deemed relevant by the user, making it more likely that vendors will strive to satisfy those objectives. In addition, publication reinforces the user's control of the acquisition process, as noted above, adding to the user's psychological negotiating leverage. When the evaluation standards are published, users also tend to devote additional care to the specifics involved. As a result, the standards are often more detailed and clear than when no public articulation is made.

Despite these advantages, publication of the evaluation standards also involves certain negative factors. First, publication generally eliminates or reduces the user's flexibility; that is, the user's ability to utilize unstated subjective factors in evaluating completed proposals. Second, because the published standards may inadvertently be incomplete or otherwise defective, publication may permit one or more vendors to utilize the deficiency to its advantage (e.g., by claiming that the user must judge the bids on the basis of the published, deficient standard rather than on the basis of the correct factor). Third, by formalizing the evaluation process, publication increases the likelihood that disgruntled vendors will file bid protests or other complaints about the procurement process. Finally, because publication may focus on the evaluation standards deemed most relevant by the user, the process makes it easier for vendors to slant their proposals toward the user's "hot buttons." (See Chapter 2). In effect, while publication of the evaluation standards may be beneficial to the user by permitting vendors to appreciate the points considered important by the user, the availability of this information can increase the effectiveness of vendor marketing ploys.

On balance, the authors recommend the publication of limited evaluation standards at least in larger transactions. This compromise approach optimizes the benefits available from publication, and minimizes the disadvantages. Thus, the user enjoys increased vendor competition, highlighting of broad acquisition objectives, reinforced control, and the incentive to draft detailed standards. On the other hand, by publishing only limited standards, the user retains meaningful flexibility and minimizes the effectiveness of vendor complaints and marketing ploys.

To implement the limited publication approach, the user focuses on the broad evaluation factors that will be employed. These are carefully defined and published either as part of the RFP or as a separate document. The more detailed evaluation factors, and the specific criteria on which the user's decisions will be based, are left unpublished.

As this overview suggests, users have considerable flexibility in determining the evaluation factors that should be published. Some users prefer to limit the published information to a broad list of relevant criteria, such as price, performance, maintenance, delivery and installation dates, and legal considerations. Other users extend this approach somewhat, by adding additional detail or subcategories within each factor. Still other users employ a more comprehensive approach, providing a textual description of each evaluation factor which discusses certain of the quantitative or qualitative measures deemed relevant by the user. In each case, however, the published information stops short of explaining the precise standards that will be utilized to grade each proposal. By adopting this approach, the user is able to encourage voluntary vendor commitments that go beyond the unpublished minimum standards that the user may have accepted internally.

Of course, where the RFP employs liquidated bid adjustments, as outlined in the Alternative Approaches section, above, the published evaluation standards must take these adjustments into account. Although liquidated bid adjustments limit the user's flexibility in the areas covered by the adjustments, they need not restrict the user's decision making in other relevant areas for which detailed evaluation standards are not published.

Regardless of whether the user adopts the limited publication procedure, the RFP should include certain minimum information concerning the evaluation process. Among the matters that should be specified are the following.

Evaluation Group. With rare exceptions, the RFP should indicate what user individuals, group, or committee will make the evaluation decision. Although this information may lead to informal lobbying (which can be specifically prohibited by the RFP), it adds formality to the user's appraisal process and offers reasonable fairness to competing vendors.

Responsiveness of Bids. The RFP should indicate the minimum standards that must be met for a vendor proposal to be considered by the user, and how "nonresponsive" bids will be treated by the user. Generally, the user should retain the right to waive minor (or other, if desired) irregularities and deficiencies in submitted proposals.

Final Decisions. The RFP should indicate that the final decision in the procurement will be made by the user, in its sole discretion, based upon its evaluation of all factors deemed relevant by it (including factors not specified in the RFP or other published evaluation standards). Despite any evaluation factors that may be published as a courtesy to competing vendors, the user should retain control of the decision making process. Of course, governmental users may be forced to temper this control to the extent required by applicable procurement regulations.

Partial Acceptance. If the user desires to have the right to split its contract award among various competitors, that fact should be noted in the RFP.

Rejection of All Bids. Unless the approach is clearly rejected by the user as unacceptable, the RFP should reserve the right for the user to reject all bids and/or to withdraw the RFP in its entirety. Some users prefer to expand this reservation by indicating that, in such an event, the user may elect to negotiate or contract with any competing vendor or any other party, in the user's sole discretion.

One government agency employed the following provisions to cover a number of the areas discussed above, The same RFP also contained extensive additional information detailing how the agency would evaluate various one-time costs, price/performance factors, and similar items.

SECTION IV

EVALUATION

4.0 BID EVALUATION

All bids will be evaluated by an evaluation committee composed of members from the Department of General Services (EDP Division), State University System, and the Department of Highway Safety and Motor Vehicles. Bids which do not meet the mandatory requirements of this RFP shall be rejected. Bids meeting the mandatory requirements shall be further evaluated on total overall costs for 60 months. The term "overall costs," as used in this sub-paragraph shall be interpreted to include, but not be limited to, such cost elements as installment purchase, maintenance, installation, transportation, training, site preparation, and any other one-time costs for 60 months.

4.1 *ESSENTIAL ITEMS*

4.1.1 Equipment bid shall be equal to or greater than that shown in Section V, Exhibit 1.

4.1.2 The Evaluation Committee will evaluate the technical content of a bid to determine the technical acceptability of the bid based on hardware capability, reliability, modularity, expandability, and software compatibility with existing application system and programs. The evaluation committee will also review the bidder's final submitted contract to ensure that it is responsive to the State's need and complies with the Terms and Conditions set forth in the contracts attached hereto and those specified within the RFP.

4.2 *TOTAL COST FACTORS*

4.2.1 For purposes of evaluation, the installment purchase method of acquisition shall be used for selecting and awarding a contract to a single supplier with the exception of Attachment C (Licensed Software) which may be awarded to a separate contractor. Total overall 60 months costs shall be considered. Total overall cost will include both one-time and life cycle costs to the State.

* * *

4.3.4 Requirements costing will be used to evaluate bidder response to desired items, features, and System performance. Desired items, features, and System performance levels will be assigned predetermined costs, as defined in Section V. The cost assigned is considered to be the cost which would be incurred by the State to develop or otherwise acquire the item or feature, or the value of the System hours which are not available to the State due to System Failure or Preventive Maintenance.

4.3.5 The requirements costing technique considers all one-time and life-cycle costs for mandatory requirements and desirable items, features, and System performance levels. Bidder proposed costs shall be used when bidder responds to a desired item or feature. The predetermined cost shall be used for those desired items to which the bidder does not respond.

4.4 *REJECTION OF PROPOSALS*

The State reserves the right to reject any and all bids received by reason of this RFP. The State does not intend to pay for information solicited or contracted for prior to entering into a contract with the successful Contractor. The State reserves the right to reject any bid which fails to meet the mandatory requirements as stated. The State reserves the right to reject any bid which does not comply with the technical or cost requirements of this RFP. The State reserves the right to contract for any portion of the equipment proposed by reason of this RFP, or to substitute equipment from other sources if in the best interest of the State. System support and training shall not be affected by the State not contracting for all items included in the bid.

The State reserves the right to waive minor deviations in bids providing such action is in the best interest of the State. Minor deviations are defined as those that have no adverse effect upon the State's interest and would not affect the amount of the bid by giving a bidder an advantage or benefit not enjoyed by other bidders. If no valid bids are received by the State, the State reserves the right to negotiate on the best terms and conditions and at the best possible price.

Review Committee

Regardless of whether the user elects to publish the membership in its RFP materials, the user must determine the individuals who will serve on its evaluation and selection review committee. Although the makeup of the committee can be delayed until the RFP has been issued, or the bids have been received, the authors recommend that the individuals be selected earlier, so that they can participate in formulating the RFP.

Considerable flexibility exists in establishing the review committee. The only significant constraints are the following:

- The committee should not be so large that meetings are difficult to schedule or meaningful discussions are impracticable.
- The committee should be large enough to ensure that all relevant interests and skills are represented. In no event should the committee membership be made up exclusively of operations or technical staff members or procurement department representatives.
- The committee should be as objective as possible. Consequently, user representatives with close ties to one or more vendors or obvious biases generally should not be assigned to the review committee.

Many users permit their negotiating team to serve as the proposal review committee. This approach has merit, as it increases the team's familiarity with all aspects of the transaction. However, the negotiating team may not have the technical breadth necessary to do a thorough job in some areas. Moreover, some users feel that this approach creates a conflict of interest that should be avoided (i.e., by permitting the selection decision to be made by the same individuals who will negotiate with the vendor).

If the review committee is to function soundly, it must have the technical and professional representation necessary to perform a detailed analysis of all aspects of the competing vendor proposals. In addition to competent representatives from the applicable operating and technical departments, the committee should include members with financial and legal skills. Legal experience is particularly important if the RFP includes legal/contractual issues, as the authors generally recommend.

Where the scope of the transaction is so significant that all necessary disciplines cannot serve effectively on a single review committee, the user may elect to establish separate committees or subcommittees in selected areas (e.g., technical, financial, and legal).

This approach can also be utilized where the RFP specifies a split submission and/or review process, as discussed above. Although these specialized evaluation processes can be highly beneficial by increasing the level of expertise involved in the review process and strengthening the user's focus on specific areas, overall control of the review process must remain with a single executive or, preferably, group. If this central control is not maintained, a balanced assessment of competing considerations will be difficult or impossible—particularly where trade-offs must be made among technical, legal, and financial factors.

Bid Compliance

As suggested above, the user's preliminary review of vendor proposals should include a determination of which proposals, if any, fail to meet the minimum bid requirements imposed by the RFP. Proposals that fail to meet these requirements should be categorized and handled according to the user's perdetermined procedures for such matters. In most procurements, the following alternatives should be considered in handling proposals that fail to meet minimum requirements: (1) the omission is waived by the user as immaterial and the proposal is processed; (2) the proposal is rejected, without any opportunity for the vendor to cure the problem; (3) the proposal is returned to the vendor for correction and resubmission within a specified time limit. Regardless of the approach employed, the user should have a formal process for the timely return, rejection, or acceptance-by-waiver of all nonresponsive proposals. This process should include a standard notice forwarded by certified return receipt mail to the vendor that submitted the deficient proposal, with copies to all other competing vendors.

Multistage Reviews

As noted above, many users employ a multistage review process in evaluating vendor proposals. This procedure requires that vendor proposals be submitted and evaluated in separate substantive sections (ordinarily, technical, financial, and legal). Depending upon the user's preference, this review can be conducted concurrently or sequentially. In the concurrent approach, the separate sections are evaluated by different user committees or subcommittees during the same time period, with each group focusing on its area of expertise. Under the sequential alternative, the separate proposal sections are reviewed in order, with subsequent sections of a particular proposal being reviewed only if the previous section meets the user's requirements (or qualifies the vendor for a berth among the ZOC contenders).

The multistage or split review process offers a number of user benefits, including the following:

First, by separating several areas (e.g., technical, financial, and legal), it highlights them and increases the relative importance of each. This benefit is particularly helpful in focusing additional vendor attention on such nonoperational areas as finance and legal.

Second, the split review process generally results in a more comprehensive and less biased evaluation of each of the separate areas. Users that employ the split process ordinarily devote considerably more attention to establishing criteria for, and reviewing vendor responses on, each of the separate areas.

Third, despite its additional complexity, the split review process can reduce the total time required for the evaluation procedure. Thus, separate user committees or subcommittees can concurrently review different sections of the RFP submissions. (Of course, this benefit will not occur where the split review process employed by the user requires that each section of the proposals be reviewed sequentially.)

On the other hand, the split review process includes several disadvantages. Among these are the following:

First, as suggested above, the divided review process adds complexity to the evaluation procedure. Where sequential split review is imposed, the review process may require substantial additional time.

Second, unless the process is carefully coordinated, the split review procedure may result in divided value judgments and a loss of relative priorities. Thus, user subcommittees may focus on their respective areas of expertise, with little regard for the problems or priorities of other areas. This tendency places a significant burden on the user to coordinate the various evaluation efforts and assign relative priorities or rankings to competing issues.

Third, the split review procedure increases the complexity of the user's RFP document and the related drafting process. It requires additional skill and resources that many users simply do not possess.

Although the split review process can be useful in a wide variety of transactions, the authors find it most helpful in large or complicated acquisitions where the financial and legal factors deserve increased attention by the vendor and user alike. The sequential variation is particularly useful where the user must narrow a large field of competing vendors at a relatively early date. This benefit results from the fact that the sequential split review process permits the user to judge all vendors on one substantive area and eliminate (or tentatively eliminate) all but three or four, before proceeding to evaluate the vendor proposals in other areas. This approach can reduce the total evaluation effort. (But it can also result in inappropriate decisions. For example, a vendor eliminated from further competition in the user's analysis of the initial substantive area may offer good commitments in the other separate areas. Consequently, any elimination of vendors on a stage-by-stage basis should be tentative, with the user reserving the right to reassess the elimination of any vendor as later substantive areas are considered. Because of the potential problems posed by the elimination of vendors on a stage-by-stage basis, some users that employ the sequential split review procedure do not eliminate vendors at any stage of the review; rather, these users rank all of the vendors separately on each stage.)

The Apples-to-Apples Problem

One of the most pervasive problems plaguing the evaluation process is the difficulty of making apples-to-apples comparisons of competing vendor proposals. Yet few areas are more important to the integrity and success of the user's RFP effort.

Control of the problems in this area must begin with the user's RFP document. As suggested earlier in this chapter, the RFP should impose standard formats, tables, and exhibits wherever possible. The failure to adopt such an approach may well undermine the value of the entire RFP process.

However, imposing these standard submission requirements in the RFP is not enough. The user's review committee must carefully study each submission to ensure that the proposals actually involve comparable data. Where deviations exist, they should be highlighted and summarized on a separate evaluation exhibit. If practicable, the user should require the vendors involved to submit additional information that will eliminate the apple-to-oranges comparison problem. Alternatively, the user should supply the necessary adjustment based upon the best information available to it. Where the desired comparability cannot be achieved, the user should either disqualify the irregular proposal or clearly identify it in a manner that will not permit the irregularity to become lost during further stages of the evaluation process.

The Quantification Problem

One of the more difficult problems in the evaluation process relates to the quantification of nonfinancial factors. Most major equipment acquisitions involve a number of matters that offer some unstated and apparently unquantifiable value (or detriment) to the user. Vendor representatives are well known for their ability to highlight these factors and attempt to turn them into hot buttons or subtle influences in the user's decision making process. (See Chapter 2.) The vendor's effort is often successful, in large part because the user either cannot or does not place a clear value or price on the factors involved. Among the many examples of such factors are the alleged "value" of maintaining an existing vendor relationship, doing business with a long time customer of the user (or affiliate of a user board member), or acquiring equipment and associated prestige from an acknowledged industry leader such as IBM. Soft dollar vendor concessions, such as education and conversion assistance, may also be involved.

Because vendor sales ploys based upon these factors can be devastatingly successful, the user should strive to quantify the value or cost of each matter wherever possible. Quantifying the value or amount permits the user to place the item in perspective and to assess the relative benefit or detriment involved.

Some equipment factors are quantifiable without significant difficulty. For example, when pressed to do so, most users can assess the value of vendor soft dollar concessions (e.g., training, programming assistance, and extra technical manuals). Although other factors are more difficult, precision is seldom required. What is required is a serious effort at placing a value on a particular subjective matter. Users reluctant to make a serious effort at quantification can sometimes be drawn into the process by an exchange such as the following.

"How much is it worth to you to do business with your incumbent vendor?"

"Well, a lot, I guess."

"Okay, but is it worth $500,000 on this transaction?"

"No, of course not!"

"Is it worth $300,000?"

"No, I guess not."

"How about $50,000?"

"Yes, it's probably worth that not to change vendors, and to have a little security."

"Well, then, would you say its worth $100,000?"

This process can continue bracketing the issue until the user representative feels comfortable with the value assigned.

Vendor Ranking Matrices

If the user is to maintain objectivity and derive optimum value from the evaluation process, it must develop and employ one or more ranking or grading systems. These systems must permit the user to keep a written record of its relative evaluation of the performance or responsiveness of each vendor on each relevant factor.

Within this broad purpose, the user can select from a variety of ranking or grading systems. The following are among the mechanisms employed by many users:

One-to-Ten Rank. In this procedure, the user ranks each vendor on a one-to-ten scale on each relevant issue. Of course, as in the case of prioritizing user objectives (discussed in Chapter 4) other numerical scales can also be employed.

Plus-and-Minus Rank. Here, the user ranks each vendor proposal as "plus" or "minus" (favorable or unfavorable) on each issue. Some users employ a middle-of-the-road rank, often symbolized by a slash, for proposals that are neither favorable nor unfavorable on a given issue. This ranking technique is particularly helpful for fringe factors that do not lend themselves strongly to more detailed assessment. (See the discussion of soft dollar benefits, above.)

Textual Commentary. In this evaluation technique, the user employs textual commentary to document its judgment of competing vendor proposals. Although this unconstrained technique permits user bias and self-serving remarks to creep into the evaluation process, it also allows more detailed explanation of relevant user assessments. Many users combine this textual approach with a numerical ranking technique on important criteria.

Financial Figures. In many areas, the best ranking or grading tool is the price, cost, value, or bottom-line amount of a particular item, problem, or concession. If the user employs liquidated bid adjustments in its RFP process (as discussed earlier in this chapter), relevant financial figures must be modified by the amount of any applicable adjustment. Financial figures can be used separately or combined with one of the numerical ranking techniques noted above.

Weighted Criteria. In most acquisitions, the relevant factors being considered and ranked by the user will not all be equally important to the user. Rather, various issues will be more or less critical than others. Because of this fact, any ranking or grading system utilized by the user must include a weighting that properly reflects the user's relative priorities on different issues. Although many techniques are available for this purpose, the authors prefer the technique in which the user assigns percentages or points to each section and subsection of the RFP, and then grades all competing vendors in the same manner that a college professor grades an examination that includes weighted questions.

Total Life Cycle Costing. Where the user employs the total life cycle costing (TLCC) approach discussed in the Specifications section of this chapter, above, the RFP evaluation process must include the detail and breadth necessary to assess all relevant TLCC factors. Where an extensive TLCC review is being conducted, the user must take particular care to ensure that the various life cycle cost components have been identified and quantified as accurately as possible. This difficult and admittedly somewhat subjective process may require that the user broaden the membership of its review committee for this purpose, or assign specific tasks to subcommittees or designated user departments. Where the TLCC approach is related to, or includes, the use of liquidated bid adjustments, the user must also ensure that the two evaluation standards are approximately coordinated.

The "Fuzz Word" Problem

Most vendor proposals include a number of open ended, vague words and phrases that are subject to varying interpretations. The authors often refer to these sales-oriented euphemisms as "fuzz words." Fuzz words can generally be classified into two categories: (1) phrases that add ambiguity; and (2) phrases that add marketing "fluff." Examples of the first category include: "in accordance with vendor's policies," "best efforts," "assist the user in," and "be responsive to the user's needs for." Examples of the second classification include: "promptly," "thoroughly," "the vendor's fine history of," and "excellent."

To maximize the objectivity of the evaluation process, the user's review committee should strive to identify these and other "fuzz words" in each vendor proposal and isolate them from consideration. Several techniques can be employed for this purpose. Some users highlight the words by underlining or by utilizing a yellow marking pen. The identified words are then viewed with great care as the proposal is evaluated. Other users obliterate the words by lining through them with a pen or black marker. The fuzz words are then simply ignored, and the proposal is evaluated without them. Still other users identify the fuzz words, list or cross-reference them, and provide them to the vendor in the request for information (RFI) format discussed in Chapter 4. In the RFI, the vendor is asked to clarify or otherwise respond to each fuzz word phrase in writing. (Although this technique seldom adds any meaningful substance to the proposal, it often has an interesting psychological impact on the vendor marketeers who drafted the response to the user's RFP.)

The "Bird in the Bush" Problem

In addition to fuzz words, many vendor proposals include a variety of promises about future products, enhancements, and opportunities that will be available to the user doing business with the vendor. Among the most frequent promises are those relating to new equipment or equipment components, software programs or enhancements, and related vendor services such as training, field upgrading, or conversion assistance.

These promised items are often most important to the user's business. Indeed, they can become key factors in the user's decision to do business with a particular vendor. The difficulty is that these admittedly relevant factors often begin to resemble a mirage as the acceptance date passes. Unless the vendor is willing to firmly document the promised availability of such factors—to the extent that the vendor's failure to deliver will be a material breach under the contract—the factors should be disregarded or, at least, viewed with a healthy degree of skepticism. (Some users employ identification systems such as those suggested for the fuzz words, above, to encourage objectively in this area.)

The fact that certain future developments are promised by a vendor in somewhat general terms does not necessarily mean that they should be wholly disregarded by the user. Perhaps the best admonition in this area is the old saying that "a bird in the hand is worth two in the bush."

Proposal Versus Contract Cross-check

Regardless of whether the user's RFP requires the vendor to submit a contract with its proposal, or to agree to the user's contract or model provisions in its proposal, the user's evaluation process should include a cross-check of the vendor's promised deliverables against the vendor's proposed contract documents. Although this cross-check can occur at virtually any stage of the negotiation process, the user's negotiating position is enhanced if the analysis occurs early during the proposal review procedure. Early identification of instances in which the vendor's proposed contract fails to reflect the deliverables promised in the proposal enhances the user's ability to gain negotiating concessions and include the omitted items in the final documents.

One of the more effective methods of implementing this cross-check is to mark each paragraph of the proposal to indicate the section of the contract where the proposal commitment appears. An alternative method is to tape paragraphs of the proposal on the left side of a page, and related sections of the contract on the right side of the same page. Indeed, some users require that each vendor submit such an assessment as part of its RFP, identifying and explaining any areas where the contract fails to reflect promises contained in the RFP.

6
GENERAL LEGAL PRINCIPLES

To achieve optimum success in any business objective, a negotiator must have thorough knowledge of the subject matter involved. A solid appreciation of negotiating practices and procedures will help, of course, but negotiating skills can never replace a lack of substantive understanding. Where major equipment is being acquired, this substantive knowledge must encompass general legal principles as well as technical matters associated with the equipment itself. Although finer legal points should obviously be left to the user's attorney, a good business negotiator will never delegate responsibility for understanding general legal principles to the legal member of the user's negotiating team. Rather, the experienced negotiator will ensure that he or she has a solid understanding of the legal concepts that govern the acquisition at hand.

This chapter is designed to provide an overview of the general contractual principles that are applicable to most major equipment acquisitions. The basic concepts discussed in this chapter are supplemented by the following chapter, which outlines the legal principles relating to patents, trade secrets, and proprietary rights. Many of the conceptual issues analyzed in these two chapters are applied in a more practical context in Chapter 8, which reviews a number of general contractual provisions, and in the following chapters, which discuss specific types of acquisition agreements in more detail.

One caveat should be noted at the outset. Although this chapter is designed to provide a good understanding of the contractual principles which apply to equipment acquisition agreements, it is not intended to constitute a course in business law. For example, the chapter does not cover such legal areas as torts (e.g., what happens when the new equipment explodes and kills, falls on, or invades the privacy of an innocent customer) or litigation (e.g., how to sue your vendor, what pleadings to prepare, and what problems of proof and evidence exist). At the same time, the legal concepts that are discussed in this chapter are, by necessity, extremely general. As every law professor tries to impress on his or her first year students (with varying degrees of success), legal principles cannot be applied in a vacuum; they must be molded to specific facts and problems. Consequently, the legal principles discussed in this chapter are intended as general background information, not as solutions for specific controversies. For additional information beyond the areas covered in this chapter, and for assistance beyond the areas covered in this chapter, and for assistance in applying the concepts discussed here, the reader is referred to competent legal counsel, and to the several good books and courses on general business law.

THE PURPOSE OF AN AGREEMENT

Virtually every book on business law and contracts contains a definition or observation concerning the "purpose" of a contract. Many of the definitions are quite long and complex, and some encompass detailed lists of the many purposes served by a good contract. Although these definitions are all perfectly acceptable, the authors prefer a more succinct statement that runs to the heart of why people, companies, and nations enter into binding legal documents. *The purpose of a contract is to prevent problems.* Note that this encompassing definition does not dwell on the fact that a contract documents the understanding of the parties, or that it provides a back-drop for enforcement of rights and remedies. A contract does these things and more. But, in most transactions, we enter into a contract with one goal in mind: to consummate a business transaction in a clearly defined manner, *without problems.* If we didn't care about such *problems* as misunderstandings, overlooked details, and the failure of others to comply, we could probably avoid the entire concept of a "contract."

As a problem avoidance mechanism, a good contract should serve a number of uses—or, put another way, minimize a number of actual and potential problems. For example, a well-drafted legal agreement should:

- prevent misunderstanding and surprise by accurately describing the responsibilities of the respective parties;
- provide protection against default by either side, by describing events of default, periods for cure, and realistic and certain remedies;
- prevent confusion in the future, by describing the transaction and responsibilities in terms that can be understood long after the initial staff participants have resigned or retired;
- provide protection against unanticipated disasters and other events, by covering such areas as risk of loss, insurance, strikes, and other acts of God;
- prevent or at least reduce the likelihood of future litigation, by accurately describing the transaction and the rights, responsibilities, and remedies of the respective parties;
- provide a background for contract fulfillment and administration, by outlining the trans-action and the responsibilities of the parties in a logical, organized manner;
- avoid disagreement over performance in key areas (e.g., delivery and acceptance by speci-fying detailed written standards);
- reduce the effectiveness of, and the problems associated with, vendor sales ploys (see Chap-ter 2) by providing an organized process to document the transaction;
- provide a "litigation document" by which either party can enforce its rights in the event of continuing default by the other party.

(Note that none of the purposes or uses listed above includes "provide a method whereby a weaker or unsuspecting party will sign a form document quickly and easily, permitting the ven-dor to successfully and promptly close the sales transaction." This tongue-in-check "use" is based upon the vendor "form contract ploy" described in Chapter 2. Clearly, a legal document should *not* be used for such purposes.)

To meet the objectives outlined above, most equipment contracts will cover a number of com-mon areas. In the broadest possible overview, these areas might be summarized as follows:

1. The Parties: Who is agreeing with whom?
2. The Transaction: What is being bought, sold, or otherwise provided and how will trans-action occur?
3. The Price: What is being paid, and on what terms?
4. The Conditions: What conditions are being imposed on the rights or the obligations of the respective parties, and how do they arise or dissolve?
5. Other Obligations: What other obligations are being imposed on the parties as part of, or in connection with, the transaction?
6. Default and Remedies: If a party fails to comply with its obligations under the agreement, what rights does the other party have?
7. The Signatures: Who has executed the agreement on behalf of the respective parties?

From a practical standpoint, the seven points outlined above could be condensed even further by considering items 4, 5, and 6 to be part of item 2, which might be called the "description of the transaction." In most agreements, it is this description that serves as the heart of the document and provides the greatest number of problems for the user. The problems arise because the description of the transaction far too frequently covers the matters that are important to the vendor, but overlooks a number of issues that are essential to the user.

As this statement suggest, no agreement can meet the basic purpose of avoiding problems unless it is complete and comprehensive. To meet this goal, it must fully and fairly document the transaction from and for both sides.

LETTERS OF INTENT

For various reasons, some vendors and vendor sales personnel have a predilection for letters of intent or "agreements to agree," as they are occasionally called. Vendor appreciation of letters of intent probably relates to the value of the "form contract" ploy explained in Chapter 2: The letter of intent represents a simple, fact method of committing the user to the transaction, without negotiating terms, conditions, or pro-user concessions. If a vendor sales representative cannot gain a signed contract from the user, the marketeer will often strive for the "next best thing": a signed letter of intent.

Letters of intent pose a number of special problems for the user. First, letters of "intent" sometimes prove to be far more binding than the user realizes or desires. Almost by definition, a letter of "intent" should not be a binding legal agreement among the parties. When a document prepared as an unbinding letter of intent proves to be a binding agreement, it is likely to exclude a number of critical areas that would have been covered if the parties had set out to negotiate and draft a binding contract. Although the courts may imply some of the missing provisions, the language supplied (e.g., provisions from the vendor's standard form agreement, local industry practice, or the Uniform Commercial Code) may be inadequate to protect the user.

Second, even where a letter of intent is not binding, it generally represents a moral commitment by the user that can be utilized to the vendor's advantage in subsequent negotiations on the binding agreement. When the user executes a letter of intent, it moves closer to a final commitment and, accordingly, suffers a loss in negotiating leverage. Indeed, during subsequent negotiations, the vendor's sales representative is likely to treat the user as if the transaction has been finalized.

Third, as suggested above, because a letter of intent is short and succinct, it seldom covers all of the user issues that should be included in the final agreement. (As one annoyed manager put it, "If the letter of intent has to cover all the issues included in the final contract, why don't we just draft the contract?" The question is remarkably valid.) Pro-vendor issues omitted from the letter of intent generally find their way into the final agreement. Unfortunately, pro-user issues that are omitted often face more difficult going, as the vendor claims that such matters were not "part of the deal" that was documented in the letter of intent.

Despite these problems, letters of intent may be appropriate or unavoidable in some situations. For example, they may help a vendor hold preexisting prices open to a user after the effective date of a new price increase. They may help hold a system in the delivery queue and preclude it from being delivered to another customer. They may also help a local vendor branch manager meet a commission or other quota, thereby permitting this manager to offer alternative concessions to the user.

Where a letter of intent must be used, it should be just what the name denotes: an expression of *intent,* not a formal, binding agreement. With a few exceptions, the only good letter of intent in an equipment acquisition is a nonbinding one. Any letter of intent executed by the user should be prepared or carefully reviewed by the user's legal counsel. Under no circumstances should a user execute or accept a letter of intent prepared by the vendor without review by the user's counsel.

In most situations, the letter of intent should be short and to the point, merely indicating that the user intends to enter into an agreement with the vendor covering certain equipment and/or services or other products, provided that the vendor and the user can and do negotiate and execute a mutually agreeable contract covering the terms, conditions, and prices involved. The letter of intent should avoid reference to any vendor form agreement either by agreement name or form number. Instead, the letter should use generic terminology in referring to the type of agreement or transaction (e.g., "an agreement for the lease of . . ." or "an agreement for the purchase of . . ."). In some instances, the user may wish to insert several of the key parameters of the proposed agreement into the letter (e.g., the term of a lease, the total purchase price, or a key vendor soft dollar concession). Although this approach may be advantageous to the user, in that it may morally commit the vendor to the matter involved, the user should remember that it too may become morally committed as a result. Consequently, this approach is advisable only if the user is convinced that it will not wish to seek a more favorable commitment on the issue during the formal contract negotiations. In addition, the user should recognize that any effort to place key concessions into the letter of intent may result in "sins of omission." Because no effort to include key issues in the letter of intent is likely to be all-inclusive, any pro-user concessions that are omitted from the letter may be denied or negated by the vendor when negotiations on the final agreement begin.

Because of this risk, and the corresponding risk that the letter may prove to be legally binding, some attorneys believe that a letter of intent should be as detailed as possible, covering every subject and concession that may ultimately be included in the final agreement. Although this approach has merit, and is often followed in certain types of transactions (e.g., real estate and option arrangements), it is seldom practicable in major equipment acquisitions. In the equipment industry, letters of intent are generally employed as items of expediency and as methods of obtaining a quick, early user commitment. As the remarks quoted above suggest, if the user had the time and talent necessary to prepare an extensive letter of intent, it could, and probably should, instead draft, negotiate, and execute the final agreement.

Regardless of the type of letter of intent used, it should include an initial or final paragraph that clearly specifies the nonbinding nature of the document. Many attorneys and users attempt to be coy about this point, preferring to rely upon implicit legal principles or indirect language to preclude the letter from being legally binding. These individuals are often supported by the vendor's sales representative, who may caution that the letter will be unacceptable to the vendor or to some assignee financial institution if the letter directly states that it is nonbinding. Unfortunately, all of these rationalizations involve more wishful thinking and salesmanship than sound logic. The authors strongly recommend that any letter of intent include a direct statement such as the following:

This letter of intent is a nonbinding document and has no legal effect. In the event that the binding agreement referred to above is executed by the Vendor and the Customer, the terms and conditions of such agreement shall control and take precedence over this letter of intent. In the event that the above-referenced binding agreement is not executed by the Vendor and the Customer, for no reason or for any reason whatsoever, this letter of intent shall be null and void and neither the Vendor nor the Customer shall have any liability or obligation to the other arising from or in connection with this letter of intent or the transaction proposed herein.

USE OF LEGAL COUNSEL

Although many legal agreements may be insignificant enough to permit execution by the user without prior legal review, most major equipment agreements deserve—indeed, require—meaningful review by competent legal counsel. As the Preface to this volume indicates, the authors consider an equipment acquisition to be "major" if it involves any of the following elements: (1) a significant finanicial commitment by the user (whether for a single item or group of related items); (2) equipment that is critical to the user's operations or business; or (3) equipment that poses significant legal, operating, or other risks to the user or its customers or employees. Any agreement for the acquisition of equipment that meets one or more of these factors can create serious financial, legal, and operational problems for the user. As such, the agreement should not be executed without prior legal review.

Despite the compelling arguments supporting review by counsel, billions of dollars of equipment is acquired each year through contracts that have had little or no review by legal counsel. Major multinational companies are among the worst offenders in this regard, particularly those that have procurement or technical officers charged with reviewing and approving the contracts involved. Much like the situation involving negotiations, described in Chapter 1, these users simply fail to see the reason to devote the time and expense necessary for meaningful legal review. Indeed, some of these users also fail to see the value of that review, having been shackled with inside or outside attorneys who have little concept of how to properly document an equipment acquisition transaction.

Benefits of Review

Legal review admittedly requires time and money. It also requires a certain amount of education and effort, as the transaction is explained to the user's counsel and his or her suggestions are considered. By definition, it also involves the painful process of dealing with lawyers—those pompous, degreed aristocrats who understand nothing about the user's business or the acquiring department's operating problems.

To make all this time, expense, and suffering worthwhile, the user should expect—and get—some meaningful benefits. Among the benefits that should be derived from legal review are the following:

- A better, more comprehensive agreement that contains fewer misunderstandings and more accurately describes the transaction that the user expects to achieve.
- A document that will provide the user with stronger and more specific remedies in the event problems arise during the contract term.
- A better understanding of the transaction itself (which generally results as the user's technical staff attempts to describe and explain the transaction to legal counsel as part of the briefing process).
- An organized process that slows the transaction down and deflates the effectiveness of vendor ploys and other marketing practices that are based upon a "sense of urgency."
- A document and an acquisition process that can be relied upon by the user with less fear of subsequent problems, surprises, and liability.

Adequacy of Review

For any review by legal counsel to be meaningful to the user, it must involve four key elements: (1) competent counsel; (2) adequate time, both for the review and for the negotiation of changes;

(3) a thorough explanation of the entire transaction; and (4) commitment by the user to support the recommendations of its counsel through serious bargaining. If any of these elements is missing, the legal review may be more illusory than real—and may offer the user only a false hope of security.

Dealing with incompetent counsel is a problem in any environment, particularly where the user's staff does not have the ability to seek alternative assistance from another source. Where the problem individual cannot be replaced with competent counsel, the user may still gain an improved position by embarking on an education program designed to improve the technical understanding and the professional expertise of the attorney involved. This approach is often particularly useful where the lawyer is part of an inside legal department. Whether the weak-link attorney is a member of the user's legal department or its outside law firm, the problem should also be communicated to a senior partner or other lawyer who can and should assist in the training process.

The problem of time is somewhat easier to control Although adequate time for legal review seldom exists in a pure sense, the acquiring user department can allocate reasonable time for review when the acquisition timetable is drawn up—if adequate incentive exists to do so. In addition, the user's operating staff can increase the effectiveness of the time that is available by providing the user's lawyer with advance copies of all relevant documents and by avoiding such useless exercises in wishful thinking as dropping by the attorney's office, with the vendor's sales representative, so the attorney can "look over the documents." No lawyer worth his or her degree can perform an adequate review of a major equipment contract while the vendor and user staff representatives wait across the desk engaging in small talk.

Similarly, no attorney can competently review a complex transaction without a thorough understanding of the facts involved. In this regard, the burden for educating the user's lawyer falls squarely on the user's technical and operating staff. Although any good attorney will share this burden by asking thoughtful questions designed to round out his or her understanding, the lawyer cannot ask about matters that are never brought up in the first place. Perhaps more importantly, the user's attorney cannot suggest protection or negotiate a concession for an issue that remains safely embedded in the mind of one of the user's technical staff.

The issue of negotiating commitment is one that is discussed throughout this volume. Regardless of the brilliance of the user's attorney, the lawyer's legal review will provide protection to the user only if the user has, and is willing to employ, the negotiating leverage necessary to achieve changes in the agreement. If the user has already lost that bargaining power by the time that legal review is commenced (see Chapter 4), or if the user has no intention of pursuing the changes recommended by counsel, the user would often be better off omitting the review process. After all, if the user will not obtain any of the benefits of legal review, it might as well not incur the time, expense, and frustration involved.

One final caveat should be made concerning the legal review process followed by some inside legal departments. In these departments, the attorney performs a perfunctory review of the vendor's form agreement and stamps it "approved as to form." At the risk of offending a number of very fine attorneys, the authors generally find that this approach offers little meaningful assistance—or protection—to the user. The suggestion made by the "approved as to form" stamp is that the lawyer has approved the agreement as a binding obligation of the user organization, but expresses no opinion about the substance, terms, or conditions of the document. This approach may be fine for an agreement covering the purchase of a $5,000 copy machine, but it has little place in a major equipment acquisition. Adequate review of a complex equipment agreement must involve more than "form." It must involve review and participation in the substance of the entire transaction. Anything less is an abdication of professional responsibility, either by the lawyer who suggests it or the user executive who demands it.

BASIC CONTRACT REQUIREMENTS

For many years, law students have defined a contract as a promise, or a set of promises, among two or more parties, that is enforceable under the law. This concept of enforceability is sometimes expressed by saying that the law must either recognize a duty to perform the promise or provide a remedy in the event a breach of the promise occurs. By tradition several basic "elements" are said to be necessary for a contract to exist. These essential elements are as follows:

- Mutual assent or agreement (often expressed as an "offer and acceptance").
- Sufficient "consideration."
- Two or more parties having the minimum legal capacity necessary to contract.

Some legal commentators also add that, at least to be enforceable, the contract must be for a legal purpose and not capable of being declared void by statute or judicial interpretation.

These essential elements are equally important for the business executive as for the law student. In the context of major equipment acquisitions, the relevance of these elements has little to do with the principal contractual documents. (Unless the lawyers have committed egregious errors, the main agreements will almost certainly qualify as binding contracts.) Rather, an understanding of the elements that constitute a basic contract is necessary to appreciate when a side letter, amendment, or marketing representation qualifies as a binding agreement—*and when it does not*. Without this knowledge, a user representative is likely to be highly vulnerable to vendor marketing ploys and sales practices. (See Chapter 2.)

Mutual Assent

The concept of mutual assent carries with it the need for two or more parties. As legal scholars observe, "a man cannot make an agreement with himself." Although this point seems self-evident in theory, many users tend to overlook it in practice, as they convince themselves that a one-sided vendor marketing pitch or user request constitutes a binding agreement.

Mutual assent also requires that the parties agree upon something with reasonable and mutual definiteness or, as it is sometimes put, that they agree "on the same thing, on the same terms, at the same time." For example, an agreement for the user to purchase "some" automated teller machines produced by the vendor lacks the necessary definiteness. Likewise, no contract will result where the user agrees to buy one amount of goods and the vendor agrees only to sell another amount.

Mutual assent also requires some affirmative manifestation of agreement, communicated by and between the parties. Thus, a mental decision to accept an offer, without more, cannot constitute an agreement. On the other hand, a party that accepts an offer, but in doing so accidently agrees to pay too much, will generally be held to be bound by the higher price that was communicated to the other party. This concept of manifestation of assent forms the basis for the legal fact, recognized by every first year law student, that an offer by one party can be withdrawn by that party until it is accepted by the other party.

As this statement suggest, mutual assent also includes the idea of a "bargain" between the parties. Whether it is stated as an "offer" and an "acceptance" or not, mutual assent is based upon the exchanging of something given for something requested. Thus, the law says that an unsolicited or gratuitous promise, given with nothing requested or expected in return, generally cannot form the basis for a binding contract.

Consideration

Consideration is routinely defined as some legal benefit to be received by the party making the promise, or some legal detriment to be incurred by the other party, which was requested by the party making the promise in "payment" (or "consideration") for the promise made. Ordinarily, the law provides that nothing will be valid consideration unless it is intended to be. (This is simply another way of saying that the consideration must be bargained for.)

With rare exceptions, the *amount* of consideration required for an agreement is irrelevant. As law students say, "the law will not inquire into the adequacy or fairness of consideration," *assuming it is present*. However, if the consideration is blatantly inadequate (or, more frequently, missing), a court may find that a contract specifying the existence of consideration and reciting its adequacy may serve some value, but it generally will not overcome a clear lack of consideration.

Although money, or an agreement to pay money, is perhaps the most obvious example of consideration, one promise can be valid consideration for another promise. Likewise, consideration can arise from forbearance or the acceptance of a legal detriment, as well as from the modification, creation, or destruction of a legal right.

Third-party payments and promises can also provide adequate consideration. Thus, a user's promise to lease one of the vendor's machines from a lessor that will buy the machine from the vendor will generally provide adequate consideration for a promise or commitment made by the vendor to the user. Where a dispute has arisen between a vendor and a user, the user's agreement not to sue the vendor (often called "forbearance on the claim" by the user) will generally provide adequate consideration to settle the dispute in a binding agreement. However, the dispute must be a valid one. Forbearance on a claim that is neither honestly nor reasonably disputed provides no consideration, just as fulfillment of a moral duty to pay or do something, without more, offers a similar empty result.

Lawyers sometimes speak of "unilateral" contracts and "bilateral" contracts. The distinction between the two types of agreements essentially relates to the issue of consideration (or, more often, the issue of how that consideration is expressed). In a unilateral contract, *one* party makes a *promise* to do or pay something, and the other party accepts by *actually doing* or paying something. For example, the user says "I will pay you $1,000 if you will send me a new component" (the promise) and the vendor delivers the new component to the user (the action). In a unilateral agreement of this nature, the promise to pay does not become legally binding, and the contract does not really exist, until the *action* by the other party occurs.

In contrast, where a bilateral contract is involved, *each* party *promises* performance of some kind; that is, mutual promises are exchanged one for another by both sides. For example, the user says "I will pay you $1,000 if you will send me a new component" (the user's promise) and the vendor replies "I will send you the new component for $1,000" (the vendor's promise). In a bilateral contract, the mutual promises become legally binding, and the contract comes into existence, when the mutual promises are given or agreed upon.

As these examples suggest, most complex commercial agreements are bilateral contracts based upon mutual promises of the respective parties. However, equipment acquisition transactions often include a number of less significant unilateral contracts, principally with respect to minor matters and changes to the main agreements.

In a few instances, the law allows certain substitutes for the consideration normally required for a contract to exist. Historically, the common law used to provide that a contract made "under seal" was enforceable without legal consideration. This concept, which is now outdated in most American jurisdictions, forms the basis for the word "(SEAL)" which is still found at the end of the signature lines of a great many form agreements.

Today, perhaps the best example of a consideration substitute is the concept of "promissory estoppel." Under this theory, no consideration is required for a binding, enforceable agreement where the following elements are present: (1) one party makes a promise that it should reasonably expect will induce substantial action or forbearance by the other party; (2) the promise actually induces the action or forbearance; and (3) injustice can be avoided only by enforcing the promise.

Parties

As noted above, the requirement for mutual assent necessitates that the bargain involve two or more parties. The legal concepts associated with the adequacy of capacity to contract have little relevance in equipment acquisitions. (For example, many of the principles deal with questions of minimum age and relative insanity, and offer such fine distinctions as whether the contract is "void" or merely "voidable.") However, one associated concept is relevant in the present context: the legal authority of an individual to bind his or her corporation by signing an agreement.

As Chapter 4 suggests, care should be taken to ensure that any contract executed by a corporate entity is properly signed by an officer having the legal authority to bind his or her corporation. Under general legal principles, the authority of corporate officers can be *actual* (express or implied) or *apparent*. (In addition, authority can be derived from subsequent ratification by the corporation of an action that was beyond the officer's power at the time the act took place.) Actual authority is based upon the relationship that exists between the corporation and the officer involved. Express actual authority generally flows from statute, the articles of incorporation, the bylaws, or one or more specific resolutions by the board of directors. For example, the by-laws of a corporation generally enumerate those officers who have the power to execute documents on behalf of the corporation. This type of provision is usually supplemented by one or more board resolutions that list the titles and/or names of officers empowered to execute certain types or sizes of agreements.

Implied authority generally arises by legal interpretation in various instances where express actual authority does not exist. Implied authority is sometimes said to be "presumptive" authority that exists "by virtue of office" or title or "by custom." Thus, even if no express authority exists, the president of a corporation will generally be held to have implied authority to execute contracts on its behalf. Although vice presidents and even lower officers may be found to have implied authority in some instances, relying upon the concept of implied authority to contract at these levels is not advisable.

Apparent authority is somewhat more complex—and often very beneficial to the user. Apparent authority generally exists where a corporation manifests to another party that an officer, employee, or agent may act upon its behalf, and bind it, and the other party in good faith believes that the individual has the corporate authority to do so. Where these factors exist, the lack of actual authority (express or implied) is said to be irrelevant, and the corporation is "estopped" from denying the authority of the officer, employee, or agent acting on its behalf. The theory behind apparent authority (sometimes called ostensible authority) is that a corporation should be responsible for the representations of its officers, employees, and agents. Thus, if the corporation "clothes its agent with the appearance of authority" that misleads another party, the corporation should not complain when the other party claims that it believed that the agent had the authority to bind the corporation.

For the doctrine of apparent authority to apply the party ostensibly misled must be able to claim in good faith that it believed that the corporate officer actually possessed the requisite authority. Thus, a user may face difficulty in relying on the doctrine where the vendor's form agreement indicates that it must be "accepted by the vice president, sales" in the vendor's main office location. (Note that this language could also be employed to defeat a user claim that it believed that a side letter signed by the vendor's local marketing officer was binding.)

Apparent authority can also run in favor of the vendor. Thus, the vendor may be able to claim that an agreement or change order signed by the user's assistant vice president is binding by virtue of apparent authority, even though the officer lacked any actual authority to bind the user. Because of this risk, some users advise all vendors, at the outset of negotiations (e.g., in the RFP or other written notice) that no document or representation made by the user will be valid unless executed by a user officer with a specified title or above.

THE CONCEPT OF PRIVITY

One of the more annoying principles of contract law involves the concept of "privity." With the exceptions allowed third party beneficiaries (discussed below), for a party to enforce rights under a contract it must be "in privity with" the other party or parties to the agreement.

When a user and vendor execute a contract for the sale and purchase of an assembly-line robot, the two firms are both parties to the contract and are said to be "in privity with" or to "enjoy privity with" one another. If the vendor fails to deliver the equipment, the user can sue the vendor and presumably recover damages. On the other hand, if the vendor fails to deliver the equipment and the user is therefore unable to construct and deliver certain goods to or for its end-user customers, serious doubt exists as to whether those customers can sue the *vendor*. The customers probably can sue the *user*, and the user may be able to sue the vendor (assuming that no contractual limits on consequential or indirect damages prohibit such a move). In terms of legal theory, the customers will be blocked from suing the vendor for breach of contract (sometimes called a suit "on the contract") because the customers lack privity with the vendor; that is, the customers were not parties to the contract with the vendor. (Technically, a suit for negligence or some similar "tort" could be brought by the customers, or some other party not in privity, against the vendor. However, for such a suit to be successful, the vendor must have committed some type of act or omission that is recognized as a tort under the law—a rather unlikely occurrence in the present context. Examples of torts include negligence, slander, libel, and assault.)

The principal exception to the requirement for privity involves certain contracts for the benefit of third parties, or "third party beneficiaries" as they are generally called. For example, consider a contract where A pays certain amounts to B, in return for B's promise to render certain services to C. If B fails to perform, the question becomes whether C can sue B to enforce C's "rights." Under the English common law, C is out of luck because C lacks privity with B—or as one commentator put it, C is a "stranger" to the contract between A and B.

Under almost all American jurisdictions, certain third party beneficiaries are entitled to enforce their rights under a contract between two other parties even though they may lack privity under the agreement that is involved. The basic rule gives a third party beneficiary such rights if it is a "donee beneficiary" or a "creditor beneficiary" under the agreement. A person or firm is a third party donee beneficiary when the party receiving the benefit of a promise under the contract (the "promisee") intends the promise to benefit the donee as a gift. This intention is best shown by demonstratiing that the promise could only result in a benefit to the third party (and not to the promisee). A person or firm is a third party creditor beneficiary when the party receiving the benefit of the promise (again, the "promisee") intends the creditor beneficiary to receive the benefit in payment or satisfaction of a real or supposed duty or obligation owed by the promisee to the creditor.

Using the example above, C would be a third party donee beneficiary if A intended the service to be performed by B to benefit C as a gift from A to C. On the other hand, C would be a creditor beneficiary if A owed C certain money (or other obligations) and, in paying B, intended B's performance of services to C to relieve A of its obligation to C.

Third parties that do not qualify as donee or creditor beneficiaries are said to be "incidental" beneficiaries. Such firms cannot enforce rights under a contract, even though they may be benefitted by performance under the contract, or harmed by a failure of performance. The reason is because the firms lack privity under the contract and also fail to qualify as third party beneficiaries.

In the context of major equipment transactions, the concepts of privity and third party beneficiaries are particularly relevant in situations involving third party leasing, turnkey arrangements, and parent/subsidiary relationships. In the first two categories, the user may need to be a third party beneficiary under an agreement between the original equipment manufacturer (OEM) and the lessor or the turnkey firm. In the last category, a subsidiary of a parent company may wish to be a third party beneficiary under an agreement between the vendor and the subsidiary's parent company. Because both donee and creditor beneficiaries involve the element of intention (intention for the contract to benefit the third party benficiary), many user attorneys add an express provision to the agreement indicating that certain entities are intended to be third party beneficiaries under the contract. Although this approach probably offers at least some value, it may not be adequate to overcome a situation that blatantly fails to qualify for donee or creditor beneficiary status.

ORAL AND WRITTEN COMMITMENTS

Many lay persons fail to appreciate that an oral contract can be just as valid and binding as a written contract. In fact, the formality of a *written* agreement is unnecessary to the validity of a contract except in those instances where an applicable statute provides otherwise. (However, as explained below, the rules relating to the validity of an oral contract are not necessarily the same as those relating to the use of oral understandings to modify an existing written agreement.)

In most states, the principal bar to oral agreements is the statute of frauds, which in most jurisdictions may actually involve a variety of separate statutes. Although a lengthy legal treatise could be written on the types of oral agreements that fall within or without the statute of frauds, only one aspect of the statute deserves discussion in the present context: the law which provides that contracts for the sale of goods at a price of $500 or more must be in writing in order to be enforceable. In most states, this provision is included in Section 2-201 of the Uniform Commercial Code (UCC), which is discussed in more detail below. This section typically states that, except as otherwise provided, "a contract for the sale of goods for the price of $500 or more is not enforceable by way of action or defense unless there is some writing sufficient to indicate that a contract for sale has been made between the parties and signed by *the* party against whom enforcement is sought or by his authorized agent or broker." Various statutory provisions and judicial interpretations usually speak to the issue of when a writing signed by *one* party is "sufficient" to prove the existence of a contract that is enforceable *against that party*. The principal exceptions to this provision involve oral contracts where partial performance has taken place (e.g., payment has been made and accepted, or the goods have been delivered and accepted). Other exceptions usually apply to unique goods that are specifically manufactured for the buyer and are not suitable for sale to others (depending on when repudiation of the contract occurs) and, between merchants, certain order confirmations that are not rejected within a limited time.

In the context of the present discussion, this UCC provision is relevant for two reasons. First, it emphasizes that, to be enforceable, most major equipment contracts must be made in writing—or, at least, documented by a writing signed by the party against whom the contract is to be enforced.

Second, it points out that certain oral contracts for the sale and purchase of huge amounts of equipment can be valid if they meet one or more of the exceptions found in Section 2-201 of the UCC. The exceptions that are most relevant in this regard are those relating to: (1) partial performance; (2) unique, especially manufactured goods; and (3) writings signed by only one party (the user)—the party against whom the contract will be enforced.

Although not part of the statute of frauds, a related legal concept deserves mention here. This principle is known as the parol evidence rule.

Where a contract is documented in a writing that is intended to be the complete and final expression of the understanding reached by the parties, "parol evidence" or prior oral or written negotiations or agreements by the parties—or of contemporaneous oral agreements—will not be admitted in a court of law. The theory behind the parol evidence rule is that, once an agreement is formalized in writing, it should be considered final and should not be subject to possibly fraudulent and perjured claims about what the parties "really" agreed upon. In essence, the parol evidence rule says that the final written agreement should speak for itself.

For the parol evidence rule to be applicable, four conditions must generally be met. First, the contract involved must be documented in writing. Second, the contract must have "legal efficacy"; that is, it must not be an obvious sham. Third, the written agreement must be an "integration"—in effect a writing that finally incorporates all previous negotiations, plans, and understandings. Finally, the parties to the agreement must *intend* that the contract serve as a final integration that incorporates their total understanding. (These conditions generally exist in the typical vendor/user purchase agreement.) Where these conditions are met, no other written or oral evidence on the subjects agreed upon will be admissible. (In most states, the parol evidence rule has been codified as Section 2-202 of the UCC.)

Of course, like all good legal "rules," the parol evidence rule contains a number of exceptions. Perhaps the most basic exception provides that parol evidence *will* be admissible to show whether the agreement ever became an enforceable contract. Thus, a user can introduce parol evidence to prove such matters as whether the agreement was ever executed or intended to become valid, whether the agreement was only to become effective upon the happening of an event (a "condition precedent"), and whether the contract should be rescinded for fraud, duress, mistake, or undue influence.

The second exception to the parol evidence rule permits the introduction of written or oral evidence to show that the parties only intended the written agreement to be a *partial* integration of their understanding on the subjects involved. Where this exception is available, the user can introduce evidence of (for example) a collateral oral agreement made at the same time and for the same consideration as the principal agreement.

The third exception to the rule permits certain parol evidence to be admitted for purposes of *interpreting* the principal agreement and showing local custom and usage. The demonstration of local custom and usage can be made to define words used in the contract or to add certain terms of performance that are not inconsistent with the terms documented in the written agreement. Thus, while the parol evidence rule may preclude a user from introducing a vendor sales brochure to prove the level of performance "sold" by the vendor, the user may be able to get the material admitted by finding an ambiguous vendor representation in the contract, relating to performance, and then utilizing the brochure as evidence to "interpret" the ambiguity or to show local industry (vendor) custom.

While the exceptions to the parol evidence rule offer some assistance to a user that is fighting or threatening a contract suit, the exceptions should certainly not be relied upon at the time the contract is being drafted or negotiated. The effect of the parol evidence rule is strong—particularly when coupled with the typical integration provision found in most agreements. From a planning and negotiating perspective, the user should assume that, in any future dispute, the court will hold that any matter not included in the written contract is not part of the binding agreement between the parties.

MODIFICATION

No discussion of contract law would be complete without considering how existing agreements can be legally modified. Perhaps the best rule in this area is that, because modifications are themselves agreements, they are valid and binding only if they meet the basic requirements necessary for a contract to exist. Thus, for a modification or amendment to be valid, it must involve mutual assent, sufficient consideration, and two or more parties. (See the discussion of Basic Contract Requirements, above.) As in the case of the primary contract itself, estoppel principles may take the place of consideration in some instances. In addition, in most states Section 2-209 of the UCC provides that a contract subject to Part II of the UCC (essentially relating to the sale of goods) may be modified without need for consideration, subject to certain other restrictions noted below.

Most written agreements contain a provision that indicates how amendments may be made (e.g., "This agreement may be amended only pursuant to a written document signed by both parties hereto.") One of the great popular fallacies is that these provisions are effective and binding. In most instances, exactly the opposite is true. An agreement can be legally modified by any subsequent "contract" that is binding on the parties (i.e., that would have been a contract in the first place). Consequently, *in the absence of statute,* an oral agreement can amend a written agreement even if the written agreement states that it can only be amended in writing. Consequently, both the user and the vendor must be cautious to ensure that a subsequent written or oral exchange does not modify or amend a written agreement. (Engineering change orders can be a significant problem in this regard—so much so that some defense contractors preclude their engineers from discussing development projects with government (user) representatives, in order to minimize allegations of oral amendments to the principal agreement.) As the previous discussion of capacity to contract suggests, the question of whether a written or oral amendment is valid may turn on whether the corporate officer who agreed to it had actual or apparent authority to bind his or her firm. Thus, some protection in this area may be derived by notifying the vendor that certain user employees have no actual or apparent authority to bind the user. Some attorneys unknowingly adopt this approach by specifying that any amendment or agreement made by the user must be agreed to by an officer holding a certain title or higher. However, the effectiveness of this approach may be limited if the officers executing the amendment have actual authority to bind their respective companies.

The principle that an oral amendment can modify a written or oral agreement is subject to the statute of frauds, discussed above. Thus, UCC Section 2-209 provides that the statute of frauds requirements of Section 2-201 (quoted above) must be satisfied "if the contract as modified" is within the provisions of Section 2-201. Because the law tends to treat every modified or amended contract under the UCC as a new agreement, most amendments to a contract for the sale of goods for a purchase price of $500 or more will be subject to the limitations on oral agreements imposed by Section 2-201, as outlined above. However, the exceptions to that section will also be available to take the amended agreement "out of" the statute, thereby permitting an oral amendment to be effective in some instances.

STATUTORY ASSISTANCE: THE U.C.C.

First promulgated more than three decades ago by the American Law Institute and the National Conference of Commissioners on Uniform State Laws, the Uniform Commercial Code (UCC) governs a variety of commercial relationships. Although the UCC has been adopted throughout the United States, most states have made minor changes to the so-called "model act." As a result, the UCC is "uniform" in terms of the general statutory scheme, but different in numerous particulars, from state to state.

The UCC is composed of ten articles, and is organized as follows:

Article 1—General Provisions
Article 2—Sales
Article 3—Commercial Paper
Article 4—Bank Deposits and Collections
Article 5—Letters of Credit
Article 6—Bulk Transfers
Article 7—Warehouse Receipts, Bills of Lading, and Other Documents of Title
Article 8—Investment Securities
Article 9—Secured Transactions; Sales of Accounts, Contract Rights and Chattel Paper
Article 10—Effective Date and Repealer

Most sales and purchases of commercial goods are governed by Articles 1 and 2 of the UCC. However, Article 9 may also be relevant in such situations, if the sale and purchase involves a "secured transaction" made on credit. Similarly, a transaction involving credit may also be governed by Articles 3 and 4, which provide the basic statutory scheme for notes and relationships among banking institutions.

Although a thorough explanation of the UCC is beyond the scope of this book, several sections of the UCC have been noted in earlier portions of this chapter. Additional sections are outlined below.

To facilitate discussion, the terms "vendor," "user," and "equipment" are used in the following explanation, in lieu of the words "seller," "buyer," and "goods," which are the terms of art used in the Code. Under the definitions included in the UCC, a "seller" is a person (or party) who sells or contracts to sell goods and a "buyer" is a person (or party) who buys or contracts to buy goods. "Goods" are defined in the Code as all things (including specially manufactured goods) which are movable at the time of identification to the contract for sale, other than the money in which the price is to be paid, investment securities, and "things in action."

Users are cautioned that the discussion of selected provisions of the UCC in this chapter is not intended to cover all possible matters or to be relied upon in connection with any specific transaction. The UCC is an extremely complex statutory scheme that includes a number of important provisions that are not discussed in this chapter. The interpretation of the UCC and its applicability to a specific acquisition should always be made by a competent attorney familiar with all relevant factors involved.

Applicability

Subject to certain limitations not particularly relevant here, the UCC applies to virtually all contracts for the sale of "goods." Despite this broad applicability, however, the parties to an agreement can "contract around" the UCC in most areas and thereby change the statutory scheme through mutual agreement documented in the contract. The important point for purposes of this discussion is that, in the absence of specific agreement between the parties, the UCC will ordinarily apply to a major equipment acquisition.

The existence of the UCC as a "fall back" statutory scheme can have severe consequences for the user. First, most standard vendor agreements clearly indicate that the contract will be governed by the law of a particular state. Vendor attorneys like this approach because they can specifically rely upon the UCC provisions of that state (which may or may not be the same as the UCC provisions familiar to the attorney for the user in his or her home state). With this knowledge of the UCC, the vendor's attorney can omit many provisions from the vendor's standard form agreement and merely permit the subject areas involved to be governed by the relevant UCC provisions. This approach permits the vendor's form agreement to be shorter than it might otherwise be. In addition, it often lulls the user and his or her attorney into a false sense of security, because certain of the onerous commercial terms imposed by the UCC are never specifically included within the text of the agreement presented to the user. Second, although the UCC contains certain pro-user provisions, these provisions can be made inapplicable by disclaimers and other specific language included in the vendor's form agreement. As a result, while the vendor's attorney carefully relies upon the pro-vendor provisions of the UCC, the lawyer makes the pro-user provisions inapplicable by specific language contained in the vendor-user agreement.

As a result of these vendor legal strategies, a user that fails to devote adequate attention to the UCC, and to its impact on a specific acquisition, may find that the Code has produced unintended results—results that could have been modified by mutual agreement prior to the time that the contract was signed. The UCC essentially permits the vendor's attorney to create contractual consequences that are not specifically stated in the text of the agreement executed by the user. Because many business executives pride themselves on being able to "read and understand" a vendor contract, the importance of this fact cannot be overemphasized. Unless the business executive reads the UCC of the applicable state along with the vendor agreement, the executive will neither be reading nor understanding the terms and conditions that will govern the acquisition involved.

The UCC and Acceptance

One of the most dangerous areas of the UCC involves user acceptance or rejection of goods supplied by the vendor. The statutory scheme in this area is outlined generally below.

Rejection. Under Section 2-601 of the UCC (subject to certain exceptions), if the equipment supplied by the vendor fails in any respect to conform to the contract, the user may reject all of it, accept all of it, or accept any commercial unit or units and reject the rest. However, Section 2-602 sets forth specific standards that must be followed in effecting any rejection. Under this provision, the user's rejection of the equipment must be made within a reasonable time after the delivery or tender of the equipment by the vendor. Moreover, the rejection will be ineffective unless the user "seasonably" notifies the vendor of the rejection. After rejection, any exercise of ownership by the user with respect to any commercial unit is deemed to be "wrongful" as against the vendor. This provision can have severe consequences where the user has provided notice of rejection but continues to attempt to make the equipment perform. The user has no further obligation with respect to equipment rightfully rejected, other than a duty to hold the equipment with reasonable care at the vendor's disposition for a time sufficient to permit the vendor to remove the equipment that has been delivered to the user.

The UCC provides that a user may be deemed to have waived its objections by failing to "particularize" the defect involved. Under Section 2-605, the user's failure to state in connection with its rejection any defect which is ascertainable by reasonable inspection precludes the user from subsequently relying on the unstated defect to justify rejection or to establish a breach of contract. This provision poses serious danger to an unsuspecting user who forwards a general rejection notice to the vendor, without outlining each and every defect that has been discovered to date. Fortunately, this provision is only applicable in two instances: first, where the vendor could have cured the defect if the user had stated it "seasonably"; and, second, where the vendor, after the user's rejection, has made a request in writing for a full and final written statement of all defects on which the user proposes to rely.

Acceptance. In its statutory scheme, the UCC also governs the facts which constitute "acceptance." Pursuant to Section 2-606, "acceptance" occurs when the user: (1) after a reasonable opportunity to inspect the equipment signifies to the vendor that the equipment is conforming or that the user will take or retain the equipment in spite of its nonconformity; or (2) fails to make an effective rejection, as discussed above (but acceptance pursuant to this provision does not occur until the user has had a reasonable opportunity to inspect the equipment); or (3) does any act inconsistent with the vendor's ownership (but if the act is wrongful as against the seller, it will be an acceptance only if ratified by the seller). In another provision that can be particularly dangerous to the user, Section 2-606 specifically provides that acceptance of a part of any commercial unit will be deemed to be acceptance of the entire unit. This provision can have severe consequences for the user where interrelated components or systems are involved.

Revocation of Acceptance. The UCC provides some opportunity for a user to subsequently complain about equipment that has been accepted pursuant to the Code. However, the user faces a fairly substantial burden of proof in attempting to do so. Under Section 2-607, acceptance of equipment by the user precludes rejection of the equipment accepted. If the acceptance was made with knowledge of a nonconformity, it cannot be revoked because of the nonconformity unless the acceptance was made by the user on the reasonable assumption that the nonconformity would be seasonably cured. (However, acceptance does not of itself impair any other remedy provided by certain portions of the Code for the nonconformity involved.) The UCC provides that the user bears the burden of establishing any breach with respect to equipment that has been accepted.

To effectively revoke acceptance in whole or in part, the user must comply with the strictures of Section 2-608 of the Code. This provision states that the user may revoke its acceptance of "a lot or commercial unit" if the nonconformity "substantially impairs its value" to the user, if the user has accepted the equipment on the reasonable assumption that its nonconformity would be cured and it has not been seasonably cured by the vendor. The same right to revoke acceptance is also available to the user if the user accepted the equipment without discovery of the nonconformity, but only if the user's acceptance was reasonably induced either by the difficulty of discovering the nonconformity before acceptance or by the vendor's assurances concerning the equipment. (This provision of the Code is often relied upon by the user attorneys seeking to validate a subsequent user rejection of equipment deemed to be accepted pursuant to the Code.) In either event, the user's revocation of acceptance must occur within a reasonable time after the user discovers or "should have discovered" the ground for the revocation and before any substantial change in condition of the equipment not caused by its own defects. A user that revokes acceptance has the same rights and duties with respect to the equipment involved as if it had rejected the equipment in the first place.

The UCC and Warranties

The UCC contains a number of interesting sections that govern and, in some instances, create warranties by the vendor. These provisions are outlined below.

Section 2-312 of the Code provides a general warranty of title. Pursuant to this section, each contract for the sale of equipment is deemed to include a warranty by the vendor that the title conveyed is good, the transfer of the equipment is rightful, and the equipment is delivered free from any security interest or other lien or encumbrance (of which the user had no knowledge at the time of contracting with the vendor). This warranty can be modified or excluded *only* by specific language in the user/vendor agreement or by circumstances which give the user reason to know " that the person selling does not claim title in himself or that he is purporting to sell only such right or title as he or a third person may have."

Section 2-312 also provides that, unless otherwise agreed, a vendor who is a merchant regularly dealing in equipment of the kind covered by the contract warrants that the equipment will be delivered free of the rightful claim of any third person by way of infringement or the like. However, this warranty is subject to the caveat that a user who furnishes specifications to the vendor must hold the vendor harmless against any such claim which arises out of the vendor's compliance with the user's specifications.

Section 2-313 of the Code specifies the circumstances in which a vendor of equipment will be deemed to have created an "express" warranty relating to the equipment. That provision states that the following express warranties will be deemed to be created by a vendor under the Code:

1. An affirmation of fact or a promise made by the vendor to the user, which relates to the equipment and becomes "part of the basis of the bargain" between the vendor and the user, creates an express warranty that the equipment will conform to the affirmation or promise made by the vendor.

2. Any description of the equipment which is made "part of the basis of the bargain" between the vendor and the user creates an express warranty that the equipment will conform to the description.

3. Any sample or model of the equipment which is made "part of the basis of the bargain" creates an express warranty that the whole of the equipment will conform to the sample or model.

For purposes of this provision of the Code, it is not necessary that the vendor use formal words such as "warrant" or "guarantee" or that the vendor have a specific intention to make a warranty. However, Section 2-313 cautions that an affirmation by the vendor "merely of the value of the goods" or a statement by the vendor purporting to be merely the vendor's opinion or commendation of the goods does not create a warranty. This caution can have particularly serious consequences for a user hoping to utilize Section 2-313 to its advantage in a controversy with a vendor.

Although the express warranty provisions of the Code provide some assistance to users, the more valuable portions of the Code are often those which create implied warranties in certain circumstances. The UCC essentially provides two implied warranties: (1) a warranty of merchantability; and (2) a warranty of fitness for a particular purpose.

Section 2-314 establishes the implied warranty of merchantability. Pursuant to that provision, a warranty that the equipment shall be "merchantable" is deemed to be implied in a contract for the sale of equipment if the vendor is a "merchant" with respect to equipment of the kind sold. (As noted below, this implied warranty may be excluded or modified in the user/vendor agreement.) For purposes of this implied warranty, to be "merchantable" the equipment: (1) must be able to pass without objection in the trade under the contract description; (2) in the case of fungible goods, must be of fair average quality within the description; (3) must be fit for the ordinary purposes for which the goods are used; (4) must be (within the variations permitted by the agreement) of even kind, quality, and quantity within each unit and among all units involved; (5) must be adequately contained, packaged, and labeled as provided in the agreement; and (6) must conform to the promises or affirmations of fact (if any) made on the container or label for the equipment. The Comment of Section 2-314 specifically explains that this listing of factors does not purport to exhaust the meaning of "merchantable" or to negate any concepts of "merchantability" that may arise by usage of trade or through case law. Indeed, Section 2-314 itself expressly provides that, unless excluded or modified as discussed below, other implied warranties may arise "from course of dealing or usage of trade."

Section 2-315 provides the Code's implied warranty of fitness for a particular purpose. That provision essentially states that, where the vendor at the time of contracting has reason to know any particular purpose for which the equipment is required and the vendor also has reason to know that the user is relying on the vendor's skill or judgment to select or furnish suitable equipment, the agreement will be deemed to include an implied warranty by the vendor that the equipment will be fit for that purpose. (However, as noted below, this implied warranty can also be excluded or modified through specific contractual language.)

Because of the fact that the implied warranties imposed by the UCC can create substantial risks for the vendor that may be difficult to foresee or measure, most vendors make every effort to exclude or modify these implied warranties in any equipment agreement. Section 2-316 of the Code provides the specific requirements that must be met for the exclusion or modification of the implied warranties imposed by the UCC. Subject to certain exceptions noted below, to exclude or modify the implied warranty of merchantability or any part of it, the user/vendor agreement must include disclaimer language which specifically mentions "merchantability." In addition, where the agreement is written, the disclaimer "must be conspicuous." In order to exclude or modify an implied warranty of fitness for a particular purpose, the exclusion must be in writing and must also be "conspicuous." Section 2-316 specifically provides that language to exclude all implied warranties of fitness for a particular purpose will be deemed to be sufficient if the language states, for example, that "there are no warranties which extend beyond the description on the face hereof."

These rules concerning the exclusion or modification of warranties are subject to several exceptions. First, unless the circumstances indicate otherwise, all implied warranties will be deemed to be excluded by expressions such as "as is," "with all faults," or other language which in common understanding calls the user's attention to the exclusion of warranties and makes plain that there is no implied warranty. Second, if the user before entering into the agreement has examined the equipment or a sample or model of the equipment as fully as the user desired, or if the user has refused to examine the equipment, no implied warranty will be deemed to exist with regard to defects which an examination "ought in the circumstance to have revealed" to the user. Third, an implied warranty can also be excluded or modified by "course of dealing or course of performance or usage of trade."

Because of the fact that conflicts may exist between express and implied warranties or between warranties and various models or technical specifications, Section 2-317 attempts to specify which matters should be given priority. Pursuant to that provision, exact or technical specifications will always be deemed to displace an inconsistent sample or model or general language of description. In addition, a sample from "an existing bulk" of equipment will always be deemed to displace inconsistent general language of description. Finally, express warranties will always be deemed to displace inconsistent implied warranties other than an implied warranty of fitness for a particular purpose. Although the Code generally makes all warranties cumulative unless the result would make construction of the contract impossible or unreasonable, the interpretative priorities imposed by Section 2-317 must be considered with care when judging the relative importance of inconsistencies between agreement language and vendor sales practices.

The UCC and Risk of Loss

Although a detailed discussion of the relevant provisions is beyond the scope of this volume, the UCC also includes a number of provisions which govern shipping and risk of loss. Because these provisions will govern any purchase of equipment, unless contrary language is included in the agreement, they should be carefully studied by the user, its legal counsel, and risk managers. Among other things, these provisions specifically define such terms as "F.O.B." (which means "free on board"), "F.A.S." (which means "free alongside"), "C.I.F.", and "C. & F." The legal subtleties of these terms can have significant consequences for the user, above and beyond mere shipping instructions.

For example, under Section 2-319 of the Code, when a contract specifies "F.O.B. the place of shipment," the vendor must ship the equipment from that location and bear the expense and risk of putting the equipment into the possession of the carrier. In contrast, where the contract specifies "F.O.B. the place of destination," the vendor must at its expense and risk transport the equipment to the destination location and, at the location, tender delivery of the equipment to the user. This distinction clearly indicates that the term "F.O.B." is intended to govern responsibility and risk of loss as well as price or shipping expense.

The term "F.A.S." (normally used in connection with a specific vessel) is also a delivery term under which the vendor must at its own expense and risk deliver the equipment alongside a particular vessel in the manner usual in that port or on a dock designated and provided by the user. In addition, the vendor must obtain and tender a receipt for the equipment in exchange for which the carrier is under a duty to issue a bill of lading. Depending upon the specific utilization of the terms "F.O.B." and "F.A.S.," the user may have responsibility to advise the vendor of certain instructions for making delivery (including, in some instances, the name and location of the ship or other carrier).

The terms "C.I.F." and "C. & F." likewise have substantial legal consequences under the Code. Pursuant to Section 2-320, the term "C.I.F." means that the equipment price includes in a lump sum the cost of the equipment and the insurance and freight to the named destination. In contrast, the term "C. & F." (sometimes merely written as "C.F.") means that the equipment price includes the cost of the equipment and freight to the specified destination.

Under the Code, a C.I.F. contract is deemed to be a shipment agreement where the risk of subsequent loss or damage to the equipment passes to the user upon shipment, assuming the vendor has properly performed all of its obligations with respect to the equipment. Delivery of the equipment to the carrier is deemed to be delivery to the user for purposes of risk and title. Thus, although insurance is stipulated by a C.I.F. agreement, for the user's benefit, the user may face the risk of loss in the event that the insurance coverage proves to be inadequate. (A similar problem arises where the contract involves a shipment "F.O.B. place of shipment," due to the fact that the user will be required to seek damages or recovery from the carrier in the event that the equipment is damaged during transport.) A C.I.F. agreement does impose certain obligations on the vendor, including the obligation to obtain a policy of insurance, including any war risk insurance of a kind and on terms then current at the port of shipment in the usual amount to cover the equipment covered by the bill of lading. This insurance must provide for payment of loss to the order of the user. Unfortunately, the UCC language concerning the vendor's obligation to provide insurance does not clearly detail the amount and type of coverage that the vendor is obligated to procure in a given situation. The problem of inadequate insurance is particularly difficult to judge where delicate, lightweight components are involved or where replacement of the equipment could prove to be difficult or impossible, regardless of the purchase price.

Pursuant to Section 2-320, the term "C. & F." or its equivalent has the same effect and imposes upon the vendor the same obligations and risks as a C.I.F. agreement, except with respect to the obligation to provide insurance. Under a C. & F. agreement, title and risk of loss still pass to the user on shipment. Some agreements that have C. & F. clauses include separate covenants by the vendor to provide insurance during shipment. This approach is not inconsistent with usage of the term "C. & F." (as opposed to "C.I.F.") and may actually be a more desirable method of specifying the exact insurance coverage desired by the user.

With respect to the international marketplace, a caveat should be mentioned concerning the French contract term "C.A.F." This term has exactly the same meaning as the term "C.I.F." because the "A" does not stand for "and" but rather for "assurance" (which means "insurance"), the term "C.A.F." should not be read as "cost and freight" or otherwise confused with a C. & F. agreement.

The UCC and Holders in Due Course

Where a user is financing an acquisition of equipment, it will normally sign a promissory note or other obligation to pay and deliver it to the vendor or to some financial institution. In turn, the vendor or financial institution may assign or sell the user's note or other obligation to another entity (often an investor or yet another financial institution). By the time problems arise with the equipment, the user may find that it is making payments to a post office box in a town that it has never heard of.

If the user threatens to stop making the installment payments as a result of the equipment problems, it may find itself face to face with the holder in due course sections of the UCC. To the inexperienced user, these statutory "hell or high water" provisions can have a shocking effect.

Under Section 3-305 of the UCC, a holder in due course of a note or other negotiable instrument takes the instrument free from all claims to it on the part of any person *and* free from all defenses of any party to the instrument with whom the holder has not dealt (subject to fraud in the inducement and certain other limited exceptions). Although other sections of the Code and numerous judicial interpretations place limitations on the conditions under which a holder takes an instrument "for value" and with or without "notice" of defenses, the basic concept is very simple: a holder in due course (such as a bank) that accepts a valid assignment of the user's promissory note to the vendor generally receives the note without being subject to any defenses or claims that the user may have against the vendor. Put another way, the user is obligated to make payments to the bank or other assignee, "come hell or high water." (The user may have similar obligations, for different reasons, under various lease transactions, as outlined in Chapter 10.) As it applies to certain consumer transactions, the holder in due course doctrine has been modified by federal regulations and, in some states, by legislative enactment of consumer protection statutes or amendments to the UCC. These modifications—which generally expand a consumer's ability to assert product defenses against a holder in due course—are seldom applicable to arms length transactions between commercial parties.

The UCC and Remedies

As might be expected, a significant number of UCC provisions govern damages and other remedies. Although space does not permit a thorough analysis of all of these provisions in this book, the general structure of the remedial scheme provided by the Code is outlined below. As in the case of most other provisions of the UCC, almost all of the remedies imposed by the Code can be altered by mutual agreement in the user/vendor contract.

At the outset, a word of caution should be offered concerning the broad manner in which the UCC provides that remedies should be interpreted. Section 1-106 provides that the remedies provided by the UCC "shall be liberally administered to the end that the aggrieved party may be put in as good a position as if the other party had fully performed." However, this Section also provides a general limitation on certain remedies. Thus, the Section states the "neither consequential or special nor penal damages may be had except as specifically provided" in the UCC or by other rule of law.

Vendor Remedies. The vendor's general remedies for breach of contract by a user are set forth in Section 2-703 of the UCC. This provision essentially states that, where the user wrongfully rejects or revokes acceptance of the equipment, or fails to make a payment due on or before delivery, or repudiates with respect to a part or the whole of the equipment, then the vendor may take certain actions and enforce certain rights with respect to any equipment directly affected and, if the breach by the user is of the whole contract, then also with respect to the whole undelivered balance of equipment. In such circumstances, Section 2-703 permits the vendor to: (1) withhold delivery of the equipment; (2) stop delivery by any bailee (as provided in Section 2-705 of the Code); (3) proceed to take certain action under Section 2-704 of the UCC with respect to goods still "unidentified to the contract"; (4) resell the equipment and recover damages as provided in Section 2-706 of the UCC; (5) recover damages for nonacceptance (as provided in Section 2-708) or, in a proper case, recover the price (as provided in Section 2-709); or (6) cancel the contract.

The concept of equipment "identified to" a particular contract can be critical to the vendor's remedies where the equipment is being manufactured by the vendor for the user. Section 2-704 provides that where the equipment is unfinished, an aggrieved vendor may in the exercise of reasonable commercial judgment, "for the purposes of avoiding loss and of effective realization," either complete the manufacture of the equipment and "wholly identify the goods to the contract" or cease manufacture of the equipment and resell for scrap or salvage value "or proceed in any other reasonable manner." If the vendor completes manufacture of the equipment and, in the process, increases the damages that it can obtain from the user, the burden is on the user to show that the vendor's action in completing manufacture was commercially unreasonable.

Section 2-708 sets forth the measure of the vendor's damages for nonacceptance or repudiation by the user. This provision states that the measure of damages is the difference between the market price for the equipment at the time and place for tender and the unpaid contract price, together with any incidental damages provided in Article 2 of the UCC (Section 2-710), but less expenses saved in consequence of the user's breach. However, if this measure of damages is inadequate to place the vendor in as good a position as performance by the user would have done under the contract, then the measure of damages is the profit (including reasonable overhead) which the vendor would have made from full performance by the user under the contract, together with any incidental damages provided in Section 2-710, due allowance for costs reasonably incurred, and due credit for payments for proceeds of resale. Under this provision, in most jurisdictions the normal measure of damages for standard priced equipment would be list price less cost to the dealer or list price less manufacturing costs to the manufacturer. In all cases, the vendor may recover incidental damages (unless otherwise provided in the user/vendor agreement). Under Section 2-710 of the Code, "incidental damages" to an aggrieved vendor include any commercially reasonable charges, expenses, or commissions incurred in stopping delivery, or in the transportation, care, and custody of equipment after the user's breach, or in connection with return or resale of the equipment, or otherwise resulting from the breach.

The UCC also provides specific remedies for a vendor who seeks to recover the purchase price for equipment ordered by the user. Under Section 2-709, when the user fails to pay the price as it becomes due, the vendor may recover, together with any "incidental damages," the price: (1) of equipment accepted by the user or of conforming equipment lost or damaged within a commercially reasonable time after the risk of loss for such equipment has passed to the user; and (2) of equipment identified to the contract, if the vendor is unable after reasonable effort to resell the equipment at a reasonable price or the circumstances reasonably indicate that such effort by the vendor will be unavailing. Where the vendor sues the user for the price, the vendor must hold for the user any equipment which has been identified to the contract and which is still in the vendor's control. However, this requirement does not apply if resale of the equipment becomes possible, in which event the vendor may resell the equipment at any time prior to collection by the vendor of its judgment against the user. Where a resale occurs, the net proceeds must be credited to the user. If the user pays the vendor's judgment, the user becomes entitled to any equipment not resold. In some instances where the user wrongfully rejects or revokes acceptance of the equipment, or fails to make a payment due or repudiates, a court may find that the vendor is not entitled to the price of the equipment under Section 2-709. In such an event, the vendor may nevertheless be awarded damages for nonacceptance under Section 2-708, discussed above.

User Remedies. Section 2-711 of the UCC sets forth the user's general remedies in the event of a breach by the vendor. The most basic portion of this provision states that, where the vendor fails to make delivery or repudiates or the user rightfully rejects or justifiably revokes acceptance of the equipment, then with respect to any equipment involved, and with respect to the whole if the breach goes to the whole contract, the user may cancel and, whether or not it has done so, may also recover so much of the purchase price as has been paid by the user. In addition to recovering the purchase price, and again without regard to whether or not the user has cancelled, the user may also: (1) "cover" and obtain damages under Section 2-712 of the UCC as to all equipment affected (whether or not the equipment has been identified to the contract); or (2) recover damages for nondelivery (as provided in Section 2-713).

The legal concept of "covering" is explained in Section 2-712 of the Code, and essentially means that the user may make in good faith and without unreasonable delay any reasonable purchase of or contract to purchase equipment in substitution for the equipment that should have been provided by the defaulting vendor. In laymen's terms, the term "cover" effectively translates as "seek reasonable replacement equipment." The UCC permits a user to recover from the vendor as damages the difference between the cost of "cover" and the contract price, together with any incidental or consequential damages (as provided in Section 2-715), but less expenses saved in consequence of the vendor's breach. Importantly, the failure of the user to effect "cover" does not bar it from any other remedy for the vendor's breach. However, as noted below, the user has an obligation to "mitigate" its damages.

Where the vendor fails to deliver the equipment or repudiates, Section 2-711 also grants the user specific additional rights to recover any equipment that has been identified to the contract (as provided in Section 2-502), or obtain specific performance or "replevy" the equipment (to the extent permitted by Section 2-716).

A user that rightfully rejects or justifiably revokes acceptance of equipment in the event of a breach by the vendor is granted a security interest in the equipment in the user's possession or control. This security interest covers any payments made by the user on the price of the equipment and any expenses reasonably incurred by the user in inspecting, receiving, transporting, or caring for the equipment. Pursuant to this security interest, the user may hold the equipment and resell it in the same manner as an aggrieved vendor is permitted to sell equipment following a breach by the user (discussed above and set forth in Section 2-706 of the Code).

Section 2-713 of the Code sets forth the specific measure of damages available to the user for nondelivery or repudiation by the vendor. In such circumstances, the user's measure of damages is the difference between the market price (at the time when the user learned of the breach) and the contract price, together with any incidental and consequential damages, but less expenses saved in consequence of the vendor's breach. For purposes of this provision, market price must be determined as of the place for tender or, in circumstances of rejection after arrival or revocation of acceptance, as of the place of arrival.

The sections of the Code outlined above provide remedies for the user where it has not accepted the equipment involved, including circumstances where the user revokes acceptance. If the user has accepted the equipment and provided notification of problems (as provided in Section 2-607), the user's right to damages is governed by Section 2-714 of the UCC rather than the sections outlined above. In such circumstances, the user may recover as damages for any nonconformity in the equipment the loss resulting in the ordinary course of events from the vendor's breach, "as determined in any manner which is reasonable." Where a breach of warranty is involved, the user's measure of damages is the difference (at the time and place of acceptance of the equipment) between the value of the equipment accepted and the value the equipment would have had if it had been as warranted, "unless special circumstances show proximate damages of a different amount." In any event, the user is also permitted to recover incidental and consequential damages, as provided in Section 2-715.

Section 2-715 provides that incidental damages incurred by a user as a result of the vendor's breach may include expenses reasonably incurred in inspection, receipt, transportation, and care and custody of equipment rightfully rejected, any commercially reasonable charges, expenses, or commissions in connection with effecting "cover," and any other reasonable expense incident to the delay or other breach by the vendor. Section 2-715 specifies that consequential damages resulting from the vendor's breach may include: (1) any loss resulting from general or particular requirements and needs of which the vendor at the time of contracting had reason to know and which could not reasonably be prevented by "cover" or otherwise; and (2) injury to person or property proximately resulting from any breach of warranty by the vendor.

Regardless of the nature or source of the user's damages, the user may deduct all or any part of its damages resulting from any breach of contract by the vendor from any part of the price still due to the vendor under the same agreement. However, to take advantage of this right (which is provided by Section 2-717), the user must first notify the vendor of the user's intention to make such a deduction.

In certain instances, monetary damages may do little to place the user in the position it expected to be in when it executed the agreement with the vendor. In those circumstances, specific performance may be the only remedy that appears to be appropriate. Under Section 2-716 of the Code, the user may obtain specific performance where the equipment is unique or "in other proper circumstances." This general language is intended to emphasize that uniqueness is not the sole basis of the remedy of specific performance. The Comment to this section of the Code observes that the user's inability to "cover" is strong evidence that specific performance would be proper. The Code also grants the legal remedy of "replevin" to the user in certain limited circumstances in which "cover" is reasonably unavailable and the equipment being produced by the vendor has been "identified to" the contract. The general concept behind Section 2-716 is to grant to the user rights in the equipment comparable to the rights granted to the vendor in the price agreed to be paid by the user.

Remedies for Fraud. Under the UCC, remedies for material misrepresentation or fraud by either party include all remedies available under Article 2 for nonfraudulent breach of contract. Section 2-721 specifically indicates that neither recision or a claim for recision of the contract for sale nor rejection or return of the equipment shall be a bar to, or be deemed inconsistent with, a claim for damages or other remedy. In this regard, the Code expands the law that was previously available in many jurisdictions and permits remedies for fraud that are as broad as the remedies for breach of warranty.

Liquidated Damages. Most users are familiar with the concept of "liquidated damages." Section 2-718 of the Code specifically provides that damages for breach by either party may be liquidated (fixed) in the agreement, but only at an amount which is reasonable in light of the anticipated or actual harm caused by the breach, the difficulties of proof of loss, and the inconvenience or nonfeasibility of otherwise obtaining an adequate remedy. This section also provides that any contractual term fixing unreasonably large liquidated damages will be deemed to be "void as a penalty." Interestingly, the Comment to Section 2-718 adds that a contractual term fixing an unreasonably small amount of liquidated damages "would be subject to similar criticism and might be stricken under the section on unconscionable contracts or clauses." The restrictions placed on liquidated damages by the Code are extremely important for anyone drafting an equipment acquisition agreement. A user should never place a liquidated damages provision in such an agreement without specifically reviewing the limitations on liquidated damages that are set forth in Section 2-718 or its equivalent under local law.

In addition to setting forth strict limitations on liquidated damages, the UCC actually imposes liquidated damages of its own in certain limited circumstances. Thus, where the vendor justifiably withholds delivery of equipment because of the user's breach, Section 2-718 provides that the user is entitled to restitution of any amount by which the sum of its payments exceeds: (1) the amount to which the vendor is entitled by virtue of terms liquidating the vendor's damages in accordance with the portion of Section 2-718 which imposes the acceptable parameters for liquidated damages; or (2) in the absence of any such terms, 20% of the value of the total performance for which the user is obligated under the contract or $500, whichever is smaller. However, the user's right to restitution under this provision is subject to offset by the vendor to the extent that the vendor establishes a right to recover damages under some other provision of the Code, plus the amount or value of any benefits received by the user directly or indirectly by reason of the contract. The provisions of Section 2-718 relating to restitution to the user specifically apply to any deposits or downpayments made by the user.

Limitation of Remedies. As noted at the outset of this discussion of remedies under the UCC, the vendor and user may alter the remedy scheme set forth in the Code, subject to certain restrictions. The general provision which governs contractual modification or limitation of remedies is Section 2-719 of the UCC. Pursuant to this section (but subject to the liquidated damage provision explained above), the user/vendor agreement may provide for remedies in addition to or in substitution for the remedies provided in Article 2 of the UCC and, in addition, may limit or alter the measure of damages recoverable under Article 2 of the Code. Section 2-719 also provides that the resort by either party to a remedy provided under the UCC is optional unless the remedy is expressly agreed in the contract to be exclusive, in which event it will be deemed to be the sole remedy. (Even here, however, the Code provides a second chance by indicating that, where circumstances cause an exclusive or limited remedy "to fail its essential purpose," the aggrieved party may still resort to some other remedy provided by the Code.)

One of the most important portions of Section 2-719 relates to the limitation of consequential damages. The relevant portion of this section provides that consequential damages may be limited or excluded "unless the limitation or exclusion is unconscionable." The Code provides that limitation of consequential damages for injury to the person in case of consumer goods is prima facie unconscionable, "but limitation of damages where the loss is commercial is not." Most vendors and, indeed, many users seek to limit consequential damages in commercial transactions by appropriate contractual language. In most instances, conspicuous language limiting such consequential damages will be given legal effect. Of course, a party can also effectively avoid any liability for consequential damages resulting from a breach of a warranty provided for by the Code by disclaiming the warranty itself, as explained above.

The concept of unconscionable limitations on general damages is an interesting one. Although courts are more willing to find such limitations unconscionable where consumer goods are involved and where the vendor has a significant advantage in bargaining power, the original Comment to Section 2-719 offers some solace to commercial users. This Comment explains that, under Section 2-719, parties are left free to shape their remedies to their particular requirements. However, it adds that "it is of the very essence of a sales contract that at least minimum adequate remedies be available." The Comment then goes on to caution: "If the parties intend to conclude a contract for sale within this Article they must accept the legal consequence that there be at least a fair quantum of remedy for breach of the obligations or duties outlined in the contract. Thus any clause purporting to modify or limit the remedial provisions of this Article in any unconscionable manner is subject to deletion and in that event the remedies made available by this Article are applicable as if the stricken clause had never existed." (The UCC also imposes limitations on certain unconscionable agreements and clauses. These limitations are discussed in the Unenforceable Agreements section of this chapter, below.)

From a practical standpoint, contractual remedies can also be limited by the "statutes of limitation" that apply in the various states. These statutes essentially limit the period within which an action must be brought by an aggrieved party. Subject to certain exceptions (generally including concealed fraud or defects that were not and could not be previously discovered), the failure to bring an action within the period specified by the statute of limitation forever bars the party from seeking a legal remedy. In many jurisdictions, the legislative trend has been to adopt increasingly short statutes of limitation. Many vendors attempt to further restrict the time period within which an action may be brought by an aggrieved user by contractually shortening the applicable statute of limitation. Vendor provisions which take this approach are discussed in Chapter 8.

TERMS IMPLIED BY LAW

For any contract to be enforceable, the court must be capable of determining what "bargain" has been made by the parties to the agreement. Thus, vagueness of expression, indefiniteness, and uncertainty as to any of the essential terms of an agreement may preclude the creation of an enforceable contract.

Despite this fact, many contracts fail to include the level of detail that might be desired in interpreting or enforcing the agreement. Were the legal system to refuse to enforce any contract that might be said to be incomplete in some respect, the reliability of documented commercial transactions would be seriously jeopardized. Fortunately, the law provides that, where the vagueness, indefiniteness, or uncertainty is not fatal, the missing terms or conditions to the agreement may be implied by the court.

As is the case with many legal concepts, no clear rule explains when vagueness, indefiniteness, or uncertainty will be deemed to be fatal. However, the failure to adequately specify the price to be paid or the goods or services to be provided will normally create serious cause for concern. The failure to specify the time when performance is due or the duration during which performance is to continue can be fatal in some instances, but in other circumstances courts may be willing to imply the necessary specifics.

When a court attempts to add definiteness to an agreement, by implication or otherwise, it normally relies heavily upon the concept of "reasonableness." Thus, if an agreement which is otherwise valid fails to fix the price, the inference will be that the vendor intended to sell at a reasonable price or at the market price, if there is one. Similarly, if the contract fails to state the time when performance or payment is to be rendered, the court will normally imply a promise to perform within a reasonable time.

In seeking to determine what circumstances should be considered "reasonable" under an agreement, the court will often look to existing commercial standards in the industry involved. Trade practices, market standards, and published or quoted prices may all be particularly relevant for this purpose.

Depending upon the industry involved, substantial reliance upon trade practices may create serious risks for the user. For example, in many industries the trade practices include standard terms and conditions that favor the vendor rather than the user. Indeed, in many such industries, the vendor specifically excludes certain of these more onerous trade practices from its written agreements. By taking this approach, the vendor avoids the possible controversy that might result from presenting these practices to the user in a contract. Instead, the vendor merely relies upon the fact that a court will imply the missing trade practices in the event that they become relevant in any subsequent dispute. Some vendors adopt a slightly stronger approach by specifically indicating in the agreement that, where applicable, standard trade practices will govern.

MISTAKE

As many law students have found, the concept of "mistake" is one of the most difficult in contract law. This difficulty essentially results from the fact that, although contractual mistakes arise rather frequently, the law gives special effect only to certain mistakes in certain circum-

stances. From a public policy standpoint, the legal concept of "mistake" is based upon the prem-
ise that certain types of mistake will be deemed to be so basic to a contractual bargain that the
contract should be untied or made subject to special legal rules.

Because the legal theory of "mistake" is highly ephemeral, and because legal decisions in this
area depend substantially upon the facts of the case and local precedent, users considering this
subject should do so with particular care. From a practical standpoint, a user should never rely
upon the concept of "mistake" as a planning or affirmative negotiating tool in any equipment
acquisition. At best, the concept of "mistake" should be used only as an after-the-fact defensive
tool to remove the user from an otherwise untenable position.

The circumstances in which "mistake" will be found can seldom be predicted with impunity.
Nevertheless, the following generalizations may be helpful to an understanding of this elusive
concept.

First, if an offer is stated in ambiguous terms the law will normally find that a contract exists
upon acceptance only if both parties attached the same meaning to the terms that were critical
to the agreement. Consequently, if parties that have *objectively* manifested their agreement
totally lack *subjective* agreement on an essential contractual term, a court may invoke the doctrine of "mistake" and find that no contract exists. Specific legal decisions in this area often
depend upon the degree to which both parties were mistaken, or one party knew that the other
party was misinterpreting an essential element of the agreement but said nothing, or the party
that was mistaken was also negligent in making the critical assumption involving the mistake.
For example, a clear offer in writing that is accepted by a user that misunderstands the content
or meaning of the contract will generally not be held to involve "mistake," at least where the
user's failure to properly inform itself is negligent and the vendor is not aware of the user's
misunderstanding.

Second, a mistake in the transmission of an offer by an intermediary will generally prevent
formation of a contract if the person accepting the offer knew or should have known that a
mistake occurred in the transmission of the offer. This approach is rather soundly backed by
public policy considerations designed to preclude a person who receives an incorrect offer from
taking inappropriate advantage of an error in transmission by accepting the offer and claiming
that a binding contract exists.

Third, if the parties to an agreement are clearly mistaken as to the *subject matter* of the
agreement, the doctrine of "mistake" will ordinarily be invoked and no contract will be deemed
to exist. As in other aspects of the concept of "mistake," this general result reflects the legal
belief that no agreement can occur where a legitimate "meeting of the minds" fails to occur on
an essential element of the contract.

Fourth, where the mistake made by the parties relates to a collateral matter rather than to
an issue that is critical to the existence of the agreement, the mistake will not ordinarily affect
the validity of the agreement. However, the mistake may provide at least some relief from
enforcement of the agreement pursuant to its terms. Ordinarily, enforcement of the contract will
not be modified unless the mistake is nonnegligent and unless prompt notice has been given by
the mistaken party before the other party has substantially changed its position. In reaching
decisions in this area, courts will often attempt to determine whether the allegedly mistaken
party knew of, or should have known of, the mistake at the time that it entered into the agreement involved.

CONDITIONS PRECEDENT AND SUBSEQUENT

When speaking about the various promises of the respective parties to a contract, both lawyers
and laymen often refer to the "terms and conditions" of the agreement. Although this termi-

nology is normally used more by force of habit than by conscious decision, the language does have operative legal effect. Many contracts include both "promises" (terms) and "conditions." The distinction between the two can be particularly important where the promise or condition is not fulfilled.

If the contractual language involves a promise on the part of one party, its failure to occur will generally be deemed to be a breach of contract, for which the other party may obtain an appropriate legal remedy such as damages. On the other hand, if the language involves a condition and not a promise, the failure of the condition to occur merely discharges the party having the conditional obligation. Being discharged by the failure of the condition, the party involved is no longer responsible for performing and the other party has no right to seek damages as a result. In certain unusual instances, the contractual language may involve both a condition and a promise, in which case one of the parties may be discharged from further performance but the party may also have a right to obtain damages from the other party.

In interpreting a stated provision in an agreement as a condition or a promise, the form of expression utilized will normally be deemed to be controlling. Thus, if the court finds that the words are those of condition, the language will be given that effect. In contrast, if the court finds that the words are those of promise, they will normally be construed as promissory only. In situations where interpretation is difficult, the language will normally be interpreted as a promise, thereby creating a right of action for damages.

In most well-drafted commercial agreements, any conditions involved are relatively easy to identify. Language such as "if," "on condition that," "provided," "when," and "after" is often used to signify the creation of a condition or conditional promise.

Contractual conditions are ordinarily classified as "conditions precedent" or "conditions subsequent." Conditions precedent involve facts or events, occurring subsequently to the making of a valid contract, that must exist or occur before a given contractual promise or action must be fulfilled (and, therefore, before the beneficiary of the promise or action has a right to performance or a right to a judicial remedy for nonperformance). Conditions subsequent involve facts and events that occur after a breach of contractual duty and that terminate the right to immediate performance as well as the right to seek a judicial remedy for nonperformance. Put more simply, if the conditioning event must occur before the promisor's duty to perform becomes present and required, it is normally referred to as a "condition precedent." In contrast, if the conditioning event causes the discharge of an existing duty of performance, it is generally referred to as a "condition subsequent."

Substantively, it makes little difference whether an event is referred to as a condition precedent or a condition subsequent. From a procedural standpoint, however, the difference can be critical. In most jurisdictions, the burden of proving that a condition precedent has occurred rests with the plaintiff promisee (in effect, the beneficiary of the promise that was subject to the condition precedent). However, the burden of proving the occurrence of a condition subsequent ordinarily rests with the defendant promisor.

BREACH OF CONTRACT

Under general contract law, any unjustified failure to perform when performance is due is deemed to be a breach of contract which entitles the injured party to seek damages or some other legal remedy. However, not every failure to perform gives rise to the same level or degree of breach. If the breach of promise is slight or insubstantial (often called a "partial breach"), the plaintiff's damages will normally be restricted to compensation for the defective performance. However, if the breach is material (often referred to as a "total breach"), the plaintiff will ordinarily have a right to claim damages for total failure of performance or, alternatively, merely seek compensation for the defective performance (as in the case of a partial breach).

Material or Total Breach

A material or total breach by the promisor generally excuses the injured promisee from his own duties of performance under the agreement and also gives the promisee a right of action for damages. The word "material" is a much better descriptor than the word "whole" in this context. For a material or total breach of contract to occur, a total failure of performance by the defendant is not required. Rather, the breach must "go to the essence" of the contract or "go to the whole of the consideration" of the agreement. Put another way, the defendant's failure to perform must be of such importance that without it the plaintiff will not obtain substantially what it bargained for.

Partial Breach

If the breach is not sufficiently serious to reach this level, the breach is said to be "partial" and the plaintiff can only seek damages for the defect. This distinction is critical when counseling a plaintiff as to its rights under an equipment acquisition agreement. If the vendor's breach of contract does not qualify as a "material" or "total" breach, the user will still be obligated to perform its own obligations under the agreement and must merely elect to proceed against the vendor for damages for any defect or nonperformance. In contrast, if the vendor's breach is "material" or "total," the user no longer has any obligation to perform its own promises under the agreement and can elect to terminate the agreement and sue for damages or seek other remedies. Alternatively, where a "material" or "total" breach is involved, the user may elect to treat the breach as "partial," leave the contract in effect, and sue the vendor for an appropriate measure of damages. (This alternative to treat the breach as "partial" is not applicable where the vendor also repudiates the agreement. The law interprets any present repudiation of a contract as a "material" or "total" breach. Repudiation is "present" rather than "anticipatory," as discussed below, if the repudiation is made when or after performance under the contract is due.)

Actions for Recovery

In virtually all jurisdictions, only one legal action is allowed to recover damages for a single breach of contract. Any damages not included in a judgment resulting from such an action will ordinarily be lost to the plaintiff. Where successive breaches are held to exist, successive legal actions may be brought. However, if the plaintiff delays suit until several breaches have occurred, damages for all of the breaches of contract to date must be included in the action brought against the defendant. These generalities are subject to subtle interpretations in certain areas, and specific legal advice should always be sought. For example, a material breach with respect to one installment of an installment sales agreement may entitle the plaintiff, if it so elects, to recover damages for breach of the entire agreement (and, indeed, many contracts so provide). In some jurisdictions, a plaintiff suing for the breach of a single installment payment may be required to bring an action for the full amount due or risk losing the right to do so at a later time. Where the breach of contract is by repudiation, the plaintiff must generally bring an action for all damages resulting from failure of the entire agreement.

The rule that damages for all past breaches must be recovered in a single action does not apply where several existing claims held by a plaintiff arose out of breaches of separate contracts. In such an event, the breaches relating to each contract may generally be pursued separately. Even here, however, care must be taken where the agreements may be considered to be "linked," either by express language or by implication. Again, the law of the relevant local jurisdiction should be carefully reviewed.

Anticipatory Repudiation

Under the early common law, it was impossible for a breach of contract to occur before the time for performance was due. Under these decisions, a promisor could announce that it did not intend to perform its future obligations under an agreement and, if the time for such performance was not yet due, have no liability for breach of contract.

In the United States today, this judicial approach has been replaced almost universally by the doctrine of "anticipatory repudiation." This doctrine essentially provides that an immediate action for damages exists for an anticipatory repudiation of a bilateral contract. (Despite the weight of the terminology involved, an anticipatory repudiation is no more than an announcement by a promisor under an agreement that, in the future, when it is obligated to perform, it will not render its performance.)

After an anticipatory repudiation has occurred, the plaintiff is no longer required to continue its own performance under the agreement or to maintain its present ability to perform its own obligations. In this regard, an anticipatory repudiation is generally considered to be a "material" or "total" breach of the agreement.

From a practical standpoint, the doctrine of anticipatory repudiation can be extremely important to the user. First, because an anticipatory repudiation will be treated as a "material" or "total" breach, a user involved in a dispute with a vendor can make a powerful threat by asserting that the vendor's statements or actions amount to an anticipatory repudiation of the agreement. If a court were to concur with the user's claim, the user would no longer have any obligation to perform under the agreement and could also seek various legal remedies against the vendor. Second, in any contractual dispute, it is most important that the user have a clear indication of whether it is still obligated to perform under the agreement (even though the vendor has breached, or threatened to breach, its own obligations under the contract). Where the user is able to invoke the doctrine of anticipatory repudiation, it will be released from its own obligations to perform and, as a result, will have greater flexibility in seeking alternative sources of replacement equipment. The doctrine of anticipatory repudiation is particularly important from a timing standpoint, because the user can claim an immediate "material" breach and need not wait until the specific time for the vendor's performance has arisen under the agreement. In this regard, the doctrine can be helpful to a user claiming a "material" or "total" breach under a series of linked agreements. Thus, the user may effectively claim that an actual breach by the vendor under one agreement should be interpreted as an anticipatory repudiation of the vendor's obligations under all of the other linked agreements.

The actions required for anticipatory repudiation vary from jurisdiction to jurisdiction and from agreement to agreement. In general, the repudiation must be positive and unequivocal. An expression as to future inability to perform will not ordinarily be held to be anticipatory repudiation. Likewise, a denial of liability based upon a good faith belief about a disputed fact will not be held to involve anticipatory repudiation. Subject to certain exceptions, the fact that a party does not appear likely to be able to perform in the future will not be deemed to be anticipatory repudiation and cannot be interpreted as an intention to repudiate the agreement. The principal exception to this general rule occurs where the likely future inability to perform is caused by some clear, voluntary act of the promisor that is so substantial that ultimate nonperformance is almost certain. Anticipatory repudiation may be manifested by conduct as well as by words. Perhaps the classic example of the former type of repudiation involves the situation where the vendor sells the equipment to be delivered under the contract to a third party.

The doctrine of anticipatory repudiation does not apply to unilateral, unconditional promises (for example, the doctrine does not apply where the maker of a promissory note declares, prior to the maturity of the note, that he does not intend to pay the note at maturity). In addition, the doctrine does not apply where a contract that was originally bilateral has been fully performed on one side. In such circumstances, no real reason for applying the theory exists.

Waiver

No discussion of default would be complete without a review of the doctrine of "waiver." The law has long recognized that, absent contractual terms to the contrary (and sometimes even in spite of such terms), the conduct of a party may be deemed to modify his prior agreement. Thus, where the conduct of one or both parties after signing a contract indicates that certain provisions were not given effect by the parties, a court may hold the provision to be inoperative and of no legal effect. Where such a judicial conclusion is reached due to the inaction of one party to the agreement, the party's conduct is generally referred to as a "waiver," and the party is said to have waived its rights under the agreement.

Because of the doctrine of waiver, inaction by a user in asserting its rights under an equipment acquisition agreement can be fatal. Even where the user's inaction merely results from an oversight or lack of attention, a court may conclude that the user's failure to file timely objection to a vendor default or nonconformity should preclude the user from objecting to a subsequent, similar problem. The doctrine of waiver often poses particular risks where a user has accepted equipment deliveries on a delayed basis, or equipment that includes minor defects, over a long period of time and then attempts to claim a default when the latest shipment arrives.

To avoid these problems, most parties specify in their agreements that a waiver will be effective only if made in writing and signed by the party to be charged with the waiver. Similarly, knowledgeable parties provide that waivers cannot be implied by action or inaction and that the waiver of a single breach or nonconformity cannot be deemed to be a waiver of any subsequent problem of a similar nature. Although language of this type will normally suffice, a blatant course of dealing clearly indicating a waiver of rights may still be accepted as such by a court.

REMEDIES

Because of the broad applicability of the UCC in the United States today, the remedies available for a breach of contract for the sale of goods will normally be governed by relevant provisions of the UCC or by provisions of the user/vendor agreement which take precedence over those provisions. Although an overview of the remedy provisions of the UCC is provided earlier in this chapter, several additional points concerning remedies for breach of contract should be noted at this juncture.

First, any breach of contract gives the injured party a right of action and a right to a verdict in its favor. However, if no actual loss has been suffered by the injured party due to the breach, or if the amount of the actual loss is too speculative to be proved with reasonable certainty, the party will only be entitled to a judgment for nominal damages. (In one classic case, the judgment entered was for "six cents and costs.") This rule can be particularly important in equipment acquisition disputes. Although a user may have suffered substantial damages, proving the amount of the damages effectively may be difficult, especially where the user has not kept detailed records following the breach.

Second, as noted in the discussion of the UCC, above, consequential damages can be recovered only for injuries or damages that the defendant had reasonable cause to foresee as the probable result of a breach at the time that the contract was made. Any other consequential damages will be deemed to be "remote" and not compensable. In the relatively rare instances where a vendor has not limited its liability for consequential damages by specific contractual language, the doctrine of foreseeability may still preclude the vendor from being liable for a substantial portion of the consequential damages incurred by the user.

Third, as suggested in the UCC discussion, above, liquidated damage provisions may be subject to substantial interpretation and narrow construction. In most jurisdictions, the fact that the parties refer to "liquidated damages" in the contract will not be deemed to be controlling if the court finds that the damages are "in the nature of a penalty" and therefore prohibited. Generally, if the court concludes that the liquidated damages were intended in the nature of a penalty in excess of any loss likely to be sustained, the plaintiff's recovery will be limited to the loss actually sustained and the liquidated damages will be stricken. If the contract is for an item of equipment or other matter of a certain value, or a value easily ascertainable, and the parties have fixed a sum in excess of that value as liquidated damages, the sum so fixed will normally be held to be a penalty. Likewise, if certain terms of the contract involve fixed or ascertainable values, and other terms do not, and the same amount of liquidated damages is applied to a breach of any one of the terms, the liquidated damages will be held to be in the nature of a penalty and not recoverable.

Fourth, a party injured by a breach of contract has an affirmative obligation to minimize ("mitigate") the loss incurred as a result of the breach. Thus, a potential plaintiff must take reasonable action to avoid any further loss that can be precluded without undue risk, expense, or humiliation. In most jurisdictions, expenses incurred in a reasonable effort to minimize further loss will be recoverable whether or not the plaintiff's basic action for breach of contract is successful.

Fifth, a suit for specific performance will generally not be available to a plaintiff if there is an adequate remedy at law. In effect, an action for specific performance will be permitted only where the plaintiff's loss cannot be compensated in damages. This distinction is readily apparent in the various legal decisions involving sales of land and sales of equipment. Except where otherwise prohibited by the agreement, specific performance is often permitted in connection with the sale of land, due to the fact that each parcel of real estate is considered to be unique. On the other hand, specific performance is seldom permitted in connection with the sale of equipment, on the theory that substitute or replacement equipment can be obtained elsewhere. The principal exception to this rule relates to "unique" equipment that simply cannot be adequately replaced. (See Chapter 8.)

IMPOSSIBILITY OF PERFORMANCE

Under certain limited circumstances, the "impossibility" of performing may be held to be an adequate excuse for nonperformance of an obligation under a contract. Acceptable defenses based upon impossibility of performance generally fall within one of three categories: (1) the defendant asserts that supervening events have made its own performance impossible; (2) the defendant asserts that performance of the agreed-upon equivalent (by the plaintiff) has become impossible; or (3) the defendant asserts that the purpose for which it entered into the contract has been frustrated.

Generalities concerning impossibility of performance are as dangerous as those relating to the legal concept of "mistake" (discussed above). However, the following broad principles can be noted for purposes of this discussion.

First, "subjective" impossibility will seldom be held to be an adequate defense for nonperformance. On the other hand, "objective" impossibility may be an acceptable defense under certain circumstances. In this regard, "subjective" impossibility of performing a promise refers to impossibility that is due wholly to the inability of the individual promisor. "Objective" impossibility refers to impossibility that is due to the fact that the promise simply cannot be performed (by any promisor).

Second, in many jurisdictions, "impossibility" has been interpreted to include "impracticability" due to extreme and unreasonable consequences (such as expense, injury, or loss). In judging whether "impossibility" or "impracticability" of performance should be viewed as an adequate defense for nonperformance, courts often attempt to interpret the agreement to assess which party (if any) was expected to bear the risk that a given set of circumstances might come to pass.

Third, in many jurisdictions, impossibility of performance will be held to be an acceptable excuse for nonperformance of a contractual duty in four situations: (1) where the subject matter covered by the contract has been destroyed or ceases to exist (for example, where the mine in a mineral requirements contract runs out of ore); (2) where incapacity, illness, or death of an essential person occurs in a contract for personal services (for example, where a specific consultant named in a consulting agreement dies); (3) where performance under a contract that was lawful when made subsequently becomes illegal (for example, where a seller of goods cannot perform due to the fact that the government has subsequently made the sale illegal); and (4) where future events prevent the accomplishment of the contractual purpose intended by both parties (the classic example involves a party who paid to rent a room to view a coronation parade that was subsequently rerouted along another street). Note should be made that, in the first of these four categories, the mere destruction of equipment proposed to be sold will not ordinarily be deemed to be an acceptable defense for the vendor. In such instances, the courts will merely look to the agreement and to existing precedent to determine which party should be held to have the risk of loss involved.

Fourth, impossibility of performance may be temporary or partial. Where the impossibility of performance is found to be partial, it may constitute an excuse for nonperformance only during the period that the impossibility exists. For example, if a named consultant under a consulting agreement is unable to perform due to illness, this fact may not be adequate to release the consultant from performing once he or she has returned to good health.

UNENFORCEABLE AGREEMENTS

In certain situations, the law provides that otherwise binding agreements cannot be enforced. In some instances, the entire contract will be held to be unenforceable, either by one party or by both parties. In other situations, only certain provisions of the agreement will be held to be unenforceable. Ordinarily, all or the applicable part of an agreement will be held to be unenforceable where illegality, duress, unconscionability, or fraud is involved.

A contract may be found to be illegal if its formation or performance is criminal, tortious, or contrary to public policy. The latter category can encompass a broad range of equitable principles, although these principles are normally invoked more in consumer contracts than in commercial agreements. The law involving illegal agreements is complex, and seldom applies to equipment acquisition contracts.

The concepts of duress and unconscionability are often blended by the court in determining that a specific agreement or provision is unenforceable. Section 2-302 of the UCC provides that, if a court as a matter of law finds that the contract or any clause of the contract was unconscionable at the time the agreement was made, the court may refuse to enforce the contract, or may enforce the remainder of the contract without the unconscionable clause, or may limit the application of the unconscionable clause in order to avoid any unconscionable result. In most jurisdictions, the decisions based upon unconscionability have been grounded upon other legal and equitable principles rather than on the specific authority of Section 2-302. The legal concept of "adhesion contracts" has often been used for this purpose. Contracts of adhesion are those agreements in which one party with superior bargaining strength forces the other, weaker party to accept the contract (often a standard form agreement) on a "take-it-or-leave-it" basis. Courts relying upon this doctrine often refer to the fact that a true "meeting of the minds" never occurred or to the fact that the weaker party never really "accepted" the form offer. Although the adhesion contract doctrine has remarkable applicability in many equipment purchases by commercial users, most courts have been reluctant to apply the doctrine to commercial settings. Rightfully or wrongfully, these courts assert that businesses should be capable of judging whether or not to enter into an agreement, regardless of any disparity in bargaining power that may exist. In the real world, of course, this assumption is often woefully incorrect.

Contracts induced by fraud are generally held to be either void or voidable. In contract law, fraud normally includes known misrepresentation, concealment, and certain types of nondisclosure (i.e., where no privilege to withhold the information exists). If the fraud is in the inducement (for example, fraudulent representations concerning the value of the property in order to induce a party to sign), the contract will generally be held to be voidable at the option of the defrauded party, but not void. On the other hand, if the fraud goes to the contract itself (for example, where a party is induced to sign a document that it does not intend to execute as a contract), then the contract will generally be held to be void "ab initio." In most instances, the normal remedy for a contract that is voidable due to fraud is recision of the contract. However, in some circumstances, the defrauded party may effectively seek a decree reforming the contract to properly express the agreement that the party intended at the time that the contract was signed.

Because fraud in the inducement permits an aggrieved user to declare the agreement void and unenforceable and thereby rescind the contract, claims of fraud can be particularly effective in equipment acquisition disputes. However, claims of fraud are serious matters that require substantial documentation in order to be proven in a court of law, particularly where two commercial parties are involved. The mere fact that an item of equipment failed to perform as represented by the vendor's marketing representative is seldom adequate ground for a claim of fraud in the inducement, especially where the user/vendor agreement contains an appropriate "integration" clause limiting the effect of any oral representations or prior written agreements.

7
PATENTS, COPYRIGHTS, TRADE SECRETS, AND OTHER PROPRIETARY RIGHTS

The equipment acquired by a user often involves a number of "proprietary rights" held by the owners or developers of the hardware, software, or processes involved. Although the protection of these proprietary rights would initially appear to be of greater interest to the vendor than the user, infringement of these rights by a third party may create substantial competitive problems for the user. In addition, if the user acquires equipment that infringes upon the proprietary rights held by another, the user may face liability or removal of the equipment from its own operations. In order to judge the degree to which a user/vendor agreement provides appropriate protection to the user in circumstances such as these, the user and its professional advisors must have a general understanding of the laws involving patents, copyrights, trade secrets, and other proprietary rights.

This chapter explores three categories of proprietary rights: (1) patents; (2) copyrights; and (3) trade secrets. An overview of each of these areas is provided below:

- *Patents:* Federal patent law grants statutory protection for a period of 17 years to persons who invent or discover any new and useful process (including an art or method), machine, manufacture, or composition of matter, or any new and useful improvement thereof.
- *Copyrights:* Federal copyright law grants an author or other copyright owner exclusive control for 50 years (or more) of the right to reproduce a form of expression (sometimes phrased as "any original modicum of authorship"). Innovation or creativity is not a prerequisite for protection and it is not a violation of the copyright for the same idea to be expressed in other words.
- *Trade Secrets:* The laws of most states provide, either by statute or common law, that a person may protect processes, programs, procedures, formulas, patterns, devices, and compilations of information which are used in the person's business and which give the owner some opportunity to obtain business advantage over competitors who do not have the trade secret. Almost by definition, a trade seret must be kept "confidential," either by practice or by agreement.

Federal statutes and the statutes of most states also provide protection to certain trademarks and service marks. This protection generally runs only to a given logo or mark, and any associated business goodwill. Although these marks may be extremely valuable when used to describe and market a given item of equipment, software, or other matter, the protection provided by trademark and service mark statutes does not run to the underlying equipment, program, or process that may be described by the mark. The law relating to trademarks and service marks is not reviewed in this chapter.

Although the following discussion provides a general explanation of the law of patents, copyrights, and trade secrets in the context of major equipment acquisitions, two caveats should be noted at the outset. First, the law of proprietary rights is highly specialized, whether it involves statutes or common law. Indeed, long before designation and specialization programs became generally acceptable for lawyers, patent law was one of the few areas in which attorneys were permitted to announce their specialized training. Although a general understanding of patents, copyrights, and trade secrets is essential to any attorney or business executive attempting to negotiate a major equipment acquisition, persons who do not specialize in this unique field should have a healthy respect for its many pitfalls. Few areas of the law offer more unusual concepts and exceptions. Consequently, a user facing a difficult or close question in the proprietary rights area, or a user attempting to protect its own proprietary rights, should always rely upon the services and advice of a competent professional who specializes in the respective proprietary field. Second, the law of proprietary rights has changed considerably in recent years, both through the enactment of new statutes and through the issuance of new judicial decisions. Rapid developments have particularly occurred with respect to the protection of software and firmware. Indeed, as this text is moving to typesetting, several cases are pending that may create further developments in this field. Because of these rapid changes, and the likelihood that further changes will occur in the near future, users should recognize that the legal concepts set forth below may need to be updated before being applied to an actual transaction.

PATENTS

The present Patent Act was adopted by the Congress in 1952, based upon federal statutory concepts dating back to 1870. As noted above, the Act essentially provides that "whoever invents or discovers any new and useful process, machine, manufacture, or composition of matter, or any new and useful improvement thereof, may obtain a patent therefor," subject to the conditions and requirements of the Act. Under this law, the term "process" includes an "art or method" and "a new use of a known process, machine, manufacture, composition of matter, or material." Even if an invention or discovery is "new and useful," and otherwise meets the requirements for patentability, a patent may not be granted if the process or other matter would be obvious to a person having ordinary skill in the particular art involved.

Once a patent is granted, any application of the ideas and principles underlying the process or other matter is protected for a statutory period of 17 years. This protection essentially grants the patent holder the right to exclude other persons from making, using, or selling the patented invention for the statutory period of protection. Unlike the copyright and trade secret laws, this protection even extends against a claim by another person that he or she independently developed the same product. Comparable patent rights can also be obtained in most other countries.

Because patent rights effectively grant a lawful monopoly to the protected invention, they can be extremely valuable. However, because of this monopoly, the patent laws are generally strictly construed.

Practical Problems

Despite the substantial value of the monopoly resulting from an effective patent, the federal patent laws create several practical problems for vendors and other inventors of patentable products. These problems are discussed below.

First, the federal Patent Office is overwhelmed with work and, in recent years, has been unable to process patent applications within any reasonable timeframe. In areas involving rapidly-changing technology, a patentable product or process may be outdated before the patent application has been processed and the patent granted.

Second, filing an application for a patent may involve disclosures which make it more likely that an otherwise secret process will be illegally used by a competitor. While the patentable product or process could be kept confidential and protected through trade secret law (discussed below), certain critical matters relating to it may have to be published in connection with the patent application. In theory, a patentable invention may be protected as a trade secret, even if a patent application has been filed, until the patent is issued. However, this theoretical protection often dissolves in actual practice.

Third, federal patent protection is granted on a "first reduced to practice" basis rather than on a "first to file" basis. Thus, where two inventors create the same product or process, and a dispute over the right to a patent results, the patent will generally be granted to the party that can produce accurate records that it developed and "reduced to practice" the product or process involved. The fact that the other party filed its application for a patent for the same product or process first will have no effect.

Because of this statutory priority, and because of the two problem areas noted above, some vendors conclude that it is to their advantage to delay filing a patent application until they are able to introduce the product or process and gain practical advantage in the marketplace. In the interim, these vendors protect the product or process by relying upon trade secret law. Indeed, in particularly fast-changing areas of technology, some vendors forego the patent process entirely, relying upon marketplace advantage and constant innovation to keep them ahead of the competition. Other vendors use this marketplace strategy, but still have their lawyers file patent applications, in the event that the product or process proves to be longer-lasting or more valuable than initially expected.

Functional Duplication

Although the patent laws grant monopoly protection to a patented product or process, they do not preclude "functional duplication" in which a competitor produces a functionally compatible or equivalent item. By using different hardware (and, in some cases, software) techniques, many vendors are able to achieve exact functional compatibility without infringing another vendor's patent rights.

This ability to achieve functional duplication of a patented product has been essential to the growth of "plug compatible" equipment in the data processing industry. Indeed, many small, aggressive vendors have become industrial success stories by tearing down a newly-released, patented product and duplicating the function through a technique that does not involve patent infringement. Of course, in some instances, efforts at functional duplication do not go far enough, and the resulting product or process is held to infringe an existing patent.

The ability to achieve protection against functional duplication is a high priority for many vendors, particularly those with substantial market power and significant legal resources. In certain industries, this protection has been achieved through the successful prosecution of many related patents (sometimes referred to as a "comprehensive patent program"). In this approach, the vendor applies for a large number of patents covering separate segments of a process or individual components of a new product. The approach is successful because of the fact that a vendor attempting functional duplication finds that it is effectively unable to achieve success without infringing at least one of the patents held by the original vendor.

In other industries, vendors have resorted to software and firmware technology to protect against functional duplication of the equipment involved. In this approach, the vendor recognizes that it may well be possible for a competitor to create a functional duplicate of its equipment.

However, the vendor places critical components of the system in software or in firmware (generally in an electronic "chip" of some type). The processes contained within the software or firmware are then protected by trade secret law, or more recently, by new developments in patent and copyright law. This approach, which has been particularly successful in the data processing industry, is not essentially different from that used by vendors in more traditional situations. In effect, the vendor employing this approach is merely placing the key competitive ingredient in a component of the equipment that can be more effectively protected than the entire system.

Many vendors also protect against functional duplication by market innovation. Thus, regardless of whether these vendors apply for patents on their products, they utilize their substantial research and development positions to create constant advances in the areas involved. Thus, as soon as a competitor is able to create a functional duplicate of an existing product or process, the market leader is able to announce an enhancement or new product that leaves the functional duplicate outclassed and undersold.

Software Protection

For many years, computer programs and other software processes were not believed to be patentable. However, beginning in 1968, the United States Court of Customs and Patent Appeals (CCPA) began holding that certain types of stored computer programs utilized in building an automatic device could be patented. To those familiar with data processing, this approach seemed to be consistent with the patent laws, due to the fact that, in many instances, hardware and software are effectively interchangeable engineering equivalents; that is, many of the processes included in data processing equipment can be controlled by hardware elements or by software elements, or both, depending upon the engineering strategy utilized by the inventors.

Despite the logic of this analysis, the Patent and Trademark Office disputed these holdings by the CCPA, asserting that computer programs are merely mathematical algorithms that do not fall within the statutory classes of patentable subject matter. During the 1970s, the Patent and Trademark Office pursued a number of cases involving this issue all the way to the United States Supreme Court. Arguments concerning the likely outcome of a decision by the Supreme Court proliferated, but the Court did not directly confront the issue until 1981.

Finally, in a 1981 case known as *Diamond v. Diehr,* the Supreme Court affirmed the position taken by the CCPA and held that "a claim drawn to subject matter otherwise statutory (i.e., patentable) does not become nonstatutory (i.e., unpatentable) simply because it uses a mathematical formula, computer program, or digital computer." The *Diehr* case involved an industrial process for molding rubber that utilized a stored computer program for calculating the molding time that was critical to the success of the process. In a companion case, *Diamond v. Bradley,* the Supreme Court again affirmed the CCPA and held patentable a general purpose digital computer that employed a firmware-stored microprogram used for controlling access to a "scratch pad" memory.

Although many commentators rushed to suggest that these two decisions settled the issue of whether computer programs may be protected through patent law, the cases left many questions unanswered. In the first place, both cases were extremely close. In the *Diehr* case, the Supreme Court affirmed the CCPA's position by a five-to-four decision. In the *Bradley* case, the CCPA's position was affirmed by an evenly-divided Supreme Court. Justice Potter Steward was one of the five Supreme Court justices voting in favor of the Diehr patent. He has since retired. Also in the *Bradley* case, Chief Justice Burger excused himself from voting because he owned Honeywell stock (and Bradley and a colleague worked for Honeywell). In addition, since these close votes occurred, Justice O'Connor has joined the Supreme Court. Consequently, if the *Diehr* or *Bradley* cases were reheard today, no assurance can be provided that the Court's decisions would be the same.

Even assuming that the same decisions would be rendered today, the specific holdings in the *Bradley* and *Diehr* cases are somewhat limited. Writing for the majority in the *Diehr* case, Justice William Rehnquist noted that the two inventors did not seek to patent a mathematical formula. "Instead," he explained, "they seek patent protection for a process of curing synthetic rubber. Their process admittedly employs a well-known mathematical equation, but they do not seek to preempt the use of that equation. Rather, they seek only to foreclose from others the use of that equation in conjuction with all of the other steps in their claimed process." In effect, Justice Rehnquist suggested that *a new combination of steps in a process can be patented*, even though all of the steps are well known and have been previously used before the new combination of steps is discovered. However, he also cautioned that a mathematical algorithm or formula is like a "law of nature," and cannot be made the subject of a patent. On balance, the *Diehr* case suggests that *the post-algorithm steps in the process* to be patented must be "significant" in order to satisfy the statutory conditions for a software patent to be granted.

The *Bradley* decision offers little guidance, due to the fact that it merely affirmed without any substantial clarification the CCPA's holding that the invention in question met the statutory requirements for a patent to be issued. In the *Bradley* case, the Patent and Trademark Office had refused to issue a patent, on the grounds that the only novel aspect of the invention was an algorithm. In reversing the Board of Appeals of the Patent and Trademark Office, the CCPA held that what the computer does in a specific situation (i.e., the process or apparatus) must be distinguished from how it does it (i.e., the formula or algorithm).

Assuming that the *Diehr* and *Bradley* cases are not reversed by the Supreme Court in a future decision, they do provide that *at least some* computer programs can be patented. Knowledgeable experts in the field have observed that the more physically fixed a computer program is in the hardware, the more likely it will be held to be patentable. On the other hand, the more readily programmable the software is by the user, and the more that the software can be isolated from the hardware or the essential industrial process that is involved, the more likely it will be considered to be an algorithm that is not subject to patentability. In this regard, programs embodied in firmware that control a particular industrial process may well have an edge in the patent application process.

In October, 1981, the U.S. Patent and Trademark Office released its new Guidelines on Computer Inventions (comprising §2110 of the Manual of Patent Examining Procedures). The Guidelines discuss the impact of the *Diehr* and *Bradley* cases on examiners' decisions on patent applications dealing with computer program inventions.

The Guidelines provide that computer program patent applications should be rejected (on the ground that they relate to "nonstatutory subject matter") where the claims pertain only to a mathematical formula or algorithm, a method of calculation, a method of doing business, an abstract intellectual concept, or a collection of printed matter. By way of example, the Guidelines suggest that a patent application based on a "bare set of [program] instructions" should be rejected because it merely defines the abstract intellectual concept of a programmer.

In contrast, the Guidelines explain that patent applications that define a process, apparatus, or composition of matter (or an improvement of any such items), *and* involve the operation of a programmed computer, are acceptable so long as they do not directly or indirectly recite a mathematical algorithm. However, the Guidelines go beyond this generality by also suggesting that examiners should accept patent applications that directly or indirectly recite mathematical algorithms or formulae "if the claim implements or applies the formula in a structure or process which, when considered as a whole, is performing a function which the patent laws were designed to protect, e.g., transforming or reducing an article to a different state or thing."

At the present time, at least, the relationship between the algorithm and the resulting process appears to be the key to patent protection in a close case. Thus, the Guidelines suggest that applications which merely apply a mathematical algorithm to derive a number or value do not present statutory subject matter capable of being patented. On the other hand, the Guidelines suggest that applications based on the use of a mathematical algorithm or formula for deriving a tangible structure or producing a physical result do present acceptable statutory subject matter. On the basis of these contrasts, it seems likely that a software program patent application will stand the best chance of acceptance under the Guidelines if the claims emphasize the particular structure or physical result achieved from utilizing the program.

One of the more interesting areas yet to be decided by the Supreme Court is whether a machine that functions primarily by way of a patented software program will be held to infringe the patent on a machine that is essentially equivalent, but that functions by way of patented hardware. A strong argument can be made that this type of infringement should be found (subject, at least, to the general legal principles relating to functional duplication, discussed above) because the decision to employ hardware or software for a particular process is essentially an engineering decision, based upon economic and engineering judgments. Federal court cases below the Supreme Court level presently suggest differing results on this question. It remains to be seen whether the Supreme Court decisions in *Diehr* and *Bradley* will create judicial consistency in this area.

COPYRIGHTS

The federal Copyright Act of 1976 was the first substantial recodification of the copyright laws since 1909. (Despite the title of the 1976 Act, it became effective on January 1, 1978.) The law was further amended in 1980, in order to provide specific protection for computer programs. Pursuant to the 1976 Act, copyright protection is available for "original works of authorship fixed in any tangible medium of expression." Among the works of authorship protected are "works . . . expressed in words, numbers, or other verbal or numerical symbols or indicia, regardless of the nature of material objects, such as . . . film, tapes, disks, or cards, in which they are embodied." The Copyright Act protects the *form* in which an idea is expressed. However, it does not protect the *idea* that the expression conveys or any process that may be described by the expression. Unlike the patent laws, the Copyright Act provides no protection against the independent development of the same work or expression by another author.

Obtaining copyright protection is remarkably easy. To perfect the copyright, the author need only include the necessary copyright notice on all publicly distributed copies of the work. However, distribution of the work without the requisite notice may cause the materials involved to be donated to the public domain. If the number of copies distributed without the notice is relatively small or certain steps are taken to obtain the return of copies distributed without the notice, perfection of the copyright may still be possible in certain circumstances.

Although copyright registration at the federal level is required before the owner can sue for infringement and obtain the various remedies provided by the statute, registration is not necessary to perfect the copyright. The copyright itself is perfected by inclusion of the necessary notice, regardless of whether the work is actually filed with the Copyright Office (administered by the Library of Congress).

The owner of a copyright holds exclusive, transferable rights to make reproductions, to prepare derivative works, to distribute copies, and (depending upon the type of work involved) to perform or display the work publicly. However, the law contains various exceptions for what is known as "fair use" and for limited use by libraries and archives. These exceptions were clarified in the 1976 Act, particularly with respect to photocopying.

The duration of a copyright for a work made for hire is 75 years from the year of the work's first publication, or 100 years from the year the work was created, whichever period is shorter.

If the work was created by one or more individuals, the copyright endures for 50 years beyond the death of a sole author or for 50 years beyond the death of the last surviving author of a jointly-authored work.

The 1976 Act specifically provides that the federal copyright laws preempt state control over "all legal or equitable rights that are equivalent to any of the exclusive rights within the general scope of copyright . . . in works of authorship that are fixed in a tangible medium of expression and come within the subject matter of copyright." (However, the common law and various state statutes continue to govern certain works that are not deemed proper for copyright protection at the federal level.) This preemption of state law by the Copyright Act has created substantial concern with respect to the protection of trade secrets, as discussed below in this chapter.

Software

Despite the broad recodification of the federal copyright laws that occurred in the 1976 Act, substantial uncertainty remained concerning the copyright protection available for computer programs. As a result of lobbying from the computer industry, the 1976 Act was amended in 1980 to provide specific protection for computer programs. The 1980 amendments added a new definition which defines a "computer program" as "a set of statements or instructions to be used directly or indirectly in a computer in order to bring about a certain result." Although the 1980 amendments provide copyright protection for "computer programs," as defined, the amendments do not extend copyright protection to concepts, ideas, and specifications. Only the program images are protected.

In adding this specific protection for computer programs, the 1980 amendments also included two limitations on the program owner's exclusive rights. These limitations provide that no copyright infringement will exist if the *owner* of a copy of the program makes *or authorizes another person* to make a further copy or adaptation of that program, but only if the copy or adaptation (1) "is created as an essential step in the utilization of the computer program in conjunction with a machine" and is used in no other manner; or (2) "is for archival purposes only" and "all archival copies are destoyed in the event that continued possession of the computer program should cease to be rightful." The word "owner" in the language quoted above is important. As originally proposed, the 1980 amendments would have authorized a "rightful possessor" of the computer program to make or authorize the copies outlined above. (In a software license agreement, the licensee generally only obtains the use of the software package as a "rightful possessor" and not as an "owner.") The 1980 amendments provide that any exact copies prepared in accordance with the provisions noted above may be leased, sold, or otherwise transferred, along with the copy from which the authorized copies were prepared, "only as part of the lease, sale, or other transfer of all rights in the program." The amendments also specifically provide that "adaptations so prepared may be transferred only with the authorization of the copyright owner."

Although the 1980 amendments add valuable protection for software programs, some commentators still believe that copyright protection may not be practicable for certain types of programs. The principal practical difficulty with software copyrights is that, to enforce the rights, the owner must register the program with the Copyright Office. This registration process includes filing the program with the Copyright Office, where it can be examined by the public (although not copied). Long programs actually have an advantage in this regard, due to the fact that only the first and last 25 pages must be filed. However, if a short program is involved, public disclosure of the critical algorithms could spell competitive disaster for the program developer. Because of this problem, some commentators urge that state trade secret law offers better practical protection. However, as noted below, the preemption provisions of the new federal copyright law create countervailing risks.

Written Materials and Circuits

To the extent that they represent literary or pictorial works, printed descriptions of equipment, including electrical circuits, technical drawings, and user manuals may all be protected under the Copyright Act. As noted above, however, any ideas, systems, processes, concepts, or discoveries relating to the equipment are not protected by the copyright laws, notwithstanding the fact that they may be described or illustrated in the literary or pictorial work that is protected by the copyright. In addition, of course, no copyright protection exists for the equipment itself.

Some controversy exists as to whether the federal copyright laws provide protection for "geometric patterns," such as those used in designing the layout and topography of semiconductor "chips." Although geometric patterns would appear to be subject to protection as pictorial or graphic works under the 1976 Act, such protection is probably barred under Section 113 of that law, which states that the 1976 Act does not afford greater rights with respect to "useful articles" than were provided under the prior federal copyright law. Prior law, including applicable judicial decisions, denied copyright protection for geometric patterns. Efforts were made to change the effect of the prior law and these decisions by specific language in the 1976 Act, but the proposed changes were tabled as a result of disagreement within the semiconductor industry. Although arguments in favor of certain types of protection can be made, the legislative history behind the 1976 Act suggests that copyright protection for semiconductor "chips" may be limited, unless such "chips" can be shown to comprise a "computer program" that is otherwise subject to protection under the federal copyright laws. Depending upon the substance and use of the device, firmware may be subject to similar problems.

Doubt also exists as to whether the algorithms contained in a computer program can be separately protected (without the full program) under the copyright laws. Although the form of expressing the algorithm is probably subject to protection, the idea represented by the algorithm—and thus the formula itself—may not be capable of being protected by the Copyright Act unless the separate algorithm can be shown to be a "computer program" under the Act.

Data Collections

Collections of data, including computer data bases, printed directories, statistical indices, and other compilations, were generally believed to be protected under the 1909 Copyright Act. However, the wording included in the 1976 Act created some concern as to whether computerized data bases would be protected. Most commentators now believe that, as a result of the 1980 amendments to the 1976 Act, data bases are clearly subject to federal copyright protection, so long as the compilations involved can be displayed in some tangible form, even if they are stored intangibly (for example, in magnetic media).

TRADE SECRETS

Although specific protection is provided by some state statutes, most trade secret rights stem from the common law. Perhaps the most widely quoted definition of a trade secret in this country is that set forth in Section 757, Comment b, of the Restatement of Torts (promulgated by the American Law Institute in 1930). That definition essentially provides that a "trade secret" may consist of "any formula, pattern, device, or compilation of information which is used in one's business, and which gives him an opportunity to obtain an advantage over competitors who do not know or use it." As the Comment explains, the trade secret may be "a formula for a chemical compound, a process of manufacturing, treating or preserving materials, a pattern for a machine or other device, or a list of customers." Under the Restatement of Torts definition, a trade secret differs from other secret information in a business in that it is not simply information "as to single or ephemeral events in the conduct of the business." Rather, a "trade secret" is "a process or device for continuous use in the operation of the business."

By definition and terminology, secrecy is the key characteristic of a "trade secret." The owner's ability to protect the device or program is lost when this secrecy is no longer maintained. Trade secrets must be clearly marked and protected as "proprietary" from their very creation, or the inventor's trade secret rights may be lost forever.

A person who independently develops a product, program, or process that is the trade secret of another may nevertheless use it, sell it, or license it, without infringing the trade secret held by the original developer. Indeed, if the new developer makes his trade secret public, the attendant publicity will destroy both the trade secret rights held by the original developer and those held by the subsequent developer.

The remedies available to the owner of a trade secret vary from state to state. In some states, intentional unauthorized use of a trade secret may be a criminal offense. In other states, the owner of the trade secret may be able to obtain damages or an injunction against further use or disclosure, if a party obtains the trade secret by improper means or discloses or uses it in violation of a contractual agreement. Under contract law alone, a party that violates a nondisclosure agreement or that wrongfully copies or misuses a program or other trade secret can be held liable for damages or, in some instances, enjoined in a civil injunctive proceeding.

Because trade secret rights do not offer protection against independent discovery of the secret by fair and honest means (including separate invention and accidental disclosure), a product that is protected as a trade secret can be commercially marketed only through the use of a nondisclosure agreement with each user. This nondisclosure agreement must not only govern the use and prohibited misuse of the trade secret time by the user, but must also require the user to exercise due care in preventing the accidental disclosure of the trade secret.

Software

Although trade secret rights may be used to protect equipment, they are more frequently employed in connection with software and firmware. In order to preserve the trade secret, a software "license" is generally used to impose restrictions on the disclosure, reproduction, use, and transfer of the program. By limiting the use of the program and by limiting the number of copies of the program (and any related documentation) that are available, the vendor minimizes the likelihood of accidental disclosure, as well as the risk of unlawful misappropriation or sale to a competitor by an employee of the user. (Limiting the number of copies of the program and limiting the number of sites at which the program can be utilized by the user also offers economic advantages for a vendor that wishes to impose additional site charges in its fee structure. Although some vendors argue that these additional site fees are justifiable purely on the basis of the additional risk of accidental disclosure, in most instances the additional fees are based upon profit motivations rather than an assessment of the increased risks associated with the additional usage of the program materials.)

Users faced with nondisclosure provisions of this nature should carefully review the obligations imposed by the vendor to ensure that the user is not required to assume an impossible burden of protection. Although it may be appropriate for the vendor to assume that the user will take reasonable steps to protect against improper disclosure of the program materials by the user's employees, the user should not be required to undertake an "insurance" role, in which it effectively guarantees that none of the user's employees will make any inappropriate use or disclosure of the vendor's program.

Preemption

As suggested above, the preemption provisions of the 1976 Copyright Act raise questions concerning the continued viability of trade secret protection for works that can be copyrighted. Under the 1976 Act, all legal and equitable rights that are "equivalent" to any of the exclusive rights within the general scope of copyright are governed exclusively by the Act, regardless of whether created before or after January 1, 1978 (the effective date of the 1976 Act) and regardless of whether published or unpublished. Some commentators have suggested that trade secrets should not be preempted by this language, because they involve at least some element (for example, an agreement to maintain secrecy) beyond the rights of reproducing, displaying, performing, and distributing the protected work, as specified in the Copyright Act. But other commentators and at least one court have argued that the preemption provisions preclude trade secret protection under state law where the trade secret is in a form that could be protected by the federal copyright laws. The preemption issue is made more complicated by the fact that language in the 1980 amendments to the 1976 Act raises questions as to whether the preemption provisons apply to certain uses of computer programs in conjunction with data processing and similar information systems.

Speculation concerning the ultimate judicial resolution of the preemption issue would offer little value in the present context. For purpose of this discussion, note should simply be made that the preemption issue raises serious questions about the interrelationship and compatibility of federal copyright protection and trade secret protection. If the preemption provisions of the 1976 Act are interpreted broadly, the continued usefulness of trade secret protection for computer programs and a number of other products could become doubtful.

Because the preemption provisions specifically exclude products and other matters that are not capable of being copyrighted, novel ideas, processes, systems, concepts, and discoveries that are not entitled to copyright protection under the 1976 Act can still be protected by trade secret law, without regard to the preemption issue. Thus, even if preemption is upheld, the algorithms contained in a computer program may still be capable of being protected pursuant to trade secret law. This protection would be based upon the argument that the algorithm itself merely comprises a mathematical expression or idea that cannot be copyrighted or patented (as explained above). If accepted, this argument would offer trade secret protection for the algorithm (which, in most instances, is the critical or unique element of the program) even though the actual program may be capable of being copyrighted. Likewise, trade secret protection may continue to be available for "geometric patterns" that cannot be copyrighted as pictorial or graphic works due to the fact that, as noted above, the 1976 Copyright Act does not afford greater protection to "useful articles" than was provided under prior law. This interpretation could continue to permit trade secret protection to be available for the layered geometric patterns or "topography" used in the design of semiconductor "chips."

USER PROTECTION

A user acquiring hardware or software that is subject to patent, copyright, or trade secret rights, or that may involve components or processes that are subject to such rights, should carefully consider several issues. These matters are discussed below.

Protection Against Infringement

At the most basic level, a user should obtain appropriate representations and warranties from the vendor that the hardware or software being acquired does not infringe any proprietary rights held by another. These representations and warranties should be contained in the written user/vendor agreement.

Fortunately, most vendor form agreements contain representations and warranties of this nature. Unfortunately, however, the vendor provisions often fall far short of providing the user with adequate practical protection in the event infringement is held to exist. For example, many such provisions simply provide that, in the event of any such infringement, the vendor will defend against the infringement litigation and, in the event that an adverse judgment or injunction is issued, the vendor will remove the infringing product. The rather obvious difficulty with this approach is that many such agreements do not provide that, in the event of any such removal, the vendor has any obligation to reimburse the user for the cost of the removed product or, perhaps more importantly, for any loss that the user may incur as a result of the removal.

Other vendor agreements take a somewhat more realistic approach, but still fall short of the mark. In these contracts, the vendor agrees to provide certain reimbursements to the user in the event that the hardware or software is removed following a finding of infringement. However, the reimbursements often bear little relation to the loss that the user would incur as a result of the removal. Indeed, in many situations, the user may be faced with only a nominal payment when it has not even fully depreciated the equipment on its books.

Users considering infringement provisions should generally devote attention to several critical areas. First, the provision should provide a warranty against infringement. Second, the provision should expressly indicate what actions the vendor must take in order to defend any claim of infringement. Third, the contract should describe the options that will be available to the vendor or the user in the event that a judgment of infringement is issued.

In this regard, the relevant provision should clearly indicate whether any choice of options is to be made by the vendor or by the user. In most situations, the options available should depend upon the specific judicial findings of infringement and the resulting remedies. For example, the user may not wish to permit the vendor to remove an infringing product if the judicial remedy against the vendor merely requires the vendor to pay a royalty to the patent owner. On the other hand, removal of the hardware or software and reimbursement to the user may be absolutely essential if the remedy upon infringement involves an injunction against further use of the product by the vendor or the user. In general, the user should strive to control any choice of options that may be available in the event that infringement is held to exist. In any event, however, the vendor should be required to bear any and all litigation expenses and indemnify and hold the user harmless from any such expenses and any damages that may ultimately be assessed.

Certain vendor provisions include an exception indicating that the vendor will not be responsible in the event that the infringement results from a modification to the hardware or software made by the user without the permission of the vendor, or from some special use to which the user places the product. Although these provisions are fair and equitable in concept, they may include specific language that poses undue risks for the user. In reviewing provisions of this nature, the user and its professional advisors should seek to limit the scope of any such exception, to clarify the conditions under which the exception will be held to exist, and to minimize the possibility that the vendor will be able to claim the benefit of the exception when the product is merely used for its intended purpose.

Rights to Patentable Products

In many situations, the user is acquiring equipment that is being manufactured to its own specifications. In other circumstances, the user may be involved in a joint development effort, in which the user and the vendor are responsible for various components of the hardware, software, or firmware involved in the product. Joint development efforts occur more often than many users realize—for example, where a user asks a vendor of an existing product to modify it slightly for the user's own operation or application.

Regardless of whether the product results from a custom order, a joint development effort, or the creation of a customized application for an existing product, the user may have certain claims to any proprietary rights that may result. Far too frequently, the user overlooks this fact until after the product is developed and protected by the vendor.

Some vendors argue that any proprietary rights that may result from such development efforts should be owned by the vendor. Knowledgeable users often counter this argument by pointing out that the applicable agreements generally require the user to pay any additional manufacturing or development costs incurred by the vendor. Thus, these users assert, the user should be entitled to the proprietary rights to any product that may result or, at least, entitled to some portion of the royalties from the product.

From a practical standpoint, the issue of whether the vendor or the user should be entitled to the benefits of any resulting proprietary rights is a matter of business judgment to be negotiated between the parties. For purposes of the present discussion, the point is that the ownership of such rights should be carefully spelled out in the applicable user/vendor agreement. The failure to specify the ownership of these rights in the applicable agreement, or the failure to provide appropriate protection to the user where the vendor claims such rights in the agreement, will almost always have a detrimental impact on the user. Users involved in decisions of this nature should recognize that, in many circumstances, a product that is not expected to have substantial commercial value may prove to be an overnight success. Although the user may be willing for the vendor that creates and markets the product to receive all or part of the royalties that may result from a new patent or other proprietary right, the user may also wish to retain a nonexclusive license to utilize the product at no charge. Alternatively, the user may prefer to specify that the user's purchase price for the developed product will be reduced by all or some percentage of the royalties that may be received by the vendor.

Protection Against Inadvertent Disclosure

Particularly where trade secrets are involved, most vendors require that the user of a licensed product agree to maintain the confidentiality or secrecy of the product. The contractual language employed for this purpose varies considerably from agreement to agreement. In some form contracts, the duty imposed on the user by the vendor essentially amounts to a guarantee that none of the user's employees will ever make any improper use or disclosure of the licensed product. Indeed, these provisions may even impose liability for improper use if the product is stolen from the user by a third party. In other vendor contracts, the language is less onerous. For example, many vendor agreements require that the user take "reasonable steps" to ensure that its employees will not make any unauthorized use or disclosure of the licensed product.

Regardless of the approach taken by the vendor, the user should ensure that the relevant contractual language is carefully reviewed by its attorneys *and* by the operations managers who will actually be responsible for the security of the program or other product. Where the language amounts to a guarantee by the user, it should generally be restricted to circumstances within the user's control. Where the language is more limited, it should nevertheless be studied to ensure that the user can implement the practical safeguards necessary to avoid liability for inadvertent disclosure by the user's employees.

Where the user agrees to take "reasonable steps" to limit any improper use or disclosure of a licensed product, it should require its employees to enter into standard nondisclosure agreements as part of its normal personnel processing. Moreover, the user should adopt formal procedures designed to protect programs and other products that are subject to trade secret or copyright restrictions. For example, where software is involved, access to the magnetic media and any related documentation should be strictly controlled. To the extent that additional copies of the program or documentation materials are permitted under the license agreement, all such copies, including the magnetic media, should be clearly labeled with a "proprietary" or "confidential" legend. Unnecessary copies of the materials, including copies no longer required as a result of revisions or updates, should be protected under archival storage methods, returned to the vendor, or destroyed. (The vendor's license agreement with the user may specify the proper disposition of such materials.)

The implementation of responsible security procedures may effectively preclude any improper use or disclosure of the product licensed to the user. Perhaps more importantly from the user's standpoint, the adoption of internal safeguards may reduce or eliminate the user's liability to the vendor in the event that one or more user employees violates the security procedures and discloses the protected product to other parties. Although the existence of proper procedures will not necessarily guarantee that the user will be able to avoid responsibility in such events, the *lack* of any reasonable safeguards will almost always increase the likelihood that the user will face liability for the wrongful actions of its employees.

Protection Against Practical Problems

Where patents and other proprietary rights are involved, protection against infringement does not necessarily guarantee the user that the product or process being acquired is covered by an effective patent or other proprietary right. Many vendors point out that a user should not concern itself with the question of how the vendor has chosen to protect its proprietary rights in a product. In many situations, this argument is quite reasonable. However, in some situations a user may have substantial reason for wanting the product or process to be protected by an effective patent or other proprietary right. For example, a user is likely to desire such protection where it is paying a premium for an advanced, state-of-the-art machine that should give it a competitive edge in the marketplace. If the equipment being acquired by the user is not covered by a patent or other proprietary right, it may be easier for a competitive machine to be introduced, possibly at a considerably lower price, by another vendor. In such circumstances, the user would lose its competitive advantage, not only in terms of access to the equipment capability involved but also in terms of its capital investment in the equipment. Although functional duplication could result in a similar situation, the existence of a patent normally reduces the user's exposure to such risks (depending somewhat upon the industry and technology involved).

Where an affirmative patent, copyright, or similar warranty is desired by the user, appropriate language should be included in the agreement. In considering such a warranty, the user should assess issues comparable to those outlined under the Protection Against Infringement discussion, above. In addition, the user should carefully consider the degree to which any proprietary right covers the essential elements of the equipment being acquired by the user. For example, many items of equipment are covered by one or more patents. However, if the user is to receive the full protection of a patent warranty from the vendor, the patent or patents involved must cover the essential processes or functions that cause the equipment to have special value to the user. A user having particular concerns in this area should normally have the applicable patents reviewed by a competent patent attorney who is familiar with the user's special business needs.

Regardless of whether a patent, copyright, or similar warranty is obtained, the user should normally consider whether its acquisition and use of the product may be adversely affected by any changes or innovations introduced by the vendor or its competitors that are designed to achieve product superiority or monopoly. Thus, if an item of equipment can be effectively utilized only because of the fact that it functionally duplicates or provides compatibility with other equipment supplied by another manufacturer, the user should carefully review whether this compatibility and usefulness can be adversely affected by new developments introduced by the other manufacturer. Perhaps the best example of this situation exists in the "plug compatible" components used in the computer industry. In data processing, dozens of manufacturers have introduced equipment that is "IBM plug compatible"; that is, equipment which is capable of being used interchangeably with the mainframe computers and operating systems offered by IBM. To the extent that the "compatibility" involved results from the benign or willing participation of IBM, the plug compatible manufacturers have little problem. However, to the extent that a vendor such as IBM has the ability to remove this compatibility by making minor changes to software, firmware, communications interfaces, or other "black boxes," a user that purchases the "compatible" unit may find that the compatibility has been removed suddenly by the dominant vendor. Although few users in this area have the resources to trace their concerns to the patent protection level, a study of the patents and other proprietary rights held by the various parties can substantially improve the user's ability to assess its future risks.

Software Contracts

Users entering into data processing software contracts must consider a number of significant negotiating and drafting issues. Many of these matters are included in the general contract checklist in Appendix A. Although a detailed discussion of these issues is beyond the scope of this volume, several excellent resources are available to users preparing software agreements. Among the best are *Computer Contract Negotiations,* written by the authors of this book (New York; Van Nostrand Reinhold Co., 1981) and *Data Processing Contracts,* prepared by Dick H. Brandon and Sidney Segelstein (New York; Van Nostrand Reinhold Co., 1976). In considering these resources, the user should carefully distinguish the types of software contracts involved. For example, the user protection required in a custom software development contract is generally much more extensive (and difficult to draft) than the protection in a contract for a proven application package. The importance of the software to the user's operations should also be considered. Thus, a contract for an operating system or application that is essential to the user's effective utilization of a new system may deserve far greater attention than a license agreement for a minor application that has little importance to the user's business.

8
GENERAL CONTRACT PROVISIONS

Regardless of the degree to which the user follows all stages of the negotiation process outlined in Chapter 4, the user's team will have occasion to negotiate specific contractual provisions with the vendor. Effective negotiation of contractual provisions requires special skills in several areas. First, the user's negotiating team must have the legal and technical expertise necessary to know what provisions should be sought and, within each provision, what language should be utilized. Second, the team must possess the negotiating skills necessary to achieve the desired provisions and language, or at least some acceptable compromise, at the bargaining table. Third, the user's negotiating team must develop and apply a sound contract negotiating "philosophy" that will govern the user's attitude (and, hopefully, the vendor's attitude) toward the bargaining process.

This chapter is designed to assist the user in determining a contract negotiating philosophy and in applying that philosophy in negotiating and drafting specific contractual provisions. Toward this end, the initial portion of this chapter focuses on two different negotiating philosophies, outlining the benefits and risks inherent in each. The remaining sections of the chapter cover selected general contractual provisions in some detail, with emphasis on substance and negotiating technique. Later chapters build on Chapter 8 by keying on specialized types of equipment contracts and provisions (e.g., third-party leasing and used equipment agreements) in more detail. Thus, the present chapter avoids discussing all possible permutations of a given provision, such as payment or delivery, when the specialized variations are explained later in this volume.

The contractual provisions selected for discussion in Chapter 8 and later chapters are not intended to represent all relevant subjects that should be included in a major equipment agreement. Appendix A presents a comprehensive checklist that offers a more detailed listing of the subjects that should be covered, or at least considered, in a good equipment contract. Even with this type of checklist, users must study each individual transaction to determine whether special circumstances mandate that yet other subjects be covered. Several other professional books offer both checklists and example provisions for computer contracts that are also generally applicable to other types of major equipment agreements. Perhaps the most comprehensive of these volumes is *Data Processing Contracts* by Dick H. Brandon and Sidney Segelstein (New York: Van Nostrand Reinhold Co., 1976). This volume contains a compilation of more than 250 specific contract provisions, with comments concerning purpose, importance, and fallback alternatives.

Because of the availability of these alternative sources of information, Chapter 8 and the remaining portions of this book focus on the conceptual and negotiating factors involved in each substantive provision discussed. Although example language is suggested in some instances, the key concern is that the user have the informational background and negotiating skills necessary to understand the reasons for and nuances of each provision, as well as the negotiating skills necessary to achieve it at the bargaining table. The provisions selected for inclusion in this book therefore share one or more common factors: (1) the provisions are of critical importance in virtually all agreements; or (2) the provisions are valuable but also somewhat unusual; or (3) the provisions offer an opportunity to demonstrate a particular negotiating technique that may be useful in achieving not only the specific section but other provisions as well.

In pursuing the remainder of this book, users should keep several caveats in mind. First, any example provision is just that: a sample intended to facilitate discussion and stimulate thought. An example provision should never be included in any contract without being reviewed and tailored to the specific transaction by a competent professional. Second, a checklist can never include all items or subjects that a user should consider in drafting a contract or an individual provision. At best, a well-drawn checklist can only indicate those areas that other users and professionals have generally found to be important or, at least, worthy of consideration. A checklist can and should serve as a reminder and encourage the production of additional ideas. It should never be considered to be a failsafe listing of all relevant issues. Third, although general strategies can be suggested for negotiating and drafting specific provisions, these suggestions are seldom directly applicable to any transaction and, in a given setting, may even exacerbate the user's dilemma rather than force an appropriate compromise. Thus, all suggestions must be considered and applied in the context of a specific transaction and a specific negotiating environment. Despite the value that suggestions may play, they are little substitute for cold, hard experience at the bargaining table. Finally, all of the tools offered in the remainder of this book—example provisions, checklists, and specific negotiating strategies—are only as valuable as the negotiators selected to apply them. Example provisions and contract checklists in the hands of the inexperienced, without professional guidance and advice, are much like blasting caps in the hands of children: apparently harmless, possibly interesting, and actually highly dangerous.

CONTRACT NEGOTIATING PHILOSOPHY

The user's contract negotiating philosophy should be developed before the team moves to the bargaining table to discuss specific agreement provisions. To be successful in the formal bargaining process, all members of the user's team must have a clear understanding of how the user intends to approach the negotiations, what it expects to achieve, and how aggressive it intends to be in advocating and attempting to reach its negotiating goals. Unless the user's team has considered and discussed these and other questions necessary to formulate a negotiating philosophy, the team is likely to be inefficient and ineffective at the bargaining table.

Negotiating philosophy varies from transaction to transaction, and conceptual agreement on what philosophy is best in each situation is indeed hard to achieve. Some negotiators feel that the user should avoid any aggressiveness, whether to preserve the vendor/user "relationship" or to create a calm, businesslike atmosphere. Others take the opposite extreme, arguing that the user should employ a hard-line position and even tactical deception wherever possible. Both of these approaches can achieve benefits for the user under certain conditions. Under other circumstances, both can cause severe disappointment or even failure.

In the final analysis, each negotiating team must formulate its own negotiating philosophy in each acquisition or other transaction. No negotiating philosophy is or should be the same; each must be tailored to the parties, the transaction, and the individual negotiators.

Despite the uniqueness of each negotiating philosophy, the philosophies applied by various users can be categorized for instructional purposes. Although many additional categories can be highlighted, two should serve as appropriate examples: (1) the professional negotiating philosophy; and (2) the adversary negotiating philosophy. Of course, each of these philosophies contains a wide variety of permutations. Although any generalizations in this area should probably be avoided, the authors suggest that the professional philosophy should be employed where possible, particularly in larger and more complex transactions.

The Professional Negotiating Philosophy

The professional philosophy is set around the following axioms:

1. In any major business transaction, both parties have a right and, indeed, an obligation to determine the goals and objectives that they wish to achieve in the transaction.

2. The goals and objectives desired by one party may create actual or potential costs or risks for the other party. Where this circumstance occurs, the party facing such costs or risks has a right and, indeed, an obligation to identify the costs and risks and to limit or protect against them or, alternatively, to require additional consideration for accepting them. (This statement may be a verbose method of communicating the old adage that "there is no free lunch.")

3. Responsibilities, costs, and risks should be discussed, understood, and allocated in an honest and open business manner. Although the advocacy and sales process almost always results in the use of puffery and convincing argument, both sides should avoid efforts designed to foster or permit misunderstanding and deception, regardless of source or reason.

4. Honest mistakes and misunderstandings may occur in the negotiation of any complex business transaction. Neither party should falsely claim such problems, but where these problems occur both parties should work honestly toward their resolution.

5. The best contract is one which accurately sets forth the mutual understanding of the parties on all relevant issues. Such a contract invariably involves compromise, both in substance and specific language. This type of contract should be the negotiating goal. (This axiom might be called the "Holiday Inn" principle, to parody the advertising line used by that firm in the late 1970s: for both sides, "a good contract should be like a good motel room: no surprises!")

6. A good contract must nevertheless contemplate that one or both parties may fail to perform their obligations under the agreement for any number of reasons, including reasons beyond their control. Therefore, the contract should include clear standards of performance and remedies. Such an approach may actually reduce the likelihood of litigation, by specifying the mutual obligations of the parties on all relevant issues.

The professional negotiating philosophy recognizes that, in an ideal world, the best method of achieving optimum and mutual success at the bargaining table is for both parties to work together, in a professional atmosphere, to agree on how responsibilities, costs, and risks will be allocated, and to document the resulting compromise in a clear contractual agreement. The philosophy requires that each party treat the other as a professional to be respected for his or her honesty, expertise, and mutual desire to fairly document and consummate the transaction. In this regard, the philosophy requires a cooperative negotiating environment rather than an adversary one. It also requires that each party be willing to listen and respond to the concerns expressed by the other side, without becoming incensed or incited toward a "killer" response. In the professional philosophy, neither side "wins" in the traditional sense. Indeed, it might be said that neither side wins unless both sides win. As a result, negotiating factors such as aspiration level and psychological negotiating leverage must be directed away from achieving victory at all costs and toward achieving an acceptable, fully-understood, and well-documented compromise. Ploys and manipulative strategies and tactics have no place in negotiations governed by the professional philosophy. Despite this fact, advocacy, sound reasoning, and effective, forceful communication play strong roles under the professional philosophy as well as under other approaches.

For example, in the professional philosophy, the salami tactic explained in Chapter 3 is replaced with what might be called an "all encompassing" tactic. In the latter approach, both sides theoretically avoid holding items back (only to spring them later once concessions on other related issues have been reached). Instead, both parties outline their respective goals and objectives in all areas, or at least major related areas, at one time. This approach optimizes the opportunity for understanding and for an honest assessment and trade-off of the specific responsibilities, costs, and risks that may be involved.

Similarly, the professional philosophy mandates against a section-by-section review and discussion of the contract. Instead, it encourages consideration of broad concepts (as suggested in Chapter 4) and, at a minimum, the discussion and review of groups of interrelated sections and obligations. In this regard, the philosophy recognizes and deals with one of the most basic and dangerous facts involved in negotiating and drafting equipment contract provisions: the boundaries of any contract provision are more or less arbitrary; contract sections do not live in a vacuum—rather, they are invariably linked to one another in a flexible, working environment that may vary depending upon the obligations being considered at any given point in time. Because of this fact, it is neither sound nor professionally possible to allocate responsibilities, costs, or risks, or to draft actual contract language, unless all interrelated sections are identified and considered concurrently.

Where the professional philosophy is used, the parties generally follow a critical path that includes the steps shown below:

1. Each party reviews its own acquisition goals and prioritized negotiating objectives (see Chapter 4).
2. Each party in turn presents an overview of the responsibilities that it believes must be assigned in the transaction. (These responsibilities are generally based upon the goals and objectives of the parties.)
3. Each party announces the actual and potential costs and risks that it believes would be involved if it accepted the various responsibilities proposed by the other party.
4. The parties propose and negotiate alternative allocations of responsibilities, costs, and risks, striving to achieve a compromise on each issue or each group of interrelated issues.
5. The parties reach and announce a buy/no-buy decision on each proposed allocation of responsibilities, costs, and risks. For example, after all realistic alternatives have been proposed on a given issue or group of issues, the user must decide (through what amounts to a form of cost-benefit analysis) which, if any, of these alternatives is both technically acceptable and affordable.
6. The parties then agree upon and draft the specific contractual provisions necessary to document the understandings reached above.

In reality, of course, the professional negotiating philosophy is seldom as easy to apply as it is to describe. Several problems may arise.

First, the professional philosophy provides that the user's opponent should be treated as a respected professional, but the vendor may in fact be engaging in wholesale use of the ploys explained in Chapter 2. This frequent occurrence is a serious blow to the user's ability to employ the professional philosophy in the contract bargaining process. Nevertheless, the user can still make an effort to use its advocacy of the professional principles noted above to seize and maintain control of the negotiations. This approach is most successful where the user firmly rejects all vendor ploys and other comments and formally announces that the user will continue to discuss contractual provisions and, indeed, continue to participate in negotiations, only if the parties mutually agree to proceed along the lines specified in the professional philosophy. As noted in Chapter 4, agendas and other control steps can be valuable user tactics in this effort.

Second, where the vendor appears willing to pursue the professional philosophy, the user may be lulled into a false sense of security and, based primarily on a lack of information, agree to inadvisable compromises. Because of the innate information and negotiating advantages generally enjoyed by the vendor, the honesty element of the professional philosophy can pose serious risks for the user if the vendor wishes to be unethical or purposefully misleading. When these conditions occur, the user must be willing to abandon the professional philosophy and move to an approach that requires less mutual cooperation. (Note that the professional philosophy does not preclude use of hard-hitting tactics, for example when progress seems unlikely.) When the vendor appears to be proceeding ethically, the user must nevertheless remain alert to the possibility of deception. Adequate user preparation is one of the best defenses in this area.

Third, the approach involved in the professional negotiating philosophy is often scorned by vendors and users alike, because it appears to require an inordinate amount of preliminary time and effort. Attorneys and other negotiators whose equipment contract experience is less limited than they would like to admit may also attack the professional philosophy on the ground it fails to allow the hard-hitting approach that they believe is necessary to do the job. Because of these perceptions, causing the parties to agree on and continue to follow the professional approach may be difficult. The only effective solution to this problem comes from experience—experience proving the value involved. In the interim, the user can only hope to outline the approach and express the fact that, despite any other appearances, the professional philosophy will save time in the long-run (and probably in the short-run) by resulting in an agreement that does an optimum job of reflecting and documenting the mutual understanding of the parties on all relevant issues.

Fourth, the professional negotiating philosophy requires both good conditions and universal participation for optimum success. As suggested above, the professional approach works best when both parties understand the philosophy and are dedicated to it. Because the professional philosophy eschews ploys and deceptive tactics, breaking deadlocks and disagreements often requires finer bargaining skills than many negotiators possess. Moreover, because the philosophy mandates an overriding commitment toward honesty and compromise, it often creates psychological problems for negotiators who are overly concerned with pride and saving face. In essence, the professional philosophy is a more difficult (and less flamboyant) negotiating approach than many users would like to admit. Because of this fact, effective implementation of the philosophy requires skill, dedication, and practice.

The Adversary Negotiating Philosophy

Where the professional negotiating philosophy does not seem advisable or effective due to vendor opposition or any other reason, the experienced user is likely to adopt a negotiating philosophy that is substantially less cooperative and more aggressive. The adversary negotiating philosophy offers perhaps the best example of such an approach. (Obviously, a wide spectrum of philosophies exists between the professional and adversary approaches.)

Like the professional philosophy, the adversary philosophy has a series of axioms, which might be explained as follows from the user's viewpoint:

1. Despite the unprofessionalism of the approach, in this transaction the vendor is attempting (or may attempt) to minimize any serious discussion of, or binding commitment by it to, responsibilities, costs, and risks that the user believes are critical to its participation in the transaction.

2. Because of this fact, any representations by the vendor concerning these responsibilities, costs, or risks must be viewed with skepticism and should be accepted only after independent verification.

3. Because of its concern over avoiding commitments and limiting liability, the vendor's negotiators may use ploys and deceptive strategies and tactics in an effort to optimize the agreement from the vendor's perspective.

4. Where a user mistake or misunderstanding occurs, the vendor is unlikely to point it out or offer to correct it. Consequently, every provision must be viewed with great care. Moreover, if the vendor misses something, the user should not feel compelled to correct it.

5. Because of the vendor's attitude, the user is justified in employing any tactics and strategies that seem productive, including efforts that are as deceptive as those used by the vendor.

6. The best contract under these conditions is one that increases the vendor's commitments, reduces the provisions which limit the vendor's liability, and changes the blanket commitments usually sought by the vendor from the user. The user should fight as hard as possible on all relevant issues and compromise as rarely as possible.

7. Because the vendor is involved in an adversary position, the contract should be drafted as a litigation weapon that can be accessed and employed when the vendor fails to meet any condition specified in the agreement. Indeed, the contract may be more important as a tool to be used in, or in threatening, litigation, than as a means to document the mutual understanding of the parties on key issues. Consequently, the user should take advantage of every opportunity to achieve a negotiating victory on substance or language.

While the professional negotiating strategy stresses the importance of achieving mutual understanding on all relevant issues, the adversary philosophy admits that mutual understanding is unlikely to be achieved. Therefore, the adversary approach emphasizes the importance of achieving the user's position at the expense of the vendor's position. In the adversary philosophy, winning is everything, and winning means "getting yours before your adversary gets his (and perhaps gets yours, too)." Put another way, the professional philosophy is based on the original statement of the Golden Rule: "Do unto others as you would have them do unto you." In contrast, the adversary philosophy is based upon the contemporary restatement of the rule that is sometimes attributed to the more capitalistic in our society: "He who has the gold, makes the rules; do unto your neighbor before he does it unto you."

Besides the fact that some find the adversary philosophy to be filled with greed and deception, the approach contains serious weaknesses. Among these are the following.

First, the adversary philosophy places too much attention on winning—on "achieving your own position"—and not enough focus on allocating all relevant responsibilities, costs, and risks in a clear and mutually-agreed-upon manner. As a result, the adversary philosophy often causes the user to win the battle (e.g., achieve a particular provision) and lose the war (e.g., obtain a contract that covers all issues with no surprises).

Second, the adversary philosophy is a battlefield of ploys, strategies, and tactics. In this environment, the vendor's experience generally gives it the superior soldiers, equipment, and battle plan. Few user negotiators have the skills necessary to recognize and deflate vendor ploys, aggressively employ their own strategies and tactics, and achieve bargaining superiority in a heated adversary context.

Third, the adversary process seldom causes the discussions to focus on the relevant issues. Because both sides are actively involved in strategic moves designed to achieve negotiating victory, there is seldom any honest discussion of overriding concepts or of groups of interrelated issues. As a result, key points may become lost in the shuffle. Where this happens, it is almost certain to create greater risk and hardship for the user than for the vendor.

Despite these problems, users must sometimes employ the adversary philosophy (or some less extreme variation of it), particularly where the vendor refuses to accept and honestly participate in the professional approach. When the adversary philosophy must be employed, the user's negotiating team must pursue it aggressively. Although the user's team may make efforts to switch to the professional approach at key points during the negotiations, the team must recognize when those efforts fail, and quickly return to the adversary philosophy. As suggested above, the adversary approach effectively turns the bargaining table into a battleground. If the user is to achieve success, or at least equality, in this environment, it must take and maintain an aggressive stance. Indecision and vacillation have no place where the user must employ the adversary negotiating philosophy.

Even so, where the user must utilize the adversary approach, it can and should employ several safeguards that will reduce some of the risks involved. First, members of the user's negotiating team must recognize and avoid the tendency to let "winning" dominate common sense. Just as anger must be controlled and directed to be used effectively in negotiations, the user's negotiators should remember that their purpose should be to achieve all of their acquisition goals and negotiating objectives, to the extent possible, and not merely to prove their negotiating prowess or avoid any compromise.

Second, the user's negotiating team should ensure that, wherever applicable, groups of interrelated issues and provisions are considered together. This suggestion is particularly important where the user's drive to "win" a given point might otherwise cause it to achieve full success on one provision while completely losing or ignoring two other related provisions.

Third, the user's negotiators should be especially alert to any vendor ploys. In any aggressive environment, the best offense is often a good defense, and major equipment negotiations are no exception. The user's team must not become so wrapped up in its own offensive efforts that it becomes more vulnerable to the vendor's deceptive techniques.

EQUIPMENT LISTS AND RELATED PROVISIONS

One of the most important aspects of reviewing a major equipment contract involves verification of the product list. Unfortunately, this task is often overlooked or inadequately performed. Improper review may cost the user several hundred thousand dollars, or more. Consider the following example based upon an actual user experience.

In the example situation, a major manufacturer structured a proposal involving the conversion of a number of existing items of equipment to a long-term step-payment lease. The proposal also included adding several new pieces of equipment to the same lease. As often happens in complex proposals, the list of components changed a number of times during the negotiations as the vendor and user worked to structure a transaction that would be attractive financially to the user.

In an effort to document the savings promised by the vendor, the user, at one point during the negotiations, obtained the initials of the vendor's salesperson and top financial representative on a spread sheet showing the various components and financial advantages in the lease. Further negotiations ensued, however, and additional changes were made in the components. In fact, various items of equipment were moved in and out of the proposal during the last few hours of negotiations as the agreements were being prepared for signature and hand delivery to the vendor's offices in another state. (As usual, the vendor had created a false sense of urgency).

What happened next is difficult to explain. The only certain fact is that the user executed the final agreement without verifying the equipment list on the actual execution copies. When the invoices began to be received on the new lease arrangement some months later, the user realized that the vendor was claiming that certain items of installed equipment were not included in the new lease. Rather, these items were being invoiced separately at the vendor's rental rates. Upon review of the new lease agreement, the user discovered that these items of equipment were simply not included in the equipment schedule for the agreement. At that point, the user also determined that it had apparently executed a separate rental agreement covering at least some of the "missing" equipment at the time that it signed the long-term lease agreement.

Negotiations to resolve the problem between the vendor and the user began several months later and proceeded on a generally unsatisfactory basis for some time. The vendor stood firm and pointed to the executed agreements as the only binding legal documents involved. The agreements, of course, indicated that the items of equipment had not been included in the new lease arrangement. The user pointed to the initialed spread sheets which indicated that the equipment in question had been included in the new lease. The vendor countered with the fact that a number of changes had been made (for very believable, specific reasons) after the spread sheets were signed. The step-payment schedule and financial arrangements in the lease were carefully analyzed and both parties based arguments upon certain variations in the figures. The matter remained at a standoff.

Following some high level telephone calls, the situation improved somewhat and the vendor and user compromised the amounts involved. Although the user might have faced an additional expense over the lease term of $200,000 to $300,000, it was able to arrange a compromise of this problem and a number of other invoicing problems at considerably less expense. Nevertheless, the compromise cost the user substantial amounts of time and money. (The problem also endangered the vendor's relationship with the user.)

Although it is possible to argue "mutual mistake," "fraud in the inducement," and a number of other legal points in connection with problems such as these, the final legal documents frequently speak for themselves. Moreover, it is often difficult to prove that the figures and components contained in preliminary or interim proposals and spread sheets were, in fact, used to prepare the final legal documents. This is particularly true where the contract simply reflects different equipment than the spread sheets.

To be sure, errors in equipment schedules can sometimes be corrected quickly and easily by mutual agreement, particularly where both sides recognize that a basic misunderstanding has occurred. Unfortunately, the errors often result from misunderstanding on the part of only one side, ordinarily the user. (After all, the user seldom shares the vendor's familiarity with system components and numbers. Far too frequently, the user's personnel refuse to admit that this problem exists.)

When an equipment list problem occurs, the user ordinarily ends up finding out that the transaction is considerably less attractive financially than it first appeared. Although negotiations may result in an appropriate compromise or reform of the agreements, these "after the fact" negotiations alone can be costly in terms of legal fees and management time. In addition, if litigation becomes necessary, both costs can soar. The user-vendor relationship is likely to be damaged and the managers involved may be strongly and appropriately criticized by their superiors or their board of directors.

These problems can be avoided by applying a very simple, although often time-consuming, rule: All equipment schedules must be verified in detail by the user's technical staff and reviewed by its senior operations or production management. At a minimum, this verification and review should include a comparison of all previous vendor proposals and spread sheets with the final equipment lists to be included in the contract or lease. Every component necessary must be separately verified. Cables, small items of equipment, and peripherals cannot be overlooked. The user's technical or operations personnel should sign off on the equipment lists and the lists should then be reviewed by management and by the attorneys and financial representatives involved. Although signature of each equipment schedule that is attached as a separate exhibit or addendum to the contract may not be necessary from a legal standpoint (if they are incorporated into the main agreement by reference), good documentation methodology provides for these papers to be separately signed or initialed for identification purposes at the time the main agreements are signed.

Verification of equipment lists is not only necessary with respect to new equipment being acquired or existing equipment being converted to another acquisition method. Verification is also critical when equipment is being traded in or removed in the future as part of a new system proposal. Far too many users simply indicate in a contract that a specific system, perhaps documented only as "the ABC 9999 system" will be removed or traded in as of a specific date. Although it should not have to be said, this type of documentation is wholly inadequate, particularly when the user has a number of other ABC 9999 systems installed at the same site. In a situation such as this, the user's technical experts must designate the precise items of equipment (by serial number where possible) that are deemed to be included in the listed system.

The necessity of verifying and reviewing equipment lists is perhaps best appreciated when a user is forced to do so and finds that, contrary to its initial reaction, the verification takes literally hours or days to accomplish. This time period is particularly likely to be necessary when complex existing equipment is being converted to another acquisition method or used equipment is being traded in or removed at some time in the future. Time consuming or not, however, verification is absolutely essential.

One final caveat should be noted. Some users have a tendency to feel that verification of equipment schedules is part of their attorney's responsibilities. Although an attorney should certainly ensure that, to the best of his or her knowledge, the equipment lists are accurate and reflect the substance of the transaction as he or she understands it, the attorney's primary role should be to see that the equipment lists are in fact verified by the technical and operations personnel who have the ability to perform such a review. Even where the attorney has substantial experience in the relevant technical area, it is doubtful that the lawyer can, or should, be close enough to the substance of the system and the transaction to be able to personally verify the schedules. However, the attorney should be certain that the copies of the contract retained for his or her file include written approval of the equipment schedules by the user's technical personnel.

VENDOR CONFIGURATION WARRANTIES

Although the user's technical personnel should be capable of determining whether the equipment schedule for a system includes all components necessary for the equipment to perform according to published specifications and the user's needs, it may be advisable to include a "vendor configuration warranty" in the acquisition agreement.

Problems sometimes arise when the vendor's sales representative inadvertently omits one or two system components on the contract equipment schedule. Unlike the more basic problem discussed in the equipment list comments, above, this type of error usually affects one or two minor parts of an extensive system. With luck, the error is discovered before the system is up and running and the additional components are supplied on a timely basis. In other situations, the error may not be noticed until the acceptance tests are being performed and extensive delays may result.

In either event, the vendor usually invoices the user for the extra cost of the additional components. If the user complains, the vendor explains—quite correctly—that the additional parts were not included in the contract or in the contract price. Consequently, the vendor goes on, the user should not expect to get something for nothing.

In some respects, the vendor's argument is a fair one. Unless the user pays for the other required components, it will get "something"—two more minor components perhaps—for nothing. On the other hand, the user may be paying more for the same "something" it ordered in the first place—a system that will perform according to basic specifications. Regardless of what the equipment schedule says, the user generally relies upon the vendor's representations that the system, as configured and priced in the contract, will perform certain tasks or meet certain needs. In effect, the user expects to acquire a functioning system, not a list of individual components that may or may not perform a given job. Moreover, even where the user's technical personnel carefully check the equipment schedule, they are likely to rely upon the expertise of the vendor's representatives. In the final analysis, after all, the vendor's sales and technical staff is far more familiar with the various components necessary to configure a particular system. Viewed in this context, it seems unfair for the user to pay more than it bargained for in order to get one or two additional components necessary for the system to meet the predetermined specifications.

One method of reducing the user's exposure in this area is to include a "vendor configuration warranty" in the acquisition agreement. In this provision, the vendor simply warrants that the system components listed in the equipment schedule comprise all items necessary for the system to operate according to certain preagreed specifications. Although a particularly good contract may provide for these specifications to be the benchmark standards previously established for the user's own business operations, a more basic document may include the vendor's published operating specifications for the system as a whole. One effective method of pursuing the latter approach is to provide that the system (and each component for which separate specifications are published) will meet the glowing operating characteristics and specifications contained in the vendor's marketing materials or sales proposal. Many users implement this approach by attaching the vendor's glossy marketing sheets to the agreement and incorporating them by appropriate reference. (Regardless of the technique utilized, the user should strive to cover all relevant specifications; for example, space and power requirements, physical and operating characteristics, performance standards, modularity, compatibility, software, memory, timing, maintenance, and the like.) Where the user contracts for *results* rather than *resources,* as discussed in Chapter 4, the vendor configuration warranty should be an integral part of the vendor's overall commitment (warranty) to supply all necessary equipment and software to meet certain specified end user needs.

RISK OF LOSS AND INSURANCE BEFORE ACCEPTANCE

Many lease and purchase agreements provide that the user will bear the risk of loss and the burden of obtaining insurance prior to the acceptance date. In most situations, this approach is inconsistent with the fact that, during this preliminary period, the user has not (or, at least, should not have) yet accepted the system or become obligated to pay the purchase price or lease payments. The irony of this situation is that, if the system is damaged or destroyed before acceptance, the user will be liable for the damage and, indeed, could be liable for the full purchase price, even though the user would not at that point be liable if the system were not damaged or destroyed.

The vendor generally takes the position that this approach is fair because the user can simply purchase insurance to protect itself. In support of this position, the vendor also explains that the only real risk is during shipment and that period will be covered (in some allegedly automatic fashion) by the insurance provided by the common carrier responsible for transporting the equipment. (See Chapter 6.)

There are several difficulties with this position. First, the risk of loss is not limited to the transportation period. For example, the equipment could be damaged or destroyed before delivery to the carrier or after delivery to the user's site (or to a temporary warehouse or vendor storage site).

Second, someone must ensure that the carrier is given proper instructions concerning packing and insurance. For household goods and electronic equipment alike, the standard insurance or liability payments offered by common carriers (often expressed as so many cents per pound) are simply not adequate. Where increasingly lightweight electronic components are involved, the shortfall could be catastrophic for the user. The vendor is the logical party to guarantee that adequate insurance will be provided. The vendor is far more likely to accept this obligation seriously if it is legally required to do so in the agreement and if it will be legally liable for the risk of loss if the insurance proves to be inadequate.

Third, if a problem arises and insurance payments are required, the vendor should be forced to look to the insurance company rather than the user. If the user has the risk of loss, and an insurance claim is contested, the vendor may be able to force the user to pay for the loss or damage, thereby leaving the user to sue the insurance company (if necessary) at the user's expense.

Finally, the user may simply fail to obtain the necessary insurance when coverage is required. Risk management is a weak link in many organizations, particularly where newly acquired equipment is involved. Although many blanket policies will cover "after-acquired" equipment for a nominal time, the applicable period may not be adequate to provide protection through the acceptance date. In other situations, this type of "automatic" coverage may be unavailable or too limited to offer full protection. Unfortunately, many risk management departments are not notified of insurance coverage requirements before the equipment acquisition contract is executed (sometimes because of oversight and the usual rush to close the transaction, and sometimes because of a misguided belief that the common carrier's coverage will suffice). This delay can result in serious coverage gaps and liability for the user.

These points strongly indicate that the vendor, not the user, should be responsible for the risk of loss prior to acceptance. The only realistic exceptions to this rule should be if the user has carefully reviewed the risks and procured full and adequate insurance, or if the user wishes to accept liability for loss or damage caused by its agents or employees (a fair exception, in the authors' opinion).

Standard vendor risk of loss provisions are also generally deficient in another important area: They fail to explain what happens to the contract, the delivery schedule, and the like if the equipment is, in fact, damaged or destroyed before acceptance. This type of disaster can create absolute havoc for the user, particularly where the vendor is unable to supply an immediate replacement. Most users naively believe that, in the event of such a problem, the vendor would simply release the user from the agreement, thereby permitting the user to regroup and pursue alternative equipment sources. Although the law may provide this result in some states, particularly where an extreme delay would be involved, the user is more likely to find that it would remain bound under the original agreement, at least for what the law would call a "reasonable" time. Unfortunately, this time could be totally unreasonable from the user's standpoint. (Ironically, most standard contracts covering the purchase of a residence cover this area far better than any vendor form agreements.)

Because of the serious delays and risks faced by the user in this area, appropriate contractual language should be used to define the parties' relative rights and obligations in the event of loss. In some instances, the user may wish to utilize a provision that specifically permits cancellation of the agreement in the event of a loss prior to acceptance. In other instances, the user may prefer to utilize a catch-all provision that permits cancellation in the event of a failure by the vendor to meet any contractual deadline (with a reasonable grace or "cure" period), regardless of the reason. However, in the latter approach, the user should ensure that any general provision specifically includes delay or nonperformance due to loss or damage, lest a court of law imply otherwise. In addition, the user should be certain that any provision of this nature is consistent with, or carefully excepted from, any force majeure or "Act of God" section. Otherwise the general force majeure language may prevail and preclude cancellation by the user. (See Appendix B.)

The following example language may be helpful in drafting an appropriate provision relating to risk of loss and insurance prior to acceptance. Although this example has been extracted from a user lease agreement, the essential points may also be utilized in a purchase or rental contract.

Risk of Loss and Insurance Through Acceptance Date. Through 11:59 p.m., local time at Lessee's site, on the Acceptance Date, as specified in Section _____ of this Agreement:

(a) The Lessor shall bear the full and complete risk of loss, damage, theft, or destruction (whether partial or complete) of, to, and/or from the Equipment or any item(s) thereof; and

(b) The Lessor shall maintain, at no expense to the Lessee, public liability, property damage, all risk, and fire and extended coverage insurance on the Equipment. Such insurance shall provide:

(i) public liability/bodily injury coverage of not less than $500,000 for each person and $1,000,000 for each accident; and

(ii) third party property damage coverage of not less than $1,000,000 for each accident; and

(iii) coverage of an amount not less than that reasonably required to repair or replace the Equipment.

Such insurance shall be maintained from the date this Agreement becomes effective through the Acceptance Date, and shall include coverage during shipping, delivery, installation, and testing.

Loss On or Before Acceptance Date. In the event the Equipment or any material part of such Equipment is damaged, lost, stolen, or destroyed before acceptance by the Lessee pursuant to Section _____ hereof, the Lessor shall cause the applicable item(s) of Equipment to be promptly repaired or replaced, at no expense to Lessee, if such repair or replacement can be accomplished by a date necessary to comply with the dates specified in Schedule _____. However, in the event such repair or replacement cannot be accomplished by a date necessary to allow compliance with such dates, Lessor shall so notify Lessee and Lessee shall have the right and option (to be exercised within ten (10) calendar days following the earlier of (i) Lessee's receipt of written notice from Lessor that such repair or replacement cannot be so accomplished or (ii) the earliest installation date specified in Schedule _____) to either:

(a) terminate this Agreement, in which event Lessor shall promptly return payment previously tendered by Lessee hereunder and neither party shall have any further liability to the other hereunder; or

(b) accept delivery and installation of the Equipment, as is, together with Lessee's ratable portion of all insurance proceeds paid or payable thereon as a result of the loss, damage, or destruction, in which event this Agreement shall remain in full force and effect; or

(c) adjust the dates specified in Schedule _____ to such dates as may be mutually agreed upon in writing by Lessee and Lessor, as to which dates time shall be of the essence, in which event this Agreement shall remain in full force and effect and Lessor shall cause the necessary repairs to be made at Lessor's expense.

DELIVERY PROVISIONS

The delivery section of a major equipment contract can be particularly valuable to the user, not only as a guide to the delivery obligations of the respective parties but also as an early indicator of nonperformance by the vendor. Consequently, the provision should be drafted with the care accorded to such related provisions as those governing installation and acceptance. In addition, the delivery provision should be tailored to meet the needs of the specific transaction. For example, the delivery safeguards for used equipment (see Chapter 9) may need to be more detailed than those for new equipment, especially if a broker or other third-party source is involved. Similarly, delivery standards may need to be accorded more importance where site improvements or other major expenditures are tied to delivery rather than acceptance or where the vendor's delivery obligation otherwise assumes increased importance compared to installation and acceptance. Several aspects of a good delivery section are discussed below.

All or Nothing

The section covering the delivery schedule should indicate that all items of equipment, including any necessary software and documentation, must be delivered before the delivery deadline will be considered met. Where staged delivery is acceptable, this requirement can be expressed in terms of specified systems or groups of components.

Unless this language is included, the vendor may be able to claim that the delivery schedule has been met because "substantially all" components have been delivered. The law permits this interpretation in many states and the question of "substantial" compliance would be one of those elusive fact questions that are risky to litigate—or threaten to litigate. The potential problem is that the system may be substantially delivered—from an objective viewpoint—but the one or two pieces that the user needs most for its new project may not be there for months. The same reasoning, of course, often applies to software and documentation.

The following example indicates one method of minimizing this risk:

No item of Equipment shall be deemed to be "delivered" pursuant to Section _____ hereof unless and until all items of Equipment listed in Schedule 1 hereto [the Equipment Schedule] have been delivered pursuant to said Section _____. Except as may otherwise be specified in Schedule 1, all programs, software, and documentation to be furnished to the Customer pursuant to this Agreement shall be deemed to be items of Equipment for purposes of this Section _____ and Section _____, relating to delivery.

Packing and Preparation for Shipment

Particularly where used equipment is being acquired from a broker or dealer, packing and shipping standards should be specified. Even where the vendor has the risk of loss during delivery (as the authors recommend, where possible), this type of provision is advisable whenever damage in transit could seriously impair the user's implementation schedule.

As amazing as it may seem, some vendors (especially smaller brokers and dealers) do not take the time and expense to pack or ship equipment—especially sensitive electronic equipment—properly. The primary reason is that these vendors have traditionally passed the risk of loss on to the carrier (who carefully limits or avoids it, contractually) and the unsuspecting user in the vendor's standard form contract. Consequently, extremely expensive data processing equipment is sometimes tossed in a cardboard box or shoved—often unpadded—onto a common freight truck for a 3,000 mile journey across the country. With luck, the resulting mess only needs cosmetics like repainting and dent removing. More likely, however, substantial repairs are required, resulting in lost time and money for the user.

Although solid contractual language will not guarantee that the vendor will ensure proper packing, it will certainly gain the vendor's attention and serve as an appropriate incentive. Moreover, if a problem does arise, the language will give the user reasonable recourse. In this regard, the user should not fall for the common vendor suggestion that matters of this sort—including liability for loss during shipment—are issues that are handled by the carrier and not by the vendor. The carrier may well be ultimately responsible for such matters, but someone must be responsible for ensuring that the carrier is given appropriate instructions and properly carries them out. Because the vendor and not the customer is generally responsible for having the equipment delivered to the carrier, the authors believe that this responsibility should rest with the vendor. As noted above, if the vendor has this responsibility, it is more likely to oversee the carrier's functions with appropriate diligence and interest.

The following language serves as an example of a packing provision utilized in a used equipment agreement:

> The Equipment shall be dismantled, crated, and prepared for shipment under the direct supervision of the Equipment manufacturer's field engineering personnel. The Equipment shall be crated and packed in materials, and pursuant to procedures, meeting or exceeding the manufacturer's then current standards for comparable components. Seller shall in any event exercise normal and reasonable care in dismantling, packing, and crating the Equipment in order to avoid damage to the appearance or operating condition of the Equipment. The Equipment shall be shipped to the Customer's site, as indicated in Section _____, by commercial carrier approved in advance by Customer. Handling, shipping, and unloading of the Equipment shall, in any event, meet or exceed the manufacturer's then-current standards for comparable components.

Notice of Shipment

The Delivery section should also include a requirement that the vendor notify the user of the impending and actual shipment dates. These notices can assist the user in scheduling site preparation and installation plans. In addition, the notices can provide quieting reassurance that the system is in fact on the way. In a more serious vein, the notice requirements can also serve as an indicator of actual or potential default by the vendor, in effect giving the user one more "checkpoint" to determine whether the vendor is meeting its deadlines. Consequently, this type of provision is particularly useful when tied to a section specifying that the equipment must be shipped by a stated date.

Users may wish to consider the following example designed for inclusion in a used equipment contract:

> Seller shall notify Customer of the impending shipment of any item of Equipment not later than two (2) business days prior to actual shipment. The Seller shall also notify Customer by telegram of the actual shipment of any item of Equipment on the date of shipment, including in each telegram the waybill number, transportation method and carrier, and expected date of delivery. Each such telegram shall be confirmed by written notice sent to the Customer by certified mail on the date of shipment.

ACCEPTANCE PROVISIONS

One of the most important provisions in any equipment acquisition document is the section governing acceptance. This provision describes the performance specifications or tests that must be met for the equipment or other products to be accepted by the user. Acceptance in this context has (or should have) considerable legal significance in that the user will generally be liable for the payment of the purchase or rental price only if the products successfully complete the specified acceptance standards. The acceptance date may also affect other contractual matters, such as risk of loss, insurance, and initiation of maintenance. Standards established for acceptance purposes may also be used in related provisions covering ongoing system performance (for example, rental credits, maintenance credits, and mandatory equipment replacements).

Unfortunately, few vendor standard form agreements include an acceptance test that is adequate from the standpoint of the user. Some vendors still exclude any acceptance provision or require that the user agree in the original contract (in advance of delivery and installation) that it has accepted the equipment. The latter practice is particularly popular among smaller and less sophisticated third-party leasing firms, brokers, and dealers. Most vendor agreements include some form of acceptance provision that, at least on first glance, appears to be reasonable. For example, one frequently utilized acceptance clause specifies that the equipment will be deemed accepted (or, alternatively, that payments will begin) when the system "is installed and ready for use." A more generous variation on this phrase provides that the equipment will be deemed accepted when the system "is installed and ready for use in accordance with the vendor's published specifications therefor." In both examples, some vendors strengthen their position by stating that acceptance will occur when, in the opinion of the vendor's field engineering personnel, the equipment meets the specified standards (for example, "the rental period shall begin when the vendor's field engineering representative certifies that the equipment is installed and ready for use").

When pressed to do so, many vendors will offer an alternative acceptance provision that is more favorable to the user. For example, some computer vendors will offer the standard acceptance section used in the General Services Administration (GSA) procurement documents for data processing equipment. (See Appendix B.) Other vendors will suggest the basic GSA approach, but will offer an acceptance addendum that modifies the GSA language in several important respects, generally by reducing the required uptime percentage or reducing the length of the acceptance testing period. Although some of these vendor alternatives are reasonable for small and medium acquisitions, they may require significant modification for more complex or critical transactions. Moreover, the alternative acceptance provisions offered by other vendors include risks and potential problems that mandate careful user review and modification (or outright rejection).

One of the more onerous examples of the latter type of provision provides that, notwithstanding any other language in the agreement, the user will be deemed to have accepted the equipment if it utilizes the system for any business production or profit purpose. This language should be rejected for several reasons. First, any reasonable acceptance provision should require that the system be tested by processing the user's normal business work. Yet language such as that noted above could mandate immediate acceptance when the first business data is entered into the system. Second, if acceptance is delayed due to minor or major problems, the user may be seriously inconvenienced. Consequently, if the user is able to minimize this inconvenience by utilizing the system for any business purposes during this period, it should be permitted (indeed, encouraged) to do so. Any other approach raises serious questions as to whether the vendor is more interested in meeting the user's needs and building a good relationship or in tricking the user into prematurely accepting the system. Third, many acceptance tests require that, once the system meets the test, the rental period will be deemed to begin as of the first day of the successful test period, rather than as of the end of that period. The difference is not critical, but it can require the user to pay rent for an additional 30 to 60 days, depending upon the duration of the minimum acceptable test period. If the user is required to pay rental and/or maintenance charges during the successful test period, which is itself a matter to be negotiated, the user certainly should be permitted to make productive business use of the equipment during this time.

As in other portions of an acquisition agreement, the acceptance section must be tailored to meet the specific needs of a particular transaction. In some acquisitions, the size, importance, and immediate reliability of the system permit use of relatively simple acceptance language (perhaps the vendor's alternative provision or the standard form language with minor additions and changes). In other transactions, elaborate acceptance language is mandated by the complexity of the system (including hardware, systems software, and custom or converted applications programs), the importance of system reliability, and the cost exposure involved in the user's processing or production. Preacquisition benchmark tests may be available for incorporation into some acceptance provisions. (See Chapter 5.) In other situations, the unique aspects of some software programs and conversions may make the development of any test criteria quite difficult.

The first step in developing any acceptance test should be to determine the basic goals expected to be achieved by the test. Conceptually, any sound acceptance test should determine or "test" two factors: (1) performance; and (2) reliability. A test which covers one of these factors, but not the other, will leave the user exposed to unacceptable risks. In testing these two factors, the acceptance provision must consider all "people, products, and services" involved in the transaction. Thus, the acceptance provision must test both performance and reliability for: (1) hardware; (2) operating software; (3) applications software; (4) special software; (5) hardware maintenance; and (6) software maintenance. Because any acceptance test is only as good as its weakest link, if the test fails to cover any one of these items (assuming it is applicable in the transaction), the entire test may be invalidated and the user exposed to unreasonable financial and operating risks. As one experienced manager put it, "the difference between a complete acceptance test and an incomplete one is very simple: one optimizes your ability to receive your $6 million investment; the other gives you a chance to receive a few boxes of components that net out at about six cents a pound."

Performance

The performance section of the acceptance test should be designed to determine whether the products being tested will perform in accordance with standards specified in the acquisition agreement. The key to the validity and the value of the performance portion of any acceptance test is the standards definition. If the user fails to specify meaningful standards, the performance test may be more perfunctory than real. Indeed, the test may pose substantial dangers for the user by creating a false sense of comfort and security.

Although a wide variety of performance standards are possible, most can be categorized into one of two categories: (1) standards based upon published specifications; and (2) standards based upon other agreed upon specifications. The first category most often includes manufacturer's published specifications, while the second generally includes benchmark tests of varying descriptions. Regardless of the type of test used, it must cover all hardware and software supplied by the vendor. As noted below, in some instances the test may also need to include certain components supplied by other sources or already included in the user's system.

A two-stage performance standard often offers advantages for the user. In this approach, the initial stage requires that, following product installation, the vendor successfully perform all standard published test and installation procedures for the system, as specified in certain vendor documents referenced in the contract. These procedures generally include the minimum or standard operating specifications published for the system by the vendor. Assuming that this test is met, the second performance stage requires that the vendor successfully repeat, on the installed products at the user's site, one or more benchmark tests that were previously conducted at another installation (perhaps to induce the user to enter into the acquisition agreement) or otherwise specified in the acquisition agreement. Whether a repetition of a previously-conducted benchmark test or the initial performance of some other test of agreed upon specifications, this stage of the performance standard must be designed with care to ensure that it is meaningful to the user.

Far from being deterred by benchmark tests, many equipment sales representatives consider them to be exceptional marketing opportunities. The reason for this view is that few users have the time or expertise necessary to design a strict, detailed test that is uniquely applicable to the user's business requirements. As a result, the vendor sales representative creates and suggests a test that the vendor knows it can achieve, even if the test has little relevance to the user as a true test of specific system performance. Because of this risk, any benchmark test or other agreed upon specification standard should be carefully reviewed by the user's technical staff before it is included in the acquisition agreement. The legal and other nontechnical members of the user's negotiating team should also carefully consider any such standard, applying a reasonableness review, in order to guard against the risk that the written standard included in the contract omits key practical details necessary to preserve the integrity of the test. Benchmark tests are discussed in more detail in Chapter 5 of this volume.

Reliability

The reliability section of the acceptance test should be designed to determine whether the products being tested will meet the specified performance standards over a stated period of time with an acceptable failure or downtime rate. In effect, the performance section of the acceptance test indicates what specifications the products must meet when they are installed. The reliability section indicates how long the products must meet these or similar specifications without failure or without some level of failure that is deemed to be unacceptable.

In designing the reliability standard, two factors are paramount: (1) duration; and (2) frequency. The duration factor must specify how long the test will be conducted and how long the products being tested will be "up" or "down." The frequency factor must indicate how often the products will be permitted to fail, regardless of the duration of the failure.

Put in a somewhat different manner, virtually all users would be willing to accept a reliability standard that required the equipment or other products to be "up" 100% of the time, throughout the installation (not merely acceptance) period. The problems arise when the vendor and user attempt to negotiate some more realistic version of this obviously unattainable standard.

For the reliability section of any acceptance test to be meaningful, it must be performed over a reasonable period of time (generally three to six weeks) under conditions that duplicate the user's business conditions. For example, if the user has acquired a new system that must meet the user's peak month-end, quarter-end, or year-end production requirements, the reliability test should be designed to overlap at least one of these peak periods. Similarly, if the user requires consistent operation, twenty-four hours per day, seven days per week, the reliability test should utilize the same schedule.

The reliability standard must also include a reasonable up-time factor. Like the GSA "standard of performance" for data processing systems, many acceptance tests include a minimum system "effectiveness level" that is specified as a percentage. For example, the effectiveness level may be computed by dividing "operational use time" during the relevant period by the sum of that time plus "system failure downtime." (As in all portions of any acceptance test, definitions are critical.)

Gaining mutual agreement on the effectiveness level to be employed is seldom an easy task. Many vendors will agree to an effectiveness level of 90% or 95%, although some will do so only after long and drawn out negotiating efforts by the user. Although these percentages sound rather impressive initially, they may or may not be adequate to meet the user's minimum needs. For example, some users readily accept a 90% effectiveness level even though their business operations demand an uptime of 98%. The difference between the two percentages can be critical in determining the operational or financial success of the system installation. Consequently, the user should ensure that its technical personnel (and often its end user personnel) seriously consider whether the minimum effectiveness level proposed by the vendor will provide an adequate test of equipment performance for acceptance purposes.

In some installations, a single effectiveness percentage may not test all user requirements. For example, the user may need only a 90% overall uptime percentage, but may also require minimum response and access times on various communications, edit, and response functions. For the reliability test to be meaningful, minimum standards must be stated for each of these separate requirements. In some acquisitions, it may be practical to specify all of these standards in the acceptance provision itself. In other situations, the user may establish a complex set of test standards in a "performance" addendum or in the RFP document (which can then be incorporated into the agreement by reference). Where the user has unique processing requirements and a strong technical staff, it may specify some or all of its minimum performance standards in the form of a test program, formula, or algorithm.

The formula or algorithm approach is particularly advantageous because it also facilitates the user's ability to specify "mean time between failures." Although most users recognize the importance of applying an "effectiveness level" performance standard, they sometimes fail to appreciate the equal importance of including a standard that limits the number of failures that can occur within a specified period. While excessive aggregate system downtime is generally more of a practical problem and risk than frequent intermittent failure, the latter problem can create havoc where it occurs, particularly if it requires reruns or manual starts. Thus, a sound acceptance test should include some method of specifying and measuring the acceptable frequency of failure.

Regardless of the tests employed, for the reliability standard to be valid it must require that the new system or other products be operated in a realistic hardware and software environment; that is, with all peripherals and communications devices that will form a part of the relevant equipment network. For example, if the new system is designed to be part of a communications or distributed processing system, the reliability standard will serve little purpose if it is applied in a sterile operating environment, separate and apart from the equipment and software with which it will be connected and for which it was acquired. If the reliability standard is to provide any serious value to the user, it must be set and described in the user's full operating framework, even if this approach requires use of existing hardware or software products supplied by another vendor.

Most vendors argue that the reliability test should not involve any equipment supplied by another source (or even previously-installed equipment provided by the primary vendor). This argument may be reasonable in certain circumstances where it would not be meaningful or necessary for the new equipment to be tested in a complex system or network environment. The key question in this area should generally be whether the user's needs dictate that the new equipment "prove itself" in a particular operating environment. For example, if a user is ordering several hundred new terminals or a new series of minicomputers to be integrated into an existing communications network, the user will gain little solace from testing the equipment in an artificial "off-line" mode. On the other hand, if the user is procuring additional terminals or minicomputers of a type that has already proven itself in the user's processing system, separate testing (and, indeed, reduced testing) may be reasonable for both the user and the vendor.

Where the products will be operated in an environment that practically necessitates use of an acceptance test which includes products other than those supplied under the agreement, both parties must take a realistic, problem-solving approach toward drafting the acceptance provision. The vendor must recognize that the user really has no interest in acquiring the equipment if it cannot be utilized effectively within the system and in the manner intended by the user. Despite the tendency of some vendor marketeers to think otherwise, the user has a right and, indeed, an obligation to specify how and where it expects to use a product and to refuse to accept it if it fails to serve the purpose intended by the parties.

On the other hand, the user must appreciate that this broad but realistic approach may create substantial additional risks for the vendor. Even if the vendor agrees with the user's concerns outlined above, the vendor is in business to make a profit. In most instances, it cannot and will not accept the possibility that it will be exposed to serious contractual or financial liability for equipment, software, or other reasons that are beyond its control.

When considered together, the concerns held by the user and the vendor suggest the following conclusions. First, the user has every right to specify that the equipment or other products must perform within an existing or other system environment. Second, having specified that fact, the user has the corresponding right to expect that the acceptance test (either the performance standard or the reliability standard or both) will meaningfully measure this specification in the total system environment. Third, the vendor has the right to bid or not bid under these circumstances. Fourth, the vendor has the right to impose reasonable safeguards in this environment to ensure that it is not penalized inappropriately for matters beyond its control (e.g., downtime on components supplied by another vendor). Fifth, both parties must determine and allocate the risks and costs of nonperformance. For example, consider the following alternatives if the vendor's products fail to meet the test: (1) the vendor is held liable for damages; (2) the user may cancel the contract without liability to the vendor; (3) the user may cancel the contract but only after reimbursing the vendor for certain out-of-pocket expenses; and (4) the user may cancel the contract and the vendor must reimburse the user for certain out-of-pocket expenses. Various combinations of these alternatives may be appropriate in a given transaction, depending upon such factors as the uniqueness of the user's system and the risks accepted by each party during the sales or RFP stage of the transaction. The alternative or alternatives selected will have a substantial effect on the vendor's willingness to employ acceptance testing that includes products not covered by the acquisition agreement.

Where the user intends to require "full system" testing involving previously-installed components or products supplied by other vendors, it can improve its negotiating position by gaining early vendor commitments concerning the compatibility of the new products in the broader system environment. To maximize its bargaining position in this area, the user should ensure that its RFP emphasizes that the new equipment must be capable of reliably operating as part of the user's existing system or network. The user can then stress this factor in evaluating the vendors' proposals and in pursuing the negotiations. This approach will generally cause the vendor to make strong oral commitments concerning compatibility that cannot be evaded when the user insists that the promises be verified as part of the acceptance test program.

In drafting the acceptance test provisions, the user should involve all members of its negotiating team. In most situations, however, primary drafting and approval responsibility will fall to the user's legal counsel and its technical experts—for, to be effective, an acceptance provision must be capable of both being drafted and interpreted in legal language and being implemented in technical terms. In this regard, the acceptance provision, or a relevant addendum or schedule, must specify the exact details and procedures to be followed in each phase of the acceptance testing. This goal can often be achieved by having the user's technical staff explain to the user's attorney, in laymen's terms, precisely how they propose to accomplish the test procedures, step by step. The lawyer can then draft these steps into appropriate legal language that can be reviewed and approved by the technical personnel and the full negotiating team.

After the standards for each phase of the acceptance test have been drafted, the user's team should ensure that all stages are consistent and, to the extent desired, sequential or overlapping. Having described the test itself, the team must also ensure that the acceptance provision meshes properly with other sections of the acquisition agreement. For example, either the acceptance test section or another provision must detail the remedies or penalties that will be imposed if the vendor fails to meet one or more stages of the test within the times and conditions specified in the agreement. (Generally, the user should grant the vendor a reasonable time to cure initial nonperformance, while at the same time reserving the right to terminate the agreement and/or pursue other remedies if the nonperformance reaches levels that are unacceptable to the user.) As in other provisions where vendor deadlines are involved, the acceptance test provision should also be coordinated with any force majeure language to preclude undue harm to the user or the vendor in the event unforeseen "acts of God" preclude satisfactory completion of the established tests. Finally, the user's negotiating team must consider whether the acceptance test provision, or another contract section, should include a continuing performance standard that goes beyond the acceptance period. Where such a continuing performance standard (e.g., rental or maintenance credit or "lemon" replacement) is employed, it must be consistent with the initial acceptance test. In many circumstances, the section governing the continuing performance standard can incorporate definitions and test formulae from the initial acceptance provision. Five example acceptance tests are set forth in Appendix B.

REMEDIES

Virtually any major equipment contract should have one or more sections that specify the remedies that will be available to the parties in the event of default, nonperformance, or the failure of a condition or event. Depending upon the preferences of the parties and drafting considerations, these remedies may be set forth in a single section or spread among various substantive provisions (e.g., delivery, acceptance, or payment), or both.

Before negotiating specific language, the user should consider the threshold question of whether the agreement should attempt to specify all remedies that the parties anticipate may be desired in the event of default. Some attorneys believe that specifying all relevant remedies in an agreement is a waste of time and paper. These lawyers argue that the law provides adequate remedies in all but the rarest of practical instances, and the effort to specify additional, detailed remedies in the contract itself is seldom needed. Other attorneys take the opposite extreme, arguing that no binding agreement is complete unless it specifies all possible remedies and, indeed, indicates that the specified remedies shall be deemed to be exclusive—a practice that is designed to override and preclude the general legal remedies (noted above) that might otherwise apply.

In contrast to these two polar positions, the authors recommend a flexible approach that tailors the remedies in any contract to the transaction involved. Although there may be theoretical merit in including all possible remedies in a written agreement, practical constraints generally preclude such a practice. On the other hand, leaving the contract devoid of all specific remedies and thereby relying on the law to provide reasonable remedies in each case is seldom likely to provide the level of protection or response expected by the parties in a given instance. Contractual remedies implied or otherwise provided by law do a fine job of handling basic business transactions; however, they seldom provide the practical remedies actually desired by the user in the event of vendor default. Indeed, in some instances remedies supplied by law may provide results that are significantly more favorable to the vendor than those desired by the user. The Uniform Commercial Code (UCC), discussed in Chapter 6, offers one example. In other instances, the size, scope, and applicability of remedies provided by law may not be known until the governing court has ruled in the user's suit against the vendor. This uncertainty and the delays and costs of any litigation virtually mandate the inclusion of at least some specific remedies in the formal contract documents.

As the first step toward preparing the remedy provisions of any agreement, the user's negotiating team should compile a written list of all vendor obligations under the transaction. Adjacent to each obligation, the team should specify two items: (1) the results (generally, the "harm" or "damage" to the user) that will occur if the vendor fails to meet the obligation specified in a complete and timely manner; and (2) the remedies desired by the user in each such event. This list can be compiled from a section-by-section analysis of all contract documents, with vendor obligations being summarized to the left of the listing and the results and remedies being set forth on the right.

In some instances, the user may list escalating remedies that grant the vendor several opportunities to perform while providing increasingly strong alternatives to the user. In other situations, the user may prefer alternative remedies that give the user the ability to select one of several actions depending upon the user's needs at the time of the vendor's nonperformance.

The approach outlined above is designed to force the user to specify all of the practical remedies it wishes to have if various events occur. In this context, the term "remedies" is extremely broad, covering far more than mere damages or injunctive relief. In effect, a "remedy" for this purpose is intended to be whatever the user may answer to the question of "If the vendor fails to do X (or "does Y"), what do you want to occur?" It is only when the user's attorney has the practical answers to many repetitions of this question that adequate drafting of any remedy section can begin.

As this list of obligations, results, and remedies is prepared and studied by the full negotiating team, the user's attorneys can determine which remedies should be specified in the agreement and which may be safely left to the law. Once this decision is reached, the remedies to be included in the contract can be drafted and circulated throughout the negotiating team for review.

For purposes of considering available remedies, the following categories are helpful: (1) special remedies; (2) damages; and (3) specific performance. The relative value of these remedies to the user varies, depending upon such factors as the type of transaction involved and the user's special needs. The practical value of the remedies also varies over time, with some remedies offering more immediate benefits and others providing later solutions if the problem or dispute continues. (See Fig. 8-1.) Each of the remedies categorized above is discussed below. The legal concepts underlying these remedies are explored in more detail in Chapter 6.

Special Remedies

As used by the authors, the category of special remedies covers a wide range of actions that do not include damages or specific performance. This category provides the user's first line of defense and satisfaction in any situation where the vendor fails to meet the standards imposed by the contract. As such, the category includes remedies that answer the pragmatic question of: "Okay, the vendor has failed to do X (or "has done Y"); since you obviously don't want to sue at this point, what do you want to do (or "cause the vendor to do")?" Thus, most special remedies are practical ones that must be spelled out in the applicable agreement and, absent such

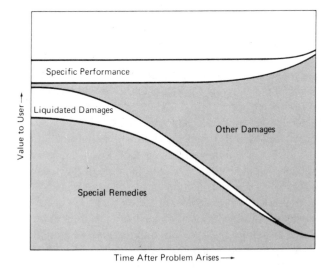

Fig. 8-1.   Relative value of various contractual remedies to the user.

specific treatment, will probably not be available to the user (or will not be available at the time or in the manner stated). Examples of special remedies include the following:

- The vendor fails to meet a specified delivery deadline; the user is given the right to cancel the agreement after stated notice to the vendor.
- The system fails to pass the benchmark performance stage of the acceptance test, due to inadequate capacity; upon demand by the user to the vendor, the vendor is obligated to supply additional equipment within a stated period, at no cost (or at an agreed upon cost) to the user.
- The equipment fails to meet the continuing performance standard during the term of the lease; upon demand by the user to the vendor, the vendor is obligated to replace the defective or inadequate component within a stated period, at no cost to the user and with indemnification by the vendor for any depreciation or ITC loss suffered by the user as a result of the replacement.
- The vendor fails to provide the specified standard of support for certain software; upon demand by the user to the vendor, the vendor is obligated to provide the software object or source code to the user within a stated period, at no cost to the user.
- The vendor fails to provide the specified minimum response time to remedial maintenance calls over a stated period; upon demand by the user to the vendor, the vendor is obligated to assign a full-time maintenance person to the user's site for a stated period.

From the standpoint of providing immediate, realistic satisfaction to the user, without the expense and delays inherent in litigation, special remedies such as those set out above are generally far superior to damages or specific performance. The reason is very simple: Special remedies can be tailored to meet specific user needs, without requiring the user to allege a "breach" of the agreement, which can and usually does create relationship problems and, as noted above, litigation expense. Where special remedies such as those set out above are included in the contract, the user must allege a breach of the agreement only where the vendor fails to comply with or provide the special remedy set forth in the agreement. Ordinarily, the vendor will comply with the special remedy in such an instance, thereby saving the user the time, aggravation, and expense of actual or threatened litigation.

In proposing special remedies, the user should carefully consider the impact of the remedy on the vendor as well as the user. In this regard, the user must trace a thin line between remedies that will offer little benefit to the user or little incentive to the vendor and remedies that will provide meaningful benefit to the user but unacceptable costs or risks to the vendor. In negotiating special remedies, the user should consistently ask the vendor what it will be willing to do to support its commitment in the event it fails to meet its stated contractual obligation. This inquiry can be enhanced by comparing the amounts that would be expended by the user and by the vendor at the future point in the transaction when the remedy would become applicable. In most instances, the vendor will have placed much less "at risk" than the user at any point in the process, particularly where the user is responsible for site preparation. (See Fig. 8-2.) This point can and should be used as a negotiating argument that, given the user's financial and practical commitment, the vendor should at least be willing to agree to the suggested special remedy.

In applying this approach, the user may find that the vendor is reluctant to offer any meaningful remedies or deadlines. One effective user response to this vendor reaction may be for the user to start at an obviously weak extreme and then work toward a more realistic deadline, grace period, or remedy. For example, the user's negotiator may suggest that "surely" the vendor would agree to a delivery date of X, a grace period of Y, and a remedy that of Z. Once the vendor's representative agrees that the vendor would certainly be willing to agree to those standards, the discussion has at least been opened. Despite the fact that the user broke the vendor's silence through the use of a weak extreme, the user now has an opportunity to step the vendor

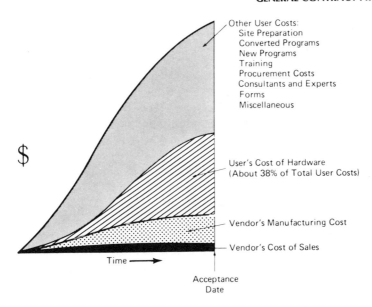

$

Other User Costs:
  Site Preparation
  Converted Programs
  New Programs
  Training
  Procurement Costs
  Consultants and Experts
  Forms
  Miscellaneous

User's Cost of Hardware
(About 38% of Total User Costs)

Vendor's Manufacturing Cost

Vendor's Cost of Sales

Time ⟶

Acceptance
Date

Fig. 8-2. Relative financial expenditures and commitments of vendor and user prior to acceptance date for data processing equipment.

up to a more realistic solution. (To implement this approach with maximum safety, the user should always initially suggest an obviously weak proposal rather than one which the vendor may claim was a serious user offer.)

Where the vendor balks at the user's efforts to negotiate meaningful special remedies, the user's team may find it effective to switch from a discussion of special remedies to a demand for strict damage remedies. When this approach is implemented effectively, it often causes the vendor's representatives to adopt a more realistic viewpoint and recognize the comparative value of employing special remedies.

Damages

Damage remedies can be subdivided into several categories: (1) actual; (2) consequential; and (3) liquidated. Punitive damages are also applicable in some instances, but many states limit or preclude their applicability in contract cases. Moreover, because punitive damages are seldom awarded in any suit unless the defendant's actions were so unconscionable as to be abhorrent to the court, they are hardly a viable remedy for planning or drafting purposes. Each of the other categories of damages is discussed below.

Actual Damages. Actual damages (sometimes called "standard" damages) represent one portion of "compensatory" damages, which are effectively designed to recompense a party for what it should have received, or expected to receive, in a contractual bargain. Contract law is filled with cases that define just what standard damages may be available in a given default situation. Ordinarily, standard damages will be provided upon default to permit a party to recover what it expended on the contract, what it expected to receive in the transaction (including the payment necessary to permit the party to "cover" itself by procuring the goods or services from another at a higher price), or what the other party unjustly received in the transaction. The damages available in a given instance vary according to the type of contract (e.g., goods or services) and statute involved (e.g., the Uniform Commercial Code).

From a drafting standpoint, the user's attorneys should have primary responsibility for determining the types of actual damages that would be available to the user in various events. The user's attorneys must also provide drafting guidance for any contractual provisions specifying or modifying the actual damages that would be available at law. Ordinarily, the authors do not recommend specifying actual damage remedies in the contract itself, preferring instead to rely upon the prevailing body of common and statutory law for this purpose. The authors generally recommend that, except where expressly specified otherwise by the user's counsel, the contract should merely provide that, in addition to the special and other remedies set forth in the agreement, the user shall have such other remedies as may be available at law or in equity (except as specifically limited by the contract).

In some instances, it may be advisable for the contract to limit the actual damages that might otherwise be available. The best and most appropriate method of implementing this approach where desired is to use contractual language that provides an obligation and a related special remedy. If the obligation is not met, but the party complies with the special remedy, no actual damages should be made available. However, if the obligation is not met, and the special remedy is also not complied with, actual (and perhaps other) damages should be available. This approach is fair and businesslike for all concerned. It permits the user to specify its desired initial special remedy, while precluding the vendor from being exposed to actual or other damages. Because of this fact, the approach often causes the vendor to be more willing to agree to specific contractual obligations and special remedies than would be the case if the vendor were immediately exposed to monetary damages for the same events.

Vendors sometimes attempt to limit actual damages in other ways, generally by placing a dollar ceiling on the total amount of any award. Users should be extremely reluctant to accept this approach under any circumstances, particularly where the limit is specified as the total amount paid by the user under a relatively small contract. First, contractual damages are often much like an insurance policy: They are more valuable in a calamity than in a minor problem. The user is more likely to sue, and more likely to need a substantial recovery, in the very situation when a dollar recovery limit would become applicable. Second, if the vendor is overly concerned about limiting its actual (and not merely consequential) damages, the user may need to reevaluate its entire relationship with the vendor. After all, if the vendor wishes to limit its liability, who is going to limit the user's liability? Yet, as between the user and the vendor, who should be responsible (or, at least, more responsible) if the vendor breaches its obligations under the agreement?

Consequential Damages

Consequential damages represent the other portion of compensatory damages and effectively include all other reasonably foreseeable losses resulting from the breach of contract. Like many other legal distinctions, the line between actual (or standard) damages and consequential damages is difficult to draw. The question of how far consequential damages go is equally difficult, although the textbook answer is generally that consequential damages will be available to cover all losses which both parties (thinking objectively as "reasonable persons" under the law) should have foreseen, at the time the contract was made, as likely resulting from the breach.

As this general definition suggests, consequential damages can cover substantial chains of events and significant amounts well above the amounts of any actual damages. Because of this risk, virtually all vendors attempt to limit or preclude any consequential damages. Where this practice occurs, as it usually does, the user bears the full risk of any consequential losses, even though (by definition) both parties reasonably foresaw the risk at the time the contract was signed.

This result can create a serious dilemma for the user, particularly where it may itself face liability for consequential damages in contracts with its own customers or end users. Where the user has such agreements, it can and should attempt to limit its liability for consequential damages by placing its own limit or restriction on such damages in each such agreement, thereby shifting the risk of loss to its customers or end users. However, where the user is unable to shift the risk of loss in this manner, it must face the very basic question of whether it is willing to accept the risk of consequential losses and, if so, whether any practical steps (usually technical or operational) can be taken to reduce this risk from a practical standpoint.

Despite the general folklore otherwise, some users do have the bargaining power necessary to remove or delimit the limitation of consequential damages provision that appears in most vendor agreements. Large national or multinational users should therefore make every effort to remove or restrict such a provision, particularly where their bargaining power exceeds that of the vendor.

Where the user is unable to gain the removal or restriction of the consequential damage limitation, the user's negotiating team should at least turn the provision around so that it "cuts both ways" and protects both the vendor and the user. Although the vendor's representative will generally argue otherwise (e.g., "Why are you worried about being liable for consequential damages? Your only real contractual obligation is for payment of the price. Don't you intend to pay?"), in a major contract dispute the user may be held liable for consequential damages (e.g., the user's improper failure to accept the equipment and pay the purchase price allegedly damages the vendor's business reputation and leads to the vendor's bankruptcy). Therefore, if the vendor has the right to limit its liability for consequential damages, the user should have a similar right. Even so, the mutual limitation of liability for consequential damages is more likely to provide substantial protection to the vendor than the user.

Liquidated Damages

Unlike actual and consequential damages, which will be imputed from common law or statute even if not specifically referenced in the contract, liquidated damages will be available only if established in the agreement. Liquidated damages are specified in an agreement when the parties wish to establish a fixed amount in advance that will be payable in the event a default or other designated event occurs in the future. Liquidated damages must be reasonable in amount (when compared to the default or other event); that is, they cannot be so unconscionable as to be considered "in the nature of a penalty." If a party successfully alleges that the liquidated damages were or are a penalty, the court may strike the entire liquidated damage provision, rather than reduce the amount, thereby leaving the user with no remedy at all. In most jurisdictions, liquidated damages can be specified only where the parties are not aware, at the time the contract is signed, of the actual damages that would be sustained in the event of default. This restriction is imposed because of the legal theory that liquidated damages are acceptable, and not penal, only when mutually established by the parties to provide a reasonable and agreed upon monetary remedy for a default for which the actual damages are unknown as of the date the contract is signed. Once liquidated damages have been specified, they are the remedy. The user cannot waive the liquidated damages and pursue other alternatives except in narrow instances that must be carefully documented to comply with prevailing legal principles.

Within these and certain other legal constraints, liquidated damages can offer significant value to users in most equipment contracts. Liquidated damages are particularly popular remedies for the vendor's failure to meet a specified delivery, installation, or acceptance deadline. Proving actual damages in such an instance is difficult or impossible, and litigation at that stage of the transaction would seldom be advisable. Liquidated damages in such a situation provide a pre-agreed remedy that reduces the user's frustration, grants the user some monetary relief, and (perhaps most importantly) provides a negative financial incentive for the vendor to perform.

Ordinarily, liquidated damages in such a situation should be specified as "X dollars per day" in order to provide a reasonable remedy that cannot be interpreted as a penalty. A cap on the total amount of liquidated damages may be imposed for the same reason. Ideally, the amount of the daily or other periodic payment should be adequate to serve the three purposes noted above. For bargaining purposes, the user may wish to suggest a dollar figure that would permit the user to obtain alternative processing or production through a time-sharing or similar service (obtaining alternative equipment at the outset may be prohibitive in some instances). However, even where the user cannot achieve such an amount in the contract, a lower liquidated damage provision may still serve as a good "carrot and stick" for the user. All other things being equal, a vendor facing delivery and scheduling problems among two or more users will ship the system to the user having a liquidated damages provision in the contract. As the saying goes, "the squeaky wheel gets the grease," and few things squeak better than a good liquidated damages provision.

Vendors and their attorneys generally have one of two reactions to liquidated damage provisions: (1) they agree to them readily, but attempt to reduce the amounts and effectiveness of the provisions to a very low level; or (2) they resolutely refuse to consider them, often asserting that the vendor has an "absolute" policy on the matter. As noted above, liquidated damage provisions are subject to a number of legal technicalities that vary from jurisdiction to jurisdiction. Therefore, if the vendor adopts the first approach noted the user's attorney must devote special care to ensure that, at a minimum, the provision will be legally valid under applicable state law. (Because the vendor will generally attempt to specify that the law of its home state will govern the agreement, the user's attorney is likely to be at a disadvantage in this effort.)

Where the vendor's representative resolutely refuses to discuss liquidated damages, the user can apply any number of negotiating tactics. Among those that can be particularly effective are the following.

1. Ask the vendor to explain in detail why it will not consider any liquidated damage provision. ("Company policy" is not an adequate answer.)
2. Ask the vendor if it would agree to a liquidated damage provision if the applicable deadline or other vendor commitment were moved back or coupled with a more substantial grace period. (The user can employ extremes here to make its point: "Well, wouldn't you agree to such a provision if we moved the delivery date out 12 months?")
3. Ask the vendor why it is not willing to stand behind its commitment to deliver (or whatever), implying or stating that, if the vendor itself is concerned about believing its delivery (or other commitment) why should the user believe it?
4. Ask the vendor if it would accept a token liquidated damages amount of $1.00 per day, then work the vendor up from there. (Because liquidated damages may prove to be the only remedy in such a situation, the user should be careful not to compromise on an inadequate amount.)
5. Deadlock the negotiations. One effective approach to such a deadlock is to assert that the user has a "policy" of not doing business with a party that is unwilling to stand behind its contractual commitments.

Because of the legal constraints imposed on liquidated damages, the provisions employed should be carefully reviewed by the user's attorney. The user's technical staff should also consider the provisions to ensure that liquidated damages are appropriate in the particular situation, and to ensure that the amounts are reasonable and adequate.

One of the more difficult legal issues involving liquidated damages concerns the question of whether a user can obtain both liquidated damages and other damages or remedies for the same default. As suggested above, in most jurisdictions liquidated damages are the user's exclusive remedy for the default for which they are specified. In an effort to avoid this problem, some user attorneys draft the liquidated damage provision in a manner that emphasizes that the liquidated damages are for the vendor's delay after the specified (e.g., delivery) deadline and not for the vendor's default if the deadline is exceeded by a certain maximum period. Under this approach, liquidated damages are specified for each day that the vendor exceeds the indicated deadline, up to a specified maximum number of days and maximum liquidated amount. If the vendor still has not performed by the time that the maximums are met, the liquidated damages stop accruing and the user is given certain alternative remedies that it may then invoke (e.g., cancellation or pursuit of general legal remedies). Although the authors strongly support this approach, they caution that its effectiveness depends upon careful drafting and a solid understanding of applicable local law.

An example of a liquidated damages provision appears in Appendix B. The legal concepts which govern liquidated damage provisions are discussed in more detail in Chapter 6.

Specific Performance

When monetary damages are inadequate in the eyes of the law, or where the right to specific performance is clearly set forth in the agreement, a court may order a party to perform or comply with an agreement. Such an action is generally said to be brought "in equity" rather than "at law" and, as a result, a number of special "equitable principles" may govern a party's right to relief. Because specific performance may indeed be the only meaningful remedy in a given instance, the authors recommend that it be preserved rather than excluded; that is, except where the user's attorneys recommend otherwise, the contract should provide that, in addition to the remedies specified, the user shall have the right to petition a court to compel specific performance.

Where the user contemplates that specific performance may be appropriate, and particularly where it may not be the sole remedy, the user should consider directly specifying the performance through a special remedy or through some other direct language in the agreement. The user's attorneys should devote particular attention to any such provision to ensure that the user's rights can be enforced judicially.

WARRANTY PROVISIONS

Particularly where new equipment is involved, most vendor form agreements include some type of warranty provision. In some instances, the length of the warranty period may be negotiable, either directly (by stating a longer period) or indirectly (by adding other related provisions, such as a refurbishment warranty). The substance of the equipment warranty may also be negotiable, particularly as it relates to any exclusions.

One of the more frequent vendor warranty exclusions involves "expendable" parts of various kinds. For example, consider the following excerpt from a major electronic equipment manufacturer's standard agreement: "Expendable items such as ribbons, brushes, resistors, diodes, capacitors, transistors or other like components are excluded from this warranty." Excluding certain truly "expendable" items from the vendor's warranty may well be acceptable. Ribbons, platens, and perhaps motor brushes fall into this category. But, as the above example indicates, some vendors go much farther and attempt to exclude electronic components that are integral parts of the equipment—components that should not fail at all for many years and certainly should not fail within the warranty period. This type of broad exclusion should be deleted or narrowed by an appropriate user amendment.

Most vendor contracts also contain one or more provisions designed to limit or preclude any and all implied warranties. While express warranties are created by actual statements in the relevant documents, implied warranties are imputed or "implied" by law based upon the facts and circumstances surrounding the transaction.

Although other implied warranties may occur, the most frequent ones are those implied through the Uniform Commercial Code (UCC), which governs the sale of goods in virtually every state. (As Chapter 6 explains, each state adopts its own version of the UCC, so differences in the statute occur among the states. In addition, applicable case law interpreting the UCC varies from jurisdiction to jurisdiction.) The UCC provides two implied warranties for contracts governed by it: (1) the implied warranty of merchantability, which essentially states that the goods shall be of not less than fair or average quality and generally suitable for their apparent purpose; and (2) the implied warranty of fitness for a particular purpose, which effectively provides that the goods shall be suitable for one or more particular purposes intended by the buyer and known to the seller. The UCC also provides that these warranties can be disclaimed in whole or in part, and most vendors do this through appropriate bold face provisions in each and every contract. (See Chapter 6.)

From a practical standpoint, any user attempt to eliminate these disclaimers of implied warranties is unlikely to be successful or worth the effort. Most vendors are appropriately concerned about accepting unknown warranties implied by law, and resolutely refuse to eliminate the disclaimer provisions under any circumstances. In most instances, the user's negotiators would be far better off permitting the implied warranties to be disclaimed and focusing on improving the express warranties and other vendor commitments in the agreement.

Warranty provisions vary considerably among vendors. Consequently the user must carefully study the warranty language contained in each vendor proposal and documentation. In many cases, the warranty section of the applicable vendor agreement does not tell the entire story. Generally, the user should also consider all relevant maintenance provisions (including any addenda or schedules). In conducting this review, the user should particularly study the scope of the vendor's warranty obligation (for example, whether the vendor will effectively "maintain" the equipment during the warranty period or merely replace equipment shown to be "defective" in workmanship or materials). The user should also consider the general interrelationship, if any, between the vendor warranty provision and any vendor/user maintenance agreement.

The latter item can be particularly interesting from a negotiating and financial standpoint. Ordinarily, when a user is presented with an equipment purchase agreement, it is also presented with a vendor maintenance agreement. Although the purchase agreement includes a warranty provision, traditionally covering parts and labor in the event there is an equipment malfunction during the warranty period, the maintenance agreement is often set up to commence upon acceptance of the equipment by the user. Depending upon the breadth of the applicable warranty language, this approach effectively requires the user to pay maintenance fees during the warranty period—that is, during the period that the vendor is (or should be) stating that there will be no problems with the equipment. At a minimum, the user should carefully consider whether this approach is fair and acceptable when viewed in the context of the entire transaction. In many instances, the user will conclude that this issue should be negotiated with the vendor.

To maximize its negotiating opportunities in this area, the user should ask the vendor to explain the scope of its equipment warranty. In most instances, the vendor will oblige by offering a glowing description of the warranty. Once the vendor has completed its description, the user should ask why the warranty is not good enough to negate the need for maintenance during the warranty period. Occasionally, the vendor will agree that maintenance is not necessary and allow the maintenance fees to become effective at the end of the warranty period. More frequently, however, the vendor will explain that the warranty is not designed to cover preventive maintenance that will still be necessary during the warranty period.

At this point, the user's response depends upon the language of the warranty provision. If the warranty contains the broad language discussed below, the user should challenge the vendor and ask why the warranty provision will not supply all necessary service during the applicable period. (This type of broad warranty language generally turns on two important vendor commitments. Consider the following example: "Vendor will maintain the Equipment in good working order for one year at no additional charge to Purchaser. At the Purchaser's request, Vendor will make all necessary adjustments, repairs, and parts replacements.") If the warranty contains narrow language, the user should attack both the narrowness of the warranty and the effective date of the maintenance fees. (In this type of narrow provision, the vendor generally limits its warranty to defects. Consider the following example: "Vendor warrants that the Equipment delivered under this Agreement shall be free from defects in material and workmanship under normal use and service.")

In the latter situation, the vendor is not likely to agree to alter its standard warranty language. However, the vendor may compromise on the issue of when maintenance payments begin. To guard against the narrow language of the warranty provision, the user should strive to have the maintenance agreement become effective at the acceptance date but have the maintenance fees effective at the end of the warranty period. If the vendor steadfastly refuses to agree that the warranty does (or should) cover preventive maintenance, the user may wish to seek a compromise where the user would pay maintenance fees during the warranty period, but the fees would be reduced in an agreed-upon amount roughly equal to the parts and labor coverage provided by the equipment warranty.

Despite the interesting negotiating aspects of this issue, it may not be worth pursuing in every instance. In many situations, the financial impact will not be material. (However, even in these situations, the point may be a good "red herring" that can be traded for another issue that is more important to the user.) In other instances, the vendor warranty language may give little room for maneuvering. Nevertheless, the warranty/maintenance issue should be reviewed and assessed in each transaction so that the user can make an informed decision concerning the proper course of action.

Users with a fondness for recalling legal principles may remember an old adage that says that a warranty or representation is always better than a "mere" covenant or promise (especially where the former can be said to be a "condition"). If this approach is considered correct, the user should therefore attempt to turn all of the vendor's contractual commitments into a warranty or representation (e.g., change "Vendor agrees to do X" into "Vendor warrants and represents that it will do X or cause X to occur"). In most jurisdictions, the legal difference between a warranty and a covenant is fading. Although gaining an additional warranty is generally an admirable user goal, in most jurisdictions the user should focus more on what it wants to achieve and how it wants to achieve it than on such niceties as whether the vendor has or has not made a promise or a representation. Particularly where the agreement provides clear special remedies, the distinction between such legal classifications should have little practical importance. Where local law does create important distinctions in this area, the user's attorney should be responsible for alerting the other members of the user's negotiating team to such differences and for providing any necessary advice.

Despite this caveat against becoming preoccupied with turning every vendor commitment into a warranty, specific vendor representations can and should be obtained on a number of critical subjects in most agreements. The following listing provides a menu from which various express warranties may be selected and tailored to a specific acquisition document. Special remedies (see above) should be included for each warranty, either in the warranty provision itself or in a separate remedy section of the agreement.

Compatibility: Vendor warrants that all hardware and software obtained by the user will be compatible with specified existing hardware and software (include detailed listings of existing hardware and software as well as measuring standards such as run times and benchmark tests).

Configuration: Vendor warrants that the services, equipment, and software ordered by the user will include all items, components, products, and services necessary to provide the user with all services, processing capabilities, or other results represented by vendor (attach and incorporate relevant standards, proposals, and benchmarks).

Financing and other commitments: Vendor warrants that it has obtained any required (and specified) financing or subcontractor commitments or will obtain such commitments on specified terms by designated deadlines (attach copies of relevant contracts or commitments). (See Appendix B.)

Investment Tax Credit (ITC): Vendor warrants that the equipment supplied to the user is new "Section 38" property eligible for the ITC (appropriate exclusions should be allowed to keep the vendor from being asked to warrant that the user can actually obtain ITC benefit in a particular situation).

Level of performance: Vendor warrants that the equipment (and software, in some instances) will meet a specified continuing performance standard, after acceptance, throughout the term of the agreement or some other stated period (include detailed performance standard, perhaps related to original acceptance test).

Noninfringement: Vendor warrants that the equipment or software does not and will not infringe any patent, copyright, trade secret, or other property rights held by any other person or entity (this "warranty" should generally be contained in or linked to an indemnity provision).

No refurbishment: Vendor warrants that, for a specified term, the equipment will not require any refurbishment or rebuilding at user expense (this warranty may be important for new equipment as well as used).

Quality: Vendor warrants that the products (hardware and software) and services furnished to the user will meet certain defined quality standards for a specified period of time (as noted above, this warranty must be meshed with the applicable maintenance provision).

Special standards: Vendor warrants that the equipment or software supplied to the user will meet certain specifications or standards detailed in the agreement (for example, specified ANSI standards for software).

Specific use: Vendor warrants that the products or services will be adequate to meet a specific use agreed upon by the parties and carefully detailed in the agreement (include written specifications and standards).

Title: Vendor warrants that it has (or will have), and will at all relevant times retain, unencumbered title (or other specified rights acceptable to the user) to all hardware, software, and supplies furnished to the user (exceptions for certain permitted liens may be appropriate).

Warranty pass-through: Vendor warrants that it has and will obtain and pass through to the user any and all warranties obtained or available from any manufacturer of equipment supplied to the vendor for use by the user.

PROVISIONS THAT CONTRACTUALLY SHORTEN THE STATUTE OF LIMITATIONS

More and more vendor form agreements are including a provision that contractually shortens the "statute of limitations" imposed by state law. The following language, based upon an actual vendor agreement, offers one example of the approach involved: "No action in any form arising out of this Agreement may be instituted by Vendor or Customer more than two (2) years after the cause of action has arisen, or in the case of nonpayment, more than two (2) years from the date of last payment."

Without a provision of this type, the time period within which a lawsuit may be brought is set by state statute. (See Chapter 6.) These "statutes of limitation" impose different limitation periods on various types of legal controversies and disputes. In most states, contractual disputes are governed by a four-to-six year statute of limitations. However, a number of exceptions exist and, in some states, an action to compel specific performance of a contract (rather than damages) may be restricted by a statute of limitations of only one year.

In many states, the basic statute of limitations may be extended if the legal "cause of action" involves such matters as fraud, misrepresentation, product liability, or malpractice. In cases such as these, the statute of limitations generally runs from the date the plaintiff actually discovers (or, in some statutes, "should have discovered") the defect or default involved. Under the more basic statute and cause of action, the statute of limitations generally runs from the date that the last element constituting the legal cause of action occurs, regardless of when the problem is discovered.

Why do vendor form contracts include a provision that contractually shortens the applicable statute of limitations? Very simply, because such provisions almost always favor the vendor at the expense of the user. This favoritism results because the vendor seldom needs more than two years after the user's default to resolve the matter or to bring its case to court. Why? Because in most instances the vendor only sues the user for nonpayment or for a similar specific failure to perform.

On the other hand, the user's case is generally much more difficult. If the vendor fails to perform, the user may spend months, if not years, attempting to get the problem corrected or to negotiate a meaningful settlement. In effect, the user's case and choices are less likely to be concrete than those enjoyed by the vendor.

Consequently, the authors strongly recommend that users object to vendor contractual provisions that attempt to shorten the applicable statute of limitations. The only exception to this rule should be if the user's legal counsel advises the user that, because of the user's special situation, a contractual shortening of the statute of limitations is acceptable or desirable. If the vendor absolutely refuses to remove this type of provision and the user must do business with the vendor, the user should strive to lengthen the period within which a lawsuit can be initiated.

Because contractual provisions of this type can be onerous to consumers and users alike, some states impose legal restrictions on the effectiveness of such clauses. One such statute states that "Any provision in a contract fixing the period of time within which an action may be begun at a time less than that provided by the applicable statute of limitations is void." In most situations, the vendor's form contract specifies that the agreement will be governed by the laws of a given state. If this type of provision is included in the agreement, the user will generally find that the law of the specified governing state does not include such a pro-consumer/user statute. However, if the applicable user/vendor transaction relates to the user's home state and that state has such a protective statute, the user may be able to indirectly invalidate a provision such as the clause quoted at the beginning of this section merely by changing the governing law provision to apply the law of the user's home state. In any event, of course, the user should seek the advice of its attorneys before taking any action in this important area.

FINANCIAL CONCESSIONS

Users with limited experience in major equipment negotiations frequently fail to devote appropriate efforts toward negotiating and documenting hard and soft dollar concessions from the vendor. Although some vendors refuse to negotiate direct price reductions, many substantial vendors will provide some form of financial savings to a user that negotiates effectively.

Soft dollar concessions, in the form of vendor-supplied benefits or third-party payments, can be as valuable to the user as direct reductions in the price of the equipment. However, the user must actively seek these advantages through aggressive negotiations. Once gained, the concessions must also be documented in the formal user/vendor agreement. Leaving these important matters in the form of oral promises ("you can trust me") or side letters from the local vendor office ("we always do it this way") is foolhardy, unprofessional, and unacceptable.

Because possible concessions are sometimes overlooked in the heat of negotiations, the following paragraphs present a checklist of areas that may be pursued by a user interested in maximizing its hard and soft dollar savings. Although this list is by no means all inclusive, it covers many of the more popular methods of achieving negotiated financial benefits for the user.

Acceptance testing: Permission by the vendor for the user to utilize the equipment and/or software during the acceptance test phase without making rental, lease, or purchase payments (and without having the user be arbitrarily deemed to have "accepted" the products by virtue of such use).

Conversion: Provision of free or reduced-rate software conversion services by vendor personnel, including guaranteed vendor conversion efforts or specified levels of vendor assistance and support.

Delivery: Payment of all or certain delivery fees (or return fees in a lease) by the vendor.

Documentation: Provision by the vendor of additional copies of manuals and documentation without charge; updating services for manuals without charge; license rights to permit the user to reproduce manuals for its own use.

Education: Provision by the vendor of free training and/or an education "credit" for the user's personnel (may cover software or services as well as hardware; concessions may include course fees, materials charges, and travel expenses).

Installation: Provision by the vendor of installation services at no or reduced charge, including "special" services such as non-prime-time installation, connection of equipment made by others, or site design work; reimbursement of payment by the vendor of all or some site preparation expenses (especially where extensive site renovations are required to meet unusual vendor requirements).

Insurance: Payment by the vendor of insurance costs that would otherwise be the user's responsibility (especially in connection with transportation and delivery and with rental/lease agreements).

Maintenance: Acceptance by the vendor of reduced maintenance fees, or no-fee increase guarantees, for preliminary periods of use; waiver of maintenance fees during acceptance and warranty periods; provision of additional maintenance services (beyond principal period) at no or reduced charge.

Price: Direct or indirect price reductions through credit, trade-in, payment drag (delay), volume discount, residual value, concurrent use, test site, or nonchargeable use methods (including waiver of "extra use" charges).

Software: Provision of conversion support or conversion efforts by the vendor (as noted above); waiver or reduction of license fees for all user sites or for "additional use" sites; provision by the vendor of fixes and updates at no or reduced charge; provision of "canned" or "custom" applications software or software assistance at no or reduced charge.

Systems and support: Provision by the vendor of special on-site systems/support personnel at no or nominal charge; analysis and provision of user system plan (periodic or one-time basis); analysis of system usage on periodic basis at no charge.

Taxes: Payment by the vendor of taxes, license fees, or filing fees (including UCC) that would otherwise be the responsibility of the user.

The above items are only a starting point. Prior to entering into meaningful negotiations, the user should carefully review its list of objectives to select additional issues that may provide financial savings to the user if properly negotiated. Other users and professional consultants should also be considered as sources of further information relating to hard and soft dollar concessions.

PRICE INCREASE AND CANCELLATION PROVISIONS

Relatively sophisticated users are generally aware of the fact that they should carefully scrutinize any provision of a contract that provides for price increases during the applicable rental, lease, maintenance, or license term. Ironically, these same users derive substantial comfort from a provision that permits either party to cancel the agreement upon 30- or 90-days notice to the other party. (Usually such a provision is only applicable following the initial term—often 12 months—of the agreement.) These users look at the cancellation clause from their own side only and do not appreciate the fact that the clause also permits the vendor to cancel upon providing the required notice to the user.

The basic problem, of course, is very simple. If the vendor determines that it is advisable to increase the rental, maintenance, or other price above the ceiling specified in the agreement, the vendor simply provides written notice to the user of the vendor's intention to cancel the agreement. To be sure, the vendor would be ill-advised to pursue this approach if the vendor seriously believed that the user could afford to cancel the agreement. In many instances, however, the user has little, if any, choice and must determine some method of keeping the agreement intact. (Consider, for example, the problem facing the user when the vendor threatens to cancel vendor-supplied maintenance on an equipment system acquired by the user under a third-party lease that mandates that the vendor must maintain the system throughout the term of the lease or the user will be in default.) In most situations like this, the user and the vendor renegotiate what is technically a "new agreement." The old agreement is terminated pursuant to the termination notice delivered by the vendor. And, of course, the new agreement provides for the increased price that the vendor wanted to implement in the first place.

Perhaps the most surprising fact about this scenario is that so many users fail to recognize the possibility that it may occur. Most users that get caught off-guard in this area simply miss the fact that the vendor may be able to get around the "price increase ceiling" provision by cancelling the agreement. Other users simply cannot bring themselves to believe that "their vendor," with which they have such a "good relationship," would ever use such a devious, underhanded method to increase prices. A few users gain some degree of reassurance from theorizing that this type of "indirect" effort to "get around the price increase limitation" is not permissible. These users generally argue, usually in vain, that "this kind of price increase just isn't permitted by the intent of the contract."

Legally, some argument may well exist that the vendor should not be able to do something indirectly that it cannot do directly. In a given court of law, a user with substantial equity on its side might be able to prevail in such an argument, particularly if the user could provide evidence of vendor representations and warranties about price increase limitations. Nevertheless, this approach is not secure from a legal viewpoint. Moreover, very few, if any, users would seriously contemplate an expensive court battle on such an issue. From a practical standpoint, then, most users would be ill-advised to rely on legalistic arguments to bail them out of this problem.

However, a user can take two separate steps to provide protection against this vendor tactic. One step should be taken before the contract is signed. The other step can be taken after the agreement has been signed and the vendor has threatened to cancel.

The first step simply requires that the user limit the vendor's right to cancel. In most instances, the user is interested in its own right to cancel. As noted above, many rental and maintenance agreements provide for cancellation by either party upon 30- or 90-day notice to the other party, following the initial term of the agreement. This type of cancellation provision is extremely important to many users, and the flexibility accorded by this right to cancel is one of the reasons why a user may elect to rent equipment, rather than to purchase or lease it, even though the rental price will generally exceed comparable prices for less-flexible acquisition methods.

By way of contrast, in most situations there is absolutely no need for the vendor to have the same right to cancel. Indeed, giving the vendor the same right to cancel may place the user in an extremely tenuous situation from an equipment availability standpoint, as well as from a financial or pricing standpoint. Where the user is required to have the vendor maintain certain equipment (as in the third-party lease example noted above), the user should obtain a written commitment from the vendor that the vendor will continue to maintain the equipment throughout the term of the applicable lease. Even where the equipment is purchased, the user would be well-advised to obtain a written commitment from the vendor to maintain the equipment, subject to the terms of the vendor's regular maintenance agreement or pursuant to the terms of a "master maintenance agreement" executed by the two parties, throughout the "expected life" of the equipment in the user's hands. Similar considerations apply in the case of software licensed by the user from the vendor.

Even where the vendor insists upon some right to cancel following the initial term of the agreement, the user should strictly limit that right to specified situations necessary to meet the vendor's needs. One of the most effective negotiating techniques in this area is to continue to press the vendor as to precisely why the vendor requires such a right to cancel. In many situations, the user will find that the vendor's only real concern is economic; that is, as suggested above, the vendor wants the right to cancel in order to have the flexibility to increase prices. Assuming that the vendor has some noneconomic reason for requiring the right to cancel, and assuming that this reason is acceptable to the user following additional verification and consideration, the user's attorney should draft a separate provision governing the vendor's right to cancel. This provision should strictly limit the vendor's right to cancel to those situations outlined by the vendor.

If the user has already executed an agreement that provides the vendor with what turns out to be an unacceptable right to cancel, the user can still implement one strategy that may alleviate the situation. If the vendor threatens to cancel the contract in order to get around a price increase limitation provision, the user should respond by threatening to throw the vendor out. To be sure, this approach generally requires a certain degree of gamesmanship and negotiating skill. Most users caught in this trap will be unable literally to throw the vendor out. Indeed, if the vendor has played its cards right, the user will probably be unable to permit cancellation of the agreement. Nevertheless, if the user is to have any serious chance to keep the vendor from successfully implementing this ploy, the user must remain calm, keep a straight face, and tell the vendor to "pack up and remove" the applicable equipment, software, or maintenance crews. If the user is willing to stone face the vendor on this point, right up to the brink of cancellation, the vendor will frequently back off and continue the agreement at the old price, at least for a while. The likelihood of the vendor's relenting on the indirect price increase ploy is greater if the user is extremely vocal about the vendor's "bad faith." The user can also increase its chances for success by convincing the vendor that this type of tactic may get the vendor a few extra dollars for now, but it will also get the vendor literally "thrown out" at the user's earliest possible convenience. Despite the fact that the user may not have serious legal precedent to back up its claim, the user may also be able to gain some negotiating equity by alleging that, from a technical legal standpoint, the vendor cannot indirectly avoid the price increase limitation provision by threatening to cancel the agreement.

The best approach, of course, is to cover this matter adequately in the initial agreement. Nevertheless, a user caught with this problem should make every effort to negotiate an equitable solution. The user may not be successful in every instance, but vigorous user negotiations will generally turn out to be worth the time and effort—at least on the average.

PROVISIONS FOR AN ERA OF VENDOR PRICE CUTTING AND NEW EQUIPMENT INTRODUCTIONS

Despite the general inflationary trend to the contrary, during recent decades, some types of equipment have experienced a history of reduced prices and improved price/performance ratios. Perhaps the best examples involve data processing hardware and other equipment that is substantially based upon electronic components, where a combination of price reductions and new equipment introductions has brought significant price/performance improvements over a period of years.

Users of equipment in these industries generally rejoice at each new round of price cuts and new system introductions, and move ahead to complete pending acquisition plans. Despite the joy of the majority, however, some users are seriously disturbed at the price reductions or new equipment introductions. This limited category of users is generally comprised of firms that made binding equipment commitments just prior to the new price/performance announcements. In these companies, the announcements may lead to competitive disadvantage, pointed questions from directors or shareholders, and job terminations for the managers who "should have known about" or considered the possibility of the new announcements.

From a practical standpoint, most good operations or production managers know roughly when to expect many price/performance announcements, or at least when to be cautious. Other announcements come as a total surprise. Consequently, achieving complete protection against price/performance announcements is probably impossible, even during the first few months after an acquisition agreement is signed.

Nevertheless, a sophisticated user can achieve some protection in this area by negotiating and drafting certain key contractual provisions. Most of these provisions are actually useful in any major equipment agreement. Because of their complexity and length, however, they are seldom utilized in full unless the user has particular reason to suspect the need for protection against the adverse effects of vendor price reductions or new equipment introductions. Thus, these provisions are often overlooked or consciously omitted in an era of stable equipment inventories and/or rising equipment prices.

The following sections present a general discussion of the recommended approaches in this area. The accompanying provisions represent "baseline" examples rather than actual wording and, consequently, should be tailored to the needs of a particular transaction before being incorporated into a vendor/user agreement.

Guaranteeing the Price

At the outset, the user should ensure that it will enjoy the benefit of any price reduction that may be announced by the manufacturer (or by some other vendor if the acquisition involves a third party) within a selected period of time. For minimum protection, the user should obtain price protection through the date the equipment is actually accepted by it, and perhaps through any warranty period.

One method of obtaining at least some protection is for the user to employ a "most favored nation" provision in which the vendor guarantees that the system has not been—and will not be—sold or leased to any other customer during a stated period at a price more favorable than that paid by the user. An example of this type of provision appears in Appendix B. If the time period covered by the most favored nation provision encompasses the period when the system is being offered or provided at the reduced price, the user should be able to claim the benefit of the reduction and demand a rebate from the vendor.

However, this provision may not be adequate in some situations. First, the clause may only cover prior sales and leases rather than future ones. Even if the provision is prospective, the period involved may not be adequate to cover the price reductions.

Second, the provision will probably apply only to past and future sales or leases made by the vendor that is supplying the system to, and contracting with, the user. For example, if a broker or dealer is furnishing the equipment, the provision will only apply to other transactions made by that broker or dealer. If the manufacturer cuts prices, and the broker or dealer does not, or does not do so within the period covered, the provision provides no relief.

Third, many users do not have the bargaining power to obtain a most favored nation provision.

This provision is extremely valuable, for it guarantees that the user is getting the best price offered to any company within the stated period. Although this protection is an excellent goal to strive for, protection against price cuts can be obtained through a provision that is more specific and, consequently, less difficult to obtain.

The following provision offers good basic protection by allowing the user to obtain the benefits of any official price reduction announced prior to a specified date, while preventing the detrimental effect of any increase. Unlike the most favored nation clause, however, it does not guarantee that the equipment will not be sold or leased to another firm at a price below the new or old published price list.

If the Vendor's published or other regularly-established price for any item of Equipment shall be less than the price for such item of Equipment set forth in this Agreement at any time between the effective date of this Agreement and the date the Equipment is accepted by the Customer hereunder [or "the expiration date for the warranty provided in Section _____ of this Agreement"], then the Vendor shall immediately notify the Customer of such fact and the price for such item of Equipment purchased hereunder shall automatically be deemed to be reduced to the lowest such published or other regularly-established price during such period. In the event any such reduction occurs after payment for the Equipment by Customer, the Vendor shall rebate the difference in price to the Customer within thirty (30) calendar days after the change in price first occurs. If the Vendor's published or other regularly-established price for any item of Equipment shall be greater than the price of such item of Equipment set forth in this Agreement during the above-referenced period, the price for such item of Equipment set forth in this Agreement shall prevail and no reduction in price required above shall be offset by any such increase in price.

Substitute or Upgraded Equipment

Price protection alone, however, may not be adequate protection for the user's needs. If the user is striving to achieve state of the art processing capabilities and is concerned about obsolesence and residual values, it may not want the system at any cost if the equipment has been rendered obsolete by a new generation or even a model of greater price/performance capability.

Obviously, the risk of obsolesence exists with any system that is purchased or leased over a long term. (Rental arrangements, even though more expensive, offer the usual alternative for those firms willing to trade additional expense for greater flexibility.) Nevertheless, the user should at least have the right to ask that the new system remain "state of the art" until it is accepted for use, and for a specified period thereafter. Such a request makes sense from the standpoint of processing capability, residual value, and vendor/user relationship. It also makes sense from a job preservation standpoint. If the user's new, expensive system becomes obsolete as a result of a new generation, before it is even installed or out of the warranty period, the user's senior management and/or board of directors may ask some particularly pointed questions concerning the competence and judgment of the user executives who handled the transaction.

Many sophisticated users ask for "upgrade protection" as a matter of course, even when price cutting strategies are not in vogue. This protection is particularly apt when the vendor has represented orally, as a major part of its presentation, that the user's new system can be upgraded into several other levels. If the user intends to rely upon this capability, the vendor's representations must be carefully documented as part of the contract.

Users should respect the fact that upgrade provisions are difficult to draft. Because of the uncertainties that may be involved in future vendor products, both the user and the vendor are likely to have practical and legal concerns about the specific language used in the upgrade section. For example, the user generally wants assurance that the vendor will not be able to avoid the provision by the all-too-common industry practice of "renameplating." On the other hand, the vendor often has a valid claim that the upgrade provision should not be so broad as to apply to a new vendor system. (This example should remind perceptive users that their tax advisors should carefully review the language and substance of any upgrade section.)

The following provision is a relatively complicated example of an upgrade section from a user/vendor computer contract. Note should be made that many vendors will not agree to the "at any time during the term of this Agreement" language included in this example unless the term is nominal in length. However, a high aspiration level in negotiations is a key ingredient for ultimate financial and contractual optimization.

Vendor hereby expressly represents and warrants to Customer that the Vendor _____ central processor leased hereunder, as it exists as of the date of this Agreement, has the capability of being field upgraded to a Vendor _____, or _____ central processor, or incrementally to each such central processor, as said central processors are offered by Vendor as of the date of this Agreement or at any time during the Term hereof. At any time during the Term of the Agreement, Vendor will allow Customer to increase the central processing capabilities of the Vendor _____ central processor leased hereunder to a Vendor _____, _____, or _____ central processor, or incrementally to each such central processor, as such central processors are offered by Vendor, as of the date of this Agreement or at any time during the term hereof, by adding modules to or retrofitting such central processor. In this regard, Vendor expressly represents and warrants that the Vendor central processor leased under this Agreement is or will be field upgradable to Vendor _____, _____, or _____ central processors as such central processors may be enhanced or modified at any time during the term of this Agreement by adding modules to or retrofitting such central processor. In the event Customer requests any field upgrading pursuant to this paragraph, the following provisions shall apply:

(i) Customer shall provide written notice to Vendor of Customer's intention to increase the data processing capabilities of the central processor leased hereunder to the equivalent of certain specified Vendor central processors. Within thirty (30) days after receipt of this notice, Vendor shall consult with Customer or its agents in good faith in order to determine the method or alternative methods of implementing the increased capabilities.

(ii) In the event that alternative methods of implementing the increased capabilities are available, Customer shall have the right and option to determine which method shall be utilized. Customer shall notify Vendor in writing of the method to be used in increasing the data processing capabilities of the central processor.

(iii) The additions, replacements, or retrofitting shall be accomplished according to a schedule that is mutually-acceptable to Customer and Vendor and that shall minimize the amount of system down time and interruption of Customer's utilization of the equipment; provided that, in any event Vendor shall have shipped the necessary modules or equipment for enhancing or retrofitting the central processor then leased hereunder by not later than a period of sixty (60) days in excess of Vendor's then published normal delivery lead time for the central processor system to which the equipment leased hereunder is to be field upgraded or replaced, calculated from the date Customer first notifies Vendor in writing of the method to be used to increase the data processing capabilities of the central processor.

(iv) The purchase or lease price for such additions or retrofitting shall be Vendor's then published price for such additions or retrofitting; provided that, such price shall not exceed the difference between: (A) Vendor's published purchase or lease price for the equipment then leased hereunder, calculated as of the date Customer gives written notice to Vendor of the method to be used to so increase the data processing capabilities of the equipment; and (B) Vendor's published purchase or lease price for the equipment with such increased data processing capabilities, calculated as of the date Customer gives written notice to Vendor of the method to be used to so increase the data processing capabilities of the central processor.

(v) Customer may, in its sole discretion, obtain the additional modules and/or retrofitting required for such increased data processing capabilities by: (A) adding such modules and/or retrofitting as additional equipment pursuant to the terms and provisions of this Agreement; (B) outright purchase of such modules and/or retrofitting; or (C) any lease arrangement selected by Customer and available as of the date Customer provides written notice to Vendor of the method to be used to increase the data processing capabilities of the central processor leased hereunder.

(vi) In the event Customer elects to purchase such modules and/or retrofitting or lease such modules and/or retrofitting through a lease agreement that does not provide for maintenance, Vendor agrees that, upon Customer's request, Vendor will provide maintenance services for any and all equipment included in the purchase or lease of such modules and/or retrofitting, based upon Vendor's then current policies and prices for such services. In any event, the Vendor warranties, representations and obligations contained in this Agreement shall apply to any and all equipment included in the purchase or lease of such modules and/or retrofitting.

Upgrading alone, however, may not be the answer. If the original equipment manufacturer (OEM) significantly changes the system and renumbers the models or introduces a new generation, the user may need the right to substitute the "old" system for the new one.

At this point, the vendor obviously has a right to be cautious, particularly if it is a broker, dealer, or lessor. The vendor's objectives are to sell or lease its existing models, not some proposed model that has not even been announced. In addition, once the new system has been introduced, the vendor hardly desires a stockpile of used older models, although such equipment can be profitable in some situations. Even if the vendor will agree to trade, the trade-in period and price are likely to be viewed strictly. Indeed, the vendor's sales representative may plead ignorance about the vendor's future announcements.

All of these points are relevant; however, none are adequate reasons to omit a trade-in clause if the user is dealing with an OEM, either directly or through a third party leasing company. The crucial point from the user's standpoint is simple. Although the provision should be carefully drafted to protect the user and vendor, only the OEM knows when a new system will be introduced. Although the local salesman may not know, someone in the OEM organization knows the game plan and the schedule for new systems.

If the OEM "cannot" provide the user with a reasonable trade-in option, the user should seriously ask if this means that introduction of a new system is imminent. If the introduction of new equipment is not planned, the trade-in option will not cause the OEM harm, at least in this particular transaction. If a new introduction is planned, the OEM should be willing to advise the user of that fact or, at least, offer the user a fair trade-in option.

If a trade-in option is not possible, the user should consider one or more of the following:

1. Utilizing a current system on an "interim" rental or "consignment" basis;
2. Allowing current system purchase option credits or accruals to apply fully to a new system offering;
3. Returning the current system to the vendor "in full satisfaction" for any current long-term obligations on the system.

Where a broker or dealer is involved, the user's position is less strong. The broker or dealer, after all, may not know that a new system is on its way. In this situation, the user's best argument is to convince the broker/dealer that it, rather than the user, should bear the risk of any such introduction in order to obtain the user's business. If resale of the equipment is required, the broker/dealer would be far more capable of handling it than the user would be.

Like upgrade provisions, trade-in sections must be carefully tailored to fit the specific transaction involved. (As noted above, the user's tax advisors should carefully consider the impact of any trade-in on the Investment Tax Credit.) The following computer contract provision offers one example:

In the event that the Vendor, at any time between the effective date of this Agreement and the date the Equipment is accepted by the Customer hereunder [or "the expiration date for the warranty provided in Section _____ of this Agreement"], publicly announces or introduces or sells, leases, or rents to any customer a data processing system, configuration, or central processor (the "New System") that has not been publicly announced or introduced by the Vendor as of the effective date of this Agreement, and such New System: (i) represents a new generation of data processing equipment; or (ii) offers enhancements or processing volume or speed not included or available in the Equipment purchased hereunder, or (iii) otherwise represents processing methodology or state of the art technology more advanced than the Equipment purchased hereunder; then, in any such event, the Vendor shall promptly notify the Customer of the introduction or availability of such New System and the Customer shall have the right and option to require the Vendor to substitute all or part of the Equipment purchased hereunder for all or part of the components of the New System. In the event the Customer elects to exercise this option, the following terms and conditions shall be applicable:

(i) Customer shall notify Vendor of its intention to require replacement and substitution of designated items of Equipment not later than thirty (30) days after the date that the Vendor so notifies the Customer of the introduction or availability of the New System; and

(ii) Customer shall purchase the substituted components of the New System at Vendor's then published prices for such components, less any discounts generally-available to comparable customers and less a trade-in credit equal to _____ percent (_____%) of the purchase price for the replaced item of Equipment purchased hereunder (as specified in Schedule _____ of this Agreement). The Vendor and the Customer shall equally share the costs of removing, delivering, transporting, and installing each replaced item of Equipment and each substituted component of the New System. Such costs shall include all expenses detailed in Section _____ [relating to Delivery and Installation]. The purchase price for all components of the New System substituted hereunder shall be due and payable thirty (30) days after the later of: (a) the date Customer receives a proper invoice from Vendor covering such components; or (b) the date all such substituted components of the New System and all remaining items of Equipment purchased hereunder have been accepted by the Customer pursuant to the Acceptance Standard set forth in Section _____ of this Agreement.

In the above example, a variety of additional subparagraphs would normally be included to detail such matters as the timing of the substitution (delivery schedules may be difficult) and installation (avoid prime time), maintenance and vendor warranties on the substituted equipment, Investment Tax Credit and depreciation impact, and the like. In addition, most vendors will require a more detailed definition of the "New System" to prevent this section from applying to certain types of systems in a different size range.

Cancellation of the Order

Some users would prefer to cancel an order if the price for the system has been significantly reduced or if a new generation of equipment has been introduced. This is particularly likely to be the case where the user has considered a number of closely-competitive bids or where state of the art processing and residual values are deemed important.

Unlike the previously-mentioned areas, cancellation is likely to be a much more sensitive issue for the vendor. A price reduction guarantee and an upgrade/trade-in provision still allow the vendor to make the sale or lease. The income may be reduced, but it will be there. In comparison, cancellation will cause a reversal of the transaction income. Indeed, it may result in a technical "loss" for the vendor when overhead and other costs of sale are included. In addition, the accounting policies of some vendors may cause a sale-with-cancellation clause to be no sale at all until the right to cancel has expired. Under this approach, the vendor and its marketeer cannot claim the income and resulting profit until the expiration of the cancellation period.

Nevertheless, cancellation is not an unreasonable request if it is mandated by the user's needs. Again, the OEM is probably the only party that knows when a new system is likely to be introduced. If no new introductions are planned during the relevant period, the OEM has nothing to risk. Price reductions are less within the OEM's control than new system introductions, but they are considerably more within the OEM's control than the user's. If one party must bear the risk of economic loss, it should be the OEM rather than the user. Even if the OEM is not willing to bear all of the financial risk, some compromise may be possible. For example, the vendor might accept cancellation during the stated period upon payment of a nominal dollar amount rather than the usual "termination value" in the lease or the damages or "lost profits" that might be due to the vendor upon breach of a purchase contract by the user.

As in the case of the trade-in alternative, cancellation is likely to pose a greater risk to a broker or dealer than to the OEM. The reasons are similar: Like the user, the broker/dealer may be unable to predict when a price cut or new system introduction is likely to occur.

The following language might be employed as a cancellation provision in a user/OEM data processing agreement:

In the event that the Vendor, at any time between the effective date of this Agreement and the date all items of Equipment are delivered to the Customer's site [or "the date the Equipment is certified by the Vendor as fully installed and ready for use at the Customer's site"]:

(a) publicly announces or introduces or sells, leases or rents to any customer a data processing system, configuration, or central processor (the "New System") that has not been publicly announced or introduced by the Vendor as of the date of this Agreement, and such New System: (i) represents a new generation of data processing equipment; or (ii) offers enhancements or processing volume or speed not included or available in the Equipment purchased hereunder; or (iii) otherwise represents processing methodology or state of the art technology more advanced than the Equipment purchased hereunder;

(b) publicly announces, publishes, or otherwise regularly establishes the price for the configuration or system of Equipment purchased hereunder, or for the central processor included in such Equipment, at a level more than ten percent (10%) below the level established and set forth in Schedule _____ to this Agreement for such configuration, system or central processor;

Then the Vendor shall notify the Customer in writing of any such event within thirty (30) days thereafter and Customer shall have, for a period of sixty (60) calendar days after receipt of such written notice from Vendor, the right and option to cancel and rescind this Agreement in full. Such option shall be exercised by the provision of written notice to Vendor prior to the expiration of the sixty (60) day period referenced above. In the event Customer so elects to cancel and rescind this Agreement, the Vendor shall remove all items of Equipment from Customer's site within thirty (30) days after Vendor's receipt of Customer's election to exercise its option to cancel and rescind hereunder. Customer and Vendor shall equally share the expense of de-installing, crating, removing, and transporting the Equipment; provided, however, that Customer's share of such expenses shall not exceed $_____.

Residual Value Guarantees

Price cuts and new system introductions usually have a significant impact on the residual values of existing systems. Residual values are a sensitive subject, as any comptroller or tax advisor knows. Leasing companies and brokers have made and lost fortunes as residual value estimates have been accurately and inaccurately made over the years.

From a practical standpoint, a vendor is unlikely to be willing to guarantee the residual value of the user's leased equipment or the "estimated" resale value of its used purchased hardware. First, a residual guarantee may have seriously adverse tax consequences in a long-term lease. Second, although many brokers and dealers "make a market" in used computer equipment, few are willing to accept the tremendous risks involved in guaranteeing resale or residual values several years out. Even where an OEM has formulated a good faith estimate of future resale values, the estimate may be drastically affected by a variety of factors outside the OEM's control, including price cuts and new system introductions by competing firms.

From a practical standpoint, these considerations make the use of a residual or resale guarantee rather difficult. Put very simply, a user ordinarily must have a tremendous bargaining advantage to convince a vendor to accept such a provision. The risks are simply too great on the vendor's side. As one vendor put it, "a residual guarantee isn't a concession, it's an insurance policy." (Residual value insurance policies were indeed available on some types of data processing equipment and transactions during the late seventies—for example, "walk-away leases"—and may be again in the future. However, the scope and value of the coverage varies greatly.)

In most situations, the user's basic goal concerning residual values can be indirectly achieved through use of an alternative provision governing price protection, upgrading, or trade-in rights. Although these provisions will not preclude eventual loss on resale or termination of the lease term, they should offer realistic protection from near-term price cuts and new system introductions.

Nevertheless, some brokers and dealers may agree to a limited residual or resale guarantee where adverse tax results are not involved. Such provisions are more likely to be accepted where the term of the guarantee is relatively short (two or three years) and the equipment involved appears to be either an "old reliable" workhorse of the industry or "first day" technology. (The vendor's key being a comfortable feeling with regard to the "futures" involved.) In these circumstances, an experienced broker or dealer may be willing to bet on the resale value, and back its bet with a guarantee, in order to obtain the user's business. As might be expected, a broker/dealer may be more willing to place this bet where its profit margin on the overall transaction is adequate to absorb some loss on the guarantee. As suggested above, a broker or other vendor may also be willing to offer a limited residual guarantee if residual value insurance can be obtained at a price that is acceptable within the context of the specific transaction. If the policy does not include unrealistic exclusions or conditions, the use of such insurance is beneficial to the user because it offers an independent source to back up the vendor's own guarantee.

Users considering any type of residual guarantee or right-to-buy should ensure that their attorneys and accountants carefully review the impact of such a provision for tax and accounting purposes (including the dictates of Financial Accounting Standards Board Statement No. 13 (often called "FASB 13")).

A relatively simple resale guarantee provision used by a substantial broker follows.

In the event that, at the end of the Term of the Agreement, the "fair market value" of the Equipment, calculated pursuant to Section _____ hereof, is less than $_____, then the Vendor shall pay to the Customer, in cash, not later than thirty (30) days after receipt of an invoice from Customer therefor, the difference between said sum of $_____ and such "fair market value" of the Equipment on such date; provided, however, that this provision shall not be applicable if the Equipment on such date is damaged or destroyed (as defined in Section _____ hereof, relating to casualty loss) or the Equipment has otherwise been materially reduced in value as a result of Customer's failure to comply with any provision of this Agreement.

PROPERTY TAX REIMBURSEMENT PROVISIONS

Many of the lease and rental agreements covering major equipment contain a provision obligating the user to pay any sales, use, and related taxes that may be imposed on the equipment during the term of the agreement. The provisions governing this obligation usually state that the user will pay the taxes "and any penalties that may be imposed thereon."

At the outset, the user should determine whether it is willing to accept the financial burden associated with this type of provision. Ideally, the user may prefer for the vendor to bear the property tax costs relating to the equipment. In many instances, this item is negotiable and the vendor may be willing to make a concession in order to gain the user's business. Where the vendor does agree to pay the property taxes, the user is relieved of the administrative burden involved and also of the uncertainty associated with future assessment and/or tax increases. However, to compensate for these matters and the cost of the tax itself, the vendor may adjust the equipment price in a manner that causes the user to pay more than it would have if the user had paid the property taxes directly. The user should therefore carefully assess the vendor's proposal to determine the impact of property tax costs, either directly upon the user (where the user pays the taxes) or indirectly upon the user (where the vendor pays the taxes). In this regard, proposals from competing vendors may need to be adjusted so that the tax aspects of the proposals are consistent.

Assuming that the user agrees to pay the property taxes, it should ensure that this obligation does not extend to tax penalties resulting from any act or omission of the lessor or its agents. Of course, the vendor sales representative will assert that only the user's negligence would result in such a penalty. In many states, however, this allegation is simply untrue: The lessor's failure to act can also result in a penalty assessment.

In one example, a large regional firm was leasing a significant equipment system from a third party leasing company. State law required the owner of the equipment to file a return each year, giving such information as the equipment price and location. Although the user persistently tried to convince the lessor to file the return, on behalf of the lessor's equity investors, the lessor failed to do so. As a result, the State levied a 25% penalty on the amount due and refused to accept payment of the basic tax unless the penalty was also paid. To avoid defaulting under the terms of the lease, the user paid the tax ($40,000) and the penalty ($10,000) and, through the assistance of legal counsel, sought reimbursement for the penalty from the lessor. Although the user in this example was successful, users should rather obviously avoid becoming involved in the same situation.

The best protection in this area is a special provision indicating that the user will not be responsible for penalties caused by the lessor. Although the exact language must be carefully tailored to the language of the particular lease, the following proviso serves as a good example:

"provided, however, that Lessee shall not be required to pay or otherwise be liable or responsible for, and Lessor hereby indemnifies and holds Lessee harmless against, any penalty, additional tax, or interest that may be assessed or levied as a result of the failure of the Owners to file any return, form, or information statement that may be required to be filed by any governmental agency."

"FORCE MAJEURE" OR "ACT OF GOD" CLAUSES

Most vendor agreements contain a "force majeure" or "act of God" provision. This well-known clause is designed to protect a party against unforeseen circumstances beyond its control. The standard vendor clause generally reads somewhat like this: "Vendor shall not be liable for any failure or delay in performance due in whole or in part to any cause beyond Vendor's control."

Despite the fact that attorneys and laymen alike often view this provision as "standard boilerplate," the clause should never be accepted by the user in this format. Although the provision may appear to be innocent enough, it can cause serious problems for the user.

The basic problem with the standard vendor clause is that it does not provide any remedy or recourse to the user if the vendor is unable to perform. Most vendors would readily concur with this point, noting that this is precisely the purpose of the provision. The difficulty is that no time limit is placed on this effect.

Consider an example where the user has signed a contract to purchase a new corporate aircraft from the vendor. The agreement contains the standard force majeure clause set out above. After the contract is executed, a strike hits the vendor's plant and the vendor is unable to perform. Alternatively, the vendor's plant is destroyed by fire and no other airplanes are available for delivery. (This list of alternative "acts of God" could go on and on.) The delivery deadline comes and goes. Six weeks pass. Ten weeks. The user threatens to invoke the damages clause in the agreement for nondelivery. The vendor cites the force majeure clause and claims no liability. The user threatens to cancel the contract and order an alternative jet from another manufacturer (despite the delivery delays associated with such a move). The vendor replies by explaining that, although the vendor is not required to perform (due to the force majeure clause), the user cannot cancel because the vendor is not in default. Indeed, the vendor threatens to sue for damages if the user tries to cancel the order.

Simply put, the question is how long can the vendor continue to hide behind the protection of the force majeure clause before the user can cancel the order and seek other means of meeting its hardware requirements. The standard force majeure clause does not answer this question. Although a court might be willing to offer a user some relief from this type of "deadlock," the vendor's force majeure clause suggests that no time limit should be placed on the period within which the vendor's nonperformance should be excused.

This problem can be handled easily if the user drafts a force majeure provision that is fair and equitable for both parties. To achieve this goal, the user should recall the basic purpose of such a clause.

Force majeure provisions are a standard part of our way of doing business. A vendor quite rightly should be able to avoid liability for certain types of nonperformance where the delay or failure is beyond the vendor's control. From a policy standpoint, the delay may injure the vendor and the user. But, since the event causing the delay was unexpected and beyond the vendor's control, neither party should suffer all the loss. Consequently, the vendor's nonperformance should be excused and the two parties should share the loss.

The problem is that the user may suffer a disproportionate part of the loss. If the strike drags on, or if the fire delays delivery for six or eight months, the user may be literally forced out of business, or suffer millions of dollars of loss, unless alternative hardware can be obtained. On the other hand, the vendor should be able to sell the equipment ordered by the user to some other party once the strike is over or the plant rebuilt.

Consequently, the force majeure clause should include a provision that will permit the user to cancel the contract if the vendor has failed to perform after a specified period, even if the delay or failure in performance is otherwise covered by the general force majeure provision. This type of "drop dead out" is particularly important where the equipment has not been delivered. At this stage, the user is especially subject to harm, and the vendor is best able to bear more of the risk from the "act of God." A similar approach may be appropriate at other stages of vendor performance, although the user's ability to justify an exception to the general force majeure clause weakens as the vendor has more and more investment in the user's specific project.

Some vendors attempt to argue against this type of force majeure cancellation right by asserting that the equipment ordered by the user is being manufactured especially for the user. In theory, this argument is valid: If the user has purchased a truly unique product designed or made solely for the user and the vendor has already invested substantial sums in the project, the user should not be able to "walk away" promptly if the vendor's performance is delayed by an "act of God." Even where the product is unique, however, the user should be able to use a "drop dead out" if the vendor has only a minor investment in the project. Similarly, it may be fair to allow the user to get out later upon reimbursement of the vendor's costs in the unique project. In most situations, however, the vendor is not manufacturing a unique component or system especially for the user. Even if the vendor places a "Built for XYZ User" tag on the equipment as it rolls through the plant, the system is likely to be fungible. If the user does not accept the equipment, it can, and likely will, be sold and delivered to another user with no changes to the system and little or no additional expense to the vendor.

In addition to modifying the force majeure clause to provide a "drop dead out" for the user, the user should also ensure that the basic vendor provision cuts both ways and protects the vendor and the user against unexpected events. After all, strikes, fires, and floods can hit users as well as vendors. For example, consider such user obligations as having the site ready for delivery and installation, providing maintenance space, and providing adequate power.

In most instances, this drafting change can be made by replacing the words "Vendor shall not be liable" (in the force majeure clause) with the words "Neither party hereunder shall be liable." In other agreements, it may be necessary to go beyond the force majeure clause to fully protect the user. For example, consider the user's obligation to return a system at the end of a lease. If the lease provides that the lease will be automatically renewed if the user fails to return the system by the stated deadline, the user should modify this provision to indicate that this type of automatic renewal will not occur if the user is excused by the force majeure clause from its failure to return the system on time. Second, consider the user's obligation to begin acceptance testing or to accept delivery. The agreement may provide that, if the user is not ready to begin acceptance testing or to accept delivery by the deadlines mentioned in the agreement, acceptance testing will be deemed waived and the system will be deemed accepted. Assuming that the user feels compelled to accept this type of provision (which many vendor agreements contain and which the authors do not recommend), the provision must be modified to ensure that automatic acceptance will not occur where the user cannot perform due to an "act of God." An example of a force majeure section appears in the General Provisions included in Appendix B.

ASSIGNMENT, MOVEMENT, AND OTHER "FLEXIBILITY" PROVISIONS

One of the more subtle dangers in vendor form agreements involves what the authors refer to as "flexibility—or, more accurately, the lack of flexibility. Flexibility in this context relates to the user's ability to pursue alternative methods and equipment in the future by assigning, subleasing, or moving its existing equipment.

Two basic problems exist in this area. First, many users refuse to appreciate the desirability of achieving this flexibility at the outset, when the contract is originally negotiated. These users essentially believe that they have accurately assessed their future plans and that no future contingencies will create a need for flexibility. Second, other users foresee a need for future flexibility, either because of existing plans or potential changes in circumstances, but fail to appreciate all of the contract changes that may be necessary to achieve this flexibility. These users aggressively negotiate minimal sublease or assignment rights and ignore the related but equally critical sections of the agreement.

Flexibility is generally a goal that should be pursued in any important acquisition where the documents otherwise create permanence or an ongoing vendor/user relationship (for example, a long term lease or a purchase agreement with associated licenses or maintenance agreements). In these situations, flexibility protects the user against known conditions or unexpected contingencies that may suggest or dictate that the user sublease, assign, or move the system, or permit others to use it. Flexibility in this context often takes the place of an even more desirable, and more difficult to achieve, provision permitting the user to cancel the agreement and return the equipment to the vendor with little or no penalty.

Many users believe that their good "relationship" with the vendor assures them of the ability to negotiate adequate flexibility in the future, regardless of contractual language to the contrary. In many situations, this assumption proves to be correct. Vendors often agree to subleases, assignments, and similar matters to enhance their relationship with a user.

The difficulty arises when the action desired by the user will have an adverse economic impact on the vendor. For example, the user may propose to sublease the equipment and/or sublicense the software to a firm that is seriously considering acquiring a similar system directly from the vendor. If the vendor agrees to the sublease, it will lose the sale. If the user proposing the sublease is committed (locked in) to the vendor under other agreements and systems, the vendor is likely to refuse to approve the sublease.

In other situations, the user may wish to assign the equipment to its proposed new facilities management firm that is known for using equipment manufactured by a competing vendor. If the vendor approves the assignment, it faces the risk of losing the user's account and site. On the other hand, if it precludes the assignment, the facilities management takeover may prove to be impossible and, consequently, abandoned. Similar circumstances may exist where the user desires to achieve flexibility in order to acquire equipment from an alternative vendor. In both examples, the vendor is likely to block the action desired by the user, especially if this approach can be implemented by relying on a relatively innocuous clause in the standard vendor agreement. Vendors that have a record of not taking advantage of these opportunities should not be overlooked. Dramatic earnings declines or increases in competition may cause these vendors to adopt radically different business policies overnight. Users that believe that this type of vendor action is "shortsighted" and therefore unlikely should carefully review the unfortunate experiences of their colleagues. Most users are reluctant to admit defeat in this area, but many will admit that their vendor has at least tried to implement the approaches noted above on one or more occasions.

To protect against these risks, the user must strive to achieve maximum flexibility before the agreement is signed. In implementing this goal, the user must assess all aspects of the agreement to determine those provisions that may reduce or eliminate the desired level of flexibility. Many of these provisions are interrelated in subtle ways.

At a minimum, the user should review all vendor contractual provisions covering the right to assign and/or sublease, the right to move, and the right to operate the equipment. Software or other license and sublicense rights must also be considered in this assessment, as must rights relating to documentation and user manuals. Many of the important sections appear in the license and maintenance agreements that accompany the main acquisition contract (or in the schedules or exhibits to those agreements). Consequently, the user must not only coordinate all relevant flexibility provisions within a given agreement but must also coordinate corresponding provisions among several related agreements.

In considering assignment, subleasing, and sublicensing provisions, the user's attorneys should devote particular attention to the issue of continuing user liability. Depending upon the contractual language and state laws involved, an assignment may be with or without "recourse" (that is, continuing liability of the original user for the actions or nonpayment by the assignee).

In addition, the user should carefully consider whether its flexibility provisions will preclude the vendor from extracting unreasonable fees or assessments in the event of a desired transfer.

To achieve maximum protection, it is not enough for the user to merely provide that the vendor cannot refuse to approve a given transfer or assignment. Rather, the user must also seek to ensure that the vendor cannot indirectly prohibit the transfer through extremely high fees or other means. Refurbishment and other maintenance "policies" established by the vendor are among the matters that must be reviewed in this area.

Although the provisions utilized to achieve the necessary level of user protection must generally be based upon the specific documentation and system involved, as well as the user's particular needs, the following example sections may provide drafting guidance. These provisions are based upon language designed for a vendor/user rental or lease agreement.

1. Relocation. Following prior written notice by User to Vendor, User may move or relocate all or any part of the Equipment from one (1) location to another location within the fifty (50) United States or District of Columbia. Vendor shall supervise the de-installation, packing, unpacking, relocation, and re-installation of any Equipment relocated hereunder. All Equipment so relocated shall be packed and transported in accordance with Vendor's then-current standards therefor. Vendor shall not charge for such services if the Equipment is relocated to another site of User or any of its parent, subsidiary, or affiliate companies. User shall pay for Vendor's services in connection with any other relocation at Vendor's then-published rates therefor, subject to the provisions of Section _____ hereof [*the "most favored Nation" pricing provision*].

2. Right to Use. The Equipment may be used or operated only by: (1) the directors, officers, employees, and agents of User or any of its parent, subsidiary, or affiliate companies; and (b) any other person or entity (including the directors, officers, employees, and agents of such entity) designated in writing by User.

3. Transfer of Maintenance. In the event User proposes to, or does, sublease, sublet, sublicense, or otherwise transfer or assign all or any part of the Equipment or the right to use or operate all or any part of the Equipment, to any other person or entity, including without limitation any parent, subsidiary, or affiliate company of User, Vendor agrees that it shall upon written request from User, agree to maintain such Equipment, and to assist in its removal and transfer to such other person or entity; provided, however, that: (a) the transfer or use is not prohibited by the terms of this agreement; and (b) the transferee or other user shall enter into an agreement with Vendor agreeing to be bound by the terms and provisions of, and to make all payments required by, the then-current maintenance agreement between Vendor and User covering such Equipment; and (c) notwithstanding any other term of such maintenance agreement, no price or penalty shall be charged or imposed by Vendor for such transfer, or for the privilege of such transfer, and the transferee shall not be required to pay to Vendor, for such maintenance, any amount greater than the amount that User would have paid to Vendor therefor if the Equipment and maintenance had not been so transferred.

4. Assignment and Sublease by User.

(a) This Agreement may be assigned in whole or in part, and all or any part of the Equipment may be subleased, by User, to any parent, subsidiary, or affiliate company of User upon written notice to, but without the consent of, the Vendor. Upon any such assignment and an assumption of liability hereunder by the assignee, the User shall be released from any further liability pursuant to the assigned portion of this Agreement.

(b) This Agreement may be assigned by User, and all or any part of the Equipment may be subleased, to any person or entity other than a parent, subsidiary, or affiliate of User, following prior written consent from Vendor, which consent shall not be unreasonably withheld. In the event of any such assignment, User shall remain liable to Vendor for the financial performance of the assignee hereunder unless Vendor, User, and the assignee enter into a novation agreement providing for the release of User. Vendor agrees that it shall not unreasonably refuse to enter into such a novation agreement.

5. Transfer of Software. In the event User proposes to, or does, sublease, sublet, sublicense, or otherwise transfer or assign all or any part of the Equipment, or the right to use or operate all or any part of the Equipment, to any other person or entity, including without limitation any parent, subsidiary, or affiliate company of User, Vendor agrees that it shall upon written request from User, agree to transfer to such other person or entity the software licensed to User for use by User on, or in connection with, such Equipment, including any license thereto, any future releases, fixes, and enhancements, and any related manuals and documentation therefor; provided, however, that: (a) the transfer or use is not prohibited by the terms of this Agreement; and (b) the transferee or other User shall enter into an agreement with Vendor agreeing to be bound by the terms and provisions of, and to make all payments required by, the then-current software license or other software agreement between Vendor and User covering the software for such Equipment; and (c) notwithstanding any other term of such software license or other software agreement, no price or penalty shall be charged or imposed by Vendor for such transfer, or for the privilege of such transfer, and the transferee shall not be required to pay to Vendor for such software, any amount greater than the amount that User would have paid to Vendor therefor if the Equipment and software had not been so transferred.

6. Transfer of Documentation and Manuals. The right of User to sublease, sublet, sublicense, or otherwise transfer or assign all or any part of the Equipment, or the right to use or operate all or any part of the Equipment, or any related maintenance services or software licenses or agreements, shall include the right to sublicense, transfer, or assign any Vendor manuals and documentation, provided or to be provided to User, relating to such Equipment, maintenance, or software; provided, however, that upon written request the transferee thereof shall enter into an agreement with Vendor providing for the confidential treatment by such transferee of such manuals and documentation, which agreement shall be on terms and conditions comparable to those then binding User and Vendor with respect to such matters.

VENDOR PROVISIONS BASED UPON "THEN-STANDARD TERMS, POLICIES, AND PRICES"

One of the authors' favorite vendor provisions states that some critical user need—such as maintenance, software, or equipment upgrades—will be "provided by the Vendor in accordance with the Vendor's then-standard terms, policies and prices." This type of phrase is frequently found in vendor form agreements. In addition, vendor attorneys are likely to suggest this language in responding to a user's demand that a particular matter be documented in the agreement. For example, the user may assert, "Our senior management says we have to provide for upgrade capability. You've said we can go to the ABC-999 with no problem, but we need to document that in the agreement." The vendor's attorney responds with a provision that states: "Subject to Vendor's then-published terms, policies and prices, Vendor will, upon user's written request, upgrade the Equipment to Vendor's ABC-999 system as such system is then configured and made available to Vendor's standard customers."

The basic problem, of course, is that the user has no way of telling what the vendor's terms, policies, or prices will be at the relevant point in the future. When confronted with this criticism, the vendor is likely to respond that, whatever policies may be in effect, they will be fair: "Really," the vendor's representative will say, "you don't expect that we would adopt policies that would cause us to risk losing our good customers, do you?" For many users, this is enough. After all, it makes sense.

However, the problem is that the vendor may adopt policies that are designed to *keep* customers. Consider the problem of software transfers and relicensing in the context of the language set out above. In general, a vendor will adopt "second user" or software transfer restrictions (contractual and/or financial) only when it is in the vendor's best interest to do so. In most cases, this has been when the vendor was faced with the actual or prospective loss of customers to third-party/used equipment sources. One of the more effective ways for a vendor to freeze out competition from third-party sources of the vendor's used equipment is for the vendor to adopt software transfer or licensing restrictions, or fees, that "equalize" the marketplace (that is, that make the effective used equipment price, coupled with the software fee, higher than the vendor's competing bid).

A similar game can be played with maintenance availability and refurbishment costs. A user intends to buy a used version of the vendor's equipment from a third-party source. The user proposing to sell the equipment has an agreement stating that, if the system is sold or moved, the vendor will continue to supply maintenance for the system "in accordance with the vendor's then-standard terms, policies and prices." When the second user contacts the vendor (hopefully before signing an unconditional purchase agreement), the second user finds the vendor's "policy" now requires refurbishment (at a healthy price) of all relocated equipment if the vendor is to maintain it at the new site. A more subtle version of this technique does not require refurbishment, but permits the vendor to inspect the hardware at the new site to determine if refurbishment is required. If the vendor determines that refurbishment is necessary, the second user must have it performed or the vendor will refuse maintenance. The uncertainty associated with this approach can inhibit a proposed second user from even pursuing the contemplated purchase.

Other variations of the then-standard prices tactic also exist. For example, some equipment manufacturers effectively tie equipment upgrade and/or software enhancement capability to the purchase of one or all upgrade components from that manufacturer. In the late seventies, one well-known minicomputer manufacturer used a "configuration chip" in its systems. If a user desired to upgrade to the manufacturer's more powerful operating system, a new "configuration chip" had to be obtained from the equipment manufacturer. This chip was available free to users that bought all their peripherals or add-on products from the manufacturer. However, if a user desired to obtain its peripherals or upgrade equipment from third-party sources (often at substantially lower price), the user still had to buy the necessary new configuration chip from the equipment manufacturer. (Unlike most other hardware, the chips—which were "set" to accept a given equipment configuration and system—were not available from third-party sources.) Of course, in this situation, the chip was available only upon payment of a rather meaningful fee that, interestingly enough, made it uneconomical for the user to acquire its additional equipment from any source other than the manufacturer. Standard terms, policies, and prices—but not terribly acceptable or helpful to the user.

The best way to minimize the risks associated with this language is for the user to refuse to accept this type of terminology in any vendor agreement. To the extent that some variation of the language is necessary to consummate the transaction, the following suggestions may reduce any adverse impact that may result.

First, the user should condition or limit the language to cover all, or at least the most onerous, contingencies. Where the vendor may utilize future price as a hammer, the user should set a limit on the amount. Where software transfer rights may be the vendor's wedge, the user should provide that no such vendor policies or prices shall preclude the user from being able to transfer the system and software to any other party, without any transfer, relicensing, or similar fee or penalty.

Second, the user should strive to narrow the application of the troublesome vendor language. If the vendor is legitimately concerned about being able to charge high standard prices for a given item or service in the future, the user should draft language that specifically meets that concern. The vendor's general language (such as that quoted above) should then be deleted.

Third, the user should change the standard vendor language to relate to present terms, policies, and prices, and attach a copy of the relevant vendor materials. In some instances, the vendor will agree to use present rather than future terms, policies, and prices. This approach can provide reasonable certainty for the user, but only if the relevant terms, policies and prices are carefully analyzed and spelled out in, or attached to, the agreement.

In summary, the user should recognize two things. First, the vendor may now have, or may adopt, terms, policies or prices that are not in the user's best interest. Second, even if it seems unlikely when the agreement is signed, the user's future requirements may necessitate taking some contingency action (such as upgrading or selling the equipment) that will be governed by the contractual language referenced above. Consequently, the user should treat such language seriously and take appropriate action to limit any adverse effects that might otherwise result.

9
USED EQUIPMENT ACQUISITIONS

Used equipment offers potential benefits to many users. However, the acquisition of used equipment also poses significant risks that are not present (or, at least, not so pervasive) in new equipment transactions. The problems associated with used equipment can be particularly critical when the system involved is being acquired from a small broker or dealer or from another user that is relatively inexperienced in disposing of used equipment.

The additional risks involved in used equipment transactions should not preclude a user from considering the used equipment alternative. Rather, the potential problems should encourage the user to recognize and take the additional steps necessary to document the transaction and minimize the user's exposure.

This chapter is dedicated toward helping the user appreciate the special problems associated with used equipment acquisitions. The initial portion of the chapter reviews several key factors in selecting a used equipment source or "vendor." Subsequent parts of the chapter analyze various legal and financial matters that deserve careful consideration in negotiating and drafting a used equipment agreement.

VENDOR SELECTION

Because of the special risks inherent in any used equipment acquisition, selecting the used equipment source or "vendor" deserves high priority in the acquisition process. In most industries, myriad sources of used equipment exist, and the benefits and dangers involved in a used equipment transaction can vary considerably depending upon the type of vendor selected by the user. Particularly where the user acquiring used equipment has little experience in negotiating and drafting equipment acquisition agreements, or where the user has never acquired used equipment before, special care must be employed when evaluating and selecting the used equipment source.

The first step in the evaluation process involves the identification and consideration of all viable alternatives. Perhaps the most obvious source of used equipment is the manufacturer or original vendor of the equipment involved. Although almost all manufacturers would prefer to sell or lease new equipment to a user, many manufacturers will quote and provide used equipment where clearly asked to do so by the user. (In this discussion, the term "new" applies both to equipment that is completely new in the lay sense and to equipment that is "new manufactured." The latter category of equipment, which is referred to by different names by various manufacturers, generally covers units that have some new and some rebuilt parts. Although "reconditioned" or "refurbished" in a sense, the equipment is sold or leased (and generally warranted) as new in the lay sense. For many years, IBM has been one of the most frequent suppliers of this type of equipment. Some IBM systems are only available as "new manufactured" equipment, while other systems (usually the latest state-of-the-art units) are available as new in the common or lay sense).

Brokers and dealers are probably the most well-publicized sources of used equipment. Brokers generally operate as finders or agents for users (or even other brokers or dealers) seeking to acquire or dispose of new or used equipment. Brokers thus function much like real estate agents, in that they seldom take an equity position in the equipment involved. Instead, they operate and profit by putting (for example) buyer and seller together. Despite this similarity, the real estate analogy is often inaccurate because the equipment broker seldom simply takes a fixed commission that is well-known to the parties on both sides of the transaction. Rather, the equipment broker ordinarily contracts with the acquiring user to provide the stated equipment. Immediately thereafter (or perhaps before if an option can be arranged), the broker contracts with the disposing user to acquire the same equipment. Ideally, these contracts are arranged so that the broker never takes possession of the equipment and does not have an obligation to pay the disposing user for the equipment until the acquiring user has paid the broker. The broker then keeps its profit (which can be a significant percentage of the total price paid by the acquiring user) and remits the amount due to the disposing user.

Dealers operate in a similar fashion, except that they actually take an equity or investment position in the equipment involved. Indeed, many dealers maintain considerable inventories of used equipment. Although these dealers face substantial financial exposure if new equipment introductions or other factors drastically reduce the value of their used equipment inventories, the dealers strive to minimize this risk by studying future market conditions, using aggressive sales techniques, maintaining high margins, and moving the equipment in and out of inventory as rapidly as possible.

Third-party lessors offer another source of used equipment. As equipment becomes available off an existing lease, the lessor generally must make arrangements to release or sell the system to another user. In this regard, the lessor occupies a position not unlike that of an equipment dealer.

Other users also serve as sources of used equipment. Despite the fact that most used equipment changes hands through other sources, direct user-to-user transactions are becoming increasingly popular, particularly as user sophistication in acquiring and disposing of equipment continues to grow.

Each of the sources mentioned above has different strengths and weaknesses, as does each firm within a particular category. The following factors should be considered in analyzing the relative qualifications of each potential source.

Determining Whether the Vendor Has the Financial Resources to Complete the Transaction

As the above discussion suggests, the financial resources of used equipment vendors vary tremendously, from the firm standing of a top manufacturer to the questionable position of a broker doing business out of his or her home or walk-up office. Practically-speaking, it is always nice, but seldom necessary, for a used equipment source to have significant financial standing. What is necessary, however, is a financial position that will permit the used equipment vendor to consummate the transaction in a timely and professional manner. Many brokers (and, indeed, some dealers) are totally unable to advance funds in a used equipment transaction, even for such routine matters as shipping and insurance. Although these brokers may prove to be reasonable sources for certain equipment and for certain users, their weak financial condition may preclude them from accepting any meaningful financial obligation under the agreements involved, thereby placing additional demands and financial exposure on the acquiring user. For example, where the broker's financial condition is weak, the broker is likely to press the user for a large downpayment and for certain advances or commitments for delivery expenses. Where a broker's financial position is reasonably good, the user generally has a realistic opportunity to negotiate financial concessions. On the other hand, where the broker's financial condition is weak, the broker may not have a choice: It may be economically impossible for the broker to agree to handle a particular matter.

Where the success of a used equipment transaction depends upon the availability of financing, either for the acquiring user or a vendor that is a broker, dealer, or lessor, the user should ensure that the vendor has the ability to obtain the required financing. In some instances, of course, the acquiring user's financial condition may be the primary or sole consideration in obtaining financing from other sources. In other situations, the vendor's financial standing may be a key factor. Even where the acquiring user will be ultimately liable on any note or other obligation, the involvement of a marginal broker or dealer may cloud the transaction in the eyes of a bank or other source that is being asked to provide financing for the acquisition. (A similar situation often exists in residential real estate mortgage lending, where a bank may refuse to provide a construction and permanent loan commitment to a credit-worthy borrower because the general contractor selected to build the home has a questionable reputation or weak financial standing. Obviously, the bank is more likely to take such a position where the credit standing of the borrower is only marginally acceptable.)

Financial standing is also important in connection with user remedies and vendor liability. Because of the special risks associated with used equipment acquisitions, the relevant contract must include realistic sections dealing with vendor noncompliance. However, if the vendor selected by the user has a weak financial standing, the value of the user's carefully-negotiated contractual provisions dealing with vendor promises, warranties, and default may be virtually meaningless. As users have discovered far too often in the past, the best contractual provisions are of little assistance if the vendor is in, or on the verge of, bankruptcy. Moreover, in the event vendor bankruptcy or other default occurs prior to delivery, the user may be in the unfortunate position of having advanced significant funds of its own to the broker or other source as a "downpayment" on the equipment. Thus, the user may not only be unable to recover damages for the vendor's default, but may also be unable to gain the return of its downpayment.

In judging the relative financial position of a potential used equipment source, the user should consider the following factors:

- The total amount involved in the transaction and the total potential liability that might be faced by the vendor and the user in the event of nonperformance or other default.
- The total amounts that should be, or may have to be, expended or advanced by the vendor and by the user at various stages of the transaction.
- The alternative methods available to reduce the user's potential financial exposure in the transaction. Such methods may include vendor performance bonds and letters of credit, vendor insurance, and user checks made payable directly to the ultimate source of the equipment (for example, to the disposing user where a broker is involved) or payable jointly to the ultimate source and the intermediate broker or other party.
- The availability of the same or similar equipment through alternative sources having a more substantial financial condition.
- The degree to which the transaction will involve a continuing relationship and/or continuing potential liability between the user and the vendor after delivery and acceptance of the equipment.

In making these assessments, the user should, at a minimum, analyze the vendor's financial statements. Where the vendor is a public company, the user can and should obtain copies of the vendor's annual and quarterly reports to shareholders, and Form 10-K and 10-Q (and perhaps even Form 8-K) reports to the Securities and Exchange Commission. Where the vendor is not a public company, the user should review financial statements certified by the vendor's independent certified public accountants (assuming that certified statements are in fact available). In addition, and certainly where certified financial statements are not available, the user should contact bank references and one or more of the nationally-recognized credit assessment organizations. The user's commercial bank can often provide informal but meaningful assistance in evaluating and researching the financial condition of a potential vendor.

Determining Whether the Vendor Has the Proven Experience and Expertise Necessary to Meet the User's Needs

Regardless of the type of vendor selected, the principals and representatives of the firm should have the expertise necessary to handle any specific needs that the acquiring user may have. For example, if the acquiring user is experienced in purchasing or leasing used equipment, or has retained experienced experts to provide advice and guidance, the user may have little or no need for a vendor that can offer "one stop shopping" and handle all aspects of the transaction from A to Z. Such a user might well be able to consider acquiring used equipment directly from another user or from a small broker, dealer, or lessor. On the other hand, if the acquiring user has neither the time nor the experience to handle a complex used equipment transaction on its own, the user would probably be best served by doing business with a vendor that is an original equipment manufacturer or a substantial broker, dealer, or lessor with a strong reputation for full service and honest dealing.

Even where the acquiring user has the expertise necessary to deal directly with a disposing user, the relative experience of the disposing user may be an important factor. If the disposing user is inexperienced in used equipment transactions, it may tend to adopt unrealistic negotiating positions (both financial and legal) and thereby extend the bargaining phase of the acquisition process or even preclude eventual agreement. Of course, in some instances the relative inexperience of a disposing user may permit the acquiring user to take the lead in negotiating and documenting the transaction, just as so many equipment vendors do in dealing with inexperienced users.

Where the acquiring user determines that the assistance of a broker, dealer, or lessor would be appropriate, the user should carefully consider whether the potential vendor has had experience in the particular type of transaction being considered. For example, some brokers and dealers are quite capable of handling small or moderate transactions involving equipment manufactured by one or two major firms, but totally incapable of handling a larger or more complex acquisition or any acquisition involving other makes of equipment.

Where the user recognizes that systems support and related matters are keys to the success of the acquisition, the user should seriously assess whether the potential vendor can or should provide the required assistance. Ordinarily, where systems support, programming assistance, and other matters are involved, they must be provided by the original equipment manufacturer or distributor or by another source (for example, a systems house or software supplier) that does not have responsibility for the hardware side of the transaction. In order to maximize flexibility in considering alternative vendor sources (and thereby optimize competition), a user considering a used equipment transaction should review the possibility of obtaining these support services from parties other than the vendor that will be supplying the hardware. If the user determines that the only realistic alternative is for the hardware vendor to supply or arrange the support services, the user should probably lean toward executing a used equipment and systems contract with the original equipment manufacturer rather than another type of used equipment vendor. With the possible narrow exception of certain turnkey suppliers, used equipment sources other than original equipment vendors seldom have the experience or the patience to provide both used equipment and meaningful systems and software support.

Determining Whether the Vendor's Business Approach Is Compatible With the User's Needs

If the used equipment acquisition is to be successful, the user must ensure that the vendor's business approach is reasonably compatible with the user's needs. "Compatibility" in this regard can involve several factors.

First, the vendor must be capable of offering acquisition (lease or purchase) terms that are within the range deemed acceptable by the user. If business or financial considerations effectively preclude the user from purchasing the equipment, the user should avoid doing business with a disposing user, unless the acquiring user can also involve a third-party lessor or convince the disposing user that a direct lease transaction would be mutually beneficial.

Second, the vendor must be willing to work with the user and the user's experts and advisors to ensure successful delivery, installation, and operation of the equipment. If the vendor refuses to cooperate with designated manufacturer representatives in connection with such matters as diagnostics, installation, and acceptance testing, the user should seriously consider refusing to do business with the vendor (unless, of course, the user can do without such cooperation or compensate for the lack of cooperation through other sources).

Third, the vendor should be willing to negotiate and document an appropriate acquisition agreement. In most situations, the user should avoid doing business with a vendor that either insists upon using its own one-sided agreement, without amendment, or prefers to "document" the transaction with only a handshake or a short bill of sale. As this volume repeats again and again, major equipment transactions are far too important and complex, both financially and legally, to be documented through any medium other than a negotiated, mutually-acceptable contract. The special risks and circumstances inherent in used equipment transactions heighten the need for contractual detail.

Maximizing Competition

Throughout the vendor evaluation process, the user should strive to maximize actual and apparent competition among alternative firms. Both types of competition can be enhanced by actively considering and encouraging a reasonable number of competing vendors. As noted in Chapters 4 and 5, one of the more effective methods of enhancing competition is through the use of a sound RFP procedure.

Regardless of the techniques employed, the key is to avoid any action or commitment that may permit a single vendor to believe that it has an inside track or that it has effectively eliminated the competition. Because so many major equipment transactions are based upon the "relationship" between the vendor and the user (or, more accurately, between the sales or staff personnel of the respective parties), subtleties can be extremely important. Consequently, all user personnel should be cautioned to take extra steps to ensure that all user/vendor conversations and commitments are objective and arms length, and not tarnished by the bias and subjectivity of personal friendships and warm business meetings. Although the user need not resort to rudeness to optimize competition during the selection process, the user can and should combine a crisp and professional manner with an occasional pointed inquiry or remark to remind every potential vendor that the successful equipment source will be selected only on the basis of objective analysis and documented "deliverables."

FINANCIAL CONSIDERATIONS

Many of the financial considerations involved in used equipment acquisitions are similar to those present in comparable lease and purchase transactions of new equipment. As in the case of new system acquisitions, third-party leases involving used equipment pose the most complex financial problems. Purchases are generally less difficult, except possibly where trade-ins or upgrades are involved. Because other financial considerations are covered elsewhere in this volume, the following section focuses on several financial factors that are particularly relevant in used equipment transactions.

Evaluating Used Equipment Prices

With one possible exception noted below, analyzing the fairness of used equipment prices is one of the more difficult tasks facing the user. The basic problem exists because, in most instances, the user does not have or seek to obtain adequate information concerning the "market price" of the equipment involved.

Where new equipment is being acquired, the user can obtain published list price information and, for many vendors, can also derive "standard discount" data that permit at least some assessment of the going price for the equipment. Where used equipment is involved, the user may be unable to obtain any published prices on the desired system. At the same time, the user is likely to be faced with a wide variety of prices on systems that are similar to, but nevertheless different from, the equipment configuration required by the user. Finding conflicting prices on alternative systems, the user must attempt to allocate the sales or lease price quoted by each vendor to various components with a view toward disposing of the unneeded equipment (at a profit or loss) and retaining the desired items.

Some exceptions to this scenario do exist. For example, used "market" prices are published for most IBM computer equipment and available to the public. In addition to these generic "blue book" listings that supposedly represent market prices rather than specific broker/dealer quotations, many brokers and dealers regularly issue newsletters, press releases, or price lists that specify the IBM or other used equipment prices quoted by their own firm. Although these sources are far from perfect and may in fact tend toward the "high retail" side, they do offer guideposts to a user that might otherwise be awash in a sea of conflicting price quotations and alternative equipment configurations.

Regardless of whether such blue book listings are available, a user faced with assessing used equipment prices should employ several strategies to maximize the potential success of its evaluation efforts.

First, the user should strive to collect all available pricing information on the same or similar equipment. In most instances, the best price sources are the original equipment manufacturer; competing brokers, dealers, and lessors; "want ad" or display listings in trade publications; and where available, the used equipment price lists noted above.

Second, the user should have its technical staff carefully dissect and evaluate each price quotation in order to assess the operating differences among various systems. This task is difficult and time consuming, but absolutely critical. Two used systems may have exactly the same equipment list at first glance, but widely different prices. The reason may become apparent only if the technical specifications of the components are evaluated by a member of the user's staff who is fully cognizant of the operating characteristics and catalog numbers of the various equipment models offered by the manufacturer involved. This type of detailed technical evaluation can generally be facilitated by requesting that each price source, including the original equipment vendor, explain and review its quoted amounts, component by component.

Third, the user should quantify any nonequipment price considerations, such as delivery, installation, and software costs, in order to assess the true or effective cost of various alternatives. At the most obvious level, two proposals involving equal used equipment prices are not likely to be equal if one of the quotations requires the vendor to pay all delivery and installation expenses and the other requires the user to pay such amounts. Less obvious but even more important is the situation where one proposal includes the operating system software (at no extra charge) and the other imposes a hefty software license or "second user" fee. In recent years, several second tier equipment manufacturers have attempted to impose various fees and other marketing practices in order to eliminate or strictly control the third-party market for their used equipment. The goal of these policies was and is to permit the manufacturer to gain or maintain a monopoly, or at least a significant advantage, in transactions involving its used equipment, thereby allowing the manufacturer to maintain reasonably high prices on used equipment and also to minimize competition from used equipment in situations where the manufacturer is attempting to sell or lease new equipment. Software license or "second user" fees and software or firmware "reinitialization" charges are among the more popular techniques utilized by computer manufacturers to implement these goals. Because these charges can drastically change the financial benefits of acquiring used equipment (or, at best, acquiring used equipment from any source other than the original manufacturer), a user considering the acquisition of used equipment should investigate the potentiality of these charges being assessed at an early stage in the decision process. Where possible, the user should obtain a written commitment from the original equipment manufacturer concerning the lack of or amount of any such charges.

Where prohibitive "second user" or similar fees are or may be involved, the user should determine whether any loopholes exist in the vendor's stated policies. In some instances, users have avoided "second user" license fees by forming a leasing subsidiary and having the leasing subsidiary acquire the used equipment and then lease it to the applicable user division. Of course, execution of this approach is facilitated if the user already operates a leasing subsidiary or department (as, for example, many financial institutions do). The leasing alternative has provided an "out" for some users because of the fact that, in order to maintain good business relations with the leasing industry, vendors adopting "second user" and similar policies have often included an exception for transactions handled by or through third-party lessors.

Fourth, where possible the user should seek the advice of an independent contract negotiator or advisor. This individual can usually offer additional insight concerning the reasonableness of various prices (assuming the user has completed the technical review noted above). In addition, a professional negotiator can assist the user in implementing RFP procedures and negotiating strategies that are likely to reduce quoted prices and also shed light on the relative firmness of alternative price proposals.

Minimizing Downpayment and Expense Risks

Many used equipment vendors, particularly smaller brokers and dealers, attempt to require substantial downpayments or "deposits" from the acquiring user. Downpayments of 25% or more are commonly demanded—and received—by some brokers and dealers. Where possible, the acquiring user should avoid any significant downpayment in order to minimize the financial risks associated with the preacceptance phase of the transaction. As noted above, the financial condition of used equipment vendors, as a category, is generally less substantial than that of new equipment firms. Indeed, the financial standing of many smaller brokers and dealers may be weak or questionable at best. Placing a considerable deposit at risk with such a vendor is simply not sound business practice.

Where a downpayment is required, the acquiring user should follow several guidelines to reduce its risks.

First, the user should strive to minimize the amount of the downpayment or deposit, in order to reduce its exposure (as noted above) and in order to give it maximum flexibility in the event the user should determine, for any reason or for no reason, to forfeit the deposit and walk away from the agreement (assuming such action could be taken without further liability under the contract).

Second, the user should protect the deposit by placing it in escrow or, if a substantial disposing user is involved, by having the deposit held directly by the disposing user. (From a practical standpoint, similar protection can probably be obtained by having the downpayment held directly by the equipment manufacturer, assuming that such an entity is also the used equipment vendor.) If the funds are placed in escrow, maximum protection will generally be achieved by having the acquiring user's bank or attorney serve as escrow agent. Although having the funds held in escrow by the broker or dealer may be preferable to having the deposit held (commingled) by the broker or dealer in its general operating account, the authors recommend utilizing a party other than the broker or dealer as an independent escrow agent. Where the deposit is to be held directly by the disposing user and a broker or dealer is involved, it may be advisable for the acquiring user to make its deposit check payable to the order of both the disposing user and the broker or dealer. Both parties would normally then be required to acknowledge receipt by endorsing the check prior to its deposit.

Third, the acquiring user should ensure that the ultimate disposition of the deposit is clearly specified in the acquisition agreement. Myriad problems can arise during the period between the date the deposit is paid and the date the equipment is accepted. Loss or damage to the equipment, delay in delivery or acceptance, default, and permissible termination of the agreement can all necessitate return or seizure of the deposit. Consequently, contractual provisions relating to these and similar matters must either cover, or cross-reference to other sections that cover, the disposition of the deposit. Where both a disposing user and a broker, dealer, or lessor are involved, it may be prudent for the acquiring user to extract a binding commitment from both such parties concerning the return of any such deposit.

Although the acquiring user is seldom asked to advance out-of-pocket expenses in an amount as large as the usual downpayment, the user should nevertheless attempt to avoid or at least minimize any exposure relating to such expenses. The authors strongly recommend that the acquiring user refuse to advance any expense funds or similar amounts to or on behalf of the used equipment vendor. The acquiring user's internal staff costs and its own out-of-pocket expenses, plus the amount of any downpayment, represent enough of a financial risk and commitment for the user without absorbing the financial risk (and cost of funds) that should be borne by the vendor. Moreover, if problems arise during the early stages of the transaction, the acquiring user's negotiating position will be substantially enhanced if the broker, dealer, disposing user, or other vendor has expended funds on various aspects of the transaction.

Validating Bids and Identifying Equipment

Because of the manner in which many brokers and dealers operate, they may submit proposals that involve equipment that they have not yet formally placed under option or other contract. As a result, two or more brokers or dealers may submit apparently competitive bids that actually involve the same installed system. Before placing any serious reliance on a bid or financial proposal, particularly one submitted by a broker, dealer, or lessor, the acquiring user should determine whether the proposal is backed by available equipment. At the same time, the user must determine whether two or more proposals actually involve the same equipment.

At the outset, the acquiring user should insist that all bids or other proposals specify the serial numbers for all equipment being proposed or, at least, for any major item or component. Ideally, the proposals should also indicate the site or other location where the equipment is installed or stored. In the latter situation, the acquiring user can seek independent verification from any disposing user that the broker, dealer, or lessor actually has, or will have, certain rights to acquire or otherwise dispose of the equipment. The user should also require each competing vendor to warrant and represent that it has title to, or certain enumerated rights to acquire, the equipment and that, in the event the vendor's proposal is accepted and an agreement is executed, the vendor can and will supply the proposed equipment by not later than a specified date.

Where the broker or dealer does not yet have title to the equipment, particular care must be taken to determine the scope of the vendor's rights to acquire the equipment. Written representations concerning these rights can and should be obtained from the vendor and the disposing user. In addition, where possible the user should obtain and review a copy of the relevant contract between the vendor and the disposing user. (In fairness, these parties may be reluctant to supply a copy of the contract unless the price is obliterated. However, a strong argument can be made that the user has every right to know the vendor's "cost of goods sold.")

If the vendor has executed a purchase contract with the disposing user, the acquiring user should carefully review all conditions and obligations to ensure that the vendor seems likely to be able to obtain valid title. The user can secure additional protection in this area by gaining representations directly from the disposing user and by entering into an agreement with the disposing user that grants the acquiring user the right to assume the vendor's rights and obligations under the vendor/disposing user contract if the vendor defaults under that agreement. At a minimum, the disposing user and the vendor should agree to provide the acquiring user with prompt notice of any such default.

Where the broker or other vendor merely has an agency or option arrangement with the disposing user, additional care is required. Here, the acquiring user must document the type of agency involved in order to determine whether it is exclusive or nonexclusive and, if exclusive, whether it is technically an "exclusive agency" or an "exclusive right of sale." Rather obviously, if the broker is only one of several nonexclusive agents, another broker may sell the same system to another party, leaving the user with no equipment to acquire. If the broker has an exclusive agency, but not an exclusive right of sale, the disposing user still retains the right to dispose of the equipment on its own (absent a contrary contract commitment), again potentially leaving the acquiring user high and dry.

Although seldom practical due to timing problems, one of the best ways to maximize protection for the acquiring user is for that party to contract directly with the disposing user, either in a triparty agreement which includes the broker or other vendor or in a user/user contract that is supplemented by one or more contracts between one or both users and the broker or other vendor.

Even where the vendor has apparently solid rights to acquire or sell the equipment, the user must recognize that the vendor may attempt to market it to two or more users simultaneously. Although this competition is obviously good for the vendor, it is likely to leave at least one acquiring user in a bad position. Consequently, it may be advantageous for the user to have the vendor represent that: (1) it is not marketing the equipment to any other user; and (2) it has not executed and will not execute without informing the user in writing, any contract or proposal to sell, lease, or otherwise transfer the specified equipment to any other person or entity. A reasonable time limit on these representations may be appropriate.

To optimize its position, the acquiring user may wish to require each bidding vendor to post a deposit or a bond to support its representation and warranty concerning the availability of the proposed equipment. In the event the bidder does not have title or rights to the equipment, or otherwise fails to deliver the equipment in accordance with its proposal (and without substitution), the deposit or bond can then be forfeited to the acquiring user. Although the amount of such a deposit or bond may or may not be adequate to compensate the user for its damages in such an event, the mere existence of such a deposit or bond requirement is likely to minimize problems such as those mentioned above. A carefully-drafted proposal "agreement" can also be used in addition to, or in lieu of, the deposit or bond approach to permit the acquiring user to sue the defaulting bidder for damages or other relief in the event the user suffers serious injury from such a default.

LEGAL CONSIDERATIONS

Most of the sections of a used equipment agreement are essentially the same as those in a corresponding agreement (e.g., purchase, direct lease, or third-party lease) for new equipment. However, because of the special risks associated with used equipment, a used equipment acquisition agreement must cover matters that might be omitted, or covered in less detail, in a similar contract for new equipment. As the more general contractual provisions are covered elsewhere in this volume, the following section focuses on several of the factors that require unique treatment in a used equipment contract. (As always, the reader should recall that the subjects discussed below do not represent all of the legal issues that should be documented in a used equipment agreement. Users should consult their legal counsel for specific advice in these and other areas.)

Describing the Equipment

One of the more basic risks in any used equipment contract involves the failure of the acquiring user to completely or accurately identify the equipment involved. To avoid the risks associated with this failure, the user should employ several procedures.

First, the user should carefully describe the components being acquired, by manufacturer's part number, description, and (where applicable) serial number. Unless the user feels extremely secure with some other arrangement, the contract should clearly provide that the vendor does not have the right, without prior written permission from the user, to substitute any equipment under the agreement or to assign its obligations to any other person or entity. (Assignment of the vendor's right to receive payments may be permitted upon reasonable notice and other conditions.)

Second, the user should make certain that it understands the exact operating specifications that are associated with the described equipment. As suggested above, equipment with the same general model number may or may not include exactly the same technology or operating characteristics. Where compatibility with the user's existing equipment is required, special care must be exercised to ensure the existence of that compatibility.

Third, the user should determine that the equipment involved will, in fact, operate as a system, or as a subsystem, without the need for any other equipment or components at additional (and unexpected) cost. This risk is often most serious, but also most obvious, where the user is acquiring used components from one or more brokers or dealers and the equipment involved is not, at the time of acquisition, installed and operating as a system at another user location. A similar but lesser risk exists where the equipment is being operated as a system by the disposing user, but the acquiring user intends to utilize the components in a different system. Perhaps the least serious and least obvious, but most annoying, risk involves the failure to specify and acquire the minor components necessary to fully utilize the equipment. Among the items included in this category are maintenance log books, cables, connectors, manuals, schematics, maintenance racks, and diagnostics.

These risks can be reduced by careful staff work and by involving the manufacturer's engineering and sales staff (even if another vendor is being utilized to supply the used equipment). Many manufacturers will supply advice and guidance (either free or at a charge) to users seeking used equipment from other sources. Where this service is not available for reasons of cost or lack of cooperation, indirect advice can still be obtained if the manufacturer can be induced to submit its own used equipment proposal containing a detailed equipment and specification list. Where the equipment is being obtained from a source other than the manufacturer (and, in effect, is installed at another user site), indirect assistance can also be obtained by studying the contracts and equipment lists (and, ideally, the vendor proposals and user analyses) that covered the initial acquisition of the equipment by the disposing user. However, because all of these sources may overlook some of the minor items referenced above, the acquiring user should also generally include broad "catch all" language in the equipment description section of the contract. Such a phrase might state "Except as may be specified in Schedule A hereto, the Equipment shall include all necessary cables, connectors, maintenance logs and racks, logics, manuals, schematics, and diagnostics applicable to the listed Equipment, together with all related components necessary to allow operation of the listed Equipment." Depending upon the acquiring user's site plan, for interconnected components it may also be advantageous to add: "The length of all cables shall be as specified in Schedule A." As in the case of new equipment, the acquiring user may also wish to consider requiring a "configuration warranty." (See Chapter 8.)

Documenting Software Availability

As noted above, some manufacturers have adopted marketing policies that directly or indirectly impose substantial license or other fees on "second users" of certain equipment, particularly when that equipment happens to be acquired from a source other than the manufacturer. Although reinitialization and firmware fees are also employed, the most popular vendor strategy in this area involves the imposition of a software license fee on the "second user" that was not directly imposed on the user that initially acquired the system from the manufacturer. In theory, at least, this fee is designed to be imposed on the use of the manufacturer's operating system software in connection with any used system (perhaps above or below a stated minimum equipment configuration), regardless of the source from which the used system is or was acquired. In practice, however, the manufacturer quotes a "bundled" used equipment and software price that is more than the equipment-only prices quoted by other used equipment sources, but less than the equipment-plus-software (second user) license price involving those sources. In taking this approach, the manufacturer simply notes that its bid includes the license fee. (The manufacturer may alternatively use an unbundled approach in its bid, quoting equipment and software separately, and still enjoy the same aggregate bottom line result.) In some situations, the manufacturer may not even have a formal "second user" or similar policy. Nevertheless, the manufacturer's marketing representative may directly or indirectly threaten that such a policy exists or may be instituted in the future.

Because problems of this nature can drastically alter the relative financial advantages of alternative vendor proposals, the user must carefully cover the availability of software in the used equipment acquisition documents. The best method of handling the availability of operating system software is generally in a binding agreement between the acquiring user and the equipment manufacturer (assuming that the latter is in fact the legal licensor of such software). In some instances, the user may already have, or appear to have, rights to the software by virtue of an existing license or agreement (for example, relating to an already-installed system previously supplied by the manufacturer). However, the user should not assume that its rights under such an existing license or agreement will be broad enough to permit the use of the software in connection with the used equipment to be acquired in the proposed transaction. Consequently, the user should optimize its position by: (1) having its attorney render an opinion concerning its software rights; and (2) seeking a commitment from, and preferably a binding, separate license or agreement with, the manufacturer relating to the use of such software.

Where no prior software rights enter the picture and the user is acquiring the used equipment from a source other than the manufacturer, the user should strive to execute a license or other agreement directly with the manufacturer to ensure the availability of the software. In many situations, the software license can be included in an agreement between the user and the manufacturer that covers a variety of matters, from deinstallation diagnostics to installation and acceptance testing (assuming that the used equipment will be acquired from a source other than the manufacturer but the manufacturer will provide services similar to those noted above). Placing the software license into such an agreement generally makes it easier for the user to show the "consideration" (payment) legally necessary for the agreement to be binding, even though the user may not in fact be making a separate payment for the license. In effect, the user pays for the various installation services and not for the software, but the agreement involved does not allocate the total amount paid by the user under the contract to the various services and software provided by the manufacturer. Of course, regardless of whether the user receives the software at no charge or at separate cost, the software license must be drafted in a manner that will prevent the manufacturer from unilaterally revoking the license or assessing new or additional fees in the future.

Even where the user is able to execute an appropriate software agreement directly with the manufacturer, the user may also wish to include certain software availability representations in its used equipment contract with the nonmanufacturer vendor. This approach is highly advisable, and perhaps mandatory, where the user is unable to consummate a clearly binding software agreement with the manufacturer before signing the used equipment contract. Several approaches can be employed in this regard. First, the acquiring user may insist that the used equipment vendor warrant that the user will be able to obtain and use the specified operating software at no additional cost to the user, or at a maximum stated cost. This approach may or may not include express penalty language indicating that the vendor will bear any such cost in excess of that specified in the contract. Second, the user may ask the vendor to give "negative assurances," in effect stating that the vendor is unaware of any facts or policies that would preclude the user from being able to obtain and use the software at no additional cost or at a stated maximum cost. Third, the user may require the vendor itself to sublicense or agree to provide specified software to the acquiring user, either at no cost or at a cost specified in the used equipment agreement. Fourth, the user may simply ask for the right to cancel the used equipment agreement, at no penalty or on terms specified in the contract, in the event the user cannot execute an acceptable software agreement with the manufacturer within a stated period of time (generally prior to delivery of the equipment to the acquiring user).

Documenting Equipment Condition

Almost by definition, the condition of used equipment is seldom likely to be equal to that of comparable new equipment. Regardless of whether the used equipment utilizes current state-of-the-art technology, it may or may not have been maintained properly by the disposing user. Moreover, the system may have suffered damage or unusual operating conditions that adversely affect its current performance. Because of these and similar risks, the acquiring user must devote special attention toward determining and documenting the condition of the equipment being acquired. The following guidelines should be helpful in this regard.

First, the acquiring user should obtain and study the original maintenance logs for the equipment. Assuming they have been diligently kept, such records offer good insight into operating problems and general maintenance levels. Ideally, this review, and a visual inspection of the equipment itself, should be conducted at the disposing user's site before the acquisition agreement is executed. However, if timing and marketing pressures necessitate that the agreement be signed prior to any such inspection, an inspection and cancellation provision should be included in the agreement. Normally, such an inspection period should be reasonably short, out of fairness and consideration for both sides. The following language may be considered as one example of this approach:

14. *INSPECTION BY BUYER; CANCELLATION.* This Agreement is expressly conditioned upon satisfactory inspection of the Equipment and any associated maintenance or other log

books by the Buyer at the Seller's site. Such inspection shall be completed by Buyer not later than ten (10) calendar days following the execution of this Agreement by both parties hereto, and shall be in addition to any other maintenance standards or acceptance tests provided for in this Agreement. In the event Buyer reasonably determines for cause, following such inspection, that the Equipment appears to be unsatisfactory, Buyer may, upon provision of prior written notice to Seller during such ten (10) day period (during which period Seller shall have the right to cure by full performance acceptable to Buyer), terminate this Agreement, in which event neither party shall have any further obligation to the other party hereunder. Acceptance of the Equipment by the Buyer as a result of such inspection shall not prejudice Buyer's other rights under this Agreement or be deemed to constitute a waiver by Buyer of any such rights.

A similar inspection section may also be drafted, but providing for inspection at the acquiring user's site within ten days following delivery of the equipment. Although such an approach may be pragmatic when time is short, and may also enhance the acquiring user's bargaining power at the time of the inspection, predelivery inspection is generally better for all concerned. Moreover, predelivery inspection precludes the acquiring user from relying upon and anticipating the delivery of equipment that immediately proves to be unacceptable. Predelivery inspection is also less likely to lead to actual or threatened litigation in the event the acquiring user rejects the equipment for questionable cause. Indeed, a relatively brief predelivery inspection period is generally so acceptable to both parties that it may be possible for the acquiring user to obtain the right to cancel the agreement with or without cause as a result of the inspection. (The example provision set out above uses a "for cause" approach that is less desirable from the standpoint of the acquiring user.)

Second, the user should determine that the equipment has been, and will be until shipment, covered by a valid and adequate maintenance agreement with the manufacturer or another acceptable maintenance source. If any significant gap exists between the date the equipment goes off maintenance at the disposing user's site and the date the equipment goes on maintenance at the acquiring user's site, the manufacturer or other maintenance firm either may refuse to provide maintenance services to the acquiring user, or may do so only after inspection and, in some cases, reconditioning or refurbishment. The maximum permissible gap period in this regard varies among manufacturers and among types of equipment. For electronic components, 30 days may be the maximum period. Ordinarily, the acquiring user should require the disposing user and any intervening vendor to warrant that the equipment has been maintained under an acceptable maintenance agreement. Language based on the following may be used for this purpose: "Seller hereby represents and warrants that, except as may be otherwise specified in Schedule B to this Agreement, the Equipment is now, has been at all times since its installation at Seller's site(s), and shall be at all times until the Acceptance Date hereunder, under continuous maintenance pursuant to one (1) or more maintenance agreements with the manufacturer of such Equipment." The acquiring user may also wish to specify that the vendor, and not the acquiring user, will be responsible for obtaining and paying for any such maintenance until the acceptance date.

Third, the acquiring user should determine that, once equipment is delivered and installed at its site, the equipment will be accepted for maintenance by the manufacturer or other maintenance firm at standard terms, rates, and conditions, and without further inspection, reconditioning, or refurbishment. The obvious time for this determination to be made (to the extent possible) is before the equipment is delivered to the acquiring user. Fortunately, many manufacturers will inspect used equipment at the disposing user's site for a reasonable fee and provide a written commitment concerning the availability of maintenance for the equipment at the acquiring user's site. Although the desired level of formality is often difficult to achieve, this type of inspection should be made pursuant to a binding engineering, maintenance, or other contract between the acquiring user and the manufacturer, in order to maximize the user's legal rights against the manufacturer in the event later problems arise or the manufacturer changes its position to the user's detriment.

Because conditions can change as a result of deinstallation and shipment, care must be taken to document the condition of the equipment at the time the manufacturer's assessment is made. In many instances, hard copy printout of the "diagnostics" run on the equipment may be available and, in such case, may be incorporated into the manufacturer's report to the acquiring user. This approach provides clear evidence of the condition of the equipment at the time the manufacturer's tests were conducted.

Unfortunately, some manufacturers and distributors employ second user maintenance policies in a manner similar to the second user software policies discussed above—again for purposes of making it more difficult or more expensive for an acquiring user to obtain used equipment from a source other than the manufacturer or distributor. Where major equipment is involved, the policies generally require, or at least threaten, expensive refurbishment or reconditioning before the equipment will be accepted for maintenance. (As in the software area, threats from the vendor's local sales representative may be as effective as any formal policy or requirement for reconditioning.) One of the more thoughtful methods of presenting such a threat is through a standard vendor letter or provision that states: "User understands and agrees that vendor cannot warrant the condition of used equipment obtained from other sources and that, to remain eligible for continued maintenance by vendor in the future, such equipment may be required to be refurbished by vendor at user's expense."

Although less frequently employed in major equipment transactions, some manufacturers and distributors utilize a "lifetime first user warranty" to achieve similar marketing results. This approach has been particularly popular among local distributors of certain types of small business equipment (e.g., desktop copiers). Where this technique is employed, the vendor offers the first user (purchaser) a "lifetime warranty" that provides free maintenance as long as the user purchases its operating supplies from the vendor. Assuming that the supplies are reasonably priced (which may or may not be a valid assumption), the principal problem arises when the user attempts to sell the equipment and recalls that the "warranty" is not transferable. At that point, the vendor may offer one of several alternatives: (1) it will transfer the warranty to the acquiring user, at a healthy fee; (2) it will provide continued maintenance at its high published prices for such services (after all, most of its customers get "free" maintenance under the "lifetime warranty"); or (3) it will buy the machine from the disposing user, "inspect and refurbish" it, and resell it to the acquiring user (after extracting a nice profit on the transaction).

Despite the maintenance representations received or to be received from the equipment manufacturer, the acquiring user should also attempt to place some burden concerning equipment condition and maintenance availability on the disposing user. If the acquiring user wishes to take a particularly strict and conservative approach, it may require the disposing user or other vendor to affirmatively represent and warrant that the equipment is in good operating condition, that all engineering change orders for the equipment have been fully implemented, and that, following installation at the new site in accordance with manufacturer's specifications, the equipment will be accepted for maintenance by the manufacturer in accordance with the desired (and specified) standards and time deadlines. This approach places a heavy burden on the disposing user or other vendor for, if the equipment is not so accepted, the disposing user or vendor may be liable for damages to the acquiring user.

If the acquiring user wishes to take a more reasonable approach, it may make acceptance for maintenance by the manufacturer a condition of the contract, in effect providing that, if the equipment is not so accepted for maintenance, the acquiring user may terminate the agreement or take other limited actions short of suing the disposing user for unlimited damages. Under the "condition" approach, the acquiring user may still provide that, in the event the condition is not met, the disposing user will expend specified resources or funds in an effort to correct the problem and permit the condition to be met. The following example provision should be helpful to users considering this area:

16.3. This Agreement and the purchase and sale contemplated herein are expressly conditioned upon all items of Equipment being accepted for maintenance by the manufacturer at Buyer's site, at standard published rates and terms, without payment by Buyer of any reconditioning, refurbishment, transit damage, or warehouse deterioration charges. In this regard, Buyer agrees to execute with the Equipment manufacturer(s) such agreements relating to installation, software, and maintenance as may be reasonably necessary to allow Seller to comply with its obligations hereunder. In the event that all items of Equipment are not so accepted for maintenance within thirty (30) calendar days after the delivery of all items of Equipment to Buyer's site, Buyer shall have the right and option to cancel and terminate this Agreement, and cause all items of Equipment to be returned to Seller at Seller's expense, whereupon Seller shall promptly return Buyer's downpayment to Buyer and, thereafter, neither party shall have any further liability to the other party hereunder; *provided that* the following terms and conditions shall be applicable:

(a) Following execution of this Agreement by both parties hereto, Seller shall, within fourteen (14) calendar days, request that the Equipment manufacturer(s) perform the necessary tests and inspections, upon delivery of the Equipment to Buyer, to ascertain the amount of any reconditioning, refurbishment, or other repairs that may be necessary for acceptance of the Equipment for maintenance.

(b) In the event that one (1) or more items of Equipment require reconditioning, refurbishment, or repair, and the estimated expense therefor does not exceed Fifteen Thousand Dollars ($15,000.00) in the aggregate, then Seller shall notify Buyer of the estimated expense. Buyer shall then have the option either: (1) to require Seller to pay such amount and cause the necessary reconditioning, refurbishment, or repairs to be performed; or (2) to cause the necessary reconditioning, refurbishment, and repairs to be made (at Buyer's initial expense) and to delete from, or receive as a credit against, the Purchase Price for the Equipment the full amount of the charges for such reconditioning, refurbishment, and repairs; or (3) to cancel and terminate this Agreement as provided above in this Section 16.

16.4. In the event the Buyer elects to have one (1) or more items of Equipment maintained by a source other than the manufacturer of that item of Equipment, the term "manufacturer" in this Section 16 shall be modified to mean the maintenance source actually selected in good faith by the Buyer.

Fourth, the user should design and document an acceptance test specifically for the used equipment being acquired. Although the general standards used in drafting any acceptance test will be applicable (see Chapter 8), special consideration must be given to several factors. For example, the acquiring user may wish to include the deinstallation diagnostics (run at the disposing user's site) as a part of the acceptance test. The results of any special benchmark tests run at the disposing user's site may also be included in the acceptance test. The acquiring user may also wish to specify that, as part of the acceptance test, the equipment must perform in accordance with certain published manufacturer specifications. Although published specifications for new equipment may be used for this purpose in a particularly strict agreement, a more reasonable approach may be to reference published specifications for refurbished or reconditioned equipment (assuming that such specifications are in fact so published by the manufacturer). Finally, because of the reliability questions frequently associated with used equipment, the acquiring user should include a sound reliability phase in any acceptance test. In designing this aspect of the acceptance test, the user should devote considerable attention to the minimum performance period (for example, 30 days) and the minimum acceptable uptime percentage (for example, 90 percent). The user's decisions on these factors may also be relevant in designing any continuing performance warranty or rental credit provision that may be considered for inclusion in the agreement.

Providing Adequate Delivery Standards

Where the used equipment is being acquired from a vendor other than the manufacturer, the user should include strict and specific delivery standards in the agreement. Such standards are desirable in all used equipment agreements, but they are absolutely mandatory where the vendor is another user or a relatively small broker, dealer, or lessor.

The acquiring user's primary goal in this area should be to ensure that the equipment will be deinstalled, packed, shipped, unpacked, and installed in accordance with stated minimum standards—generally the minimum standards specified by the original equipment manufacturer. Perhaps the best method of ensuring this minimum is to require that the original equipment manufacturer or its approved maintenance agent either directly handle, or at least supervise, all deinstallation, packing, unpacking, and installation activities. Even in this instance, the agreement should reference the minimum permissible specifications.

Where direct involvement by the manufacturer is not practical, the acquiring user should nevertheless specify that all matters be handled in accordance with minimum standards stated or referenced in the acquisition agreement. Language similar to the following may be used as a basic provision:

A. The Equipment shall be dismantled, crated, and prepared for shipment under the supervision, and pursuant to the current standards, of the Equipment manufacturer(s). The Equipment shall be crated and packed in materials meeting or exceeding the manufacturer(s) then current specifications. Seller shall in any event exercise normal and reasonable care in dismantling, packing, and crating the Equipment in order to avoid damage to the appearance or operating condition of the Equipment.

B. The Equipment shall be shipped to the Buyer's site by commercial carrier approved in advance by Buyer. Handling, shipping, unloading, and installation of the Equipment shall meet or exceed the manufacturer(s) then current specifications.

Depending upon its special needs, the user may also wish to specify the type of delivery method (e.g., air freight), the carrier, or the type of vehicle (e.g., padded van). Where the user intends or requires that all components be shipped on a single van or other vehicle, this fact should be specified in the contract. Whether included in the delivery section of the agreement or elsewhere in the contract, the user may require that the equipment be delivered to an interim location for cosmetic (surface cleaning and painting) or other refurbishment prior to final delivery to the user's site. Where cosmetic or other refurbishment is required or desired, of course, the contract should include detailed information concerning the work to be performed and the parties responsible for supervision and costs.

Providing for Clear Passage of Title

Although liens and title problems can also affect new equipment, these difficulties are much more likely to occur in used equipment transactions. Consequently, the user should ensure that the acquisition agreement includes strong warranties of title and "no liens." The applicable provision or provisions should include the following considerations.

First, the agreement should specify when title to the equipment will pass to the user. The authors recommend that title pass on the acceptance date, in order to permit proper meshing of the provisions relating to risk of loss, insurance, payment, and title. If payment is not actually made on the acceptance date, the agreement can grant the vendor a security interest in the equipment until the full purchase price is paid.

Second, the agreement should provide that, when title passes to the user on the acceptance date, it will pass free and clear of any liens or encumbrances. In effect, the agreement should provide that, at the closing on the acceptance date, the vendor will have, and will pass to the user, "good and valid legal title to the equipment, free and clear of any and all liens and encumbrances of whatever kind and description."

Third, the user may wish for the vendor to make a similar warranty as of the date the acquisition agreement is executed, which warranty would apply to the full period between the execution of the agreement and the acceptance date. This approach may be too strict for most brokers and for many dealers due to one of two reasons: (1) The vendor may not have acquired title to the equipment at the time the agreement is signed; or (2) the vendor may have acquired title to the equipment but may have borrowed money to do so, using the equipment as collateral for the loan (thereby giving rise to a lien on the equipment). Nevertheless, by asking for the warranty noted above, the user will generally force the vendor to describe its equipment acquisition plans and, in the process, disclose potential lien problems that may concern the user. Where the vendor's acquisition method precludes it from making the desired warranty for the full period suggested above, the user may nevertheless require that the contract detail exactly how and when the vendor will acquire title and/or create and satisfy any liens or encumbrances. If liens are to be permitted during the period between the date of the contract and the acceptance date, the user should consider requiring the lienholder to join in the acquisition agreement for purposes of agreeing that, in the event of default by the vendor, the lienholder will permit the user to satisfy the lien and proceed with the acquisition (including any situation where the lienholder may have already "foreclosed" its lien and taken title to the equipment).

Providing Adequate Remedies

User remedies are important in any acquisition agreement (see Chapter 8), but the special risks associated with used equipment require that particular consideration be devoted to the section or sections dealing with remedies. As in other types of equipment agreements, the remedy provisions in a used equipment contract must be tailored to the size of the transaction and the reputation and financial standing of the vendor involved. (In theory, the reputation of the used equipment vendor might be said to be irrelevant to the relative strength or weakness of the user remedies contained in the agreement. After all, contractual remedies are theoretically designed to provide protection in the event unforeseen problems arise. And vendors with good or bad reputations can suffer unforeseen problems and default under the agreement. Consequently, this line of reasoning suggests all contracts should include maximum remedy provisions regardless of whether the vendor is deemed to be reliable or not. Although this approach is both logical and philosophically correct, it ignores the realities of most negotiated transactions. Practically, few users have either the time or the patience to optimize each and every provision in a major equipment agreement. Compromises are made for a variety of reasons, including relative business priorities, negotiating strategies, and time constraints. Consequently, most users must strive to achieve less than optimum provisions in many situations, tailoring the relative strength or weakness of a given provision to the specific circumstances surrounding the transaction.)

From a substantive standpoint, certain of the remedies included in a used equipment contract deserve special attention. The following observations may be helpful in tailoring more general user remedies to a used equipment agreement.

Risk of Loss. Although most users seldom devote serious attention to risk of loss provisions, the fact remains that equipment—new and used—is sometimes lost or damaged during or prior to delivery and installation. Arranging for the replacement of used equipment is generally more difficult than providing for the replacement of new equipment, due to the fact that the used system is more likely to be "unique" at a given point in time. The difficulties involved in replacing a damaged or destroyed used system are increased where the equipment involved is relatively rare (either due to a low installed base or high current demand) and where the equipment is being acquired through a relatively small broker, dealer, or lessor that may not have access to a broad used equipment market. Even where a replacement system can be located, it may not be available at the same price that the user paid, or agreed to pay, for the equipment that was damaged or destroyed. Although discounts and delivery position premiums may pose similar problems in the case of certain new systems, the financial risks associated with replacement used equipment are generally much higher.

As noted above, the financial condition of the used equipment vendor is often less than fully desirable. Where the vendor has some financial weakness, it is less likely to be able to bear any uninsured loss or damage that may occur to the equipment being acquired by the user. Moreover, even if adequate insurance proceeds are available, the vendor may be unable to arrange for replacement equipment on its own financial position if the proceeds are delayed due to controversy or other reason.

These problems generally dictate that the user devote particular attention to the risk of loss provision in any used equipment contract. Although the precise form of the risk of loss provision will vary depending upon the vendor and equipment involved, the following suggestions will apply in most situations.

First, the agreement should clearly allocate the risk of loss, both before and after acceptance. As noted in Chapter 8, the authors strongly recommend that the vendor have the full risk of loss through the acceptance date. If this approach is absolutely unacceptable to the vendor, then the vendor should have the risk of loss at least through delivery of the equipment to the user's site.

Second, the agreement should require the party that has the risk of loss to obtain, at its expense, appropriate broad coverage insurance in an amount not less than the reasonable replacement value of the equipment. Because of price fluctuations in the used equipment market, it may be difficult to obtain the full degree of insurance protection needed in the event the cost of the replacement equipment is considerably above the contract price for the equipment that is damaged or destroyed. Nevertheless, every effort should be made to require the highest reasonable coverage available. Coverage during transportation of the equipment is particularly critical. Standard commercial carrier coverage will not be adequate. Consequently, the party responsible for consigning the equipment for shipping must take responsibility for obtaining the necessary special insurance coverage. (The importance of this special coverage is one reason why the vendor, and not the user, should be responsible for both the risk of loss and the necessary insurance prior to acceptance. If the vendor clearly has this responsibility, it is much more likely to obtain the required special coverage.) Of course, any insurance obtained by the vendor should name the user as a loss payee, to the extent that its interest may appear. The user should always require a certificate or other evidence of insurance from the vendor.

Third, the user should review its own insurance coverages to determine whether it may have, or be able to arrange, backup or umbrella coverage in the event the vendor either fails to obtain insurance or obtains such insurance in an inadequate amount. In addition, the user must arrange for its own insurance following the acceptance date or other point where the risk of loss shifts to the user.

Fourth, the user should consider the interrelationship of the risk of loss, delivery and installation deadline, and force majeure provisions in the agreement. In general, the user should ensure that, if the equipment cannot be, or is not, replaced within a stated time following the damage or loss, the user will be permitted to terminate the agreement at no penalty and receive a full refund of its deposit. (See Chapter 8.) Several variations on this approach are also possible. For example, the agreement may grant the user the option to terminate if the equipment is totally destroyed or seriously damaged. The agreement may also provide that, in the event the equipment cannot be replaced within the specified maximum time frame, due to the failure of the vendor to obtain the required insurance, then the user may not only terminate the agreement and receive the return of its deposit, but the user may also hold the vendor liable for any damages suffered by the user as a result.

Delivery, Installation, and Acceptance Deadlines. Many of the problems noted above concerning the risk of loss to the equipment are also applicable to any failure by the vendor to deliver the equipment as required (either in terms of failure to meet required delivery or acceptance deadlines or in terms of delivering equipment that fails to perform). Again, the basic questions involve the financial and practical ability of the vendor to stand behind its contractual commitments in the event of serious problems. The following suggestions may be helpful in reducing the risks involved in this area.

First, the contract should include interim performance deadlines (for example, deadlines for shipment, delivery, installation, and acceptance). These multiple checkpoints permit the user to declare a default at the earliest stage of vendor nonperformance, thereby reducing the user's potential loss, as well as the delay likely to be involved in procuring replacement equipment.

Second, the user should consider the possibility of requiring a performance bond, letter of credit, or guaranty of performance from an independent source willing to make a financial commitment concerning the vendor's performance. Although this type of indirect "insurance" is often difficult or at least expensive to obtain, it may be practical in some situations. For example, a parent company or affiliate may be willing to guarantee the performance of its vendor subsidiary. The individual entrepreneurs in a small broker or dealer firm may be willing to personally guarantee the vendor's performance under the contract. The disposing user may even be willing to make certain commitments to the acquiring user concerning the performance of an intervening broker or dealer.

Third, the user should avoid the possibility that a poorly drafted force majeure clause will excuse vendor nonperformance. As suggested in Chapter 8, the user should be certain that it has the absolute right to terminate the agreement after a certain "drop dead" deadline, even if the vendor's nonperformance at that time is due to an event that would otherwise fall within the force majeure provision.

Fourth, the user should consider conditioning any grace period for the correction of vendor nonperformance upon the vendor's compliance with certain conditions. For example, if the vendor fails to ship the equipment by the deadline set forth in the agreement, the contract may grant the vendor a ten day grace period within which to cure this failure, before the user may declare a default. However, the provision granting this grace period may state that the user can immediately declare a default unless the vendor: (1) certifies to the user in writing the reasons for the delay, the actions being taken to correct the problems, and the date by which the problems will be corrected; and (2) posts a "deposit" of $1,000 with the user guaranteeing that the problems will in fact be corrected by the specified date. In the latter case, care must be taken that the "deposit" amount not be deemed to be the user's exclusive remedy or an impermissible "penalty." In a situation involving failure to meet the required acceptance tests, the provision might require the vendor to execute a contract with the manufacturer providing for its systems or field engineering representatives to correct or at least diagnose the problem. The purpose, in each case, is to require the vendor to take immediate action and make a financial commitment to correct the deficiency involved.

Performance. A user acquiring used equipment should consider the advisability of requiring a continuing performance standard, above and beyond the initial acceptance test. Continuing performance standards are beneficial to the user in any major equipment agreement, but they are particularly valuable in a used equipment context, where the age and relative condition of the equipment create a higher risk of postacceptance failure. Rental or lease credit provisions, such as those employed in new equipment transactions, can sometimes be tailored to a used equipment environment. Where the equipment is being acquired from the original equipment manufacturer, or from a substantial dealer, it may be practicable to include a provision requiring the vendor to repair or replace the equipment at no charge to the user if the continuing performance standard specified in the agreement is not met over a period of time. (The key in this regard, of course, is to ensure that the vendor involved has the capacity to replace or repair the equipment if called upon to do so.) In other instances, the user may be able to back the continuing performance standard with a performance bond, letter of credit, or guaranty, as suggested above. However, the most likely method of supporting a continuing performance standard is to place a portion of the purchase price in escrow for the duration of the performance period (for example, twelve months). Ideally, the escrowed funds should be handled by an independent escrow agent charged with distributing the funds to repair any equipment defects.

Documenting the Rights to Move and Transfer

In addition to covering the availability of software and maintenance for the used equipment being acquired, the user should also document various other areas where the original manufacturer may be able to condition or preclude the sale, lease, or other transfer of the system to the user. Many manufacturer/user agreements give the manufacturer considerable control over all nonhardware "products" sold, licensed, or leased to the original user. In addition, such agreements often grant the manufacturer indirect control over the hardware itself. In order to preclude later problems with the manufacturer, including the imposition of unexpected costs at a subsequent date, the user acquiring used equipment should consider and document the areas noted below.

First, the user should ensure that the disposing user has the right to move the equipment. Some manufacturer, lessor, and other vendor agreements state that the equipment may not be moved without the prior written consent of the vendor. (This condition is sometimes imposed in software, maintenance, and documentation agreements and provisions, in addition to or in lieu of hardware contracts.)

Second, the user should ensure that it can and will legally obtain all relevant documentation relating to the equipment being acquired. Again, some vendor agreements preclude or condition the transfer of such material, or do so if the transfer involves duplication of the documentation.

Third, the user should review the contract, lease, or other documentation covering the original acquisition of the equipment by the disposing user in order to determine: (1) whether any other conditions exist that might preclude, or increase the cost of, the transfer of the equipment to the acquiring user; and (2) whether any benefits exist that can or should be transferred to the acquiring user. Benefits are most likely to be available if the used equipment transfer will involve the assignment or sublease of an existing contract or lease with the manufacturer or other original vendor. However, warranties, lease or rental credits, and other continuing performance provisions may be available and transferable in other situations as well.

Fourth, the user should require the disposing user and any intervening broker or dealer to represent and warrant that: (1) They have complied with any and all terms and conditions of any agreement or license with the manufacturer (or other applicable vendor) relating to, precluding, or affecting the assignment, sublease, or other transfer and relocation of the used equipment (including such enumerated items as hardware, software, and documentation) to the acquiring user; and (2) the equipment (including the enumerated items noted above) can be so assigned, subleased, or transferred and relocated to the user without payment by the user of any penalties, charges, or fees to the manufacturer other than certain amounts that may be specified in the agreement. In this regard, the acquiring user may require that copies of all approvals and consents be attached to the used equipment agreement as exhibits.

Fifth, the user should obtain an estoppel letter or other written consent from the equipment manufacturer agreeing that the equipment may be assigned, subleased, or transferred and relocated, as described above, without penalty or additional charge (except as may be specifically identified). Ideally, this commitment should be included in a general services or support agreement between the acquiring user and the manufacturer, in order to ensure valid consideration and proper privity between the parties. However, the acquiring user may elect to require the disposing user or intervening broker, dealer, or lessor to provide an estoppel letter from the equipment manufacturer as part of the disposing user's (or other vendor's) obligations under the used equipment agreement. Where an assignment or sublease is involved, the acquiring user should obtain the written consent of the manufacturer, lessor, or other party agreeing to the transaction. In some situations, it may be prudent for the acquiring user to execute a novation agreement with the manufacturer, thereby releasing the prior user from its obligations under the original document and giving the acquiring user privity with the manufacturer or other original vendor. The user's counsel can generally advise when and if a novation agreement is preferable to an assignment or sublease.

10
THIRD-PARTY LEASING

Third-party leasing offers significant advantages to many users. Like a challenging golf course, however, leasing has its share of sand traps. Indeed, some lessees begin to think that even the "fairways" of the leasing game bear striking resemblance to the Great American Desert. Even when an oasis begins to appear (compliments of the lessor's marketing representative), it often turns out to be a mirage—after the contract has been signed.

Things don't have to be like this if the user is willing to spend the time and resources necessary to analyze the leasing transaction and tailor the deal to the user's specific business objectives. This chapter is designed to provide an overview of some of the methods of maximizing user protection in a third-party leasing environment. The discussion assumes that the user has already selected a vendor and equipment appropriate to its needs, and that the user has decided to utilize some type of third-party lease for at least part of the acquisition. In practice, of course, the user will probably spend countless man-hours evaluating the relative advantages and disadvantages of various vendors, systems, and acquisition methods.

The first portion of this chapter tackles the question of how to select a third-party leasing company—and how to ensure a healthy degree of competition among potential lessors. After setting the state in this manner, subsequent pages zero in on some of the specific considerations that may affect an optimum user-oriented third-party lease. One word of caution should be mentioned: third-party lease financing is an extremely complex undertaking. Great care must be taken to ensure that all aspects of the transaction, whether financial, tax, legal, or business, are properly assessed and negotiated. The best safeguard against the many pitfalls is to secure appropriate professional assistance at the outset of the negotiations. In this regard, one of the best available resource materials on third-party leasing is a text entitled *Legal and Financial Aspects of Equipment Leasing Transactions,* by Richard M. Contino (Englewood Cliffs, NJ: Prentice-Hall, Inc., 1979). No user negotiating team should engage in any leasing transaction without utilizing this treatise as its bible.

VENDOR SELECTION

Selecting a third-party leasing company can be almost as difficult—and as critical—as selecting the equipment itself. Unfortunately, many users do not devote adequate time or resources to selecting the leasing company. As a result, some of these users select firms that do not have the capital, expertise, or business flexibility necessary to optimize the user's transaction. Other users select a "big name" leasing firm that has excellent talent and financial resources; however, in the process these users pay considerably more than they might have if they had considered a more aggressive, but less well-known, lessor.

These problems can be avoided, or at least minimized, by analyzing the qualifications of each potential leasing company well in advance of the negotiations. Ideally, only well-qualified firms should be invited to bid on the user's request for proposal. Practially, however, it can be advantageous to permit less-qualified firms to bid, provided their strengths and weaknesses have been carefully examined.

Although the lessor qualification requirements will vary somewhat among users and among transactions, the following factors should be considered in analyzing any third-party leasing company.

Determining Whether the Lessor Has the Ability to Provide the Financing

The leasing company should either have the equity capital for the system, or the proven ability to raise the equity capital promptly through committed investors. If the lease is to be "leveraged" with third-party debt, the leasing company must have the necessary contacts and expertise to obtain the debt financing at an acceptable interest rate and within the desired time frame.

Regardless of the attractiveness of the "deal" from a financial standpoint, the user will have nothing but trouble (and perhaps wind up having its equipment "repossessed") if the lessor is unable to obtain the necessary financing. Although the user's credit rating may be critical here, the financial standing and experience of the leasing company are also important.

Determining Whether the Lessor Has Staying Power

The leasing company should have the financial stability to remain in business for at least the term of the lease, including the renewal period. The lessor's ability to perform during the lease term can be very important. If the lessor goes out of business, the generous upgrade and trade-in provisions in the lease may become meaningless. Other lease obligations imposed on the lessor may also become unenforceable. Without backup support for a lessor's performance obligations, the user can find itself in difficulty.

Probably the best measures of the necessary financial stability are the lessor's earnings history and management expertise. To be sure, negotiating with a lessor that enjoys almost unconscionable profit levels may be somewhat challenging. But an extremely profitable lessor may be a sound contractual partner, assuming that the lessor's profits were honestly earned and that the user is able to negotiate a favorable transaction. On the other hand, an overly aggressive leasing company that readily gives out deals that are "too good to be true" may not have a particularly long life expectancy—and, as a result, the deal that seemed too good to be true may end up being exactly that.

The prudent user will ask for copies of the lessor's financial statements and appropriate bank references. Where large public leasing companies are involved, the user should obtain copies of the firm's annual and quarterly reports to shareholders, and Form 10-K and 10-Q reports to the Securities and Exchange Commission. Management quality should also be analyzed, using these reports and individual resumes for source material.

Determining Whether the Lessor Has the Proven Experience and Expertise Necessary to Meet the User's Needs

The principals and representatives of the leasing company should have the expertise necessary to deal with the user's specific business and financial needs. For example, a lessor with a fine track record on small transactions may or may not be able to handle a large transaction involving multiple systems and sites. The small firm, however, may be able to furnish more customized service and advice on a large or small acquisition. On the other hand, the complexities and financial requirements of the transaction may mandate use of a large, sophisticated lessor.

Some leasing firms may offer special expertise in dealing with the practical and regulatory problems involved in the user's business. Other firms may have little experience with the user's business but, alternatively, may have superior abilities to package and optimize the financial side of the transaction. One group of companies may specialize in simplifying the transaction for the user that has little or no experience in third-party leasing ("one stop shopping"). Another group of firms may handle only the most complex transactions.

The key is to objectively select a lessor that meets the user's special interests and needs. (Note the word "objectively." This selection criterion requires an objective assessment of the lessor's credentials and special abilities, not a biased prejudgment based upon "gut reaction" and the warmth of the salesman's "relationship.") The best protection in this area is to obtain a client list from the potential lessor. Although the lessor will tend to give out "favorable" references, each reference should be contacted, not merely to obtain a general favorable/unfavorable reaction but also to receive comments on the lessor's strengths and weaknesses in areas that are particularly important to the user. Where possible, the user should make special efforts to obtain comments from other users in the same industry that have acquired similar systems through similar transactions.

Determining Whether the Lessor's Business Approach is Compatible With the User's Needs

The lessor must be willing to do business in a manner that will enhance the user's management objectives and operating needs. For example, some lessors will not offer competitive one- or two-year leases. Quite clearly, the user that requires this type of lease should not waste time negotiating with firms that only offer five- to seven-year leases. Other lessors specialize in larger systems. If the user even conceptually anticipates adding or swapping out components during the lease term, it should not seriously consider leasing from a lessor that finds such small additions and deletions to be an unprofitable annoyance. On the other hand, a user that does not require that type of flexibility may be able to save money by engaging a lessor with more restrictive standards.

The leasing company should also be willing and able to design a lease agreement and payment stream that will meet the user's specific requirements. A lessor that does not have the ability to offer a number of payment alternatives, including step payment programs and the like, may not be capable of meeting the user's income and financial statement goals. Perhaps more importantly, the lessor's inability to offer this type of flexibility may be indicative of other deficiencies in expertise or innovation.

The lessor should also be willing to negotiate appropriate changes in its standard lease form. Virtually without exception, standard lessor and lender lease financing forms are drafted to maximize the protection afforded to those parties and, as a result, the protection afforded to the user is minimized. This type of drafting is perfectly acceptable legal practice, assuming the user makes the changes necessary to equalize the transaction and protect the user's interest. Most form documents, particularly third-party leases, need to be tailored to the individual transaction in order to reflect the agreements involved and protect the interests of all the parties.

In most situations, a user should simply refuse to do business with a leasing company that insists upon using its standard documents and no others. Any exceptions to this user policy should be made only after detailed review of the lessor's documents by the user's attorneys, accountants, and operations executives. (In fairness, it should be noted that the financing required for most third-party leases mandates that the lease documents be acceptable to any lending institution involved. Although less flexibility may be available with respect to certain forms and provisions that are critical to protect the lender's interest, even here negotiations are possible and, indeed, may be advisable to protect the user's interest.)

Assessing Whether a Broker Is Also Involved

The user should determine at the outset whether it will be dealing directly with the leasing company as a "principal" or with a "broker." In many situations the prospective entity offering to put the lease financing together may look like a principal lessor; that is, it may be called the "XYZ Leasing Company," but in actuality it may be a broker. In other words, the XYZ Leasing Company may merely intend to locate a "regular" leasing company or other interested party to purchase the desired equipment and lease it to the user. Depending upon the user's circumstances, the interposition of an independent broker between the user and the actual lessor may only add to the cost and the negotiating problems involved in the transaction. An independent broker may have little incentive to provide assistance once the lease is signed and his or her fee is paid. Yet the broker may add indirect fees and expenses to the proposal, increase possibilities for misunderstandings, and create time delays. On the other hand, a competent independent broker may provide valuable technical or financial assistance and free the user's executives for other responsibilities. The broker may also be able to locate necessary equipment that cannot be made available through any other source. (Since the adoption of the Economic Recovery Tax Act of 1981, more and more firms have entered the brokerage side of the equipment leasing business—principally to assist in designing programs to transfer ITC and other tax benefits from one company to another. As a result of the 1981 Tax Act, a larger number of business corporations with operations in other areas can be expected to serve as equipment lessors, in order to obtain ITC and other tax benefits, with or without the assistance of a broker intermediary.)

Where the services of a broker are desired, the user should also consider whether the assistance could be better provided by the leasing company itself. Some lessors maintain significant in-house inventories and offer "full-service" broker/dealer/lessor programs. Other lessors offer brokerage activities, but do not maintain equipment inventories. Still other lessors avoid both broker and dealer services and rely almost entirely upon established brokers, dealers, and manufacturers as equipment sources. As suggested earlier, the user should select the type of lessor most capable of meeting the user's special needs in a given transaction.

Maximizing Competition

Regardless of whether brokerage services are necessary, the user should talk with a number of alternative third-party leasing sources. The keys to success at this stage of the acquisition process are to evaluate available leasing sources and maximize competition.

During the user's evaluation process, the various leasing sources are likely to quote a variety of interest or lease rates and some users may be tempted to terminate discussions with those firms quoting higher rates. Nevertheless, at this stage the user must avoid any temptation to let such tentative rates influence the selection of potential lessors. In many instances, the overall quality and financial stability of the leasing company and the substance of the transaction will be more critical (or sensitive) to the user in the long-run than a minor savings in interest rate. Perhaps more importantly, interest or lease rates quoted at an early stage of the proceedings often have a habit of changing rather substantially before the deal is closed. Whether quoted as "firm" or "tentative," particularly low rates often increase significantly as the other "higher rate" competition is eliminated from consideration by the user. On the other hand, high initial rates sometimes decline as the various leasing companies attempt to meet the competition. Of course, changing economic conditions can also influence rates as negotiations progress.

Dealing with a number of leasing companies can be a time consuming and frustrating task for the user's executives, lawyers, and accountants—particularly when lending interest rates start changing overnight. However, whether outside assistance is utilized at this stage or not, the expenditure of time and resources necessary to properly evaluate the available leasing sources should be viewed as a mandatory and valuable part of the acquisition process.

FINANCIAL CONSIDERATIONS

Because most users view third-party leases as alternative methods of financing an equipment acquisition, the financial aspects of the transaction should be considered at an early stage in the acquisition process. Through step-payment and other plans, lease transactions offer a great deal of financial flexibility.

At the outset, the user should ensure that the "lease" documents accurately reflect the type of legal, tax, and accounting transaction desired by the user. To put it mildly, the fact that the parties agree to provide equipment to the user and call the transaction a "lease" is not binding for tax, accounting, or SEC reporting purposes. Rather "substance" prevails over "form." And the "substance" of the transaction depends upon a number of critical factors that must be weighed individually and collectively by the user's attorneys and accountants. (A detailed analysis of these factors is beyond the scope of this text.)

Once the user has reviewed its budgeting goals and restraints and analyzed the desired "substance" of the lease, it should consider the following financially related issues.

Reviewing Other Acquisition Methods

Perhaps the most basic financial consideration is whether all components of a system should be placed on the lease. Most users should undertake a lease-versus-rental analysis on different components of the system. (See Fig. 4-5.) In some cases it may be advantageous to use a third-party lease to acquire some items of equipment—like a central processor—but a rental agreement to acquire other components—such as disk drives—directly from the vendor. The user's operations division should perform an evaluation to determine which components are likely to be replaced or upgraded during the term of the lease. The flexibility and costs involved in the upgrading or trade-in provision of the lease can then be compared to the corresponding flexibility and cost in the rental approach. Rentals may be particularly advisable where the state of the art in the component is undergoing rapid change or the user anticipates other reasons for a swap-out at an early date. Some users may find it advantageous to purchase selected components outright, while placing others on a third-party lease, and renting the remainder. This approach can also create problems for some users, and each potential situation must be carefully evaluated to determine the viability of a particular combination in the context of the user's needs.

Including Software and Services

Another item that deserves careful review concerns software and services expenses that may be included in the amount being "financed" under the lease. In some instances, a user may have no objection to—and may, in fact, be interested in—including these costs in the total amount financed under a third-party lease. Indeed, the user may achieve a cash flow advantage by following this practice, assuming the technique does not create tax problems. Where "firmware" is involved, including such costs in the lease financing may seem to be the only logical alternative for many users. Other users may prefer to pay cash for software and services as they receive them. Disregarding any special cash flow considerations, the long-term lease financing of non-capital items may be an expensive and unnecessary practice. In either event, however, the user should ensure that the lease agreement clearly indicates whether any software or service dollars are included and, if so, accurately defines the quality and extent of these services.

Including an Unamortized Balance

If the lease involves a trade-in or an upgrade of equipment, the user should determine whether any unamortized balance on the old hardware should be rolled forward into the new lease or paid off in cash. In terms of total cash outlay, many users find it advantageous to pay off the unamortized balance on the spot. This is due to interest costs and the fact that, downstream in the lease, the unamortized balance on the old equipment simply adds to the unamortized balance on the new equipment and the user may later on end up owing considerably more than the components are worth. On the other hand, some users prefer to include the unamortized balance in the new lease, generally for purposes of improving cash flow or maximizing current earnings.

Evaluating the Lease "Price"

Negotiating the financial aspects of an equipment purchase is a difficult task in itself. But the financial side of an acquisition involving a third-party lease can make the straight purchase transaction seem like child's play. A major problem when a third-party lease is involved is the user's inability to decipher and correctly analyze the financial terms proposed by the third-party lessor. In essence, the user often has no way of knowing whether the proposal offered by the lessor and, indirectly, by the manufacturer is good or bad.

The best protection in this area begins with recognition of some of the more popular financial ploys used in the third-party leasing arena. Not all third-party lessors engage in these practices, but many are widespread. The user should be particularly alert to these and other vendor efforts if the third-party lessor and the manufacturer have maintained a "warm working relationship" for a period of years. Although such a close relationship can facilitate the user's acquisition, there is a chance that the marketing representatives from the two firms have devised a variety of deceptive (or at best misleading) sales practices during previous transactions. Several of the more frequently used vendor techniques are discussed below.

The most popular trick is very simple. The manufacturer and lessor salesmen represent that the system is being sold to the lessor (for lease to the user) at one price—say $1.6 million—when it is actually being sold for a lower price—perhaps $1.5 million. The interest rate on the transaction, however, is calculated on the higher price rather than the actual price. The user's comptroller checks the figures and sees the rate is, in fact, fair and competitive—assuming the lessor's purchase price is $1.6 million. The only problem is that the rate should only be charged on the actual price of $1.5 million, not on the higher price. And, of course, the user is also paying an "extra" $100,000 for the system.

Several variations of this ploy also exist. For example, the lessor may offer to roll the unamortized cost of the user's existing leased equipment into the new transaction at a substantial savings over the termination penalty shown in the user's present lease. Alternatively, the lessor and manufacturer may offer to ease the transition into the lease by taking the user's present rental equipment "off rent" for several months. In both situations, the user's financial people or top management may approve this approach because of its favorable impact on the user's cash flow.

In many cases, those supposedly "free" dollars may actually be right there in the new lease too. When this happens, the lessor and the manufacturer simply come up with two sets of numbers—one for the user's use and one for theirs. The user firmly believes the lessor is buying the system for $1.6 million and "giving" the user a concession worth $100,000 (the savings over the termination penalty or the off-rent savings, for example). In fact, however, the lessor is paying the manufacturer $1.5 million and simply adding the "free" $100,000 into the lease, bringing the total amount financed under the lease agreements to $1.6 million.

The scheme can favor the manufacturer, too. For example, the difference between the false $1.6 million price and the lessor's actual $1.5 million price can be used to hide $100,000 of manufacturer services in the amount financed under the lease. The user still believes that the system is costing $1.6 million. The manufacturer's salesman, however, is enjoying the commission or "points" associated with the sale of the services. Interestingly, the manufacturer's salesman may turn around and convince the user that, because the user's business is so valued, the vendor is offering the user $100,000 of "free" support services.

The key, of course, in all these variations is the difference between the actual price of $1.5 million and the false price of $1.6 million. The "slush fund" that results can be used to benefit the manufacturer or the lessor, or both. In fact, when that "warm relationship" exists, the lessor's and manufacturer's salesmen may alternate deals, with one party taking the hidden benefits in this deal and the other getting the break in the next transaction.

There are a few affirmative defenses that can reduce the user's risk in this area. First, the user should let the lessor and manufacturer know that the user will expect to receive a copy of the executed purchase contract between the two parties. This won't guarantee protection, of course, because kickbacks and credits outside the contract are possible. But it may help keep some marginal salesmen honest—or force the "funny numbers" into a kickback format (interesting federal tax questions and risks arise when the contract shows one price, for user consumption and ITC purposes, but the "actual" price paid by the lessor is less).

Second, the user should learn all it can about the current selling price for the system it is about to lease. (This is considerably easier for new equipment than for used.) The user can contact other customers and friends in the applicable user's group and discuss alternative proposals with brokers and professional negotiators. If the price to be paid by the lessor is more than the best price available (that is, at less than the maximum discount), the user should obviously start trying to figure out why.

Third, if the user is being offered "free concessions," it should ask whether all or part of the cost of these concessions (retail or "wholesale") is being hidden in the total amount being financed under the lease. In effective equipment negotiations, the user can occasionally get something for nothing. However, it must always take extra steps to ensure that its "gifts" really are free.

Fourth, the user should do its best to "break the deal apart." The lessor should be asked to explain every dollar of the amounts included in the lease. The user must go over the transaction again and again. This often-difficult exercise has two important goals. First, it may let the user uncover a supposed "freebie" that has been incorporated into the lease costs. Second, it may cause the user to realize that it is lease financing some items—such as support services—that it would prefer to pay for in cash as the services are provided.

Finally—and perhaps most basically—the user should not believe everything the lessor (or the manufacturer) tells it. The user must have a healthy skepticism and demand numerical proof rather than grammatical reassurance. Despite the user's long-standing "relationship" with the lessor's or manufacturer's local salesman, the user must recognize that third-party lease transactions offer an excellent opportunity for hidden profits. The user should have no objection to the lessor making a reasonable return—but it should strive to preclude an unreasonable profit at the user's expense—especially if the profit results from misrepresentations that the user failed to perceive.

Avoiding the "Annuity Switch Game"

One of the more subtle financial ploys used by some vendors is the "annuity switch game." The full impact of this financial manipulation can best be appreciated by reviewing an actual negotiating situation in which this factor became a point of controversy.

In this particular negotiation, the user had appropriately pressed the lessor to break out the financial aspects of the lease in terms of the lessor's acquisition cost, the annual percentage rates on equity and senior debt funds, the lessor's residual position at the end of the initial lease term, the lessee's actual amount to be financed, and the like. As a result of this discussion, the "effective annual percentage rate" on the amount to be financed soon became a topic of discussion.

After the effective rate had been determined, the financial negotiations continued in an open and straightforward manner.

When it came time to run the final numbers for the execution copies of the acquisition documents, both sides ran a calculation for the monthly payment. Both negotiators used the same present value amount, interest rate, and term. However, each negotiator obtained a different monthly payment.

The payment calculated by the lessor was higher, as might be expected. Both parties then reran the numbers, carefully entering each figure into their respective calculators. The results were the same as before: The lessor's payment was higher. At this point, the lessor's marketing representative borrowed the calculator from the lessee's negotiator and reran the figures in plain view of everyone to prove that the lessee's negotiator had made a mistake somewhere down the line. Interestingly, the lessor's representative came up with the same payment calculated by the lessee's negotiator. At this juncture, the lessor's salesman was temporarily at a loss for words.

The lessee's professional negotiator carefully reacted by appearing defensive and confused. He suggested that perhaps the parties should review the entire deal in an effort to locate the problem. This approach—often known as giving the opponent enough rope to hang himself—was used in order to prevent the lessor's representative from being able to "explain away" the discrepancy in payments later in the negotiating session. In pursuit of this goal, the lessee's negotiator routinely replayed the basic ingredients of the deal, waiting for positive reinforcement on each point from the lessor's representative:

"The term is 84 months, right?"

"Right."

"The amount to be financed is $2.1 million, check?"

"Check."

"Your effective annual percentage rate is eight percent (8%), right?"

"Absolutely."

The lessee's negotiator then went off on an apparent tangent by expressing strong doubt that the lessor could actually perform with an eight percent (8%) annual rate. The reaction by the lessor's salesman was exactly as planned: he countered with strong reassurances of the lessor's ability to live with the eight percent (8%) rate.

To allow the lessor to save face during the coming events, the lessee's negotiator suggested he and the lessor take a walk away and have a little "informal communication." Once away from the formal negotiating session, the lessee's negotiator explained the Annuity Switch feature of his calculator to the lessor. (On the calculator involved, with the Annuity Switch set in the "BEGIN" position, the calculator would automatically calculate monthly payments for an "annuity due," i.e., payments in advance, the type of payment arrangement contemplated.)

The lessee's negotiator then demonstrated how the payment difference occurred by putting his Annuity Switch to "END," which permitted calculation of monthly payments for an ordinary annuity (or payments in arrears). The negotiator explained that, with the switch in this position, he could come up with exactly the same payments that the lessor came up with on his calculator, which did not have an Annuity Switch—its "automatic" payment calculations were done only for payments in arrears.

The lessor backpedaled by saying his management had approved the "monthly multiplier" that determined the monthly payments, as presented, and he did not have the authority to "cut the rate." The lessee's negotiator at this time reminded the lessor's negotiator of his strong reaffirmation of the annual percentage rate that was just made in the formal session and suggested that any reneging at this time could "blow the deal." The lessor's negotiator reacted by immediately calling his company, apparently advising them of the new events. After completing the call, he came back with a very honest statement: "You know, I've been in the leasing business a long time; I have placed major deals with primarily Fortune 500 companies, and no one has ever caught the payment in advance, payment in arrears subtlety, probably because I didn't realize that I was unknowingly charging too much for this type of transaction. No wonder our company's profits are looking so good."

The lessor's marketing representative then elected to return to the formal session, apologize for the minor discrepancy, and provide the lessee with the lower payment amount.

How significant was the difference? A look at some real numbers suggests the dollars that might have been left on the table by an unsophisticated lessee. Taking an 84 month term lease with an amount to be financed of $2.1 million, at 8 percent (8%), and calculating the monthly payment as an ordinary annuity (with the Annuity Switch in the "END" position), the monthly payment would be $32,731. Using the same term, the same amount to be financed, and the same interest rate, but running the calculations for an "annuity due," which is the case with a normal third-party lease requiring monthly payments in advance (with the Annuity Switch in the "BEGIN" position), the monthly payments become $32,514 a month. The difference in the switch is a savings of $217 a month for 84 months. The raw dollar savings amount to $18,228 (84 × $217). If the user were to invest that $217 per month for 84 months at an internal rate of return of ten percent (10%), it would end up with $26,464 in its pocket, instead of the lessor's pocket.

Avoiding "Precommencement Rental Days"

Some lessor salesmen candidly admit that they make their entire commission from a seldom-recognized technique that involves something known as "precommencement rental days." To fully appreciate the way this lessor technique is implemented, the user should consider the following contractual language taken from a lessor form agreement. The user should recognize that it may be easier to catch the problem language in this controlled environment than in an actual acquisition. Here, the user is aware that the provision contains something unusual to look for. In addition, the particular language is not part of a "boiler plate" provision in a lengthy, printed lease document that contains even more onerous language (that normally tends to divert attention from seemingly innocuous areas of the agreement):

2. ADDITIONAL DEFINITIONS:

(a) The "Installation Date" means, as to the Equipment designated on any Equipment Schedule, the date specified as the Installation Date in such Schedule, or if no such date is so specified, the date which is determined by the manufacturer of the Equipment or other organization designated by lessor, in writing, to install the Equipment ("Maintenance Organization") to be the date of installation of such Equipment.

(b) The "Commencement Date" means, as to the Equipment designated on any Equipment Schedule, where the Installation Date for such Equipment falls on the first day of the month, that date, and, in any other case, the first day of the month following the month in which such Installation Date falls.

3. TERM OF LEASE:

(a) The term of this Agreement, as to all Equipment designated on any Equipment Schedule, shall commence on the Installation Date for such Equipment, and shall continue for an initial period ending that number of months from the applicable Commencement Date as is specified on such Equipment Schedule (the "Initial Period"); thereafter, the term of this Agreement for all such Equipment shall be automatically extended for successive three-month periods unless and until terminated by either party giving to the other not less than six months' prior written notice. Any such termination shall be effective only on the last day of the Initial Period or the last day of any such successive periods.

(b) Notwithstanding any right lessee may have to terminate any Equipment Schedule under any provision thereof or Rider thereto, during the Initial Period specified in such Equipment Schedule, lessee agrees that it shall not terminate this Agreement as to any Equipment Schedule during said Initial Period for the purpose or with the intent of replacing the Equipment described on such Schedule with other equipment of the same type.

(c) Any notice of termination given by either party under Paragraph 3(a) or under any Supplement annexed hereto may not be revoked without the written consent of the other party.

4. RENTAL:

As to all Equipment, the monthly rental payable by lessee to lessor is as set forth in the applicable Schedule. Rental shall begin on the first day of each month. If the Installation Date does not fall on the first day of a month, the first payment shall be a pro-rata portion of the monthly rental, calculated on a 30-day basis, due and payable on the Installation Date. In addition to the monthly rental set forth in the Schedule, lessee shall pay to lessor an amount equal to all taxes paid, payable or required to be collected by lessor, however designated, which are levied or based on such rental, on this Agreement, or on the Equipment or its use, lease, operation, control or value, including, without limitation, state and local privilege or excise taxes based on gross revenue, any penalties or interest in connection therewith or taxes or amounts in lieu thereof paid or payable by lessor in respect of the foregoing, but excluding taxes based on lessor's net income. Personal property taxes on the Equipment shall be paid by lessee. Lessee agrees to file, in behalf of lessor, all required property tax returns and reports concerning the Equipment with all appropriate governmental agencies, and, within not more than 45 days after the due date of such filing, to send lessor confirmation of such filing. Interest on any past-due payments shall accrue at the rate of 1% per month, or if such rate shall exceed the maximum rate allowed by law, then at such maximum rate, and shall be payable on demand. Charges for taxes, penalties and interest shall be promptly paid by lessee when invoiced by lessor.

In considering the above language, pay particular attention to the provisions dealing with the "Installation Date," "Commencement Date," "Term," and "Rental." Ignoring the unusual possibility that the equipment will be installed on the first day of a month, when do rental payments begin? When does the term ("Initial Period") begin? How many full payments are made? How many pro-rata payments? How does the pro-rata payment relate to the full payments?

Before pursuing the point further, remember that a third-party leveraged lease is basically a type of financing instrument that allows a user to "purchase" (actually, "use") equipment with someone else's money. A third-party lease is ordinarily longer than a rental agreement, normally is less expensive, and does not involve a payment for overtime use.

Assuming that the lease can be treated as such under appropriate accounting principles, "usage" of the system does not necessarily equate to the making of "payments." That is, the financing of the equipment will be spread over a given term at a specified interest rate (step-payment schemes are often popular), regardless of whether the user has access to the equipment—even though in practice the user prefers to match the total payment period to the total usage period.

The basic problem with the lease provision reprinted above is that it includes a period of "precommencement rental days." The "financing" period of the lease is the term of the "Initial Period" referred to in Section 3(a). In essence, the cost of the equipment is "financed" over this period. However, the lessor also collects one extra pro-rata payment if the Installation Date does not fall on the first day of a month. (First-day-of-the-month installations are a rare occurrence—perhaps due to chance, perhaps due to design.)

For example, if the Installation Date falls on the second day of the month, the pro-rata payment covers 29 days. Consequently, the lessee pays (for example) 60 full payments and one pro-rata payment only slightly less than a full payment—in essence 61 payments. The "financing," however, has been analyzed on the basis of 60 payments.

Of course, the pro-rata payment gets smaller as the Installation Date occurs later in the month. But the point is that the user/lessee still leaves from one to thirty days of payment dollars on the table. (Incidentally, some interesting and subtle lessor ploys can come into play here. By manipulating the Installation Date and Commencement Date, the lessor can appear to offer the user, for example, a week's free "usage," only to collect a pro-rata payment for almost three weeks time in return.)

If the pro-rata payment is not part of the lease "financing" (and in most situations it is not), it flows through as "extra" income to the lessor. Indeed, the amount of this payment can provide a significant boost to a lessor in an otherwise highly competitive transaction.

Most users simply miss this point completely. Other users question the purpose of the pro-rata payment, but acquiesce when the lessor presents a "reasonable" explanation. In most situations, the lessor explains that the pro-rata payment is to cover the lessee's use of the system between the Installation Date and the Commencement Date (when the first full rental payment is generally due).

The problem is that the lessor is trying to have the user to equate "usage" with the making of "payments" in a financing lease context. The lessor's approach would be fine in a rental agreement. Indeed, the pro-rata payment would even be acceptable in a third-party lease if the payment was included in calculating the payment/financing stream under the lease. In most situations, though, the pro-rata payment is flowing straight through to the lessor's bottom line. From the user's standpoint, the key test should be whether the pro-rata payment consists of part of the payment/financing stream or merely an extra (and "unjustified") usage payment to the lessor. The user's financial officers and accountants can analyze this situation quite easily.

In all fairness, it should be noted that this extra "precommencement" payment can be important to the lessor. Although the user has every right (indeed, every obligation) to question this type of payment, the user should be aware that eliminating the amount may cause the lessor to try to change other financial aspects of the transaction in order to achieve the same profit margin or rate of return. The user's duty, of course, is to analyze when such a change is acceptable and when it is not. In essence, this requires that the user engage in the difficult task of evaluating the fairness of the lessor's potential profit. (This thankless task is somewhat easier if alternative bids have been received.)

One final caveat should be noted. Some lessors justify the "precommencement" payment on the ground that it reimburses them for interest and other costs incurred by them between the date they must pay the manufacturer for the system and the date any debt financing for the purchase is advanced by the lender. Although this theory could be true in a particular situation, it is not likely. In many transactions, the lessor does not pay the manufacturer for the equipment until 60 or 90 days after it has been accepted by the lessee. Indeed, because of this fact, the delay between the date the lessee's payments begin and the date the manufacturer is paid by the lessor can be a viable source of interest-related income for the lessor—or an equally viable source of savings for the lessee.

Locking in Money and Interest Rates

In many third-party lease transactions, the lessor borrows a substantial portion (e.g., 60% to 80%) of the purchase price for the equipment from a third-party lender. If the lessor cannot obtain these funds for some reason, or if the funds can only be obtained at a prohibitive interest rate, the lease proposal may be impossible to implement. The user should make every effort to guard against this possibility, and to provide appropriate remedies in the event proper financing cannot be timely arranged. This step is particularly important in an era of rising interest rates and/or tight credit.

When either of these conditions exists, and in other situations where the lessor has low-balled the user on the rental rate, the interest rate on the debt financing portion of the acquisition funds has a remarkable habit of moving upward between the date of the preliminary financial discussions and the date of closing. In some situations, this increase may be virtually impossible to avoid. For example, when interest rates are increasing rapidly in the national money markets, most lessors are likely to insist upon the right to increase the lease or rental rate to compensate for increases in the debt interest rate. Indeed, the user should recognize that permitting this type of increase (provided it is adequately understood and documented) may be essential to the acquisition of any debt financing and, therefore, critical to the viability of the lease transaction itself. In other situations, the increase may be less justified, either because the lessor has intentionally low-balled the initial rate and failed to disclose the likely increases or because the lessor has nudged the final rate due to greed rather than market interest rate factors. In either situation, the user should ensure that the agreement covers this matter in a manner that is fair to the lessor and the lessee. Many third-party leases include a provision that allows the lessor to increase the effective interest rate—and consequently the lease payments—in the event that the debt financing cannot be obtained at the rate specified in the lease. Signing this type of provision is somewhat like signing a blank check, especially if no maximum rate is set by the lease. The lessor can represent that a very favorable rate will be obtained and then face no penalty whatsoever if a substantially higher rate "becomes necessary."

Assuming that a rental adjustment clause is required by all of the leasing companies being considered by the user, the user should at least insist that the provision cut both ways; that is, if a higher interest rate will result in higher lease payments, a lower interest rate should result in lower lease payments.

This type of rate increase provision is often accompanied by a clause allowing the lessor to get out of the lease if the financing cannot be obtained on certain terms. On the other hand, in this type of pro-lessor document, the user has no option to get out and select another leasing company, even though the present lessor may have difficulty arranging financing at anywhere near the proposed rate. Needless to say, where this type of provision is insisted upon by the lessor, the user should require a similar escape clause. Indeed, some type of financing escape provision should probably be included in any third-party lease where any required debt financing has not been firmly arranged, regardless of the "reputation" or past favorable performance of the lessor.

The problems associated with an increased rental rate may be insignificant compared to the havoc that can occur if the lessor fails to obtain any required debt financing, particularly if the entire system is up, running, and fully converted. Technically, if the lessor fails to pay the vendor, the vendor can come in and repossess the equipment. Presumably, most vendors would not take such a step unless all else failed, but the user could be forced into the difficult position of having to choose among raising a substantial amount of cash quickly, hastily obtaining alternative third-party financing (perhaps at a higher interest rate), or negotiating a less-than-acceptable rental or lease arrangement directly with the vendor. (Problems in this area can also create some significant tax difficulties, particularly if the user intended to claim the ITC on the system.) Although these risks may be minimized by doing business with a reputable leasing company, every lease should specifically cover this possibility.

One method of "separating the men from the boys" in this area is to insert a clause in the lease providing for a type of "financing performance bond" or liquidated damages in a meaningful amount in the event the lessor is unable to supply the specified financing within the desired time frame and predetermined maximum rate. At a minimum, the user "escape" clause suggested above should be included in the lease. In addition, the user may wish to require that a firm debt financing "commitment" (from the financial institution that will supply the funds) be attached to the lease prior to its execution by the lessee.

LEGAL CONSIDERATIONS

Like all complex equipment acquisition agreements, third-party leases involve a variety of important legal considerations. Many of the key legal points are similar to those involved in purchase and rental agreements. Other issues are unique to third-party lease agreements. The following section summarizes some of the more important legal considerations involved in third-party lease agreements. (However, the reader should keep in mind that these issues do not represent all of the legal factors that should be documented in a third-party lease transaction. Users should consult their legal counsel for specific advice on these and other areas.)

Reducing Risks from Equipment Failure

One of the user's most serious problems in any third-party lease is how to minimize its risks in the event the leased equipment malfunctions. A perfect solution to this problem is seldom available. However, a number of methods can be used to reduce the user's risks or, at least, minimize its financial exposure.

The available approaches depend upon the type of third-party lease transaction involved. Because of space limitations, the following discussion focuses upon a transaction where a third-party lessor is purchasing new equipment from the manufacturer and leasing that equipment to a user. (Actually, the purchaser may be a group of investors who accept an assignment of the contract to purchase and then lease the system to the third-party leasing company that, in turn, subleases the equipment to the user.) Although some of the suggestions set forth in this discussion may be applicable to other types of third-party lease transactions, other solutions may not be.

In the event the lease is to be structured as a "leveraged" lease (that is, the lessor proposes to put up only a portion of the equipment purchase cost, with the remainder being borrowed from a third-party lender), the third-party lessor must ensure that the flow of lease payments (which will be assigned to the lender) will continue to be made regardless of whether the user/lessee may have a claim against the lessor or the manufacturer (e.g., if the equipment malfunctions).

The key point for the user to remember in this area is to avoid demanding a provision that will be rejected out of hand by the lender providing the financing. The bank wants a clean, uninterruptible stream of payments. Although it might in theory agree to look to the lessor (rather than the user) for those payments if the equipment malfunctions, few lessors have a financial position that will enable them to satisfy the payments on one lease, not to mention dozens of leases, and, therefore, this type of arrangement is unlikely to be acceptable to the lender. Moreover, when it extends its loan, the lender is generally relying on the credit of the user, not the lessor. Consequently, most banks will not accept this alternative.

Given the fact that the lender will usually demand a clean payment stream, the user's efforts should be directed toward the other two primary participants in the transaction: the lessor and the manufacturer. Both of these parties stand to gain substantially if the lease agreement is executed and both can be expected to make realistic concessions to induce the user to sign the agreement. The goal should be to cause these parties to agree to one or more provisions that will give them a significant incentive to make the system perform at acceptable levels throughout the lease term.

Getting the Manufacturer Involved. Many users overlook the fact that concessions can be obtained from the manufacturer in a third-party lease transaction. Three approaches are usually available.

First, and probably most desirable, the user can contract directly with the manufacturer pursuant to a purchase contract and any related agreements (e.g., maintenance). These documents can and should contain all manufacturer warranties and commitments to the user (see below). Once this agreement is executed, the right to buy included in the agreement is assigned to the lessor, which then takes title to the equipment and leases it to the user. This partial assignment is made pursuant to a section of the manufacturer/user agreement that contemplates and approves such an assignment. By treating the lease transaction as just what it is—a type of financed purchase—this approach permits the user to have full "privity of contract" with the manufacturer and to be certain of receiving all manufacturer warranties and commitments. The approach also permits the user to sign the document that specifies the purchase price for the equipment, thereby reducing at least some aspects of the "funny numbers" game described above.

Second, the lessor can execute the purchase agreement with the manufacturer but include in the agreement various representations, warranties, and commitments to be passed on to the user in the lessor/user agreement. In addition, the user can be made a third-party beneficiary under the manufacturer/lessor contract. Where this approach is used, the "pass through" of items to the user should be documented in both the manufacturer/lessor agreement and the lessor/user lease.

Third, the user can enter into a separate agreement with the manufacturer at the time the lease agreement is signed (the "consideration" being the manufacturer's inducement of the user to sign the lease, thereby causing the lessor to buy the equipment from the manufacturer). This agreement can cover a variety of matters, including the degree of support to be provided by the manufacturer if the equipment malfunctions. Similar protection can be incorporated into any maintenance agreement that is signed by the manufacturer and the user. However, the term of any such agreement must be equal to the term of the lease or the protection may not be effective for the full period required. Most manufacturers will not enter into a maintenance agreement for that length of time. Consequently, a separate user-manufacturer agreement may be a more effective vehicle than a maintenance agreement for obtaining this protection.

The following paragraphs summarize several of the more basic provisions that should be included in a separate manufacturer/user agreement. Most of these provisions can also be included, with minor modification, in a manufacturer/user purchase agreement if the user adopts the first approach noted above.

Warranty pass-through. As noted above, the user-manufacturer agreement should provide for the acquiescence by the manufacturer in the pass-through of the manufacturer's equipment warranties from the lessor to the user. Alternatively, the agreement should include a commitment by the manufacturer that the user may claim directly against the manufacturer under its equipment warranties. The user should also be made a third-party beneficiary under the manufacturer-lessor purchase agreement. Some users prefer to be made the lessor's "attorney-in-fact" for purposes of dealing with the manufacturer on warranty matters. (This approach effectively involves the grant of a limited power of attorney in the lease from the lessor to the user, as lessee.)

Maintenance continuity. If desired by the user, the manufacturer should agree to furnish maintenance to the equipment, at the user's request, throughout the term of the lease. Although the user will probably have to agree to price increases during the term, it must be assured that the system will in fact be maintained. (Failure to have the system maintained by the manufacturer may be a user default under the lease.) Careful wording of this provision will include guidelines on the type of maintenance (referencing manufacturer's specifications), the terms and conditions of service, and so on. Maintenance provisions should be meshed with applicable equipment warranties to ensure full protection without unnecessary overlap.

Refurbishment protection. Some maintenance agreements allow the manufacturer, at its discretion, to require that the system be "refurbished" by the manufacturer (usually at an off-site location) at the user's expense. (Certain maintenance agreements cover this indirectly by indicating that the system will be maintained according to the vendor's "then-existing policies.") Needless to say, this possibility presents a serious risk to a user under a third-party lease. Consequently, the user-manufacturer agreement should include a warranty by the manufacturer that no refurbishment will be required during the term of the lease or, if refurbishment is required, it will be performed at the manufacturer's expense. Where possible, this provision should also require that the manufacturer limit the usage interference caused by the refurbishment. For example, the manufacturer might agree to supply an equal system during refurbishment, perform the refurbishment at the user's site, or simply replace any component requiring refurbishment. (Particularly where the user will claim the ITC or where the user might indemnify the lessor for tax losses, the user's tax counsel should review the tax impact of any potential replacement.) Regardless of the approach employed, the user should ensure that the maintenance agreement language is not inconsistent with this provision.

Lemon replacement or refurbishment; maintenance credit. Although the necessary standards are sometimes difficult to articulate, the agreement should provide for refurbishment—or better, replacement—of the system or an applicable component, if the system or component experiences a given failure level. Although this concession may be more likely to come from the manufacturer than from the lessor, the lessor may be willing to agree to some variation of this provision (particularly if the lessor has a strong relationship with the manufacturer). Standards based upon manufacturer's specifications, hours of downtime, or the original acceptance test criteria (see below) may be used in this provision. In all fairness to the manufacturer, an objective, quantifiable standard should be used. As noted above, tax counsel should review the tax impact of any equipment replacement.

A similar approach can be used to require the manufacturer to provide a credit against maintenance payments if the system is not able to meet specified standards over delineated periods. This approach is probably more feasible (but less desirable) in most cases than requiring the manufacturer to pay a portion of the lease payment in the event of continued malfunction.

Reduced limitations on liability. Both the lease and any agreement with the manufacturer will seek to limit the user's recourse against the lessor and the manufacturer. Although third-party lender requirements may create some inflexibility, it may be possible to strip away some of the standard limitations on the liability of the lessor and the manufacturer. This technique will not necessarily ensure that the system will work, but it will increase the user's bargaining power in the event of system failure. Simply put, the lessor or manufacturer will be more willing to go to considerable lengths to cure a problem if it faces an above-average risk of liability. The typical prohibition against the user's claiming consequential damages for equipment problems is difficult to remove from a lease (see Chapter 8), but other liability limitation provisions can generally be productively altered through effective user negotiations.

Maintenance response. Depending upon the user's particular needs, some effort should be made to increase the manufacturer's response under the applicable maintenance agreement. (Because most maintenance agreements can be effectively amended by the manufacturer every twelve months or more often, care should be taken to ensure that this provision will survive for the full term of the lease.) This type of provision might include a requirement that the manufacturer respond to any emergency maintenance call within specified time limits, or that a specified number of maintenance engineers be assigned to the user's site, or that any replacement component be made available at the user's site within eighteen hours after the engineer recommends replacement, and so on.

Getting the Lessor Involved. Many users do not realize that a number of third-party lessors will agree to accept at least some responsibility for excessive equipment failure during the lease term. Although policies vary widely among third-party leasing companies, the more sophisticated leasing firms are generally more likely to seriously consider this type of provision.

Many leasing companies try to convince the user that financing arrangements absolutely preclude the lessor from accepting any liability for inadequate performance. Although there may be a connection between financing and lessor liability, the lessor's marketing representative usually overplays this point in an effort to hide behind protection that actually relates to the lender more than the lessor. As suggested above, the key is to select provisions that will bind the lessor but not adversely affect the bank or other source of lessor financing. The following paragraphs summarize some of the provisions that may be possible to include in the third-party lease agreement between the user and the lessor.

Term extension credit. The lease should include at least some economic incentive for the lessor to cause the equipment to perform satisfactorily. As noted above, any arrangement where the user is able to withhold payments which have been assigned to a lender by the lessor will usually be unacceptable. However, the user may be able to obtain a rental credit that can be applied at the end of the lease, to extend the lease term at no additional charge. For example, if the equipment fails to meet objective criteria for more than a specified period each month, the lease term will automatically be extended by an equal (or greater or lesser, as may be provided) amount of time at no additional rental. Although this term extension is usually less desirable than the lessor's waiving or, in the case of a lease assignment, paying a current lease payment, it may provide at least some long-time economic benefit to the user and serve as an incentive for the lessor to encourage adequate system performance. This type of provision is relatively acceptable to many lessors because it does not require a cash payment or credit by the lessor during the lease term.

Lease payment credit. Although a lease payment provision is considerably more difficult to obtain than the related term extension credit, it may be possible to have the lessor agree to it. In this type of provision, the lessor agrees to pay, or reimburse the user for, an amount equal to some portion of the monthly lease payment if the system fails to meet specified performance criteria during the period. The bank or lease assignee is generally willing to accept this arrangement because the user is still obligated to make the lease payments; the lessor, however, provides a cash credit to the user in the event of excessive malfunction. Needless to say, lessors dislike this type of provision because of the potential cash exposure involved. Some lessors may agree to this type of provision if some limitation is placed on maximum credit payable in any twelve (12) month period or if the credit is based on the maintenance payment rather than the lease payment. From a technical standpoint, any provision of this type will usually be more acceptable under an "operating" lease than under a "finance" lease.

Specification warranty. If the lessor can obtain similar assurances from the manufacturer, the lessor may be willing to warrant that the system will meet manufacturer's specifications during the lease term. Any representation or warranty that the lessor is willing to make strengthens the user's negotiating position in the event of system malfunction. Although the lease payments may still have to be made to the bank or other assignee, the legal exposure faced by the lessor will again provide the desired incentive.

Acceptance. Perhaps the most basic protection against serious later equipment malfunction is a comprehensive acceptance test performed before the user's obligations begin under the lease. Far too many third-party leases do not include an acceptance test or, alternatively, include a test that is woefully inadequate. To be sure, even a comprehensive acceptance test will not guarantee that the equipment will function at a reasonable level for the entire lease term. However, the lack of an adequate acceptance test significantly increases the risk that the equipment will not be fully debugged initially and that extensive problems will occur throughout the lease period.

The acceptance test problem is particularly acute in the third-party leasing context because of the division of interests inherent in such transactions. The vendor is, by definition, interested in getting the equipment up, running, and turned over to the user so that it can receive payment from the lessor. The lessor's interest is in having the lease payment stream begin. The user should analyze both the vendor-lessor contract and the lessor-user lease agreement to ensure that the acceptance criteria dovetail in the two documents. The lease should not become effective or, at a minimum, the user's payment obligations should not begin, until the entire system has met detailed performance specifications, including operation for a given period with less than the percentage of downtime which is acceptable to the user during the performance period. Likewise, the vendor should not be entitled to payment from the lessor until the same standards have been met. (Acceptance tests are discussed in more detail in Chapter 8.)

Other provisions. As suggested above, variations of certain provisions applicable to a user-manufacturer agreement may also be included in the third-party lease. Consider, for example, the provisions relating to warranty pass-through, lemon replacement or refurbishment, reduced limitations on liability, and the like discussed earlier.

In summary, the user should not overlook the manufacturer and the lessor in a third-party lease transaction. Although both parties will attempt to avoid any responsibility for equipment performance during the lease term, both parties have a serious stake in having the lease executed by the user. Third-party lender requirements must be taken into account, but an astute user can achieve at least some economic protection against the risks of equipment malfunction by negotiating concessions from the manufacturer and the lessor.

Covering Relevant Federal Income Tax Consequences

Federal income tax considerations are often the single most important technical factor in a third-party lease. A user should not enter into any third-party leasing arrangement without having the entire transaction, including all legal documents, specifically approved by its tax lawyers and accountants. Nothing can take the place of this review, regardless of any time delays that may result. It should go without saying that the warm, self-serving assurances offered by the lessor's marketing representative should not be relied upon for this purpose.

Tax Lease Qualification. The user's tax advisors should ordinarily review the transaction to ensure that it will be treated as a true lease rather than an installment sale (or a loan), thus allowing the deduction of lease payments for tax purposes. The Economic Recovery Tax Act of

1981 created a "safe harbor" lease election which assured that a three-party financing lease transaction would be characterized as a true lease for investment tax credit, cost recovery, and other federal income tax purposes. If the transaction qualified for the "safe harbor," no other factors were required to be taken into account in determining whether the transaction was a lease for federal tax purposes. The "safe harbor" provision was adopted to make it easier for tax benefits (particularly those flowing from the new tax rules relating to "recovery property" depreciated under the Accelerated Cost Recovery System) to be distributed to corporations that could use the benefits to offset current tax liability.

To qualify for the "safe harbor," all the parties to the lease were required to characterize it as such and elect to treat the lessor as the owner of the leased property. In addition, several other requirements had to be be met. For example, the lessor had to be a corporation (other than a Subchapter S corporation or a personal holding company), a partnership composed of permissible corporations, or a grantor trust with a grantor and beneficiaries that were permissible corporations (or permissible partnerships). The lessor also had to have a minimum "at risk" investment of not less than 10% of the adjusted basis of the leased property at the time it was first placed into service and at all times during the term of the lease. The term of the lease (including extensions) could not exceed the greater of 90% of the useful life of the property (for purposes of Section 167 of the Internal Revenue Code) or 150% of the ADR class life of the property at January 1, 1981. The leased property had to be "qualified leased property." To be "qualified," the equipment had to be new "Section 38" property that was leased within three months after its acquisition or, in the case of a sale-leaseback transaction, purchased by the lessor within three months after the acquisition of the equipment by the lessee. In a sale-leaseback, the purchase price for the equipment could not exceed the adjusted basis of the equipment in the hands of the lessee at the time of the lessor's purchase. For purposes of these qualified property rules, the time that the equipment was "acquired" was deemed to be the later of the time of the actual acquisition or the time that the equipment was placed in service.

If the user/lessee acquired the equipment from the lessor *during* the lease term, the "safe harbor" requirement concerning the lessor's 10% minimum investment was no longer met, and the user/lessee would be treated as the owner of the equipment. Consequently, on any subsequent disposition of the equipment by the user/lessee, the property was subject to ITC and recovery allowance recapture under the Internal Revenue Code. (ITC recapture is discussed in more detail later in this chapter.)

As this book was moving to printing, the "safe harbor" leasing rules were radically altered by the 1982 tax act. These changes, and the lack of new regulations at press time, made it impossible for this volume to focus on the post-1982 rules for tax leases. Readers should consult their tax advisors for the latest guidelines in this complex area.

Prior to the 1981 tax act, and after the adoption of that law if the "safe harbor" requirements were not met, a lease transaction was required to meet more stringent conditions to qualify for an IRS ruling characterizing it as a true lease for tax purposes. These conditions generally included the following: (1) the lessor at all times had to have a minimum "at risk" investment in the equipment equal to 20% of its cost; (2) the lessor had to be able to show that the transaction was entered into for profit, apart from its tax benefits; (3) the lessee could not have a contractual right to purchase the equipment at less than its fair market value and the lessor could not have a contractual right to cause any party to purchase the equipment; (4) the lessee could not have furnished any part of the purchase price of the equipment (or loaned or guaranteed any indebtedness created in connection with the acquisition of the equipment by the lessor); and (5) the use of the equipment at the end of the lease term by a person other than the lessee had to be commercially feasible to the lessor.

As the above summary indicates, one of the principal changes created by the 1981 "safe harbor" rules related to the lessee's ability to purchase the property at the end of the lease at a preagreed (and possibly bargain) price. Without this "safe harbor," a tax lease could only provide that the lessee could purchase the equipment at its fair market value at the end of the lease.

Tax Benefit Indemnification. The issue of tax indemnification must also be addressed. Various federal income tax benefits may play key roles in determining the lessor's return on a third-party lease. As a result, most lessors insist that the user/lessee indemnify the lessor against the loss of all or certain of these benefits. In most instances such an indemnification provision covers the loss or recapture of ITC or depreciation benefits. Because these provisions are generally designed to place the lessor in the after-tax position it would have been in prior to the loss of benefits, the loss of $250,000 in benefits may require an indemnification payment of $500,000.

Tax indemnification provisions are generally quite complex and should be reviewed and approved only after consultation with the user's professional tax advisors. The key to making decisions in this area is to recognize that tax losses generally occur, and thus indemnification responsibilities arise, in any of three ways: (1) through changes in applicable law; (2) through acts or omissions of the lessor; and (3) through acts or omissions of the user/lessee. These three factors should be considered when determining which party should be liable for the loss of tax benefits.

Ideally, the user should attempt to avoid any liability for any tax loss. However, this approach is unrealistic from a practical standpoint. Consequently, most experienced users accept liability for any loss of tax benefits caused by an act or omission of the user, but attempt to avoid any further responsibility. This is a realistic and fair approach. Under no circumstances should the user agree to be responsible for any loss of tax benefits resulting from an act or omission of the vendor. Indeed, the vendor should accept responsibility for any such loss, not only by sustaining its own economic injury but also by indemnifying the user against any such loss. The issue of which party should bear responsibility for a tax loss caused by a change in law is more difficult. The user's best argument is that this entire risk should be assumed by the lessor (and that the lessor should indemnify the user against any such loss) on the theory that the lessor is in the leasing business and therefore should assume the normal risks that a law or regulation affecting that business may be changed. Where this approach is unsuccessful, it may be beneficial for the user to argue that both parties should assume their own risks of a change in law, with neither party agreeing to indemnify the other against any resulting loss of tax benefit. Particularly where this compromise is adopted. the user's attorney must employ special care in drafting the tax indemnification provisions to ensure that the user does not accidently assume (through sloppy drafting) responsibility for indemnifying the lessor against loss of tax benefits caused by a change in applicable law.

Investment Tax Credit. As most users are aware, the ITC provisions of the federal Internal Revenue Code provide for certain tax credits in the event capital is invested in certain qualifying equipment pursuant to Section 38 of the Code and the related regulations. However, few users appreciate the numerous problems that can arise in an ITC-based acquisition. This discussion provides an overview of some of the basic financial, tax, and contractual factors that may be involved in an acquisition where ITC is, or is said to be, available.

At the outset, it should be noted that the ITC regulations are typically complex and fraught with pitfalls. Where a user intends to claim the ITC or must indemnify against ITC loss, it should always have the details of the applicable transaction reviewed by its tax counsel or tax accountants. (Such a review can be conducted only if the user's tax advisor is furnished with full details of the proposed transaction, including relevant contingencies, and if appropriate time is allocated for review and drafting.) The discussions here are by their nature general and based upon tax laws and regulations in effect when this text was prepared for printing. Consequently, the following comments should not be considered complete or relied upon in formulating any ITC benefit or decisions.

Financial benefits. The basic value of the ITC to the user is financial. As a credit against federal income taxes, the ITC effectively reduces the cost of the equipment to the user, regardless of whether the credit is claimed by the user or by the lessor. Although further changes in the ITC are under consideration in Congress, the credit currently allowable is 10% of the eligible equipment investment, subject to a number of conditions. (A three-tier investment tax credit ranging from 15% to 25% is also available for certain expenditures incurred in rehabilitating qualified buildings and historic structures. This alternative credit is obviously beyond the scope of this book.)

Although some managers simply overlook the fact until it is too late, the user's ability to gain any financial statement benefit from a tax credit may be limited. Consequently, before a user relies upon the alleged savings that it can enjoy from "taking the ITC," the user should firmly ascertain that its tax position will actually permit it to obtain financial benefits from the credit. Generally, this analysis can only be conducted by the user's chief financial officer and tax advisor. Despite this warning, the history books are replete with stories of the user manager who proudly arranged for his firm to receive the ITC on a large acquisition (that was priced accordingly) only to learn that the ITC was virtually useless (at least for awhile) due to the user's tax loss position. Complex tax regulations permit a user to apply unsed ITC to its federal income tax liability for other years. Under these regulations, unused ITC may be carried back for several preceding tax years and the balance still unused in those years may be carried forward for a number of other years.

Where the user cannot directly benefit from the ITC, it may still be able to derive an indirect benefit by asking the lessor to retain the ITC. Although the ITC is directly available only to the owner of the eligible equipment, the owner can elect to pass the credit on to the equipment lessee—assuming certain procedures are followed and the equipment is considered qualifying "new" property both to the owner/lessor and to the lessee. (The safe harbor lease qualification provisions, discussed above, included in the Economic Recovery Tax Act of 1981 were designed to facilitate the transfer of ITC and other tax benefits to firms that could use the benefits to offset taxable income.) This flexibility permits either the owner/lessor or the user/lessee to enjoy the ITC benefit. When the lessor retains the ITC, the credit benefit, or a substantial portion of it, should then be indirectly passed on to the user in the form of a lower lease rate. Even where the user believes that it can take full advantage of the ITC, the user should seriously consider asking the owner/lessor to quote "both ways": one quote where the ITC is retained by the owner/lessor and the other quote where the ITC is directly passed to the user/lessee. From a practical standpoint, the authors have seldom seen a lessor that retains the ITC pass all of the resulting financial benefit through to the user. As a result, a good rule of thumb is that, where the user can effectively use the ITC benefit on its own tax return, it will gain maximum financial advantage by taking the ITC itself rather than permitting the lessor to take it and pass through some financial value to the user.

The amount of equipment investment subject to ITC varies. Prior to the Economic Recovery Tax Act of 1981, the determining factor was the estimated useful life of the eligible equipment to the party claiming the credit. Pursuant to the 1981 Act, the key element for "recovery property" is the applicable Accelerated Cost Recovery System (ACRS) recovery period, rather than the useful life. (Under that Act, "recovery property" is simply depreciable tangible property that is used in a trade or business or held for the production of income.) For eligible equipment that is 10-year or 5-year property under ACRS, 100% of the investment qualifies for the ITC. For eligible equipment that is 3-year property under ACRS, only 60% of the investment qualifies for the credit. (Several exceptions to these general rules exist for certain narrow categories of property.)

A user considering the potential value of ITC benefit must also consider the possibility that the ITC may be lost during the useful life of the eligible property; that is, that the user may suffer "ITC recapture." Under the 1981 Act, ITC recovery occurs, and the tax liability of the user or other party is increased, if "Section 38" property is disposed of, or otherwise ceases to be "Section 38" property before the close of the applicable "recapture period," for equipment placed in service after 1980. (For this purpose, the "recapture period" is the period consisting of the first full year after the equipment is placed in service and the four succeeding full years, or the two succeeding full years in the case of 3-year recovery property.) The amount of the increase in tax is determined by applying the applicable recapture percentage (specified in the Internal Revenue Code) to the decrease in the investment credit that would have resulted from reducing to zero the qualified investment employed in computing the credit for the equipment in previous years. The increase in tax due to recapture is limited to investment credits that were actually used to reduce federal income tax liability. Where the investment credits were not used to reduce tax liability, adustments are made in ITC carrybacks and carryforwards. (Special ITC recapture rules apply to certain qualified energy property.)

As noted above in connection with the "safe harbor" lease election, if the user/lessee acquires the equipment being leased from the lessor and then disposes of it, the user will be subject to the ITC and recovery allowance recapture rules (set out in Sections 47 and 1245 of the Internal Revenue Code) as if the user had been the owner of the property for the entire term of the lease. However, any investment tax credit or recovery allowance recaptured by the vendor/lessor will not be recaptured again by the user/lessee.

Eligible property. Although the ITC can also be claimed on certain other types of property, most major equipment must qualify as "Section 38" property to be eligible for the investment tax credit. In general, "Section 38" property must be *either* (1) tangible personal property (other than air conditioning and heating units) *or* (2) other tangible property (excluding buildings and their structural components) that is used as an "integral part of manufacturing, production, or extraction or of furnishing transportation, communications, electrical energy, gas, water, or sewage disposal services." (Certain additional uses for "other tangible property" are also specified in the Internal Revenue Code, primarily in connection with railroad rolling stock, storage facilities for bulk commodities and petroleum, agricultural structures, and certain elevators and timber property.) In addition, the property must be *either* (1) "recovery property," as that term is used in Section 168 of the Internal Revenue Code (added by the Economic Recovery Tax Act of 1981 in connection with the Accelerated Cost Recovery System), regardless of useful life *or* (2) any other property with respect to which depreciation (or amortization in lieu of depreciation) is allowable and which has a useful life (determined as of the date the property is placed in service) of three years or more. As noted above, "recovery property" is any depreciable tangible property used in a trade or business or held for the production of income.

To qualify for the investment tax credit, the property cannot be used in any manner prohibited by the Internal Revenue Code. For example, equipment that would otherwise qualify as "Section 38" property will be excluded from eligibility if it is used predominantly outside the United States (subject to certain exceptions). These prohibited uses should be carefully considered by a user assessing the availability of the ITC.

The Economic Recovery Tax Act of 1981 also added a new "at risk" requirement for ITC property. Under this provision, ITC is not allowed for amounts invested in qualifying property to the extent that the invested amounts are not "at risk." This rule applies to property placed into service after February 18, 1981, unless it was acquired pursuant to a binding contract entered into on or before February 18, 1981. Fortunately, the "at risk" limitation applies only to individuals, tax option (Subchapter S) corporations, and certain closely-held corporations (e.g., personal holding companies) engaged in business activities that are subject to the "at risk" rules of Section 465 of the Internal Revenue Code. In general, amounts are not considered to be "at risk" if: (1) the taxpayer is protected against loss of the invested amount; (2) the amount was borrowed and the taxpayer is not personally liable for repayment of the debt; (3) the lender has an interest other than as a creditor; or (4) the lender is a related party to the borrower. The "at risk" ITC rules are rather complex, and include a number of exceptions relating to energy property and other matters. The rules also provide for the recapture of ITC where the taxpayer ceases to meet the "at risk" requirements during the applicable recovery period.

Most users tend to think that the ITC is only available on "new" equipment. From a practical standpoint, this assumption is valid. Technically, however, ITC benefit is available on used equipment that otherwise qualifies under the above tests, subject to an important limitation: The investment in used equipment that can be taken into account in a given year is limited to $125,000 (for tax years beginning 1981 through 1984; and $150,000 thereafter). (A controlled group must apportion the used equipment limitation among its members in accordance with their purchases of used property.) Other conditions may also further restrict the amount of the used equipment investment that may be utilized in calculating the ITC.

In reviewing these and other issues, the user should ensure that it refers to the latest available tax regulations. Articles and books containing ITC discussions should be carefully updated in light of the 1981 and 1982 tax acts and any subsequent laws or regulations.

Legal problems. The very complexity of the ITC area suggests that sound legal advice is required whenever the user expects to claim the ITC benefit. Competent professional guidance is important not only in handling the complicated tax regulations, but also in drafting certain provisions of the acquisition document. If the user plans to take advantage of the ITC, a number of points should be covered in the vendor/user agreement.

First, the vendor should warrant that the equipment will qualify as "new" Section 38 (ITC) property, eligible for the investment tax credit. Because of the dollar limitation on the amount of used property investment that is eligible for the ITC, the user must ensure that the warranty differentiates between "new" and "used" ITC property.

In fairness to the vendor, the user should recognize that the vendor is really unable to warrant that the user will actually be able to obtain the benefits of the ITC on the user's tax return. The ultimate use of the property is in the hands of the user and, as the general discussion above indicates, certain user actions may cause the property to become ineligible or otherwise invoke the ITC recapture provisions. Moreover, the user's tax position may itself change, thereby precluding the user from deriving any value from the ITC. These problems do not and should not preclude the vendor from warranting that the equipment is "new" and "eligible" for ITC purposes; rather, the problems require that the warranty provision be drafted in a manner that is fair for the vendor and the user.

Where the user is receiving the ITC through a third-party lease, the manufacturer of the equipment should provide the requisite warranty to both the user and the lessor. (This approach may necessitate a manufacturer/user agreement, in which event the user should ensure that the legal "consideration" for the agreement is carefully documented.) Ideally, the lessor should provide a similar warranty to the user/lessee or, at a minimum, pass on the manufacturer's warranty to the user.

Second, the user should carefully consider the ITC impact or any vendor actions that require or otherwise involve the replacement or removal of any equipment or any substantial part of the equipment. The user should ensure that the replacement items are also "new" and "eligible" for ITC purposes, as suggested in the warranty mentioned above. In addition, the user should ensure that the vendor will hold the user harmless against any ITC recapture or other loss of ITC benefit that results from the failure of the equipment to meet all applicable tests and standards, including all terms and conditions of the relevant agreement. Perhaps the best method of dealing with these matters is to cover each one separately in the applicable sections of the agreement and also include a blanket warranty or indemnification by the vendor that it will not take any action, during or after the agreement term, that would cause the user to suffer any ITC or depreciation recapture not previously agreed upon by the user in writing.

Third, the user should recognize that tax consequences may not be the only problems that arise if the vendor violates its warranty that the equipment is "new" Section 38 property. If the equipment is "used" rather than "new" for ITC purposes, the user may need to consider a number of additional contractual provisions necessary to cover the acquisition of used hardware. (See Chapter 9.) For example, if the equipment is used rather than new, the user may want the vendor to warrant that the equipment will not require rebuilding or refurbishment for a specified number of years. The user may also require the vendor to warrant that the used equipment has been refurbished at the factory immediately prior to shipment to the user. The user may demand to inspect the equipment (or the applicable maintenance logs) at the previous site, or require that diagnostics be completed before and after shipment. The list goes on and on. The important point is that, if the equipment is not "new" Section 38 property, the user should know in advance, while it can still add appropriate contractual protection (and determine whether it should be paying the "new" price or the "used" price for the equipment).

In this context, it should be noted that the ITC warranty issue can be an effective way to "smoke out" a vendor that is not clearly specifying whether the equipment is new or used. Although many users may wonder why this point is even relevant, it should suffice to note that some vendors do purposefully or inadvertently misrepresent—or fail to clearly and voluntarily represent—the new versus used condition of the equipment being acquired by the user.

Finally, if the user plans to receive the ITC benefit as a lessee, the lease agreement should clearly specify that the owner/lessor will pass on any and all available ITC benefit to the lessee. (Unnecessary hedging by the owner/lessor should not be tolerated in this provision.) The tax regulations require that the election of a lessor to pass ITC benefit on to its lessee must be made by the lessor's filing a statement with the lessee. This statement or "ITC election form" must contain certain specified information and must be signed by the lessor and accepted in writing by the lessee. The lessor must file the election statement with the lessee on or before the due date (including extensions) for the user/lessee's tax return for the tax year in which possession of the equipment is transferred to the lessee. Generally, the applicable lease agreement should provide that the lessor will provide the necessary, executed ITC election forms to the user on or before the acceptance date.

As complicated as the ITC provisions may be, they offer substantial advantage to many users, regardless of whether the ITC benefit is taken by the user or by the lessor. The key to obtaining this advantage is to appreciate the complexity of the ITC area and seek competent professional guidance.

Limiting Miscellaneous Costs

The third-party lease should be carefully studied to determine which party will be liable for such routine items as insurance, state and local taxes, and the costs of arranging any necessary financing. Insurance and taxes are fairly standard items, but the lease provisions should be analyzed for any ambiguous or inappropriate wording. For example, if the lease provides that the user will pay all state and local taxes, including "any penalties," the provision should be amended to delete any taxes on the lessor's income, as well as any withholding and similar taxes relating to the lessor's employees. As noted in Chapter 8, the provision should also indicate that the lessor will pay any penalties that may result from the lessor's failure to file any information returns that may be required under local law. In addition, where the user is responsible for paying property taxes on the leased equipment, the user should be permitted to dispute any tax amounts deemed unreasonable by it, assuming certain stated precautions are taken by the user to protect the equipment from liens or forced sale (escrow of the disputed tax amounts, for example).

More importantly, any "costs of financing" section may need to be amended to specify exactly what costs, if any, the user must pay. Although the user may ultimately bear these costs through the lease payments, care should be taken to ensure that no unexpected costs of this nature are imposed directly on the user in addition to the lease payments. For example, some lessors attempt to use this type of provision to cause the user to pay the lessor's attorneys' fees and other costs of obtaining financing, including travel, presentation costs, and the like. Occasionally, brokers' fees and mortgage banking commissions are also imposed in the same fashion.

Maximizing Flexibility

Due to the longer term involved in most third-party leases, the user should strive to maximize whatever flexibility may be possible. As noted above, this may be done to some extent by renting certain components and leasing others, and by including acceptable upgrade and trade-in provisions in the lease. Careful consideration should also be given to the question of modifications. The lease and maintenance agreements should allow the user to obtain all desired software and hardware modifications, yet give the user the opportunity to decline certain changes that may be detrimental to its operations. The cost and ownership of such modifications should be specified and the user should retain flexibility in financing any major upgrades.

Regardless of the user's present business plans, the lease arrangements should also cover moving and subleasing the equipment and, if appropriate, renting machine time to others. Few equipment installations are static; economic and business needs can change during the term of a third-party lease. Earnings can decline; business can increase; the company can be acquired by another firm. As suggested in Chapter 8, the lease and maintenance agreements should allow the user (with appropriate protection to the lessor) to move the equipment, to sublease the equipment, or assign the lease and maintenance agreements, and to rent the equipment or otherwise allow it to be operated by other parties, such as a facilities management firm. In this regard, software as well as hardware should be considered.

Every term-oriented agreement (rental, lease, maintenance), whether for hardware, software, services, time sharing, or facilities management, should have a renewal provision (initial term extension) contained in the original agreement. This renewal provision should provide for certain basic points such as the method of renewal, the renewal payment amounts, the renewal term, any new termination considerations, and other factors that may need to be changed from the initial term of the agreement.

Many users feel that, by waiting until near the end of the initial term, they will be able to negotiate a more favorable price, due to the fact that the equipment may be worth less on the open market. This approach can be beneficial at times. If the user agrees to a preestablished renewal rate at the outset of the initial term, and the value of the equipment drops substantially before renewal, the lessor may be unwilling to accept a lower renewal price than previously agreed.

Although this risk does exist, preoccupation with this possibility causes many users to overlook the more serious alternative. If a renewal provision is not included in the initial lease agreement, and the user still needs the equipment or service at the end of the term, the lessor may be able to demand an excessive price for the renewal period. Indeed, the renewal rate is particularly likely to be above the going market rate where the user is literally "over a barrel"; for example, where no alternative equipment or services are available within the time frame required or where the swap-out costs (primarily deinstallation, installation, freight, and possibly programming) involved in obtaining alternative equipment or services are substantial. (Both of these problems are likely to arise when the desired renewal period is relatively short.) If a user executes an agreement without predefined and very specific, renewal provisions, the user is effectively giving the lessor a potential blank check, payable at the end of the initial term, in the event the equipment is still needed and the lessor wants to "hold up" the user. The best and only time to negotiate a favorable renewal provision is during the initial agreement negotiations, not months or years later, when the user is at the mercy of the lessor. The primary reason for negotiating a renewal provision when the user is still a prospect (and merely contemplating doing business with the lessor), is that the user has more leverage to negotiate favorable terms and conditions on renewal provisions.

Given the significant expense that can result from failing to include a renewal provision at the outset, little excuse exists for omitting such a provision from any lease agreement. Even if the prenegotiated renewal price turns out to be above the market rate at the time of renewal, it may be considerably less expensive than the lessor's "extortion rate." Moreover, if the preagreed renewal price is significantly above the market at renewal time, the user still has the option of renegotiating the preagreed rate with the lessor or seeking alternative equipment or services from other sources. In essence, a renewal provision gives the user an opportunity to optimize the renewal arrangements, but also provides a known fallback position. Many users base the renewal rate upon a specified percentage of the original lease payment. Although this is an acceptable approach to determining the payment to be used during one or more renewal periods, a creative user may wish to consider using a formula or algorithm that establishes the rent for the renewal term by calculating a "fair lease value" based upon fair market value at the end of the term and some preagreed rate of return tied, for example, to the average prime rate of a specified bank over a designated period. (Because some particularly pro-user renewal provisions can affect the "substance" of the lease for tax and financial reporting purposes, the user's attorneys and accountants should review the terms of any renewal provision. Renewal periods that clearly go beyond the economic life of the equipment and renewal rates at excessively low prices are particularly likely to be troublesome.)

To some users, "flexibility" suggests that the third-party lease should also grant the user an option to purchase the system at the end of the term, at a fixed or formula price. Although some third-party leases include an option to purchase as one user alternative at the end of the term, the purchase price is generally stated in "fair market value" language. This approach is used because of the adverse tax and financial accounting results that can occur if the lease includes a fixed, formula, or nominal purchase price.

If the user requires the right to buy the system at the end of the term, a purchase option should definitely be included in the lease agreement. (The provision should be a true "option," where the user has the "right," but not the obligation, to purchase the system.) The terms of the option, and particularly the price, should be reviewed carefully by the user's attorneys and accountants (including the user's independent auditors if the transaction is of material size).

Limiting Redelivery Responsibilities

Many third-party leases contain language such as the following: "At the expiration of this Lease, lessee shall, at its expense, deliver the equipment, at an address specified by lessor, and in the same condition as received, less normal depreciation and wear." The basic problem with this language is that it places no limitations on the lessee's obligation to redeliver the equipment. For example, legally the lessee can be required to deliver the system from its site in Atlanta, Georgia to the twenty-third floor of an office building located in Los Angeles, Honolulu, or Hong Kong.

Ideally, the lease should not require the user to bear the expense of redelivering the equipment at the end of the lease term. In most instances, the next lessee of the equipment will contract in its lease to pay for the delivery of the equipment to its site; consequently, the prior user should not have a similar obligation except, perhaps, for delivery to an interim refurbishment site.

If the user must bear the expense of redelivery, however, the agreement should limit the maximum expense that the user may be required to pay and, within the limit, restrict the user's liability to expenses actually incurred. The user's obligation for insurance and/or risk of loss upon redelivery should also be carefully examined in order to minimize or eliminate the user's potential liability.

Coordinating Risk of Loss, Insurance, and Acceptance

Because of the multiple parties involved in a third-party lease transaction, it is imperative for the user to coordinate all contractual provisions relating to risk of loss, insurance, and acceptance. These provisions must be coordinated both within each agreement and between the lease agreement and the vendor/lessor purchase agreement.

Far too many third-party lease transactions provide that the user will bear the risk of loss and the burden of obtaining insurance prior to the applicable acceptance date. In most situations, this approach is inconsistent with the fact that, during this preliminary period, the user has not yet accepted the equipment. Consequently, the user should insist that the vendor, or possibly the lessor, bear full responsibility for insurance coverage and risk of loss prior to the acceptance date. (See Chapter 8.)

Similarly, the user should ensure that the acquisition documents specifically cover the possibility that the equipment may in fact be seriously damaged or destroyed prior to the acceptance date. Although risk of loss and insurance coverage are generally mentioned in most third-party lease documents, these agreements usually fail to specify what happens to the contracts, the delivery schedules, and the like if the equipment is destroyed prior to delivery or acceptance. (Ironically, most contracts for the sale and purchase of a new house include this topic.) Therefore, the user should ensure that the lease documentation includes a specific provision governing this possibility. Although this type of provision is important in purchase agreements, it is particularly important in third-party leases due to the multiple parties involved and the "hell or high water" provision likely to be required by any participating financial institution.

Drafting Indemnification Provisions

Most third-party leases include a standard provision in which the lessee indemnifies the lessor against virtually anything and everything that might go wrong during the term of the lease. If a third-party lender is involved, certain types of lessee indemnification may be unavoidable. Nevertheless, most standard-form indemnification provisions go far beyond what is necessary and what is prudent to the lessee. Consequently, the lessee should strive to narrow the scope of the required lessee indemnification. (See the ITC discussion, above.) The preferred method of achieving this limitation is to restrict any user indemnification responsibility, particularly in the tax area, to the user's own acts and omissions. An alternative and less desirable method of reducing the user's indemnification responsibilities is to exclude indemnification for various acts or omissions of the lessor or the vendor and their respective officers, directors, employees, and agents. In this regard, the user should be particularly cautious with respect to such words as "directly," "indirectly," and "solely." In addition, where at all possible the user should seek to include some counter- or cross-indemnification provisions running from the lessor and/or vendor to the lessee.

Providing for "Quiet Enjoyment"

One of the most basic provisions in any third-party lease should be a "quiet enjoyment" provision. This provision essentially states that, if the user abides by its obligations under the lease, it will not be disturbed in its "quiet enjoyment" of the leased equipment. A sample pro-user provision might read: "Provided that the Lessee has duly performed its obligations pursuant to this Agreement, the Lessee shall have the right to use and possess the Equipment during the term of this Agreement, including any renewals hereof, without disturbance, interference, or interruption by the Lessor or any person claiming by, through, or under the Lessor, including without limitation any assignee financial institution."

This type of provision has two basic purposes. First, it contractually precludes the lessor from harassing the user during the term of the lease. Second, and more importantly, it attempts to ensure that any assignee of the lessor (claiming by, through, or under the lessor) must honor the user's rights under the lease. In this context, for example, the provision would provide protection to the user if the lessor had financial problems and its creditors gained the lessor's position under the lease.

The user may also want to attempt to obtain the specific concurrence of any assignee financial institution involved (or any other party that may hold a lien on the equipment). This agreement can often be achieved as part of the assignment documents.

In connection with this general area the user should also obtain a warranty from the lessor (and, perhaps, from the equipment manufacturer or other vendor) that the leased equipment is and will remain free from any and all liens, claims, or encumbrances, other than liens and security interests contemplated in the lease arrangements (such as any third-party debt) that are consistent with the "quiet enjoyment" provision.

Additional protection for the user's right to use the leased equipment can also be obtained by ensuring that the user has the right to defend any lawsuits or other claims involving the use or ownership of the equipment. Generally, such a provision will provide that the lessor must furnish the user with prompt notice of any such suit or claim. In addition, the provision will usually grant the user the right to participate in the suit or, at least, to concurrently defend its right to use the equipment.

Judging "Walk-Away" Leases

One of the more interesting (and dangerous) third-party leasing options is the so-called "walk-away" lease. Although a number of variations of this option are available, the basic approach involves a long-term third-party lease where the user has (or is supposed to have) the ability to terminate the lease at an earlier date (usually after two or three years) at no penalty. The advantage of this approach, assuming it works, is that it permits the user to obtain equipment at third-party lease rates for a shorter term than most lessors are able to offer. In effect, the walk-away term of two to five years is more like a rental term; but the lease payments are more like those associated with a five- to seven-year third-party lease.

This rather strange hybrid receives its name from the fact that the lease the user enters into is actually a long-term lease (usually five to seven years) that the user can supposedly "walk-away" from at the end of the desired shorter term. The critical point is that, despite any other representations by the lessor, the legally binding term of the lease is the full five to seven years, not the shorter walk-away period.

Despite its potential advantages, the walk-away lease offers a number of serious risks for the user. If a user is not fully aware of the dangers inherent in this type of leasing arrangement, it may well find that its marvelous "walk-away" lease has turned into a "crawl-away" lease—or worse.

Perhaps the most important step in walk-away leasing is for the user to know exactly what it is getting. Although many lessors are perfectly honest from the start, some are not particularly candid in marketing a walk-away lease. These less scrupulous lessors market a seven-year term/three-year walk-away lease as a simple "three-year lease." The user reacts favorably to the lessor's offer of a three-year lease at seven-year rates and the papers are presented for signature. Only then (if at all) does the user read the documents and realize that it must sign a full seven-year lease with an appended "early termination option."

This marketing approach has two basic problems. First, it involves marketing deceit ("fraud" might be a more correct, if less polite, word). If the lessor's marketing representative is willing to misrepresent the basic nature of the lease, the user might well ask what else the lessor has confused or hidden in the transaction. Second, the approach opens the user up to serious potential financial liability. As this fact suggests, the approach also exposes the user's management (and perhaps others) to serious subsequent criticism. (The important point, incidentally, is that the user should never unknowingly accept the financial risks involved in this type of leasing. The user should recognize the risks at the start, through an honest explanation from the lessor's marketing representative.)

The dangers lurking in the early termination walk-away option can best be appreciated by reviewing an example of the language used in several popular walk-away leases. This language was extracted from an "early termination option" addendum to a relatively standard, pro-lessor third-party lease. The addendum was accompanied by an "election of early termination," a desirable exhibit that specifies the exact form of notice that the user must supply in the event of early termination pursuant to the walk-away provision. The basic third-party lease involved had a term of seven years and made no reference to the walk-away option, except to the extent that it incorporated the early termination addendum by reference. The addendum language provided the user with the right to terminate the lease after a specified term for any reason other than certain causes specified in the addendum. The basic pro-user language is relatively simple and clear.

NOW, THEREFORE, it is hereby agreed as follows:

1. Lessor hereby agrees to allow the lessee to terminate the Lease Agreement after _____ months for any reason other than:

(a) Insolvency and/or financial default of the manufacturer, lessor or any party or parties to the Lease; or

(b) War, invasion, acts of foreign enemies, hostilities (whether war be declared or not), civil war, rebellion, revolution, insurrection, military or usurped power or confiscation, or nationalization or requisition or destruction of or damage to property by and under the order of any government or public or local authority, or ionizing radiations or contaminations by radioactivity from any nuclear waste from the combustion of nuclear fuel, or the radioactive, toxic, explosive or other hazardous properties of any explosive nuclear assembly or nuclear component thereof; or

(c) An assignment of the Lease by lessee; or

(d) A sublease of the Units by lessee; if such sublease occurs other than with the written consent of and in cooperation with lessor; or

(e) The occurrence of any Event of Default under the Lease.

The essence of the risk faced by the user appears in three other provisions in the addendum:

This Agreement is made with reference to the fact that the lessee has entered into or will enter into a Computer Equipment Lease dated the same date as this Agreement (the "Lease"), with _____ as the lessor. As an inducement for lessee to enter into the Lease, lessor has agreed to enter into the Agreement. However, lessee specifically understands that _____ lessor intends to assign the Lease and the right to receive the Lease payments to a financial institution as security for a loan to lessor and the obligation of lessee to make the payments provided for in the Lease to the financial institution shall not be affected in any manner whatsoever by this Agreement.

Under the terms of the Lease the lessee will continue to be obligated to the financial institution to whom the Lease is assigned notwithstanding the fact that lessee elects to terminate the Lease pursuant to the terms of this Agreement but lessor hereby agrees to indemnify and hold the lessee harmless from the required payments of the Lease which are due subsequent to the termination of the Lease pursuant to this Agreement.

Notwithstanding anything contained herein, this Agreement shall not be construed to affect or modify the Lease or any of the rights or obligations of lessor, lessee, or the lender and/or financial institution contained or referred to therein and is in all respects subject thereto.

These provisions make several things quite clear. Despite anything to the contrary in the walk-away addendum:

1. The user is legally obligated to make any and all payments required by the lease for the full seven-year term of the lease.
2. The lessor intends to assign the lease to the financial institution that provides the debt financing for the equipment, and the user's legal obligation to make all lease payments will, therefore, run in favor of this financial institution and not in favor of the lessor. (And, in light of the standard pro-lessor "hell or high water" provision in the lease, the user will have no right to offset or deduct any claim the user has against the lessor from the amounts owed the assignee financial institution.)
3. The only escape the user has from its legal obligation to make all payments under the lease for seven years is the lessor's representation that it will step in and pay the user for ("indemnify and hold the user harmless from") all lease payments required to be made by the user after the user's walk-away option is exercised.

Make no mistake about the important point: If the lessor for any reason fails to reimburse the user for the lease payments, the user must continue to make them. Perhaps more important from a technical and operations standpoint, if some disaster occurs after the walk-away option is exercised, the user may still be liable to the assignee financial institution for any loss or for the failure of the next user to comply with the terms of what will amount to a sublease or assignment under the initial seven-year lease.

In this regard, note that, despite the walk-away addendum, in the example above the lease itself was not modified and remained in full force and effect as to the financial institution. Unless the initial user was released by the lessor and the assignee financial institution from the user's obligations under the lease (for example, insurance, risk of loss, operation, nondisclosure, and the like), the user would be technically responsible to the assignee financial institution for all such obligations—even though the lessor or another user would then be operating the system.

In this type of situation, of course, the lessor will be obligated to hold the user "harmless from the required payments of the lease which are due subsequent to the termination of the lease" pursuant to the walk-away addendum. Despite representations by lessors to the contrary, some doubt exists as to whether this indemnification language covers, or is intended to cover, user obligations under the lease other than the obligation to make the basic "required payments of the lease"—that is, the lease rental payments.

As this discussion suggests, the basic user risk under a walk-away lease is that the lessor will not be financially able to, or for some other reason will not, indemnify the user after the walk-away date. Consequently, a user executing this type of walk-away lease is relying on the lessor's financial standing, and willingness to honor its obligations. In some respects, the user's position is as if it had guaranteed the performance of the lessor after the walk-away date.

The financial risk faced by the user in a walk-away lease can be particularly significant in high technology industries where prices are subject to sharp reductions as new generations of equipment are introduced. In a walk-away lease, the lessor (and any insurance carrier providing walk-away backup) essentially counts on being able to release the equipment at an adequate price after the walk-away date. If residual values and lease prices drop substantially, the lessor may be faced with significantly lower lease prices after the walk-away date (assuming the equipment can, in fact, even be released to another user).

More sophisticated lessors appear to mitigate this user risk by providing insurance to cover the lessor's indemnification obligation under the walk-away addendum. The example addendum quoted in this discussion includes the following provision:

> As security for the performance by lessor under this Agreement, lessor agrees to obtain insurance to cover its indemnification obligation provided for herein and to provide lessee with evidence of such insurance coverage. The lessor further agrees to assign its interest under the policy to the lessee as additional security for the indemnification provided for herein.

Although this type of provision is certainly better than no insurance coverage at all, two basic problems still exist. First, as suggested above, some question exists as to the lessor's indemnification obligation for matters and costs other than the basic lease payments. If the lessor is not responsible for such matters, insurance coverage for those items will also be nonexistent.

Second, the insurance will only be as good as the coverage. Yet few users take the time and trouble to ask for a copy of the relevant policy, analyze the scope of the coverage, and amend the addendum to provide basic pro-user insurance provisions (no modification or cancellation of coverage without user permission and the like). Some policies contain a loophole that precludes payment of the policy proceeds if the lessor fails to use due diligence in remarketing the system involved. Even assuming that the necessary level of remarketing effort is adequately defined in the policy (an assumption that may well be invalid), this approach may leave the user's insurance coverage totally dependent upon the lessor's efforts.

Yet another user risk exists, regardless of whether insurance coverage is offered by the lessor; despite the language of the addendum, the lessor may be slow in honoring the obligation to step in and make the lease payments after the walk-away date. In this scenario, the lessor has the basic financial ability to make the necessary payments, through insurance proceeds or otherwise. However, the lessor purposefully drags its feet in making the required payments. As a result, the user makes the payments to avoid being declared in default under the lease. (As noted above, the user is legally obligated to make all such payments.) The user continues to attempt to obtain reimbursement from the lessor (or the insurance carrier, if appropriate) and, eventually, the lessor provides the funds to the user, without interest. In the meantime, of course, the lessor enjoys the use of the user's funds and/or receives additional time to remarket the system.

The user loses two things: first, the time value of the funds advanced by the user before reimbursement by the lessor; and second, the nights of sleep wondering whether the lessor will or will not perform under the walk-away addendum. Technically, the user should have a legal right to receive interest on the delayed payments; however, collection of the interest by legal process will seldom be cost effective. Moreover, some question may exist as to whether the lessor is liable for the interest, assuming that the user is reimbursed for the payments within a reasonable time. The basic language in the example provision only covers the required lease payments and no time limit is specified for the lessor's obligation to make such payments.

Assuming that the basic concepts of a walk-away lease seem appealing, the following suggestions may help reduce the user risks associated with this hybrid acquisition vehicle:

First, the user should be certain that a walk-away lease is the only real alternative. Other short-term acquisition approaches should be considered and weighed carefully in light of the risks involved in the walk-away approach.

Second, the user should try to deal with a well-respected leasing firm that has the financial standing and business reputation to stand behind its walk-away obligations.

Third, the user should carefully draft the language governing the lessor's walk-away obligation to ensure that all possible user liabilities are covered and that lessor payment, plus any interest, must be made within a specified period.

Fourth, the user should insist upon meaningful insurance coverage to back up the lessor's indemnification obligation. The user's risk management advisors should be asked to review the coverage to ensure that the policy provisions are adequate, that the user is named as an insured, and that the coverage cannot be cancelled or modified without advance notice to the user.

Fifth, the user should consider requiring the lessor to post a performance bond to back up its obligations. In some instances, a carefully considered performance bond may offer more complete protection than "insurance" coverage.

Sixth, the user should ensure that all relevant lease provisions (covering, for example, the right to use, right to move, right to assign, right to sublease, and software arrangements) are consistent with the contemplated early walk-away by the initial user. In this regard, the user should remember that the prime lease will continue in effect, despite any obligation by the lessor to reimburse the user for the lease payments after the walk-away date. If the lessor is really willing to protect the user from liability after the walk-away date, the lessor's indemnification duties must cover all user obligations under the lease, and not merely the user's payment obligation.

Finally, to preclude surprises and subsequent criticism, all members of the user's negotiating team should fully appreciate and approve the walk-away concept—and the accompanying risks. A detailed memorandum prepared by the user's financial and legal advisors may be the best method of handling this.

11
MASTER CONTRACTS AND USER FORM AGREEMENTS

Increasingly today, larger users are turning toward "master" or "general procurement" agreements to document all of their equipment transactions with a particular vendor. Other users are promulgating their own "standard form agreements" to impose on smaller vendors. In some instances, these standard agreements take the form of a master procurement document. In other situations, separate standard agreements are prepared for various types of transactions—for example, purchase, lease, and rental alternatives.

Although their use is not without potential pitfalls, master contracts and user form agreements can both offer significant benefits for the sophisticated user—particularly where the user has both the resources to prepare competent documents and the bargaining power to impose them on vendors. This chapter focuses on master contracts and user form agreements, outlining the benefits and pitfalls of each and detailing the substantive issues that should be considered in drafting such documents.

MASTER CONTRACTS AND GENERAL PROCUREMENT AGREEMENTS

Benefits

Properly prepared, master contracts and general procurement agreements can offer significant benefits for many users. Although master contracts have been employed by corporate users in private industry for a far shorter period of time, such documents have been utilized effectively by federal and state agencies for many years. The principal opportunities offered by master contracts are summarized below.

First, because significant dollars are or will be involved during the term of the agreement, the user's bargaining power is almost always optimized in master agreement negotiations. Perhaps more importantly, because the agreement covers everything from large systems to small components, the user's negotiating position is enhanced with respect to all products and services offered by the vendor, not just the more expensive items that might otherwise be involved in a single transaction.

Second, because master agreements are both comprehensive and important to the parties, the documents are likely to be carefully negotiated and drafted. Despite the fact that the vendor will certainly attempt to optimize its own position under the master agreement, this thoroughness of negotiation and drafting will generally inure to the benefit of a sophisticated user.

Third, the size and importance of most master agreements ordinarily increases the likelihood that higher levels of the vendor's marketing and management staff will be directly involved in negotiating the contract. The involvement of these key people generally places the negotiations on a higher, more professional plane. In addition, this involvement facilitates major vendor commitments that simply could not be made at the local or branch office level.

Fourth, to the extent that master agreements permit supplemental orders to be placed by the user's operations or other personnel during the term of the agreement, the master document approach reduces the likelihood that the equipment ordered will be subject to terms and conditions that are unfavorable to the user. Thus, assuming that the master agreement has been properly drafted, the terms and conditions of all supplemental orders will be governed by the master agreement and not by some pro-vendor form agreement thrust into the hands of a local manager. Because both the user's local manager and the vendor's marketing representative recognize that the entire user-vendor relationship is governed by the master agreement, both individuals are less likely to engage in inappropriate negotiations that may result in an undue advantage for the vendor.

Fifth, although the preparation of a master agreement requires a substantial commitment of time and resources by the user and the vendor, the master contract may actually save time and aggravation later on. This savings results because all subsequent purchases during the applicable term will be governed by the general procurement document. Because of this fact, extensive negotiations need not occur in connection with each additional acquisition by the user. Although certain specific details may need to be negotiated and separately documented in the individual order placed by the user, the general terms and conditions, which ordinarily include those most likely to require extensive discussions, will already be set forth in the master agreement.

Pitfalls

Despite these and other benefits, master agreements should not be employed by all users or in all situations. The potential pitfalls involved in using master agreements include the following.

First, because of their breadth and complexity, master agreements require considerable drafting and negotiating expertise. They also require substantial time and effort to prepare. If the user lacks the requisite skills in these areas, or cannot devote the time and talent necessary to achieve its negotiating objectives, the user would be well advised to avoid the general procurement approach and focus on attempting to optimize its position in a less complicated manner.

Second, master agreements can be particularly dangerous for the inexperienced user, facilitating efforts by the vendor to execute the "Form Contract Ploy" (described in Chapter 2) on a comprehensive, long-term basis. Under this ploy, the vendor's sales representative suggests that a naive user simply execute a master form agreement that will cover all of the user's transactions with the vendor for a specified period. All equipment, software, services, and other items acquired by the user from the vendor during this period will then be documented or ordered through a one-page "order" that incorporates all of the terms and conditions of the master agreement. In theory, this approach seems logical enough to many users. Indeed, the documentation system is the same as that employed in many master agreements that provide proper protection to the user. The problem arises when the user signs the vendor's standard form master agreement with few or no changes. A similar problem occurs where the user negotiates a few changes to the vendor's standard form master agreement, but the changes are essentially limited to those affecting the initial equipment order that the user signs concurrently with the master agreement. Later, if and when the user becomes more sophisticated and attempts to negotiate a more favorable position on a specific order, the vendor will politely reply that the master agreement is still in effect and, therefore, will govern the terms and conditions of the proposed new acquisition. This long-term variation of the "Form Contract Ploy" can seem particularly attractive where the vendor offers price or discount concessions if the user will sign the vendor's standard form master agreement. Users faced with this marketing approach should pursue the discount offer, but document it pursuant to a fully-negotiated master contract that protects the user as well as the vendor.

Third, master acquisition agreements can be a waste of time and money in some transactions. Not every vendor relationship is worth the effort of drafting and negotiating a master agreement. For a contract to be a true general procurement document, it must be capable of covering all future transactions between the user and the vendor (for example, purchases, leases, and rentals of hardware; equipment trade-ins and upgrades; associated software licenses; unique systems and services work performed by vendor personnel; and maintenance of both hardware and software). Where the user's anticipated relationship with a vendor is reasonably small, it makes little sense for the user to spend the time and effort necessary to draft and negotiate a complex master agreement. (In situations where a true master agreement is not justified, the user may nevertheless determine to impose a standard form user agreement, as discussed later in this chapter.)

Where the expected user-vendor relationship does not justify the drafting and negotiating of a true master agreement, some benefit may still be derived by using what might be called a "limited" master contract. This type of document can be crafted to cover multiple acquisitions, but with a much more limited scope than a true general procurement agreement. Thus, a limited master agreement might be drafted to cover several related equipment orders over a period of months or years, or a series of equipment conversion efforts associated with the expansion of a user manufacturing facility. In some instances, "limited" master agreements of this nature require the same commitment of drafting and negotiating resources that is involved in a general procurement document with a broader scope. In other circumstances, the limited approach may substantially reduce the time and resources necessary to prepare the agreement.

Fourth, master agreements may be inappropriate in some situations for strategy reasons. Even where the user has the sophistication and time necessary to draft and negotiate a master contract, the user may recognize that, for various reasons, it will be better able to optimize its negotiating position if it postpones the master agreement for some period of time. For example, if the user expects to expand its relationship with the vendor at some point in the future, the user may have a superior bargaining position if it waits and negotiates the master agreement at the time it intends to announce or place a new and significant order with the vendor. Despite the fact that a master agreement is designed to cover all aspects of the user-vendor relationship over a stated period, the fact remains that the vendor is much more likely to be conciliatory if the master agreement is negotiated in connection with a major transaction. From a psychological standpoint, it makes little sense for the initial order under a master agreement to be a few thousand dollars worth of equipment. On the other hand, the user must be aware that negotiating a master agreement as part of a major equipment acquisition may place severe time pressures on the user's negotiating team. Although these pressures can be turned to the user's advantage, the user must make certain that its efforts to achieve a sound master agreement are not tarnished by the vendor's successful use of various "sense of urgency" ploys. (See Chapter 2.)

Fifth, the form contract advantages of a master agreement can prove to be detrimental to the user under certain circumstances. While the user may benefit from the fact that subsequent orders under the master agreement will merely be documented by a one-page order form, this approach may cause user personnel to pay little or no attention to the terms and conditions that will actually govern a particular procurement. Thus, when future orders are placed under a master contract, the user's staff may ignore the terms and conditions of the agreement, simply assuming that the contractual provisions contained in the master agreement will be appropriate to the transaction. Where the master agreement has been carefully drafted and administered, this assumption may of course be quite valid. In other situations, however, subsequent transactions may require special terms and conditions that supplement or modify the master agreement for purposes of the specific order. If the user's staff does not consider the substance of the master agreement each time that a supplemental order is placed, with or without assistance from the user's counsel, any necessary supplemental language may be omitted.

Content

Assuming that the user determines that execution of a master agreement would be advisable, a number of special factors must be considered in negotiating and drafting the contract. Several of the more critical issues are noted below. In general, all of these factors are applicable to true master agreements and, on a narrower scale, to various types of limited master agreements.

Scope. At the outset, the user must carefully determine the scope of the master agreement. As noted above, a true general procurement agreement should be capable of covering virtually all transactions anticipated between the user and the vendor during the applicable term of the agreement. In determining the scope of the agreement, the user's negotiating team should generally discuss, analyze, and list in writing all relevant transactions that might occur during the proposed term of the agreement. In addition, the user's team should determine the degree to which the user's negotiating position will be enhanced—both on a short-term and long-term basis—by the inclusion or exclusion of specific potential transactions in the master agreement. These steps must be completed before drafting of the agreement commences.

Once the scope has been determined, it must be described in the master contract. Regardless of whether the desired scope is broad or more limited, this drafting effort is a dangerous and difficult task that requires linguistic precision. In order to reduce the risk that the scope provision will include errors in coverage, the user should have the draft language carefully reviewed by all members of the user's negotiating team and by additional staff representatives from the operating departments for which the equipment will be procured. In each case, the draft language should be "tested" by comparison to potential transactions that may occur in the future.

The following scope provision provides one example. This provision was utilized in a general procurement document for a multinational telecommunications firm. The scope was clearly intended to be very broad. For purposes of the agreement, the word "products" was defined in a separate definitions section to include virtually any equipment, software, service, or supply item offered by the "Supplier" under the agreement. Obviously, where the scope of the general procurement agreement is intended to be more limited, the provision will generally be more complex.

(A) *Applicability.* This Agreement is applicable to the procurement by Customer in any State of the United States or the District of Columbia from Supplier of any of Supplier's Products that have been announced on or before the effective date of this Agreement and, unless Supplier notifies Customer in writing to the contrary prior to the date of an Order therefor, any of Supplier's Products announced after such effective date.

Term. In connection with assessing the appropriate scope of the master agreement, the user must also determine the term. This decision requires that the user consider both the term itself (i.e., the number of months or years) and whether either party will be able to terminate the master agreement prior to the end of that term, with or without penalty. The question of renewals must also be considered.

Generally, it makes little sense to negotiate a master agreement that can be terminated (and, thus, avoided) by either party on short notice. On the other hand, conditions do change and it may be equally disadvantageous for the agreement to have an unreasonably long term. Although each master agreement must be considered on its own, the authors often recommend 24 to 36 months as a typical or average fixed term for a general procurement agreement. Of course, where a limited master contract will be utilized in connection with a specific project, such as the expansion of a manufacturing plant, the term of the master agreement should generally coincide with the project or some segment of the project.

In one master procurement agreement, the authors used the following approach to describe the term of the contract:

1. TERM OF AGREEMENT.

(A) *Initial Term.* This Agreement shall become effective as of the _____ day of _____, 19 _____, and, except as otherwise provided herein, shall continue in full force and effect through the _____ day of _____, 19 _____ (hereinafter referred to as the "Initial Term" of this Agreement.)

(B) *Renewal Terms.* Following the Initial Term specified above, this Agreement shall be automatically renewed for _____ (_____) consecutive renewal terms of twelve (12) calendar months each (hereinafter referred to individually as a "Renewal Term" or collectively as the "Renewal Terms"), unless any or all such Renewal Terms are canceled by Customer as follows:

(1) *Cancellation During Initial Term.* During the Initial Term, Customer may cancel all Renewal Terms by giving written notice of such cancellation to Supplier at least thirty (30) days prior to the date of expiration of the Initial Term.

(2) *Cancellation During Renewal Term.* During any Renewal Term, Customer may cancel all succeeding Renewal Terms by giving written notice of such cancellation to Supplier at least thirty (30) days prior to the date of expiration of the Renewal Term then in effect.

(3) *Effect of Cancellation of Renewal Term.* Upon cancellation of any or all Renewal Periods, as provided above, the canceled Renewal Period(s) shall be terminated, null, and void as of the date of expiration of the Initial Term or the Renewal Term in effect on the date notice of cancellation was given as provided herein. Neither the cancellation nor nonrenewal or any Renewal Term hereunder shall affect either:

(a) The obligation of either party hereunder to the other party hereunder pursuant to any accepted Order, and each such Order shall continue in effect as if such Renewal Term(s) had not been canceled; or

(b) The obligation of either party hereunder to the other party hereunder pursuant to any right or cause of action that accrued prior to the effective date of such cancellation or nonrenewal.

Orders. After the user has determined the scope and term of the agreement, it must decide how orders will be placed under the master contract and how language contained in these orders will interrelate with language contained in the master contract itself. Although the approach employed will ordinarily depend upon the user's business needs and internal control procedures, the authors generally recommend that individual orders under a master contract be placed by the execution of a one or two page order or specification form that becomes a part of, and is subject to all the terms and conditions of, the master agreement. Where this procedure is used, a sample order form should be included as an exhibit to the master agreement.

Depending upon the breadth of the master contract, it may be advisable to formulate separate types of order forms for each category of product, such as hardware, software, and services. Where separate order forms will be employed for such purposes, a sample copy of each form should be included as an exhibit to the agreement. The function of all forms should be clearly marked in order to avoid confusion.

Despite the fact that the order form is included as an exhibit to the master agreement, the agreement itself should include a provision that sets forth the basic information that must be included in each order. Where certain types of orders require special information, the agreement should reference this fact and specify the additional information required. The following provision offers one example of this approach:

3. FORM OF ORDERS

(A) *Basic Information.* Each Order hereunder shall be written on Customer Form _____, as the same may be amended by Customer from time to time, and shall contain the following minimum information, to the extent the same is applicable:

(1) The incorporation of this Agreement by reference;

(2) The applicable term of any license, rental, lease, maintenance, or service period;

(3) A complete list of the Products covered by the Order specifying the quantity, type and model number, and description for each;

(4) The list price and, if different, the actual price of each Product; any additional charges and costs, including without limitation, periods and charges for overtime use, nonstandard services and special features; the total amount payable by Customer; and the list purchase price and, if different, the actual purchase price of each Product subject to the purchase option provisions of this Agreement;

(5) The location at which the Products shall be delivered and, if different, the location at which the Products shall be initially installed or used;

(6) Any applicable site specifications for the Product;

(7) The date(s), if any, by which Customer shall complete preparation of the installation site or perform other specified obligations and the date(s), if any, by which Supplier shall inspect Customer's installation site to determine its compliance with Supplier's site requirements;

(8) The date(s) by which Supplier shall ship the Products;

(9) The Delivery Date for the Products and, if applicable, any interim delivery schedule;

(10) The Installation Date for the Products;

(11) The maintenance schedule for the Products;

(12) The terms and conditions of any supplemental agreements or licenses, including without limitation any software licenses that may be applicable; and

(13) Any special terms and conditions agreed upon by Supplier and Customer.

(B) *Additional Information for Service Orders.* In addition to the minimum information specified above, each Service Order shall contain the following additional minimum information, to the extent the same is applicable:

(1) The maintenance schedule to be provided, including without limitation the Principal Period of Maintenance; and

(2) A point of contact at which Supplier shall receive notification from Customer of the need for Remedial Maintenance.

Whenever individual orders will be subsequently completed under a master document, a question arises as to whether special terms or conditions included in an order can or should take precedence over conflicting terms in the master agreement. Regardless of the approach agreed upon by the user and the vendor, it is absolutely critical for this matter to be covered, both in the master agreement *and* in the preprinted wording on the individual order forms. Unless each order will be reviewed in advance by the user's legal counsel, the safest and strongest position for the user may be to provide that the master agreement will control in the event of any conflict between the terms of the master agreement and an individual order. Alternatively, the user may adopt this approach, but add an exception that permits certain provisions of an order to take precedence over conflicting language in the master agreement only where the master document specifically states, in one of its provisions: "except as may be specified in the applicable Order." Where the master agreement can be modified by terms and conditions included in a subsequent order, the user should adopt strict internal control procedures to ensure that any such modifications are reviewed and approved prior to the time that the order is submitted to the vendor for acceptance under the agreement. If the user fails to adopt internal controls for this purpose, it may find that it is faced with a supposed "master " agreement that actually has been modified separately for each order. Where this type of modification is permitted to occur, it greatly increases the likelihood that the vendor's marketing representative will utilize various ploys to counteract some of the protection built into the master agreement by the user's negotiating team. Obviously, this risk is greatest where the separate orders are not reviewed by the user's negotiating team, management, or legal counsel.

The following language offers one example of a provision designed to describe the interrelationship of orders with a general procurement agreement. This approach permits language contained in the order to take precedence over conflicting language in the master contract, but only for purposes of the specific transaction documented in the order. Again, each order form should contain language compatible with that used in the master agreement.

(B) *Interrelationship with Orders.* This is a general procurement agreement that contemplates the future execution by Supplier and Customer of one (1) or more Orders. Each Order shall contain the minimum information specified in this Agreement and shall automatically be deemed to include, without the necessity of reference or incorporation, all the terms and provisions of this Agreement. All transactions between Supplier and Customer during any term of this Agreement shall be governed by this Agreement and any applicable Order; *provided, however, that:*

(1) The parties hereto may otherwise agree in a writing executed by both of them; and

(2) Whenever the provisions of an Order conflict with the provisions of this Agreement, the conflicting provisions of the Order shall control and take precedence over the conflicting provisions of this Agreement, but only for purposes of such Order and, except for such Order, the terms and conditions of this Agreement shall not be deemed to be amended, modified, cancelled, waived, or released.

The master agreement should also include language that limits the vendor's ability to reject a valid order placed by the user. For convenience, this same provision should also specify the manner in which orders will be placed by the user and reviewed and acknowledged by the vendor. The effective date of each order must also be specified in some manner. In order to reduce the risks that valid orders will be placed by user personnel having only apparent authority (see Chapter 4), the agreement should also specify the titles of the user officers who will be entitled to execute orders on behalf of the user. The following provision includes example language in each of these areas. It also clearly indicates that the vendor has no authority to make changes, amendments, or modifications to any order submitted by the user without the prior written consent of the user.

4. ORDERS.

(A) *Order Acceptance.* Supplier agrees to notify Customer in writing of Supplier's acceptance or rejection of each Order within ten (10) days of Supplier's receipt of the Order. Supplier shall have the right to reject any Order for failure of Customer to: (i) provide all ordering information required by this Agreement on said Order; or (ii) correctly state prices or other amounts on the Order; or (iii) allow reasonable time for Supplier to manufacture, ship, supply, or install the Product requested in the statement of dates on the Order. Supplier shall indicate in its written acknowledgment to Customer whether the Order was accepted or rejected, and if rejected, Supplier shall detail its reasons for such rejection and shall indicate the modifications necessary to make the Order acceptable to Supplier. Acceptance of any Order by Supplier will bind Supplier to honor dates, amounts and other ordering information shown on the Order, including supplemental provisions contained therein. An Order will be deemed to be null and void and rejected by Supplier if it has not been accepted by Supplier without modification or amendment within ten (10) days after the date the Order was executed by Customer, or its Parent, Subsidiary, or Affiliate.

(B) *Effective Date of Order.* The effective date of an Order shall be the date upon which the Order is accepted and executed by the later of Supplier or Customer without modification or amendment.

(C) *Customer Order Authority.* Each Order placed hereunder shall be executed by a Vice President or higher officer of Customer or, in the case of an Order placed by a Parent, Subsidiary, or Affiliate of the Customer pursuant to the partial assignment provisions hereof, by a Vice President or higher officer of the Parent, Affiliate or Subsidiary placing the Order. Unless so executed by a Vice President or higher authority, an Order placed hereunder shall not be valid or binding upon Customer or Customer's Parent, Affiliate, or Subsidiary.

(D) *Order Modification, Substitution, or Amendment.* Supplier shall make no changes, amendments, modifications, additions, or deletions to any Order offered by Customer, including without limitation substitutions or cancellations of any Product before or after delivery, without the written consent of Customer. Supplier's sole right shall be to accept or reject each Order as the same is offered by Customer. Unless approved in writing by Customer, any such change, amendment, modification, addition, or deletion made by Supplier to any such Order shall immediately cause such Order and any Related Order to be null and void.

Definitions. The size and complexity of most master agreements absolutely mandate use of "terms of art" and a separate definitions section. Among the terms that must be carefully considered are those defining the various items of hardware, software, supplies, systems support, and services that may be provided under the master agreement. Separate but interrelated definitions may be helpful in this regard. For example, anything covered by the agreement may be defined as a "product," whether hardware, software, supplies, or services. A "component" or "item of equipment" may then be defined as the hardware parts of a "system" that includes both software and hardware.

Any definitions drafted by legal counsel for purposes of the master agreement should be carefully reviewed by all members of the negotiating team, particularly those having technical expertise in the type of equipment being acquired. Although the terms of art selected by legal counsel need not necessarily be those used by the staff that will be responsible for operating the equipment, counsel should avoid terms that are clearly inconsistent with trade usage. In addition, every effort should be made to avoid definitions that may have ambiguous meanings or cause unintended results.

The definitions included in any master agreement must be crafted to the specific transactions and type of equipment involved. However, the following excerpts from the definitions section of a general procurement agreement may provide drafting assistance to attorneys and other members of the negotiating team.

DEFINITIONS.

(A) *Acceptance Date.* For any hardware or software product hereunder, Acceptance Date is the first day after the applicable Product successfully completes all phases of Acceptance Testing provided for in this Agreement or the Order. In the event Customer waives Acceptance Testing of any such Product in writing, the Acceptance Date for such Product shall be the date that Supplier delivers its written certification to Customer that such Product is installed and ready for use in accordance with all applicable specfications. For any maintenance, support, or other service Product for which Acceptance Testing is not required hereunder, the Acceptance Date shall be the first day of the applicable maintenance, support, or service period, as specified in the applicable Order.

(B) *Acceptance Testing.* Acceptance Testing is the performance and reliability evaluation standard that must be met by Supplier's hardware and software Products acquired by Customer hereunder, as set forth in Paragraphs 13 and 45 of this Agreement.

(C) *Affiliate.* An Affiliate is any company, partnership, or joint venture more than fifty percent (50%) of the voting shares of which, or interest in which, are owned by any Parent of Subsidiary of Customer.

(D) *Component.* A Component is any integral part of a "System," whether hardware or software, and whether offered by Supplier or any other source.

(E) *Component Failure Downtime.* Component Failure Downtime for a Component after the applicable Component and System have successfully passed any required Acceptance Testing is the accumulated time during which the Component is inoperable due to its failure.

(F) *Control Software.* Control Software is any software Product offered by Supplier (including revisions released by Supplier during the term of this Agreement or the applicable Order) which is designed to control or supervise basic System operation or process commonly encountered applications.

(G) *Conversion.* The Conversion of a Product is the exchange of a leased, rented, or licensed Product for another leased, rented, or licensed Product, which conversion may involve replacement or on- or off-site modification of a currently-installed Product.

(H) *Delivery Date.* Delivery Date is the date by which all items and parts of the applicable Product(s) shall be delivered to the destination specified in the Order.

(I) *Effectiveness Level.* The Effectiveness Level for a System or Component is the factor computed by dividing the Operational Use Time of the System or Component by the sum of that time plus System or Component Failure Downtime, as specified in Paragraph 13 of this Agreement.

(J) *Enhancement.* Enhancement is any improvement to or change in any Supplier software Product that improves or otherwise alters its basic function.

(K) *Installation Date.* The Installation Date is the date by which all items and parts of the applicable Product(s) shall be installed and prepared for Acceptance Testing at the location specified in the Order. Preparation for Acceptance Testing shall include completion of the System Audit specified in Paragraph 12(H) of this Agreement. Installation Date for purposes of Paragraph 44 is defined in that Paragraph.

(L) *Operational Use Time.* Operational Use Time for Acceptance Testing of a System or Component is the accumulated time during which the applicable central Processing Unit (CPU) or Component is in actual operation, measured in accordance with the provisions of Subparagraph (A) (3) (b) (ii) of Paragraph 13 of this Agreement.

(M) *Order.* An Order is any written order for any Supplier Product issued pursuant to this Agreement.

(N) *Parent.* A Parent is any company, partnership, or joint venture that owns more than fifty percent (50%) of the voting shares of Customer.

(O) *Preventive Maintenance.* Preventive Maintenance is maintenance performed, or required to be performed, by Supplier on a scheduled basis to keep the Product in good operating condition in accordance with Supplier's published specifications therefor and any additional specifications contained or referenced in any Supplier Order, and in accordance with the Effectiveness Level specified in Subparagraph 37(J) of this Agreement. Preventive Maintenance shall include but not necessarily be limited to: (i) calibration, testing, and any necessary adjustments, cleaning, lubrication, replacement of worn, defective, or questionable parts, and minor circuit updating and modifications; and (ii) maintenance and engineering services necessary to retrofit or otherwise install engineering changes, modifications, and improvements (including the latest Supplier engineering revision and any and all reliability improvements) made to any Product by Supplier at any time during the maintenance term for that Product; and (iii) automatic update services for any and all manuals and documentation furnished with any Product subject to maintenance under this Agreement or any Order.

(P) *Principal Period of Maintenance.* The Principal Period of Maintenance is that period of time during which there shall be no additional or overtime charge for any maintenance services performed by Supplier.

(Q) *Product(s).* Product(s) is any equipment, software, service, or supply item offered by Supplier. For this purpose, "equipment" includes any hardware Product; "software" includes any program, programming aid, routine, subroutine, translation, compiler, diagnostic routine, Control Software or Special Software; "service" includes any programming service, preventive maintenance, remedial hardware maintenance, software maintenance, conversion service, consulting service, or support service; "supply item" includes any cards, paper, ribbons, magnetic tape, other magnetic storage media, and similar items that are used or required to operate the Products acquired by Customer under this Agreement or any Order.

(R) *Related Order(s).* Related Order(s) is any Order(s) that is related to one (1) or more other Order(s) where: (i) either such Order specifies that the two (2) or more Orders are so related; or (ii) either such Order specifies that one (1) or more such Orders is conditioned or contingent upon the execution or performance of the other Order(s); or (iii) the Order(s) is for Products that are necessary to the reasonable or intended operation or use of any other Product ordered by Customer within thirty (30) days before or after the date Customer executes the other Order.

(S) *Related Product.* A Related Product is any Product(s) that is related to one (1) or more other Products by virtue of the fact that the Products were ordered pursuant to one (1) or more Related Orders.

(T) *Remedial Maintenance.* Remedial Maintenance is maintenance performed, or required to be performed, by Supplier upon the written or oral request of Customer to place the applicable Product back into good operating condition, in accordance with the standards specified in the definition of "Preventive Maintenance" herein, after it has become inoperative or subject to malfunction.

(U) *Special Software.* Special Software is any software Product offered by Supplier that is custom-developed by Supplier for operation as, or as an integral part of, a unique Customer application.

(V) *Subsidiary.* A Subsidiary is any company, partnership, or joint venture more than fifty percent (50%) of the voting shares of which, or interest in which, are owned by Customer.

(W) *System.* A System is any collection or aggregation of two (2) or more Components that is designed to function, or is represented by Supplier as functioning or being capable of functioning, as a functional entity. A System may be offered by Supplier or any other source and may include Components offered by Supplier and those offered by one (1) or more other Suppliers.

(X) *System Failure Downtime.* System Failure Downtime is the accumulated time during which the applicable System or Component is inoperable due to Component or other Product failure, measured in accordance with the provisions of Subparagraph (A) (3) (b) (iii) of Paragraph 13.

(Y) *Upgrade.* Upgrade, when applied to software, is any improvement in the software that relates to operating performance but does not alter the basic function of the software. When applied to leased or rented hardware, Upgrade is the exchange or conversion of such hardware for one (1) or more other Products, as specified in Paragraph 44 of this Agreement.

Specific Tailoring. In many instances, the user will need to devise some method of making certain provisions of the master agreement applicable only to certain types of transactions or products. Despite the value of having all transactions with a vendor covered by a single master agreement, not every sentence or paragraph will necessarily be equally applicable to every product that is acquired. Although many types of exclusionary language can be devised, one approach is to organize the agreement around various types of orders, as noted above. Thus, a "purchase order" may apply to equipment and related products acquired by purchase; a "rental order" may apply to lease or rental transactions; and a "software order" or "license order" may apply to software transactions. Although this approach interjects additional complexity into the definitions section of the agreement, it permits ready use of simple exclusionary or inclusionary language where required to limit the applicability of a particular sentence or provision. For example, a paragraph of limited application may be introduced with, "Except for a Rental Order . . ." or with, "For a software Order. . . ."

Organization. The organization and content of a general procurement agreement should be tailored to the user's business needs and the types of transactions and equipment that will be covered by the document. As in the case of most complex legal agreements, the keys to drafting success are comprehensive treatment of the subject matter, clear wording, and an organizational format that can be understood by all of the parties involved. The following outline sets forth the format utilized in a general procurement agreement involving electronic equipment. The master contract covered equipment, software, services, and certain related supplies. (This outline is presented for purposes of demonstrating organization and format. It should not be relied upon as representing a comprehensive listing of all issues covered in a master agreement.)

1. Term of Agreement

   A. Initial Term
   B. Extension

2. Definitions

3. Scope of Agreement

   A. Initial Order
   B. Subsequent Orders
   C. Future Discounts
   D. License
   E. Implementation Schedules
   F. Technical Support
   G. Maintenance
   H. Charges
   I. Training
   J. Documentation
   K. Software Modification
   L. Resource Scheduling
   M. Software
   N. Systems Interfaces
   O. Joint Ventures
   P. Communication Lines
   Q. New Product Development Updates

4. Pre-Order Product Evaluation

   A. Benchmark Testing
   B. Products For Testing

5. Forms of Orders

   A. Basic Information
   B. Special Instructions

6. Ordering Procedure

   A. Order Acceptance
   B. Effective Date of Order
   C. Order Authority
   D. Order Modification, Substitution, or Amendment
   E. Order Termination
   F. Order Severability

7. New Equipment/Substitution of Used Equipment

   A. New Equipment Warranty
   B. Substitution of Used Equipment

8. Taxes

   A. Sales and Use
   B. Property
   C. Other
   D. Duty to File

9. Purchase Option

   A. Price
   B. Transfer of Title
   C. Discontinuance from Lease or Rental

10. Transportation

    A. Invoicing
    B. Packing Cases
    C. Maximum Charges

11. Delivery

    A. Delivery Schedule
    B. Delivery Authorization
    C. Delivery of All Items
    D. Notice of Change or Delay

12. Insurance and Risk of Loss Through Acceptance Date

    A. Responsibility and Coverage
    B. Action in Event of Loss
    C. No Limitation of Liability

13. Site Preparation and Installation

    A. Site Specifications
    B. Site Preparation
    C. Site Inspection
    D. Alterations
    E. Permits
    F. Access
    G. Installation
    H. System Audit
    I. Early Acceptance Testing

14. Installation Procedures

    A. User Obligations
    B. Timely Performance Prior to Final Acceptance
    C. Installation Team
    D. Progress Reports by Vendor

15. Acceptance Testing Procedures

    A. Hardware Testing
    B. Operations Software Testing
    C. Application Software Testing
    D. System Acceptance Testing

16. Insurance and Risk of Loss After Acceptance Date

17. Invoices and Payments

    A. System Acceptance
    B. Payments
    C. Limitation on Additional Charges
    D. Application of Charges
    E. Proration of Charges
    F. Reduction Before Acceptance
    G. Increase During Term
    H. Invoicing Standards
    I. Credits
    J. Delivery of Invoices
    K. Security Interest
    L. Records and Disputes

M. Order Records
N. Invoice Term and Conditions

18. Indemnity

    A. By Vendor
    B. By User

19. Field Modifications

    A. Modification
    B. Discontinuance of Charges
    C. Notice
    D. System Unavailability

20. Corporate Authority Warranties by Each Party

    A. Corporate Organization
    B. Corporate Authority

21. Performance Warranties

    A. System Warranty
    B. Component Warranty
    C. Redundancy Warranty
    D. Catastrophic Failure Warranty
    E. Configuration Warranty
    F. Software Release Warranty
    G. Data Base Error Correction
    H. Parts Availability
    I. Minimum Acceptable Level of Performance
    J. Response Time

22. Patent Warranty

    A. Patent Indemnity
    B. Use of Infringing Products
    C. Discontinuation of Payments
    D. Equal Treatment
    E. Remedies for Infringement

23. Title

    A. Warranty of Title
    B. Title to Leased, Rented and Licensed Products
    C. Title to Purchased Products

24. Survival of Representations and Warranties

25. Defaults By User; Remedies of Vendor

    A. Defaults by User
    B. Remedies of Vendor
    C. Limitation and Mitigation of Damages

26. Defaults by Vendor; Remedies of User

    A. Defaults by Vendor
    B. Remedies of User
    C. Limitation and Mitigation of Damages

27. General Provisions

    A. Independent Contractor Status
    B. Quiet Enjoyment

    C. Limitation on Promotions and Advertising
    D. Confidentiality
    E. Site Rules and Regulations
    F. Assignment and Sublease
    G. Releases and Waivers
    H. Disaster Availability
    I. Force Majeure
    J. Notice
    K. Nonwaiver
    L. Partial Invalidity
    M. Successors and Assigns
    N. Paragraph Headings
    O. Entire Agreement
    P. Rights Upon Orderly Termination
    Q. Applicability of Uniform Commercial Code
    R. Governing Law
    S. Relocation of System or Components
    T. Nondiscrimination
    U. Disclaimer of Implied Warranties

EXHIBITS

    A. Hardware Acquisition List
    B. Software Acquisition List
    C. Software Modification
    D. General Contract Schedule
    E. Vendor Training Courses
    F. Vendor Documentation Schedule
    G. Performance and Reliability Specifications
    H. Equal Employment Opportunity Compliance Requirements
    I. Trade-in Schedule
    J. Installation Support Personnel

USER FORM AGREEMENTS

Although such documents have been employed by state and federal agencies for many years, *user* form agreements are relatively new in many industries. The idea of a user form agreement is relatively simple: The contract is a standard form which sets forth the terms and conditions on which *the user* is willing to acquire certain equipment, software, or services. In this regard, the document is not unlike the standard form agreement proposed by many vendors. The significant difference is that the user form agreement either optimizes the position of the user at the expense of the vendor, or at least sets forth a fair and equitable agreement that protects the interests of both sides to the transaction.

Benefits

Properly prepared and employed, user form agreements can offer significant benefits for the user. The principal user benefits are explored below.

First, form agreements permit the user to document its goals and objectives in an organized manner, prior to engaging in direct negotiations with a vendor on a specific acquisition. As a result, the user's negotiating team is better able to assess the terms and conditions that should be included in the form document. The user's attorneys are also able to work with the negotiating team to prepare, review, and revise the form agreement, without the usual "sense of urgency" associated with pending transactions. Senior management can also be brought into the review process in a more orderly fashion. Other user departments that need to review specific portions of the agreement can perform their responsibilities in a more comprehensive and systematic manner. In effect, preparation of a form agreement permits the user to consider and structure the business, technical, legal, and financial aspects of the transaction prior to the time that emotion, a sense of urgency and the heat of battle impinge upon the acquisition process.

Second, although the preparation of user form agreements may itself require a fair commitment of time and other resources, such agreements generally save considerable time and money over the longer term. Assuming that the form agreements receive a reasonable amount of use (discussed below), they should obviate the need for separate drafting efforts in connection with each acquisition. Even where the user form agreements must be tailored somewhat in order to be accepted by a particular vendor or to be applicable in a specific transaction, the user's lawyers will ordinarily be able to implement the necessary changes with considerably less time and effort. Indeed, time can also be saved where the form agreements cannot be used at all. Even if the various forms are not applicable to a particular transaction, the substantial number of provisions contained in the forms can serve as an excellent user "data base" from which another document can be constructed by the user's advisors.

Third, form agreements can be included as part of the user's vendor evaluation process. In this regard, the applicable form agreements can be published in the user's RFP, either as a mandatory or as an aspiration-level contract. The user can then base part of its acquisition decision on the vendor's willingness to accept the user's standard agreement. Even if the vendors prove to be unwilling to accept the user's form in full, this approach permits the user to begin negotiations on all principal factors when the user has maximum negotiating leverage—at the outset of the RFP process. (Despite these benefits, including form contracts in the user's RFP can have a negative effect on the level of voluntary vendor concessions. The relative advantages and disadvantages of including form contracts and lists of legal/contractual issues in user RFPs are explored in Chapter 5.)

Fourth, particularly where the user has a reasonable amount of bargaining power resulting from the volume of its equipment purchases, user form agreements can reduce the barrage of vendor form agreements with widely-differing terms. To the extent that this plethora of vendor agreements can be reduced, the user will save both time and money in the review process. *In addition, the user will minimize the risk that one or more over-zealous managers will execute the standard vendor form, without adequate legal or financial review.* Where the user has a solid form agreement program, user managers recognize that they will be able to execute a document and move ahead with the procurement process much more rapidly if they utilize the standard user form. After some degree of "training," most vendor sales representatives will come to the same conclusion from their own perspective: They will have a better opportunity to close the sale and execute the agreement if they accept the standard user form rather than their own one-sided agreement.

Fifth, form agreements permit larger users to implement their own *fait accompli* strategy with their existing and potential vendors. (See Chapter 3.) When a relatively small vendor is advised by a fairly large user that the vendor will be able to supply equipment or services to the user *only* if the vendor agrees to utilize the user's standard form agreement, the *vendor* must determine whether it wishes to spend the time and money necessary to review and negotiate the agreement. This decision is not unlike that faced by many users when the vendor presents its own form agreement—the roles are simply reversed. Although the idea of employing user form agreements as a *fait accompli* strategy may appear to be somewhat onerous, the approach can actually be beneficial to both the vendor and the user. Many smaller vendors, and a remarkable number of larger ones, do a very poor job of preparing their own standard form agreements. Many such agreements are prepared by the vendor's president or chief financial officer, with little or no advice of counsel. Other such agreements are prepared or reviewed by the vendor's lawyers, but the attorneys do not have adequate training in the equipment acquisition field. Although the user's standard form agreement may be somewhat more preferential to the user than to the vendor, it will often do a far superior job of documenting the acquisition transaction on a basis that is comprehensive and fair to *both* sides. Even if concessions must be negotiated in order for the agreement to be acceptable to the vendor, the documentation of the overall transaction will be improved by beginning with the user's standard form agreement and including any changes or addenda that may be appropriate.

Finally, form agreements permit user staff personnel to employ the "Unfortunately, I'll Have to Get Any Changes Approved by Corporate" ploy. (This ploy is described from the vendor's perspective in Chapter 2.) When implemented as a strategy from the user's perspective, this negotiating approach permits the user's representative to emphasize his or her own willingness to do everything possible for the vendor, but continually stress the problems of dealing with the user's corporate headquarters or legal departments. By stressing the problems of getting any changes to the user form agreement through "corporate" or "legal," the user staff representative can encourage the vendor to set forth all of its objections at one time. In this regard, the user negotiator may explain "I don't want to go to headquarters for approval on this thing too many times, so let's make sure we have all of your demands before I stick my neck out." In addition to causing the vendor to disclose its entire "shopping list" of changes to the user's form agreement at the outset of the negotiations, this approach enables the user representative to employ the "limited authority" negotiating technique. It also permits the user negotiator to hide behind the shield of the user's "standard way of doing business." Moreover, because the vendor is placed in the position of proposing changes to the user's standard agreement, the vendor marketing representative is constantly forced to justify his or her negotiating position.

Pitfalls

Despite these benefits, user form agreements can create risks and disadvantages if they are not drafted and utilized effectively. Several of the problems associated with user form agreements are highlighted below.

First, the preparation of good user form agreements requires a substantial commitment of time and resources. Many users do not have the necessary resources (particularly in terms of drafting expertise) to prepare a comprehensive set of form agreements. Other users are unwilling to commit the necessary time and money to do the job. Despite the longer-term benefits that will be derived from utilization of the form agreements, these users either cannot or will not make the "up front" commitment of resources necessary to derive these subsequent benefits. Still other users commit a nominal amount of time and resources to a standard form agreement project, but refuse to provide the effort and funds necessary to complete the job. The result of this half-hearted commitment is generally disaster. The form agreements are inadequate and, as a result, the user becomes disenchanted with the entire concept of employing user form documents. Indeed, user management may even view the failure as further indication of the fact that extensive negotiations on any equipment acquisition are an unnecessary expense. Actual experience strongly suggests that, unless the user is prepared to make the commitment necessary to prepare and utilize thorough standard form agreements, the user would be better served by continuing to negotiate vendor-supplied agreements or to draft new agreements for each transaction.

Second, some users misunderstand the purpose of user form agreements. Based upon their experience with vendor standard form documents, these users assume that their own form agreements should be comprised of an extreme set of pro-user provisions that will be onerous to the vendor. Unfortunately, this approach merely reverses the roles of the protagonist and the antagonist. Few intelligent vendors will be likely to submit to a blatantly pro-user agreement. Indeed, where the user presents such a document, the vendor may simply refuse to consider it and deadlock its sales efforts until the user agrees to accept the vendor's form. (This approach is particularly likely—and effective—if the vendor recognizes that the user's form agreement program is relatively new and may not be fully supported by senior management. When this occurs, the vendor's marketing representative does everything possible to advise senior user management that the vendor has no pride of authorship in its own agreement, but the user's approach is totally unacceptable and commercially unreasonable. Successful implementation of this vendor strategy has destroyed a number of budding user form agreement programs.) As suggested below, the user's form agreement program is unlikely to be successful unless the form documents provide a reasonable and equitable division of responsibility and risk. The user should not assume that it will obtain substantive benefits from a standard form agreement only if the agreement includes strong pro-user provisions that are onerous to the vendor. Compared to vendor form agreements, the user will obtain meaningful substantive benefits if the user form agreement merely describes and documents the transaction in a reasonable, even-handed manner.

Third, user form agreements that are not properly drafted may actually pose more risks than benefits to the user. If the user's lawyers and other advisors do not have the necessary drafting expertise, or do not have an adequate understanding of the technical and business aspects of the transactions in which the agreements will be used, the form contracts may be substantively deficient from the user's standpoint. Although this risk always exists in connection with any contract prepared by the user, it is compounded in a standard form program because each copy of the agreement contains the same weakness or error. Because of this risk, many users embarking on standard form agreement programs have the documents prepared or reviewed by outside legal counsel and/or by negotiating experts in the respective field, even where the user has a strong internal legal department. Other users have initial drafts of the agreements prepared internally, but circulate the drafts to the user's external attorneys or consultants for review.

Fourth, a user form contract program must be properly administered and implemented in order to be safe and effective. Regardless of the quality of the form contracts themselves, the user's form contract program may create more risks and problems than benefits if the contracts are not properly used. The principal risks in this regard are that the form agreements will be employed in the wrong transactions, that they will be used without change where minor amendments are appropriate, and that they will create a false sense of security for the user's operations and legal personnel.

Few form agreements will be applicable to all transactions contemplated by the user. Because of this fact, many users prepare a wide variety of standard form agreements. In this approach, each agreement focuses on a specific type of transaction and/or equipment. In one user form agreement program, the following types of contracts were prepared:

1. Hardware Purchase (New)
2. Hardware Purchase (Used)
3. Hardware Lease/Rental (New)
4. Hardware Lease/Rental (Used)
5. Hardware Maintenance
6. Software License (System Software)
7. Software License (Application Software)
8. Software Development (Original and Enhancements)
9. Software Maintenance

10. Third Party Lease
11. Independent Consultant

Although having an adequate number of different agreements applicable to specific transactions reduces the problems of drafting and applying a single agreement to a multitude of acquisitions, it does not necessarily guarantee that the user's staff will apply the correct agreement to the right transaction. In this regard, subtle interpretive problems can often arise. For example, where the user is acquiring electronic typewriters, should the user's form agreement for data processing systems or its form agreement for office equipment be utilized? What about advanced word processing systems? Microcomputers? Minicomputers? In order to reduce the potential risks in this area, the team responsible for developing the user form agreements should ordinarily be charged with determining the transactions in which specific agreements should be employed. In larger form agreement programs, some users develop transaction indices which key a given type of transaction and equipment to a specific user form agreement. Other users require that decisions in this area be made by the user's legal department. Indeed, a strong argument can be made that no user form agreement should be used and executed without prior review and approval by the user's legal or purchasing department. At a minimum, this review should ensure that the proper agreement is being utilized in the proper transaction and that the agreement has been validly executed. This review procedure can also be employed to ensure that the transaction itself has received all applicable corporate approvals.

This type of consolidated review can also reduce the likelihood that a standard form agreement will be used without change where minor amendments are in fact dictated by the transaction or equipment involved. When standard form user agreements are promulgated, user staff personnel often tend to pay less attention to the documentation side of the transaction. As a result, user representatives sometimes assume that a particular type of form agreement can be employed in virtually all relevant transactions, without change. The fact of the matter is that no form agreement can ever apply effectively to all possible transactions. Specific problems or user business goals may dictate changes. Where these changes occur on a relatively frequent basis, they can be incorporated into the next regular draft of the applicable form agreement or, alternatively, set forth in standard addenda that can be affixed when necessary. (Standard addenda are frequently employed by vendor legal and marketing personnel.) Of course, form agreements simply should not be used in some equipment acquisitions. Where the complexity or uniqueness of the acquisition or other special factors dictate, the necessary legal documents should be drafted specifically for the acquisition involved. However, the user's form agreements can still be used as part of the drafting data base of example provisions and ideas.

One final caveat should be noted concerning the use of provisions excerpted from standard form agreements. As most experienced lawyers recognize, law students and new attorneys have a tendency to "build" contracts by pulling provisions from existing agreements. This drafting technique is not dangerous in and of itself. Indeed, most lawyers continue to use the approach throughout their practices. The danger occurs when the provisions are pulled and reemployed without proper understanding or thought. An even greater problem occurs when business executives without legal training attempt a similar approach. The existence of user form agreements may increase the risk that these problems will occur. Because of this fact, the implementation of any user form agreement program should include appropriate precautionary reminders that provisions taken from a resource form agreement should not be inserted into another document without a clear understanding of the purpose and applicability of the provision.

Content

Almost by definition, user form agreements should be well-prepared and as thorough as necessary to deal with the transactions involved. From a substantive standpoint, such agreements should include the same types of provisions that would be included in any other properly prepared contract. Consequently, reference should be made to other chapters of this book, and to the checklist contained in Appendix A, for a review of provisions that may be relevant to a particular type of major equipment acquisition.

Although the substance of user form agreements should be essentially the same as that in similar contracts drafted for specific transactions, users should consider several special factors when drafting and designing the organization of form agreements. These matters are discussed below.

First, as explained above, user form agreements should be comprehensive but fair. Although some users naively believe otherwise, a user form agreement program will stand little chance of success if the agreements contain pro-user provisions that are obviously onerous to the vendor. In certain industries (such as data processing), vendor form agreements are notorious for being one-sided in favor of the vendor. Rather than attempting to employ a similar approach, the user should limit its efforts to crafting form agreements that fairly and even-handedly describe and document the transactions involved. Taking any other approach will provide little substantive benefit to the user in the final analysis, due to the fact that few vendors will execute such agreements under any circumstances. The user will ordinarily stand a much greater chance of obtaining realistic concessions and gaining a fair and reasonable agreement if it poses an equitable standard form document. This approach also increases the likelihood that the vendor will accept the user's form agreement program and that the user's standard agreements can be routinely executed without significant negotiating sessions and subsequent changes. (Users should remember that one of the principal benefits of a standard agreement program—saving time—will be lost if the user is forced to engage in lengthy negotiations with each vendor over the standard user forms. Where these negotiations result in material changes to the user's form, this loss of time is of course exacerbated.)

Second, user form agreements should be designed to "fit the transaction." As suggested above, few form agreements can effectively apply to a wide range of acquisitions. Rather than attempting to narrow its total number of form agreements to an unrealistic level, the user should create a variety of standard forms that specifically apply to particular transactions and types of equipment. This approach may actually be far easier than many users assume. If the user's drafting team creates several basic agreements in key substantive areas, these documents can generally be tailored to other transactions and types of acquisition without significant effort. Indeed, some users create basic form documents and then supplement them with addenda that apply to specific types of equipment or transactions. Other users employ "modules" of provisions that can be moved in blocks from one type of agreement to another type of agreement. The "module" approach permits the basic agreement to be built very quickly. The user then need only add additional specific provisions where necessary.

When the user is not prepared to create the breadth of standard form agreements that may be necessary to deal with its total procurement needs, it should ordinarily develop its form agreement program in stages. In this approach, the user creates form contracts for specific segments of its equipment acquisition program, but continues to draft original agreements, or modify vendor form agreements, in other areas until the form agreement program can be extended.

Third, user form agreements should be capable of relatively easy modification. Although any changes to the user's forms must be properly controlled, the form agreement program will be enhanced if the user is able to accommodate vendor requests for changes with minimum difficulty. As suggested above, certain changes may be capable of being documented in standard form addenda that can be removed from an existing set of preprinted forms and applied where necessary. Standard agreements can also be established on advanced word processing machines, thereby creating substantial flexibility in a "form agreement" context. Many users keep alternative provisions in a word processing "library." When specific vendors require changes that the user recognizes that it has prenegotiated in earlier transactions, these alternative provisions are simply inserted in the "standard" form where appropriate. Other users that do considerable business with one or two vendors create specific variations of their standard form agreements that are used for all transactions between the user and the specific vendor.

Fourth, to be effective, the user form agreements must be thoroughly understood by all user representatives involved in the acquisition process. Some legal and procurement departments prepare complete form contract packages, in which the agreements are supplemented with summaries of the documents, procedures for use, and guidelines for subsequent contract administration. As explained in Chapter 5, some users integrate their form contracts into a comprehensive RFP that includes various form documents and "modules" that can be utilized in a variety of different acquisitions. These packages may also include form letters for correspondence to the vendor and various internal approval documents. Other users provide educational sessions for all staff members that will be involved in completing or utilizing the form contracts. These sessions appear to be most effective where the contracts and any supplemental materials are distributed to the user's staff in advance of the training meeting, so that staff members have an opportunity to ask questions during the session. Where practicable, at least one of the lawyers involved in drafting the agreements should be present for these sessions.

Fifth, user form contracts should be structured to facilitate contract administration. (See Chapter 13.) Personnel involved in the user's contract administration program should assist in drafting and organizing the form agreements. To facilitate the monitoring of vendor performance, the form agreements should include clear deadlines and firm remedial provisions. Interim deadlines should be used where applicable, in order to provide early warning of potential vendor defaults.

Sixth, the content of all user form agreements should be prereviewed and preapproved, both by the user's internal staff and by its outside advisors. As suggested above, for form agreements to be effective, they must be predeveloped, ahead of specific acquisition negotiations. They must also be firmly supported by senior management. If the user's management is unwilling to stand behind the form agreements in face of vendor criticism, the user's form agreement program will probably fail before it ever begins. If the user's form agreements are subjected to continuing vendor complaints, the user should have the documents carefully reviewed by independent counsel or other outside consultants experienced in equipment negotiations. If these advisors determine that the form documents require modification, appropriate changes can be made. Otherwise, the user's management and staff should be prepared to stand behind the form documents and to provide the support necessary for them to gain vendor acceptance.

12
RENTAL AND INSTALLMENT PURCHASE CONTRACTS

RENTAL AND DIRECT LEASE AGREEMENTS

Although many equipment manufacturers offer both "rental" and direct "lease" arrangements, the law seldom if ever distinguishes between a "rental" agreement and a "lease" agreement. In both types of contract, the vendor permits the user to utilize the equipment for a specified term in return for payment of a periodic availability charge. From a practical standpoint, however, many vendors and users tend to employ the word "rental" when referring to an agreement that covers a reasonably short term, and the word "lease" when referring to a contract that covers a longer term. Although the vendor's standard form rental and lease agreements may be different, this difference generally stems from the vendor's willingness to offer varying terms depending upon the length of the agreement, and not because rental and lease agreements involve different legal principles.

In contrast, however, direct lease agreements must be distinguished from third-party leases. In the former, the user acquires the equipment directly from the manufacturer or other vendor and enters into a lease agreement with that party. In the latter, the manufacturer or other vendor sells the equipment to a third-party leasing firm (or to its investment syndicate), which then enters into a third-party lease or sublease arrangement with the user.

Third-party leasing is explained in more detail in Chapter 10. The following discussion focuses on rental and direct lease agreements.

Use and Cost Considerations

Rental and direct lease agreements offer a number of advantages to the user. In general, such agreements minimize the user's commitment to the equipment, and therefore maximize the user's flexibility. Where the agreements are signed directly with the manufacturer, they also eliminate the need to document manufacturer concessions in a separate "side agreement," as often occurs in third-party leasing arrangements.

Many users also find the terms and conditions of rental agreements to be advantageous. For example, rental agreements often include maintenance at no extra charge, resulting in one stop "shopping" and documentation. Some users also conclude, rightfully or wrongfully, that, because the vendor still owns the equipment, the level of service provided will be higher than in purchase or third-party leasing alternatives.

The financial aspects of rental and direct lease agreements may also offer benefits to the user. Rental payments are generally deductible business expenses and, in some agreements, may also be applicable as purchase option credits. Because the accounting and tax treatment for most rental and direct lease arrangements is relatively settled, these agreements seldom pose problems in these areas for the user.

On the other hand, rental and direct lease agreements also offer certain disadvantages. Compared to other acquisition methods, the cost of the rental alternative is almost always high. Moreover, depending upon the specific agreement terms, the rental price may be subject to increase on short notice (for example, 90 days). Unless purchase option credits are involved, rental arrangements also offer no opportunity for the user to build "equity" in the equipment or to receive any residual value. (Of course, if the equipment offers substantial residual value *risk*, the user may well *prefer* the rental alternative, as it reduces the user's exposure to fast-changing technology.)

As suggested in Chapter 4, users may find it advantageous to acquire certain types of equipment on a rental basis at the same time that they acquire other types of equipment through a purchase, third-party lease, or installment purchase arrangement. Where this approach is employed, the user should normally utilize the rental acquisition method for equipment that will only be needed for a short period of time. For example, the rental technique is most appropriate where the user is acquiring equipment to fill temporary overload problems associated with high-volume production or the failure of other equipment. The rental approach may also be preferred where the equipment involved is undergoing rapid technological change. In this circumstance, the rental approach places the principal risk of obsolescence with the vendor rather than the user. If new, state-of-the-art equipment is released, the user can cancel the rental agreement on short notice, or await termination of the rental period, and order the new equipment. (Indeed, the user may be able to include an "upgrade" provision in the rental agreement, at little or no additional cost. However, this approach does not immunize the user from technological advances announced by other vendors.) In contrast, where the release of a new generation of equipment does not create problems for the user (for example, where basic "work horse" equipment will do), the higher acquisition cost involved in the rental method will generally dictate use of the purchase or third-party lease technique.

Rental arrangements may also be preferable where the user faces reduced capital availability. From a financial standpoint, many users rent equipment simply because they cannot afford to purchase it or do not have the financial standing necessary to enter into third-party lease or installment purchase agreements on acceptable terms. Other users have the financial standing to enter into these more permanent arrangements, but prefer to preserve their capital and borrowing power for other purposes. The preservation of capital and borrowing power can be particularly important when considered in the context of temporary high-volume production demand. During the first half of the seventies, many road building and heavy equipment contractors faced serious financial problems resulting from a general downturn in the economy and the real estate industry. Many of these firms survived only because they had previously chosen to avoid purchasing any expensive earth moving equipment, limiting their use of such equipment to that which could be rented on a short-term basis. Although the daily rental costs greatly exceeded the daily costs of ownership, the rental expenses were due and payable only when the equipment was actually being put to productive use.

Negotiating Considerations

When determining to utilize the rental or direct lease alternative, the user should recognize that its decision will affect the negotiating strategies employed by it and the vendor in the acquisition. Several more important negotiating considerations are outlined below.

First, the relative willingness of a vendor to offer incentives in a rental or direct lease transaction will generally depend upon the degree to which the vendor (or its marketing representative) has an incentive or disincentive to pursue such transactions. Vendor incentives in this regard ordinarily vary over time. For example, vendors are frequently motivated to increase the size of their rental or lease base early during the life cycle of a particular system. At this stage of a model life cycle, the vendor has the greatest opportunity to optimize its longer term rental income and reduce its exposure to rental and lease cancellations resulting from new equipment introductions. A similar incentive often exists when the vendor has substantial extra cash that cannot be invested in other enterprises at a higher return than the vendor can achieve on its rental arrangements. Conversely, many vendors prefer to reduce the size of their rental and direct lease base late in the cycle of a particular system. At such points, these vendors will often offer substantial purchase concessions in order to encourage their rental and lease customers to convert to permanent ownership. This approach permits the vendor to shift the risk of a decline in residual value to the user. Similarly, many vendors attempt to reduce the size of their rental and lease base when they are short of cash or can invest their available funds in other areas at a higher rate of return. Again, when cash shortages exist (or where the cash is simply desired for another corporate purpose, such as a major acquisition or a research and development program), the vendor may create incentives to encourage its rental users to convert their equipment to direct ownership. Where the vendor's incentive to encourage or discourage rental arrangements is based upon some general corporate strategy (such as need for cash), the vendor's actions may offer substantial value for the user with little risk. On the other hand, where the vendor's incentive is grounded upon a desire to reduce the size of its existing rental base before introducing a dramatic new generation of equipment, the vendor's "special prices" may actually cost the user a great deal. Consequently, before jumping at purchase incentives for existing rental or leased equipment, the user should carefully analyze its residual value risk in light of the estimated remaining life cycle for the generation of equipment involved.

Second, as noted above in this chapter, the user's ability to extract negotiating concessions from the vendor is often dependent upon the vendor's relative maneuvering room in the transaction. Because rental and direct lease arrangements generally involve lower user commitments and firm published prices, users may find it more difficult to achieve financial and nonfinancial concessions from the vendor. A user's ability to achieve concessions will often depend upon its ability to link the rental or lease arrangement with a longer term commitment, the existence or promise of a more substantial transaction, or the purchase of other equipment. Where the vendor's willingness to offer rental or lease concessions appears to be connected to the length or size of the potential user-vendor relationship, the user can employ several strategies. For example, the user can offer to sign a "general procurement agreement" or other master contract, thereby suggesting that it intends to purchase, lease, or rent substantial additional equipment from the vendor in the months or years to come. (Obviously, in such situations, the user must be prepared to do a competent, professional job of negotiating and documenting the agreement—unless, of course, the user never intends to employ it.) Alternatively, the user can convince the vendor that the rental arrangement is absolutely essential if the user's operations department is to persuade top management that the vendor's equipment should be purchased for use throughout the user company. This alternative is often particularly effective when the user is attempting to obtain concessions of a relatively nominal rental agreement, but the user might be interested in substantially increasing its relationship with the vendor in the months to come. (Some users implement this approach by encouraging the vendor to install the equipment at no charge, or at a "maintenance only" charge, during a preliminary "test" or "demonstration" period. However, users pursuing this tactic should negotiate all relevant terms of the applicable agreement. As explained in Chapter 2, many vendors use the "Try It, You'll Like It" ploy to lull users into installing trial equipment that will ultimately be governed by standard form vendor agreements.) In yet another alternative, the user can suggest that it would be willing to enter into a direct lease agreement with a longer term (rather than a rental arrangement), but only if the user has certain cancellation privileges. The longer lease agreement will often appeal to the vendor marketing representative simply because it suggests that the user-vendor relationship will be more substantial. It may also help the vendor marketeer meet a sales quota in a given area. If the cancellation provision is drafted carefully, the longer-term agreement may offer the necessary flexibility to the user, while not clouding these vendor benefits. Of course, the specific cancellation provisions should be carefully reviewed by the user's counsel.

Third, the user's ability to achieve negotiating concessions in rental and direct lease transactions will normally be enhanced if the vendor can be convinced that the user has the financial ability to purchase the equipment. As noted above, many users enter into rental and lease arrangements because they do not have the financial standing to buy the equipment involved. Vendors are perhaps justifiably less willing to offer financial and nonfinancial concessions to user accounts that may have weak financial standing. Consequently, the user may find that its negotiating position is improved if it indicates that it is considering either purchasing or renting the equipment, and that its rental-purchase decision will be based upon factors other than the user's ability to generate the capital required for the purchase alternative.

Legal Considerations

Users drafting rental and direct lease agreements should remember that such documents essentially involve elements of both purchase agreements and third-party leases. However, where the rental or direct lease agreement is executed with the manufacturer or other vendor, there is no necessity for complex services or other side agreements with such firms, as in the case of third-party lease transactions. Soft dollar and financial concessions can and should be documented directly in the rental or lease agreement.

Among the more important provisions in any rental or direct lease agreement are those relating to purchase option credits, termination, and flexibility. Provisions relating to acceptance, term, insurance and risk of loss, rental credits, and property taxes are also important. These and other relevant provisions are discussed below. However, this review of legal considerations is not intended to be exhaustive. Most of the provisions explained in Chapter 8, and many of those included in Chapter 10, are directly or indirectly applicable to rental and lease agreements. Appropriate reference should be made to these chapters and to the general contract checklist contained in Appendix A. Users interested in a more comprehensive treatment of equipment leasing may also wish to study *Legal and Financial Aspects of Equipment Leasing Transactions,* by Richard M. Contino (Englewood Cliffs, NJ: Prentice-Hall, Inc., 1979).

Purchase Option Credits. Rental and direct lease agreements frequently include a so-called "purchase option" that permits the user to buy the leased equipment at some point into the lease or rental term, often at a discount of some kind that is calculated by using "purchase option credits." The basic difficulty posed by purchase option credits is that, when the user proceeds to exercise its purchase option, the credits either do not exist, or include some "apparent misunderstanding" that reduces their value to the user. Although vendor ploys in this area vary considerably, they often follow the "Trade-In Credit" ploy described in Chapter 2.

The principal problem with most purchase option credits is that they are not properly documented in writing. If the user is particularly naive, the vendor will not even offer to place language guaranteeing the credits into the contract. (In this approach, the vendor is likely to emphasize the vendor's "POC Policy" as if it were etched in granite.) When this occurs, of course, the purchase option "credits" only exist through the continued generosity of the vendor. Alternatively, the vendor may attempt to include the credits in a "side letter" rather than in the formal user-vendor agreement. As other portions of this volume explain, "side letters" that do not prove to be valid legal obligations of the vendor pose significant future risks for the user. In most instances, the only valid reason that a vendor marketing representative has for including a "commitment" in a side letter rather than in the formal agreement is to avoid having the commitment reviewed at the vendor's corporate headquarters—where it would probably be rejected out of hand. In those rare instances where the inclusion of purchase option credits in a side letter appears to be justifiable for other reasons, the user should accept this approach only following assurances from counsel that the side agreement will be a binding legal obligation of the vendor.

If the user follows basic contracting principles, the vendor will include the purchase option credits directly in the agreement. However, the vendor's first choice will be to employ vague language that does not pin down the amount of the supposedly guaranteed credit. For example, the provision may simply state: "If the user elects to purchase the equipment during the Rental Term, the purchase price paid by the User shall be reduced by the purchase option credits attributable to the Equipment in accordance with the Vendor's policies." Again, the rather obvious problem with this approach is that only the vendor has any control over its "policies" and, therefore, the amount of the credits.

If the user rejects this approach and demands more detail, the vendor's marketing representative may finally "give in" by offering a "guaranteed" purchase option credit "formula." Although this formula may at first appear to be a firm guarantee, two problems often exist. First, the "guaranteed formula" may be more flexible than it initially appears. This flexibility for the vendor, and the concurrent risk for the user, ordinarily results from the inclusion of one or two hedge phrases in an otherwise complicated and valid formula. (The phrase "pursuant to vendor's policies" is again often employed for this purpose.) Second, and perhaps more likely, the credit is frequently applied against a purchase or lease price that is not specified in the original rental or direct lease agreement. Because the price is not specified in the original agreement, the price that is eventually quoted by the vendor often turns out to be substantially above the then-market rate for the equipment involved. This point represents the critical danger, and no user should seriously value any purchase option credit without being aware of this risk.

Perhaps the best example of this problem occurs when the vendor explains that, in order to use its purchase option credits, the user must pay the full then-published list price for the equipment, even though the vendor has been routinely discounting the system to other users by 10% –20%. In a variation on this example, the vendor offers the user a discount from list, but quietly reduces the amount of the discount because purchase option credits are involved. Consequently, the user pays the full list price for the system, less a very small discount, and the vendor's sales representative proudly explains that the purchase option credits will be deducted from this discounted amount. Assuming that the vendor is offering the equipment at a greater discount at the time, the user will either be getting the standard discount (without knowing it) and not getting the full purchase option credits, or the user will be getting the purchase option credits, but not getting the full discount routinely offered to other users.

Despite the risks that may be involved in a vendor's offer of purchase option credits, the user can take several steps to "lock in" the value being offered by the vendor. First, in assessing the vendor's proposal, the user should place only limited value on the offer of purchase option credits. To be sure, the credits should be sought and tied down if they are available. But the user should recognize that the credits will provide financial benefits only if the purchase option is exercised and the credits are applied in full. The ultimate value of the credits may be limited if, for example, the user desires to change vendors or the risks set forth above cannot be minimized through solid documentation. This recognition by the user is particularly important where it is comparing alternative proposals from competing vendors that may not offer purchase option credits.

Second, the user should make every effort to ensure that the purchase option credit provision in the contract is as specific as possible. All "hedge" provisions should be eliminated, and the final language should be carefully reviewed and approved by the user's operations manager and legal counsel.

Third, the user should attempt to lock in the price against which the purchase option credits will be applied. Where the credits will be applied against the equipment being rented, it may be possible to specify the original purchase price for the equipment in the agreement (i.e., the purchase price for the equipment on the date the rental agreement was executed). Where the credits may be applied against other equipment, or against the *future* purchase price of the equipment being rented, the drafting problem is more difficult. In this situation, the user should devote maximum attention toward describing the "base" or "list" price against which the purchase option credits will be applied. The user should also specify that the credits will be fully available despite the application of any other discount from, or credit against, the base or list price. A "most favored user" provision is often helpful in providing protection in this area. (See Appendix B.)

Fourth, the user should optimize its ability to employ the purchase option credits in alternative transactions. Some vendors will permit purchase option credits to be applied against *any* purchase of equipment made by the user from the vendor, not merely the equipment on which the credits were accrued. Other vendors will allow the user to sell or assign its purchase option credits to another user, thereby permitting that party to apply them against the purchase price of the rented equipment (or other vendor equipment). In some instances, the credits can be assigned as part of the sublease of the equipment by the user. In other situations, the credits can be transferred separately from the rental agreement under which they were accrued. Where flexibility of this nature is desired by the user, it must be documented in the rental or lease agreement.

Finally, when the time comes to apply the purchase option credits, the user should initially negotiate the best possible deal *without* the credits. (Accurate information concerning current prices should be sought from professional negotiators and other users in connection with this effort.) Then and only then should the user consider or subtract the purchase option credits. If the price offered by the vendor, as reduced by the purchase option credits, is greater than that which the user could obtain through an open-market purchase of the same equipment without the credits, the user should obviously pursue the latter approach. Indeed, if the user announces its intention to utilize an open-market purchase in lieu of applying the purchase option credits, it may be able to convince the vendor to reduce the base price against which the credits will be applied—even if that price is specified in the rental agreement. The user's efforts in this regard will often be more successful if the user protests loudly and threatens to call off its negotiations with the vendor.

Termination. Although a rental or direct lease agreement should obviously specify the term of the contract, as noted below, it should also indicate whether the user has the right to prematurely terminate the rental or lease arrangement and, if so, under what conditions. In this regard, the user should focus on three areas: termination due to purchase of the equipment by the user; termination due to a change in business needs; and termination due to damage or destruction of the equipment.

Users are often surprised to find that the vendor will not readily agree to a "purchase off lease" during the term of the agreement. Although the vendor's recalcitrance may be based upon various marketing strategies, it often stems from the fact that the vendor has assigned the lease document (and the associated payment stream) to a third party or to the vendor's captive finance company. After the assignment is made, the vendor may be unwilling or unable to terminate the lease arrangement without payment of a penalty (such as the present discounted value of the interest factor employed in computing the lease payments). The vendor's reluctance in this area is often directly related to whether the vendor or its assignee has already accrued (booked) the future interest income, or the full rental payment stream, on the transaction.

Where the user's business objectives may require a purchase off lease during the term of the agreement, the user should ensure that the lease documents contain appropriate termination values or language that specifically excludes any penalty for premature purchase of the equipment. One approach that often meets the vendor's goals as well as those of the user involves the inclusion of a "schedule of termination values" in the lease. This schedule generally provides for the payment of a slight premium by the user in the event that the lease is terminated as a result of the purchase of the equipment by the user during the lease term. This approach is quite routine in third-party lease agreements.

Where the user's business needs dictate that the user have the flexibility to prematurely terminate the rental or lease agreement for other reasons (e.g., changes in business needs, production volumes, or equipment requirements), a specific provision to this effect should be included in the user-vendor contract. As in the case of walk-away leases (discussed in Chapter 10), clear, unambiguous language is often essential to enforcement of the user's rights to early termination. Where the vendor refuses to give the user any early termination rights, headway can sometimes be made by focusing on trade-in and upgrade rights. (See the discussion of "flexibility," below.)

Regardless of whether the user believes that it may affirmatively decide to terminate the rental or lease agreement prior to the end of the initial term, it should consider the possibility that termination may be necessary as a result of damage to or destruction of the equipment. At a minimum, any lease or rental agreement should cover termination due to casualty loss. The relevant language should normally be integrated with the contractual provisions covering risk of loss and the obligation to procure insurance (discussed below). Some longer-term lease agreements include a separate schedule of casualty termination value—again, using the same approach employed in many third-party leases.

In considering the subject of termination, the user should also ensure that its rental or lease agreement does not contain dangerous provisions for automatic renewal. Although fewer and fewer vendors are employing such practices, some form agreements still include provisions that state that the rental or lease agreement will be automatically renewed at the end of the initial term or some other period, unless the user furnishes so many days prior written notice to the vendor. Some users actually prefer this type of automatic renewal provision for certain equipment. On the other hand, most users prefer to reverse the obligation so that the rental or lease agreement will automatically terminate unless it is renewed pursuant to appropriate written notice from the user to the vendor. (Where this approach is employed, the user should be certain that the renewal notice requirement is reasonable. The user should also adopt appropriate suspense procedures to ensure that renewal decisions are considered and documented in an orderly manner.)

Default. Because title to the equipment remains with the vendor (or, in some instances, an assignee of the vendor), rental and lease agreements generally provide "repossession remedies" to the vendor in the event that the user fails to make payments when due or otherwise fails to abide by its obligations under the contract. Although any rental or direct lease agreement should provide appropriate protection to the vendor in this regard, the remedies set forth in the agreement should be reasonable and lawful. For example, the user should not accept archaic boilerplate remedies that essentially permit the vendor to take possession of the equipment without notice, by force or other unlawful means, or without liability to the user for any damage caused by the vendor's repossession. Likewise, the user should not condone unreasonable provisions that permit acceleration of the full rental or lease payment stream without notice in the event of some minor default by the user. Any acceleration provision should be reasonable, and should be exercisable only after due notice to the user and the expiration of a grace period specified in the contract. The acceleration provision should also specifically permit the user to cure the alleged default during the grace period. Where a longer-term lease agreement is involved, and the user expects that the document may be assigned by the vendor to a financial institution or a captive finance company, the user should remember that the assignee will generally be entitled to receive full payment regardless of any problems that the user may experience with the equipment. This "hell or high water" payment obligation must be carefully considered by the user when drafting the lease agreement. Advice concerning hell or high water provisions, quiet enjoyment provisions, and the correction of operating problems in the context of such provisions, appears in the third-party leasing discussion in Chapter 10. Related provisions of the Uniform Commercial Code (dealing with the rights of a "holder in due course") are reviewed in Chapter 6.

Flexibility. Regardless of the duration of the rental or lease term, the agreement should provide adequate flexibility to the user in its future operations. Because the vendor will retain title to the equipment, and may well intend to re-lease the equipment immediately following the term of its agreement with the user, the vendor has a substantial interest in protecting the value of the equipment. Consequently, many rental and direct lease agreements impose specific restrictions on the use, movement, and sublease of the equipment. To the extent that these restrictions are reasonable, do not interfere with the user's existing and anticipated operations, and do not give the vendor inappropriate control over the user's future equipment decisions, they may be acceptable. However, to the extent that these so-called vendor protection provisions create the opposite effect, they deserve careful review and modification by the user.

Many such vendor provisions are overboard, prohibiting far more than is reasonably necessary to protect the vendor's ownership of the equipment. In reviewing such provisions, the user should carefully consider its own future plans, identify all relevant contingencies that may occur, and then draft alternative language that permits appropriate user flexibility. In conducting this review, the user should be careful not to limit its assessment to current operations. Objectives and strategies change in any business environment. Although the user may not require a given level of flexibility today, its operations may be substantially impaired if it is unable to attain that flexibility in the future. The time to negotiate flexibility is at the onset of a lease or rental agreement, not halfway through the term. As outlined in Chapter 8, the lease or rental agreement should allow the user to have certain rights to move the equipment, sublease the equipment, assign the lease or rental agreements, and allow the equipment to be operated by other parties. Where software and/or maintenance agreements are involved, the flexibility provisions should also cover these critical areas. The degree to which the user should remain liable for the making of payments or the taking of other action under the rental or lease agreement should normally be subject to negotiation between the parties.

Depending upon the user's specific business goals, it may also be advantageous for the rental or lease agreement to contain a provision that permits the user to add or delete equipment over the rental or lease term. Although this type of provision is generally more important in longer-term lease agreements than in shorter-term rental contracts, it can also be helpful in the latter situation. The principal opportunity offered by this approach is that it permits the user to have equipment flexibility without the annoyance of negotiating a separate agreement or amendment each time that an equipment change becomes necessary. Assuming that the user negotiates a good rental or lease agreement at the outset, it can rest assured that any equipment added during the term will be governed by the same provisions. Of course, if the user does a poor job of negotiating the initial agreement, the ability to have subsequent equipment governed by the same terms may turn out to be more of a disadvantage than an advantage.

Regardless of whether the user believes that it may need flexibility rights during the rental or lease term, it should ensure that the agreement contains two basic provisions. First, to the extent that the agreement conditions any flexibility right (such as the right to use or the right to sublease) upon receipt by the user of approval from the vendor, the contract should specifically indicate that this approval shall not be unreasonably withheld. This is one of the easiest drafting changes that can be made. In most instances, the words "such approval not to be unreasonably withheld" can merely be appended to an existing sentence. Second, where the user is part of a larger company, or may become part of such a company during the rental or lease term, the agreement should provide appropriate flexibility throughout the entire user organization. Thus, any restrictions on assignment, subleasing, usage, and the like should contain a specific exception for any "parent, subsidiary, or affiliate" of the user. If this exception is not included in the agreement, the vendor may have inappropriate control over the user's ability to implement intraorganizational transfers of the equipment. Although most vendors will readily agree to such transfers when they are made for normal business purposes, some vendors will threaten to withhold necessary approvals in order to obtain a user commitment in another area. This unfortunate approach is particularly likely to be employed where the user has recently changed vendors, or is threatening to do so. Appropriate protection can ordinarily be achieved by including a provision which grants the user the right to transfer or sublease the equipment to a parent, subsidiary, or affiliate of the user *without prior approval* of (but with notice to) the vendor. The specific language utilized for this purpose should anticipate both existing and future parent, subsidiary, and affiliate companies. In addition, it should ordinarily include separate definitions of "parent," "subsidiary," and "affiliate." Some vendors indicate that definitions are not necessary if the user attaches a list of its parent, subsidiary, and affiliate companies. Although this approach may be acceptable with respect to existing entities, it may create problems for the user if additional entities are acquired or organized during the rental or lease term.

Acceptance and Commencement of Rental Payments. In most situations, the rental or lease agreement executed by the user will become binding and effective upon its execution by the vendor. Although the agreement will be effective, the term for the rental or lease period (often simply and incorrectly referred to as the "term of the agreement") may not begin until a later time. Indeed, where the equipment is to be delivered and installed at a subsequent date, the term for which rental payments must be made should never begin when the agreement becomes effective.

Where the user is acquiring equipment that will not be subject to a true acceptance test, rental payments should normally begin on the date that the equipment is installed and ready for use. Although it should go without saying, rental payments should not commence on the date that the equipment is shipped, or on some arbitrary "invoice" or "billing" date eatablished by the vendor. At a minimum, payments should begin when the equipment is delivered to the user in accordance with its acquisition specifications. Where the user's agreement provides for the equipment to be installed and/or tested by the vendor or its agents, commencement of the rental period should ordinarily be delayed until after these actions by the vendor have been completed satisfactorily.

Some agreements specify that the rental payment period begins on the date that the agreement is executed, but that the user will receive "free use" of the equipment at the end of the term for a period equal to any time at the beginning of the term during which the equipment is not available and ready for use. In most instances, this type of provision should be avoided. In the first place, it causes the user's obligation to make rental payments to begin even though the equipment is not installed and ready for use. Second, it permits the vendor to receive the "time value" of any payments made by the user before the equipment is installed and ready for use. Third, it presupposes that the user will be able to make productive use of the equipment after the end of the normal rental or lease period.

Where the acceptance test will be employed for the equipment, the user's *obligation* to make rental payments should normally be conditioned upon satisfactory completion of the test. In addition, the rental payment period itself should begin on the acceptance date. Some agreements provide that, while the user's *obligation* to make payments will not begin until after the equipment has passed the acceptance test, once the equipment has passed the test the user will be obligated to make payments *from the date that the equipment was first installed*. This approach effectively requires the user to pay full rental or lease payments for its utilization of the equipment during the test period. Although the user may be willing to pay all or some portion of the payment for the test period if the user is able to make productive business use of the equipment during the test, the user should accept this type of provision only after appreciating the financial consequences involved. (Acceptance tests are described more fully in Chapter 8.)

In reaching a decision as to whether to include an acceptance test in a rental or direct lease agreement, the user should ordinarily look to the importance of the equipment to its business, the potential consequences of equipment failure, and the financial and other commitments made by the user in its agreement with the vendor. In essence, the decision should be made without regard to the fact that a rental or lease agreement is involved. The only relevance of the rental or lease acquisition alternative should generally be in connection with the user's assessment of the size and permanence of its contractual commitment to the vendor. Thus, if the user is procuring relatively inexpensive equipment through a *short-term* rental agreement, the user may feel reasonably secure in foregoing a substantial acceptance test. If problems with the equipment arise, the user can reduce its exposure by terminating the rental agreement or simply letting it run to its early predetermined conclusion. Although this flexibility exists in many situations, the user should recognize that, when it makes a decision to forego an acceptance test, it is assuming a risk that would normally be assigned to the vendor. The assumption of this risk should be made by the user only following a full assessment of its negotiating alternatives and its business needs.

Insurance and Risk of Loss. Insurance and risk of loss provisions can be particularly important in rental and lease agreements, due to the fact that the equipment ownership remains with the vendor. If the equipment is damaged or destroyed during the rental or lease term, and adequate insurance is not available, the user may find that it remains obligated to make full rental or lease payments to the vendor even though the equipment is no longer in existence or available for use.

At a minimum, the rental or lease agreement should specify which party has the risk of loss and the obligation to procure and pay for insurance coverage. Because disagreements can arise concerning the amount and types of insurance that should be obtained, the relevant provisions should ordinarily cover matters of this nature. (In this regard, the user should recognize that, in the event that insurance coverage is not available for a particular casualty, the party that has the risk of loss will normally be responsible for bearing the loss, *even though insurance proceeds are not available.*) As explained in other sections of this volume, the authors strongly believe that, wherever possible, the risk of loss and obligation to procure insurance should shift to the user from the vendor only after the equipment has passed any relevant acceptance tests. One method of implementing this approach is to provide that the user will assume the risk of loss and the obligation to procure insurance only upon the date that the user's obligation to make rental or lease payments begins.

Admittedly, this approach is not practical in every situation. Where the equipment will be delivered to the user's site well in advance of the date of acceptance, the vendor may press hard for the user to accept the risk of loss at an earlier time. Where the user must accept the risk of loss at an earlier date, it may still achieve some advantage by requiring the vendor to accept the risk of loss and the obligation to procure insurance during the transportation and delivery period. Where the vendor assumes this risk, it will be required to negotiate any necessary settlement with the carrier responsible for delivering the equipment, in the event of damage or destruction during delivery. This approach generally assures that the vendor will take an active interest in the amount and type of insurance coverage provided for the equipment during transportation.

In reviewing the risk of loss provision, the user should ensure that the agreement specifically indicates what rights the user will have in the event that the equipment is destroyed or substantially damaged during the rental or lease term. Many agreements provide that, regardless of any damage or destruction to the equipment during the term, the user will remain obligated to make all necessary payments to the vendor. Agreements of this nature often fail to specify what will happen to the insurance proceeds in such an event, and which party will be responsible for repairing or replacing the equipment with any such proceeds that may be available. Where practicable, the user's position will normally be enhanced if the agreement provides that, in the event of destruction or serious damage (which should be defined in the document) to the equipment, the user will have the right and option to terminate the agreement and cease making payments to the vendor. Where this approach is not acceptable to the vendor (or to the user), the user should make certain that the insurance proceeds will be adequate to replace or repair the equipment. In addition, the user may need to ensure that insurance proceeds will be available to reimburse the user for any operating losses that it may incur during the period that the equipment is unavailable. Alternatively, the proceeds should cover the cost of obtaining replacement equipment during the repair or replacement period.

In considering this area, the user should also appreciate that the equipment may be damaged or destroyed prior to the time that it is installed or accepted by the user. The user may well wish to have different rights in the event that this unfortunate situation occurs. For example, the user ·may be willing to accept the risk of loss during the normal lease term, and to assume the obligation to repair or replace the equipment with any insurance proceeds. On the other hand, the user may prefer to have the right to cancel the agreement if the equipment is damaged or destroyed while it is in the process of being delivered or installed.

Particularly where the equipment is being manufactured specifically for the user, the agreement should also clearly indicate which party has the risk of loss during the manufacturing or production period. In some states, the user may find that it has responsibility for certain losses that occur during the design or manufacture of equipment being produced specifically for the user pursuant to its specifications. Counsel for the user should carefully review applicable provisions of the Uniform Commercial Code in the context of the user-vendor agreement in order to determine what language should be added to the document to protect the user in such situations. Again, the authors ordinarily recommend that the vendor be required to assume responsibility for any loss during this period. This approach appears reasonable due to the fact that the vendor has the best ability to provide protection and insurance coverage during the manufacturing process. In addition, because the equipment has not yet been delivered, the user has no assurance that the equipment will even be capable of performing in accordance with contractual specifications.

Allowance for Operational Failure. Where the rental or direct lease agreement is executed between the user and the manufacturer (as vendor), the user's ability to provide for an allowance or credit in the event of operational failure is generally enhanced. Users considering this approach should carefully review the discussion of liquidated damages and special remedy provisions contained in Chapters 6 and 8. A number of alternative "lemon" clauses and reimbursement provisions are also discussed in Chapter 10, in the context of third-party leasing. Most of these provisions can be easily tailored to a rental or direct lease agreement.

Property Taxes. Any rental or lease agreement should clearly indicate which party will have the obligation for paying property taxes and for filing any necessary returns in connection with such taxes. Unless the user's RFP requires otherwise, proposals submitted by various vendors may not all include the same approach with respect to property taxes. Consequently, adjustments to the financial figures quoted by competing vendors may have to be made in order to differentiate the proposals in which the user is responsible for such taxes from the proposals in which the vendor assumes this responsibility.

As explained in Chapter 8, where the agreement provides that the user will be responsible for the payment of all property taxes during the rental or lease term, it should specifically indicate that the user will not be liable for any penalties caused by any action or inaction by the vendor.

If this approach is not taken, the user may be required to pay tax penalties resulting from the fact that the vendor (or its assignee) failed to file a required property tax return (which, in many states, can only be filed by the owner of the equipment).

INSTALLMENT PURCHASE AGREEMENTS

Like rental and direct lease agreements, installment purchase contracts involve many of the factors found in purchase agreements and third-party leases. In an installment purchase contract, the user generally buys the equipment directly from the manufacturer, but agrees to pay for the equipment over a period of time through a traditional installment sale arrangement. In this approach, the user obtains title to the equipment at the acceptance date (or some other time specified in the agreement), but the vendor retains a security interest in, or a lien upon, the equipment until the user has made all required payments under the agreement.

Because the manufacturer or other vendor may not be in a position to hold the notes on the installment purchase obligations of a large number of borrowers, the vendor may sell or assign the notes, usually at a discount, to a financial institution or to its own captive equipment financing subsidiary. This arrangement is not unlike that employed by an automobile dealer that offers its new car customers "easy financing." The customer signs an installment sales agreement that is then sold or assigned to the car dealer's bank at a discount. In most situations of this nature, the customer simply remits its payments to the bank. In the banking business, this type of transaction is known as an "indirect loan" because the bank's association with the customer is "indirect" through the dealer. This financing is contrasted with a "direct loan," where the customer borrows the funds directly from the bank, and then uses the proceeds of the loan to pay "cash" to the dealer.

From the user's standpoint, these financial factors are the principal ingredients that distinguish an installment purchase agreement from other major equipment contracts. Moreover, it is these financial factors that require the user's primary consideration in negotiating and drafting an installment purchase agreement.

Use and Cost Considerations

Installment purchase agreements offer several advantages to the user. In many respects, they provide a compromise between straight purchase and lease or rental alternatives. Although flexibility is reduced, the price of obtaining the equipment is frequently lower than in rental arrangements. While the capital outlays required for installment purchases are higher than those involved in rental and direct lease agreements, they are lower than those required for purchases that are not financed.

While the installment purchase alternative offers some of the benefits of a rental or direct lease arrangement, it also gives the user most of the benefits of outright ownership of the equipment. For example, the user is ordinarily entitled to all of the tax benefits of ownership (e.g., depreciation or "cost recovery" and investment tax credit). The user's assets are increased by the purchase price of the equipment, although its liabilities are also increased by the amount of the installment purchase obligation. Once all payments are made, the user obtains unencumbered title to the equipment, without the necessity of exercising purchase option credits or buying the equipment at some residual value. Although installment purchase arrangements ordinarily include contractual restrictions during the installment payment period, these restrictions and other user commitments are seldom as extensive as those found in third-party leveraged lease agreements, and may also be less detailed than those included in comparable rental and direct lease contracts. Depending upon whether the vendor intends to assign the user's installment purchase agreement to a financial institution, the installment purchase approach may also avoid much of the negotiating complexity found in third-party lease agreements. When no such assignment of the user's obligations will be involved, the user will generally be able to negotiate directly with the manufacturer or other vendor, without having to arrange separate financing or accept "hell or high water" provisions necessary to make the user-vendor agreement acceptable to the assignee financial institution.

Despite these benefits, installment purchase agreements offer certain disadvantages. The financing arrangements involved almost always impose more restrictions than outright purchase alternatives. For example, the restrictions associated with installment financing may preclude or substantially reduce trade-in and upgrade alternatives during the installment payment period. Restrictions may also be placed on the user's right to sell the equipment or permit others to use the equipment. Depending upon the length of the installment payment period, rental and direct lease alternatives may both offer greater short-term flexibility than the installment approach.

Although the installment alternative automatically permits the user to obtain the residual value of the equipment, this apparent benefit may prove to be a detriment in some industries. Where the risk of technological change is high, the user may be in a better position by paying slightly higher rental or direct lease rates and giving the equipment (with substantially reduced value) back to the vendor at the end of the rental period. The computer and other high technology industries have witnessed many users that paid installment amounts over a number of years only to find that, at the end of the installment purchase term, the equipment was worth virtually nothing.

Although the cost of installment financing may be advantageous for some users, it may be excessive for others. The relative advantage or disadvantage can only be assessed by a detailed comparison of alternative acquisition methods in light of the user's internal rate of return. The relative costs of the installment purchase alternative can be particularly high if the equipment being acquired is not put to productive use at the level required to justify the continuing installment payments. Where the equipment is only necessary to meet interim needs, the user's financial position may be enhanced by paying higher rental rates during the limited period that replacement or supplemental equipment is required.

The relative advantages and disadvantages of the installment purchase alternative must be carefully considered in light of federal income tax changes adopted in 1981 and 1982. The Economic Recovery Tax Act of 1981 made a number of important changes in the federal tax statutes relating to the investment tax credit, depreciation (now called "cost recovery"), and leasing. Because the law greatly expanded the flexibility available in leasing transactions, the installment purchase technique became less favorable than the leasing alternative in some equipment acquisitions. (Certain of the new tax provisions relating to leasing are discussed in Chapter 10.) Users considering the impact of the 1981 tax act should devote particular attention to the provisions which grant lessees increased flexibility in purchasing the equipment at favorable prices at the end of the lease term. Unfortunately, many of the pro-leasing changes that were adopted in 1981 were repealed or altered in the 1982 tax act.

Negotiating Considerations

In assessing the relative advantages of utilizing the installment purchase alternative, the user should appreciate that its decision may affect the negotiating strategies employed by the vendor and the user. Several more important negotiating considerations are outlined below.

First, most vendors are more willing to offer financial and nonfinancial concessions in installment purchase arrangements than in rental and shorter-term direct lease agreements. Because a purchase is involved, the vendor ordinarily has more flexibility in providing discounts from its published price schedule. Moreover, most installment purchase agreements involve a considerably larger commitment than rental and shorter-term direct lease arrangements. Because of the larger amount involved, the total dollar value of the concessions that can be offered by the vendor is increased. The larger dollar value of the transaction also permits the vendor to devote additional time and effort toward its marketing and negotiating efforts. As a result, increased non-financial concessions (including contractual changes) can ordinarily be obtained.

Second, the relative willingness of a vendor to offer concessions in an installment purchase transaction will generally depend upon the degree to which the vendor (or its marketing representative) has an incentive or disincentive to pursue such transactions. As in the case of rental and direct lease agreements, vendor incentives in this regard ordinarily vary over time. For example, vendors are frequently more willing to engage in installment purchase transactions when the vendor or its captive financing subsidiary has substantial extra cash that cannot be invested in other enterprises at a higher rate of return than the vendor can achieve through its installment purchase agreements. Vendors may also be motivated to offer favorable installment purchase terms when the installment method appears to be the only practicable way to encourage users to buy. Thus, during periods of extremely high interest rates or "tight money," many vendors offer internal installment purchase financing at relatively favorable rates in order to offset substantial reductions in sales. (In the early eighties, this approach was particularly popular with manufacturers of automobiles, smaller aircraft, and certain types of farm and earth moving equipment.) Vendors are willing to adopt this approach when the loss of interest income that they face on the favorable financing arrangements is less than the loss of profit that they face from reduced equipment sales.

Third, because the concessions that can be obtained in an installment purchase generally exceed those available in a rental or direct lease arrangement, the user may wish to consider using a combination of both methods in a particular acquisition. Thus, the user may be able to obtain greater overall negotiating concessions and also meet its other business and financial needs by acquiring certain equipment through the installment purchase method and the remainder of the equipment through the rental or direct lease method. This approach permits the user to extract additional vendor concessions that might not be available if all of the equipment were acquired through the rental or direct lease method. As explained in Chapter 4, this combination of acquisition methods may also offer other benefits to the user. Thus, the user may be able to obtain equipment with a high residual value by the installment purchase method, and obtain equipment that carries a substantial residual value risk or that may only be needed for a short period of time by the rental method.

Fourth, the user's ability to achieve negotiating concessions in installment purchase transactions may be enhanced if the user can convince the vendor that the user has the financial ability to purchase the equipment outright. In addition to reducing any concern that the vendor might otherwise have about the user's financial condition, this approach generally signals the vendor's marketing representative that, if the installment purchase alternative is to be pursued by the user, it must be made more attractive than the direct purchase method. As suggested above, many vendors have the flexibility to create this relative attractiveness by reducing the interest rate factor utilized in calculating the installment payment amounts or by offering other financial or nonfinancial concessions. As in any other negotiating environment, the vendor will be more likely to offer these concessions where they appear to be essential to closing the deal.

Legal Considerations

From a drafting standpoint, installment purchase agreements involve many elements of both purchase agreements and third-party leases. However, because installment purchase agreements are frequently executed directly with the manufacturer, there is seldom any necessity for complex services or other side agreements with such firms, as may occur in third-party lease transactions. Soft dollar and financial concessions can and should be documented directly in the installment purchase agreement with the manufacturer/vendor. Whether the installment purchase documents will include forms or provisions required by an assignee financial institution (as generally occurs in third-party leveraged lease arrangements) will normally depend upon whether the vendor intends to assign the user's obligations under the agreement to an outside financing source. Frequently any such assignment will be limited to the vendor's captive financing subsidiary, thereby increasing the user's ability to negotiate any relevant contractual changes directly with the vendor.

Among the more important provisions in any installment purchase agreement are those relating to title (including the vendor's security interest), repossession remedies, prepayment, insurance and risk of loss, and flexibility. These provisions are reviewed below in the context of installment purchase agreements. Additional information concerning these and other important provisions is included in Chapter 8. Certain of the contractual provisions discussed in Chapter 10 and the general contract checklist contained in Appendix A may also be helpful to users drafting installment purchase agreements.

Title and Security Interest. The installment purchase agreement should ordinarily provide for the user to obtain title to the equipment at the acceptance date. Under certain conditions, the user may agree to receive title at an earlier date. However, any such agreement by the user should be carefully considered in light of such matters as risk of loss, the obligation to procure insurance, and the commencement of payments under the contract.

Although the installment purchase agreement should provide for early transfer of title to the user, it should also grant the vendor or its assignee a security interest in the equipment until the user has paid all amounts due under the agreement. The extent of the vendor's security interest and any related vendor remedies in the event of user default should be specified in the installment purchase contract. The user should ordinarily agree to execute any documents that may be reasonably required to perfect the vendor's security interest in the equipment, and the vendor should normally be responsible for preparing and filing the security interest documents, including any UCC-1 filings, at the vendor's expense. However, all such documents should be subject to reasonable review and approval by the user's counsel. Once all required amounts under the agreement have been paid, the vendor should have an affirmative obligation to file releases or satisfactions of its security interest in all relevant jurisdictions, at its own expense.

Repossession Remedies. Any vendor remedies provided by the security interest should be reasonable and lawful. The user should not condone archaic boilerplate remedies that permit repossession of the equipment without notice, by unlawful methods, or without liability to the user for any damage caused by the repossession. Likewise, the user should refuse to accept provisions that permit acceleration of the full contract price without notice in the event of some minor default by the user. Any acceleration provisions should be reasonable, and should be exercisable only after due notice to the user and the expiration of a specific grace period during which the user may cure the alleged default. Where the installment purchase contract is subsequently assigned by the vendor to a bank or other third party, the assignee will generally be entitled to receive full payment regardless of any problems that the user may be experiencing with the equipment. This "hell or high water" payment obligation must be carefully considered by the user when drafting the installment purchase agreement. Advice concerning hell or high water provisions, quiet enjoyment provisions, and the correction of operating problems in the context of such provisions, appears in the third-party leasing discussion in Chapter 10.

Prepayment Rights. The installment purchase agreement should indicate whether the user will be permitted to prepay its obligations with or without penalty. Particularly during periods of high interest rates, the vendor or the assignee financial institution may agree to an installment purchase transaction only if the user may not prepay the amount due, or may do so only at a substantial prepayment penalty. This approach effectively precludes the user from paying off or "refinancing" the transaction when rates decline. In addition, the prepayment penalty may pose flexibility problems if the user decides to sell or trade in the equipment during the installment period. (As in the case of rental and direct lease agreements, the vendor's willingness to subsequently allow prepayment may depend on whether the vendor or its assignee has already booked the interest income on the installment sale.) Consequently, prepayment penalties should be avoided or severely limited. Although some marketing representatives attempt to provide oral assurances that the vendor will always permit prepayment without penalty (notwithstanding the terms of the written agreement), the user should never rely upon such self-serving comments.

Insurance and Risk of Loss. The installment purchase agreement should also carefully cover insurance and risk of loss. Because it will hold title to the equipment during the installment payment period, the user must obviously insure its own interest in the equipment during this period. However, most installment purchase agreements also require the user to provide insurance for the benefit of the vendor or any assignee financial institution. Many such agreements utilize a casualty termination schedule, similar to that found in third-party lease agreements, that clearly indicates the amount that must be paid to the vendor or its assignee in the event the equipment is seriously damaged or destroyed during the installment payment term. The amounts reflected in such casualty termination schedules are generally based upon the principal amount owed on the equipment plus an interest factor. In some instances, the practical effect of such termination schedules is to cause the user or its insurance carrier to pay what amounts to a "prepayment penalty" in the event the equipment is destroyed. This result ensues where the amount specified in the casualty termination schedule is greater than the remaining principal amount due on the equipment, plus interest accrued from the date of the last payment to the date of the casualty termination payment. Users accepting casualty termination schedules should be certain that the insurance procured by their risk management department is adequate to fully fund any payment obligation that the user may have pursuant to the schedule (unless, of course, the user wishes to self-insure a portion of this obligation). Many of the comments made earlier in this chapter concerning insurance and risk of loss in connection with rental and direct lease agreements are also applicable to installment purchase contracts.

Flexibility. In order to protect the vendor's security interest in the equipment, the vendor and any assignee financial institution will expect to impose at least some restrictions on equipment use, and therefore flexibility, in an installment purchase transaction. For example, the vendor's standard form installment purchase document is likely to preclude the user from moving or selling the equipment, or assigning the agreement, during the installment term. The vendor's standard contract is also likely to restrict the user from placing additional liens or encumbrances on the equipment (other than the vendor's security interest) during the time that any part of the purchase price remains unpaid. To the extent these and related provisions are necessary to protect the vendor's security interest in the equipment, the user should respect the underlying substance of each. However, many such vendor provisions are blatantly overbroad, and prohibit far more than is reasonably necessary to protect the vendor's lien on the equipment.

While reasonably recognizing the vendor's need to secure its position, the user should ensure that the installment purchase agreement includes provisions that permit reasonable flexibility. For example, moving the equipment out of state may void the vendor's perfected security interest if the equipment is transported into a jurisdiction where the vendor has not filed a UCC-1 form under the Uniform Commercial Code. Many vendors attempt to deal with this problem by prohibiting any movement of the equipment. This approach imposes unnecessary restrictions on the user. The user can achieve increased flexibility, without any serious risk to the vendor, by employing an alternative provision that merely requires prior notice to the vendor and mutual cooperation of the vendor and the user in preparing any additional lien documents that may be necessary. Similarly, reselling the equipment during the term of the installment payments may cause the vendor to feel insecure, particularly if the new owner is weak financially or if the transaction could be deemed to release the original user from its obligations under the installment purchase agreement. Rather than prohibiting any resale of the equipment during the installment term, the agreement should merely impose reasonable conditions, such as prior notice to the vendor and the continued primary or secondary liability of the user under the installment purchase agreement. Alternatively, the agreement might require prior vendor approval of the financial condition of the new owner, coupled with the release of the first user under the agreement.

The user's assessment of the provisions necessary to assure future flexibility should also include those relating to attachments, trade-ins, and upgrades with the same or a different vendor. For example, the agreement should permit reasonable additional equipment to be attached to the system during the installment period, regardless of source, so long as the attachment does not impair the value of the equipment or the vendor's lien. The agreement should also permit the user to trade in or upgrade the equipment (if practicable) during the installment term, without payment of any prepayment or casualty termination amounts that might otherwise be required by the agreement.

13
CONTRACT ADMINISTRATION

In any major equipment acquisition, the negotiation process continues through contract compliance and administration. (See Chapter 4.) Despite the increasing willingness of users to negotiate proposed acquisitions, most users still fail to implement strong contract administration programs. This chapter provides an overview of contract administration. After reviewing the need for administration, the chapter focuses on responsibility assignments and various steps involved in the administration process.

THE NEED FOR ADMINISTRATION

In a major equipment acquisition, contract administration has three principal goals:

- To ensure that the user complies with its obligations under the user-vendor agreement;
- To ensure that the vendor complies with its obligations under the user-vendor agreement; and
- To provide a written record of user and vendor performance for purposes of assessing compliance, enforcing rights, and making future procurement decisions.

As these goals suggest, any major equipment acquisition that is worth *negotiating* is also worth *administering* after the equipment is delivered. Indeed, where user-vendor negotiations have created a complex legal document, or a series of interrelated agreements, the need for administration is particularly high.

The user that fails to establish a meaningful contract administration program is leaving its investment in the equipment open to substantial risks. The following examples highlight some of the problems that may arise.

- Unable or unwilling to decipher the extensive user-vendor contract, the user's facilities manager fails to begin work on certain key building alterations necessary for the equipment to be installed. As a result, the user is unable to accept delivery when required by the contract, the equipment must be stored at the user's expense, the alterations are undertaken on an expensive emergency basis, and the vendor claims that purchase price is due because the user was unable to permit the acceptance test to begin on schedule.
- The insurance required under a third-party lease is not procured by the user (or is obtained with inadequate amounts or coverages); the equipment is seriously damaged and the user is faced with paying a substantial casualty termination amount under the lease, without insurance proceeds.
- The vendor consistently fails to provide remedial maintenance within the maximum response times specified in the user-vendor lease or maintenance agreement, resulting in longer equipment down-time, customer complaints, and user overtime. When the user's

operating costs get out of hand and several customers threaten to sue or discontinue service, the user attempts to make the vendor comply with its obligations. Unfortunately, the user has no detailed records of the down-time delays and the vendor's inadequate performance. Moreover, the vendor claims that, by accepting the longer response times for 12 months, the user has waived its contractual right to the shorter time specified in the agreement.

- Equipment acquired from the vendor fails to meet the required acceptance test and is eventually removed from the user's site, creating significant costs and production problems. When a special committee appointed by the user's board looks into "what went wrong," it determines that the vendor apparently failed to meet several early deadlines (e.g., shipping, delivery, installation, and conversion) under the agreement. Unfortunately, the user failed to keep records of these problems and also failed to send default notices or written objections to the vendor in connection with any of the delays.

- Two systems ago, the user utilized equipment supplied by Vendor A, but changed to Vendor B (the current supplier) because Vendor A consistently failed to meet the user's needs and to comply with its obligations under the contract. Key members of the user's operations team, who were present when this vendor change was made, are no longer employed by the user. The user again decides to change vendors, and shifts back to Vendor A. When problems arise, the user's president asks her operations director, "Didn't we have some sort of similar problems when we used Vendor A equipment a few years ago?" Fortunately or unfortunately (at this point), the operations manager is unable to put his hands on any records that explain the prior problems or the related solutions.

- The user is negotiating for the acquisition of a significant new system to be provided by its incumbent vendor. Because of the importance of the equipment to the user's operations, its negotiating team is striving to cover all relevant risks in the new user-vendor agreement. The user's operations manager is outspoken on the fact that the new contract should preclude some of the problems that he and his staff have had in dealing with the vendor. When the user's attorney asks to review the file of written records documenting these problems, the operations manager replies, with a blank stare, "*Records* of the problems?"

- Equipment supplied by the vendor consistently fails to perform in accordance with published specifications as required by the user-vendor contract. After months of working with the vendor, the user determines it has no alternative other than a lawsuit. Armed with his available files on the project, the user's operations manager meets with trial counsel. After reviewing the documents and discussing the situation with the operations manager, the user's attorney observes, "We can bring suit, John, if you really want to. I don't doubt that you've had—and are still having—some serious problems. But your files on the subject leave a great deal to be desired. Very few of your problems are documented at all, and there are virtually no written records of your efforts to place the vendor on notice. In addition, can you really show *how much* you've been damaged, in dollars and cents?"

The time to prevent problems like these is *before* they occur. The only failsafe method of reducing or eliminating these risks is a comprehensive program of contract administration. A strong contract may reduce the likelihood that problems will arise, and effective negotiations, arbitration, and litigation may reduce the extent of any problems that do arise. But good contract administration is necessary to preclude the problems in the first place.

THE ASSIGNMENT OF RESPONSIBILITY

In many user organizations, contract administration never gets off the ground because responsibility for the program is not assigned to a specific department or individual. It should go without saying that the first step in developing any contract administration program is to assign responsibility for it. This assignment should be made in writing, with a clear delegation of executive authority. Copies of the formal assignment should be supplied to all user managers involved in the acquisition, implementation, and administration process (including those responsible for the ongoing use and maintenance of the equipment). The vendor's marketing representative or project manager should also receive written notification of the contract administration program, and the individuals or departments responsible for it.

Responsibility for contract administration can be assigned to any number of departments or other functions. Although the final assignment decision will normally depend on such factors as the user's existing organization, the availability of qualified staff, the type of equipment, and the nature of the acquisition project, the following alternatives outline several responsibility assignments that have been successful in various companies.

Quality Review Committee. Particularly where larger projects are involved, many users assign executive responsibility for contract administration to a special quality review committee appointed to monitor the project. Members of the committee are generally senior user executives with broad administrative responsibilities (for example, the user's chief financial officer, chief legal officer, principal operations executive, and executive vice president responsible for the business function where the equipment will be employed). In some instances, these executives are joined by one or more managers with specific technical expertise in the business, production, or operating functions involved. However, the concept of the quality review committee approach is to separate the responsibility for *review and oversight* from the responsibility for *design and implementation.* Consequently, a majority of the committee should be made up of user managers who were not directly involved in justifying the equipment, designing the project, or implementing the acquisition. This separation of responsibilities increases objectivity and reduces the likelihood that the contract administration program will inappropriately gloss over problems.

Although the quality review committee provides an excellent high-level review board, the composition and nature of the committee generally preclude it from actually implementing the user's contract administration program on a day-to-day basis. The corporate-wide responsibilites faced by members of the committee make them valuable participants in the oversight process; but these responsibilities also keep them from having the time necessary to execute the staff assignments involved in the administration process.

For a contract administration program based upon a quality review committee to be successful, the committee must have adequate staff support. In addition, this staff must be supervised on a day-to-day basis—not merely when the quality review committee meets to give out additional assignments. Two approaches are generally employed to gain the necessary level of support and supervision. In the first alternative, staff assistance is supplied by personnel from the respective departments that are represented on the review committee (e.g., legal or operations), and one member of the committee is assigned primary responsibility (which may be executed personally or through a key subordinate) for coordinating and supervising the day-to-day activities of the staff. In the second alternative, all regular staff assistance for the quality review committee is provided by a single department that may or may not be represented on the committee (e.g., operations, procurement, or the end-user department for which the equipment was procured). If special staff assistance is required, it is provided by another applicable department (e.g., legal or finance). This approach is similar to the "User Department" technique set forth below, but it adds the objectivity and corporate-wide perspective of a quality review committee to the day-to-day administration of a single department.

Negotiating Team. Users that employ the negotiating team approach to equipment acquisitions often assign responsibility for contract administration directly to the negotiating team. Substantial support exists for this approach. The negotiating team members generally have the greatest familiarity with the project. Moreover, if contract administration is part of the negotiation process—as the authors assert—permitting the negotiating team to handle the task is most logical. On the other hand, the negotiating team approach has certain disadvantages. For example, the team may be "too close" to the transaction to be objective. Indeed, if contract administration problems result from deficiencies in the team's acquisition efforts, it may be difficult for team members to admit the problems and pose meaningful solutions. The negotiating team approach also poses staff support problems much like those faced when contract administration is handled by a quality review committee. The team members may be able to supervise the administration program, but they can seldom devote the time necessary to manage it on a day-to-day basis. Consequently, one of the alternative methods of providing staff support (discussed above in connection with the quality review committee approach) must be devised and implemented.

Purchasing Department. In many firms with established procurement procedures, the responsibility for contract administration is assigned to the purchasing department. The logic of this approach is that it centralizes departmental responsibility for both the acquisition and administration phases of an equipment transaction. Contract administration functions simply become a further chapter in the procurement procedures manual issued by the purchasing department. If the purchasing department is well organized, it may have the best ability to execute the administration program on a day-to-day basis. On the other hand, the purchasing department is unlikely to have direct and continuing contact with the equipment, once it is installed. Thus, the department must develop forms and communications procedures to ensure that it receives adequate information from the end-user department concerning equipment status, vendor performance, and similar matters. Moreover, the purchasing department may have an objectivity problem similar to that faced by the user's negotiating team: If the contract administration effort reveals that the purchasing department was responsible for problems in the acquisition process, the department may have difficulty handling its administration responsibilities.

User Department. Where contract administration responsibilities are assigned to a single department, some firms select the end-user department, rather than the purchasing department, for this purpose. The principal advantage enjoyed by the end-user department is that it is most familiar with the day-to-day operation and performance of the equipment. If problems exist, the end-user department is the first to know. In most instances, it is also the best judge of the extent of the difficulties and the practicality of the solutions. On the other hand, the user department may lack objectivity with respect to certain aspects of the acquisition/procurement process (principally in connection with the selection of the equipment and the business judgments made during the negotiations). The user department may also take a parochial view of the administration function, focusing on its own operating problems but devoting inadequate attention to problems that have more corporate-wide ramifications. Perhaps most importantly, the user department may lack training in proper contract administration procedures. Even where the user department has basic skills in this area, no procedures may exist to ensure that the contract administration record compiled by the department is "flowed up" to a central corporate location where it can be meshed (if applicable) with similar reports produced by other user departments.

Combined Responsibility. Because each of the contract administration alternatives outlined above has various strengths and weaknesses, many users employ a combined responsibility approach. In this technique, overall responsibility for managing the program is placed with a single executive or department, but critical assistance is contributed by other departments or committees (Fig. 13-1). For example, the user's purchasing department may be given principal responsibility for the contract administration effort, including such areas as day-to-day manage-

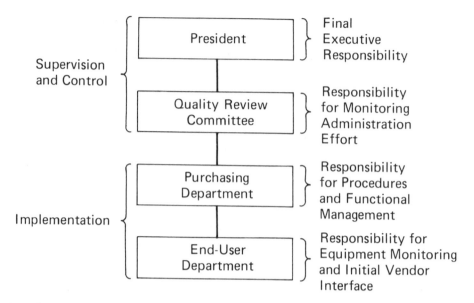

Fig. 13-1. Organizational chart depicting one method of implementing the Combined Responsibility approach to contract administration.

ment, routine staff support, permanent record keeping, and promulgation of all contract administration manuals, forms, and procedures. This approach appropriately centralizes the procedural aspects of the administration program. At the same time, the end-user department may be assigned responsibility for monitoring vendor performance and user compliance (utilizing forms and procedures promulgated by the purchasing department). The efforts of both departments may then be monitored on a periodic basis by a quality review committee or the negotiating team. This group can also assist in making critical decisions on any user-imposed sanctions that may be required to gain vendor cooperation during the administration period. Of course, direct managerial supervision of the respective department heads will also be provided by the executives to whom these individuals report.

Regardless of the exact allocation of duties that is employed, the authors support the combined responsibility approach to contract administration. In most instances, it offers the most effective and efficient method of assuring user compliance, monitoring vendor performance, and creating a permanent record of both.

THE ADMINISTRATION PROCESS

Timing and Interface with Acquisition Effort

From a planning standpoint, the contract administration process begins before the equipment agreement is signed or negotiated. Indeed, planning for contract administration should normally begin before the user's RFP is released.

This early beginning is necessary if the acquisition documents are to be structured in a manner that facilitates the administration effort. For example, if the user intends to employ arbitration (discussed below) to resolve contract disputes, appropriate language must be included in the user-vendor agreement. (Where a form agreement, or a schedule of legal/contractual issues, is included in the user's RFP, the arbitration decision must be made during preparation of the

RFP documents.) Similarly, if the contract administration effort is to be facilitated through the use of special remedies, interim performance deadlines, and written reports or certificates of compliance, these matters must be covered in the contract.

From the standpoint of direct implementation, the contract administration process begins when the "final report" on the acquisition is prepared by the user's negotiating team. As Chapter 4 explains, this report should be produced immediately after the user-vendor agreement is executed. Although the format is not important, the report should provide a summary of the final transaction, including principal user and vendor obligations, and a reference or index to each of the contract documents. Where time and resources permit, the report may also provide or at least refer to a more detailed analysis of the contract documents, perhaps including a schedule of key future events and responsibility assignments and excerpts from relevant contractual provisions. In many acquisitions, the final report can be prepared as an update to the user's negotiations position paper (described in Chapter 4).

Where the user does not employ formal contract administration procedures, the final report (or excerpts from it) can be suspensed for use in future compliance reviews. In this regard, the report can be helpful both in testing future vendor performance and in conducting a management-level "quality review" of the entire acquisition.

Where the user employs formal contract administration procedures, the final report can serve as the bridge into the administration effort. Indeed, where the responsibility for contract administration is not assigned to the user's negotiating team, the department or group having that responsibility may participate in preparing those portions of the final report that summarize the future performance obligations of the vendor and the user.

Functional Steps

From a functional standpoint, the contract administration process essentially involves five steps (Fig. 13-2), which can be outlined as follows:

- Assign responsibility;
- Define specific tasks;
- Provide documentation;
- Utilize results;
- Follow up.

Each of these steps is described briefly below.

Assign Responsibility. As the preceding section of this chapter suggests, before the user's contract administration effort can begin, direct and supervisory responsibility for it must be assigned. (Alternative approaches in assigning this responsibility are discussed above.) However, further assignments of responsibility may also need to be made *during* the administration process. As Fig. 13-2 indicates, contract administration is a "closed-circle" or "feedback" process that proceeds on several levels or sequences. For example, as problems are discovered during the contract administration period, responsibility for dealing with those problems must be assigned—often to individuals, departments, or groups that do not have responsibility for the overall administration program. Similarly, tasks must be defined, documentation provided, and results utilized as the problem is resolved. Finally, the responsible department or group must report the results of the effort, so that appropriate follow-up procedures can be instituted. If the follow-up suggests that the problem has not been resolved, the entire process may be repeated, again beginning with the assignment of responsibility.

Fig. 13-2.   One depiction of the contract administration process.

Define Specific Tasks. As most experienced executives realize, assigning responsibility is only the necessary first step in any program. For implementation to occur, specific tasks must be defined (and assigned). Because so little has been written on contract administration, many users have difficulty defining the tasks that are necessary for a successful administration program. As a result, the contract administration effort rocks along (if it exists at all) without any organization or direction. Whatever administration occurs takes place as a result of external factors, such as equipment problems, customer complaints, or contractually-imposed deadlines. Crisis management becomes the order of the day.

To avoid this syndrome, the user must *organize* its contract administration effort by defining specific tasks *before* the problems arise. (Subsequent portions of this chapter review a number of functional techniques that can be employed for this purpose.) In addition, as problems do arise during the contract administration process, the managers responsible for resolving them must likewise define the tasks that will be used to implement the solution. Weak managers prefer to "wing it," avoiding the definition of specific tasks in order to minimize recriminations if the tasks are not fulfilled. (The proverbial lack of time is the most frequent excuse.) This informal approach will seldom provide adequate results. Indeed, it may play directly into the hands of the vendor if serious problems arise.

Provide Documentation. In the contract administration area, few things are more important than documentation. If the administration program fails to provide the level of documentation necessary to verify problems, demonstrate vendor actions, and prove user compliance, it will not be effective.

The documentation aspect of contract administration should not merely generate meaningless piles of paper. Rather, it should be designed to create planned documentation that can be *used* for specific purposes and *retained* for future requirements. As suggested above, the documentation effort will generally be improved if the forms, procedures, and manuals are designed and issued, and the permanent records are maintained, on a centralized basis. (However, this centralized approach should not preclude various departments from maintaining duplicate records on specific transactions or matters.)

Utilize Results. If the contract administration effort is to have any value to the user, the results flowing from the program must be utilized. On a narrow level, the user should employ the results of the program in dealing with the correction of specific problems or the resolution of disputes. On a broader level, the user should utilize the vendor's overall contract compliance record in reaching future procurement decisions. (See Chapter 4.) Documentation is the key source in both instances, but the forms, memoranda, and reports will have little impact unless they are actively employed in the user's decision-making process.

Follow-Up. To ensure success, the user's contract administration program must go full circle—to the point of follow-up. Solutions must be monitored and assessed to ensure that they are appropriate to the problem and competently implemented. Judgments must be tested, particularly where user personnel having close relationships with vendor marketing representatives determine to waive noncompliance by the vendor.

As in other phases of the contract administration process, the necessary follow-up must occur on both a broad and narrow basis. Thus, problems that arise during the administration of a specific agreement must be corrected, monitored, *and assessed.* In addition, the vendor's longer-term compliance record with the user must be updated from time to time, in order to reflect specific contracts and user decisions (e.g., whether to permit the vendor to bid on a new system). These user decisions must themselves be tested against the conclusions that were used in reaching them and against the future actions promised by the vendor. For example, if the vendor's performance record on prior agreements has been bad, but the user grants a new contract to the vendor in return for the vendor's assurances of improved future performance, this user judgment must be tested and assessed in the broad follow-up phase for the new procurement.

Because the follow-up process often discloses weaknesses in the user's efforts and judgments, as well as the vendor's, the follow-up task is often avoided by user personnel. This is particularly true where the follow-up indicates that a decision made by a key user manager, or the user's president, was less than outstanding. Some insulation can be provided in these circumstances if the follow-up responsibility is assigned to the quality review committee rather than to individual user departments or managers. Follow-up efforts will also be improved at all levels if the user's contract administration program is formalized and strongly supported by senior management. Where the user's president employs a management style that supports candid but constructive assessments of internal problems, user managers participating in the follow-up effort will be more likely to reach difficult decisions that may be necessary to improve future operations.

Implementation Techniques

The sequence and substance of the contract administration steps outlined above are not difficult or complex. The challenge occurs in designing the forms and procedures necessary to implement these steps in actual practice.

To be effective and efficient, the procedures and forms used in any contract administration program must be tailored to the user's operations and to the transaction and equipment involved. Forms and procedures that work well in one company may only create paper shuffling in another firm. Similarly, documents that do an excellent job of measuring vendor compliance in one transaction may do a poor job in another—even within the same user organization.

Despite the fact that each contract administration effort must be designed to serve a specific purpose and user, the program can often be constructed by selecting several contract administration "modules" or techniques from prevailing user practices. Although certain of these modules may be inappropriate in one transaction, they may be highly useful in another. By picking and choosing from its library of administration modules, the user can create an administration program that meets the unique needs of a specific acquisition. (This program should *always* be documented in a contract administration manual prepared by the user.)

A number of more effective contract administration techniques or "modules" are outlined below. Although all of these techniques would seldom be employed in a single transaction, selected combinations could be used in designing a wide variety of contract administration programs.

Vendor Compliance Certificate. Where the user/vendor agreement requires that the vendor perform certain actions under the contract, a vendor compliance certificate can be used to document the date and facts of the vendor's action. Each vendor compliance certificate should be completed and executed on behalf of the vendor by its local marketing or engineering representative. For example, if the agreement requires the vendor to cause the equipment to be installed and made ready for use, the vendor should be obligated to notify the user of the completion of these tasks by delivering a vendor compliance certificate. The form of the compliance certificate should normally be determined by the user, with reasonable input and assistance from the vendor. Indeed, one of the principal reasons for utilizing a formal compliance certificate is to permit the user to establish the format of the communication from the vendor. If the user does not take this step, it may find that its files either lack any written documentation or contain potentially self-serving letters from the vendor. Each vendor compliance certificate should ordinarily be delivered in duplicate. The user should then sign both copies and return one fully-executed copy to the vendor. The user's signature on the vendor compliance certificate should merely indicate the user's acceptance of that form; in no event should the user's signature indicate that the user has accepted, or waived any rights with respect to, the vendor performance indicated on the certificate. In order to preclude any possible misunderstanding, some users include a disclaimer to this effect directly on the vendor compliance certificate.

User Acknowledgment Form. The user acknowledgment form is designed to provide a standard document in which the user can acknowledge certain vendor actions or, in some instances, specify its own compliance with terms or conditions of the agreement. In this respect, the user acknowledgment form is not materially different in purpose from the vendor compliance certificate. (Indeed, to facilitate user-vendor relations, some users refer to the user form as a "user compliance certificate.") The user acknowledgment form can be used for such purposes as indicating the user's agreement that the acceptance test was initiated or satisfactorily completed as of a specific date. However, every effort should be made to preclude this form from being used as a waiver of the user's rights under the agreement. (Waivers are discussed in more detail below.) In order to provide protection against this risk, some users include specific "no waiver" language on each acknowledgment form. The user acknowledgment form should be designed by the user and should replace any similar communication from the user to the vendor (such as the user's signature on a letter from the vendor indicating that the equipment has passed the acceptance test).

Annual Officers' Certificate. Where long-term leases, maintenance agreements, or other similar agreements are involved, an annual officers' certificate can be used to document compliance by both parties with their respective obligations under the contract. Officers' certificates are frequently used in connection with the trust indentures which govern debt securities issued by public companies. The purpose of the certificate is to require certain designated officers or managers to certify that they have reviewed the applicable agreements (or specified portions of the agreements) and that, based upon such review, they have concluded that their company has complied with all of its obligations under the document and is not in default. The value of the officers' certificate is often as much in the required review as it is in the statement that no default has occurred. Most certificates anticipate that one or more defaults may be discovered during the review process. The certificates normally provide for the default to be described in the certificate and for the certificate to indicate that the default has been cured. Where the user's contract administration program includes officers' certificates, an appropriate provision should be included in the user-vendor agreement. This provision should outline the obligation to supply the certificates and detail the format and substance of each such certificate. As suggested above, trust indentures governing debt securities offer excellent drafting guidance in this regard.

Maintenance Log/Equipment Operation Record. Wherever a significant item or system of equipment is involved, the contract administration program should include a required maintenance log or equipment operation record. This permanent written logbook should provide a detailed operating history of the equipment, with particular emphasis on preventive and remedial maintenance. The format of this record must be designed to apply to specific equipment (e.g., aircraft, data processing, or laser manufacturing). However, the record should normally include such matters as operating hours (by date and time), usage interruptions (including reasons and solutions), preventive maintenance (including time required, services performed, and parts replaced), remedial maintenance (including time required for response and solution, services performed, and parts replaced), upgrades, attachments, and refurbishment or reconditioning steps. Although many vendors supply operating or maintenance logs with their equipment, the user should not assume that these vendor-supplied materials will be adequate for the user's contract administration purposes. In some instances, the user will be required to complete the vendor's record book (for example, to keep the applicable warranty in place or comply with the vendor's maintenance agreement). This dual recordkeeping should not deter the user from developing its own, more comprehensive system. Many users design their equipment operation record so that it is supplemented by, or easily interfaces with, related malfunction incident procedures (discussed below).

Malfunction Incident Procedures. Regardless of whether the user maintains a permanent equipment operation record, it should develop malfunction incident procedures to record all operating problems with the equipment. One method of documenting equipment operating problems is to utilize a malfunction incident report designed by the user, often with meaningful input from the vendor. This report should normally include such matters as the date, time, description, and reporting individual for each problem or incident, the action taken by the user in reporting or attempting to rectify the problem (for example, calling for remedial maintenance by the vendor), the date, time, and extent of any vendor response, and the degree to which the response or other action was able to solve the problem. Where the equipment is maintained by the vendor, the malfunction incident report should normally be signed both by the user's operating representative and by the vendor's maintenance engineer. In such situations, a copy of the report should ordinarily be furnished to the vendor. The value of the malfunction incident report is the detailed record that it supplies on every operating problem. Because a separate malfunction incident report is compiled for every problem, regardless of size, consequence, or solution, the user's staff is not required to reach judgments as to which problems should be recorded for future reference. This comprehensive approach precludes the user from finding later that it failed to keep appropriate records of the early stages of a series of incidents that subsequently developed into a critical operating deficiency. As suggested above, the user's malfunction incident procedures should normally be coordinated with any equipment operation record that is maintained.

Vendor Notification Forms. When problems do arise and communications with the vendor become necessary, the user should employ vendor notification forms specifically designed for this purpose. Although serious vendor defaults should almost always be handled by letters drafted or approved by the user's legal counsel, minor problems (that would seldom be brought to the attention of legal counsel) can and should be covered by standard form communications designed by the user with the assistance of its attorneys. Because the user's failure to notify the vendor of an operating problem may later disadvantage the user in litigation or arbitration proceedings, many users compile vendor notification forms that can be used to supplement the malfunction incident report noted above. Thus, while a malfunction incident report may be used to document each remedial maintenance item, if the vendor fails to comply with any of its obligations under the agreement, a vendor notification form may be used to formally bring this matter to the attention of the vendor. Many users draft a series of notification forms that cover specific matters and that increase in the level of severity (much like standard form collection notices, which vary depending upon such matters as the amount of the debt and the delay in payment). All vendor notification forms should be approved by the user's legal counsel. The forms should not threaten legal proceedings unless the user has reviewed the matter with counsel and is prepared to bring such an action. Some users require that vendor notification forms be completed by the end-user department, but be routed through the legal department before being provided to the vendor.

Malfunction Credit Form. Where the user-vendor agreement provides for rental, maintenance, or similar credits, a standard malfunction credit form should be utilized to document the amount of the credit. Most credit provisions include relatively complex formulae that determine both the availability and amount of the credit due to the user. Each malfunction credit form should be designed to incorporate the work sheet data necessary to support the credit in light of the applicable contract language. When completed, each form should be signed by a representative of the user and a representative of the vendor, and each party should retain an executed copy of the form. Where applicable, the malfunction credit form should be integrated into the user's malfunction incident procedures and maintenance log/equipment operation record.

Customer Complaint Record. Where the equipment involved is used by, or provides services to, customers of the user, a customer complaint record should be utilized to document each problem experienced by a customer as a result of the equipment. (For this purpose, many users consider internal departments, affiliates, and subsidiaries to be "customers.") Although certain customer complaints will be indirectly documented through the user's malfunction incident procedures, other customer problems may not be. If the user does not keep an on-going record of all customer complaints, it may find that it lacks documentation concerning the early stages of what later proves to be a critical equipment problem. In addition, maintaining a complete customer complaint file may be important to any effort by the user to obtain damages from the vendor. (Damages experienced by customers may be deemed to be "consequential" or "indirect" under certain circumstances, making them difficult or impossible to recover under certain contractual provisions. However, even where the contract appears to preclude recovery of such damages, a complete customer complaint file can have a significant impact on a jury or a judge considering other aspects of the user's suit against the vendor.) Where the user follows this approach, a separate customer complaint record should be completed for each problem brought to the user's attention. Relevant correspondence or other materials may be attached to each complaint record. Where practicable, the record should include the name, address, and telephone number of the complaining party.

Insurance Review Certificate. An insurance review certificate offers an excellent method of documenting the existence and adequacy of insurance coverage on the equipment. The certificate can either be completed by user or vendor personnel or by the insurance carrier or agent providing the coverage. Better protection is generally provided if the certificate is completed by the agent or carrier (or if the agent or carrier provides formal documentation that is attached to the certificate completed by vendor or user personnel). The certificate is ordinarily delivered by or on behalf of the party responsible for maintaining insurance coverage on the equipment. Preparation of the certificate may require an appraisal of the equipment and a thorough review of the applicable user-vendor agreements (for example, to consider casualty termination schedules and the like). Where the user's contract administration program provides for insurance review certificates, the documents should not merely be completed and placed in the relevant file. To provide adequate protection, the certificates must be carefully reviewed by the user's risk management department or outside risk management consultants.

Audit Procedures. Where particularly complex procurements are involved, some users provide for periodic audits by their internal or external auditors. Federal and state agencies frequently follow this approach, opening the entire acquisition to the scrutiny of the applicable general auditor. This approach can be especially valuable where the user's contract administration program does not include a quality review committee. On the other hand, audits can also create substantial ill-will, particularly if the auditors are not experienced in equipment procurement. Even where the user does not require a full audit of each major acquisition, it may employ its internal or external auditors to review specific problems or to confirm certain financial amounts that may be due (for example, the availability and amount of purchase option credits). Where specific amounts are being confirmed by the auditors, the figures should be documented by signed certificates.

Waivers. As Chapter 6 explains, if a party fails to take timely action to enforce its rights under an agreement, a court may later find that the party "waived" those rights by accepting incomplete performance or some other default under the agreement. Because of this risk, most well-drafted agreements specifically provide that no action or inaction by either party shall be interpreted as a "waiver" and that no waiver shall be valid unless it is in writing and signed by the party charged with the waiver. Because of the risk of inadvertent waiver, the contract administration forms employed by the user should always reserve full rights to the user, even though the user may be granting a grace period to the vendor or otherwise delaying the enforcement of the user's rights against the vendor. In those rare instances in which the user actually wishes to waive its rights against the vendor, a waiver form or letter prepared by the user's legal counsel should be employed. This written waiver should be designed for the specific purpose involved, and should not be employed as a standard user form. Legal counsel for the user should always review applicable local law to determine the legal effect of each waiver, particularly in light of such matters as any requirement for contractual "consideration."

Releases. Where a vendor or user default under an agreement creates actual liability, the parties may desire to reach and document a negotiated settlement. In such instances, the user and vendor should enter into a formal release (which may be documented in a separate release or in an agreement covering other equipment). The user should never enter into a release of any claim, whether for or against the user, without having the specific release document reviewed by the user's legal counsel. Although general forms of release are readily available, they may cover far more than counsel would recommend in a given situation. Although lawyers differ in their views on the subject, the authors generally recommend that, where specific rights are intended to be reserved and others are intended to be released, the release document should include both the reservation and the release. Some practitioners assert that the release need not include a reservation of rights if the liability to be released has been appropriately described and limited in the document. Although this approach is probably correct from a technical standpoint, it increases the risk of drafting errors.

Negotiations. Where conflicts arise that cannot be settled by exchanging forms such as those discussed above, the fastest, easiest, and least expensive method of reaching a solution is by honest and reasonable negotiations between the user and the vendor. Compared to good faith negotiations, any form of arbitration or litigation is almost certain to take more time, create more problems and ill feelings, and incur more expense. Where a negotiated settlement must be sought, the user should adopt a reasonable but firm approach. In addition to reviewing earlier portions of this book relating to vendor ploys (Chapter 2), general negotiating skills (Chapter 3), and the negotiation process (Chapter 4), the user's negotiators should read *Getting to Yes* (Boston: Houghton Mifflin Co., 1981), written by two leaders of the Harvard Negotiation Project, Roger Fisher and William Ury.

Where good faith negotiations do not appear to be progressing toward a settlement, the best solution is generally to shift the negotiations to an alternate level or to alternate negotiators. Thus, if the user's operations personnel have been negotiating with the vendor's local marketing representatives, some improvement may be achieved by suggesting that the matter be discussed by the parties' attorneys or by their respective senior management representatives. Professional negotiators may also be helpful to the user in these circumstances. Changing the level of the negotiators and the players involved has a number of advantages: It minimizes personality problems, removes stale issues from the discussions, and permits concessions to be made without loss of face.

Most equipment vendors do not hesitate to intimidate users in the conflict resolution process. Consequently, the user cannot expect to achieve a fair settlement unless it maintains a high aspiration level, is well-informed about all relevant facts, and is represented by competent advisors experienced in the area involved.

In conflict resolution negotiations, perhaps nothing is more important than conveying the user's seriousness and tenacity. If the vendor believes that the user can be worn down or that senior management of the user does not really support the position being taken by the user's lawyer or staff, the vendor will normally maintain a firm position and await its victory. On the other hand, if the vendor recognizes that the user is prepared to throw significant resources against the problem in an effort to achieve success or, at least, a negotiated solution, the vendor will be much more likely to seek an orderly, fair settlement.

Special Remedies. As Chapter 8 explains, special remedy provisions can be an important tool in the contract administration process. As used by the authors, the term "special remedies" covers a wide range of user rights that do not include damages or specific performance. When properly included in the user-vendor agreement, special remedies provide the user's first line of defense and satisfaction in any situation where the vendor fails to meet the standards imposed by the contract. Special remedy provisions explain the specific rights available to the user, or the exact corrections to be made by the vendor, when a problem stated in the contract occurs. Because the specific remedy for the precise problem is spelled out in the agreement, the user can simply call upon the vendor to take the stated remedial action, without declaring a default under the agreement. Ordinarily the vendor will comply with the special remedy provision, thereby avoiding relationship problems and saving the user the time, aggravation, and expense of actual or threatened litigation. Where the vendor refuses to comply, the user can escalate matters by declaring (or threatening to declare) a default, and pursuing its other remedies or dispute resolution techniques (e.g., negotiation, arbitration, or litigation). Users employing special remedy provisions should carefully review the discussions of remedies and liquidated damages included in Chapters 6 and 8 of this volume.

Arbitration. Where a negotiated settlement cannot be reached, many users prefer to fall back upon an arbitration provision contained in the user-vendor agreement. Arbitration agreements are recognized by statute or judicial decision in almost all states today, although in some jurisdictions agreements to arbitrate future disputes (as distinguished from existing disputes) are still not enforceable. The Federal Arbitration Act also provides for arbitration of existing and future disputes where the documents involve maritime contracts, or transactions in interstate or foreign commerce when diversity or other federal jurisdiction exists. This Act makes the federal courts available for the enforcement of arbitration clauses in a substantial number of commercial agreements where the necessary jurisdictional requirements are present.

Proponents of conflict resolution by arbitration assert that it offers a fast and relatively inexpensive method of settling disputes. Many commentators believe that it is particularly applicable in highly-technical areas and in on-going, long-term contracts where minor problems can be expected to arise over the term of the relationship. These arbitration proponents note that trained arbitrators are far better equipped than judges and juries to evaluate and resolve problems involving exotic technology.

Opponents of arbitration assert that it often takes at least as along as litigation, carries considerably less weight when viewed by the parties (and, therefore, is less of an incentive toward settlement), and may be far more costly than either party expects. Arbitration opponents also suggest that, in some jurisdictions and subject areas, the availability of experienced arbitrators is extremely limited. These opponents also note that, while some users may benefit from the fact that arbitration is arguably less expensive than litigation to pursue, other users may achieve better results by pleading their case before a judge or jury.

Arbitration has a place in some agreements, and appropriate arbitration language should certainly be included in the contract where the user and its legal counsel have concluded that it will best serve the user's interests. On the other hand, including a blanket arbitration provision in every equipment acquisition agreement is probably foolish, and may create results that are neither intended nor desired by the user. The authors generally tend to use arbitration provisions only where they appear to offer benefits to the user under the specific transaction involved. In this regard, arbitration provisions appear to be appropriate in selected industries (generally by virtue of trade usage), in long-term development agreements, and in certain limited circumstances where the user recognizes that it cannot possibly afford to bring legal action against the vendor in the event of default.

Where arbitration is desired, appropriate language must be included in the user-vendor agreement (although a separate written agreement providing for arbitration will generally also be enforceable). In most instances, parties selecting arbitration have the agreement provide that all controversies or claims arising out of or relating to the agreement shall be settled by arbitration. Where this approach is used, arbitration will be the exclusive remedy and any action brought in disregard of the arbitration provision may be stayed by a court of law (assuming that the request for the stay is brought in a timely manner). The most frequent arbitration provision is that suggested by the American Arbitration Association, which reads as follows:

> Any controversy or claim arising out of or relating to this contract, or the breach thereof, shall be settled by arbitration in accordance with the Rules of the American Arbitration Association, and judgment upon the award rendered by the arbitrator(s) may be entered in any court having jurisdiction thereof.

Where appropriate, some arbitration provisions change the above reference to the American Arbitration Association rules to the rules of a particular industry association which maintains arbitration facilities for its members. By referring to applicable rules of the American Arbitration Association or an industry association, the above language avoids considerable additional detail that would otherwise be necessary (for example, the scope of the arbitration, the choice of arbitrators, and the method of enforcing the arbitration award). Some attorneys prefer to include all of these matters in the written agreement. Although the shorter approach referring to applicable rules appears to be preferable, the arbitration clause should generally include the location of the arbitration, particularly if the user and vendor maintain offices in different cities or states. Where an arbitration provision will be used, particular care should be taken in considering language that requires that the demand for arbitration be brought within a specified period. In some jurisdictions, the failure to demand arbitration within the time specified in the contract may leave the user without any remedy at all.

Litigation. As the above discussion of arbitration suggests, some attorneys believe that the user's position is enhanced if any final dispute resolution is handled by the courts rather than by an arbitration panel. Despite the risks of increased cost and substantial additional time, legal process is a more formalized procedure that may better serve the user's position under certain circumstances. For better or for worse, the legal process generally permits the user to have its day in court before a jury. Particularly where the vendor is a "deep pocket" and the user has been victimized by what amounts to an adhesion contract, the user may receive a much greater award from a jury than from an arbitration panel.

Regardless of whether it is compared to arbitration or to negotiation, litigation is time consuming and expensive. The authors feel strongly that litigation should be employed to resolve equipment contract disputes only as a last resort. On the other hand, the authors also believe that, in order to maintain a firm negotiating stance, a user should always be prepared to pursue litigation if necessary. Indeed, the user's negotiating position with the vendor may be improved if the user indicates at the outset that it is prepared to go to trial if the problem involved cannot be resolved on an amicable basis.

If litigation appears to be necessary, it should be pursued adamantly. If the user is not prepared to engage the best legal counsel available and to provide appropriate financial and managerial resources to support the lawyers' litigation effort, the case generally should not be brought in the first place. Much like "limited" wars, limited litigation may be less effective and considerably more costly than other forms of conflict resolution. When pursuing necessary litigation, the user should ensure that its legal counsel has proper training, not only in trial practice but also in the specific type of equipment involved. Although most good trial lawyers have a remarkable ability to complete the research necessary to become familiar with virtually any subject matter, the user's case against the vendor will have a far greater chance of early settlement if the user's lawyers understand the specific technical matters that are involved. In particularly complex cases, the user should consider retaining trial counsel with specific experience in equipment litigation or utilizing professional consultants or special counsel to provide the necessary technical support.

APPENDIX A
GENERAL CONTRACT CHECKLIST

This appendix presents a general contract checklist designed to be useful in drafting and negotiating various types of major equipment agreements.

Although checklists can be effective aids in drafting and negotiating optimum user-oriented agreements, the substance of each provision is the key to proper user protection. An agreement drafted with weak provisions covering all of the items mentioned in a comprehensive checklist may provide little protection for the user. On the other hand, an agreement drafted with strong pro-user versions of less than all of the checklist points may offer excellent protection.

In the final analysis, a checklist should be exactly that—a source of relevant points to consider in negotiating and drafting an agreement. Few contracts can or will contain provisions covering all of the points in a comprehensive checklist. Likewise, few checklists can cover all of the subjects that may need to be included in a particular agreement, or all of the details that may need to be noted within a particular subject or provision. Many of the items briefly referenced a checklist could be expanded to fill a page or more if space (and patience) permitted.

Regardless of the relative complexity or simplicity of any checklist, the provisions relating to the items mentioned must be carefully tailored to fit the particular transaction being considered by the user. As in the case of example contractual provisions, checklists must be used with considerable care and, in the final stages, must be applied or at least reviewed by a competent professional who is familiar with the legal, financial, and business aspects of the transaction.

Because the following checklist is designed to provide general guidance for a wide range of transactions, it does not attempt to focus on matters that would be applicable only in specific industries or transactions. Thus, the checklist should be augmented by any factors relevant to the particular type of equipment involved (e.g., aircraft, construction, or data processing). Similarly, the checklist should be tailored to the specific type of acquisition method (e.g., third-party leveraged lease, installment purchase, or rental) being employed by the user. Where the transaction requires special arrangements with third parties (e.g., subcontractors, project managers, or original equipment manufacturers), the checklist should again be expanded to include any additional issues that may be involved. Various "soft dollar" benefits that may be available are among the items that should be considered in this regard.

GENERAL CONTRACT CHECKLIST

☐ **Identification of Parties:**
   a. Legal name and address (including division).
   b. State of incorporation, if any.
   c. Short reference used in agreement.
☐ **Definition of Terms Used in Agreement:**
   a. Parenthetical definitions throughout agreement.
   b. Special definition or glossary section.
☐ **Description of Products and Services:**
   a. Hardware.
   b. Software.
   c. Systems support.
   d. Special conversions or other services.
   e. Education, training, and manuals.
   f. Comprehensive list of equipment components (including cable lengths and connectors), with quantity, catalog number, and description clearly indicated.
   g. Cross-reference to "Warranties by Vendor" provision (equipment to be warranted as new, Section 38, rebuilt, or other).

h. Reference to, and incorporation by reference of, all schedules and addenda, including vendor marketing materials and proposals and user specifications.

i. Configuration warranty by vendor and/or manufacturer that equipment ordered will perform as represented.

j. Compliance with ANSI or other standards.

☐ **Term of Agreement:**

a. Effective date of agreement as a binding contract between vendor and user ("agreement" to be void if not signed by vendor, user, and any other party within stated time).

b. Commencement date for any initial rental or lease term, or other term during which products or services will be provided.

c. Commencement date for any rental or lease payments, or other payments (beware of "precommencement rental days").

d. Dates for increases or decreases in amounts of lease/rental payments, or other payments.

e. Termination date for initial rental or lease term, or other term during which products or services will be provided.

f. Termination date for lease/rental and other payments.

g. Options and requirements at termination of term and/or lease/rental payments, including availability and length of renewal term(s), availability and price for purchase option(s), and option notice periods and conditions.

h. Termination date for agreement as a binding contract between vendor and user.

i. Early termination and cancellation dates for term, payments, and agreement, including termination/cancellation schedules and penalties (cross-reference to "Default").

j. Provision for orderly transfer of data, programs, and support upon termination of any term and/or agreement.

☐ **Acquisition of Equipment:**

a. Source, condition, specifications, and availability of all equipment, software, programs and other items to be acquired by or on behalf of user (use serial numbers where appropriate).

b. Obligations of any lessor, broker, or other party to acquire the equipment and other items at designated prices, on specified terms, and by indicated deadlines; review copies of proposed and actual third-party purchase agreements and related documents.

c. Include any obligations with respect to additional or substitute equipment.

d. Cross-reference to "Default" provision and provide prompt remedies in event vendor or any third-party fails to timely perform.

☐ **Performance Deadlines:**

a. Specific performance deadlines, with or without grace periods, for all major products and services.

b. Where practicable, interim performance checkpoints (e.g., delivery, installation, testing, and acceptance).

c. Cross-reference to "Acceptance," "Delivery and Installation," "Force Majeure," and "Default."

☐ **Payment Terms:**

a. Initial downpayment (as low as possible).

b. Interim payments (only upon satisfactory compliance with interim acceptance criteria and deadlines).

c. Final payment.

d. Penalty and interest factors in event of late payment by user (avoid if possible, or exclude where billing dispute controversy exists).

e. Price to be paid by lessor or other third-party for each item, product, or service (attach copy of relevant contract to lease).

f. Initial precommencement rental days payment (generally to be avoided).

g. Rental/lease payments during initial term and any renewal terms (watch length of minimum renewal term).

h. Relationship of use to payment due (overtime charges, unlimited use, or other).

i. Calculation of lease/rental payments in advance or in arrears (use proper calculator setting for type of annuity involved in calculations).

j. Apportionment of lease/rental payments during partial months (do not confuse with "precommencement rental days").

k. Increases or decreases in lease/rental payments during initial and renewal terms, including predetermined step increases and decreases, cost-of-living escalators, and lessor-mandated increases (include amounts, timing, notice periods, and methods).

l. Late payment and interest charges levied by lessor, including reference to rate, terms of application, prior notice, disputed billings, and applicable usury limits.

m. Other payments and amounts due from user, including UCC filing fees, legal expenses, financing expenses, and the like (limit to stated amounts or obligations; beware of broad or vague language).

n. "Most favored nation" or similar pricing provision in user/vendor agreements and any third-party agreements.

o. Comparison of lease/rental payments and other obligations to any loan agreement, stock, or debt restrictions on user's maximum financial obligations.

p. Assessment of whether lease payments must be capitalized under Financial Accounting Standards Board (FASB) Statement No. 13 and related federal securities law accounting standards.

q. Invoicing standards (tailor to user's needs).

r. Trade-in or substitution charges and/or percentage tables.

s. Termination and casualty charges or penalties and/or percentage tables.

t. Assignment of payments by lessor to financing institution (consider effect of lessor or manufacturer default on user's obligation to continue to make payments to the assignee financial institution—the "hell or high water" clause).

u. Cross-reference to "Insurance and Risk of Loss."

v. Cross-reference to "Taxes."

w. Cross-reference to "Insurance."

x. Cross-reference to "Delivery and Installation."

☐ **Taxes:**

a. Party responsible for any sales and use taxes on purchase of equipment or service.

b. Party responsible for any documentary or other taxes on financing of equipment.

c. Party responsible for any sales and use taxes on lease/rental and other payment made by user.

d. Party responsible for personal property taxes on equipment and software.

e. Party responsible for taxes on gross or net income of vendor or lessor.

f. Party responsible for any penalties imposed because of late or nonpayment of any taxes due, including situations where user is required to pay tax but lessor fails to file legally required information return.

g. Ability and method of challenging any taxes imposed, including degree of required cooperation in suit.

h. Allocation and/or return of taxes subsequently determined not to be payable.

i. Availability of Investment Tax Credit:
  1. Type of equipment.
  2. Warranty by manufacturer (passed through to user, if applicable).
  3. Warranty by lessor to user.
  4. Ability of user to take advantage of ITC in light of user's actual and projected federal income tax positions.
  5. Timing of ITC in light of installation and acceptance dates.
  6. Pass through to user of any ITC advantage retained by lessor (in form of lower lease/rental payments).
  7. Liability of user to lessor or lessor's investors in event ITC lost during lease term.
  8. Possible loss of ITC due to equipment replacements, trade-ins, and upgrades.
  9. Relationship, if any, to "safe harbor" lease provisions of Economic Recovery Tax Act of 1981, as modified in 1982.

☐ **Delivery and Installation:**

a. Shipping specifications, methods, and carriers; notification of shipment.

b. Parties responsible for crating, shipping, delivery, uncrating, floor set-up and positioning, and installation, including arrangements, payments, insurance, and risk of loss.

c. Site plan and installation environment specifications, including party responsible for necessary site modifications and vendor or manufacturer warranty of site plan and environment adequacy.

d. Shipment, delivery, and installation deadlines, including applicable schedules, liquidated damages, agreement termination, or other recourse provisions, and adjustment of dates in certain user-oriented situations.

e. Ability of user to delay or accelerate shipment, delivery, or installation upon specified terms and conditions.

f. Provisions requiring delivery, or installation of all components by required deadline(s), in order to eliminate risk of partial delivery.

g. Separately state various requirements as necessary for specific subsystems, hardware, or software.

h. Use separate agreement between manufacturer and user where necessary to ensure availability of assistance from manufacturer or to otherwise protect user's interest; provide for user to be third party beneficiary under manufacturer/lessor or similar purchase agreement.

i. Payment and reimbursement provisions for delivery and installation costs, including FOB points and caps, if any, on total costs to be incurred by user.

j. Cross-reference to "Default."

k. Cross-reference to "Payment Terms."

☐ **Acceptance Criteria:**

a. Detailed acceptance tests and criteria for:
  1. Each major hardware subsystem.
  2. Each major software, system, and support project.
  3. The system as a whole, including all equipment, software, systems, and support work.

b. Parties responsible for, and procedures to be used in, certifying completion of installation and readiness for acceptance testing.

c. Specific acceptance tests to be performed, including performance criteria and parties responsible for judging compliance.

d. Provisions for correcting deficient performance and rerunning tests in event of failure.

e. Provision for replacing equipment components or terminating agreement, with or without penalty to vendor, manufacturer, lessor, or other party in the event of continued failure to meet acceptance tests.

f. Coordinate obligations and liabilities of lessor and manufacturer; review terms of lessor/manufacturer or other third-party purchase agreement.

g. Cross-reference to "Default."

☐ **Default and Damages:**

a. Definition of "Default" by vendor, by user, and by manufacturer/lessor, or other third party; review lessor/manufacturer or other third-party purchase agreement to determine impact on the user of a default under such agreement (consider giving user the right to cure such a default).

b. Notice required and opportunity to cure both financial/payment defaults and non-financial defaults.

c. Statement(s) of legal and equitable remedies, including liquidated damages, specific performance, rights at law and in equity, actual, consequential, and punitive damages.

d. Statements of special contractual remedies, including repossession (insist upon lawful notice), assignment of software, and escrow and/or release of software source codes.

e. Remedies in event of bankruptcy, significant change in economic condition, and related financial problems.

f. Remedies and contingency provisions in event vendor, lessor, or other party fails to obtain required financing or deserved interest rate and terms.

g. Limitations on liability, including restrictions on punitive and consequential damages (such limitations should protect the user as well as the vendor, lessor, and manufacturer).

h. Cross-reference to "Force Majeure" and "Patent Indemnity" provision.

i. Cross-reference to "Warranties" and tie to limitation of warranty provisions.

j. Consider effect of lessor or manufacturer default on user's obligation to continue to make payments to any assignee financial institution (the "hell or high water" clause in a lease or installment purchase agreement).

☐ **Force Majeure or "Act of God" Provision:**

a. Include only after careful consideration.

b. Be sure provision also protects user.

c. Cross-reference to "Default."

☐ **Insurance and Risk of Loss:**

a. Responsibilities of manufacturer, lessor, or other vendor and user for risk of loss and for obtaining various types of insurance (hazard, liability) during each relevant period, e.g., shipping, installation, testing, lease term, return to lessor (separate items, such as hardware, software, programming work, and proprietary data, may require separate coverage); coordinate risks and obligations under purchase agreement and lease.

b. Indication of whether and how agreement is to continue in event of loss at each relevant period, e.g., shipping, installation, testing, lease term, return to lessor. Include obligation to replace, ability to terminate, and allocation of insurance proceeds.

c. Minimum insurance requirements, including any approval of company selected, mandatory policy provisions, and proof of insurance and premium payment.

d. Basic "Casualty Occurrence" provision and payment schedule covering such areas as: notification; repair, replacement, and termination options and responsibilities; definitions; subrogation, if any; and relationship to other provisions such as patent idemnity.

e. Permission for user to insure through valid self-insurance, blanket, or master policies.

f. Where desirable, mandatory business interruption or termination insurance from manufacturer, lessor, or other vendor.

g. Cross-reference to "Payment Terms," "Title," "Indemnification," and "Term."

☐ **Manuals and Other Materials:**

a. Number of copies of manuals to be received by user and price, if any; procedures and prices for updates.

b. Permission for user to reproduce vendor manuals and training materials (indicate any restrictions and copyright notice requirements).

c. Permission for user to utilize vendor manuals or materials at multiple sites; permission, if desired, for user to sell to, or permit the use of such manuals by, third parties.

d. Coordination of obligations of vendor, user, and any other parties with respect to manuals and similar materials.

e. Cross-reference to "Education."

f. Cross-reference to "Proprietary Rights."

☐ **Education and Training by Vendor:**

a. Amount, type, and price (if any).

b. Site(s), number of participants, and times available.

c. Quality (number of instructors, background, training and the like).

d. Attach vendor's training materials or bro-

chures, if available, and incorporate by reference.

e. Provision for user to teach internally from vendor materials.

f. Cross-reference to "Manuals."

g. Cross-reference to "Proprietary Rights."

☐ **Proprietary Rights and Nondisclosure:**

a. Indication of which party or parties own various proprietary data, programs, and the like (devote special attention to programs or projects to be developed through joint efforts or to be modified by user).

b. Indication of all restrictions on disclosure for all parties.

c. Provision for licenses to user or vendor for all relevant software and other proprietary materials.

☐ **Software Source Code Availability:**

a. Provision for availability of program source codes, either directly or through source code escrow agreement or later conveyance provision.

b. Cross-reference to "Default" provision.

☐ **Transfer of Title:**

a. Indication of whether title to the equipment will be held by a specified party other than the user (generally the lessor or the lessor's investors).

b. Provision for warranty of title by manufacturer and transfer of title from manufacturer to lessor (generally in manufacturer/lessor purchase agreement) or other third party; coordinate with lease to user.

c. Provision for transfer of title to any manuals, peripherals, or programs to user, if applicable.

d. Provision for no liens upon lessor's interest in the leased equipment; include specified labels or signs to be affixed to equipment to indicate lessor's ownership.

e. Provide for filing of UCC and similar financing statements to indicate interest of lessor or secured party (lessor or other secured party to pay costs of filing and to file releases at end of term).

f. Provision for reasonable inspection of equipment by lessor or other secured party with adequate protection of user's proprietary and customer information.

☐ **Warranties by Each Party:**

a. Warranty by each party that it is a validly organized corporate entity with authority to enter into each applicable agreement (include incumbency or secretary's certificates and other documentation as required).

b. Warranty by each party that no government approvals are required to permit the party to enter into and perform pursuant to each applicable agreement.

c. Warranty by each party that entry into and performance under each applicable agreement is not restricted or prohibited by any loan, security, financing, contractual or other agreement of any kind.

d. Warranty by each party that no existing or threatened legal proceedings against it will have a material adverse effect upon its ability to perform its obligations under any applicable agreement.

e. Cross-reference to "Default."

☐ **Warranties by User:**

a. Warranties and representations concerning user's financial condition (limit strictly to warranties necessary for lease or other financing; review warranties with securities counsel for user).

b. Cross-reference to "Warranties by Each Party."

c. Cross-reference to "Default."

☐ **Warranties by Manufacturer:**

a. Pass-through and assignment to user of all equipment, software, and systems warranties in lessor/manufacturer purchase agreement or other third-party agreement (make user and/or its applicable affiliates third party beneficiaries; consider direct warranty agreement between user and manufacturer or other third party).

b. Provision for meshing all applicable warranty periods with maintenance agreement terms and prices.

c. Assessment of the scope of all manufacturer's equipment, software, and systems warranties (including all limitations) before executing any documents.

d. Provision for warranty of title by manufacturer to lessor or other vendor and pass-through of warranty (or direct manufacturer warranty) to user.

e. If applicable, appropriate "ITC warranty" by manufacturer and pass-through of warranty (or direct manufacturer warranty) to user.

f. Provision for patent indemnity warranty by manufacturer and pass-through of warranty (or direct manufacturer warranty) to user; ensure that user and/or its affiliates have direct enforcement rights;

provide related protection for software and programs supplied by manufacturer.

g. Provision for configuration warranty that equipment ordered includes all components necessary to perform as represented (pass-through to user).

h. Provision for warranty that equipment meets ANSI or other applicable standards, if desired, and that equipment will perform according to manufacturer's published specifications (pass-through to user).

i. Cross-reference to "Warranties by Each Party."

☐ **Warranties by Lessor or Other Third Party Vendor:**

NOTE: The reference to "lessor" in the following portion of this Checklist would be equally applicable to any other third-party vendor in many transactions.

a. Specific obligation of lessor to pass-through all warranty benefits available from manufacturer; review and coordinate all warranty benefits in all applicable agreements, including lessor/manufacturer purchase agreement or other third-party agreement.

b. Where practicable, separate warranties from lessor covering all subjects warranted by manufacturer.

c. Warranty by lessor that it has title to the equipment or that it has binding agreements with the manufacturer permitting lessor to obtain title by the designated date.

d. Warranty by lessor that it has obtained the specified financing required to purchase the equipment on stated terms and deadlines or that it can and will so obtain such financing.

e. Warranty by lessor that, as of the commencement date of the original lease term (or the commencement date for the payment of rentals if such date is earlier) and continuing through the initial and renewal terms, the lessor will have full and free title to the equipment subject only to specified liens relating to senior financing.

f. Configuration warranty that equipment ordered includes all components necessary for the performance represented by the manufacturer (consider pass-through to user of manufacturer's representation to lessor).

g. Reasonable limitations on warranties by lessor, particularly if such limitations may restrict or negate the right of any assignee financial institution to receive lease/rental payments (remember that it is possible to effectively guarantee the stream of payments to an assignee financial institution under a "hell or high water" clause and still make the lessor remain liable for performance of its warranties).

h. Cross-reference to "Warranties by Each Party."

i. Cross-reference to "Default."

□ **Assignment and Sublease:**

a. Specify right of vendor and user to assign applicable agreement(s) in whole or in part; provide broad assignment rights to vendor or lessor where necessary to ensure senior financing; restrict other assignment or delegation of duties by vendor; require vendor to guarantee performance in event of any assignment.

b. Provision for user assignment and sublease rights to ensure flexibility and to meet unforeseen circumstances during term; provide special assignment and sublease rights among user's parent, subsidiary, and affiliate companies.

c. Type of notice and degree of permission required, if any, for assignment or sublease by user; consider use of "such permission not to be unreasonably withheld."

d. Indication of whether assignor or sublessor remains responsible for performance after assignment or sublease.

e. Indication of whether warranties continue after assignment or sublease and, if so, to whom such warranties then run.

f. Indication of right of user to sublease, sublicense, assign, or permit use of software, programs, manuals, educational and other materials, and copyrights (including after purchase of equipment by user during or at end of lease term).

g. Coordination of all assignment rights with senior financing requirements and documents and with lessor/manufacturer or other third-party agreement.

h. Cross-reference to "Maintenance," "Right to Use," and "Right to Move" provisions.

□ **Maintenance and Parts:**

a. Minimum maintenance obligations of user during term, including whether

maintenance by manufacturer is required.

b. Warranty by manufacturer or vendor that maintenance and/or spare parts will be available to user (at standard rates and terms or better) during entire term or other specified minimum period after acceptance, including reasonable renewal periods; provide for assignment to any assignee or sublessee of user.

c. Shifts or periods during which maintenance will be required; consider limiting preventive maintenance to non-prime-shift periods.

d. Coordination of manufacturer's warranty period(s) with term and price of manufacturer's initial maintenance agreement.

e. Negotiate initial maintenance agreement with manufacturer before executing lease documents.

f. Indication of whether parts and supplies must be obtained from manufacturer or other designated source and, if so, whether adequate availability is assured; state any supply specifications.

□ **Hardware and Software Modifications:**

a. Indication of whether user may modify hardware or software.

b. Conditions or costs imposed in event of modification.

c. Cross-reference to "Warranties," "Maintenance," and "Proprietary Rights."

□ **Software Enhancements:**

a. Indication of vendor's obligation to supply software corrections and enhancements:
   1. Term.
   2. Price.
   3. Mandatory or voluntary.

b. Indication of penalty, if any, if user fails to incorporate software enhancements.

c. Time periods within which major software errors must be corrected.

d. Warranty period for all enhancements and corrections.

e. Provision that no enhancement or correction may cause system to fail to meet original performance specifications.

□ **Right To Use:**

a. Limitations, if any, on who has the right to operate and/or use the equipment, software, programs, manuals, and other materials; provide for adequate flexibility among user's parent, subsidiary, and affiliate companies; coordinate with assignment and right to move provisions.

b. Assessment of any restrictions on use that may be directly or indirectly imposed by lessor/manufacturer purchase agreement or other third-party agreement and/or any applicable software license agreements or policies.

c. Cross-reference to "Assignment," "Maintenance," and "Right to Move" provisions.

☐ **Right To Move:**

a. Indication of whether user has the right to move the equipment; specify all limitations and conditions on such right (imposed directly or indirectly by manufacturer, lessor, assignee financial institution, or other entity) and ensure that all necessary conditions can be met, if necessary.

b. Indication of whether software, programs, manuals, and other materials can be used at more than one user site or at alternative sites.

c. Provision for assistance in any move by manufacturer, vendor, and/or lessor, as may be required.

d. Indication of whether maintenance will be available at new or alternative site; review possible application of any refurbishment or other extra cost provisions in maintenance agreement.

e. Cross-reference to "Assignment," "Maintenance," and "Right to Use" provisions.

☐ **Allowance For Operational Failure:**

a. Provision for allowance or credit in event of operational failure in excess of specified limits during term or during a specified period following acceptance:

1. Allowance must be consistent with protection of any stream of lease payments to assignee financial institution.

2. Consider payment of credit by lessor or manufacturer (including credit or payment under user/manufacturer maintenance agreement).

3. Consider mandatory manufacturer replacement of components during first year if necessary; consider ITC implications.

4. Consider extending lease or other term (e.g., rental or maintenance) at no cost to user for a period equal to the aggregate failure period.

5. State methods of determining failure, calculating allowance, and notifying lessor.

b. Cross-reference to "Default," "Maintenance," and "Taxes" provisions.

☐ **Indemnification:**

a. Careful restriction of any provisions requiring user to indemnify or "hold harmless" any party; do not permit user to be obligated to indemnify vendor, lessor, or any other party for its own negligence or omission or for other matters for which the user should not be liable.

b. Provision for basic indemnification of vendor or lessor (and, more importantly, any assignee financial institution) against loss relating to the user's operation of the equipment; include exception for loss caused by the indemnified party and other appropriate exceptions (provide right to contest and limitations on time period and types of events).

c. Assessment of all indemnification obligations in light of user's existing and proposed insurance coverage.

d. Careful restriction of any provision requiring user to idemnify lessor or lessor's investors in event ITC or other tax benefits retained by lessor are lost during lease term; require corresponding indemnity from manufacturer to user in event ITC loss is caused by manufacturer.

e. Assessment of indemnification provision contained in lessor/manufacturer purchase agreement and other third-party agreements.

☐ **Covenant of Quiet Enjoyment:**

a. In any lease or rental agreement, provision for a covenant of "quiet enjoyment" running from lessor to user throughout term of lease (with usual requirement that user must comply with lease terms and make all required payments).

b. Provision for the covenant of quiet enjoyment to bind any assignee of the lessor, including any assignee financial institution, and any other secured party of the lessor (such as the manufacturer before the purchase price is paid); provide for reasonable attornment by user to such assignee or secured party.

☐ **Disaster Backup:**

(Specify availability, cost, timing, and the like.)

☐ **Deinstallation and Redelivery of Equipment:**

a. Shipping specifications, methods, and

carriers; provide for notification of shipment.

b. Parties responsible for deinstalling, crating, shipping, and delivery, including arrangements, payment, insurance, and risk of loss.

c. Deinstallation and redelivery deadlines.

d. If user is required to pay for redelivery, provision for limits on maximum shipping distance and/or maximum costs.

e. Use separate agreement between manufacturer and user where necessary to ensure availability of assistance from manufacturer or to otherwise protect user's interest.

☐ **Guarantees of Performance:**

a. Issued by user's parent, subsidiary, or affiliate companies to lessor, manufacturer, other vendor, or assignee financial institution where necessary due to credit standing, subsidiary status, or the like.

b. Issued by parent, subsidiary, or affiliate companies of lessor or other third party to manufacturer, user, or assignee financial institution where necessary.

c. Issued by manufacturer's parent, subsidiary, or affiliate companies to lessor, user, or assignee financial institution where necessary.

d. Issued by bonding company or escrow agent on behalf of one or more parties.

☐ **Financial Statements and Disclosure:**

a. If required for financing or credit status, provision for delivery of user financial reports and other information to vendor, lessor, and/or assignee financial institution during term.

b. If desired by user, provision for delivery of lessor, vendor, and/or manufacturer financial reports and other information to user and/or assignee financial institution during various periods, including negotiations, acceptance testing, and agreement term.

c. Assessment of risks involved in disclosing user's confidential insider information; review user disclosure requirements with user's securities law counsel.

☐ **Applicability of Uniform Commercial Code (UCC):**

a. Applicability to lessor/manufacturer or other third-party purchaser.

b. Applicability to any direct purchase by user.

c. Applicability to any trade-in or sale of used equipment by user.

d. Applicability to "nongoods" transactions by mutual agreement (if legally effective).

e. Applicability to lease transactions (if legally effective).

☐ **Governing law**

☐ **Notices**

☐ **Nonwaiver in Event of Nonenforcement or Delayed Enforcement**

☐ **Partial Invalidity of Agreement**

☐ **Execution of Amendments**

☐ **Entire Agreement:**

a. Integration of all representations and agreements into the written agreement, with incorporation by reference of specified manufacturer, lessor, and other vendor representations, proposals, and marketing materials, as well as the user's RFP.

b. Merger of specified provisions at closing (strictly limit or preclude where merged provision would be beneficial to user after closing).

c. Survival of specified provisions in user/lessor, lessor/manufacturer, and/or other agreements beyond closing and/or termination of lease or other term.

☐ **Third Party Beneficiary Provision:**

a. Provision for user and/or its parent, subsidiary, or affiliate companies to be third party beneficiaries under the lessor/manufacturer agreement.

b. Provision for all or certain parent, subsidiary, or affiliate companies of user to be third party beneficiaries under the user/lessor lease or other applicable agreements.

c. Careful assessment of all third party beneficiary provisions in light of governing state law.

☐ **Signature Blocks:**

a. Full legal name of each corporate party.

b. Name and title of each officer executing agreement on behalf of each corporate party.

c. Special execution requirements (e.g., corporate resolutions) imposed by any proposed assignee financial institution or other third party.

APPENDIX B
SELECTED CONTRACT PROVISIONS

The following pages set forth example contract provisions in the areas listed below. Although the general text of this volume also includes contract provisions in certain sections, the following provisions were deferred to the appendix either because of their length or because of their applicability to several chapters of text:

1. Most Favored Nation Provision
2. Acceptance Provisions (Five Alternatives)
3. Availability-of-Financing Warranty by Third-Party Lessor
4. Liquidated Damages Provision
5. General Provisions (Including General Liability and Force Majeure Sections)

MOST FAVORED NATION PROVISION

Notwithstanding any other provision of this Agreement, all of the prices, warranties, benefits, and terms granted by the Vendor to the Customer hereunder are hereby warranted by the Vendor to be comparable to, or more favorable to the Customer than, the equivalent prices, warranties, benefits, and terms that: (a) have been offered by Vendor to any of its other ___(1)___ customers ___(2)___ during the period from ___(3)___ to the effective date of this Agreement; and (b) are being and will be offered by Vendor to any of its other ___(1)___ customers ___(2)___ during the period from the effective date of this Agreement through and including ___(4)___. If at any time during the periods stated in subparagraphs (a) or (b) above, the Vendor shall contract, or have contracted, with any other ___(1)___ customer ___(2)___ for the ___(5)___ of substantially similar equipment as that listed in Schedule A hereto, on a basis that provides prices, warranties, benefits or terms to the customer more favorable than those provided to Customer hereunder, then: (i) Vendor shall within (30) calendar days after the effective date of such other contract notify Customer in writing of such fact, explaining the more favorable basis in detail; and (ii) regardless of whether such notice is sent by Vendor or received by Customer, this Agreement shall be deemed to be automatically amended, effective retroactively to the effective date hereof, to provide the same prices, warranties, benefits, or terms to the Customer; provided that Customer shall have the right and option at any time to decline to accept any such change, in which event such automatic amendment shall be deemed to be null and void effective retroactively to the effective date of this Agreement. The provisions of this section ____ shall survive the closing and termination of this Agreement.

Notes:
(1) Insert any limitation describing the type of customer or business, such as "banking or savings and loan association."

(2) Insert any geographic or other limitations, such as "located in the Commonwealth of Massachusetts" and/or "purchasing a system with a list price of $1.2 million or more."

(3) Insert earliest date Vendor will agree to accept.

(4) Insert latest date Vendor will agree to accept.

(5) Insert any descriptive limitations based upon the type of transaction involved, such as "purchase" or "lease."

ACCEPTANCE PROVISIONS

Example One

The following provision was used in an agreement covering the purchase of equipment from a large minicomputer manufacturer. Although the provision is less than perfect in several respects, it represents a substantial achievement due to the fact that the vendor is well-known for refusing to vary its standard agreements and methods of doing business.

4. **ACCEPTANCE:** Upon completion of Installation, acceptance testing will be performed in three phases, as follows:

4.1 Vendor's standard test procedures will be performed for User's personnel, verifying operation of all components of the installed system.

4.2 During the first business week following Installation, User will perform the "benchmark" tests described in Schedule A to determine that the performance of the System falls within the allowable range of Schedule B. [*Note: Schedule A should list all programs and routines to be used for the benchmark. Schedule B must be carefully reviewed by the user's technical personnel.*]

4.3 Following satisfactory performance of the benchmark tests specified in Section 4.2, above, Reliability Testing will be performed by User, with assistance of Vendor, during a period of three (3) consecutive business weeks. During this period, User will operate the system for its ordinary data processing needs, from 8 A.M. to 8 P.M., local time, Monday through Saturday. The System will be deemed to have satisfactorily passed the Reliability Test if, during this period, the equipment and the software operate free from Major Failure. Major Failure is defined for this purpose as a failure of any item of the equipment or software, or both, that prevents the User from performing meaningful work on the System, based upon User's business needs. The parties agree that User's business needs require that the System be available for normal operation for at least twenty (20) jobs (or terminals logged on) except in case of temporary failure.

If the System satisfactorily passes all three (3) phases of the Acceptance Tests outlined above, the System will be accepted by the User and the User will thereafter execute the Certificate of Acceptance attached as Exhibit E hereto and promptly deliver the same to Vendor. If the System fails to pass any or all phases of the Acceptance Tests outlined above, the Vendor shall correct the deficiency or deficiencies at its expense, within not later than five (5) calendar days after such failure, and the applicable phase of the Acceptance Test shall be repeated until all three (3) phases of the Acceptance Tests are satisfactorily passed; provided, however, that if all such phases are not satisfactorily passed by _____, 19___, [or within _____ (___) calendar days after the date Phase 1 of the Acceptance Test is begun], the User shall have the right and option to terminate this Agreement by delivery of written notice to Vendor, whereupon the provisions of the Section ____ [relating to Default] shall be applicable.

Example Two

The provision below was included in a lengthy contract for the purchase of a large scale mainframe system from a top five computer manufacturer. A separate provision covered acceptance of the conversion of several hundred of the User's existing application programs.

Section 21—Acceptance: The System will be considered ready for use upon the successful completion of Steps A through H specified below (hereinafter called the "Acceptance Tests"). The Acceptance Tests described in the following steps shall be run by a Vendor field representative in the presence of a Customer representative.

A. Vendor's complete Field Engineering Acceptance Test will first be performed on the System using the latest acceptance test software formally released by Vendor as of the test date. The results of this test will be certified by Vendor as conforming to the published results for normally functioning equipment.

B. Symbolic code for both the test routine and the language compilers used during the following tests will then be copied to disk pack. The symbolic code for the compilers, intrinsics, and [specify all appropriate operating software, compilers, and utilities] will also be loaded. All symbolics will be for the latest systems software formally released by Vendor as of the test date.

C. The Vendor field representative will then execute the following steps:
   1. Compile a new _____ compiler.
   2. Compile new _____ and _____ compilers using the _____ compiler that has just been compiled.
   3. Compile a new version of the [operating software], intrinsics, and associated program units and create a new operating system from these components.
   4. Halt/Load the System using the new operating systems software.
   5. Compile any additional language compilers necessary to compile Field Engineering Acceptance Test software.
   6. Compile a new set of routines necessary to run the Field Engineering Acceptance Test.
   7. Execute the Field Engineering Acceptance Test as set forth in Test A above, using the newly compiled routines.
   8. Within one (1) business day after the completion of Test C (7) above, the results of Test C (7), shall be compared with those of Step A. If the results are identical, Customer shall certify in writing, within one (1) business day after the comparison is made, that the System is ready for use. If the results are not identical, the testing procedure described heretofore shall be reinitiated after Vendor has taken corrective action, which action shall be completed not later than five (5) business days after the above comparison is made.

D. Upon satisfactory completion of the Tests A, B, and C, Customer will begin paying maintenance.

E. The following Performance Period shall begin within five (5) business days after satisfactory completion of Tests A, B, and C, above, and shall end when the System has met the specified "Standard of Performance" for a period of thirty (30) consecutive calendar days by operating in conformance with Vendor technical specifications at an effectiveness level of ninety-five percent (95%) or more.

F. In the event the System does not meet the Standard of Performance during the initial thirty (30) consecutive calendar days, the Standard of Performance Test shall continue on a day-to-day basis until the Standard of Performance is met for a total of thirty (30) consecutive calendar days.

G. If the System fails to meet the Standard of Performance (or if Tests A, B, and C, above, have not all been satisfactorily completed) within ninety (90) calendar days from the Installation Date, the Customer may at its option request a replacement or terminate the order upon written notice to Vendor.

H. For purposes of the Standard of Performance Test, the "Effectiveness Level" for the System shall be computed by dividing the operational use time by the sum of that time plus system failure downtime during (specified period(s) system is expected to be operational).

(Note: In the actual agreement, the published, complete General Services Administration (GSA) Acceptance Test criteria were used as the "Standard of Performance" and were inserted at this point. See Example Four, below.)

Example Three

The following provision was used in a general procurement agreement drafted for a major multinational corporation. As such, the provision was designed to apply to a wide range of transactions covered by the master document (see Chapter 11).

13. *Acceptance Testing of Hardware Products.*

(A) *Acceptance Testing.* Upon completion of installation, Acceptance Testing of all hardware shall be performed by the Supplier in the following three (3) phases. The Acceptance Testing requirements of this Paragraph 13(A) also apply to substitute, replacement, and conversion hardware Products that are acquired by Customer after any related System or Product has passed earlier Acceptance Testing.

(1) *Phase One.* Supplier shall initially perform its standard test procedures for Customer's personnel and shall certify to Customer in writing that all Components and each applicable System (including without limitation all applicable Control Software and Special Software) are operating in accordance with the Supplier's published specifications and, if applicable, the additional specifications set forth in the applicable Order. In the event the Supplier is unable to, or does not, so certify to Customer within thirty (30) calendar days from the Installation Date, the System and any applicable Component will be deemed not to have successfully completed this phase of the Acceptance Testing.

(2) *Phase Two.* With the advice and assistance of Supplier's representatives, Customer will operate the System (including without limitation all applicable Control Software and Special Software) for five (5) business days, using all software furnished by the Supplier or otherwise specified in the applicable Order, to perform: (i) Customer's routine business transactions; (ii) transactions performed during any Supplier benchmark or other demonstration included, referenced, or incorporated into the applicable Order; and (iii) such other transactions as may be specified in the applicable Order. In the event the System fails to perform all such transactions, or fails to run such software, in accordance with applicable published or represented specifications, and within two percent (2%) of applicable benchmark or other demonstration results, for a period of five (5) consecutive business

days, Customer shall operate the System for additional consecutive business days until the System so performs such transactions and runs such software for a period of five (5) consecutive business days. In the event such failure continues in whole or in part for a period of more than thirty (30) calendar days from the Installation Date, the System and any applicable Component will be deemed not to have successfully completed this phase of the Acceptance Testing.

(3) *Phase Three.* With the advice and assistance of Supplier's representatives, Customer will operate the System (including without limitation all applicable Control Software and Special Software), using all software furnished by Supplier or otherwise specified in the applicable Order, to determine whether the System and each applicable Product meet the reliability Standard of Performance specified in this Subparagraph (A) (3).

(a) *Performance Period.*

(i) The Performance Period for Phase Three shall begin on the date the System successfully completes Phase Two of the Acceptance Testing and shall end when the System has met the Standard of Performance for a period of thirty (30) consecutive days by operating in conformity with Supplier's technical specifications, as quoted in any proposal, presentation, or representation to Customer, and as otherwise generally published by Supplier, at an Effectiveness Level of ninety-nine percent (99%) or more.

(ii) In the event the System fails to meet the Standard of Performance during the initial thirty (30) consecutive days, the Performance Period shall continue on a day-by-day basis until the Standard of Performance is met for a total of thirty (30) consecutive days.

(iii) In the event the System or any Component thereof fails to meet an Effectiveness Level of ninety-nine percent (99%) or more after ninety (90) days from the Installation Date, the System and any applicable Component will be deemed not to have successfully completed this phase of the Acceptance Testing.

(b) *Effectiveness Level.*

(i) The Effectiveness Level for the System or Component shall be computed by dividing the Operational Use Time of the System or Component by the sum of that time plus System or Component Failure Downtime.

(ii) Operational Use Time for Acceptance Testing of the System or Component is defined as the accumulated time during which the applicable Central Processing Unit (CPU) or Component is in actual operation. During Phase Three of Acceptance Testing, a minimum of one hundred (100) hours of Operational Use Time with productive or simulated work will be required as a basis for computation of the Effectiveness Level. In the event the actual Operational Use Time is less than one hundred (100) hours, the initial thirty (30) consecutive day period will be extended until such minimum period of use is reached. In the event the actual Operational Use Time is in excess of one hundred (100) hours, such actual time will be used for the computation of the Effectiveness Level.

(iii) System Failure Downtime is defined as the accumulated time during which the applicable System or Component is inoperable due to Product failure. Downtime for each incident during the Performance Period shall be measured from the time Supplier is notified of Product failure until the applicable Product is returned to Customer in proper operating condition, exclusive of actual travel time required by Supplier's maintenance personnel not in excess of one (1) hour per day on the day such maintenance service is requested. System Failure Downtime shall not include any down or inoperable time that is due to Customer's failure to maintain its site environmental conditions at the level specified in Supplier's site specifications and approved by Supplier during its site inspection.

(iv) Operational Use Time and System Failure Downtime shall be measured in hours and whole minutes or the decimal equivalents thereof.

(v) Customer shall maintain appropriate daily records to satisfy the requirements of this Paragraph 13, and shall notify Supplier in writing of the date of the first day of a successful Performance Period.

(B) *Maintenance During Acceptance Testing.* Supplier agrees to provide maintenance services as set forth in the Order during all Acceptance Testing. Such services shall be provided at no expense to Customer.

(C) *Failure to Complete Acceptance Testing Successfully.* In the event the System or any applicable Component is deemed not to have successfully completed any phase of the Acceptance Testing, as provided in this Paragraph 13 above, then the Customer may, in its sole discretion, elect one (1) of the following options, which election shall be effective upon written notification of the Supplier by the Customer:

(1) Customer may terminate the applicable Order and any Related Order and request the removal of the System or Components failing to meet the applicable phase of Acceptance Testing, and any Related Product, in which event neither party shall have any further liability under the Order or any Related Order.

(2) Customer may demand, and Supplier agrees to install, within such time period as may be mutually agreed in writing by Customer and Supplier prior to Customer's election hereunder, a direct replacement of the Components or System failing to meet the applicable phase of the Acceptance Testing. Such replacements, and the applicable System, shall be subject to Acceptance Testing as provided in this Paragraph 13. Supplier shall use due care in the removal and replacement of such Product.

(3) Customer may pursue any other remedy hereunder or available at law or in equity or seek to enforce any damages, including any liquidated damages that may be specifically set forth in the applicable Order or any Related Order.

(D) *Use Shall Not Constitute Acceptance.* In no event shall use of any Product by Customer, for business, profit, revenue, or any other purpose during any phase of the Acceptance Testing, constitute acceptance of any Product by Customer.

(E) *Acceptance Testing of Software Products.* Acceptance Testing of all software Products shall be performed pursuant to Paragraph 45 (D) of this Agreement.

45. SOFTWARE.

* * *

(D) *Software Acceptance Testing.* Software furnished by the Supplier shall be subject to Acceptance Testing as follows:

(1) Following delivery and installation of the Software on the applicable System at Customer's site, Supplier shall certify in writing to Customer that the software is ready for Acceptance Testing. With Supplier's assistance, Customer shall, within fifteen (15) business days after receipt of such certification, operate the software on such System to determine whether:

(a) The software meets the specifications, performs the functions, and does not exceed the facilities usage or "run time" limits and standards set forth in the Supplier's published specifications for the software, and/or the specifications included or referenced in the applicable Order, on the applicable System; and

(b) The software is capable of running on a repetitive basis on a variety of Customer's actual data, without failure; and

(c) The documentation for the Software meets the requirements of the applicable Order.

(2) If the software successfully meets these Acceptance Tests, the Customer shall so notify the Supplier in writing within five (5) business days and the Software shall be deemed to be accepted (and the "term" of the applicable software license shall be deemed to commence). In such case, the Acceptance Date shall be the date that the software satisfactorily completes all of the tests specified above.

(3) If the software fails to meet any or all of the above-specified Acceptance Tests, the Customer shall forthwith notify the Supplier of such failure in writing and Supplier shall have fifteen (15) calendar days after receipt of such notice in which to correct, modify, or improve the software to cause it to meet each such Acceptance Test. Thereafter, the Customer shall have fifteen (15) additional business days in which to re-conduct all of the Acceptance Tests specified above. This process shall be repeated as may be necessary until the software is deemed to be accepted hereunder; provided, however, that if the software is not accepted hereunder within sixty (60) days after Supplier's initial written certification to Customer that the software is ready for Acceptance Testing, Customer shall have the right and option following ten (10) days advance written notice to Supplier (during which period the Supplier shall have the right to cure by full performance of its obligations hereunder), to declare the Supplier to be in default hereunder for purposes of Paragraph 27 of this agreement.

(4) Notwithstanding the above provisions of this Paragraph 45(D), Customer shall have the right to cause any Control Software furnished as part of an Order or Related Order for a hardware System acquired by Customer hereunder to undergo Acceptance Testing as part of the Acceptance Testing of such hardware System. In any such event, the Control Software shall be deemed a part of such System and shall undergo Acceptance Testing for the System pursuant to Paragraph 13 of this Agreement; provided, however, that such Control Software shall also be subject to the Acceptance Testing standards specified in this Paragraph 45(D). In such event, the Acceptance Tests specified in this Paragraph 45(D) shall be performed during the same period in which Acceptance Tests specified in Paragraph 13 are performed.

* * *

Example Four

The following provision was included in the General Services Administration's (GSA) Solicitation Document for ADP Systems. It represents the "standard" GSA approach to acceptance testing— an approach that is frequently adopted by private sector users with good negotiating success. Various amendments are made in GSA Solicitation Documents from time to time and the provision below (taken from the Solicitation Document dated November 14, 1978) may not reflect the most current revisions.

E.6. INSPECTION AND ACCEPTANCE

E.6.1. *Standard of Performance and Acceptance of Equipment*

E.6.1.1. General

This paragraph establishes a standard of performance which must be met before any equipment listed in the hardware unit Price Schedule—Table I-1 is accepted by the Government. This also includes replacement, substitute machines, and machines which are added or field modified (modification of a machine from one model to another) after a successful performance period.

E.6.1.2. Performance Period

The performance period shall begin on the installation date and shall end when the equipment has met the standard of performance for a period of thirty (30) consecutive days by operating in conformance with the Contractor's technical specifications and functional descriptions, or as quoted in the Contractor's proposal, which must satisfy the requirements of Section F, at an effectiveness level of ____ % or more.

E.6.1.3. Continuance of Performance Period

In the event the equipment does not meet the standard of performance during the initial 30 consecutive days, the performance period shall continue on a day-to-day basis until the standard of performance is met for a total of 30 consecutive days.

E.6.1.4. Failure to Meet Standard of Performance

If the equipment fails to meet the standard of performance after 90 calendar days from the installation date or start of the performance period, whichever is later, the Government may at its option request a replacement, or terminate the contractual document and request the immediate removal of the equipment.

E.6.1.5. Effectiveness Level Computations

The effectiveness level for a system is computed by dividing the operational use time by the sum of the operational use time plus system failure downtime.

E.6.1.6. Changes in Equipment

The effectiveness level for machines added, field-modified, or substituted or for a replacement machine is a percentage figure determined by dividing the operational use time of the machine by the sum of that time plus downtime resulting from equipment failure of the machine being tested.

E.6.1.7. Operational Use Time for System

Operational use time for performance testing for a system is the accumulated time during which the Central Processing Unit is in actual operation, including any intervals of time between the start and stop of the processing of the programs.

E.6.1.8. Operational Use Time for Equipment

Operational use time for performance testing for a machine added, field-modified, substituted or for a replacement machine, is defined as the accumulated time during which the machine is in actual use.

E.6.1.9. System Failure Downtime

System failure downtime is that period of time during which the scheduled productive workload, or simulated workload, being utilized for acceptance testing cannot be continued on the system due to machine(s) failure. If simulated workload is being used for acceptance testing, it must be consistent with the data processing requirements set forth elsewhere in this contract.

E.6.1.10. Start of Downtime

Downtime for each incident shall start from the time the Government contacts the Contractor's designated representative at the prearranged contact point until the system(s) or machine(s) is returned to the Government in proper operating condition, exclusive of actual travel time required by the Contractor's maintenance personnel but not in excess of one hour on each day such services were requested; provided that, at the request of the Contractor, the Government shall make available not only the failed equipment, but also those machines which must be utilized by the Contractor in accomplishing such repairs. The Contractor shall provide an answering service or other continuous telephone coverage to permit the Government to make such contact.

E.6.1.11. Equipment Use During System Downtime

During a period of system failure downtime, the Government may use operable equipment when such action does not interfere with maintenance of the inoperable equipment. The entire system will be considered down during such periods of use. Whenever the operable equipment is not released to the Contractor upon request, then all such usage period shall be considered system operational use time in computing the effectiveness level.

E.6.1.12. Machine Failure Downtime

Machine failure downtime for a machine added, field-modified, substituted or for a replacement machine after the system has completed a successful performance period is that period of time when such machine is inoperable due to its failure.

E.6.1.13. Minimum of Use Time

During the performance period for a system/machine a minimum of 100 hours of operational use time with scheduled productive or simulated work will be required as a basis for computation of the effectiveness level. However, in computing the effectiveness level, the actual number of operational use hours shall be used when in excess of the minimum of 100 hours. Machines added, field-modified and substitute machines are subject to the 100 hour minimum use time requirement. However, the Government shall accept such machine(s) without the addition of simulated work solely to achieve the minimum of 100 hours use time, provided the average effectiveness for the 30 day acceptance period is equal to or better than the level specified in E.6.1.2.

E.6.1.14. Date of Acceptance

Equipment shall not be accepted and no charges shall be paid until the standard of performance is met. The date of acceptance shall be the first day of the successful performance period.

E.6.1.15. Daily Records

The Government shall maintain appropriate daily records to satisfy the requirements of paragraph E.6.1. and shall notify the Contractor in writing of the date of the first day of the successful performance period.

E.6.1.16 Measurement of Operational Use Time

Operational use time and downtime shall be measured in hours and whole minutes.

E.6.1.17. Delay of Start of Performance Period

Should it be necessary, the Government may delay the start of the performance period, but such delay shall not exceed 30 consecutive days; therefore, the performance period must start not later than the 31st day after the installation date. Should the Government delay the start of the performance period, rental charges shall accrue for that period of time between the installation date and the start of the performance period and shall be paid only upon completion of the successful performance period.

E.6.1.18. Remote Devices

For remote devices the standard of performance shall be determined in accordance with paragraph E.6.1.6.13. A remote device is defined as any Contractor supplied devices which are connected to the Central Processing Unit by way of data transmission lines rather than contractor supplied direct cable connection. The effectiveness level for equipment supplied by the contractor shall be computed in accordance with paragraph E.6.1.6. and shall exclude downtime attributable to related equipment, cables, transmission lines, wires, etc., not supplied by the contractor.

E.6.2. *Guaranteed Rerun of the Benchmark Test.*

(Applicable if a benchmark test was the method of performance validation.)

E.6.2.1. Agreement

If requested by the Government, the Contractor agrees to rerun the benchmark test set forth in the solicitation on the initial ADP system installed under this contract. This rerun shall be accomplished by Contractor personnel and shall be completed prior to the start of the acceptance test period. If emulation is used in the preaward benchmark, the same emulation may be used in the benchmark rerun at the option of the Contractor.

E.6.2.2. Required Performance

If the initial installation includes all of the hardware and software proposed by the Contractor, the time to perform the benchmark reruns shall not exceed the minimum benchmark time specified for the preaward benchmark test. In those instances where the initial hardware/software configuration does not include all such items called for in the contract life, the time to perform the benchmark reruns shall not exceed the time(s) specified for the preaward benchmark test by more than _____ %.

E.6.2.3. Files, Data and Procedures

The benchmark program files, input data and processing procedures must be the same as used in the original timed benchmark test. The Contractor agrees to retain all necessary files, programs and information used in the original benchmark test for the guaranteed rerun benchmark test.

E.6.2.4. Additional Hardware and Software

If the required performance is not attained on rerun of the benchmark tests, through no fault of the Government, the Contractor shall provide whatever hardware and/or software that is necessary to meet the specified benchmark test time(s). Such additional hardware and/or software shall be provided at no cost to the Government for the duration of the system life specified in the solicitation.

Example Five

The following provisions were included in a "required" user contract that was attached to a bid solicitation document issued by the State of Florida Department of Highway Safety and Motor Vehicles. Excerpts from the RFP in which this contract was incorporated appear in Appendix C.

18. *Data Processing System Acceptance Test*

Conversion of IBM 370-115 Programs must be completed before the start of the Acceptance Test.

a. *Acceptance Testing.* Upon completion of Contractor's installation, Acceptance Testing of the System shall be performed by the Contractor in the following three (3) phases. If any single unit of Equipment is malfunctioning, a System Failure shall be declared.

(1) *Phase One.* Contractor shall initially perform its standard test procedures for the State's personnel and shall certify to the State in writing that the System is operating in accordance with the Contractor's published specifications. In the event the Contractor is unable to, or does not, so certify to the State within thirty (30) calendar days from the Installation Date, the System will be deemed not to have successfully completed this phase of the Acceptance Testing.

(2) *Phase Two.* With the advice and assistance of Contractor's representatives, the State will operate the System for five (5) business days, to perform: (i) the State's routine business transactions to include all programs and functions (including, but not limited to, OCR, Diskette Input/Output and Data Collection) running on the IBM 370-115 located at [data center location omitted]. Programs are specified in Rider G, Schedule B; and (ii) rerunning of the State's pre-award benchmark. In the event the System fails to perform all such transactions, or fails to run the pre-award benchmark in accordance with applicable published or represented specifications, and within two percent (2%) of applicable pre-award benchmark results, for a period of five (5) consecutive business days, the State shall operate the System for additional consecutive business days until the System so performs such transactions and runs the benchmark for a period of five (5) consecutive business days. In the event such failure continues in whole or in part for a period of more than thirty (30) calendar days from the Installation Date, the System will be deemed not to have successfully completed this phase of the Acceptance Testing.

(3) *Phase Three.* With the advice and assistance of the Contractor's representatives, the State will operate the System to determine the reliability Standard of Performance specified in this paragraph.

(a) *Performance Period.*

(i) The Performance Period for Phase Three shall begin on the date the System successfully completes Phase Two of the Acceptance Testing and shall end when the System has met the Standard of Performance for a period of thirty (30) consecutive days by operating in conformity with Contractor's technical specifications, as quoted in the Contractor's proposal, presentation, or representation to the State, and as otherwise generally published by the Contractor, at a System Availability Level of ninety-five percent (95%) or more.

(ii) In the event the System fails to meet the Standard of Performance during the initial thirty (30) consecutive days, the Performance Period shall continue on a day-to-day basis until the Standard of Performance is met for a total of thirty (30) consecutive days.

(iii) In the event the System fails to meet a System Availability Level of ninety-five percent (95%) or more after ninety (90) days from the Installation Date, the System will be deemed not to have successfully completed this phase of the Acceptance Testing.

(b) *System Availability Level.*

(i) Operational Use Time for Acceptance Testing of the System is defined as the accumulated time during which the System is in a non-malfunction state and actually operating. During Phase Three of Acceptance Testing, a minimum of one hundred seventy six (176) hours of Operational Use Time with productive work will be required as a basis for computation of the System Availability Level. In the event the actual Operational Use Time is less than one hundred seventy six (176) hours, the initial thirty (30) consecutive day period will be extended until such minimum period of use is reached. In the event the actual Operational Use Time is in excess of one hundred seventy six (176) hours, such actual time will be used for the computation.

(ii) System Failure Downtime for each incident during the Performance Period shall be measured from the time Contractor is notified of a System Failure until the System is returned to the State in proper operating condition. System Failure Downtime shall not include any down or inoperable time that is due to State's failure to maintain its Site environmental conditions at the level specified in Contractor's Site specifications and approved by Contractor during its Site inspection.

(iii) The State shall maintain appropriate daily records to satisfy the requirements of this Section 18 and shall notify Contractor in writing upon completion of a successful Performance Period.

b. *Maintenance During Acceptance Testing.* Contractor agrees to provide maintenance services as set forth herein during all Acceptance Testing. Such services shall be provided at no expense to the State.

c. *Failure to Complete Acceptance Testing Successfully.* In the event the System is deemed not to have successfully completed any phase of the Acceptance Testing, as provided in this Section 18, above, within ninety (90) days after the Installation Date, then the State may, in its sole discretion, elect one (1) of the following options, which election shall be effective upon written notification of the Contractor by the State:

(1) State may terminate this Agreement.

(2) State may demand Contractor to install, within such time period as may be mutually agreed in writing by State and Contractor, a direct substitute of the Equipment to meet the applicable phase of the Acceptance Testing. Contractor shall use due care in the removal and substitution of such Equipment. Such substitutions shall be subject to Acceptance Testing as provided in this Section 18 and, in the event such substitute Equipment fails to successfully complete Acceptance Testing by the agreed-upon date, the provisions of this paragraph 18.c shall again be applicable.

(3) State may permit Contractor to continue to attempt to cause the System to successfully complete the Acceptance Testing required by this paragraph 18; provided, however, that the State may revoke its election of this alternative at any time upon not less than five (5) days' prior written notice to the Contractor, in which event the State may, in its sole discretion, elect any one (1) of the other options specified in this paragraph 18.c, which further election shall be effective upon written notification of the Contractor by the State.

(4) The State may pursue any other remedy hereunder or available at law or in equity or seek to enforce any damages, in addition to those provided in Section 17 entitled "Liquidated Damages" herein.

19. *Exchange and Expansion Equipment Acceptance Testing*

a. The Contractor shall certify in writing to the State when the Equipment is installed and ready for use. The performance period (a period of thirty (30) consecutive calendar days) shall commence on the first State work day following Installation Date certification, at which time operational control becomes the responsibility of the State. It is not required that one thirty (30) day period expire in order for another performance period to begin.

b. If the Equipment operated at an Equipment Availability Level of ninety-five percent (95%) or more for a period of thirty (30) consecutive days from the commencement date of performance period, it shall be deemed to have met the State's

Standard of Performance and shall constitute a successful performance period. In addition, Equipment added to this Agreement by amendment to this Agreement shall operate in conformance with the Contractor's published specifications applicable to such Equipment at the time of such amendment.

c. During the successful performance period, a minimum of 176 hours of operational use time will be required as a basis for computation of Equipment Availability Level. However, in computing the Equipment Availability Level, the actual number of operational use hours shall be used when in excess of the minimum stated above. When it is obvious that the actual hours that may be accumulated during the performance period will be less than 176 hours, the hours may be supplemented using Contractor's diagnostic routines or simulated production operations, so as to provide a total of 176 hours.

d. Equipment shall not be accepted by the State and no payment will be paid by the State until the Standard of Performance is met.

e. When an Acceptance Test involves on-line Machines which are remote to the basic installation, the required Equipment Availability Level shall apply separately to each remote Machine.

f. Immediately upon successful completion of the performance period, the State shall notify the Contractor in writing of acceptance of the Equipment and authorize payment as specified in Rider D and Rider E.

g. If successful completion of the performance period is not attained within ninety (90) days of the installation date, the State shall have the option of (i) terminating the Equipment, or (ii) continuing the performance tests. The State's option to terminate the Equipment shall remain in effect until such time as a successful completion of the performance period is attained.

20. *Post-Acceptance Performance*

a. Following acceptance of the System, exchanged or expansion Equipment by the State, the Standard of Performance shall be measured on a calendar month basis.

b. In the event that any unit of Equipment's Equipment Availability Level decreases to less than 95% in any consecutive three (3) month period, or 94% in any consecutive two (2) month period, or 93% in any one (1) month period due to any cause attributable to the Contractor, the Contractor will at its option:

(1) refurbish, overhaul or rebuild the Equipment and provide a temporary substitute for such Equipment at no charge, or

(2) mechanically replace the Equipment.

c. In the event that the System Availability Level decreases to less than 95% in any consecutive three (3) month period, or 94% in any consecutive two (2) month period, or 93% in any one (1) month period due to any cause attributable to the Contractor, Contractor shall be liable to State for the provisions of Section 17 entitled "Liquidated Damages."

AVAILABILITY-OF-FINANCING WARRANTY BY THIRD-PARTY LESSOR

__1. Availability. The Lessor agrees and warrants that the Lessor has obtained, or will obtain by not later than _____(1)_____ _____, firm written commitment(s) for the necessary financing, including but not necessarily limited to the equity funds, subordinated debt, and senior debt financing, to allow the Lessor to purchase or otherwise validly acquire and lease to Lessee hereunder all of the items of Equipment.

__2. Rates. The Lessor and Lessee specifically understand and agree that the Monthly Rental Charges specified in Schedule ____ of this Agreement are firm prices as indicated in such Schedule and shall not be increased or decreased for any reason, including but not necessarily limited to a change in the interest rate, closing costs, or other amount(s) paid or to be paid by the Lessor, the Equipment owner(s), or any other party or person for the equity funds, subordinated debt, or senior debt financing used by Lessor to finance the acquisition of any item of Equipment for lease to Lessee hereunder.

__3. Cancellation. In the event the Lessor is unable, for any reason whatsoever, including but not necessarily limited to a change in prevailing interest rates or a change in the financial position of the Lessor, or any other person or party, excepting however a materially adverse change in the financial position of the Lessee or a violation by the Lessee of any of its warranties under Section (2) hereof (both of which shall be governed by Section

(2) hereof rather than this Section ____), to obtain:

(a) by not later than _____(1)_____ _____ _____, the firm written commitment for the necessary financing, including but not necessarily limited to the equity funds, subordinated debt, and senior debt financing, to allow the Lessor to purchase or otherwise validly acquire and lease to Lessee hereunder all of the items of Equipment; or

(b) by such date(s) as may be required to allow the Lessor to ship, deliver, and install the Equipment pursuant to Schedule 1 hereto, and to otherwise meet its obligations to Lessee hereunder (including Section ____, relating to Quiet Enjoyment), the actual funds for the necessary financing, including but not necessarily limited to the equity funds, subordinated debt, and senior debt financing, to allow the Lessor to purchase or otherwise validly acquire and lease to Lessee hereunder all of the items of Equipment; Then, in either such event, the Lessee shall have the right, provided that the Lessee is not otherwise in default hereunder (including Section (3), relating to the furnishing of certain financial information by Lessee), to cancel and terminate this Agreement at any time after such date by providing not less than ten (10) calendar days prior written notice to Lessor (during which period the Lessor shall have the right to cure by obtaining the necessary firm commitment or financing, as may be applicable, and otherwise performing its then-existing obligations pursuant to this Agreement). In the event the Lessee so elects to cancel and terminate this Agreement, upon the effective date of such cancellation this Agreement shall be deemed terminated and rescinded and: (a) the Lessor shall within five (5) calendar days thereafter return to the Lessee all amounts previously paid by Lessee to Lessor hereunder; and (b) neither party hereto shall have any liability to any other party pursuant to this Agreement, except such liability as may have accrued by virtue of any other default or damage occuring prior to the effective date of such termination pursuant to this Section _____.

Notes:

(1) Insert applicable date.

(2) The referenced Section should contain the usual warranties by Lessee, including the warranty concerning the accuracy of the Lessee's financial statements previously furnished to Lessor.

Although the exception provided allows some room for hedging by the Lessor in a close situation, removal of this exception would probably be unacceptable to any thinking Lessor. An alternative provision should provide for what happens if financing cannot be obtained due to a materially adverse change in the financial condition of the Lessee. Some standard form leases cover this by allowing either party to terminate the transaction, with the Lessee agreeing to cover certain specific costs previously incurred by the Lessor, up to a stated maximum.

(3) The referenced Section should contain the Lessee's agreement to provide additional financial data to the Lessor on a timely basis. Copies of annual and quarterly reports are probably not adequate during the interim "financing" period of the lease term. Copies of SEC Forms 8-K, 10-Q, and 10-K are probably reasonable throughout the term; in addition, copies of all new press releases, or all new financial press releases, may be reasonable during the interim "financing" period.

LIQUIDATED DAMAGES PROVISION

The following liquidated damages provision was included in the General Services Administration's (GSA) Solicitation Document for ADP Systems dated November 14, 1978. Various amendments are made in GSA Solicitation Documents from time to time and the provision below may not reflect the most current revisions.

E.7. LIQUIDATED DAMAGES (HARDWARE/SOFTWARE)

E.7.1. *Equipment (Hardware) and Software*

For non-delivery of equipment or software the Contractor shall pay to the Government, as fixed and agreed liquidated damages for each calendar day's delay beginning with the Installation Date(s) specified in Section G, but not for more than 180 days as follows:

E.7.1.1. Total System

If the Contractor does not install all the equipment and deliver the operating software, in accordance with his functional specifications, identified in Section I, Tables I-1 and I-2, including the special features and accessories included on the same order with the equipment and software, and as a result, no portion of the total system is ready for use on the Installation Date, then the liquidated damages shall be ____% of the Total Monthly Charge or ____% of the purchase price for the ordered equipment and software, depending on whether ordered for rental or purchase.

E.7.1.2. Machines

When an installation date is specified on an order for machines to be added subsequent to the initial system installation date, and the Contractor fails to install, ready for use, any such machine (including special features, any required operating software, and accessories) on or before the required installation date, liquidated damages shall be assessed. Such liquidated damages shall be computed on the basis of each calendar day of delay at a rate of ____% of the monthly charge for each machine(s) that cannot be used as a direct result of the delay or ____% of the purchase price of the machine, depending on whether the machine is ordered for rental or purchase. Liquidated damages shall cease upon the day the machine is installed and determined ready for use.

E.7.1.3. Partial Installation

If some, but not all, of the equipment and software on order is installed/delivered, ready for use, by the Installation Date, and the Government uses any such installed equipment and/or delivered software, liquidated damages shall not accrue against these items for any calendar day on which they are used. In this event, for each day's delay, the Contractor shall pay, depending on whether ordered for rental or purchase, ____% of the Total Monthly Charge or ____% of the purchase price, for each item of equipment and software not installed/delivered, as well as for each installed/delivered item which as a result cannot be used by the Government.

E.7.2. *Equipment (Hardware)*

E.7.2.1. Substitute Equipment

If the Contractor provides suitable substitute equipment, acceptable to the Government, on or before the Installation Date, no liquidated damages shall apply to ordered equipment for which substitute equipment was accepted.

E.7.2.2. Replacement Equipment

If the Contractor fails to install all the equipment identified in Section I, including the special features and accessories included on the same order with the equipment, then the Government may obtain replacement equipment. In this event, the Contractor shall be liable for liquidated damages from the Installation Date specified in Section G, until replacement Equipment is installed, ready for use, or for 180 days from the Installation Date, whichever occurs first.

E.7.3. *Software*

E.7.3.1. Operating Software

If the Contractor fails to deliver, on or before the specified delivery date, all of the ordered operating software, as set forth in Section I, Table I-2, or if the delivered operating software fails to conform to the functional descriptions set forth in Section Q, then, the provisions of E.7.1. shall apply with respect to liquidated damages.

E.7.3.2. Other Software

If the Contractor fails to demonstrate and provide written certification that the ordered software, as specified in Section I, Table I-2 with the exception of any software identified as Operating Software, has been furnished on or before the delivery date indicated in this contract and in accordance with the functional description provided by the Contractor in Section Q, then liquidated damages in the amount of 1/30th of the monthly license fee for each calendar day for each such item shall be assessed. However, such liquidated damages shall not be assessed for more than 180 days.

E.7.3.3. Replacement Software

In the event that the Government terminates the right of the Contractor to install the equipment in accordance with paragraph E.7.2.2., the Contractor shall be liable for liquidated damages for the period of time between the specified delivery date and the date the software for the replacement equipment is delivered, ready for use, or for 180 days from the delivery date, whichever occurs first.

E.7.3.4. Substitute

If the Contractor provides suitable substitute software, acceptable to the Government, on or before the specified delivery date, no liquidated damages shall apply to ordered software for which substitute software was accepted.

E.7.4. *Exception*

Except with respect to defaults of subcontractors, the Contractor shall not be liable for liquidated damages when delays arise out of causes beyond the control and without the fault or negligence of the Contractor. Such causes may include, but are not restricted to, Acts of God or of the public enemy, acts of the Government in either its sovereign or contractual capacity, fires, floods, epidemics, quarantine restrictions, strikes, freight embargoes, and unusually severe weather; but in every case the delay must be beyond the control and without the fault or negligence of the Contractor. If the delays are caused by the default of a subcontractor, and such default arises out of causes beyond the control of both the Contractor and the subcontractor, and without the fault or negligence of either of them, the Contractor shall not be liable for liquidated damages for delays, unless the supplies or services to be furnished by the subcontractor were obtainable from other sources in sufficient time to permit the Contractor to meet the required performance schedule.

GENERAL PROVISIONS

The following general provisions were included in a master procurement agreement prepared for a major United States corporation. Depending upon drafting preference, the "General Liability" and "Force Majeure" provisions contained in this section of the master document could have been set forth in separate sections of the agreement rather than being included with other so-called "general" provisions.

GENERAL PROVISIONS.

(A) **Compliance with Laws.**

(1) Supplier agrees that it will comply with the provisions of the Fair Labor Standards Act of 1938, as amended, and all other applicable federal, state, county and local laws, ordinances, regulations, and codes in the performance of this Agreement, including the procurement of permits and certificates where needed. Supplier further agrees to indemnify and hold Customer harmless against any loss or damage that may be sustained by reason of Supplier's failure to comply with the aforementioned federal, state, county, and local laws, ordinances, regulations, and codes.

(2) Unless exempt under the rules and regulations of the Secretary of Labor or other proper authority, this agreement is subject to all applicable laws and executive orders relating to equal opportunity and nondiscrimination in employment. Sup-

plier shall not discriminate in its employment practices against any person by reason of race, religion, color, sex or national origin. Supplier agrees to comply with the provisions of all such laws and orders, as well as laws and orders relating to the employment of the handicapped, the employment of veterans and the use of minority business enterprises, to the extent any such laws and orders are applicable in the performance of work or furnishing of services, materials or supplies hereunder.

(B) **General Liability Provision.**

(1) Supplier shall be deemed to be an independent contractor hereunder and shall not be considered or permitted to be an agent, servant, joint venturer, or partner of Customer. Supplier agrees to take such steps as may be necessary to ensure that each subcontractor of Supplier will be deemed to be an independent contractor and will not be considered or permitted to be an agent, servant, joint venturer, or partner of Customer. All persons furnished, used, retained, or hired by or on behalf of Supplier or any of its subcontractors shall be considered to be solely the employees or agents of Supplier or such subcontractor, and Supplier shall be responsible for payment of any and all unemployment, social security, and other payroll taxes for such persons, including any related assessments or contributions required by law.

(2) Supplier shall maintain, throughout the performance of its obligations under this Agreement, a policy or policies of workmen's compensation insurance with such limits as may be required by law, and a policy or policies of general liability insurance (including automobile liability and broad form contractual coverage) insuring against liability for injury to, and death of, persons, and damage to, and destruction of, property arising out of or based upon any act or omission of Supplier or any of its subcontractors or their respective officers, directors, employees or agents. Such general liability insurance shall have limits of not less than ONE MILLION DOLLARS ($1,000,000) combined single limit per occurrence. On or before beginning performance hereunder, Supplier shall supply Customer with a written certificate from its insurers or their agents, addressed to Customer, indicating the existence of Supplier's insurance coverage, the amount and nature of such coverage, and the expiration date(s) of each applicable policy. Supplier shall furnish to Customer such additional information concerning insurance coverage, including copies of relevant policies, as Customer shall reasonably request in writing. Supplier shall also require that each of its subcontractors maintain the insurance required by this Subparagraph. The provisions of this Subparagraph shall not be deemed to limit the liability or responsibility of Supplier or any of its subcontractors hereunder.

(3) In addition to the other indemnities provided in this Agreement, Supplier agrees to indemnify and hold harmless Customer, its subsidiaries, their respective assigns, and their respective officers, directors, employees, agents, and servants from and against any and all causes of action, claims, demands, and expenses, including reasonable legal fees and expenses, that may be made or asserted by or on behalf of any persons furnished, supplied, or retained by Supplier or its subcontractors under the workmen's compensation laws of any jurisdiction. Supplier agrees to defend Customer, at Supplier's expense, against any such claim. Customer agrees to notify Supplier promptly of any known written claims or demands for which Supplier is responsible hereunder.

(C) **Force Majeure.**

Neither party hereto shall be deemed to be in default of any provision of this Agreement, or for any failure in performance, resulting from acts or events beyond the reasonable control of such party. For purposes of this Agreement, such acts shall include, but not be limited to, acts of God, civil or military authority, civil disturbance, war, strikes, fires, other catastrophes, or other "force majeure" events beyond the parties' reasonable control; **provided, however, that** the provisions of this Subparagraph shall not preclude Customer from canceling or terminating this Agreement (or any order for any Product included herein), as otherwise permitted hereunder, regardless of any force majeure event occuring to Supplier, except that, in such event, Customer shall not cancel or terminate this Agreement to the extent that it involves an order for Products specifically produced or fabricated for Customer's unique use unless Customer shall have given Supplier ninety (90) days prior written notice of its intent to so cancel or terminate this Agreement and, during said ninety (90) day period, Supplier shall have failed to cure such delay or failure in performance or delivery.

(D) **Applicability of Uniform Commercial Code.**

Except to the extent the provisions of this Agreement are clearly inconsistent therewith, this Agreement shall be governed by the applicable provisions of the Uniform Commercial Code. To the extent this Agreement entails delivery or performance of services, such services shall be deemed "goods" within the meaning of the Uniform Commercial Code, except when deeming such services as "goods" would result in a clearly unreasonable interpretation.

(E) **Publicity.**

Supplier agrees to submit to Customer all advertising, sales promotion, and other publicity matter relating to any Product furnished by Supplier wherein Customer's name is mentioned or language used from which the connection of Customer's name therewith may, in Customer's judgment, be inferred or implied. Supplier further agrees not to publish or use any such advertising, sales promotion or publicity matter without the prior written consent of Customer.

(F) **Site Rules and Regulations.**

Supplier shall use its best efforts to assure that its employees and agents, while on Customer's premises, shall comply with Customer's site rules and regulations.

(G) **Releases and Waivers.**

Neither party shall require waivers or releases of any personal rights from representatives of the other in connection with visits to its premises and, if any such waivers or releases are obtained, both parties agree that no such releases or waivers shall be pled by them or third persons in any action or proceeding hereunder.

(H) **Notices.**

Any and all notices permitted or required to be given hereunder shall be deemed duly given: (1) upon actual delivery, if delivery is by hand; or (2) upon receipt by the transmitting party of confirmation or answer back if delivery is by telex or telegram; or (3) upon delivery into the United States mail if delivery is by postage paid registered or certified return receipt requested mail. Each such notice shall be sent to the respective party at the address indicated below or to any other address as the respective party may designate by notice delivered pursuant to this Subparagraph:

If to Supplier:
[insert appropriate name and address]
If to Customer:
[insert appropriate name and address]

(I) **Non-Waiver.**

No term or provision of this Agreement shall be deemed waived and no breach thereof shall be deemed excused, unless such waiver or consent shall be in writing and signed by the party claimed to have waived or consented. No consent by any party to, or waiver of, a breach by the other, whether express or implied, shall constitute a consent to, waiver of, or excuse for, any different or subsequent breach.

(J) **Partial Invalidity.**

If any term or provision of this Agreement shall be found to be illegal or unenforceable, then, notwithstanding any such illegality or unenforceability, this Agreement shall remain in full force and effect and such term or provision shall be deemed to be deleted.

(K) **Successors and Assigns.**

This Agreement shall inure to the benefit of, and be binding upon, the respective successors and assigns, if any, of the parties hereto, except that nothing contained in this Subparagraph shall be construed to permit any attempted assignment which would be unauthorized or void pursuant to any other provision of this Agreement.

(L) **Whereas Clauses.**

The matters set forth in the "Whereas" clauses on page one (1) hereof are incorporated into and made a part of this Agreement.

(M) Paragraph Headings.

The Paragraph and Subparagraph headings used in this Agreement are for reference purposes only and shall not be deemed to be a part of this Agreement.

(N) Survival of Representations and Warranties.

The terms, provisions, representations, and warranties contained in this Agreement that by their sense and context are intended to survive the performance thereof by either or both parties hereunder shall so survive the completion of performance and termination of this Agreement, including without limitation the making of any and all payments due hereunder.

(O) Entire Agreement.

This Agreement, together with all subordinate and other documents incorporated by reference herein, constitutes the entire agreement between the parties with respect to the subject matter contained herein and may only be modified by an amendment executed in writing by both parties hereto. All prior agreements, representations, statements, negotiations, understandings and undertakings are superseded hereby; provided, however, that Supplier hereby agrees that, except where this Agreement specifically indicates otherwise, all written proposals, specifications, brochures, and sales materials presented by Supplier to Customer in connection with this Agreement, and all other Supplier representations, commitments, and warranties referenced elsewhere in this Agreement, shall be deemed to be, and hereby are, incorporated by reference into and made a part of this Agreement.

(P) Rights Upon Orderly Termination.

Upon termination or other expiration of this Agreement, each party shall forthwith return to the other all papers, materials and properties of the other held by such party and required to be returned by this Agreement. In addition, each party will assist the other party in effecting the orderly termination of this Agreement and the transfer of all aspects hereof, tangible and intangible, as may be necessary for the orderly, nondisrupted business continuation of each party.

(Q) Governing Law.

This Agreement shall be governed by and construed in all respects in accordance with the laws of the State of _____.

APPENDIX C
EXCERPTS FROM A USER REQUEST
FOR PROPOSAL

The following pages reproduce excerpts from an actual "Specification for Acquisition of Data Processing Equipment," or RFP, that was issued by the State of Florida Department of Highway Safety and Motor Vehicles. Rather than adopting the "legal/contractual issues" approach, discussed in Chapter 5, this RFP included alternative "user form contracts" that were attached to and incorporated into the RFP. (Due to their length, these documents are not reproduced in this appendix.) As Paragraph 2.0 of the RFP stated, these contracts "set forth the terms and conditions required by the State" unless the State agreed to accept bidder-proposed changes through the unique process outlined in Paragraphs 2.3 and 2.4 of the RFP. The RFP also stressed various approaches to quantify the financial cost or value of vendor commitments to provide "soft-dollar" concessions.

SECTION I
PURPOSE AND SCOPE OF THIS
REQUEST FOR PROPOSAL (RFP)

1.0 INTRODUCTION
The State of Florida is interested in obtaining bids for a computer system with processing capabilities that shall meet the technical requirements of Section V and successfully complete all of the benchmark requirements of Section VI with required peripherals to implement and operate an on-line communications-oriented Wisconsin Vehicle/Driver Data Base System (WVDDBS) in the State of Florida.

The equipment will be located in [location omitted] Tallahassee, Florida 32301.

The State of Florida anticipates acquisition of all equipment by the installment purchase method over a period of 60 months.

1.1 The objective of the State of Florida is shown in [figure omitted] "Conceptual Hardware Overview." Some of this equipment presently exists. Detailed equipment requirements are specified in Paragraph 5.2.1.

1.2 The conditions at the [location omitted] dictate a timely response from interested bidders, a timely benchmark test, early installation of the proposed equipment and implementation of the On-line Tax Collector Network (Florida Real-Time Vehicle Information System).

SECTION II
GENERAL INFORMATION

2.0 GENERAL CONTRACTS
Attachments A, B, C, and D are contracts which set forth the terms and conditions required by the State unless the State accepts bidder proposed changes as hereinafter provided.

2.1 Attachment A is an Installment Purchase Contract containing the terms and conditions to be used for the acquisition of equipment, programming, maintenance and bidder support of the evaluation configuration. Attachment C ia a contract containing the terms and conditions to be used for acquisition of Licensed Software.

2.2 Attachments B and D are contracts that may be used to acquire additional equipment and provide for separate maintenance service. These contracts are defined as follows:

    a. Attachment B—Lease with Option to Purchase Additional Equipment
    b. Attachment D—Maintenance Service

2.3 Bidders may submit proposed written changes to Attachments A, B, C, and D which the bidder desires the State to consider in accordance with the established schedule contained in Paragraph 3.0. Bidders are required to provide the value of each proposed contract change and a brief explanation as to why the change is requested. Value shall be defined as the cost or savings to the State, and the advantage to the State of the proposed change. Proposed contract changes that do not include specific values and brief explanations as to reason for the change will be subject to rejection. The State reserves the right to accept or reject any proposed contract changes.

2.4 All bidders will be notified in writing of all proposed contract changes that are acceptable and all proposed contract changes that are not acceptable to the State. Those proposed contract changes that are acceptable to the State may be used by any bidder. The use of proposed contract changes that bidders have not been notified by the State as being acceptable to the State, will be grounds for rejecting and disqualifying the bidder's response.

2.5 It is mandatory that Attachments A, B, C, and D be submitted with the bid and signed by the bidder. All Attachments must contain the signature of a corporate official who is authorized to act on behalf of the corporation. The State, at its option, may award Attachments A and C to different bidders. Attached contracts contain blank spaces with underline to allow the bidder to provide certain specific items. Failure to supply data in all such spaces provided may subject the bid to rejection. Any spaces left blank will be assumed to be zero. The following Attachments contain space for bidder supplied data:

Attachment A:

Paragraph Number 7.a. (2)
Paragraph Number 7.a. (3)
Paragraph Number 7.b
Paragraph Number 9.g
Paragraph Number 11.a. (2)
Riders B through G

Attachment B:

Paragraph Number 7.g
Paragraph Number 9.b
Rider C

Attachment C:

Rider B, Pages 1 and 2 if applicable.

Attachment D:

Paragraph Number 7.d Rider C

2.6 METHOD OF ACQUISITION

The State shall acquire the system configuration by the Installment Purchase method. The acquisition of additional equipment may be by the Lease with Option to Purchase Method or by exchange or expansion to the Installment Purchase Contract by amendment and will be predicated on new and presently unknown requirements which may arise during the initial contract period or subsequent thereto.

2.6.1 The *Installment/Purchase Method* means the acquisition and full use and benefit of the equipment and software for sixty (60) months in exchange for payment by the State to bidder of a sum certain in sixty (60) monthly payments; and, upon the expiration of said period of time, all rights, title and interest in the equipment shall be automatically vested in the State.

2.6.2 The *Lease with Option to Purchase Method* means the acquisition and full use and benefit of the equipment for a certain period of time in exchange for payment by the State to bidder of a sum certain in equal monthly payments. At any time during said lease period the State may elect to obtain all rights, title and interest in the equipment in exchange for a sum certain.

2.7 THIRD-PARTY LEASING BIDDERS

Bids will be accepted from third-party leasing bidders provided maintenance is performed by the original equipment manufacturer representatives located in Leon County, Florida. It is mandatory the bidder shall be considered the Prime Contractor and is responsible for all terms and conditions contained herein.

2.8 INFORMATION AND DESCRIPTIVE LITERATURE

Complete product information, including technical and descriptive literature, shall be submitted with the bid. Information submitted shall be sufficiently detailed to substantiate that products offered meet or exceed the specifications. Technical characteristics shall be obtained from the manufacturer and submitted as part of the technical portion of the bid.

2.9 *LEGAL REQUIREMENT*

Any corporation conducting business with the State shall be on file with the Department of State in accordance with the provisions of Chapter 607 Florida Statutes; and all partnerships conducting business with the State shall comply with the applicable provisions of Chapter 620, Florida Statutes. Bidders shall provide their State Registration number and expiration date on the Supplemental Bid Sheet.

2.10 *SUBSTITUTION*

Delivery of substitute commodities shall be as provided for in Attachment A (Installment Purchase Contract).

2.11 *NO BID*

Any corporation in receipt of this RFP who is not submitting a bid should fill in the lower portion of page S3 on the Supplemental Bid Sheet and return to the Procurement Office identified on the cover page of this RFP.

2.12 *PROPOSAL COST ERRORS*

Bidders are expected to thoroughly examine the specifications and all instructions. Preparation of cost extensions shall be at the bidders risk. In the event of a bidders error in cost extension, the bidders unit price will prevail.

2.13 *BID OPENING*

Bid opening will be as indicated in Paragraph 3.0 (Schedule of Events) and shall include technical proposals, contracts, and cost data.

SECTION III
BIDDER INSTRUCTIONS AND SUBMISSIONS

3.0 *SCHEDULE OF EVENTS*

August 3—Release Specifications.
August 13—Bidders' Conference (9:30 A.M.) [location omitted].
August 13—Last day for written inquiries as specified in Paragraph 3.1.
August 13—Last day for bidders' first recommended changes to Attachments A thru D, as specified in Section II.
September 3—Last day for bidders' final recommended changes to Attachments A thru D, as specified in Section II.
September 28—Proposals due and closing date and time for objections to the State's RFP in accordance with Paragraph 3.14 (1:00 P.M.)
September 28—Proposal and Cost Opening (1:30 P.M.). The proposal and cost opening shown above will be a public proposal and cost opening at [location omitted].
October 1—Begin evaluating bidder proposals.
November 2—Announce Apparent Qualified Bidders.
November 9—Closing date for objections to selection of Qualified Bidders in accordance with Paragraph 3.14.
November 12—Start Benchmark of apparent low qualified bidder(s).
November 26—Notify bidders of Evaluation Committee Recommendations.
December 3—Closing date for objections to Evaluation Committee recommendations in accordance with Paragraph 3.14.
December 18—Recommendation to Governor & Cabinet.
March 18—Site preparation complete (Facilities Readiness Date).
March 31—Delivery Date.
April 14—370-115 Conversion Complete.
April 21—Installation Date.

3.1 *BIDDER INQUIRIES*

Any inquiries from bidders concerning this bid shall be submitted in writing to the Procurement Office [location omitted].

No bidder may consider any verbal instructions as an official expression on the State's behalf. Only written communications signed by a duly authorized representative of the Procurement Office identified on Page 1 may be considered valid. All questions and answers of a substantive nature will be in writing and forwarded via registered mail, return receipt requested, to all bidders being solicited.

3.2 BIDDERS' CONFERENCE
There will be a bidders' conference in [location omitted], as scheduled in Paragraph 3.0 Schedule of Events. The purpose for the bidders' conference is to discuss the contents of the bid. Attendance is not mandatory. Questions must be in writing.

3.3 BID CLOSING DATE
All copies of bids must be received by the Procurement Office identified on Page 1 no later than the bid due date and time shown in Paragraph 3.0 Schedule of Events.

Requests for extensions of the bid closing date or time will not be granted. Bidders mailing bids should allow sufficient mail time to insure the timely receipt of their bids.

3.4 ADDENDA AND ORAL PRESENTATIONS
All addenda to this RFP will be in writing with content and number of pages described and forwarded by registered mail, return receipt requested, to all bidders known to be in receipt of this RFP. The bidder shall acknowledge receipt of all addenda.

If deemed necessary by the State, bidders shall be required to supplement their bids with oral commentary. The State will notify bidders in the event such presentation is necessary.

3.5 ECONOMY OF PRESENTATION
Each bid shall be prepared simply and economically, providing a straightforward, concise delineation of bidders capabilities to satisfy the requirements of this RFP. Fancy bindings, colored displays, and promotional material are not desired. However, technical literature and photographs of bid equipment may be included in the bid. Emphasis in each bid shall be on completeness and clarity of content. In order to expedite the evaluation of bids, it is mandatory that bidders follow the instructions contained herein and use the following format for bid submission:

Bid Format

VOLUME I—GENERAL INFORMATION
1) Executive Summary.
2) Supplemental Bid Sheets (Ref. par's 2.9 and 3.12.1).
3) Exceptions from Supplemental Bid Sheets (Ref. par. 3.12.4).
4) Performance Bond.
5) Addenda Acknowledgement Forms.

VOLUME II—TECHNICAL INFORMATION
1) Bidder commitment to Prime Contractor requirement (Ref. par's 2.7 and 5.1.6).
2) Customer list (Ref. par. 3.12.2).
3) Tables A and B.
4) Training Program (Ref. par's 3.12.5 and 5.5).
5) Delivery schedule (Ref. par. 3.12.7).
6) Installation and delivery (Ref. par. 3.12.8).
7) Environmental and site requirements, including table D (Ref. par. 3.12.9).
8) Responses to all other paragraphs in Section V not listed above.
9) Descriptive literature (Ref. par. 2.8).
10) Conversion Plan (Ref. par. 5.2.3).

VOLUME III—BENCHMARK INFORMATION
Responses to each paragraph in Section VI

VOLUME IV—CONTRACTS (Ref. Section II)
1) Signed Installment Purchase Contract.
2) Signed Lease with Option to Purchase Contract.
3) Signed Licensed Software Contract.
4) Signed Maintenance Contract.

Note: Each volume shall include a contents page plus a tab index to precede each section within a volume. Multiple volumes are acceptable provided each is properly identified. There is no intent to limit or restrict a bidder from including additional information, however, it should be placed in the back of the appropriate volume and be identified. Bid organization and format specified above will provide for ease of evaluation and continuity of each bid. Bidders responses should be preceded by quoting the paragraph reference and the specific requirements from the RFP.

3.6 COST DISCUSSIONS
Prior to the public bid and cost opening as scheduled in Paragraph 3.0 all bids will remain unopened at the Procurement Office identified on Page 1. During this period, any discussion by the bidder

with any employee or authorized representative of the State involving cost information will result in rejection of said bid.

3.7 *VERBAL INSTRUCTIONS PROCEDURE*

No negotiations, decisions, or actions shall be initiated or executed by the bidder as a result of any discussions with any State employee. Only those communications which are in writing from the State may be considered as a duly authorized expression on behalf of the State. Also, only communications from bidders which are signed and in writing will be recognized by the State as duly authorized expressions on behalf of bidders.

3.8 *MINIMUM EVALUATION CONFIGURATION*

Specified in Section V, Exhibit I.

3.9 *BENCHMARK CRITERIA*

The bidder shall successfully complete all of the required benchmark problems or be subject to rejection. Any programs created by the bidder in accordance with the State's specifications shall completely fulfill the objectives of those specifications. The State shall have access to all data resulting from the benchmark.

The bidder is instructed to note that successful performance of critical items on the benchmark is a mandatory requirement and shall be satisfactorily demonstrated to the State evaluation committee.

3.10 *BENCHMARK CRITICAL REQUIREMENTS*

Problems will be released for the Wisconsin Vehicle/Driver Data Base System. (See Section VI.) The bidders must benchmark their capability to run the Wisconsin Vehicle/Driver Data Base System, at benchmark time to the satisfaction of the State. Failure to satisfactorily demonstrate at benchmark time will subject the bidder to rejection.

3.11 *BIDDER SUBMISSION*

Paragraph 3.12 plus all sub-paragraphs prescribe mandatory submissions which must be complied with in response to this RFP. Failure to comply with any of this RFP mandatory requirements will subject the bid to immediate rejection. The mandatory submissions are not the sole requirements of this RFP. All conditions and requirements throughout this RFP are considered binding. Bidders are allowed to recommend alternatives to non-mandatory items by taking exception to specific

items. The State, however, will be the final authority in determining the responsiveness of a bid.

3.12 *TECHNICAL INFORMATION* (3 Copies)

The bidder shall address the singular technical requirement of the several sub-paragraphs in Sections V and VI. Bidders must substantiate in their bid the ability to meet all of the mandatory technical requirements of this RFP.

3.12.1 *SUPPLEMENTAL BID SHEET*

Bidders are required to return a completed Supplemental Bid Sheet with their bid. It must be signed by a representative who is authorized to contractually bind the bidder.

3.12.2 *CUSTOMER LIST*

Each bidder's response shall include a list of five (5) customers within the Continental United States having equipment similar to that being bid for evaluation. The list should include organization, address, phone and contact individual.

3.12.3 *ADDENDA*

Any addendum or answers to questions supplied by the State to participating bidders shall include an Addendum Acknowledgement Form. This form shall be signed by a company representative, dated and returned with the bid.

3.12.4 *BID EXCEPTIONS*

Should a bidder wish to take exception to any item (except Sections V and VI), he must identify that item on the Supplemental Bid Sheet and explain the objection. If appropriate, an alternative should be offered. *Alternate software for the Wisconsin Vehicle/Driver Data Base System will not be allowed, except as provided for in Paragraph 4.2.1.7.* Any exception to Section V should be addressed in the technical response. All items not listed as exceptions are considered to be acceptable as presented. The State of Florida will be the final authority in resolving any differences.

3.12.5 *TRAINING*

Bidders shall identify training courses referenced in Paragraph 5.5. Bidders shall complete Rider C1 of Attachment A for proposed training courses and include costs therein.

3.12.6 *MAINTENANCE*

The prime contractor shall be the primary point of contact for all maintenance requirements. It shall be the responsibility of the bidder to insure that sub-contractors if used, are responsive to the needs of the State in responding to maintenance schedules and remedial maintenance.

3.12.7 *DELIVERY/INSTALLATION*

DELIVERY SCHEDULE: All equipment shall be delivered, installed and ready for use not earlier than [date omitted], and not later than [date omitted]. Delivery Dates beyond [date omitted] are not acceptable.

3.12.8 *INSTALLATION AND DELIVERY DATES*

a. Equipment
  (1) The Contractor shall install equipment ready for use on the installation date specified in Paragraph 3.0.
  (2) Installation shall be accomplished in such a manner as to not interrupt current key entry, and OCR operations and supporting programs.
  (3) Installation dates may be changed in accordance with the terms and conditions of Attachments A & C.
  (4) The State agrees to have the site prepared in accordance with the Contractor's written minimum site and environmental requirements and in accordance with the provisions of Attachment A and the Facility Readiness Date specified in Paragraph 3.0.
b. Software
  The Contractor shall supply the System Control Program in accordance with the delivery schedule in Paragraph 3.0. Other software products contained in Section V will be delivered in accordance with Paragraph 3.0 or contracted for separately to include delivery schedule. (See Paragraph 5.3.) Bidders will provide all appropriate software costs on Attachment C, Licensed Software.
c. Manuals
  Three complete sets of instruction manuals concerning operation and use will be supplied with the bid.

3.12.9 *SITE ENVIRONMENTAL REQUIREMENTS*

The bidder shall provide the site environmental requirements for the Equipment bid in response to Section V. The power and cooling specifications for equipment bid shall be submitted on Table D.

3.12.10 *COST INFORMATION*

Cost data shall be submitted on the following:

a. All Contract Riders from the Installment Purchase Contract (Attachment A).

b. All Contract Riders from the Licensed Software Contract (Attachment C).
c. Table A—One-Time Charges.
d. Table B—Optional Equipment and Software.

3.12.11 Table C—Cost Evaluation Matrix will be prepared by the State and will use the bidder submitted cost data plus the additional cost data developed by the State for power, cooling, one-time charges, construction, etc., based on the bidders proposal.

3.12.12 Tables A and B shall conform to those supplied within the RFP. Contract Riders shall conform to those supplied within the contracts.

In addition to the Equipment and software requirements contained in Section V, bidders are requested to bid any optional equipment and software that the bidder considers to be applicable or necessary to the State's overall objective. Bidders will use Table B for optional equipment and software.

3.12.13 *PERFORMANCE BOND*

All bidders shall, at no cost to the State furnish a Performance Bond in the amount of $500,000. Such Bond shall be issued from a reliable surety corporation, licensed to conduct business in the State of Florida. Performance Bond will be returned to the successful bidder upon satisfactory completion of the Acceptance Test as specified in Attachment A (Installment Purchase Contract). If the successful bidder does not satisfactorily complete the Acceptance Tests specified in Attachment A, the bidder shall forfeit the performance bond to the State. Performance Bonds furnished by bidders who are not awarded the contract will be returned.

3.13 *MULTIPLE BIDS*

A bidder may submit more than one bid. At least one of the bids shall be complete and comply with all requirements of this RFP. However, additional bids may be in an abbreviated form, using the same format, but providing only that information which differs in any way from that contained in the initial bid. Each bid must be separately bound and contracts must be separately identified.

3.14 *INFORMAL DEPARTMENTAL HEARINGS*

Should there be any bidder objections to be tendered regarding:

a. The State's Request for Proposal specifications, or

b. Evaluation committee's determination of apparent qualified bidders, or

c. Evaluation committee's recommendations following the Pre-Award Benchmark,

the Evaluation Committee will convene an informal hearing to consider said objections.

This action will be initiated in accordance with Part I, Chapter 287 Florida Statutes; Chapter 23, Florida Statutes; Rules 13A-1, 13E-3 and 13-4 of the Department of General Services and provisions of this RFP.

The time for affected persons to present evidence and argument on all issues under consideration is specified by the Schedule in Section 3.0 of this RFP.

Objections must be submitted in writing to:

[Name and location omitted]

SECTION IV
EVALUATION

4.0 *BID EVALUATION*

All bids will be evaluated by an evaluation committee composed of members from the Department of General Services (EDP Division), State University System, and the Department of Highway Safety and Motor Vehicles. Bids which do not meet the mandatory requirements of this RFP shall be rejected. Bids meeting the mandatory requirements shall be further evaluated on total overall costs for 60 months. The term "overall costs," as used in this sub-paragraph shall be interpreted to include, but not be limited to, such cost elements as installment purchase, maintenance, installation, transportation, training, site preparation and any other one-time costs for 60 months.

4.1 *ESSENTIAL ITEMS*

4.1.1 Equipment bid shall be equal to or greater than that shown in Section V, Exhibit I.

4.1.2 The Evaluation Committee will evaluate the technical content of a bid to determine the technical acceptability of the bid based on hardware capability, reliability, modularity, expandability and software compatibility with existing application system and programs. The evaluation committee will also review the bidders final submitted contract to insure that it is responsive to the State's need and complies with the Terms and Conditions set forth in the contracts attached hereto and those specified within the RFP.

4.2 *TOTAL COST FACTORS*

4.2.1 For purposes of evaluation, the installment purchase method of acquisition shall be used for selecting and awarding a contract to a single supplier with the exception of Attachment C (Licensed Software) which may be awarded to a separate contractor. Total overall 60 months costs shall be considered. Total overall cost will include both one-time and life cycle costs to the State.

The following cost factors will be considered in determining costs to the State for installing and operating the proposed new computer system:

4.2.1.1 *HARDWARE (BIDDER)*
Equipment Cost
Maintenance 24 hrs., 7 day
Shipping (In and Out)
Movement of Existing if required
Test time rentals and travel
Rigging and Drayage
370/115 Termination Charge (if applicable)
Maintenance charges in the evaluation will include the maximum maintenance price increases as proposed by the bidder for the 60 month evaluation period.

4.2.1.2 *SITE COSTS*
Power use by KWH and Peak Demand
Air conditioning Modifications
Power stabilization equipment
Solid state frequency convertor
Continuous power equipment (UPS)
Room modifications
Cabling
Plumbing
Office space, maintenance spare parts, etc.

4.2.1.3 *TRAINING, EDUCATION, MANUALS*
User education
Travel
Programmer Training
Operator Training
Analyst Training
Manuals:
    Language
    Guides

Control Languages
Logic Manuals
Equipment specifications
Operating system

4.2.1.4 *SOFTWARE*
Maintenance (Estimate if per hour)
Licensing fees
One time charges
Systems support cost
Conversion tools

4.2.1.5 *CONVERSION COST*
4.2.1.6 *All desirable items, features and System performance levels* as specified in Section V.

4.2.1.7 *LOST DEVELOPMENT TIME*
A conversion, simulation, or emulation of the Wisconsin Vehicle/Driver Data Base limits the State's ability to share mutual software enhancements with the State of Wisconsin and would result in additional State support requirements. Therefore, for those bidders who submit a convertor, simulator, or emulator, the following costs shall be added to each bid:

Additional Manpower Support	$130,000
Documentation	50,000
Mutual Software Enhancements	130,000
Total	$310,000

4.3 *COST EVALUATION*

4.3.1 To determine the "total overall cost" of the bid, over the stated term, three costs will be evaluated, to wit: One-time costs, "life-cycle" costs and cost of desired items as proposed by bidders or by pre-established dollar amounts as indicated in Section V.

4.3.2 One-time costs to be considered in the evaluation include equipment transportation and installation, renovations to the physical facility, acquisition and installation of additional/special power, acquisition and installation of additional/special chilled water/air-conditioning cooling units, etc.

4.3.3 Recurring "life cycle" costs of the equipment to be considered will include recurring costs of monthly installment purchase payments, equipment maintenance costs, environmental and support equipment maintenance costs, power consumption and heat loss, both of which will be translated by the supplied rates into dollar amounts. The life cycle cost evaluation will con-

sider the "power-on/cooling-on" period to be 720 hours per month. Rates to be employed are as follows:

a. Cooling
   1. to air—$.008/KBTU/HR
   2. to water—$.004/KBTU/HR
b. Power
   1. 60 Hz—$.04/KWH
   2. 400 Hz—$.04/KWH

4.3.4 Requirements costing will be used to evaluate bidder response to desired items, features and System performance. Desired items, features and System performance levels will be assigned predetermined costs, as defined in Section V. The cost assigned is considered to be the cost which would be incurred by the State to develop or otherwise acquire the item or feature, or the value of the System hours which are not available to the State due to System Failure or Preventive Maintenance.

4.3.5 The requirements costing technique considers all one-time and life-cycle costs for mandatory requirements and desirable items, features and System performance levels. Bidder proposed costs shall be used when bidder responds to a desired item or feature. The predetermined cost shall be used for those desired items to which the bidder does not respond.

4.4 *REJECTION OF PROPOSALS*
The State reserves the right to reject any and all bids received by reason of this RFP. The State does not intend to pay for information solicited or contracted for prior to entering into a contract with the successful Contractor.

The State reserves the right to reject any bid which fails to meet the mandatory requirements as stated.

The State reserves the right to reject any bid which does not comply with the technical or cost requirements of this RFP.

The State reserves the right to contract for any portion of the equipment proposed by reason of this RFP, or to substitute equipment from other sources if in the best interest of the State. System support and training shall not be affected by the State not contracting for all items included in the bid.

The State reserves the right to waive minor deviations in bids providing such action is in the best interest of the State. Minor deviations are defined as those that have no adverse effect upon the State's interest and would not affect the amount of the bid by giving a bidder an advantage or benefit not enjoyed by other bidders.

If no valid bids are received by the State, the State reserves the right to negotiate on the best terms and conditions and at the best possible price.

SECTION V
FUNCTIONAL AND TECHNICAL SPECIFICATIONS

5.0 *TECHNICAL REQUIREMENTS*

5.1 WISCONSIN VEHICLE/DRIVER DATA BASE SYSTEM

5.1.1 *CONCEPT AND FACILITIES*
The Wisconsin Vehicle/Driver Data Base System is a Data Base/Data Communication (DB/DC) Support System which operates under the OS/370 MVS control program with TCAM. The system is a control program itself that schedules and supervises the processing of data to and from the data base. Both batch and telecommunications programs can be processed concurrently under the system.

5.1.2 *SYSTEM FACILITIES*
The DB/DC Support System provides a file organization and an access method for random and sequential processing of the data base. Within the data base there are large volume data files with multiple external indexes. The system also provides a recovery scheme to insure file integrity in either the batch or the on-line update environment. It can handle concurrent batch and on-line update of the data base thus eliminating operations scheduling problems for batch programs.

The system includes terminal support and a program scheduling facility capable of directing the processing of multiple step terminal-to-program interaction requests. These terminal requests are processed by teleprocessing programs that communicate with the data base through a standardized interface. The purpose of the standardized interface is to isolate the application system from the physical structure of the data base.

The DB/DC Support System is designed to accommodate all the application areas sharing the data base. It is designed to be responsive to the changing requirements of any application system.

5.1.3 *MAJOR SYSTEM COMPONENTS*
The DB/DC Support System is comprised of six major components. These are:

a. Terminal control component with queuing for data communications.
b. Data base input/output handler consisting of a data base access facility and related recovery restart facilities.
c. Data base dictionaries that describe each data item and its location; tables that describe the physical data files and their relationships are also present.
d. Teleprocessing program scheduling.
e. Batch interface facility that allows batch programs to retrieve data directly from the data base.
f. Utilities, i.e., peripheral support programs such as file load, recovery, etc.

5.1.4 *DESIGN CONCEPTS*
An understanding of four basic concepts is a prerequisite to an understanding of the DB/DC Support System. These concepts include the following:

Transaction
Data Element
Agenda
Modular Structure

An explanation of the above is contained within the benchmark material.

5.1.5 *BIDDER REVIEW*
Prospective bidders may review available documentation for the Wisconsin Vehicle/Driver Data Base System in [location omitted], during the period 8:00 A.M. to 4:30 P.M., on Monday through Friday, provided that at least 24 hours of advance notice of the visit is furnished. Requests to review should be directed to:

[Name and location omitted]

Because of limited space an appointment time will be reserved. Except in relation to a benchmark as provided in Section VI, no documentation will be removed from [location omitted].

5.1.6 *SINGLE BIDDER RESPONSIBILITY*
It is mandatory that the bidder responding to this RFP shall bid all equipment, programming, and services as specified and must be the single point of contact for the following activities:

1. Submission of a plan for the physical installation of the Processor and peripherals contained in the bid. The bidder shall respond with both a written plan, by phase, including dates installation will begin and dates of installation completion as well as scale drawings for each phase of proposed equipment in place showing, to scale, the relationship(s) to existing equipment and physical facility.
2. Delivery of the Processor(s) and peripherals contained in the bid.
3. Delivery or recommended source of all mandatory software (as specified in Section 5.3) in their current release.
4. Equipment and programming ready and operational for acceptance testing.
5. Maintenance (Preventive and Remedial) for all equipment.
6. Maintenance for System Control Program.
7. Training for Data Center Managers, Analysts, Programmers, Operators and other Agency personnel.
8. Systems Analyst support for program conversion, System Control Program installation, application planning, etc.
9. Current reference manuals for processor, peripheral and System Control Programs.
10. 370/115 Conversion.

5.2 *MANDATORY TECHNICAL REQUIRE-MENTS*
The technical requirements for the purpose of this RFP include paragraphs 5.2 through 5.5.

5.2.1 *EQUIPMENT* (Minimum Evaluation Configuration—Exhibit I)

5.2.1.1 For the purpose of this RFP, the words expandable and/or upgradeable mean:

a. Expandable—Additional capacity attained through addition to or expansion of installed equipment.
b. Upgradeable—Additional capacity through exchange of unit(s) of Equipment for unit(s) of greater capacity.

Both terms require plug compatible units currently installed at a minimum of 5 user locations.

5.2.1.2 The Equipment proposed shall be minimally configured as follows:

a. 4,000,000 bytes of directly addressable memory, with the ability to be expandable and/or upgradeable to a minimum of 16,000,000 bytes of addressable memory. A uniprocessor, AP or MP configuration is acceptable in the expanded configuration if all processors function under a single control program and all files and all memory are accessible by each processor.
b. A minimum of eight (8) input/output channels, to be configured as two (2) byte multiplexer, and six (6) block multiplexer channels, with the ability to be expandable and/or upgradeable to a minimum of twelve (12) input/output channels, to be configured as two (2) byte multiplexer and ten (10) block multiplexer channels, or equivalent capability.
c. A minimum of 1.6 billion bytes of disk storage equivalent to IBM-3330-11s with string switch feature with the ability to be expandable and/or upgradeable to a minimum of 4.8 billion bytes.
d. A minimum of 3.8 billion bytes of disk storage equivalent to IBM-3350-A, B and C2Fs with string switch feature with the ability to be expandable and/or upgradeable to a minimum of 11.4 billion bytes.
e. Communications controller(s) with a minimum capacity to allow operation of Network Control Programs (NCP) in Partition Emulation Programs (PEP) environment or equivalent 100K for user code supporting 183 4800 baud full duplex synchronous lines with the ability to be expandable and/or upgradeable to a capacity to allow 200K for user code supporting 458 4800 baud duplex synchronous lines.

Communications controller(s) must attach to two (2) channels of the CPU to provide alternate path capability.

f. A two channel magnetic tape system consisting of the following:

(1) Two (2) tape drives with 6250/1600 BPI dual density capability and transfer rates at 6250 BPI of 1,250,000 bytes per second and at 1600 BPI of 320,000 bytes per second and equivalent to IBM 3420 Model 8.
(2) Four (4) tape drives with 6250/1600 BPI dual density capability and transfer rates at 6250 BPI of 470,000 bytes per second and at 1600 BPI of 120,000 bytes per second and equivalent to IBM-3420 Model 4.

g. A minimum of two (2) printers with separate control units equivalent to IBM-1403-N1. The Department requires high quality OCR and non-OCR printing.

h. A minimum of the following card reader equipment:

   (1) Card reader capable of reading a minimum of 1,000 cards per minute equivalent to an IBM 2501 Model B2.

   (2) Card reader capable of reading a minimum of 600 cards per minute equivalent to an IBM 2501 Model B1.

i. All tape control and disk storage control units to be equipped with two channel switch feature.

j. Any required system console device(s).

k. Any required power and/or coolant distribution unit(s), including any solid state motor generator/frequency convertor unit.

l. Any required interconnecting cables, including peripheral controller cables.

Exhibit I depicts the equivalency of a minimum acceptable configuration.

5.2.2 INTERNAL PERFORMANCE

The internal performance of the proposed CPU(s) shall be sufficient to pass the Benchmark.

5.2.3 EQUIPMENT COMPATIBILITY

The equipment bid must replace the currently installed IBM System/370 Model 115 with a CPU(s) capable of:

1. Channel interfacing to the two (2) currently installed IBM 3886 Model I Optical Scanners.

2. Producing print of sufficient quality to be acceptable to the 3886's.

3. Channel interfacing to the forty-four Telex 3270 video display terminals currently installed on the System/370 Model 115.

4. Channel interfacing the IBM 3540 Diskette Input/Output unit.

The equipment must be installed between 4:30 P.M., Friday and 8:00 A.M., Monday in order to avoid interruption of data entry operations normally available from 8:00 A.M. to 4:30 P.M. each workday.

Any program conversion necessitated by the replacement of the System/370 Model 115 shall be the responsibility of the bidder. The bidder shall include in his bid a detailed plan for the conversion effort as specified in Rider G of Attachment A. Such plan shall include personnel requirements, time required, schedule of events and cost to the State.

The System/370 Model 115 is operating under DOS/VS utilizing CICS and BTAM to support key entry and document reading operations. The inventory of modules/programs operational on the 115 are; (1) 10 3270 CICS Screen Maps. (2) 42 COBOL programs and (3) 4 assembler modules. Source listings and documentation will be supplied with the benchmark material.

5.2.4 SOFTWARE COMPATIBILITY

5.2.4.1 The Department plans to use the Wisconsin Vehicle/Driver Data Base System. It is mandatory, therefore, for the selected bidder to be capable of accomplishing one of the following:

1. Execute the Wisconsin Vehicle/Driver Data Base Systems as is on the equipment configuration bid, or

2. Convert the Wisconsin Vehicle/Driver Data Base System to run on the equipment configuration bid. Should this option be selected, it is mandatory that the bidder be responsible for the conversion effort and the conversion plan (including personnel to be provided, time required, schedule of events and costs to the State) be contained in the bid. Should any bidder propose an emulator or simulator to execute the Wisconsin Vehicle/Driver Data Base System it is mandatory that the bidder cite in his bid a minimum of five (5) present users of the emulator or simulator. The references cited must be users of the specific emulator or simulator on a similar configuration. Additionally, it is mandatory that the emulator or simulator be usable on any expansion system which the bidder includes in his proposal.

5.3 SOFTWARE

Compilers that must be provided or source identified:

ASSEMBLER
ANSI COBOL
FORTRAN IV—Level H
PL/1 OPTIMIZED

Communications package that must be provided or source identified:

TCAM or equivalent (it must be modified to interface with the Wisconsin Vehicle/Driver Data Base System)

Network Control Program (NCP) in Partition

Emulation Program (PEP) environment (or equivalent)
270X Emulation

Communications package must be able to address a minimum of 1,000 terminals:

Utilities that must be provided or source identified:

General purpose sort/merge
Basic utilities support

System Control Program must be capable of performing:

Local batch
Remote batch
A teleprocessing monitor processing on-line transactions
Demand (Time Sharing)
(If multiple CPU's are bid they must operate as a single system.)

5.4 PHYSICAL FACILITY

5.4.1 The equipment bid in response to Section V must be installed and operated in the available space identified in Exhibit II. Each square indicates the location of a 2' by 2' raised floor tile. A scale size drawing will be supplied with the benchmark package.

5.4.2 The physical facility is at grade level, with the top of the raised flooring measuring 12" from the building floor. Removable 2' by 2' tiles are employed on pedestals. The underfloor area is used as a cable trace and air conditioning plenum. For the purpose of RFP, no power, air conditioning or chilled water is presently available.

5.4.3 Installation/conversion must be accomplished in a minimum of two phases.

5.4.3.1 *Phase I*

Phase I must include but not be limited to the following equipment:

1 Central Processing Unit
1 Bank of 3330 type disk storage (.8 billion bytes)
1 Bank of 3350 type disk storage (1.9 billion bytes)
1 card reader
1 high speed line printer and control unit
1 system printer
1 system console
2 tape control units
6 tape units

Connection of CPU to IBM 3272s in support of Telex 277 key entry operation.

Connection of CPU to IBM 3886 OCR equipment.

Connection of CPU to IBM 3540 Diskette Input/Output Unit.

During the period the above equipment is undergoing checkout it is mandatory that both the key entry and document reading functions not be disrupted. It is also mandatory that should malfunctioning occur when the key entry and document reading functions are converted to the newly installed equipment that either malfunction be corrected or re-connection to the IBM 370/115 be accomplished without interruption of: (1) the normal key entry operation, as defined in paragraph 5.2.3, and (2) document reading operations for more than 48 hours.

5.4.3.2 *Phase II*

This phase will consist of removal of the IBM 370/115 and associated equipment and the installation of the balance of the equipment, not installed in Phase I, relative to this acquisition.

Upon completion of Phase II the contractor shall certify equipment ready for acceptance testing. Acceptance testing will be carried out as specified in contract.

5.5 TRAINING

[Data center name omitted] personnel are presently using [Vendor name omitted] equipment and have no formal training in either hardware or software of any other bidders involved in this procurement. It is mandatory therefore that responding bidders propose a training program both on site and off site for Data Center Managers, Analysts, Programmers, Operators, Systems Programmers and other Agency personnel. The details of the program and associated costs, if any, must be included on Rider C-1 of Attachment A. The Contractor's proposal shall designate a curriculum for the training program including but not limited to:

Communication Processing training for 5 persons in the equivalent to the following IBM training courses.

Course Number	Description
10053	OS/VS BTAM Macros & Facilities
G3606	TCAM Facilities & Planning
E3123	ACF/TCAM Coding

E7913	ACF/TCAM SNA Workshop
G3631	3704/3705 NCP Coding Fundamentals
G3632	3704/3705 NCP Coding for SS/BSC
E3031	3704/3705 ACF/NCP Control & Flow
E3084	TCAM SNA Control & Flow

Control Program training for 2 persons in the equivalent to the following IBM training courses.

Course Number	Description
A3754	OS/VS VSAM for System Programming
H3762	OS/MVS Structure & Supervisor Services
H3770	MVS Measurement and Tuning
H3620	JES 2 Internals
H3769	TSO for MVS Systems Programmers
H3764	OS/MVS Installation & Maint.

The State requires training for 40 Applications Programmers however the State conducts its own training of applications programmers for the following IBM training courses.

Course Number	Description
10004	OS/VS JCL
10067	VSAM—Using Access Method Services (OS/VS)
10014	VSAM—Coding in COBOL
SR20-4193	TSO Command Language for Applications Programmers

If the bidder is proposing conversion, emulation or simulation he must bid an equivalency of the above courses. Conversely if a bidder is not proposing conversion, emulation or simulation he should omit the above application programmer courses from his bid.

5.6 *DESIRABLE ITEMS*

5.6.1 *PROGRAMMING PRODUCT SUPPORT*
The State places value on the presence of Programming Product Support personnel, above the mandatory requirement, as specified in the contract residing within 50 miles of Tallahassee as of the first day of each of the contract periods specified

below. If the bidder does not agree to provide such additional support the amounts applicable to the periods for which such support is not provided shall be added to the bidders bid. These personnel would not primarily be assigned in support of this acquisition, but would be available from time to time for consultation or other support activities. The level of additional support in manyears for the period of this acquisition (60 months) is shown below. Please note that cases such as paragraphs 5.6.1.2a and 5.6.1.2.b reference the same period and are addressing the need for 2 persons for ½ manyear each and that should a bidder respond by offering 1 person on a full time basis for this period the State will only consider this as ½ manyear. A manyear is defined as 2,088 manhours.

5.6.1.1 *PROJECT MANAGER*

a. ½ manyear from month 25 through 36. If not agreed to the State will add $17,173.50 to the bidders bid.

b. ¼ manyear from month 37 through 48. If not agreed to the State will add $9,187.82 to the bidders bid.

c. ¼ manyear from month 49 through 60. If not agreed to the State will add $9,830,97 to the bidders bid.

5.6.1.2 *OPERATING SYSTEMS ANALYST*

a. ½ manyear from month 1 through 12. If not agreed to the State will add $12,500 to bidders bid.

b. ½ manyear from month 1 through 12. If not agreed to the State will add $12,500 to bidders bid.

c. ¼ manyear from month 13 through 24. If not agreed to the State will add $6,687.50 to the bidders bid.

d. ¼ manyear from month 13 through 24. If not agreed to the State will add $6,687.50 to the bidders bid.

e. ½ manyear from month 25 through 36. If not agreed to the State will add $14,311.25 to the bidders bid.

f. ¼ manyear from month 25 through 36. If not agreed to the State will add $7,155.63 to the bidders bid.

g. ½ manyear from month 37 through 48. If not agreed to the State will add $15,313.04 to the bidders bid.

h. ¼ manyear from month 49 through 60. If not agreed to the State will add $8,192.48 to the bidders bid.

5.6.1.3 *COMMUNICATIONS ANALYST*

a. ½ manyear from month 1 through 12. If not agreed to the State will add $12,500 to the bidders bid.

b. ½ manyear from month 13 through 24. If not agreed to the State will add $13,375 to the bidders bid.

c. ¼ manyear from month 13 through 24. If not agreed to the State will add $6,687.50 to the bidders bid.

d. ¼ manyear from month 25 through 36. If not agreed to the State will add $7,155.63 to the bidders bid.

e. ¼ manyear from month 25 through 36. If not agreed to the State will add $7,155.63 to the bidders bid.

f. ¼ manyear from month 37 through 48. If not agreed to the State will add $7,656.52 to the bidders bid.

g. ¼ manyear from month 49 through 60. If not agreed to the State will add $8,192.48 to the bidders bid.

5.6.2 *SYSTEM AVAILABILITY, RELIABILITY AND MAINTAINABILITY*

It is desirable that each bidder submit with his proposal, maintenance data extracted from vendor maintenance logs, system utilization, and system failure data for ten (10) current users (commercial or government) utilizing the bidder's equipment being proposed, which has an activity level similar to the State's requirements defined herein, for the period [dates omitted]. The name of each user, a contact person and telephone number of the contact person shall be included for each of the ten users. Data shall be submitted as follows, for each user for each month, [dates omitted]:

a) Operational Use Time
b) System Failure Downtime
c) Number of Systems Failures
d) Preventive Maintenance Hours
e) Number of Preventive Maintenance Periods
f) System Availability Level

5.6.2.1 *SYSTEM AVAILABILITY LEVEL*

Although the State has identified a minimum System Availability Level of 95% as mandatory, a higher System Availability Level is desired. Using the data provided by the bidder, the State shall compute a combined average System Availability Level for the ten users. The State shall add to the

bidder's proposal, a cost to be determined as follows:

(Installment Purchase Cost + 60 months maintenance cost) (1.00 − combined average System Availability Level) = Cost to be added to bidder's proposal.

Bidder's not submitting data for ten users shall have a cost added to their bid based on a 95% System Availability Level.

5.6.2.2 *SYSTEM RELIABILITY*

Using the bidder supplied data the average number of System Failures per year will be calculated. The State shall add to the bidder's proposal a cost to be determined as follows:

(Hourly System Cost) (average number of System Failures per year) (5) (.167) = cost to be added to bidder's proposal.

Note 1: The hourly system cost is computed as follows:

$$\frac{\text{(Installment Purchase Cost + 60 Mos. Maint. Cost)}}{720 \times 60}$$

Note 2: An average recovery time of 10.02 minutes per System Failure is assumed.

Bidders not submitting data for ten users shall have a cost added to their proposal which is determined by using 540 as the average number of System Failures per year.

5.6.2.3 *SYSTEM MAINTAINABILITY*

Using the bidder supplied data, the average number of Preventive Maintenance hours per year will be calculated. The State shall add to the bidder's proposal a cost to be determined as follows:

(Hourly System Cost) (average number of Preventive Maintenance hours per year) (5) = cost added to bidder's proposal.

Bidder's not submitting data for ten users shall have a cost added to their proposal which is determined by using 208 as the average number of Preventive Maintenance hours per year.

5.6.3 *PRICE PERFORMANCE*

It is desirable that each bidder propose a System that will exceed the Benchmark contained in Section VI of this RFP with a maximum transaction rate of 15 transactions per second on Phase V. The State attaches a value of $100,000 to this additional capability. For those bidders that do not attain the 15 transactions per second rate, the State shall add to their costs in accordance with the following:

$$\frac{(15-n)}{(5)} \; (\$100,000) = \text{Cost added to bidder's proposal}$$

n = Number of transactions processed per second (maximum of 15 being credited)

5.6.4 The State desires that a Single Bidder execute Attachments A and C to the RFP. The State has assigned a value of $125,000 to this item based on the additional coordination cost to the State if a single bidder does not sign both Contracts. A bidder that does not sign both Contracts will have $125,000 added to its bid.

SECTION VI
BENCHMARK INFORMATION

6.0 *BENCHMARK PLAN*

6.1 *BENCHMARK PROBLEM*

1. Each bidder must be prepared to run a benchmark upon satisfactorily meeting the requirements of this RFP.
2. The bidder shall advise the State of the recommended location for benchmark in their bid. The bidder must submit three proposed start times for execution of the benchmark with a minimum of 90 hours between each. The State will schedule benchmark activities in a manner which reflects the best interests of the State.
3. The equipment used for processing the benchmark problem must be the same type components as bid. The bidder shall submit, with his proposal, a working diagram of his benchmark equipment configuration for approval by the State.
4. Failure to complete the benchmark in accordance with Paragraph 6.2 and 6.4 shall constitute nonresponsiveness and shall remove the bidder from further consideration.
5. Due to the limited time the bidder will not be required to benchmark the OCR, diskette input/output, nor key entry capability. How-

ever, an affirmative statement regarding the capability to accomplish these functions must be made. Furthermore, these functions will be part of acceptance testing.

6.2 *BENCHMARK OBJECTIVES*
The benchmark demonstration will afford the bidder an opportunity to physically demonstrate the ability of his proposed computer system(s) to process the Wisconsin Vehicle/Driver Data Base Package.

The benchmark demonstration shall provide a measurement of the potential throughput of the bidder's proposed equipment using the WVDDB/DC package.

Performance requirement of 10 transactions (as defined in the Wisconsin Vehicle/Driver Data Base Package) per second with a response time not to exceed 5 seconds is required. If this performance criteria is not achieved the bidder shall be considered nonresponsive. The transaction rates of 10 transactions per second apply to Steps I, IV and V of benchmark.

Failures of equipment and/or bidder supplied software during the benchmark shall subject the bidder to disqualification.

6.3 *ADDITIONAL INFORMATION*
The actual benchmark package will be submitted to bidders separately from this specification.

Copies can be obtained from [name, location, and phone number omitted] for a deposit of $1,000 refundable upon return of the benchmark package. A cashier's check shall be made payable to the Department of Highway Safety and Motor Vehicles. The benchmark package is proprietary to the State and must be returned.

6.4 *BENCHMARK PROBLEM*
The Department of Highway Safety and Motor Vehicles will furnish two (2) levels of test data, as follows, to be used in the benchmark demonstration:

1. To be used by bidder for testing the system.
2. To be provided by the Department of Highway Safety and Motor Vehicles on the date of the benchmark.

The following is a brief abstract of individual problems required on the benchmark.

6.4.1 *PHASE I—WISCONSIN DATA BASE PACKAGE*

This is a complete data base system written in IBM assembler and PL/1. It uses three user SVC's. It will be capable of monitoring its own performance.

6.4.2 *PHASE II—YARDSTICK*

This is a Fortran program designed to measure the relative CPU power.

6.4.3 *PHASE III*

Demonstrate capabilities equivalent to TSO.

6.4.4 *PHASE IV*

Run concurrently Phase I, Phase II and Phase III.

6.4.5 *PHASE V*

Run two levels of the Wisconsin Data Base:

1. One similar to production environment.
2. One similar to test environment concurrently with Phase II and Phase III.

Table A
One-time Charges

BIDDER _____ Bid Number _____

ONE-TIME COST SUPPLIED BY BIDDER

1. Equipment Transportation Costs $_____

2. Equipment Installation Costs $_____

3. Equipment Return Transportation Costs $_____

4. Bidder's Support Costs $_____

5. Programming Costs $_____

6. Training Costs $_____

7. Other One-Time Costs (Identify) $_____

TOTAL ONE-TIME COSTS SUPPLIED BY BIDDER $_____

ONE-TIME COSTS CALCULATED BY THE STATE

1. Air-Conditioning (Construction Cost calculated in increments of 15 tons at $20,000.00 per 15 ton increment) $_____

2. Power (Construction cost calculated in increments of
   30 power connections at $6,000.00 per 30 power connections) $_____

3. UPS construction cost calculated in accordance with
   the following table:
       100 KVA UPS—$175,000.00 $_____
       200 KVA UPS—$250,000.00 $_____
       400 KVA UPS—$300,000.00 $_____ $_____
4. Cost of solid state frequency convertor including transportation and installation ($85,000.00 per unit) $_____

5. Plumbing (Construction costs on the basis of
   $25,000.00 per liquid cooled CPU) $_____

6. Other (if applicable) $_____

TOTAL ONE-TIME COSTS CALCULATED BY
THE STATE $_____

GRAND TOTAL ONE-TIME COSTS $_____

BIBLIOGRAPHY

BOOKS

American Bar Association Section of Science and Technology (Bigelow, Robert P., ed.). *Computers and the Law: An Introductory Handbook,* 3rd Edition. Chicago: Commerce Clearing House, 1981.

Auer, Joseph, and Harris, Charles Edison. *Computer Contract Negotiations.* New York: Van Nostrand Reinhold Co., 1981.

Brandon, Dick H., and Segelstein, Sidney. *Data Processing Contracts.* New York: Van Nostrand Reinhold Co., 1976.

Cohen, Herb. *You Can Negotiate Anything.* Secaucus, N.J.: Lyle Stuart, Inc., 1980.

Contino, Richard M. *Legal and Financial Aspects of Equipment Leasing Transactions.* Englewood Cliffs, N.J.: Prentice-Hall, Inc., 1979.

Fisher, Roger, and Ury, William. *Getting to Yes.* Boston: Houghton Mifflin Co., 1981.

Ilich, John. *The Art and Skill of Successful Negotiation.* Englewood Cliffs, N.J.: Prentice-Hall, Inc., 1973.

Karrass, Chester L. *The Negotiating Game.* New York: Thomas Y. Crowell Co., 1970.

Mandell, Ludwig. *The Preparation of Commercial Agreements.* New York: Practising Law Institute, 1978.

Nierenberg, Gerard I. *Fundamentals of Negotiating.* New York: Hawthorn Books, Inc., 1973.

Nierenberg, Gerard I., and Calero, Henry H. *How to Read a Person Like a Book.* New York: Hawthorn Books, Inc., 1971.

Sippl, Charles J. *Data Communications Dictionary.* New York: Van Nostrand Reinhold Co., 1976.

PERIODICALS

Computer Law and Tax Report (CLTR). Warren, Gorham & Lamont, Inc., 210 South Street, Boston, MA 02111.

Computer/Law Journal. Center for Computer Law, 530 West 6th Street, 10th Floor, Los Angeles, CA 90014.

Computer Negotiations Report (CNReport). Sunscape International, Inc., 1513 E. Livingston Street, Orlando, FL 32803.

The Business Lawyer. Section of Corporation, Banking, and Business Law, American Bar Association, 1155 E. 60 Street, Chicago, IL 60637.

INDEX